FROMMER'S
NEW ZEALAND
ON $45 A DAY

SUSAN POOLE

With
Alice Garrard

GW00417604

4TH EDITION

PRENTICE HALL

New York □ London □ Toronto □ Sydney □ Tokyo □ Singapore

Published by Prentice Hall Trade Division
A Division of Simon & Schuster Inc.
15 Columbus Circle
New York, NY 10023

ISBN 0-13-331612-2
ISSN 1045-9111

Manufactured in the United States of America

CONTENTS

MAPS

ABOUT THIS BOOK

In a world of fast disappearing budget travel destinations, New Zealand continues to offer exceptional value. Still, the scoffers will say that *New Zealand on $45 a Day* is a fantasy. Not so. Consider the following.

First of all, as with all Frommer budget guides, the cover price quoted is meant to take care of only your *basic* daily travel expenses: that is, a roof over your head and three square meals a day. Transportation, entertainment, sightseeing, shopping, and any other expenses are in addition to that $45 a day. Of these, your getting-there transportation will be the single largest expense item, and I have included some money-saving tips to help you trim that as much as possible. This book will, however, point out best buys in each of these categories to help you hold down *all* costs.

As to specifics, that $45 U.S. translates into NZ$72 at the exchange rate used throughout this edition of NZ$1.60 for $1 U.S.! Thus, in many cases what would be "moderate" in New Zealand currency becomes "budget" in U.S. dollars. Throughout this guide, I'll give you both New Zealand prices and their U.S. dollar equivalents so you can make your own comparisons.

Two other factors must also be taken into consideration: the first is a 12.5% Goods and Services Tax (GST) that applies across the board to both accommodations and meals; and the second is fluctuating economy with a current inflation rate of 4% to 5%. While the GST is likely to be around for the foreseeable future, stringent steps are being taken by the current government to reduce the inflation rate quickly, which should at the very least *halt* the upward climb of prices and quite possibly bring about some reduction. With political and economic conditions so uncertain, it is impossible to predict the exact course of prices over the life of this book, but what can be stated with some degree of certainty is that *value for dollar* will continue to be high for the traveler to New Zealand.

Let's look at those basic expenses in detail. You'll find good accommodations listed that average about NZ$55 ($34.40) single, NZ$65 ($40.65) double. Since each accommodation may elect to *include* or *exclude* GST in its rates, you'll need to take particular notice of this when reading those listed in this book and make the necessary 12.5% adjustment. On a per-person basis, unfortunately it is as true in New Zealand as it is in other parts of the globe that two people traveling together will travel more cheaply than those on their own.

With breakfasts averaging NZ$6 ($3.75), lunch NZ$10 ($6.25), and dinner NZ$21 ($13.25), a couple will come in just under the U.S. $45-per-person figure. But one of the joys (in terms of the pocketbook) of traveling in New Zealand is that almost all the "best-buy" accommodations come in the form of motel flats with complete kitchens, which means you can save as much or as little as you choose on the cost of meals. The bed-and-breakfast accommodations that are the mainstay of budget travelers in Europe have been relatively scarce in New Zealand in past years but are now beginning to appear in more and more locales. You'll find many recommended in these pages, and a stay in any one will, of course, eliminate the breakfast cost from that $45 budget.

A blessing that has *not* changed over the years is New Zealand's tipping policy. You'll seldom find a service charge added to your hotel or restaurant bill—it's strictly on a "when and if you want to" basis, with never any obligation. That's a big budget bonus, but I'll confess that when a taxi driver or porter shifts heavy baggage with a smile or restaurant service has been especially good, my American training takes over and I reach for a 15% tip. Feel free to let your conscience be your guide—no Kiwi is going to give you less than top-notch service whether you tip or not!

And last, but by no means least, no matter *how* you budget your sightseeing, you'll be treated to some of this world's most magnificent scenery at absolutely no cost—Mount Cook, Milford, Doubtful, and Marlborough Sounds, the Coromandel Peninsula, the Bay of Islands, the Southern Alps, glaciers, rushing rivers, moonlike thermal crater scapes, sheep and kiwi-fruit farms, and caves and dells filled with glowworms.

One final word: I have researched all prices in this book as close to press time as possible, and I feel secure in assuring you of their accuracy *as long as the currency exchange rate remains intact*. If there is a drastic change, you may look for upward changes in the prices quoted here, *especially in the second year of the book's life*, 1991. It's a virtual certainty, however, that even if that occurs, price *categories* will remain the same and what is budget today will be budget tomorrow, even if "budget" takes on a slightly different definition.

You have undoubtedly bought *New Zealand on $45 a Day* with finances uppermost in your mind. Well, they have been my foremost consideration too, but far more than currency has played a part in the preparation of this book. What you'll find in its pages is a guide to the *total* New Zealand travel experience—a sort of love letter to that country's inordinate sense of decency and order, its gorgeous landscape, and its endearing people. Having made the decision to visit Kiwiland, you're in for one of the travel treats of your life, dear reader—enjoy every minute!

—Susan Poole

ACKNOWLEDGMENTS

Writing this 4th edition would have been difficult—and much less fun—without the support and help of many old and new friends in New Zealand. While it's impossible to thank all of them by name, I would like to single out a few shining lights starting with the capable, enthusiastic representatives of the New Zealand Tourist and Publicity Department: Graham Palmer in Wellington; the indefatigable Marion Fisher in Auckland; Benny Goodman, Jo Downey, and Peter Reilly in Christchurch; Linda Blake in Queenstown; Sue Harraway in Dunedin; Petra Sauter and Pat Johnston in Rotorua; and Maggie Kerrigan in Los Angeles. A specially big thanks goes to NZTP staffer Kim Wong, also in Los Angeles.

Others who played an invaluable part in my research efforts include the ever-helpful Norm Barry of Auckland; Dennis and Louise Winchester in Queenstown; John and Alyse Alexander of Napier, who introduced me to the joys of sheep farming; Ellie Bates in Christchurch, who encouraged my first visit to Akaroa; Heather Cowie and Peg and Doug Graham in Hokitika, who served a terrific whitebait supper; the unsinkable Barbara Doyle of Thames and the Coromandel Peninsula; Jane and Alistair Bowden of Tauranga, who gave me a lift when I missed my bus, forgoing a soccer game to do it; Peter Hope of Whangerei, an enthusiastic Kiwi I met on the flight from Los Angeles to Auckland; Graham and Joan Hodern in the Bay of Islands; Susanne Hannagan of the Dunedin Visitor Centre; Kirsten Stöckler of the Wellington City Council; Doris and Wally Cheesman in Nelson; Prue Norling of Mount Cook Line in Christchurch; Shirley Thomas of the Information Centre in Greymouth; Kerrie Burrow of the Buller Promotion & Tourism Association in Westport; Jeff Schurr and Damien O'Connor of Westport; Margaret Davidson of InterCity in Christchurch; preservation advocate Helen Stead of Oamaru; Lorraine, Reg, and Richard Harris in Franz Josef; and Yvonne Brown in Rotorua, who enhanced my understanding of Maori culture and concerns.

Finally, I'd like to thank Steve Jensen in New York, who kept my computer purring, sometimes against its will, to the last editorial change.

A Disclaimer

Readers are advised that prices fluctuate in the course of time and travel information changes under the impact of the varied and volatile factors that affect the travel industry. The author and publisher cannot be held responsible for the experiences of the reader while traveling. Readers are invited to write the publisher with ideas, comments, and suggestions for future editions.

Readers should also note that the establishments described under Reader's Selections or Suggestions have not in all cases been inspected by the author and that the opinions expressed there are those of the individual reader(s) only and do not in any way represent the opinions of the publisher or author of this guide.

NEW ZEALAND ON $45 A DAY

There are probably as many misconceptions about New Zealand as there are people who have never been there, and one that is particularly popular with Americans is the notion that it is virtually a suburb of Australia. Don't you believe it! True, they *are* both in the southern hemisphere, and on any map they appear to be close South Pacific neighbors. But that's *1,300 miles* of Tasman Sea separating them, and their separations are by no means limited to those of a watery nature.

One of the most basic differences between the two countries is also one of the most visible—the land itself. For while Australia presents a dramatic, hot landscape of brilliant reds and oranges ringed by splendid, white-surfed beaches shading out to the deep blue of its oceans, New Zealand offers the striking contrast of lush, semi-tropical rain-forest greenery, cascading waterfalls, playful geysers, wondrous thermal grounds sporting halos of live steam, and more than 5,700 miles of glorious coastline winding in and out of island-studded bays and harbors. In fact, there is such a wealth of nature's blessings that even the most hidebound urbanite cannot escape inner stirrings of those deep ties with which all humankind is bound to the universe in which we live—New Zealand is, above all else, the perfect setting for getting back in touch with the harmony that should (and so seldom does) exist between the human race and its environment.

Surely one of the world's most beautiful countries, New Zealand is composed of two major islands plus little Stewart Island pointing off toward Antarctica. It is bounded on the north and east by the South Pacific, on the west by the Tasman Sea, and on the south by the Southern Ocean. And it's a mere speck on the map—a small country, right? Well, not all *that* small. From tip to tip, it measures a long 1,000 miles, although at its widest it's no more than 280 miles across.

Within those perimeters is such an astounding array of natural beauty, sporting activities, and sightseeing "musts" that you can banish any thought of "doing" it in a few days or just one week—you couldn't even scratch the surface in that short a time! On the North Island, you surely won't want to miss the very special Bay of Islands, rich in history and a haven of tranquility rare in this modern-day world of ours. Or a day or so along the eastern "Sunrise Coast," where New Zealand's first light of day illuminates breathtakingly beautiful headlands. Or Rotorua's steamy thermal hotpot. Or Auckland's surprisingly sophisticated urban scene. Or Waitomo's glowworms. All that takes time—and that's just a *taste* of the North Island! Then there's that marvelous ferry ride across the Cook Strait to the South Island, where golden sunsets and exotic coastal drives lure you the length of the West Coast, where the Southern Alps cover more territory than the entire country of Switzerland, where glaciers beckon you to their mountaintop source, where Stewart Island dares you to come as close as possible to the South Pole without shipping out for Cape Horn, where every day's drive is an education in the definition of "sheep station," where Dunedin unfolds its Scottish charms, and where Christchurch is waiting to show you its mirror image of England. More time.

Allow *at least ten days* just to sample the highlights—and I should issue the warning that once there, you'll want to spend months to see it all. Since most of us don't really have that kind of time, you'll find some suggested itineraries in Chapter I (see "How Long to Stay") to help you use whatever time you have to get around to the highlights that most interest you. My best advice is to study this book and any others you can lay your hands on to determine just what those highlights are—you're going to have to make some hard choices! And the chances are good that you'll go home busily planning your next trip back to see those places you missed.

No matter what your itinerary, one promise I can make unconditionally: you're going to fall head-over-heels in love with New Zealand's scenery. To that promise I can add another, just as unconditionally: even more, you're going to love its people! New Zealanders are so . . . well, civilized. They have good manners (they don't push or utter rude remarks on the street, or mark public buildings with graffiti). They have an innate sense of decency that sends them rushing to the aid of strangers and keeps them on cordial terms with the original New Zealanders. Above all, a strong respect for order pervades their daily lives. Things work as they're supposed to work—and if they don't, somebody fixes them. In short, all the human virtues we remember (or remember hearing about) are in abundant supply in New Zealand. Now I'll wager you'll hear at least once the remark from another traveler that the country is so charming because "it's 20 years behind the times." Well, for my money, all the "progress" in all the rest of the world is miles behind the sort of human progress New Zealand has managed to achieve!

And all those nice people have come up with a cornucopia of travel goodies to make your stay so easy and so comfortable you won't believe you're traveling on a budget. For example, if a rental car is beyond your means (but *do* plan for it if you can), there's one of the best public transportation systems I've run across anywhere —rail, bus, ferry, or plane, you'll travel in comfort. Stopovers can be spent in accommodations that will change forever your image of motels—they're motel *"flats,"* complete with lounge, separate bedroom in most cases, and a kitchen equipped right down to coffee, tea, and milk in the fridge!

Just one more thing. You're going to bring back many things from your New Zealand visit—memories, souvenirs, friendships—and unless I miss my guess, among them will be some irresistible expressions, which will have beguiled their way into your vocabulary. Just try not to adopt the lovable "Spot on!" Or the complimentary "Good as gold." And when tempers flare back home, what better way to cool them than with a smiling "Just don't get your knickers in a knot, mate"?

Those interested in the nitty-gritty facts and figures will want to know the following. New Zealand lies across the International Date Line and below the Tropic of Cancer, some 6,500 miles southwest of Los Angeles and 6,500 miles southeast of Tokyo. Its nearest neighbor, Australia, is some 1,300 miles to the west across the Tasman Sea. To keep track of time back home, remember that New Zealand is 20 hours ahead of Los Angeles, 17 hours ahead of New York, and 12 hours ahead of Greenwich Mean Time (example: at 5 a.m. Tuesday in New Zealand, it's noon on Monday in New York).

New Zealand's length (all islands) is about 1,000 miles, and its land area is comparable to that of Colorado, 103,883 square miles. Its population totals 3.5 million, with 818,000 concentrated in Auckland, 342,000 in the capital city of Wellington, and 321,000 in the South Island's largest city, Christchurch. Most are of British descent, and English is the official (and prevailing) language, although the more than 400,000 Maoris also use their native (Polynesian) tongue. The parliamentary form of government recognizes the Queen of England as head of state, and she's represented by a governor-general, with a locally elected prime minister and members of parliament.

All the above is, of course, a very general overview of New Zealand. Now let's get down to specifics, and where better to begin than at the beginning, with a look at its history.

1. A Brief History

As to its very beginning, you have your choice of two theories on just how New Zealand came about. Geologists will tell you that its islands are the relatively young remnants of a continental mass separated by violent shifts in the earth's crust. Its location on a major fault line accounts for frequent earthquake activity, volcanic mountains, the drowned glacial valleys of Fiordland, and the string of mountain ranges that stretches, with a few interruptions, from the alpine peaks of the South Island up to the blunted headland at Cape Reinga.

But ask any Maori and you'll get a far different story. Now, maybe this theory won't be as authentic, but it's a lot more fun.

According to Maori legend, in the days of the gods and demi-gods, the frail fifth son of a woman named Taranga was thrown into the sea by his mother, who felt the infant was too weak to survive. He was rescued, however, by Rangi, the Sky Father, who raised him through childhood, then returned him to his amazed mother, complete with a full set of magical abilities and the enchanted jawbone of his grandmother. The overjoyed mother doted on Maui, her restored offspring, to such an extent that his brothers quickly developed an oversize case of sibling jealousy, which really wasn't eased much when Maui pulled off such astonishing feats as snaring the sun in the pit from which it rose each morning, then smashing its face with that all-powerful jawbone until it was too weak to do anything but creep across the sky, thus giving all the people longer days in which to fish and eliciting buckets of gratitude and respect for Maui.

Needless to say, when Maui set out to fish, his was always the record catch, while his nonmagical brothers barely brought home enough to feed their families—much to the consternation of their wives, who duly complained to Maui. With a condescending (and irritating) wave of his hand, Maui promptly promised his sisters-in-law one load of fish so large it would go bad before they could eat it all. They were delighted; but their husbands were frustrated, angry, and determined to beat Maui to the punch with one last fishing expedition, which they launched at dawn.

The clever (and probably obnoxious) Maui, however, had hidden under the flooring mats of his brothers' canoe, armed with a special fishhook whose point was fashioned from a chip of the precious jawbone. It wasn't until they were well out to sea that he made his appearance, which sent the brothers into a rage. But their luck was running true to form, and when Maui assured them that it would turn in their favor if they'd only sail out of sight of any land, they grumpily agreed, and sure enough, they soon filled the canoe with fish. It was so full, in fact, that they began to take on water, and the brothers were all for turning back for home. To their consternation, the arrogant Maui insisted they sail still farther into the unknown waters and

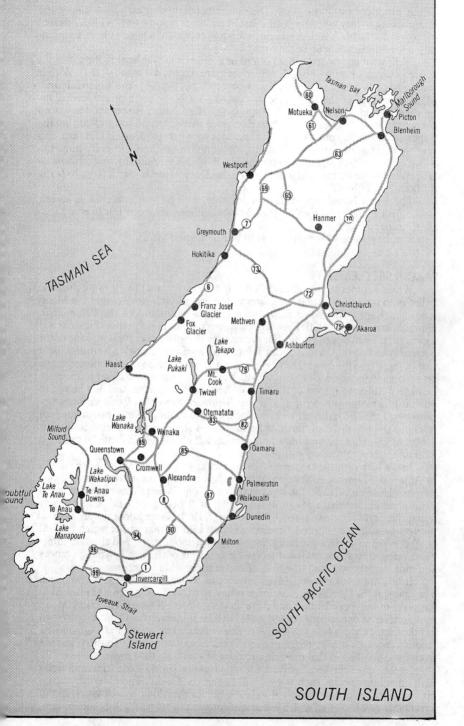

SOUTH ISLAND

calmly produced his magic hook. Their protests fell on deaf ears, so—bailing and complaining—they sailed on until at last Maui struck his nose until it bled, smeared his blood on the hook as bait, and threw his line overboard while chanting an incantation for "the drawing up of the world."

Well, what he hooked turned out to be a gigantic fish, as large as the gable of a *whare runanga* (meeting house), whose very size rendered it *tapu* (sacred). With it came a large wedge of land, which we know today as New Zealand's North Island. Maui, respectful of the *tapu,* quickly departed for home for a priest, leaving his brothers behind with strict orders not to cut up the fish until his return. He was no sooner out of sight than the brothers disobeyed that order, scaling and cutting the huge fish. Now, the gods were much angered at such flagrant disregard for *tapu,* and they set that great fish to lashing about, throwing cut-up chunks in every direction —which is a perfect explanation for the North Island's mountains and offshore islands! And while we may call it the North Island, any Maori knows it is really *Te Ika a Maui,* "the Fish of Maui."

The South Island is actually Maui's canoe, with Stewart Island as its anchor stone. And up in Hawke's Bay, that famous fishhook has been transformed into Cape Kidnappers.

So take your pick—geological fault line or magical Maori.

MAORI SETTLEMENT

When it comes to New Zealand's first inhabitants, again there is more than one belief as to how they settled here. From the mists of prehistory comes the Maori legend of Kupe, who sailed from the traditional homeland of the Polynesians, Hawaiki, around A.D. 950. Even legend doesn't tell us exactly where Hawaiki was located in the vast South Pacific, but present-day authorities believe it was one of the Society Islands group that includes Tahiti. One version of Kupe's adventures has it that he murdered the carver Hoturapa, and with the murdered man's wife and canoe set off on a long, wandering voyage, which eventually brought the pair to the place he named Aotearoa ("land of the long white cloud"). Another says that he was in pursuit of a mammoth octopus when he happened onto New Zealand. Both versions agree that he returned to Hawaiki, taking with him sailing instructions for reaching the uninhabited "Fish of Maui." From some historians comes another explanation—that the first Maori canoes to reach New Zealand came by accident, after having been blown off course at sea.

In the 12th century, two more Maori canoes are said to have touched the shores of Aotearoa. A young Polynesian, Whatonga, was swept out to sea during canoe races, and his grandfather, Toi, went in search of him. When the two were reunited somewhere in the Whakatane region in the Bay of Plenty, they found people already living there and the newcomers intermarried with those we know simply as moa-hunters because they hunted a meaty, wingless bird by that name, which reached heights of up to 13 feet. Nothing more is known about them, and they are sometimes referred to as the Archaic Maoris. Descendants of the two Polynesian canoes and moa-hunters now form the basis of two of today's Maori tribes.

It was not until the mid-14th century that Maoris arrived in great numbers. They came from Hawaiki because of devastating tribal wars, which had erupted in the wake of overpopulation and severe food shortages. If we are to believe Maori tradition, seven ocean-going canoes sailed in a group, which has come to be known as "the fleet." Others sailed in groups of one or two; some came singly. On making landfall, canoe groups kept together, settling in various parts of the country, and it is from these first canoes that most modern-day Maoris trace their roots.

By the time "the fleet" arrived, the moa had been hunted to extinction, along with other bird species, such as giant rails, swans, and geese. There were, however, bounteous supplies of fish and seafood to be had for the taking, as well as berries and a few other edible plants, which were supplemented by tropical plants such as taro, yams, and kumara (a kind of sweet potato) that had come in the canoes from Hawaiki. Dogs and rats had also been canoe passengers and became an important source of protein. The cultivation of these imported vegetables and animals gradually led the Maoris to become an agricultural society living in permanent villages centered around a central *marae* (village common or courtyard) and *whare runanga* (meeting house). It was in these villages that the distinctive Maori art forms of wood carving and tattooing evolved, along with a strong sense of family loyalty and total harmony with their environment. It was this culture that thrived at the time of Capt. James Cook's first contact with New Zealand's Maoris.

EUROPEAN DISCOVERY

The first recorded sighting of New Zealand by Europeans came on December 13, 1642, when Abel Tasman, scouting new trade territory for the Dutch East India Company, spied what he described as "a great high, bold land" in the Hokitika region of the South Island's west coast. Sailing north in his two tall-masted ships, the *Heemskirk* and *Zeehaen,* he entered Golden Bay on December 18, where he encountered the Maoris without ever setting foot on land. As the two ships lay at anchor in the peaceful bay, several war canoes put out from shore and shouted challenges from a safe distance. The next day, however, they were bolder and attacked a cockboat rowing from one of Tasman's ships to the other, killing four sailors in the brief battle before withdrawing. Tasman, dismayed at this hostility and disinclined to seek reprisals, fired at the retreating canoes and put out to sea. For many years afterward, lovely Golden Bay was known as Murderer's Bay, as it was christened by Tasman on that December day.

As it turned out, this was his only glimpse of the Maoris since bad weather prevented his entering Cook Strait, so he proceeded up the west coast of the North Island, failed to find a suitable landing spot, and left what he charted as a vast southern continent to sail on to Tonga and Fiji. But for that bad weather and the hostile Maoris, the first European exploration of New Zealand would almost certainly have been Dutch. But that distinction was left for an Englishman more than a century later.

THE COMING OF CAPTAIN COOK

When Capt. James Cook left England in 1768 on the 368-ton bark *Endeavour,* he was under orders from King George III to sail to Tahiti to observe the transit of the planet Venus across the sun, a once-a-century happening. But the Yorkshireman carried "secret additional orders," which he opened only when his initial duty was accomplished. King George had directed him to sail southwest in search of the "continent" reported by Tasman. If he found it uninhabited, he was to plant the English flag and claim it for the king; if not, his instructions were to take possession of "convenient situations" but only with the consent of the indigenous people. In addition, he was to study the nature of the soil, its flora and fauna, and to make charts of its coastal waters.

It was on October 7, 1769, that New Zealand was first sighted by the surgeon's boy, Nicholas Young, from his perch in the mast. Naming the headland (in the Gisborne area) Young Nick's Head, Captain Cook sailed into a crescent-shaped bay and put down anchor. A rather kindly man, Captain Cook made every effort to cultivate Maori friendship, communicating by way of a young Tahitian chief named Tupea who had come along as guide and interpreter. The Maoris, although they understood and could converse with Tupea, remained hostile even in the face of gifts the captain offered. Nor would they permit him to put aboard the food and water his men so badly needed. Disappointed and bitter, Cook weighed anchor after claiming the country for King George and naming the beautiful bay Poverty Bay because, as he noted in his journal, "it afforded us no one thing we wanted."

Sailing north, Captain Cook rounded the tip of the North Island and went on to circumnavigate both islands during the next six months, charting them with amazing accuracy, missing only such details as the entrance to Milford Sound (which is quite invisible from the open sea) and the fact that Stewart Island was not a part of the mainland (he mistakenly believed Foveaux Strait to be a bay). In addition, he recorded the flora and fauna as instructed and brought back sketches of the indigenous people, who grew more friendly as word of the gift-bearing Pakehas (fair-skinned men) spread. He also recorded details of Maori customs and described the "Indians" as "a brave, open, warlike people." Even today, the journal he kept so meticulously makes fascinating reading.

Captain Cook returned to New Zealand for a month in 1773 and again in 1777. Until his death at the hands of indigenous people in Hawaii on February 14, 1779, he ranged the length and breadth of the South Pacific, sailing as far north as the Arctic Circle and as far south as Antarctica. He and the *Endeavour* have in fact become as much a part of New Zealand legend as those early Maori chiefs and their mighty canoes.

EUROPEAN SETTLEMENT

Organized European settlement in New Zealand did not get underway with any success until 1840, and the *un*organized settlement that preceded it was, for the most part, a disaster.

Sealers began arriving in 1792 and virtually denuded South Island waters of what had been flourishing colonies of seals through their policies of killing cows and pups and allowing no closed seasons or limit on skins (some ships carried off as many as 60,000 per year). By 1820 they moved on to more profitable waters.

Whalers, too, discovered rich hunting grounds in New Zealand waters and arrived in droves. Oil vats soon dotted the Bay of Islands, where safe anchorage was an added attraction. Their unscrupulous methods were much like those of the sealers, and New Zealand's coastal waters were no longer a natural haven for the mammoth animals. Unlike the sealers, however, the whalers brought in their wake a multitude of land-based evils in the form of an attendant population, which Charles Darwin described after his 1835 visit as "the very refuse of Society." Consisting of escapees from Australia's penal colonies, ex-convicts, runaway sailors, and a motley collection of "beachcombers," and concentrated in the Kororareka settlement (now known as Russell), their groceries, brothels, and lawlessness earned it the nickname "hellhole of the Pacific." Ships that would have normally called in at the port stayed away in fear of the widespread practice of shanghaiing sailors for whaling vessels that were shorthanded.

Legitimate traders and merchants, attracted by the wealth of flax and trees such as the kauri, which were ideal for shipbuilding, as well as the lucrative trade in muskets and other European goods with the Maoris, while law-abiding (that is, observing such law as there was), were little better than the sealers and whalers in respecting the country's natural resources. Great forests were felled with no eye to replanting; luxuriant bushlands disappeared in flames to clear hills and valleys for man's encroachment; and when a commercial value was placed on the tattooed and preserved heads that were a part of Maori culture, even the native population was threatened for a time as chiefs eager to purchase muskets lopped off more and more heads, both friend and foe. The latter was a short-lived trade, but quite lively while it lasted.

The immigration of Europeans had a devastating impact on the Maori culture. Most destructive were the introduction of liquor, muskets, and European diseases against which the Maoris had no immunity. Muskets in particular set off decimation of Maoris on a grand scale, for they intensified the fierce intertribal warfare, which for centuries had been a part of the Maori lifestyle—tens of thousands were killed off by the fire-spouting sticks until the availability of muskets became so general that no one tribe had superiority in firepower and by about 1830 chiefs began to realize that the weapon was literally destroying *all* tribes.

Missionaries constituted the one benign group to arrive during this period, spearheaded by the Rev. Samuel Marsden, who arrived in the Bay of Islands in 1814 and preached his first sermon to the Maoris on Christmas Day with the help of a young chief he had befriended. His was a practical brand of Christianity, and when his duties as chaplain to the convict settlement in Sydney demanded his return, he left behind a carpenter, a shoemaker, and a schoolteacher to instruct the Maoris. Most of those men of the cloth who followed were of the same persuasion, and they were responsible for setting down the Maori language in writing (largely for the purpose of translating and printing the Bible), establishing mission schools (by the 1840s large numbers of Maoris could both read and write), and upgrading agricultural methods through the use of plows and windmills, for instance.

On the religious front, their progress was slow—to their credit, they were determined not to baptize any Maori until he had a full understanding of the Christian faith—and it was some 11 years before they made the first Maori convert. Nor is it surprising that it took so long, for deeply imbedded in the indigenous culture were such practices as cannibalism, infanticide, and the worship of gods of war. That the missionaries went about their conversions in much too puritanical a manner is illustrated by the fate of one who admonished a chief for fishing on Sunday: "You are a wicked, bad man . . . You have broken the Sabbath . . . you and your people will all go to hell and be burnt with fire for ever and ever." As the chief's great-grandson reported many years later, "To have put up with insult without avenging it according to its nature would have been fatal to a chief occupying a leading position and injurious to the tribe, as it would render it contemptible to its neighbors." Accordingly, "in less time than it takes to remove the feathers from a fat pigeon, the man of incantation was in an oven and prevented from creating further mischief."

By the late 1830s, however, Maoris were ready to accept the concept of a god of peace, undoubtedly influenced greatly by the vastly changed nature of warfare since the coming of the musket. They were also a literal-minded, practical people, much impressed by the missionaries' ability to cure diseases that resisted all efforts by their own healers, as well as the white man's imperviousness to Maori witchcraft. But in embracing the doctrines of Christianity, they relinquished much of the sensual beauty embodied in their own complex, age-old religious traditions. Naked bodies must now be covered; symbolic carvings of the gods of fertility must be destroyed; the reverence and fear once accorded a tribe's chief must now be transferred to this new god. It was in fact the beginning of the end of many aspects of Maori tribal society as it had existed for centuries.

As the number of British in New Zealand grew, so, too, did lawlessness, with many atrocities committed against both Maoris and settlers. The missionaries were foremost among those who complained to the British government, which was by no means anxious to recognize the faraway country as a full-fledged colony, having already experienced difficulties with America and Canada, and struggled through the Napoleonic Wars and revolts on various other fronts. As a substitute, in 1831 the Crown placed New Zealand under the jurisdiction of New South Wales and sent James Busby as "British Resident," with full responsibilities for enforcing law and order, but with such laughable means of meeting those responsibilities that he was nicknamed "the man-of-war without guns." Needless to say, he was completely ineffectual.

Back in Britain, the newly formed New Zealand Company began sending out ships to buy land from the Maoris and establish permanent settlements. Their methods were questionable to say the least, and caused increasing alarm in London. It must be noted, however, that between 1839 and 1843 the New Zealand Company sent out 57 ships carrying 19,000 settlers, the nucleus of a stable British population. In 1839 Capt. William Hobson was sent out by the government to sort things out, and by catering to the Maori sense of ceremony (and some mild arm-twisting), he arranged an assembly of chiefs at the Busby residence in the Bay of Islands. There, 150 years ago, on February 6, 1840, the famous Treaty of Waitangi, after lengthy debate, was signed with much pomp.

The treaty guaranteed the Maoris "all the Rights and Privileges of British Subjects" in exchange for their acknowledgment of British sovereignty, while granting the Crown exclusive rights to buy land from the Maoris. The fact that many of the chiefs had no idea of the treaty's meaning is clear from one chief's later explanation that he had merely signed a receipt for a blanket sent by the Queen as a gift! Nevertheless, 45 of the Maori chiefs at the assembly did sign, and when it was circulated around the country, another 500 also signed. Instead of easing things, however, the Treaty of Waitangi ushered in one of the bloodiest periods in New Zealand's history.

The British were eager to exercise that exclusive right to purchase Maori land, and while some chiefs were just as eager to sell, others wanted only to hold on to their native soil. As pressures were brought to bear to force them to sell, revolt quickly surfaced, and when Chief Hone Heke (ironically, the first to sign the treaty) hacked down the British flagpole at Kororareka (Russell) in 1844, it signaled the beginning of some 20 years of fierce fighting.

The Maoris, always outnumbered and outarmed, won the unqualified respect and admiration of the British as brave and masterful warriors. The British, on the other hand, were regarded with the same degree of respect by the chiefs, who had not expected that the Pakehas could put up any sort of real fight. At last the British emerged as victors, but out of the bloody confrontations came the basis of a relationship, which to this day is based on that same mutual respect as well as many of those same tensions.

MATTERS OF GOVERNMENT

In 1852 the British Parliament passed the New Zealand Constitution Act, and self-government was administered through a governor appointed in London, a Legislative Council appointed by the governor, and an elected House of Representatives. Elected, that is, by Pakeha landowners who argued that the Maori communal land ownership disfranchised them, as the vote was only extended to "individual landowners." That situation was corrected in 1867, and women were granted the vote in 1893, a full quarter of a century before it happened in Britain or America.

The government also pioneered such social reforms as minimum-wage laws, old-age pensions, paid vacations, labor arbitration, and child-welfare programs. Thus New Zealand became in many respects a "welfare state," its economy based on exports of lamb, mutton, butter, and eggs to England. Throughout the ups and downs of economic developments since, it has retained its humanitarian approach to government.

Today there is a population base of 3.5 million people (most of similar backgrounds) that today supports *72 million* sheep and more than 9 million cattle!

2. Maoris and Pakehas

In modern New Zealand, it is to the credit of both Maori and Pakeha that their widely differing cultures and a history encompassing long years of cruel warfare have been overcome to generate an environment that is peaceful even though not entirely trouble-free. The difficult journey has required a great deal of restraint on both sides and a willingness to put aside the past. Yet today their goodwill is being tested as Maoris and Pakehas debate the provisions of the 150-year-old Treaty of Waitangi, which functions as a Bill of Rights for Maori New Zealanders.

Maoris have seen their numbers increase from a low of 42,000 at the turn of the century to more than 400,000 today, about 12% of the population. From a people suffering from the imported alcoholism and diseases that produced a depression that afflicted the race as a whole with a debilitating lethargy, they have become a largely urban people, participating in the middle-class benefits of their Pakeha brethren while holding fast to as much of their traditional culture as survived in the early years of European settlement.

They have demonstrated a surprising adaptability to the ways of democracy, and the skills acquired through mission schools have been improved and honed to expertise, with more and more additions as industrial development moved across the country. The political arena has afforded them access to power acquired through the oratorical prowess and widespread popularity of such leaders as Apirana Ngata, Te Rangi Hiroa, and Maui Pomare, all of whom were knighted and served as cabinet members, and their Young Maori Party. Because of their political, educational, and professional achievements, Maori candidates often are elected by substantially Pakeha constituencies. They have been quick to take advantage of educational opportunities, with a high percentage of college graduates among the current Maori population. And they have managed to imbue the Pakeha population with a marvelous appreciation for their ancient culture.

To experience that culture in its purest form, the visitor these days must travel to Rotorua (a Maori center) or stumble upon a communal village. It is here that you'll find woodcarvers and mat weavers demonstrating the arts that adorn their great meeting houses with such stylized masterpieces and their bodies with such colorful garb.

Yet even deep in the heart of New Zealand's largest cities (which are home for some 76% of the Maori population), it's easy to observe the traditional lifestyle rhythm that supersedes the white man's alarm clock. When a Maori loved one dies, respect must be shown with attendance at the *tangi*, or funeral, no matter how far away it is. Ancient tribal celebrations also demand time off work, and one's family always comes first. And while the old war *hakas* (complete with foot stomping and protruding tongues) and graceful *poi* dance are mainly performed in shows staged for visitors, most Maori city dwellers have a large repertoire of such melodies as the world-famous "Now Is the Hour" (or, Maori Farewell), which was actually written by an Englishman before World War I. And in national elections, they are free to vote in the Pakeha district in which they reside or in one of the four official Maori electorates.

One sad by-product of the Maoris' move from rural to urban areas has been a gradual weakening of those tribal and family ties that have always been at the very heart of their culture. When there is no *marae* in which to gather at the end of the day, youngsters tend to lose contact with their elders, and even the elders are less closely bound together. In some of the North Island cities (where the Maori concentration is heaviest), social problems are beginning to crop up that can be traced directly to the feeling of isolation that has developed among a younger generation adrift without strong identity support systems. The Maori people have established urban *marae*, which are used daily by numerous groups. The ancient ties are gaining strength, as are the ancient teachings, which are passed down to the young from their elders.

As for their language, with its colorful and vivid imagery, well, the Maoris came very close to losing it. Living in a predominantly European culture, they were forced by circumstance and education to use the English language. However, the growth of *kohanga heo*, or language nests, has resulted in thousands of Maori preschoolers and their parents learning the beautiful Maori language from tribal elders, and its being heard increasingly in homes, schools, and universities. It also is often heard on the radio and is sometimes used to begin the evening's TV newscast with the traditional Maori greeting.

You'll find most of New Zealand's whites living in the cities, too. Or at least working in cities. More and more, as centers such as Auckland grow larger and larger, the people who work there go home at night to the same sort of small suburban satellite communities popular in the United States. Those miles of dual-lane express motorways leading into Auckland, and the sprawling shopping malls in the dozen or so communities that surround it, will have a surprising familiarity!

For most of us, though, there will be a fascinating unfamiliarity about the lifestyle of other Pakehas who live and work on New Zealand's farmlands (which bring in a whopping 60% of the country's export income from meat, dairy products, and wool). From high-country "stations," which concentrate on wool production, to lower pastures, which fatten up lamb and mutton on the hoof, most certainly we'll click our cameras at lovable sheep that seem to have been born with a one-track mind—a fun game when you're traveling is to try to find the sheep that's *not* eating!

For the farmer, it's a hardworking life of comparative isolation, with socializing more or less relegated to the occasional drop-in at the local tavern. Some of your own best socializing may very well come from just such a drop-in if your timing is good enough to coincide with one or two of the farmers'. Or better yet, if you're in the tavern when a gaggle of shearers come in at the end of a busy day.

In the North Island, the cattle that supply all that rich, yummy cream and butter and milk—as well as the ten extra pounds you'll probably carry home—spend winters and summers in the pastures, for grass grows year round in this perfect growing climate. The New Zealand dairyman is more likely to be found in city or small-town watering holes, since his grazing lands are not so spread out and towns are more plentiful up north.

Actually, about three-quarters of all those people in the cities depend on the output of these country folk for prosperity, involved as they are in the processing and marketing of farm products.

City dweller or farmer, the average Pakeha is more likely to be found messing around in boats or out tramping in the bush than in dancing and singing in the manner of the Maori neighbor.

And how do they get on with those neighbors? Very well, most of the time, thank you. Pakehas don't really participate in Maori cultural activities very much, but you can be sure they're *proud* of that culture. You can virtually count on being dragged off to a Maori concert, *hangi* (feast), or some other event by every other Pakeha with whom you spend any time. And you'll be very welcome—as I said before, New Zealanders live together with only an occasional flareup of racial tensions.

A MAORI GLOSSARY

While you're not very likely to overhear the soft, lilting sound of Maori voices speaking their native language on the streets in New Zealand, you *will* be surrounded by words and phrases, both in place names and names of objects always identified by their Maori names. It's a lot more fun to travel around New Zealand if you know, for example, that *roto* is the Maori word for "lake" and *rua* for "two"; hence, Rotorua.

The following are a few of the most commonly used prefixes and suffixes for place names:

ao	cloud
ika	fish
nui	big, or plenty of
roto	lake
rua	cave, or hollow, or two (Rotorua's two lakes)
tahi	one, single
te	the
wai	water
whanga	bay, inlet, or stretch of water

Other frequently used words:

ariki	chief or priest
atua	supernatural being, such as a god or demon
haka	dance
hangi	an oven made by filling a hole with heated stones
karakia	prayer or spell
kereru	wood pigeon
kumara	sweet potato
mana	authority, prestige, psychic force
marae	courtyard, village common
mere	war club made of greenstone (jade)
pa	stockade or fortified place
Pakeha	white-skinned person; primarily used to refer to Europeans
poi	bulrush ball with string attached twirled in action song
tangi	funeral mourning or lamentation
tapu	under religious or superstitious restriction ("taboo")
tiki	grotesque human image, sometimes carved of greenstone
whare	house

If Maori legend and language catch your imagination, you may want to look for *The Caltex Book of Maori Lore* (published by A. H. & A. W. Reed Ltd.), by James Cowan, who spent much time among the Maoris; and *A Dictionary of the Maori Language,* by H. W. Williams, grandson of Bishop William Williams, who compiled the first dictionary at Pahia in 1844.

---

3. Flora and Fauna

New Zealand has been, in a sense, one huge botanical garden during its relatively short life. Undisturbed by the destructive influence of mankind, its forests and plant life flourished, regulated by no forces save those of Mother Nature. Luxuriant ground covering, ferns ranging in size from tiny plants attached to mossy tree trunks all the way to tree-size pongas, more than 100 species of trees, and garlands of starry white clematis and blossoms of other flowering vines created hundreds of miles of cool, dim, tree-vaulted "cathedrals."

The first humans to arrive, themselves closely attuned to nature, accorded the forests due reverence, with just the proper mix of awe and fear. As Peter Hooper, one of New Zealand's best writers and a leading conservationist, says in his excellent book *Our Forests, Ourselves* (published by John McIndoe, Ltd.), "Landscape possesses *mauri*—soul or mind—and it is the outward and visible form of an inward invisible power." And an acute awareness of that quality is inescapable when one walks the present-day forests of New Zealand. Its effect can be profound. As Mr. Hooper goes on to say, "The tonic wildness of natural spaces is essential to the physical/mental/spiritual wholeness of the individual." You have my personal promise of just such a restorative experience upon entering any one of the forests, which will never be too far away throughout your visit.

In the northern quarter of the North Island you'll find the surviving stands of tall, stately kauri trees, whose hardwood trunks—unblemished by knots or other imperfections—were so prized for shipbuilding by early settlers. During December and January, North Island cliffs and lake shores are a mass of scarlet when the pohutukawa (or Christmas tree) bursts into bloom, while its kinsman, the rata, is doing likewise down in the South Island. In early spring, the kowhai, which makes no distinction between north and south but grows almost everywhere, is a profusion of large golden blossoms. The totara has always been much loved by the Maoris, who find its light, durable timber just right for making canoes, as well as for their magnificent carvings. Then there are the pines, including the rimu (red), matai (black), kahikatea (white), and *Dacrydium laxifolium* (pigmy). And the beeches—red, black, and silver. Almost all are evergreen, and seasonal color changes are subtle.

New Zealand also has an astounding array of flowering plants, a full 80% of which are not to be found anywhere else in the world. Undisputed queen of blossoms has to be the world's largest buttercup, the Mount Cook Lily. There are almost 60 varieties of mountain daisies, and a curious "vegetable sheep," which grows in mountainous terrain and has large, cushiony blooms that look like sheep even when you take a closeup look. Bright orange-and-yellow "red hot pokers" look like just that. Up to a dozen white, fringed, saucer-shaped blooms adorn a single flower stalk of the hinau, and the golden kumarahou bloom has been used over the years in medicinal herb mixtures.

An added joy in tramping the forests is the fact that you never have to be afraid to put your foot down—there's not one snake in the entire country! Nor are there any predatory animals. In fact there's only one poisonous spider, and it's rarely found anywhere except on a few scattered sand dunes.

Most of New Zealand's animals did not originate there but were imported by various settler groups. The Maoris brought over dogs (and rats, though I can't say if *that* was intentional!). Captain Cook released a pig, whose wild descendants are still about. Other importees include the red deer, opossum, hedgehog, weasel, and rabbit (which were brought over for skins and meat but became so numerous and destructive that another animal, the stoat, had to be brought in to control the rabbit population).

As for birds, the more species you see, the curiouser and curiouser they get. The kiwi, whose name New Zealanders have adopted as their own, is one of the most curious. Wingless and about the size of a chicken, it lives in hollow trunks or holes in the ground; emerges only at night to forage for insects and worms with a long, curved beak, which has nostrils at its tip; and emits a shrill, penetrating whistle. The female lays one gigantic egg and then leaves the hatching to the male! These days it's rare to see the kiwi in the wild, but you'll find them in special kiwi houses around the country, which simulate nocturnal lighting so you and I can see them during "normal" hours.

Down in the mountains of the South Island there's a comical mountain parrot that is as bold as the kiwi is shy. The kea nests among the rocks, but keeps an eye on the main roads and is quick to investigate any newcomers. It's not unusual, for instance, to see as many as three (as I once did) camped alongside the Milford Sound road—and if you stop, their antics will have you grinning in no time. But it's just as well you keep a sharp eye on them, for those cunning cut-ups are quick to steal jewelry or other shiny objects and to attack such formidable targets as automobile parts with their strong, curved beaks. Campers and trampers in the know are careful to keep their gear well beyond the reach of the mischievous little kea.

If you hear a series of pure, bell-like sounds pouring through the forest air, it's likely to be the song of the lovely bellbird. Only slightly different in sound is the handsome tui. Around swampy areas, those ear-piercing screams you hear in the night will be coming from the pukeko. And the forest-dwelling morepork's call (often heard at dusk or after dark) may give you a start—it sounds just like its name. The graceful gannet is found only on offshore islands, with one exception, Cape Kidnappers near Napier.

As curious as are some New Zealand birds, however, none of them holds a candle to the tuatara, a reptilian "living fossil" whose prehistoric ancestors became extinct 100 million years ago. It is completely harmless—that is, if its looks don't scare you to death. Shaped like a miniature dinosaur, complete with a spiny ridge down the back and a thick tail, it's protected by law and confined to offshore islets.

The richness of New Zealand flora and fauna will be within easy reach wherever you find yourself around the country, and if you should miss some particular species, there are excellent zoos as well. National parks and forests provide ample showcases for the primeval bush.

4. An Invitation to Readers

In this book, as in all Frommer guides, I invite our readers to participate in future editions. Let me hasten to say that the judgments, opinions, and comments offered here are based on personal inspections and experiences. But change is the very nature of the travel world—accommodations and restaurants appear and disappear; change managements, ownership, and chefs; improve or go to pot. Should you find any of these conditions, please do let me know about it. And don't be shy about sharing with me any especially good discoveries or suggestions of your own—some of the best listings in this book have come from Readers' Selections that I have followed up. You have my word that each and every letter will be read by me, personally, although I find it well nigh impossible to *answer* each and every one. Be assured, however: I'm listening! Just write: Susan Poole, Prentice Hall Travel, 15 Columbus Circle, New York, NY 10023.

5. Frommer's Dollarwise Travel Club—How to Save Money on All Your Travels

In this book we'll be looking at how to get your money's worth in New Zealand, but there is a "device" for saving money and determining value on *all* your trips. It's the popular, international Frommer's Dollarwise® Travel Club, now in its 30th successful year of operation. The club was formed at the urging of numerous readers of the $-A-Day and Frommer Guides, who felt that such an organization could provide continuing travel information and a sense of community to value-minded travelers in all parts of the world. And so it does!

In keeping with the budget concept, the annual membership fee is low and is immediately exceeded by the value of your benefits. Upon receipt of $18 (U.S. residents), or $20 U.S. by check drawn on a U.S. bank or via international postal money order in U.S. funds (Canadian, Mexican, and other foreign residents) to cover one year's membership, we will send all new members the following items.

(1) Any two of the following books
Please designate in your letter which two you wish to receive:

Frommer $-A-Day® Guides
  Europe on $40 a Day
  Australia on $30 a Day
  Eastern Europe on $25 a Day
  England on $50 a Day
  Greece on $35 a Day
  Hawaii on $60 a Day
  India on $25 a Day
  Ireland on $35 a Day
  Israel on $40 a Day
  Mexico (plus Belize and Guatemala) on $35 a Day
  New York on $60 a Day

New Zealand on $45 a Day
Scandinavia on $60 a Day
Scotland and Wales on $50 a Day
South America on $35 a Day
Spain and Morocco (plus the Canary Is.) on $40 a Day
Turkey on $30 a Day
Washington, D.C. & Historic Virginia on $40 a Day

$-A-Day Guides document hundreds of budget accommodations and facilities, helping you get the most for your travel dollars.

Frommer Guides

Alaska
Australia
Austria and Hungary
Belgium, Holland & Luxembourg
Bermuda and The Bahamas
Brazil
California and Las Vegas
Canada
Caribbean
Egypt
England and Scotland
Florida
France
Germany
Italy
Japan and Hong Kong
Mid-Atlantic States
New England
New York State
Northwest
Portugal, Madeira & the Azores
Skiing USA—East
Skiing USA—West
South Pacific
Southeast Asia
Southern Atlantic States
Southwest
Switzerland and Liechtenstein
Texas
USA

Frommer Guides discuss accommodations and facilities in all price ranges, with emphasis on the medium-priced.

Frommer Touring Guides

Australia
Egypt
Florence
London
Paris
Scotland
Thailand
Venice

These new, color-illustrated guides include walking tours, cultural and historic sites, and other vital travel information.

Gault Millau
    Chicago
    France
    Hong Kong
    Italy
    London
    Los Angeles
    New England
    New York
    San Francisco
    Washington, D.C.

Irreverent, savvy, and comprehensive, each of these renowned guides candidly reviews more than 1,000 restaurants, hotels, shops, nightspots, museums, and sights.

Serious Shopper's Guides
    Italy
    London
    Los Angeles
    Paris

Practical and comprehensive, each of these handsomely illustrated guides lists hundreds of stores, selling everything from antiques to wine, conveniently organized alphabetically by category.

A Shopper's Guide to the Caribbean
Two experienced Caribbean hands guide you through this shopper's paradise, offering witty insights and helpful tips on the wares and emporia of more than 25 islands.

Beat the High Cost of Travel
This practical guide details how to save money on absolutely all travel items—accommodations, transportation, dining, sightseeing, shopping, taxes, and more. Includes special budget information for seniors, students, singles, and families.

Bed & Breakfast—North America
This guide contains a directory of more than 150 organizations that offer bed-and-breakfast referrals and reservations throughout North America. The scenic attractions and major schools and universities near the homes of each are also listed.

California with Kids
A must for parents traveling in California, providing key information on selecting the best accommodations, restaurants, and sightseeing attractions for the particular needs of the family, whether the kids are toddlers, school-age, preteens, or teens.

Caribbean Hideaways
Well-known travel author Ian Keown describes the most romantic, alluring places to stay in the Caribbean, rating each establishment on romantic ambience, food, sports opportunities, and price.

Frommer's Belgium
Arthur Frommer unlocks the treasures of a country overlooked by most travelers to Europe. Discover the medieval charm, modern sophistication, and natural beauty of this quintessentially European country.

Frommer's Cruises
This complete guide covers all the basics of cruising—ports of call, costs, fly-cruise package bargains, cabin selection booking, embarkation, and debarkation—and de-

scribes in detail more than 60 ships cruising the waters of Alaska, the Caribbean, Mexico, Hawaii, Panama, Canada, and the United States.

Frommer's Skiing Europe
Describes top ski resorts in Austria, France, Italy, and Switzerland. Illustrated with maps of each resort area. Includes supplement of Argentinian resorts.

Honeymoon Destinations
A special guide for that most romantic trip of your life, with full details on planning and choosing the destination that will be just right in the U.S. [California, New England, Hawaii, Florida, New York, South Carolina, etc.], Canada, Mexico, and the Caribbean.

Manhattan's Outdoor Sculpture
A total guide, fully illustrated with black-and-white photos, to more than 300 sculptures and monuments that grace Manhattan's plazas, parks, and other public spaces.

Marilyn Wood's Wonderful Weekends
This very selective guide covers the best mini-vacation destinations within a 200-mile radius of New York City. It describes special country inns and other accommodations, restaurants, picnic spots, sights, and activities—all the information needed for a two- or three-day stay.

Motorist's Phrase Book
A practical phrase book in French, German, and Spanish designed specifically for the English-speaking motorist touring abroad.

Paris Rendez-Vous
An amusing and *au courant* guide to the best meeting places in Paris, organized for hour-to-hour use: from power breakfasts and fun brunches, through tea at four or cocktails at five, to romantic dinners and dancing 'til dawn.

Swap and Go—Home Exchanging Made Easy
Two veteran home exchangers explain in detail all the money-saving benefits of a home exchange, and then describe precisely how to do it. Also includes information on home rentals and many tips on low-cost travel.

The Candy Apple: New York with Kids
A spirited guide to the wonders of the Big Apple by a savvy New York grandmother with a kid's-eye view to fun. Indispensable for visitors and residents alike.

The New World of Travel
From America's #1 travel expert, Arthur Frommer, an annual sourcebook with the hottest news and latest trends that's guaranteed to change the way you travel—and save you hundreds of dollars. Jam-packed with alternative new modes of travel that will lead you to vacations that cater to the mind, the spirit, and a sense of thrift.

Travel Diary and Record Book
A 96-page diary for personal travel notes plus a section for such vital data as passport and traveler's check numbers, itinerary, postcard list, special people and places to visit, and a reference section with temperature and conversion charts, and world maps with distance zones.

Where to Stay USA
By the Council on International Educational Exchange, this extraordinary guide is

the first to list accommodations in all 50 states that cost anywhere from $3 to $30 per night.

(2) Any *one* of the Frommer City Guides
Amsterdam and Holland
Athens
Atlantic City and Cape May
Boston
Cancún, Cozumel, and the Yucatán
Chicago
Dublin and Ireland
Hawaii
Las Vegas
Lisbon, Madrid, and Costa del Sol
London
Los Angeles
Mexico City and Acapulco
Minneapolis and St. Paul
Montréal and Québec City
New Orleans
New York
Orlando, Disney World, and EPCOT
Paris
Philadelphia
Rio
Rome
San Francisco
Santa Fe, Taos, and Albuquerque
Sydney
Washington, D.C.

Pocket-size guides to hotels, restaurants, nightspots, and sightseeing attractions covering all price ranges.

(3) A one-year subscription to *The Dollarwise Traveler*
This quarterly eight-page tabloid newspaper keeps you up to date on fast-breaking developments in low-cost travel in all parts of the world bringing you the latest money-saving information—the kind of information you'd have to pay $35 a year to obtain elsewhere. This consumer-conscious publication also features columns of special interest to readers: **Hospitality Exchange** (members all over the world who are willing to provide hospitality to other members as they pass through their home cities); **Share-a-Trip** (offers and requests from members for travel companions who can share costs and help avoid the burdensome single supplement); and **Readers Ask . . . Readers Reply** (travel questions from members to which other members reply with authentic firsthand information).

(4)Your personal membership card
Membership entitles you to purchase through the club all Frommer publications for a third to a half off their regular retail prices during the term of your membership.

So why not join this hardy band of international budgeteers and participate in its exchange of travel information and hospitality? Simply send your name and address, together with your annual membership fee of $18 (U.S. residents) or $20 U.S. (Canadian, Mexican, and other foreign residents), by check drawn on a U.S. bank or via international postal money order in U.S. funds to: Frommer's Dollarwise Travel Club, Inc., 15 Columbus Circle, New York, NY 10023. And please remember to specify which *two* of the books in section (1) and which *one* in section (2) you wish to receive in your initial package of members' benefits. Or, if you prefer, use the order form at the end of the book and enclose $18 or $20 in U.S. currency.

Once you are a member, there is no obligation to buy additional books. No books will be mailed to you without your specific order.

NEW ZEALAND: A TOURIST SURVEY

While certainly not the most exciting words between these covers, this chapter may well be some of the most important reading you'll do before setting off on your New Zealand trip. It deals with the preplanning and "homework," which can make the difference between returning with pleasant, happy memories or with a feeling of frustration and bewilderment.

What I'll be talking about here are the details that will help you plan a trip as carefree as possible. You'll *need* to know about such things as currency, the rate of exchange, and travel documents. You'll *want* to know when to go, how long your trip should be, what sort of clothes to pack, and what you may expect in terms of accommodations, restaurants, shopping, and things to see and do.

Since finances are at the very heart of successful budget travel, let's start with a discussion of money in New Zealand.

1. The Currency

You won't have any trouble at all with New Zealand currency. It's based on the decimal system and has coins in denominations of 1, 2, 5, 10, 20, and 50 cents, and notes in $1, $2, $5, $10, $20, and $100 amounts. From 1975 until 1982 the New Zealand dollar was at near parity with the U.S. dollar, but things have changed drastically in the past years. As a result, your U.S. money is worth (as we go to press) a little more than half again as much over there as it is at home.

What this means, of course, is that you'll be able to do more, see more, buy more, upgrade accommodations, and still stay within your $45 U.S. per day allowance for room and board. As I said right up front, in terms of New Zealand money $45 U.S. is now worth NZ$72. Far be it from me to predict that this exchange rate is going to stay in effect for the entire life of this book, so my very first financial advice is to check for the current rate at the outset, *before* you do any concrete planning. Then make any necessary adjustments to the rates shown in these pages.

The exchange rate in effect as this book is written is $1 U.S. to NZ$1.60, and all conversions listed are at that rate.

Just a word or two about the money you carry with you. There's no need, I'm sure, to say that most should be in traveler's checks, *not* in cash. But because exchange rates of foreign currencies against the U.S. dollar have fluctuated more radically recently than in years past, Deak International (one of the leading international currency exchange companies) advises that as soon as you know you'll be going to New Zealand, you should start watching daily exchange rates. A variation of only a few cents can sometimes net you considerably more buying power. Of course, for safety's sake, you won't want to convert all your precious travel dollars, no matter what the rate. Deak International suggests that if the rate is exceptionally favorable before you leave home, you should convert no more than half your funds into the foreign currency, and take the balance in traveler's checks. I should also remind you that it's a good idea to keep the record of your traveler's checks separate from the checks themselves, and to be sure to record each one you cash. If the worst should happen and you lose checks, replacement will depend on your having those uncashed numbers. Banks, of course, offer the best exchange rates, not hotels, department stores, or restaurants.

Check to see if there is a bank fee for cashing the checks; in late 1989, Countrywide Bank had none, and American Express and Thomas Cook do not charge for cashing their own checks.

American Express, MasterCard, Diners Club, and VISA credit cards are widely accepted, even in remote areas.

You may be asked upon arrival to show that you have sufficient funds to cover your expected stay without having to get a job (they're pretty picky about things like that, although I must say I've personally never been questioned). Also, when leaving you will not be allowed to carry more than $100 in New Zealand currency out of the country. It would be best to convert funds into the currency of your next destination before departure time.

READER'S BANKING SUGGESTION: "Visitors intending to stay for more than a brief period might consider opening an account at a bank that offers access to automatic teller machines. With a card, there is no need to worry about traveler's checks, and cash can be obtained until 11 p.m. I found that the Bank of New Zealand offered very good service" (S. Scott, Victoria, B.C., Canada).

---

2. Preparing for Your Trip

Good preparation makes for good travel, and in this section you'll find both essential matters, such as passports and visas, and a few suggestions to make your pre-travel preparations easier and better.

Special Note: One of the first items I pack any time I head overseas is a handy calculator/currency converter. Put out by Deak International, it's credit-card size and functions as well for straight mathematical computations as it does for converting foreign currency units into U.S. equivalents. Best of all, you set the exchange rate just once and it remains constant even when you push the "off" button. As exchange rates change, it's a blessedly simple matter to set in the new rate. Retailing for $15, the "International Currency Converter" is available at most Deak International offices, or by mail or telephone from Deak International, 630 Fifth Ave., New York, NY 10019 (tel. 212/757-6915).

TRAVEL DOCUMENTS

You'll need a passport for entry to New Zealand, and it must be valid for no less than three months beyond the date you plan to depart. A travel tip about passports: It's a good idea to make two photocopies of the identification page of your passport (the one with your photo), as well as any other travel documents, then leave one copy at home and carry the other with you. You'll save yourself a lot of hassle if you and those vital papers part company and you have to have them replaced! The photocopies will not serve as valid documents, but they'll furnish the information necessary to cut through miles of red tape to get new ones.

For a stay of less than three months, you won't need a visa (providing you don't intend to work, study, or undergo medical treatment) if you're a citizen of the United States, Canada, Great Britain (allowed a six months' stay), Australia, Austria, Belgium, Denmark, Finland, Federal Republic of Germany, Greece, Iceland, Ireland, Italy, Japan, Liechtenstein, Luxembourg, Malta, Monaco, the Netherlands, Norway, Portugal, Spain, Sweden, Switzerland, and Singapore. The same applies to French nationals.

If you wish to stay beyond the limits stated above, or if your nationality is not listed, consult your nearest New Zealand Embassy, High Commission, or consulate for information on obtaining the appropriate visa. Americans who want to stay longer than three months may obtain a visa application from the consular office nearest their home. The New Zealand Embassy is located at 37 Observatory Circle NW, Washington, DC 20008 (tel. 202/328-4880), and there are consular offices in Los Angeles and New York. Still other consulates may be found at the New Zealand Tourist and Publicity Travel Office addresses shown below. No fee, but you'll need a photograph. For information on working-holiday visas, inquire at one of the consulates for current regulations.

No certificate of vaccination is currently required of any traveler arriving in New Zealand. However, officials are quick to point out that should you develop an illness or skin rash, you should see a doctor and say you've recently arrived in the country.

Three things visitors must show before entry permission is granted: a confirmed onward or round-trip ticket; enough money for their New Zealand stay—figure NZ$1,000 ($625) per person per month, or NZ$400 ($250) with accommodation already paid (credit cards are acceptable as evidence of funds)—and the necessary documents to enter the next country on their itinerary or to reenter the country from which they came.

There is no Customs duty on any personal effects you bring into the country and intend to take away with you. Also duty free are 200 cigarettes or half a pound of tobacco or 50 cigars, as well as 4.5 liters of wine or beer, one bottle of spirits or liqueur (up to 1.125 liters), and goods up to a total combined value of NZ$500 ($312.50) for your own use or that you are bringing as a gift. If you plan to take in anything beyond those limits, best contact the New Zealand Customs Department, Head Office, Wellington, New Zealand, or the nearest embassy or consulate office, *before* you arrive. Ask for their publication *Customs Guide for Travelers*.

TOURIST INFORMATION

One of the most useful things you can do in planning a visit to New Zealand is to contact the **New Zealand Tourist and Publicity (NZTP) Office** nearest you in

North America for their comprehensive publication, *The New Zealand Book*. It will be your constant traveling companion, and even before leaving home it's a perfect complement to your advance reading (like this book!). They'll also include helpful brochures. Travel consultants in each office will be happy to help with any specific queries you may have.

When you arrive in New Zealand, this same government department operates both an information service and a booking service (for transportation, accommodations, sightseeing—almost anything). Staffs in every office are experts and eager to help you in any way possible.

You'll find New Zealand addresses for the NZTP offices listed in each destination section. In North America, here are the details:

☐ **NZTP,** 10960 Wilshire Blvd., Suite 1530, Los Angeles, CA 90024 (tel. 213/477-8241)

☐ **NZTP,** 630 Fifth Ave., Suite 530, New York, NY 10111 (tel. 212/698-4650)

☐ **NZTP,** IBM Tower, 701 West Georgia St., Suite 1260, Vancouver, BC, V7Y 1B6 Canada (tel. 604/684-2117)

Before your trip, you might also want to look at one or two travel videos about New Zealand. They really make the country, its diversity, and its people come alive and help you in determining the places you most want to visit. Several good ones —and hopefully one or more of them will be available in the travel section of your local video store—include *New Zealand: A World on Its Own* (25 minutes), *New Zealand on My Mind* (produced by the NZTP, 25 minutes), and *Utterly New Zealand* with Leeza Gibbons (40 minutes).

WHAT TO PACK

When planning your New Zealand wardrobe, there is one basic tenet you can hang on to, no matter when you plan to go or what you plan to do: dress in Kiwiland, for the most part, is *informal.* Men will want to take along a jacket and tie; women, at least one dress or skirt for those restaurants or hotels that have a dress code at dinner. Otherwise, casual is the keynote.

When you plan to come will of course play a big part in your dress decisions, so study the next section carefully and remember that the seasons will be those of the *southern* hemisphere. There are, however, few temperature extremes either in the subtropical tip of the North Island or in the cooler South Island. Auckland, for example, has an average midsummer temperature of 73°F, with 57°F the midwinter average. Queenstown's summer average is 72°F, with 46°F about the lowest in winter. Generally, you can look for balmy days in the Bay of Islands, cool-to-cold down in the Southern Alps. That translates into layering: a warm sweater, long-sleeved blouses to be worn over short sleeves, sleeveless knit vests—that sort of thing. One item I've found useful is a pair of cotton knit or polypropylene "longjohns" to wear under lightweight trousers when I get down to the cooler climes. Combined with a zip-in-lining jacket, they've seen me through two fall-to-winter stays.

What you plan to do will also determine what clothes you pack. New Zealand offers some of the best tramping in the world, and if that's what you plan to do, bring along suitable clothing, sturdy boots, backpack, and the necessary utensils if you'll be camping overnight. I might add here, however, that you needn't bring along boots and heavy coats if the extent of your tramping will be an organized trek on the glaciers—both will be provided by your guide. If you travel like most people, you'll simply be moving from place to place and sightseeing, and for that just be sure the clothes you take along are comfortable, easy to pack, and washable. Incidentally, most of those great motels I'll be telling you about later in this chapter have washing and drying facilities. One item no one should omit is comfortable shoes—no place on earth is appealing when your feet hurt!

Now for one bit of advice that stems from my own experience of returning with an overstuffed suitcase that was nice and light when I left home: there's no way you're going to be able to resist those terrific natural-wool sweaters (especially the hand-knits), and you'll save yourself oodles of packing troubles if you leave the ones you now own at home, then pick up one (I *dare* you to buy just one!) and wear it during your trip. Men will no doubt be tempted in warm weather to adopt the universal New Zealand male dress of walking shorts, high socks, and short-sleeve shirts. In other words, leave some packing room—you'll be wearing some of your nicest souvenirs.

Besides clothing, there are a few other carry-alongs: a washcloth in a plastic bag, since they're seldom furnished in New Zealand accommodations; a travel alarm clock; prescriptions for any medication or glasses that are essential to your comfort and well-being; a flashlight if you'll be driving after dark; a pen for all those postcards; and any small personal items you're just not comfortable without.

Sports enthusiasts may want to bring along favorite fishing rods, golf clubs, or skis, all of which are allowed through Customs, but these items are readily available in New Zealand. Many fishing guides furnish equipment, and clubs can be rented at most golf courses. If the hostels will be your home away from home, bring along a sleeping bag or sheets and a pillowcase. Blankets and linens can be rented.

---

3. When to Come

Weatherwise, you're safe to visit New Zealand any time of the year. As I said earlier, temperatures are never extreme, although I've experienced days warmer than those midsummer averages and a degree or two below the midwinter averages quoted. One thing to keep in mind, however, is that on a visit that takes you to both islands, you'll be going from a subtropical climate in the north of the North Island to the coolness (sometimes coldness) of the South Island.

Nor is there a specific rainy season, although the west coast of the South Island can experience up to 100 inches or more of rain a year on its side of the Southern Alps, while just over those mountains to the east rainfall will be a moderate 20 to 30 inches. Rain is heavier in the west on the North Island as well, with precipitation on the whole ranging from 40 to 70 inches annually. Milford Sound holds the record as the wettest spot in the country (and also perhaps the most beautiful—a personal bias!) with an annual downpour of 365 inches; fortunately, it doesn't rain every day or all day long.

As for sunshine, you'll find more in the north and east of both islands, with the Bay of Islands and the Nelson/Marlborough Sounds area leading sun spots. Frost and snow in the North Island are mainly confined to high country such as Mount Egmont and the peaks in Tongariro National Park, so if it's snow or snow-related sports you're after, look for them in the South Island. Even there, skiing is not a year-round activity, so a little research on specific destinations is in order before you set your dates. One of my visits to Queenstown, for example, was in mid-June, and local headlines announced "One More Dump and We Ski." I'll get into that in more detail later in this chapter (see "Where to Go and What to Do").

SEASONS

Seasons, as I've said before, are those of the *southern* hemisphere, thus the exact opposite of ours. There just isn't a bad season to travel, so your own schedule and interests will set your timing priorities. A fundamental guideline, however, is that during Kiwi holiday times, accommodations can be very tight. So if you plan to come between mid-December and January 30, when New Zealand families are traveling about their country on annual "hols," or during the Easter, May, or August school holidays (see below), prebooking is an absolute must. Here's a brief season-by-season rundown and the holiday schedule.

Spring

September, October, November. This is one of the best times to visit, since Kiwis are going about their business activities, schools are in full session, innkeepers will greet you with delight—with or without a booking—and the countryside is bright with blossoming fruit trees and brand-new baby lambs.

Summer

December, January, February. Beaches and boats are primary preoccupations of the natives during these months, and resorts are booked to capacity. Advance planning will let you share these sun-filled days, although you should be prepared for slightly higher accommodation rates. It's a fun time to visit if you get your bookings under way early enough.

Fall

March, April, May. In my personal opinion, this is a great time to visit New Zealand. The weather is pleasant and just cool enough in southern parts to remind you that winter is on its way, while in the Bay of Islands region midday and early afternoons are still shirt-sleeve warm. Poplars are a brilliant gold, and more subtle foliage changes can be seen in the forests. Just remember those Easter and May (two weeks) school holidays, when bookings will be tight.

Winter

June, July, August. Okay, you ski buffs—this is the time when your ski calendar goes on a year-round basis. From about mid-June on, the slopes are a skier's dream. Booking ahead at major ski resorts is certainly advisable, but you can nearly always count on finding accommodations within an easy drive even if you arrive with nothing confirmed. Around the rest of the country, this is another season you can pretty much amble around without booking ahead—except, of course, for that aforementioned two-week school holiday in August.

HOLIDAYS

Statutory holidays are: January 1 (New Year's Day), February 6 (Waitangi Day), Good Friday, Easter Monday, April 25 (Anzac Day), June 1 (Queen's Birthday), October 26 (Labor Day), December 25 (Christmas Day), and December 26 (Boxing Day).

Holidays celebrated locally are: January 22 (Wellington), January 29 (Auckland), January 29 (Northland, that is, Bay of Islands), February 1 (Nelson), March 23 (Otago and Southland, that is, Dunedin, Queenstown, Invercargill), March 31 (Taranaki), November 1 (Hawke's Bay and Marlborough), December 1 (Westland), and December 16 (Canterbury).

School holidays last for 2½ to 3 weeks and fall in May, August, and December—and I repeat, *that's* when Kiwi families are on the move holidaying it up, so be *sure* of your bookings during those months.

SPECIAL EVENTS

Aside from seasonal and holiday considerations, your decision when to come to New Zealand may well be influenced by a special interest of your own. Well, there's *something* pretty special going on almost every month, so as a guide, here's a list of festivals, sports highlights, and other events during the year—bear in mind, however, that this is simply a *guide,* and to avoid disappointment, you should check with the NZTP for exact dates or to see if these events are scheduled during the year you plan to come.

January

Commonwealth Games (January 24 to February 3, 1990, only)	Auckland
Auckland Cup (galloping)	Auckland
Wellington Cup (galloping)	Wellington
National Yearling Sales	Wellington
Motueka Wine and Art Festival	Nelson
Men's Benson & Hedges International Tennis Tournament	Auckland
Women's International Tennis Tournament	Auckland
Anniversary Day Yachting Regatta	Auckland
NZ Power Boat Ass. Races	Lake Wakatipu
Nissan Mobile 500 Car Race	Wellington
NZ Grand Prix	Christchurch

February

Cricket	Napier
Polo	Auckland
Big Game Fishing Councils Open Contest	Bay of Islands
	Auckland
	Whitianga
	Waihau
	Gisborne
	Napier
	Invercargill
	Dunedin
	Tairua
	Whangamata
NZ Hang-Gliding Championships	Wanaka
Fruit Festival	Cromwell
Festival Week	Dunedin
Waitangi Festival	Waitangi
Waikato Racing Club	Hamilton

March

Festival of Arts (even-numbered years only)	Wellington
International Shearing Contest	Masterton
Ngaruawahia River Regatta	Ngaruawahia
National Surf Lifesaving	Taranaki
Round the Bays Run	Auckland
Interdominion Pacing and Trotting Championships	Christchurch

April through September

Rugby Season	All New Zealand

April

Auckland Racing Club Easter Festival	Auckland
Auckland Trotting Club Great Northern Pacing Derby	Auckland
Highland Games	Hastings
Fishing Contest	Taupo
Arrowtown Autumn Festival	Arrowtown
Easter Arts Festival	Alexandra

May

Fletcher Marathon	Rotorua
National Woolcraft Festival	Christchurch
Duke of Marlborough Billfish Tournament	Russell

June

National Agricultural Field Days	Hamilton
Auckland Racing Club Cornwall Cup	Auckland

July

Queenstown Winter Festival	Queenstown

August

Grand National Steeplechase	Canterbury

September

Boat Show	Whangarei

October

Blossom Festival	Alexandra
Rotorua Gallops	Rotorua
International Trout Fishing Tournament	Rotorua
Rhododendron Week	Dunedin

November

NZ Cup Carnival	Christchurch
International Trout Fishing Competition	Rotorua

December

Festival of Roses	Queenstown
Horse Racing (NZ Derby, Queen Elizabeth Handicap, and others)	Auckland

---

4. How Long to Stay

This can be a problem, for New Zealand has so much to see and do you'll have a hard time fitting in everything. But it *is* possible to plan itineraries that will hit the high spots. Travel counselors at NZTP offices are most helpful in this respect. Here are a few sample itineraries as well. You'll note that you'll have to cover some of the longer stretches by flying. Those flights, however, will be on rather small, low-flying planes, with breathtaking views of the countryside below and awesome mountain peaks that ring the landscape.

7 DAYS (NORTH ISLAND ONLY)

Day 1: Arrive Auckland in early morning; sightseeing in afternoon.

Day 2: Drive from Auckland (or take tour bus, which allows time for sightseeing) to Waitomo, tour caves and glowworm grotto, then on through wooded hills and pastureland dotted with sheep and cattle to Rotorua (221 miles).

Day 3: Full day of sightseeing; Maori concert or hangi in evening.
Day 4: Early-morning flight to Bay of Islands; launch cruise in afternoon.
Day 5: Entire day of sightseeing, or take the day-long bus excursion to Cape Reinga and the Ninety-Mile Beach.
Day 6: Drive from Bay of Islands to Auckland (234 miles, about 7½ hours), with sightseeing stops at Waipoua Kauri Forest, Dargaville.
Day 7: Sightseeing most of day; early-evening departure for overseas destination.

7 DAYS (SOUTH ISLAND ONLY)

Day 1: Arrive Auckland early morning; fly to Christchurch; sightseeing in afternoon.
Day 2: Drive along the east coast from Christchurch to Dunedin (225 miles, about 5½ hours), across part of the Canterbury Plains and through the seaside resort of Timaru and the "White Stone City" of Oamaru.
Day 3: Entire day sightseeing in Dunedin, with drive or tour-bus excursion to Otago Peninsula to see Larnach Castle, Penguin Place, and the royal albatross colony (get your visitor's permit in Dunedin).
Day 4: Early start for drive from Dunedin to Queenstown (176 miles, about 5 hours), through pleasant farmland; sightseeing in late afternoon.
Day 5: Day-long excursion to Milford Sound (bus in, fly out), including launch cruise to Tasman Sea. (If you're pressed for time, fly in and out; the cruise is included in the price.)
Day 6: Allow about 10 hours for the drive from Queenstown to Christchurch (302 miles), which passes through beautiful Kawarau Gorge, then north past breathtaking views of Mount Cook at Lake Pukaki and on across the Canterbury Plains. (*Note:* An option is an early-morning flight to Mount Cook, with flightseeing in the afternoon, flying on to Christchurch and Auckland on Day 7.)
Day 7: Sightseeing in the morning; midafternoon flight to Auckland, arriving in time for evening overseas departure.

10 DAYS (BOTH ISLANDS)

Day 1: Arrive in Auckland in early morning; sightseeing in afternoon.
Day 2: Drive or take tour bus to Rotorua via Waitomo caves and glowworm grotto.
Day 3: Full day of sightseeing in Rotorua; Maori concert or hangi in evening.
Day 4: Early-morning flight from Rotorua to Christchurch, sightseeing in afternoon.
Day 5: Early-morning flight to Mount Cook; flightseeing over glaciers, icefields, and mountains in afternoon.
Day 6: Early-morning flight to Queenstown; sightseeing in afternoon.
Day 7: Day-long trip to Milford Sound (by tour bus and/or plane) for launch cruise to Tasman Sea.
Day 8: Early-afternoon flight to Dunedin; sightseeing in late afternoon.
Day 9: Drive or take tour-bus excursion to Otago Peninsula to see Larnach Castle, Penguin Place, and the royal albatross colony.
Day 10: Sightseeing in morning; early-afternoon flight to Auckland (with plane change in Christchurch), arriving in time for evening overseas departure.

14 DAYS (BOTH ISLANDS)

Day 1: Arrive Auckland early morning; fly to Christchurch; spend afternoon sightseeing.
Day 2: Early-morning flight over Canterbury Plains to Mount Cook, in the heart of the Southern Alps; flightseeing in afternoon.
Day 3: Early-morning flight to Queenstown; sightseeing in afternoon.

Day 4: Day-long tour-bus excursion to Milford Sound for launch cruise to Tasman Sea.

Day 5: Drive from Queenstown to Dunedin (176 miles, about 5 hours), through pleasant farming country.

Day 6: Drive or take tour-bus excursion to Otago Peninsula to visit Larnach Castle, Penguin Place, and the royal albatross colony.

Day 7: Scenic early-morning flight from Dunedin to Wellington, following the east coastline and crossing Cook Strait; sightseeing in afternoon.

Day 8: Sightseeing in Wellington.

Day 9: Drive or take InterCity coach from Wellington to Napier (203 miles) through rugged—and scenic—Manawatu Gorge.

Day 10: Sightseeing in Hawke's Bay area around Napier; then drive to Taupo (96 miles) and on to Rotorua (55 miles).

Day 11: Full day of sightseeing in Rotorua; Maori concert or hangi in evening.

Day 12: Drive or take tour bus to Waitomo to tour caves and glowworm grotto; then on to Auckland (221 miles).

Day 13: Full day of sightseeing in Auckland.

Day 14: Depart Auckland for overseas destination.

All these itineraries are possible, but I strongly recommend that, if there's any way you can manage it, you plan a minimum of *three weeks* to see both islands at something like a leisurely pace. Some of New Zealand's beauty spots simply invite (almost demand) loitering, and there are several you will have to omit on a shorter visit. A month would be even better. Failing that, I personally would stick to one island per visit for the shorter time periods and take in such memorable extras as the Bay of Islands and the Coromandel Peninsula on the North Island and the Banks Peninsula and Stewart Island in the south. You will have come a long way to see New Zealand, and it would be a shame to get around at too fast a trot.

5. Where to Stay

New Zealand presents a vast supermarket of accommodation choices even in our budget range. The sheer number and variety of places to lay your weary head will add spice to your trip, and although there is no national system for inspection or grading, it is rare to come across a single one that isn't spotlessly clean, an accomplishment I have yet to see in any other country in my travels.

We'll examine the variety in detail below, but first, there are some elements they all share. Check-in time is usually around 2 p.m.; checkout, 10 a.m. There's no tipping (unless you feel especially grateful for some special service). Some hotels and motels charge an extra NZ$1 (65¢) for one-night stays, and in some resort areas, such as the Bay of Islands and Queenstown, rates go up during peak seasons. Almost all have discount rates for children. Even the most "budget" of budget accommodations will have an electric kettle (which goes by the name of "jug" in New Zealand), tea and coffee, sugar and milk, either in your room or in a centrally located public room—at no charge (they *know* it's too much to ask of guests to send them out for such necessities). All have telephones either in-room or in a public room, hall, or office available to guests, except in the case of some hostels. Almost all have laundry facilities, which means electric washing machines and either a dryer or drying rooms —and there's only a small charge for their use. With the exception of some hostels and cabins, all have good winter heating, either central or individual room heaters. There's not much air conditioning, but not much need for it either.

To the above, I'd like to add one little message from my New Zealand accommodations friends: it seems that we Americans are highly valued as guests for many reasons, including the fact that they say we always leave the premises in such good order (for once, we're the "pretty Americans"). Our one failing has to do with that "jug," and I think it's because we're so accustomed to appliances being turned on and off by thermostatic controls. Well, where the jugs are concerned, in most cases it's up to *you* to unplug it or flip the control switch on the wall socket when the water comes to a boil; otherwise, it keeps boiling away, the jug's heating element burns out, and our "highly valued" status becomes a little less so. So keep an eye on it and be sure it's turned off when you've made your tea or coffee.

I know I've told you this before, but it bears repeating: during peak travel months, *you must book ahead.* "Peak" means mid-December through January, Easter, and the two (two-week) school holidays in May and August. New Zealanders are on the road in droves during those periods—most spend their holidays within their own country, and most are as budget-conscious as we are. They do their booking months in advance, and so should you to avoid disappointment. When you have selected the accommodations you prefer, simply write as early as possible enclosing a money order or bank draft to cover the first night's lodging and an International Reply Coupon for confirmation to be mailed back to you. If you should have to cancel and you do it within a reasonable time, you'll usually receive a prompt refund, although occasionally there will be a small service charge.

The accommodations listed in this book, I rather immodestly believe, are a pretty select group, but for a complete listing of all accommodations available around the country, the NZTP Travel Department publishes an excellent *Where to Stay* guide, which you can obtain from all their offices in North America. It lists hotel, motel, bed-and-breakfast, and farm accommodations, as well as private-home-host organizations. All price ranges are included. Also, the Automobile Association covers the subject very comprehensively in a series of accommodation guidebooks: hotels and motels in the North Island, motor camps and campgrounds in the North Island, and a "South Island Handbook." If you're an AAA member at home, you'll have reciprocal privileges in New Zealand and will have no difficulty picking up all three guides. Or contact them in advance at 166 Willis St., Wellington.

BOOKING SERVICES

The **New Zealand Tourist and Publicity Travel Office** (known throughout Kiwiland as **NZTP**) has offices located in Auckland, Rotorua, Wellington, Christchurch, Queenstown, and Dunedin (you'll find addresses in the destination chapters of this book) that will make accommodation bookings in all price ranges and all locations throughout the country. They'll also make your transportation bookings. Those services are combined with their free, government-sponsored travel-information service, with one important difference—when they handle your bookings, they're acting as full-fledged, profit-making travel agents. They list only their commission clients (that is, they won't have every accommodation in this book on their lists), and they charge a small fee for each accommodation booking plus long-distance or telegram charges; and you can get two free transportation bookings, after which there is a small charge. If you go to them only for travel *advice* or for help in sorting out travel schedules and then do the actual bookings yourself, their expert staffs are at your service at no charge whatsoever.

Of course, there are bound to be times when you need that kind of help and aren't anywhere near one of those six offices. Not to worry—just look for a Public Relations Office (PRO), Visitors' Bureau, or something similar. There's no standard marking (like the international "i" symbol) used in New Zealand, but there are few places in the country that do not have some central information and booking office. If you can't find one on your own, ask a local—you may just wind up with another Kiwi friend.

YOUTH HOSTELS

You'll be way below our $45-a-day cost if you utilize New Zealand's excellent network of hostels. And aside from saving all that money, you'll be mingling with hostelers from all over the world as well as a fair few friendly natives. It's a great way to travel, and you'll find Kiwi hostels, both private and members of the Youth Hostels Association, way above average.

There are more than 42 hostels throughout New Zealand, many in choice scenic locations—you'll be paying hostel rates for a beachfront, lakefront, or mountainside room just down the way from a luxury hotel whose guests are paying an arm and a leg for the same view! The hostels vary both in size and style, and their architecture ranges from comfortable old farmhouses to slick, modern edifices.

Here's what you must do to qualify: be a Youth Hostel member (and, if you're age 5 or over, "youth" has no age limitations) with a valid membership card. In the United States, you can join through **American Youth Hostels, Inc.,** P.O. Box 37613, Washington, DC 20013, by sending $10 if you're under 18 (youth membership), $25 if you're 18 to 54 (adult), or $15 if you're 55 or older (senior). You can join in New Zealand for NZ$10 ($6.25); under age 15, free. Either card is good internationally. If you join in New Zealand, you'll receive free the invaluable New Zealand *YHA Handbook;* overseas members pay NZ$1.50 (95¢). It describes each hostel in detail, with transportation, food shops, and other useful information for each location. It also sets out all hostel rules and regulations (leave things tidy, no drugs, liquor, gambling, or animals).

You'll need to bring a sleeping bag or rent linens for a nominal fee; blankets are provided. Also, if you plan to use the fully equipped kitchens, bring your own cup, plate, and cutlery, as well as a tea towel. Managers are called wardens, and most reside in the hostel itself, and those who don't live nearby—the warden is the person to whom you show your card and pay your fee. Don't show up after 11 p.m., however, because that's curfew time, and you can be refused entry; hostels open at 5 p.m. daily; and you'll have to vacate the premises between the hours of 10 a.m. and 5 p.m., when all hostels are closed. Hostel offices are usually open to accept bookings between 8 and 10 a.m., 5 to 6:30 p.m., and 8 to 11 p.m. Your booking will be held until 7 p.m., so when you cross the Cook Strait by ferry in either direction, be *sure* it's the afternoon crossing, since the evening ferry will arrive too late for you to stay in a YHA hostel. (Private hostels may have space and be open later.)

New Zealanders are great hostelers within their own country—there are some 31,000 native members—which makes advance booking every bit as important at hostels during peak months as in any other type of accommodation. In fact, you'll be well advised to book ahead in all major resort areas or large cities at any time of the year. You can do so by sending, *at least 14 days prior to your first requested booking,* a money order or bank draft for your entire stay, along with an International Reply Coupon, directly to the warden of each hostel, or to the **YHA National Reservations Centre,** P.O. Box 1687, Auckland (tel. 09/794-224). Bookings are usually limited to three consecutive nights in any one hostel, and fees range from NZ$11 ($6.90) to NZ$15 ($9.40), half that for Juniors.

For even greater savings, request the **20/200 card,** which gives you 20 nights' accommodation in youth hostels throughout New Zealand for NZ$200 ($125), or an assured NZ$10 ($6.25) a night. The **9/99 card** gives you nine nights for NZ$99 ($61.90), or NZ$11 ($6.90) a night.

There are a number of benefits that come along with your YHA membership, such as travel insurance, discounts on rail and ferry transportation, sightseeing attractions and activities, and clothing. There's also a helpful **Travel Section** which actually offers hostel package tours. Planned with a great deal of flexibility, they're based on public transportation and the use of hostels throughout. The Travel Section issues several informative touring booklets, which outline services and tours; they are available (along with any specific information you'd like) by writing YHANZ Travel Section, P.O. Box 436, Christchurch.

National headquarters for the **Youth Hostel Association of New Zealand (YHANZ)** is in Christchurch, 28 Worcester St. (tel. 03/799-970), in the Arts Centre just across the street from the Rolleston House hostel. Hours are 8:30 a.m. to 4:40 p.m.

There are also some good privately run hostels, and you will find many listed in this book.

MOTOR CAMPS, CABINS, AND CAMPING

New Zealand is a camper's delight, whether you're toting a tent to pitch, back-packing and looking for a cabin at night, or hauling along a motor caravan. There are facilities to suit all needs, and they're all over the place. The nice thing is that you'll many times find the whole array available in a single motor camp!

On grounds that are sometimes quite extensive—and many times in prime mountain, lakeside, or beachfront locations—there are **campsites** that can cost as little as NZ$8 ($5) per person per night. **Caravan sites** with power connections run about NZ$9 ($5.65) per person per night.

Then, there are **rustic cabins or huts** that contain beds or bunks, pillows, a table, and chairs. Many times, linen and blankets can be rented; otherwise, you bring your own. You must also supply your own crockery and cutlery in most cases. Cabins come with two, four, or six beds, and on average the cost for a basic cabin is NZ$30 ($18.75) for two people. A "Tourist" cabin, which has hot and cold water and cooking facilities, will run about NZ$32 ($20) per night for two. Both cabins and campsite occupants have full use of centrally located shower and laundry facilities. There is also a centrally located modern kitchen, with hot- and cold-water sink units, fridge, and hotplates—a great place to meet fellow travelers. Needless to say, the "leave it tidy" doctrine applies.

Rubbing elbows with those "bare essentials" accommodations, almost all motor camps will have at least one block of **tourist flats.** They are rustic in decor, and you still must bring the bedding, but they have one or two separate bedrooms, cooking facilities (all have running water), and private showers. Prices run about NZ$50 ($31.25) for double occupancy.

In the chapters that follow, you'll find several motor camps listed, which I believe are outstanding, and for a complete directory, just contact the Camp & Cabin Association of New Zealand for their official publication: Secretary, C.C.A., 4A Kanawa St., Waikanae, North Island (tel. 058/34781).

Trampers will find basic, rustic **bunkhouses** or huts in all national parks, with water and outdoor cooking areas provided. Maps of their locations are furnished by park rangers, who also collect a small fee.

THE Ys

Unlike other New Zealand accommodations, both the YWCA and YMCA hostels are booked to capacity from February through November, when students fill the available space. This can be a real boon, however, especially in city areas, if you have trouble finding a room during those peak months of December through February when students are on holiday.

Most Y rooms are, as you might expect, very basic, and in a few cases have a rather grubby aspect, while others are as light and cheerful as you could wish. Beds are narrow, floors are rugless, and showers and baths are down the hall, with no water basins in rooms. There are, however, laundry rooms, TV lounges, and the usual Y facilities. Some provide full board, and all serve breakfast. You'll find Ys in Auckland, Wanganui, Christchurch, and Dunedin (see the individual chapter listings). Each has its own rate structure, but you can expect them to be in the neighborhood of NZ$17 ($10.75) or slightly higher.

Especially for the young traveler, the Ys are a pleasant travel base, since the majority of other guests are likely to be in a similar age group (although that should by no means deter those in upper age brackets). For more information, write to the YWCA of New Zealand, P.O. Box 1780, Wellington.

BED-AND-BREAKFASTS

I have always favored B&B accommodations when traveling, both because that terrific cooked breakfast will very often see me through until dinnertime (saving the cost of lunch) and because when I'm tired of my own company, there are always other guests to get to know in the lounge (I've made some enduring friendships in just this way over the years).

Unfortunately, New Zealand is not blessed with a plentiful supply of the bed-and-breakfast establishments so many travelers consider the only way to travel. They are on the increase, however, and I have managed to ferret out a number that are real gems. You'll find them described in detail in the following chapters.

When doing your scouting, you should know that B&Bs go by two names in New Zealand: **guesthouses** and **private hotels.** Both provide comfortable, homey (New Zealanders say "homely") rooms with hot and cold running water (H&C), bath and shower down the hall, and a huge cooked breakfast. And both are unlicensed (serve no liquor). Guesthouses, however, are limited to bed-and-breakfast, with dinners sometimes served guests by special arrangement, but never to nonguests. Private hotels (which are usually much larger), on the other hand, serve all meals to both residents and nonresidents. Rates in both will run about NZ$70 ($43.75) double.

One of the most reliable of several organizations that specialize in bed-and-breakfast bookings throughout New Zealand is New Zealand Home Hospitality Limited. Details are available through travel agents, or in the U.S., by calling toll free 800/351-2323 weekdays (800/351-2317 in California); in New Zealand, contact the NZTP offices in Auckland or Christchurch.

There is also an excellent directory, new in 1987, published by Moonshine Press, 27 Marine Dr., Mahina Bay, Eastbourne, Wellington, called *The New Zealand Bed and Breakfast Book,* and available in most New Zealand bookshops. Descriptions are written by the hosts themselves in such surprisingly revealing style that you get a sense of their personality from their own words.

If you have chosen Air New Zealand as your international carrier, an added bonus is that you're eligible for Hotpac discounts on accommodations, as well as a wide range of sightseeing attractions and activities. Ask for "The Go as You Please Book" and the "Good Night Book" from your travel agent or any Air New Zealand travel center in New Zealand, or call toll free 800/223-9494.

READER'S BED-AND-BREAKFAST SUGGESTION: "I especially want to inform you of an excellent group of B&Bs that have joined together to form the **Federation Travel Hotels/ Motels.** I stayed in nine of the Federation group and found them all to be very comfortable, offering full English-style breakfasts (and sometimes dinners) and maintaining a consistently high standard of excellence." (G. Grenfell, Hollister, Calif.). [*Author's Note:* You'll find several of these listed in this book. For a brochure detailing all members, write: The Secretary, NZ Hotels/Motels Federation, Inc., 123 Grey St., Palmerston North, New Zealand (tel. 063/86-928).]

MOTEL FLATS

I once wrote in a travel guide, "A motel is a motel is a motel." Well, while that was certainly true for the location under discussion, it is definitely *not* true for New Zealand! If you think you've seen enough motels to know all variations, just wait until you see them in this country—they give a new definition to the word. Get set for a rave about the best budget travel value you're likely to run across anywhere.

You'll note that the heading for this section is "Motel Flats," not simply "Motels." And therein lies the difference between New Zealand's offerings and those we're accustomed to under that latter label. Most—if not all—have been built in recent years, since tourism as a full-fledged industry has been a late bloomer in New Zealand. What this means is that all modern conveniences have been incorporated in their designs. And the last few years have seen the addition of spa pools (we know those as Jacuzzis) in most properties. All of which is a bonus, but not the biggest bonus. That comes in the form of a "flat," a fully developed, fully equipped *apartment* as opposed to the room (no matter how spacious, a room is not a flat!) and bath that comprise our motel units.

What you'll find in Kiwi motel flats are: a lounge, usually with sofas that open into beds; one or two separate bedrooms (except in the case of "bed-sitters," when the lounge becomes your bedroom at night); a kitchen or kitchenette (and here's where "fully equipped" takes on special meaning, for they come with everything from pots and pans to dishes and silverware to potato peelers to the obligatory electric jug to coffee, tea, sugar, and milk in the fridge, right down to the tea towel); and a bathroom. If you're a taker of baths, I should warn you that most bathrooms have showers rather than a bathtub, although more and more places are installing both, and in some the shower rim is built up and there's a stopper for the drain, so you can fill the "shower" and proceed to bathe in a square "tub." The units are so well planned that where there are two bedrooms, the bathroom is usually accessible to each separately, thus providing privacy for two couples or a family traveling together. There's a TV and radio in virtually every unit, telephones in most, and personal touches such as plants, paintings, and tablecloths in all. Heating is usually by means of individual heaters, and beds come with electric blankets or (most often) electric underblankets. You can count on a laundry room with automatic washer and dryer (or a drying room with a clothesline), many times with soap powder for guests' use, and most are available at a minimal charge. There are few motels (or motor inns) without an outdoor swimming pool.

It should be noted that, just like home, you'll be expected to do such elementary household chores as make beds and wash dishes. Motel flats are *not* serviced. But everything you'll need to take care of those basic jobs will be right there— dishwashing detergent, fresh linen twice a week, clean tea towels daily. Now, that's entirely to my own tastes, for I must confess to being a slow mover in the early a.m., and it's a relief to loiter leisurely, secure in the knowledge that "housekeeping" won't be pounding on the door.

A continental or cooked breakfast can be ordered the night before, with the makings brought to your room that evening so you can please yourself as to breakfast time if you're going continental, or the hot meal delivered to your unit at a pre-arranged time in the morning. Few motels have restaurants, but if you don't choose to eat in, a good restaurant will be close by.

In addition to all this, there is a bonus that goes beyond monetary values. Almost all motels are owner operated, which means there's no possibility of your running into impersonal, uncaring attitudes. To the contrary, you're very likely to leave each establishment on a first-name basis with the owners and all their family. In fact, it's one of the best ways I know to get to meet and know New Zealanders.

That, dear reader, is the description of *budget* accommodations in New Zealand! The average cost for a double in these home-like dwellings is NZ$65 ($40.75) or $20.25 U.S. per person. Singles, as I said earlier, don't fare quite as well, with an average price of NZ$55 ($34.40). And, of course, the per-person cost goes down as the number of occupants goes up: you'll pay about NZ$12 ($7.50) per extra adult, bringing the individual cost for a party of four way down.

As you can see, all New Zealand motel flats are a bargain, but the Best Western chain, which merged with Motor Lodges of New Zealand in 1989, takes things a little further and offers a bargain on top of a bargain with their **Best Western Holiday Pass.** If you stay in Best Westerns throughout your stay, you'll receive a 10% discount on all rates by presenting your card on arrival, and they have a computerized booking system that will either book ahead as you go or book the entire trip in advance if you prefer. I've found that without exception Best Westerns are tops in this type of accommodation in New Zealand, with many extras such as a higher percentage of in-house restaurants and locations that are choice for the region. In some cases their rates will be slightly higher than others in the same locality, but generally that difference is equalized by the discount program. Incidentally, Best Western motels are *individually* owned and operated, not franchised. The "chain" aspect only means that each property is rigidly inspected on a regular basis to be sure that the high standards are being maintained (those copper-bottomed pots must have *shiny* copper bottoms!).

For a directory of all 120 Best Western motels in New Zealand, write Best Western International, Inc., Attn: Marketing Services, P.O. Box 10203, Phoenix, AZ 85064. When you have selected your first night's accommodation from that directory or from this book, you can reserve in advance by calling toll free 800/528-1234 and asking for the International Desk.

Information on the Best Western Holiday Pass should be obtained *directly from Best Western in New Zealand*. Write in advance, call, or drop by their friendly office as soon as you set foot in the country: Best Western New Zealand, 97 Great South Rd., Greenlane (P.O. Box 74-346), Auckland 5 (tel. 09/5205-418). Your first Best Western host will also be able to give you full details and sign you up for the discount program.

An alternative to pre-booking at Best Western is to purchase a quantity of the **Best Western New Zealand Accommodation Passes.** Each pass costs NZ$56 ($35) plus GST (12.5%) and entitles the holder to one night's accommodation for two people at any Best Western property in New Zealand. Because of the broad range of motel types and locations, there is sometimes a small supplement that must be paid at individual motels (these are prominently listed with rates in the Best Western New Zealand Accommodations Guide). Since pass rates already include a discount, Holiday Pass discounts do not apply simultaneously—choose one or the other. Passes may be purchased through your local travel agent or direct from Best Western International in Phoenix.

Best Western New Zealand motels are participants in the **Best Western Gold Crown Club.** Holders of Gold Crown Club cards issued in the U.S. (or any other country) should request a benefits brochure to find out the additional benefits to which they are entitled.

SERVICED MOTELS

This term refers to motels just like those at home—one room and private bath —with one (very important to this tea and coffee drinker) difference: the ever-present electric jug plus tea bags and instant coffee. You'll find some scattered through the following pages, but because those in our price range tend to be small and sparsely furnished and not nearly as good value as motel flats, their numbers are few. Still, if you have a thing about not making the bed in the morning or you'd rather someone else flicked a dustcloth around, you may find them to your liking. I must say that the ones recommended here are quite on a par with their counterparts in the U.S.

LICENSED HOTELS

Most of the licensed hotels in New Zealand are luxury establishments and in a price range beyond our budget (see "Big Splurges," later in this chapter). And many of those that we could budget for, we wouldn't want to—they're relics of the days when sleeping accommodations had to be offered in order for drink to be served, and bedrooms invariably came off second (or third, fourth, or fifth) to the public drinking rooms. I've found a few whose rooms are clean, comfortable, and inexpensive. If, however, you are tempted by a listing in any of the accommodations guidebooks mentioned above, I strongly recommend that you insist on a personal inspection before plunking down a night's rent.

There is one important exception to all the above, and that is the THC hotels.

The **Tourist Hotel Corporation of New Zealand** operates about a dozen semi-luxury hotels in some of the country's remote beauty spots where commercially owned hotels would have a hard time making a go of it. The avowed purpose of the corporation is to "provide suitable accommodation in vital but remote areas." It's an admirable goal, and one that is realized in admirable style: some of the hotels have gained international recognition, such as the Château, a white-gabled, country mansion in Tongariro National Park, and the window-walled Hermitage, facing Mount Cook's majestic peak. Others of special note are at Milford Sound, Waitomo, and Franz Josef. (There are others in not-so-remote spots, such as Queenstown and Rotorua.) You may well choose one of these as your "Big Splurge" indulgence spot, since budget accommodations in off-the-beaten-track areas are sparse. Whether or not you book in, you're likely to spend some time at a THC facility somewhere along the line, for they're the very center of tourist activity in their areas—that's where you'll book many sightseeing tours, find the most pleasant public bar (and often inexpensive pub grub, as well), and go for nighttime entertainment.

You'll find the following THCs in the North Island: THC Waitangi, Paihia; THC Auckland Airport; THC Waitomo; THC Rotorua; THC Tokaanu, Lake Taupo; THC Wairakei (near Lake Taupo); THC Château, Tongariro National Park; THC James Cook, Wellington. In the South Island: THC Franz Josef; THC The Hermitage, Mount Cook; THC Wanaka; THC Queenstown; THC Milford Sound; THC Te Anau. At press time a couple of these properties were for sale, so their status may have changed by the time you pay a visit.

Pricewise, they fall into the moderately expensive category, with rates ranging from NZ$75 ($47) to NZ$150 ($93.75) double. Just as is the case with much pricier luxury hotels, however, THCs in virtually every location often offer weekend or off-season specials that bring a sparkle to bargain hunters' eyes—how about NZ$99 ($62), plus GST per person, double occupancy, for two nights, two breakfasts, and one lunch. It pays, then, to inquire about any specials offered during your visit so your itinerary can be planned to take advantage of them.

You can book THC accommodations from the U.S. by calling the **Southern Pacific Hotel Corp.** (tel. toll free 800/421-0536). In New Zealand, there's a Central Reservations Office in Wellington (tel. 04/729-179), with toll-free connections from Auckland (tel. 09/773-689) and Christchurch (tel. 03/790-718).

SPORTING LODGES

A relatively new development in New Zealand are deluxe lodges set in idyllic country surroundings. Definitely "upmarket" properties, these small retreats are—if I may coin a phrase—rustically luxurious. Well worth considering for a big splurge or two, they offer the very best in facilities, personal service, activity specials such as onsite professional guides and helipads so you can be whisked away on a moment's whim, and gourmet meals accompanied by vintage wines.

There are lodges in prime fishing country, lodges that concentrate on skiing nearby slopes, lodges that feature tramping and/or horseback riding, lodges where white-water rafting is a part of every day's activity, and . . . well, if you have a special interest, more than likely there's a host lurking somewhere in one of these lodges who'd love to cater to that and in the process pamper you within an inch of your life. If, on the other hand, your idea of perfect pampering is doing absolutely nothing but relaxing and enjoying the good life, that particular special interest is catered to in every one of the lodges.

If all that sounds like a fantasy, just take my word for it that in some of these establishments you'd have to be quite a fantasizer to dream up the extras on hand. Splurges they are—but if you're going to spend big bucks, you'll not get better value for every dollar spent than in one of these lodges. Prices in these dream spots average between NZ$250 ($156) and NZ$300 ($188), plus GST, per person per day for accommodation and meals. But, as I said, if you decide to go for it, you'll know it's money well spent.

In the United States, **Ambassador Travel,** 1035 Redondo Ave., Long Beach, CA 90804, or 3030 S. Collins Ave., Fort Collins, CO 80525 (tel. toll free 800/234-8040), can furnish details and help you find those that best fit your dreams and your "splurge" pocketbook, as can any NZTP office—in the States or in New Zealand.

FARMHOUSE AND HOME-STAY HOLIDAYS

In a country where agriculture reigns supreme, I can't think of a better place to feel the pulse of the people than on a working farm. A firsthand knowledge of just what it takes to raise all those sheep and cattle and kiwi fruit will give you more insight into New Zealand life than you could gain in any other way. Besides, what a joy to wake in the mornings to pastoral beauty and a charming country home in the midst of a host family who are delighted to have you as a guest and eager to show you around the farm!

Any NZTP office can put you in touch with several organizations that offer closeup experience on farms throughout the country. Farmhouses are also listed in the NZTP *Where to Stay* guide. There are rugged South Island sheep stations, dairy farms, farms with glowworm caves, Maori burial sites, hot springs, trout fishing, and scenery that includes magnificent mountains and coastlines. And if you want to jump in and help muster sheep on that station or groom one of the thoroughbred horses, well, you have only to let your wishes be known. On the other hand, if a day or so of quiet rusticating suits you better, that's okay too. You will have your own bedroom (sometimes with a private bath, but more often it's on a share-with-the-family basis), plus two hearty farm meals each day (dinner and breakfast), which you'll take around the family dining table.

With such a widespread network of host farms, you'll be able to stay on a farm in virtually every location you want to visit. Daily charges for bed, breakfast, and dinner, per person, average NZ$80 ($50) to NZ$100 ($62.50), plus GST.

Air New Zealand also offers a fly/drive farm holiday plan with the option of staying in the family home or in self-catering cottages on the premises. Other options include an InterCity Railways Travelpass instead of a car, and a "Go as You Please" plan that lets you arrange your own itinerary rather than pre-book the entire stay. Prices vary according to your choice of options and are quite reasonable. Bookings must be made through travel agents.

You can locate some wonderful farm-stay possibilities on the North and South Islands through **New Zealand Farm Holidays,** P.O. Box 256, Silverdale, Auckland (tel. 09/372-024). On self-drive tours, New Zealand Farm Holidays' Free & Easy Vouchers let you plan your own itinerary, selecting accommodations from the directory and calling ahead at least 48 hours in advance. Rail and coach farm tours are also available. For even more possibilities, contact **Farmhouse and Country Home Holidays,** P.O. Box 31250, Auckland 9 (tel. 09/410-8280), for their booklet of extensive listings.

Kiwi hospitality is, of course, by no means restricted to farms and rural areas—there are warm, friendly homes in cities and towns just as eager to welcome you as are the farm families. And **New Zealand Home Hospitality Ltd.,** P.O. Box 309, Nelson (tel. 054/82-424)—in the United States call the Central Reservation Office (tel. toll free 800/351-2323, 800/351-2317 in California)—can put you up with host families whose only interest is in seeing that you enjoy your time in their locality. You'll find them in beachfront and lake locations as well as in city suburbs, and all are invaluable "data banks" of local attractions, sightseeing, and history.

In most, you will be the only guest, becoming an instant member of the family. Some offer private baths; at others you'll share with the family. All serve a full cooked breakfast, and your evening meal is optional. (*Note:* Comparing notes and reporting on the day's activities over the dinner table is a decided plus when you're staying with a local family.) There are smoking and nonsmoking hosts, those with and those without pets, retired couples with no live-in children and others with lively youngsters a vital part of the family scene.

A wide variety of home-stay packages lets you choose a pre-booked holiday or a freewheeling itinerary (whether you're driving, biking, or using public transport). All packages may be booked through travel agents or any New Zealand Tourist and Publicity Office. Or write direct for their helpful brochure describing all options in detail.

According to the NZTP, farm- or home-stay guests can expect to pay about NZ$100 ($62.50) per person per night, including meals.

READER'S FARMHOUSE SELECTION: "We found **Home Hosting–Rural Tours,** in Cambridge, to be small, personal, and great value. This was definitely a highlight of our brief stay in a beautiful country. Dinner and breakfast are included, lunch is always possible, and the selection of homes in the Cambridge area is superb!" (J. Smith, Kelowna, B.C., Canada). [*Author's Note:* Full address is Home Hosting–Rural Tours, P.O. Box 228, Cambridge (tel. Joy Thomas or Helen Hicks at Maungataurtari 872).]

READER'S HOME-STAY SELECTION: "We found one home-stay organization absolutely wonderful. They put you with families throughout New Zealand, and have a choice of Budget, Medium, and Deluxe price ranges. We stayed Budget and Medium, and found the food and hosts wonderful in every case. But the best thing is that it was very inexpensive. Contact: Graeme and Judy McLean, **Hospitality Haere Mai,** P.O. Box 56-175, Auckland (tel. 09/393-869)" (C. Feldmann, Bonners Ferry, Idaho).

---

6. Where and What to Eat

Mention New Zealand and food to almost anyone and the response is "lamb." Well, I'm told by my Kiwi friends, with a groan, that the best lamb gets shipped out to the likes of you and me on our home turf. That may well be so, but I've had very good lamb in New Zealand—as well as some that wasn't so very good. No matter what the quality, however, it's served as a roast more often than not, and a well-done roast at that. Quite frankly, I've become very fond of roast **hogget** (that's sheep a little older than lamb and a little younger than mutton), and I rather suspect that that's what comes to table many times under the "lamb" label. What's not so well known outside New Zealand is their **beef,** and it's superb. Steaks and roast beef are plentiful and inexpensive. In the last year or two, venison has also appeared in more and more restaurants.

The star of Kiwi cuisine, as far as I'm concerned, however, is **seafood,** always fresh and of a wide variety. Bluff oysters are a treat on which I shamelessly gorge myself every trip—they're large and tangy, with a strong taste of the sea. Then there are the tiny whitebait, usually served in fritters, sometimes crisply fried. And the crayfish (you'll recognize the taste as that of the New Zealand rock lobster we buy frozen in the States), which is more expensive than other seafood, but worth every penny. And a fish with which I'm on a first-name basis—the John Dory—as sweet and succulent as any I've ever tasted. Up in the north of the North Island, you can sometimes find toheroa soup, a delicacy made from a small shellfish much like a cockle, which is served in a rich chowder. Trout, of course, abound in the rivers and lakes of New Zealand, but they are not sold commercially (seems Kiwis adhere to the theory that for such a sporting fish, it would be a deep indignity to be eaten by anyone who didn't land him in a fair fight!). Nevertheless, it does occasionally appear on a menu (maybe when the chef is a fisherman?).

Dairy products, too, play a starring role in the New Zealand diet, and you'll know why after your first taste of rich, creamy milk and butter that reminds you of what it *used* to taste like in this country. Both are served in generous portions in restaurants and guesthouses, so enjoy. Government subsidies keep prices low, so you can afford to indulge even for those meals you cook in motel flats. Cheeses are also delicious and inexpensive. A loaf of vogel bread (rich, whole-grain bread, which you'll find in almost any health-food store and many supermarkets), a selection of cheeses, and a bottle of good wine or beer make the perfect picnic lunch on long drives.

You'll find **meat pies** everywhere, from lunch counters in rail and bus stations to pubs to take-away shops. They're thick-crusted little pies filled with chunks of meat and gravy, and can be quite delicious. That's if they're the homemade variety, with light, flaky crusts and just the right combination of mild spices and herbs. Keep an eye out for the "homemade" sign, which is more prevalent than you might imagine, and avoid whenever you can the tasteless factory-mades.

I've been told that the traditional New Zealand **dessert** is called pavlova because it's "as light and airy as the great dancer for whom it is named," and I don't doubt that for one moment. It consists of a large meringue made of stiffly beaten egg whites, which has been baked slowly at a low temperature to form a crusty outside and soft inside. Shaped like a large cake, its top is usually filled with whipped cream and fruit (kiwi fruit when it's available)—great!

Beer is the closest thing to a national drink (though wine is gaining in popularity), and you'll have to do a bit of sampling to find your own favorite brew among the many brands—friends of mine spend a lot of time debating the merits of DB (Dominion Breweries), Lion, Steinlager, and a few others. Be cautious, however, when testing those labeled "Export"—they're more than twice as potent as American beer! If you're a dedicated beer drinker or have a large party, you'll save money by ordering a "jug of draft," which holds about five eight-ounce glasses.

In recent years New Zealand's vineyards have been producing better and better **wines.** Labels like McWilliams, Montana, Mission, Corbans, and Penfolds are surprisingly inexpensive and varied in their offerings. Prices are even lower when you buy half-gallon flagons. Spirits have risen in price somewhat when purchased by the bottle, but are quite cheap (by U.S. standards) by the drink. You may want to stock up in Dunedin, where the bottle shop at the Robbie Burns Hotel has some of the lowest prices in the country.

Alcohol is only sold in licensed premises, bottle shops, and wholesale bottle stores (the best bargains are in the latter). Wholesale does not mean they won't sell individual bottles (although some have minimum purchase requirements), so look for that name, usually in city-center shopping areas. Licensed hotels serve drinks from 11 a.m. to 10 p.m. (11 p.m. on Saturday, *never* on Sunday) in their bars and lounges, but anytime with a meal. Registered guests may be served anytime, regardless of the hour. Hotels with a Tourist House License are allowed to serve alcohol only to residents. Licensed restaurants serve drinks only with meals, and many unlicensed restaurants invite you to bring your own wine (most post a BYO notice—some don't, so it pays to inquire).

As for where to eat, the budget-wise thing to do is to breakfast at your lodging place, have pub grub at lunch (look for the "bistro" signs for pubs that serve food), and take your main meal in the evening in one of the many inexpensive and quite acceptable restaurants. A bistro lunch (which usually offers a choice of hot dishes such as pot roast, steak-and-kidney pie and stew, served with potatoes and vegetables; or cold platters) will run around NZ$8 ($5), but an even better buy are the buffet lunches where you can eat your fill for no more than NZ$5 ($3.15).

For any meal, a **Cobb & Co.** restaurant will provide good food (definitely not gourmet, but filling) at low prices. Open from 7 a.m. until 10 p.m., seven days a week, and fully licensed, they're all over New Zealand, in large cities and towns of any substantial size. You'll find addresses listed throughout this book, and they have my recommendation as dependable for both price and quality. All have the same menu, hours, and decor (colonial in nature, with much red velvet, gleaming brass hanging lamps, dark woodwork, and cozy, comfortable booths). Specialties are dishes like the old-fashioned beef-and-kidney pot pie, served with jacket potato and salad and stuffed Cobb schnitzel. Seafoods, grills, sandwiches, quiches, and hamburgers are also on the menu. Beer and wine are reasonably priced and come in pitchers and carafes as well as by the glass. Lunch prices will average NZ$8 ($5); dinner, about NZ$15 ($9.40). The restaurants are the last vestiges of the original Cobb & Co., one of New Zealand's first and largest public transport companies in the days of the coach-and-four, and placemats and menus feature interesting bits of the company's history.

New Zealand has in the last few years seen the birth of some truly **fine restaurants,** with elegant decor, polished service, and superb international cuisine. They're too pricey for budget travel, true, but—holding firmly to the belief that there comes a time in every trip when you just can't *stand* to pinch one more penny —I've listed some of the more outstanding for those "big splurge" dinners. Expect to pay NZ$40 ($25) or slightly more (without wine) at these establishments, and if you should unearth others you feel warrant that kind of expenditure, do let me know about them.

One thing that will take some getting used to is the use of "entree" to mean *not* the main course (which they call the "main course"), but a small serving of a hot dish immediately before the main course. Most New Zealanders eat an entree, main course, and dessert (or two entrees and dessert) and I usually do the same. I've never been able to manage five courses at one sitting, and unless the set dinner price covers all five, I save my money. You may want to do the same.

READERS' DINING SUGGESTIONS: "You should mention to your readers that New Zealand makes the very best **ice cream** in the world—it's so rich and creamy, made with the incredible dairy products here! Hokey Pokey is a butterscotch flavor with pieces of candy in it— too good to be true!" (D. Smith, Portland, Ore.). [*Author's Note:* Amen!] . . . "We highly recommend the NZTP's **Taste of New Zealand booklet** for an evening restaurant guide. We had no disappointments with the food" (M. Luciano, Norwich, N.Y.).

---

7. Big Splurges

As a confirmed budget traveler, I have always loved staying in the sort of small, homey places we've been talking about thus far. It takes *a lot* to induce me to "bust the budget" and spring for lodgings in large, luxury establishments. But there comes a time when I've pinched my pennies to the "nth" degree and something in my soul rebels. One short, really *big* splurge usually puts me back in touch with both my budget and my love for the personal touch so often found only in moderately priced places. It's happened to me wherever I've traveled, and New Zealand is no exception. With the thought that this affliction is not mine alone, I've listed in the chapters to come "Big Splurges" in major destinations that do the most for my budget-battered psyche and offer the best value for my carefully hoarded "bust out" dollars.

Until recently, New Zealand has been able to boast of only a few truly posh, luxury hotels. Well, that situation has now changed, with many outstanding hotels that can hold their own with any on the international scene. You can, in fact, just about tool around this little country and stay in nothing *but* those high-class hostelries while dining only in restaurants of the same caliber. For those of us on a strict budget, of course, they're much too pricey even to be considered on a regular basis. But if you are seized from time to time, as I am, by an irresistible urge to let the budget go hang and indulge in at least one night of extravagant, soul-soothing pampering, then look for the "Big Splurge" accommodation or restaurant listed nearest wherever you find yourself when the notion strikes.

One thing more, if the splurge notion strikes and you *don't* find anything listed in these pages, just ask the nearest friendly Kiwi—the locals will always know where to send you when money is no object.

---

8. Shopping

Before we get into specifics, let me say that shopping is *fun* in New Zealand, with craft, hand-knit woolens, and souvenir shops cropping up in the most unexpected places. Prices are sometimes better in these out-of-the-way shops than in tourist centers—they're best at the duty-free shops in Auckland, Wellington, and Christchurch, but selections can be very limited in both. My own credo has been to buy something that appeals wherever I find it—price variations aren't *that* wide, and there's always the possibility of not finding it again.

New Zealand wools, leathers, and knits are sold all over both islands, as are sheepskin rugs. Really bulky purchases can be mailed home, but I've found that half the fun of buying a suede coat or woolen sweater is using it there. And look for the hand-knits rather than machine-made sweaters—one of my most prized sweaters was handmade by a lovely little lady in the Bay of Islands, another by a talented knitter in Hokitika on the South Island. Both served me well as I traveled the country.

Souvenirs feature Maori carvings or designs, and there's a wide selection, from greenstone tiki figures on neck chains to carved wooden keychains to coasters, placemats, and small replicas of beautifully carved war canoes. Items made from paua shell are also very popular. You'll probably want to bring home at least one Maori concert record or tape, probably more—a marvelous way to trigger instant memories once you're back home. Pottery and ceramics will tempt you, especially in places like Nelson and Taupo, where many are made by fine craftspeople, and prices are inexpensive to moderate.

Paintings of the gorgeous scenery by New Zealand artists are on sale almost everywhere. Some are quite good, and a small oil can sometimes be found for an amazingly low price. You're almost certain to find one depicting that bit of Kiwiland you fell in love with, and, like the Maori music, a painting is instant mental transport back to a lovely experience.

Look for **Rehabilitation League Shops** in some large cities and major resorts. Their prices are competitive, and they offer an extensive selection of New Zealand crafts, woolens, and souvenirs. It's also gratifying to know that profits from the shops go to a program of vocational assessment and rehabilitation for the disabled. Indeed, the shops were initiated as outlets for disabled veteran craftsmen following World War II.

---

9. Where to Go and What to Do

The temptation in this section is simply to say "Go everywhere and do everything!" That's because New Zealand has such a wealth of sightseeing treasures and activities, especially those of an outdoor nature.

WHERE TO GO

Sightseeing highlights are pretty well covered in the sample itineraries of "How Long to Stay," above. But, given time, there are some other pretty special areas you really shouldn't miss: the Bay of Islands is a place to loiter longer; the coast from Rotorua to Gisborne is another; Stewart Island is a place unto itself of unspoiled scenery and rugged island people; the South Island's west coast with its "Pancake Rocks" is a sunlit panorama; and Milford Sound's mystical, primeval beauty begs more time than an afternoon launch cruise. All will be detailed in the following chapters—follow your heart in making additions or substitutions in your itinerary as you go along.

WHAT TO DO

Active Sports
New Zealanders are water bugs! Anytime they're not slaving away in an office or some other workplace, you'll find them in the water, on the water, or fishing the waters. As a visitor, you can participate in all sorts of **water sports.** There are pleasant beaches in the Bay of Islands, the Gisborne area, the Marlborough Sound area, and around Nelson. Surfing is especially good around the Bay of Plenty, with Tauranga offering what a Kiwi friend assures me is "the best surf of any New Zealand beach." Sailing is available to visitors in the Bay of Islands, where you can indulge in deep-sea fishing jaunts as well.

Angling for rainbow and brown trout can put dinner on the table as well as provide a day in the open. Rotorua and Taupo are trout-fishing centers, but it's hard to fish any river or lake in the country without coming up with a good catch. In Rotorua, look up Barry Jaeger in the Hunting and Fishing Office; he can point you to especially good fishing spots in the area. In Taupo, Brian Leverell at Taupo River Guides is one of the North Island's best fishing guides and will practically guarantee you at least one trout on a half- or full-day fishing trip. Down south, Tony Busch of Sportsgoods Nelson Ltd. will do the same. The season is a long one—from the first Saturday in October to the end of April (year round at Rotorua and Taupo), and you can buy a special Tourist Fishing License for a month for NZ$50 ($31.25) from most fishing tackle or sporting goods stores and NZTP Travel Offices.

In the North Island, deep-sea fishing comes into its own along some 300 miles of coastline. Waters less than an hour from shore hold such trophies as marlin, mako shark, thresher shark, hammerhead shark, tiger shark, five species of tuna, broadbill, and yellowtail. The season runs from mid-January through April, and you'll find good, well-equipped bases at the Bay of Islands, Whitianga in Mercury Bay, Tauranga, and Whakatane. Expect to pay in the neighborhood of NZ$450 ($281) to NZ$800 ($500) per day for a boat that can carry as many as four to six fisherpeople. No license required.

Trekking, or **tramping (hiking),** is another popular sport, and as you move around the country good tracks are almost always right at hand. The ten national parks, which cover more than five million acres, all have well-defined trails, and many provide bunkhouses or huts for overnight stops. Even when you're based in a city, there will be scenic walks in the vicinity; I'll tell you about some in the chapters to come, and tourist offices can furnish brochures for their area. In fact, it's possible to hike most of the 1,000-mile length of New Zealand, and if that's your inclination, contact the **New Zealand Walkways Commission,** c/o Department of Lands & Survey, Private Bag, Wellington, for details of connecting regional and local walks. Hostel wardens are also very knowledgeable about treks in their particular area. The most famous—and one of the most splendid—is the guided five- to seven-day Milford Track walk in Fiordland National Park, which draws trekkers from around the world. You can book the guided walk through the NZTP or contact park rangers if you'd like to strike out on your own. Tramping is best in New Zealand from late November through April, when temperatures are their most moderate.

New Zealand has some of the best ski terrain in the world, which, for North Americans, makes year-round **skiing** possible, since the season runs from mid-July through September—just in time to take up when our season leaves off and ends just prior to the beginning of ours. Major ski fields in the South Island are at Queenstown, Tekapo, Wanaka, Mount Hutt, and—for advanced skiers—famed Mount Cook, where you fly by skiplane to the 8,000-foot-high head of the Tasman Glacier and ski down the 12-mile run. In the north, there's good skiing at Tongariro and Turoa.

There are over 300 registered **golf** clubs in New Zealand, and members of overseas clubs are granted guest privileges in most private clubs. Clubs and a "trundler" (don't expect motorized carts) can be rented, and greens fees are low. One of the most outstanding courses is 50 miles south of Rotorua at Wairakei. You may find courses a bit crowded on weekends, much less so during the week.

READER'S TREKKING SUGGESTION: "Visitors who enjoy **tramping** should bring along good gear (boots, fleecy clothing). Also, in addition to the wealth of material available from the Department of Lands & Survey, there's a very good book on sale in New Zealand [and in the U.S.], *Tramping in New Zealand*, by Jim DuFresne (published by Lonely Planet Publications). Another good publication is *Guide to Walking Tracks of the Southern Lakes/Fiordland Area*, available from the Department of Lands & Survey, P.O. Box 478, Queenstown. Also, it cannot be stressed enough that the Milford Track must be booked well in advance, and the Routeburn Track is very overcrowded over Easter and the summer holiday break, so it should be avoided at those times if at all possible" (L. Best, Queenstown, New Zealand).

Spectator Sports

Rugby dominates the sports scene from Easter through September, with Saturday matches featuring Kiwi males from schoolboys to businessmen to members of the national team (the All Blacks, who are elevated to a status in national esteem approaching reverence), to senior citizens. International matches are held in Auckland's Eden Park, Wellington's Athletic Park, Dunedin's Carisbrook Park, and Lancaster Park in Christchurch. If you're a football nut at home and think our players are pretty tough hombres, be sure to take in at least one match and watch the lads rough-and-tumble around the pitch in knee pants—with nary a padded shoulder to be seen!

After rugby, it's **horse racing** that claims national affection in New Zealand. There are 271 days of licensed racing (133 of trotting) during the year, and race meets take place in informal beach settings or open fields with the same degree of enthusiasm as those at the larger tracks around the country. In January there's the New Zealand Cup, a highlight of the racing year—if you're there and are overcome by gambling fever, go ahead and indulge: betting is perfectly legal, both on and off the track.

Evening Activities

Except in larger cities, nightlife is quiet, quiet, quiet. Quiet, that is, when it isn't totally nonexistent. New Zealand will have little appeal for travelers who require a swinging nightlife that goes on into the wee hours. In Auckland and Wellington, supper clubs and a few nightspots offer revues or other entertainment, and there are theater productions on a sporadic basis. Dunedin has an active theater, and of course there are the Maori concerts in Rotorua and nighttime visits to Waitomo's glowworm grotto. Otherwise, do as the Kiwis do—enjoy full, bracing days of outdoor activity followed by a satisfying evening meal followed by quiet visits with friends or a little time in front of the telly followed by an early bedtime. It makes a refreshing change from our frenetic pace at home, and you may be surprised to find how ready you are for those early evenings after a day or so of heavy sightseeing.

GETTING TO AND AROUND NEW ZEALAND

1. GETTING THERE
2. GETTING AROUND

In this chapter we'll be dealing with the single largest item in any budget for New Zealand travel—the cost of getting there. While not nearly as costly as it once was, transportation across the South Pacific is the first financial hurdle in your planning. Once you arrive, you'll have a number of options as to how much or how little to spend on transport around New Zealand.

1. Getting There

You *could* go by ship, of course—one of the luxury liners that sails maybe twice a year, or a freighter making stops all across the Pacific—but for most of us, the only practical way to go is by jet plane. And although air fare cannot be called cheap, it *can* be called a travel bargain if you utilize the options wisely. More about that later.

The most important part of your holiday planning begins with predeparture research on air fares. There are differences in the types of fares and seasonal charges, and there are differences in airlines. Your first task should be to study these differences, decide on the one best suited to your needs, then telephone or visit a qualified travel agent or the individual airline offices. Be forearmed with a list of the *specific* information you need so that answers to your questions can be as direct as possible.

All direct flights to New Zealand from the United States depart from Los Angeles, and principal airlines offering this service are Air New Zealand, United, Qantas, UTA French Airlines, and Continental (a word about personal preference later on). American Airlines inaugurated service to Auckland, via Honolulu, in February 1990. Departures are from Dallas/Fort Worth.

FARE OPTIONS
Set out below are the basic types of fares available and their costs as this book is written. Remember, however, that these figures are far from cast in stone—nor are

the fare types, for that matter. Fares can change in a matter of days as airlines rush to introduce new and more competitive fare structures. Use these as a guide, then shop around carefully.

First Class

This is the costliest way to travel, of course, but the fare carries with it many extras, such as no advance-purchase requirement, stopovers en route, no penalty for changes or cancellations, a maximum stay of one year, and many in-flight comfort and service perks. In 1989 the *one-way* adult fare was $2,796, half that for children, 10% for infants. By paying $3,190, adults add interline transfers to other airlines.

Business Class

Called Pacific Class on Air New Zealand flights, this classification differs from First Class chiefly in in-flight comfort and service (seats are not as wide, menu choices not as varied). *One-way* fares in 1989 were $1,704; with the interline-transfers option, $2,022. Other conditions are the same as for First Class.

Economy Class

Regular Economy Class is the next rung down on the comfort and service ladder, but includes the same no advance purchase, stopovers en route, and other provisions as the two classes above. *One-way* fares in 1989 were $1,258; with interline transfers, $1,558.

Superpass

Good for a minimum stay of six days and a maximum of one year, this fare carries with it no advance-purchase requirement, but there's a charge for any flight changes and a cancellation penalty. Stopovers en route are permitted, and some fares for children and infants are higher than on classes above. *Round-trip* fares in 1989 were $1,320 from May through August; $1,520 in March and April and from September through November, and $1,700 from December through February.

Super-APEX Fare

Restrictions on this category include a 14-day advance-purchase requirement, cancellation penalty, and children's fares of 67% (infants, 10%). Good for one year, with no minimum-stay restriction, *one-way* fare in 1989 was $960. Four stopovers were permitted.

Promotional Fares

Every airline comes up each year with special bargain fares for limited time periods. Examples in 1989 were Air New Zealand's Kiwi Smile and Aussie Wonder *round-trip* fares of $1,170 from May through August, $1,370 in March and April and from September through November, and $1,550 from December through February. An even-greater bargain was the "Kangaroo/Kiwi Express" fare of $970 to New Zealand and $1,095 to Australia, which ran from May through August with a 14-day advance-purchase requirement.

Package Plans

There are several excellent package plans on the market that offer good value to the budget traveler. In addition to air fare, they include ground transportation,

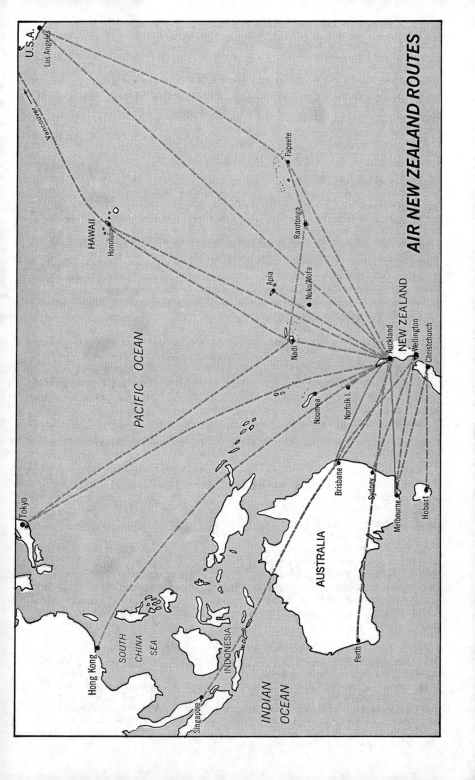

AIR NEW ZEALAND ROUTES

lodging, and some sightseeing discounts. Air New Zealand, for example, often offers a hotel accommodation package for a mere pittance above its promotional fares. That's hard to beat, as are other moneysaving packages included "Hotpac" and "Lodgepass" accommodation vouchers in good-quality motels and lodges at reduced rates. There's a good range of fly/drive, farm- and home-stay, and ski packages—for details contact Air New Zealand (tel. 213/615-1111 or toll free 800/262-1234, 800/663-5494 in Canada) or your travel agent and ask for their "New Zealand Holiday Planner" and/or the 300-page Australia/New Zealand "Silver Book" that details both group and organized packages.

GOOD-VALUE AIR FARES

Well, as I said at the beginning, getting to New Zealand can hardly be called *cheap*. However, if you choose one of the fare classifications listed above that permits en-route stopovers, you will be purchasing transportation to as many as four destinations for the same fare you would pay just to get to New Zealand—four travel experiences for the price of one. And a little beforehand research will reveal further savings in package deals that include reduced land costs at all four. So instead of just a New Zealand vacation, you could include stopovers in Australia, Fiji, and Hawaii before returning home.

A Travel Fantasy: Around the World

Well, why not! After all, you'll have come virtually halfway around the world by the time you travel from North America to New Zealand. Instead of backtracking across the Pacific, this is the perfect time to circle the globe. This is a fantasy that nags at me on each trip to New Zealand, and while I've not yet managed the free time, it's definitely in my future. Air New Zealand makes this dream trip available on an individual basis, with some restrictions, for around $2,500. Other carriers such as Pan Am, TWA, and British Airways also give flight to around-the-world fantasies. It's certainly worth thinking about.

TRAVEL TIPS

No matter which airline you choose, if you fly direct, it's going to be a *long* 13-hour flight during which you cross the International Date Line and lose one whole calendar day (which you gain, of course, on the return trip), go through four time zones, and turn the seasons upside down. There's no way your body is *not* going to suffer the pangs of jet lag! There are as many ways to minimize that malady of long-distance travel as there are long-distance travelers, but here are two strategies that work for me: first, I make it a point to get up from my seat at least once an hour when not sleeping and walk around the plane to keep my legs and feet from swelling; and second, I plan on a stopover of at least 24 hours (48 hours or more when I can manage it) en route both ways—gradually, I'm getting to know those South Pacific islands, and my body gets to make the time adjustment in easy stages. You, of course, no doubt have your own, time-tested jet-lag remedies. If they really work, drop me a line.

READERS' TRAVEL SUGGESTIONS: "I followed the 'Overcoming Jet Lag' program by Ehert and Scanlon that combines diet and avoidance of caffeine, depending on direction of travel and time zones crossed. While I was tired, I had no real jet lag going or coming" (E. Angeletti, Greenville, S.C.). . . . "I'm fine traveling east to west, but on the return trip, special diets and avoidance of alcohol and caffeine don't work for me, so I eat and drink what I like, then take one Halcion sleeping pill each night for the first few nights of my return. I try to get on the time frame of the place I'm visiting. When I come home, it takes a couple of weeks to feel energetic again" (A. Ellington, New York, N.Y.).

YOUR CHOICE OF AIRLINE

All other things being equal (fares, schedules, etc.), there is much to be said for choosing any country's national airline, since flying with the locals and the cabin crew enables you to encounter the people you'll be visiting. In the case of Air New Zealand, there was an added inducement for me—the praises sung long and loud by everyone who had ever traveled with them. Those praises, I must now admit, gave rise to my natural skepticism about the delights of almost any airline, a skepticism based on more than a few disappointments.

Well, that skepticism began to vanish before we even left the ground. The Air New Zealand crew introduced me from the very first to the unique brand of Kiwi friendliness that typifies their native land. Once airborne, the intercom crackled and the captain's welcome was surprising: "Welcome aboard, ladies and gentlemen, girls and boys. We're going to do everything we can to see that you have a good flight. In the meantime, get comfortable, look around, and maybe introduce yourself to that fellow or girl sitting next to you—who knows, you may make a friend for life." Friendlier than that, it's hard to get.

From a pampered standpoint, I love the food, which features New Zealand specialties such as lamb with a genuine "home-cooked" flavor, fresh vegetables, hot rolls, a great dessert, cheese and fruit. Breakfasts were every bit as good, and when I commented on the fresh, sweet taste of both milk and butter, my host informed me that Air New Zealand flies these supplies to departure points so that only good, native dairy products are served on all planes. Now, *that's* attention to detail!

The combination of all these factors undoubtedly accounts for Air New Zealand topping international airline passenger polls year after year. Those who sing its praises know whereof they sing—and, as I said, it's a great way to begin to experience New Zealand before you reach New Zealand!

---

2. Getting Around

When it comes to getting around New Zealand, you can pick and choose, mix and match, modes of transport. As I said earlier in this book, things *work* in this country. Bus and rail transportation are both reliable, car-rental firms are dependable, and the two major airlines furnishing domestic service cover longer stretches with ease. Driving, of course, affords the most flexibility, as you are tied to no one's schedule except your own. However, public transportation is an economical, pleasant way to go, and in one form or another will reach any destination within the country.

RAIL AND ROAD

Most rail and bus services are provided by **InterCity,** which operates all railways, most provincial buses, some suburban buses, ferry service between the North and South Islands, and many of the better sightseeing tours. For the budget traveler, they offer what is probably the least expensive way of getting around the country.

A personal word here: As a veteran of several seven-week-long jaunts around New Zealand by train and bus, I can tell you that—aside from a few early-morning departures, which are a bit hard on my late-rising psyche—this method of travel has much to offer that cannot be found otherwise. Consider: You travel with New Zealanders who are not touring, but simply going about their own business—a chance to rub elbows in the most elementary way. Consider: On many of the buses (particularly in the South Island), drivers give an excellent commentary on the countryside—not for tourists, mind you, but for Kiwis who may travel the route frequently but who seem as interested as those of us who are traveling through for the first time. Consider: Trains run along coastlines and mountain gorges with fantastic views, which are completely hidden from highways that run farther inland or on higher ground. Consider: When you leave the driving to someone else, there's no need to worry about driving on the left, keeping one eye glued to the map, or looking for road signs rather than scenic splendors. I admit it—I'm positively addicted to InterCity.

Aside from all that, a very good reason to travel this way is the money-saving **Travelpass,** available from February 1 to December 14, which must be purchased *before you leave home.* You get unlimited travel by rail, coach, and ferry for 8 days of travel in a 14-day period for NZ$275 ($172), 15 days of travel in a 22-day period for NZ$355 ($222), or 22 days within a 31-day period for NZ$440 ($275). Children 4 to 15 travel for half price; under-4s, free. The pass may be purchased in the United States or in New Zealand at an InterCity travel Center, NZTP office, or travel agency. Pass holders receive discounts on designated motels, hotels, and tours.

Mount Cook Line offers the **Kiwi Coach Pass,** which may be purchased only outside New Zealand and is good for coach service on Mount Cook Landline, InterCity, and Newmans. The cost for 7 days is $163; for 10 days, $201; for 15 days, $268; and for 25 days, $385. It may be purchased from travel agents or NZTP offices; you'll be given a certificate that you trade in for the pass when you reach New Zealand.

You should know that *all bus and rail journeys must be booked*—this is particularly important during peak travel periods. Bookings may be made at any InterCity station or through NZTP offices as much as six months in advance. Of course, I've never seen anyone just show up without a booking and be refused a seat, but I wouldn't recommend chancing that. Sometimes there is only one bus a day.

To preplan your entire trip before leaving home, write to the Passenger Manager, InterCity, Private Bag, Wellington, and tell them where you'd like to go and your time limit—they'll respond with an itinerary planned to your requirements. In New Zealand the NZTP will do the same. Both will provide you with a complete set of timetables covering rail, bus, and ferry services.

InterCity telephone numbers are listed in each destination chapter. Mount Cook Lines' U.S. sales office is at 1960 Grand Ave., Suite 910, El Segundo, CA 90245 (tel. 213/640-1200, or toll free 800/468-2665).

Buses

The InterCity service network is extensive, and there are good connections with Newmans or Mount Cook Landline to those few points they don't reach. For example, if you cross Cook Strait from Wellington to Picton en route to the South Island's west coast, you'll travel by Newmans as far as Greymouth. Your vouchers or Travelpass will not apply on those portions of your travel.

All buses are comfortable; some are carpeted and most have individual reading lights. Frequent stops for tea or refreshments are scheduled, and as I mentioned above, on many runs you'll hear an interesting, informative narrative about the country through which you're traveling. In rural areas, buses often pull up in front of T-bars alongside the road and drivers lean out to collect mail sacks to be dropped off at the next post office. All sorts of other freight travels along with you as well—a closeup look at Kiwi life outside the cities!

In addition to regularly scheduled services, New Zealand bus lines run excellent sightseeing and excursion day trips. Details are in the appropriate chapters.

Trains

All trains in the country are operated by InterCity, and all are quite comfortable, although the equipment can be anything from older suburban cars to very good overnight sleepers to sleek, modern rail cruisers. The major rail services are:

Auckland–Wellington: The *Northerner,* a part sleeper, leaves Auckland and Wellington at 7:30 p.m., arriving at the opposite terminal at 8:30 the next morning.

There are twinette sleeper cars and normal seated carriages, plus a licensed buffet car where drinks and buffet food are served.

The day trip is via the *Silver Fern,* and there's an informative commentary as you pass through fern forests, sacred Maori burial grounds, and volcanic peaks. Free morning and afternoon tea is served by uniformed hostesses and stewards, who also provide newspapers and magazines and will take drink orders to be served at your seat. There's a lunch stop at Taihape Station. Departure from Auckland is at 8 a.m., with arrival at Wellington at 7:02 p.m.; departure from Wellington is at 8:20 a.m., with arrival at Auckland at 7:30 p.m. Both run every day except Sunday, and Saturday service is subject to cancellation, so be sure to check.

Christchurch–Dunedin–Invercargill: Daily except Sunday, the *Southerner* makes this run, one train in each direction. Christchurch departure is at 8:40 a.m., Dunedin at 3:05 p.m., and arrival at Invercargill is at 6:45 p.m. Going north, trains leave Invercargill at 8:40 a.m. and Dunedin at 12:21 p.m., arriving at Christchurch at 6:35 p.m. There's a buffet car that serves drinks and buffet food, and drinks may also be ordered from the service staff in your carriage. You're given an illustrated map of the route, which passes some quite spectacular coastal scenery as well as pastoral scenes of grazing sheep and wheat fields.

The *Northerner, Silver Fern,* and *Southerner* express trains are the showpieces of the system. They're carpeted, attractive in decor, and well heated, air-conditioned, or ventilated. Comfortable trains run daily between Wellington and Gisborne (with a stop in Napier), Christchurch and Greymouth, and Christchurch and Picton. Although there are no service staff or buffet cars on these trains, refreshment stops are made en route.

BY CAR

New Zealand is a driver's paradise. You can wander at will over roads that (outside the larger cities) are virtually traffic free. Better yet, you can stop at will to take a closer look at an inviting seascape or lush fern forest. When lunchtime arrives, you can picnic at whichever scenic spot takes your fancy. Bus and train rider that I am, I usually plan to drive at least one segment of the trip just for the joy of all that freedom. And if you can possibly afford it, I highly recommend the experience. One caution, however: New Zealand distances can be deceiving—check the following mileage charts. Also, pick up a copy of *The New Zealand Motoring Book* from NZTP —it's full of useful information.

New Zealand **roads** are exceptionally well maintained, except for a few mountainous stretches in the South Island, where you sometimes wonder how they managed to carve out a road in the first place. And speaking of mountains, let me say—as one who has driven for donkey's years in all sorts of terrain—that if you're not accustomed to mountain driving, you should consider using public transportation from Hokitika to the glaciers, Queenstown, Te Anau, and Milford Sound, then resuming your journey by car from Te Anau. I've been assured by my Kiwi friends in this area that such a plan is entirely unnecessary and that driving is not that difficult in this part of the South Island. All I can say is that I feel much more secure when someone else is navigating along those mountain roads.

You must be at least 21 to rent a car in New Zealand, and must possess a current **driver's license** that you have held for at least one year from the United States, Australia, Canada, the United Kingdom, and a few other countries, or an International Driving Permit. You drive on the left and must—by law—buckle that seatbelt when the car is moving. Speed limit on the open road is 60 mph (100 k/hr), and in congested areas, towns and cities, 30 mph (50 k/hr). Drive with extreme caution when an area is signposted "LSZ" (Limited Speed Zone). Signposting, incidentally, is very good all through the country—there's little chance of losing your way.

You'll be given a set of **maps** when you pick up your rental car, and if you're a member of the Automobile Association in the States, Australia, Britain, or some European countries, you'll have reciprocal privileges with the New Zealand AA, which includes their very good maps, plus "strip maps" of your itinerary and comprehensive guidebooks of accommodations (some of which give discounts to AA members). You can contact the New Zealand AA at 342 Lambton Quay, Wellington; 33 Wyndham St., Auckland; and 210 Hereford St., Christchurch.

Nearly all New Zealand **car-rental firms** offer unlimited-mileage rates, a decided plus for budgeteers. One of the best bargains I've been able to unearth is through Maui Rentals, which provides late-model Japanese cars at one low daily rate, NZ$41 ($25.75) plus GST. That's with unlimited mileage—insurance is NZ$12 ($7.50) per day. With offices in Auckland and Christchurch, they don't even charge for pickup in one island and dropoff in the other. They also have terrific rates for caravans (more about that later). You can book through NZTP offices in the States, or contact them directly at: **Maui Rentals,** 100 New North Rd., Auckland (tel. 09/793-277); or 23 Sheffield Crescent, Christchurch (tel. 03/584-159), both open daily from 8:30 a.m. to 5 p.m. (*Note:* One reader has complained that the company limits the last day's rental to 5 p.m. that day for the return of the car, rather than a full 24 hours; check before you sign the contract.)

Letz Rent A Car, 51-53 Shortland St. (P.O. Box 2752), Auckland (tel. 09/390-145), furnishes Hondas at NZ$76 ($48) per day. Rates are even better, however, if you pre-book and prepay through their U.S. office: Letz Rent A Car, Suite 105, 1448 15th St., Santa Monica, CA 90404 (tel. 213/393-8262, or toll free 800/551-2012, 445-0190 in California). This is the reliable firm offering the Buy Back plan outlined later in this chapter.

Avis (insurance is an additional charge, but there's unlimited mileage) is at 22 Wakefield St., Auckland (tel. 09/792-650), with over 40 branches throughout the country and major airports; **Hertz** at 154 Victoria St. West, Auckland (tel. 09/34-924). Insurance is extra. Airport delivery.

READERS' CAR-RENTAL SUGGESTIONS: "The cheapest rental-car agency we found was a small agency in Christchurch called **Renny Rent a Car.** They were very nice people, as well, and we were able to see the South Island in one of their cars for a reasonable price" (L. Breihan, Austin, Tex.). [*Author's Note:* This company (113 Tuam St., 03/666-790), only operates in Christchurch.] . . . **"Southern Cross Car Rental** gave us the best deal by far, and superior service. They were extremely helpful and courteous and supply so many extras at a truly budget price" (M. L. Thie, Coupeville, Wash.). [*Author's Note:* Pickups and dropoffs may be made in Picton, Christchurch, Dunedin, Queenstown, Wellington, and Auckland.]

Motor Homes

If you want to take advantage of New Zealand's budget motor camps—or if you're simply a caravaner at heart—**Maui Rentals** offers motor homes at incredibly low rates. Their Hi-Top Campa has one double bed and an overhead single bunk and complete cooking facilities, plus hot and cold running water; it costs NZ$64 ($40) to NZ$130 ($81.25) daily, depending on season. More luxurious is the Maui Campa, which accommodates four adults and one child at NZ$79 ($49.50) to NZ$180 ($113) daily, and the spiffy Travel Home sleeps up to six adults at NZ$100 ($62.50) to NZ$200 ($125)—and you can be installed in your motor home within two hours of landing (saving that first night's hotel bill). All rentals are on an unlimited-mileage basis, and you can pick up and drop off at either their Auckland or Christchurch office at no extra fee. There's a NZ$12 ($7.50) daily insurance charge and a NZ$275 ($172) security deposit required when you book, refundable when the car is returned in good condition. In New Zealand, contact them at the addresses shown above for rental cars. North Americans can also book directly through all NZTP offices listed in the Introduction.

Mount Cook Line also offers motor home tour packages—contact a qualified travel agent or the airline itself for details.

The Buy-Back Plan

If you're going to be in New Zealand for as long as four months or more, the most feasible transport is your very own car. The problem is what to do with it when you leave. But a long-established auto firm in Auckland has solved that problem for you. **Letz Buy a Car Ltd.,** 51-53 Shortland St. (P.O. Box 2752), Auckland (tel. 09/390-145), will sell you a new or used car and guarantee to buy it back at a predetermined price when you leave (you're perfectly free to sell it elsewhere if you can get a better price). For example, if you purchase a used Honda Civic for $6,800 U.S. and drive it for six months, they will buy it back for $4,220U.S.—your maximum cost is $2,580 U.S., or just over $14.15 U.S. per day. That's a bargain by any standard! You'll get an even better deal if you pre-book and prepay through their U.S. office: Letz Buy a Car Ltd., Suite 105, 1448 15th St., Santa Monica, CA 90404 (tel. 213/393-8262, or toll free 800/551-2012, 800/445-0190 in California). If you're coming to New Zealand from Australia, you can pre-book and prepay through their office at 116 Darlinghurst Rd., Kings Cross, Sydney (tel. 02/331-3099).

BY AIR

Air New Zealand, Mount Cook Line, and Ansett fly internal routes in New Zealand. Schedules are frequent and convenient, and equipment is modern and comfortable on all three.

Air New Zealand operates some 200 flights daily, connecting 23 domestic airports, virtually covering the entire country. Planes are 767 and 737 twin jets and F27 jetprops, and on short hops you'll usually be served snacks of New Zealand cheese, crackers, and a beverage—full meals are served on longer flights.

For those whose time is limited (or those who simply want to vary their modes of travel), their **Visit New Zealand Fare** is a godsend. For NZ$370 ($231) you purchase four coupons good for any four of those 200 daily flights; six coupons cost NZ$495 ($309); children's fares are NZ$290 ($181) and NZ$405 ($253). The coupons (which are good for 60 days from the date of your first flight) *must be purchased before you reach New Zealand and must be bought in conjunction with international travel.* You don't have to book individual flights, however, until you actually reach New Zealand, and unused coupons may be turned in for a refund *before you leave New Zealand.*

Incidentally, if you're curious about the symbol that adorns the tail of every Air New Zealand plane, it's called the *Koru,* and it's an ancient Maori motif that was first seen on the prows of those mighty canoes that navigated the Pacific many centuries ago.

Mount Cook Line links New Zealand's major tourist areas to each other and to Auckland and Christchurch. Schedules are designed to connect with Air New Zealand's domestic service, as well as international flights.

Mount Cook also provides some of the most spectacular flightseeing tours to be found anywhere in the world. If you splurge (as you most certainly should) on a glacier flight, you'll be flying Mount Cook Line. And if you're on one of those short-stay itineraries, it's Mount Cook Line that can get you around to the sightseeing points that top your list. In that case, you should definitely consider the **Kiwi Air Pass,** which must be purchased *before you arrive in New Zealand.* For $499 U.S. (children pay $375 U.S.) you can take a circle trip around New Zealand, with stops at any point. Travel must be within 30 consecutive days, and must be in one direction—no backtracking. The pass is also valid on Mount Cook Line's coach service if it's substituted for air travel. The Kiwi Air Pass is valid for one month following your first flight, and you can purchase it through qualified travel agents in the U.S. or by calling toll free 800/468-2665 (in the Los Angeles area, 213/649-6185).

Relatively new to New Zealand is **Ansett New Zealand,** an offshoot of an Australian airline. It operates between seven cities at present, with expanded routes

DISTANCES BETWEEN MAJOR CITIES: SOUTH ISLAND
(In Kilometers)

	Blenheim	Christchurch	Dunedin	Franz Josef	Greymouth	Invercargill	Milford Sound	Mount Cook	Nelson	Oamaru	Picton	Queenstown	Te Anau	Timaru	Westport
Alexandra	767	455	190	373	552	202	370	242	876	223	795	93	249	307	653
Arthurs Pass	440	150	451	241	98	668	922	412	388	336	468	645	801	252	199
Blenheim		312	674	503	324	891	1,085	643	116	559	28	798	964	475	260
Christchurch	312		362	427	248	579	773	331	428	247	340	486	652	163	333
Dunedin	674	362		563	742	217	411	331	790	115	702	283	290	199	695
Franz Josef	503	427	563		179	575	769	498	469	596	579	404	560	493	280
Gore	825	513	151	509	688	66	260	378	941	266	853	169	139	350	789
Greymouth	324	248	742	179		754	860	510	290	434	352	583	739	350	101
Haast	645	738	421	142	321	433	539	356	611	376	673	262	418	418	422
Hanmer Springs	262	135	497	395	216	714	908	466	306	382	290	621	787	298	218
Invercargill	891	579	217	575	754		278	444	1,007	332	919	187	157	416	855
Milford Sound	1,085	773	411	769	860	278		550	1,150	526	1,113	291	121	610	961
Mount Cook	643	331	331	498	510	444	550		759	216	671	328	484	211	664
Nelson	116	428	790	469	290	1,007	1,150	759		675	110	873	1,029	591	226
Oamaru	559	247	115	596	434	332	526	216	675		587	316	472	84	580
Picton	28	340	702	579	352	919	1,113	671	110	587		826	992	503	288
Queenstown	798	486	283	404	583	187	291	328	873	316	826		170	335	684
Te Anau	964	652	290	560	739	157	121	484	1,029	472	992	170		489	840
Timaru	475	163	199	493	350	416	610	211	591	84	503	335	489		497
Wanaka	736	424	276	287	466	278	394	211	756	231	764	117	273	273	567
Westport	260	333	695	280	101	855	961	664	226	580	288	684	840	497	

DISTANCES BETWEEN MAJOR CITIES: NORTH ISLAND
(In Kilometers)

	Auckland	Gisborne	Hamilton	Hicks Bay	Kaitaia	Masterton	Napier	New Plymouth	Palmerston North	Rotorua	Tauranga	Wanganui	Wellington	Whakatane	Whangarei
Auckland		504	127	508	325	638	423	369	528	234	206	454	660	302	170
Bulls	509	424	382	604	834	139	208	204	30	311	397	44	151	396	679
Gisborne	504		394	180	829	449	216	599	394	287	298	468	550	202	674
Hamilton	127	394		398	452	511	296	242	401	107	107	327	533	192	297
Hicks Bay	508	180	398		833	629	396	603	574	291	302	596	730	206	678
Kaitaia	325	829	452	833		963	748	694	853	561	531	779	983	627	155
Masterton	638	449	511	629	963		233	343	109	440	526	183	101	543	808
Napier	423	216	296	396	748	233		412	178	225	311	252	334	310	593
National Park	330	432	203	474	655	305	244	222	196	183	269	122	317	268	500
New Plymouth	369	599	242	603	694	343	412		234	312	398	160	355	397	539
Paihia	241	745	368	749	108	879	664	610	769	475	447	695	901	543	71
Palmerston North	528	394	401	574	853	109	178	234		331	417	74	145	416	698
Rotorua	234	287	107	291	561	440	225	312	331		86	305	462	85	404
Taihape	422	492	295	515	747	217	285	274	108	224	310	114	238	309	592
Taupo	280	350	153	373	605	358	143	296	249	82	168	223	380	167	450
Tauranga	206	298	107	302	531	526	311	398	417	86		391	548	96	376
Waitomo Caves	202	437	75	441	527	451	307	183	342	150	151	268	463	235	372
Wanganui	454	468	327	596	779	183	252	160	74	305	391		195	390	624
Wellington	660	550	533	730	983	101	334	355	145	462	548	195		547	819
Whakatane	302	202	192	206	627	543	310	397	416	85	96	390	547		472
Whangarei	170	674	297	678	155	808	593	539	698	404	376	624	819	472	

planned for the near future. They are in the process of building their own airport facilities in several locations, and while their fares are for the most part comparable to Air New Zealand domestic fares, there is a seven-day advance-purchase "Good Buy" fare available at savings that can run as high as 55%.

SPECIAL-INTEREST TOURS

It is, I suppose, a given that if you've bought this book you plan to freewheel it around New Zealand. For that reason, I'll skip any detailed discussion of escorted coach tours. There are, however, several special-interest tours available (golf, boating, fishing, skiing, etc.) that can be both time- and moneysavers. Any NZTP office can point you to the appropriate places to book, but there are a few I'd like to mention because of their proven track record and dependability.

For those who fall in the 18-to-35 age bracket, **Contiki Holidays** has offered great South Pacific holidays for more than a quarter century. While travel is with a group, these trips could hardly be called "group tours"—schedules are such that ample freewheeling time is allowed, and for virtually every planned activity there is at least one option. Transportation and accommodations are top-notch (Contiki is presently building its own accommodations in many New Zealand locations), and activities include such unusual events as beachside barbecues, white-water rafting, and ballooning. In short, these are *fun* tours and appeal to those lively souls who are young at heart as well as in years. Best of all, they offer one of the best value-for-dollar bargains in the business—for example, in 1989 their 16-day tour of New Zealand was priced as low as $894! On some tours, there's a free stopover in one of several South Pacific islands. For details of their current offerings, contact your travel agent or Contiki Holidays, 1432 E. Katella Ave., Anaheim, CA 92805 (tel. toll free 800/ 626-0611, 800/624-0611 in California).

Jetset Tours has been getting people around Australia since the early 1960s and now covers New Zealand and most of the South Pacific as well. There are well-organized group tours, fly/drive tours, and a 300-page Australia/New Zealand "Silver Book" offering hundreds of hotels, sightseeing activities, and tours. The booking desk can arrange flights on Air New Zealand. In 1989 the company offered a Dollar Special: up to five nights at selected hotels for only $1 a night before September 30. Details may be obtained through travel agents or direct from Jetset Tours, 8383 Wilshire Blvd., Suite 450, Beverly Hills, CA 90211 (tel. toll free 800/ 453-8738).

Two other long-established operators in the South Pacific who have built solid reputations for reliability and good prices are **Ted Cook's Islands in the Sun,** P.O. Box 1398, Newport Beach, CA 92663 (tel. 714/645-8300, or toll free 800/854-3413 in the U.S. and Canada); and **Globus-Gateway** (specializing in budget prices), 95-25 Queens Blvd., Rego Park, NY 11374 (tel. 718/268-1700 collect from New York, or toll free 800/221-0090 from the eastern U.S.), and 150 S. Los Robles Ave., Suite 860, Pasadena, CA 91101 (tel. 818/449-0919, or toll free 800/ 556-5454 in the western U.S. outside California). Both are also represented by most travel agents.

INTER-ISLAND FERRY

Even if you fly the better part of your trip, try to plan a crossing of Cook Strait on the Wellington–Picton ferry in at least one direction. You'll get a look at both islands from the water, as well as the near-mystical Marlborough Sound, just as those early Maoris and Europeans did. The crossing is one of New Zealand's very best travel experiences. *If you plan to bring a car by ferry, you need a confirmed reservation.* Buy your ticket ahead to avoid a potential delay of a day or more. The rate for taking the car or caravan with you in 1989 was NZ$90.67 ($55.75); for a large vehicle, NZ$117.80 ($73.75). For more information, check the details at the end of the Wellington chapter.

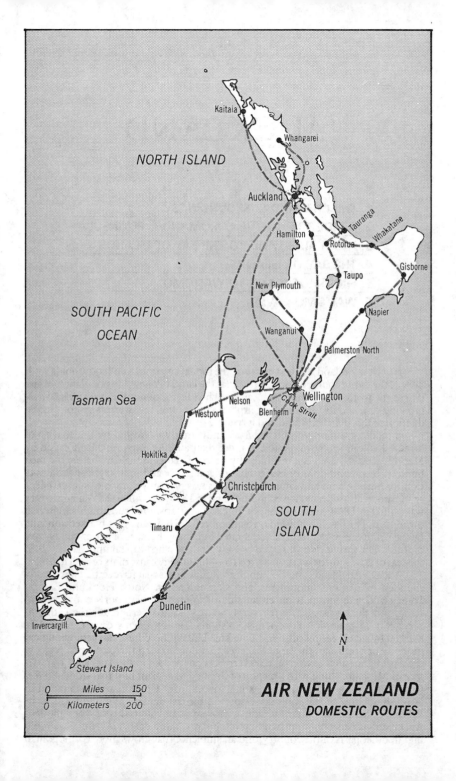

NORTH ISLAND

Kaitaia

Whangarei

SOUTH PACIFIC

OCEAN

Auckland

Tauranga

Whakatane

Hamilton

Rotorua

Gisborne

Taupo

New Plymouth

Napier

Tasman Sea

Wanganui

Palmerston North

Nelson

Wellington

Westport

Blenheim

Cook Strait

Hokitika

Christchurch

SOUTH
ISLAND

Timaru

Dunedin

Invercargill

N

Stewart Island

| 0 | Miles | 150 |
| 0 | Kilometers | 200 |

AIR NEW ZEALAND
DOMESTIC ROUTES

AUCKLAND

It is New Zealand's largest city; was the capital city until 1864; now holds a full 24% of the entire country's population; has the largest Polynesian population of any city in the world; adds many thousands each year, making it the country's fastest-growing city; and its international airport is most often the overseas visitor's introduction to this delightful land and its people.

Straddling a narrow, pinched-in isthmus that was created by the activity of some 60 volcanoes over a period of more than 50,000 years, Auckland is said by Maori legend to have been inhabited by a race of giants in the days before the moa hunters. Its present-day giants are those of commerce and industry, but the attraction for both ancient and latter-day Goliaths was probably the same—its excellent twin harbors. Europeans arrived in Auckland in 1839, and when the Waitangi treaty was signed in 1840, negotiations with the Maoris transferred the isthmus to British ownership. The flag was hoisted on September 18, 1840, an event marked annually by the Anniversary Day Regatta (celebrated in January because of better sailing conditions). The thriving town served as New Zealand's first capital until 1864, when the seat of government was transferred to Wellington because of its central location.

Today's Auckland is nestled among volcanic peaks that have settled into gently rounded hills, minor mountains, and sloping craters. North Head and Bastion Point stand like sentinels on either side of Waitemata Harbour's entrance, and Rangitoto, the largest and more recently active volcano (it erupted in the 13th century), sits in majestic splendor just offshore. Mount Eden's eastern slopes are marked by Maori earthworks, and One Tree Hill has become an archeological field monument because of the large Maori *pa* that once existed there. What is possibly the world's finest collection of Maori artifacts can be seen in the Auckland War Memorial Museum, along with a display of the moa, that giant bird that stood ten feet from beak to toe and that has been extinct for centuries. Colonial-style homes and an astonishing array of towering skyscrapers in the city center are monuments to its Pakeha development. Side by side with reminders of its history are modern Auckland's diversions—outstanding restaurants, more entertainment than you'll find in other parts of the country, and an ambience that grows more cosmopolitan every year. The city warrants a few days of your time, with much to offer that will enhance the remainder of your New Zealand visit.

1. The City and Surroundings

ORIENTATION
You can credit the Kiwi's inborn desire for a home and garden to the fact that central Auckland is surrounded by districts that have become cities in their own right—people may *work* in the inner city, but when evening comes, they're off to wider spaces. And the homeward journey will take them over at least one bridge (the place is broken out with bridges—they cross the harbor, rivers, creeks, and bays) and possibly onto the speeding motorway that runs north-south through the city. That motorway can be a blessing for the visitor unfamiliar with the territory and driving on the left, for it virtually eliminates the possibility of losing your way when you set out for the Bay of Islands, Rotorua, or other major points.

The city itself is also fairly straightforward. The main street is **Queen Street,** which ends in Queen Elizabeth's Square at Quay Street. **Quay Street** runs along the Waitemata harborfront. At the other end of Queen Street is **Karangahape Road** (pronounce it "Ka-ranga-happy," or simply call it "K" Street as Aucklanders do), a mere 1¼ miles from Quay Street. Within that area you'll find most of the city's shops, restaurants, nightspots, and hotels, as well as bus, rail, and air terminals.

The city's **bus system** is quite good, reaching all districts with convenient and rather frequent schedules. You can pick up route maps and timetables from most news agents or the Quay Street (near Commerce) bus terminal; or call the Auckland Regional Authority (tel. 797-119) for information. Fares are by zone, running from NZ$.40 (25¢) to NZ$1.20 (75¢). Children under 15 pay half fare; under 4, free. You must have the exact change. If you're going to be using the buses a lot, you can purchase a one-day Busabout unlimited bus travel ticket for NZ$5 ($3.15). Buy them on the buses or through the Auckland Regional Authority. An Inner City Shuttle bus (it's the one painted yellow, with a red band and the destination "000" —yes, that's how it's marked!) runs every five or ten minutes from the Railway Station along Customs Street, up Queen Street to Karangahape Road, then back to the station by way of Mayoral Drive and Queen Street for a fare of NZ$.30 (20¢), no matter how far you ride. One word of caution when you're planning evening activities: Auckland buses stop running around 11:30 p.m. on weekdays and Saturdays (10 p.m. on Sunday), so if your evening is going to be a late one, plan on taking a taxi home.

New in 1987 is the free **waterfront bus** that runs every two hours from the Downtown Airline Bus Terminal on Quay Street to St. Heliers Bay. Along the way you'll pass (and may disembark at) the Sea Bee Air office on Mechanics Bay, the Parnell Baths, Lilliputt Mini Golf, Kelly Tarlton's Underwater World, and the Mission House at Mission Bay. The bus itself is a curiosity—a 1972 Atlantean double-decker that holds a grand total of 66 passengers. With its open upper deck and gaily decorated interior (bright watercolor waterfront scenes), it has been dubbed the "Fun Bus" by Aucklanders.

Auckland has a high percentage of drivers per capita, and driving in the city can be a real hassle. My best advice is to park the car and use that excellent bus system as much as possible. If you must drive into the city, you can park the car for the day in **parking lots** (called car parks hereabouts) operated by the City Council. They're on Beresford Street, just off Karangahape Road; near the waterfront on Albert Street, west of Queen; on Victoria Street, just east of Queen; Britomart, off Customs Street to the east of Queen Street; downtown to the east of Queen Street; downtown to the west of Queen Street with an entrance from Customs Street West; Civic Underground on Mayoral Drive; and Victoria Street East. All are open seven days a week, 24 hours a day, and rates are quite reasonable.

Useful Information

The **New Zealand Tourist and Publicity Department** has a **Travel Office** at 99 Queen St. (tel. 09/798-180), open Monday through Friday from 8:30 a.m. to 5 p.m. and on Saturday from 9:30 a.m. to noon. Go by to pick up free brochures, any specific help you may need, and a copy of *Auckland A–Z* and the *Auckland Tourist Times* (which are also distributed free by many hotels) for a listing of current daytime and nighttime happenings. . . . The **Auckland Visitors Centre**, 299 Queen St., at Aotea Square (tel. 09/303-1889), is open from 8:30 a.m. to 5 p.m. Monday through Friday and 9 a.m. to 4 p.m. weekends and public holidays.

InterCity buses and trains arrive and depart from the **Auckland Railway Station** east of Queen Street on Beach Road (tel. 792-500). . . . Domestic **Air New Zealand** flights can be booked at the NZTP Travel Office, 99 Queen St. (for domestic flight information, dial 275-6197; for international flights, 793-930). . . . The **Airporter Express** (tel. 275-1234) gets you to and from the airport, and you need to book at least two hours before you want to travel. The **Super Shuttle** (tel. 375-210) performs a similar and equally reliable service. . . . The **Explorer Bus** (tel. 866-335) runs all day making dropoffs and pickups at five major Auckland attractions and in general is a convenient way to get around for a set fare of NZ$5 ($3.15). The **Downtown Bus Terminal** for local transportation is at 131 Hobson St. (tel. 794-420), where you can get timetables and price information, and catch a bus; hours are 7 a.m. to 9 p.m. Monday through Saturday and 9 a.m. to 5 p.m. on Sunday. . . . The **Devonport ferry** departs regularly from the Princes Wharf on Quay Street (tel. 303-3318). . . . **Mount Cook Line** is at 109 Queen St. (tel. 770-904 or 395-395). . . . **Taxi ranks** are at all terminals and on the corner of Customs Street West at Queen Street, or you can phone for a taxi (tel. 792-792 or 392-000).

The **Chief Post Office** (CPO) is between Quay and Customs Streets on Queen Street, and is open Monday through Thursday from 8 a.m. to 5 p.m., until 7 p.m. on Friday. The **United States Consulate** is at the corner of Shortland and O'Connell Streets (tel. 32-724). . . . Auckland's **telephone prefix** is 09.

Auckland International Airport

Auckland International Airport lies 13 miles south of the city just behind Manukau Harbour. You'll find the **Downtown Airline Terminal** (tel. 796-056) at 86-94 Quay St. at the corner of Albert Street next to the Travelodge Motel. Coach fare between the airport and bus station is NZ$8 ($5). If you're staying at a city hotel on the direct bus route, the driver will drop you off upon request. A **shuttle bus** connects the International Terminal to the Domestic Terminal, about a mile away for NZ$5 ($3.15). **Taxi fares** to and from the airport run about NZ$30 ($18.75) on weekdays, a little higher on weekends and at night. **Minibus transport** between the airport and downtown hotels and motels is supplied by Super Shuttle and the Airporter Express (see above) for NZ$12 ($7.50) per person one way (ask about discounts for two people traveling together).

At the International terminal, there's a **Public Information Office,** coffeeshop, licensed restaurant, bar, bank, post office, rental-car desk, and rental showers. The attractive terminal building's decor is designed to showcase New Zealand's character through the use of murals, timber, stone finishes, and wool carpets.

Special Help for the Budgeteer

Otto and Joan Spinka have operated **Touristop** since 1978, located in Auckland's Downtown Airline Terminal, 86-94 Quay St. (tel. 775-783). This knowledgeable couple specializes in offering value-for-dollar services such as bookings for accommodations, tours, rental cars, sightseeing tours, harbor

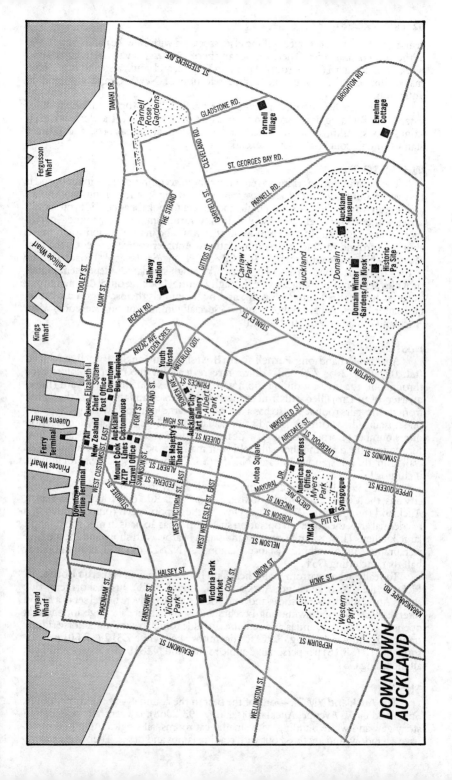

DOWNTOWN
AUCKLAND

cruises, and, well, just about anything else associated with New Zealand–wide travel at the best possible price. There's never any booking fee! They're open seven days a week from 8 a.m. to 6 p.m. (until 9 p.m. on Friday), and you'll also find magazines, maps, film, candies, coins, and a nice selection of New Zealand souvenirs at Touristop.

The Spinkas have opened a new business called **Ferrystop** in the newly renovated Ferry Building. It is also open seven days a week to provide travelers with magazines, books, film, postcards, local and international newspapers, and postage stamps (highly sought-after on weekends).

WHERE TO STAY

The most important thing to remember about accommodations in Auckland is that you should book *before you leave home*—I can think of few things worse than arriving anywhere after a 13-hour flight and having to look for a room! If you should arrive without a room already reserved, however, turn immediately to the Government Tourist Bureau. Just keep in mind that you'll be in no position to do much shopping around for budget accommodations. Another source for help is the Best Western/NZ reservation number (tel. 09/505-418). (See Chapter I for an outline of their discount Holiday Pass.) This network of high-standard, independent motels provides a 24-hour booking service through a central booking office during normal business hours (8:30 a.m. to 5 p.m.) and by the motels themselves on a rotation basis after hours. A pre-booked room is especially important on weekends, when Auckland can be very tightly booked.

Hostels

Auckland's handsome **Parnell Youth Hostel,** 2 Churton St., Parnell, Auckland (tel. 09/793-72 or 790-258), draws rave reviews for the cheerful colors used throughout, the inviting dining room with pine tables and chairs, the yard (three-quarters of an acre) filled with fruit trees and picnic tables, and the view of the harbor from the upstairs rooms. It also has a TV room, a large lounge downstairs, a smaller one upstairs filled with books and games, a laundry, baggage storage, and an enormous number of brochures on New Zealand. Videos about the country are shown throughout the day. And they will hold your mail. The hostel is a ten-minute uphill walk from the bus station. Rates are NZ$14 ($8.75) for seniors, half that for juniors, including GST.

Some 2½ miles south of the city center, but easy to reach by the Three Kings city bus, the **Mount Eden Youth Hostel,** 5A Oaklands Rd. (off Mount Eden Road), Auckland (tel. 09/603-975), is also close to the airport coach route. Located in a residential area, the hostel, in operation since 1967, has 46 beds in nine rooms and a large kitchen. There's a full-size pool and sauna nearby, with shops and inexpensive restaurants within walking distance. Seniors pay NZ$13 ($8.15), and juniors pay half that, including GST.

To really get away from it all, there's no better place than **Hekerua House,** 11 Hekerua Rd., Waiheke Island, Auckland (tel. 09/72-8371). Just a short ferry ride across Auckland harbor to the island, and you'll find the private hostel set in a Maori reserve close to good swimming beaches and shops. There's a large lounge that opens to the sundeck, and island activities include fishing, swimming, horse riding, tramping, and windsurfing. Rates for dormitory beds are NZ$12 ($7.50) per person, NZ$13 ($8.15) per person in double rooms, and NZ$10 ($6.25) for tent sites, all including GST.

The Y

The **Auckland YMCA**—one of the best in the country—at the corner of Pitt Street and Greys Avenue, Auckland (tel. 09/303-2068), is a centrally heated, five-story gray-and-white building with small, neat rooms, all singles. All are carpeted, have a window, and are fitted out with reading lamps and desks. The Y has an elevator, a laundry and shower on each floor, parking on the premises, and two TV lounges. It accepts both men and women over the age of 17, and about half of the 128 rooms are filled with permanent guests, either students or working people. Rates, which include full board (breakfast, a cold lunch during the week and hot lunch on weekends, and dinner) are NZ$30.40 ($19) the first night and NZ$22.50 ($14) per night thereafter.

Caravan Parks and Cabins

The **North Shore Caravan Park Cabins & Motels,** 52 Northcote Rd., Takapuna, Auckland (tel. 09/4191-320 or 4182-578), is a first-class location, the closest to downtown Auckland via the Harbour Bridge. There are 30 tent sites, 130 caravan sites, cabins, bunkrooms, and four motel units, as well as large bathroom and kitchen facilities. It's handy to frequent bus service, shops, and restaurants. Rates are NZ$10 ($6.25) for tent sites, NZ$15 ($9.40) for most cabins, NZ$35 ($22) for one person and NZ$45 ($28.15) for two for luxury cabins, and NZ$60 ($37.50) for one person and NZ$70 ($43.75) for two for the motel units, all including GST.

The **Meadowcourt Motel** (no, it's *not* a motel in the regular sense), 360 Great South Rd., Papatoetoe, Auckland (tel. 09/278-5612), sits in park-like grounds and is handy to both the airport and the city, as well as several entertainment complexes. There's a pool and a food store on the premises, as well as 20 tent sites at NZ$10 ($6.25), 62 caravan sites at NZ$12 ($7.50), 8 cabins at NZ$30 ($18.75), 12 tourist flats at NZ$40 ($25), and 14 motel rooms at NZ$55 ($34.50). All rates are for double occupancy, and you must add GST.

Bed-and-Breakfasts

Ascot Parnell, 36 St. Stephens Ave., Parnell, Auckland 1 (tel. 09/399-012), is one of Auckland's most pleasant and atmospheric lodgings, located just a short walk from Parnell Village, the Auckland War Memorial Museum, and the Rose Gardens, and a longish walk from the city center (with good bus service, including the airport bus, which stops right out front). Its grounds feature lovely shrubbery and flowers, with a gigantic, century-old pin oak tree that's registered as a "historic tree." The house itself dates from 1910 and, under the loving care of Alfred and Heidi Hassencamp, it is beautifully maintained to preserve what is a sort of informal elegance. Guest rooms here are especially spacious, and some family rooms will accommodate up to four people. All have private baths and direct-dial telephones. There's a pretty dining room, a TV lounge (where coffee and tea are free), and off-street parking. Singles here, including a cooked or continental breakfast, are NZ$58 ($36.25), and doubles run NZ$79 ($49.50), plus GST. Children under 12 pay NZ$10 ($6.25); each additional adult sharing a room pays NZ$19 ($12). I've had nothing but good reports from readers (who first alerted me to Ascot Parnell), and because it is so popular with overseas visitors, it is advisable to book as far in advance as you possibly can. (*Note:* Be sure to ask for an introduction to "George.")

In the Epsom section of Auckland close by One Tree Hill, **Janet and Jim Millar,** 10 Ngaroma Rd., Epsom, Auckland (tel. 09/657-336), open their three-quarters-of-a-century-old bungalow to bed-and-breakfast guests. They have four bedrooms, with two baths and two lounges, and they are especially adept at working out family accommodations (their grandchildren are frequent and welcomed visitors, so little ones are no problem here). There's a path at one end of the street that leads directly to Maungakiekie (One Tree Hill Domain), and nearby bus service takes you into the city center. Both experienced travelers, the Millars enjoy travel talk with their guests, and they'll provide the evening meal with advance notice. Early arrivals are welcome. Rates for bed-and-breakfast are NZ$35 ($22) single, NZ$55 ($34.50) double; for bed, breakfast, and dinner, NZ$50 ($31.25) single, NZ$85 ($53.25) double. GST is included.

One of our faithful readers must be given full credit for leading me to the **Cha-**

let Chevron Hotel, 14 Brighton Rd., Parnell, Auckland (tel. 09/390-290). I found it, as that reader wrote, to be a "small, clean, comfortable, and *happy*" place, run by Jane Nilsson, an enthusiastic and informative host with a genuine interest in her guests' enjoyment of Auckland and New Zealand, as well as in their comfort. The 15 rooms all have private showers, and there are two family units. It's a short walk away from Parnell Village, and there's convenient bus transportation into the city center. Rates are NZ$48 ($30) single and NZ$70 ($43.75) double for bed-and-breakfast, plus GST.

Another bed-and-breakfast establishment conveniently located is the **Aspen Lodge,** 62 Emily Pl., Auckland (tel. 09/796-698). This small, neat hotel is a short walk from Queen Street and also from the main rail and coach station (the airport shuttle stops at the hotel). The 26 rooms are on the small side, but clean and bright. Singles run NZ$40 ($25) and doubles go for NZ$55 ($34.50). Prices include GST, and the hearty breakfasts here are outstanding.

Aachen House, 39 Market Rd., Remuera, Auckland (tel. 09/5202-329), sits up on a hill overlooking Hobson Park, and is one of a pair of two-story residences built back in 1905 that were known as the "Two Old Ladies of Market Road." There's a decided Victorian air about the place, with its rounded turret wing off to one side and lots of gingerbread trim. Jean and Donald Goldschmidt are the friendly, helpful hosts. Rooms all have high ceilings, some have bay windows looking out onto nice views, and all share the three baths at one end of the upstairs hall. Downstairs, a cooked English breakfast is served in a quaint old dining room, and there's a TV lounge with tea and coffee makings. On cool evenings, the lounge is warmed by an open fire. Several bus lines into the city are just one block away, so there's frequent service. Bed-and-breakfast rates are NZ$40 ($25) single, NZ$60 ($37.50) double, plus GST.

"Old-fashioned" best describes **Remuera House,** 500 Remuera Rd., Remuera, Auckland (tel. 09/547-794). The house itself dates from 1901 and has a big bay window—in fact, large windows everywhere—and wisteria growing in the backyard. Pictures of the grandparents of host Ray King, who has an avid interest in genealogy, hang on the dining room wall. The house has comfortable rooms (singles will love corner room 5), a sun porch, a TV lounge with tea and coffee facilities, and laundry. It's ten minutes from downtown Auckland, and buses 635, 645, and 655 stop out front. Rates are NZ$36 ($22.50) single, NZ$55 ($34.50) double, and NZ$66 ($41.25) triple, including a cooked breakfast and GST.

Over on the North Shore, **Joyce and Harry Mossman,** 2 Grove Rd., Devonport, Auckland (tel. 09/459-437), are only 20 minutes from the center city via the Harbour Bridge or that delightful ferry; there is also door-to-door shuttle-bus service from the airport. The large home set amid shade trees and a spacious lawn is only a minute from Cheltenham Beach and just a little farther from shops, restaurants, and bus transportation. Their two bedrooms, each with twin beds, have H&C, private bath with shower and toilet, and a private entrance. Complimentary tea and coffee are provided, and they'll prepare an evening meal with advance notice. Rates (add GST) for bed-and-breakfast are NZ$45 ($28.25) single, NZ$60 ($37.50) double; and for bed, breakfast, and dinner, NZ$60 ($37.50) single, NZ$90 ($56.25) double.

Also within walking distance of Cheltenham Beach, **Devonport Manor,** 7 Cambridge Terrace, Devonport, Auckland (tel. 09/452-529), is a Victorian home with four guest rooms, each with a queen-size bed and firm mattress. Baths are shared, and terrycloth robes thoughtfully provided. For a harbor view, request the Chantilly Room; the Carmel Room looks out on the Devonport Domain, where soccer and cricket are played. A self-contained unit, the Cambridge Suite, has bay windows, a fireplace, a queen-size bed plus a sofa bed, a kitchenette, and bath with shower. There is also an airy common room, veranda with wicker furniture, gazebo, and laundry. The stellar breakfast includes fresh orange juice, homemade museli, and muffins, fresh fruit salad, and egg dishes. Owner Jackie Cozby of Carmel, Calif., shares the house with Mindy and Smoker, two rarely seen and never heard cocker spaniels. The house is also a walk away from North Head, which affords a fine view of the harbor and Auckland. Devonport shops are half a mile away. Room rates are NZ$55 ($34.50) and NZ$66 ($41.25) per person; the suite is NZ$88 ($55). All include GST and that nutritious breakfast.

A Licensed Hotel

Let me warn you right up front that *this recommendation is for Friday or Saturday only*—rates Monday through Thursday skyrocket out of the budget range at the **Hotel De Brett,** High and Shortland Streets (P.O. Box 237), Auckland (tel. 09/32-389). An Auckland landmark that has been completely renovated and done up in tasteful furnishings and decor, Hotel De Brett has a pricing policy that lets you spend a weekend right in the heart of the city for some of the best rates in town. And if it's after-dark doings you're looking for, you won't even have to leave the hotel, since there's nightly entertainment. There are no fewer than five bars, as well as an excellent restaurant for pricey meals, and light lunches available in two of the bars. Single or double rooms go for NZ$75 ($47) on weekends; they jump to NZ$110 ($68.75) other days. GST, of course, is additional.

Serviced Motels

One of Auckland's best accommodations is the **Smart Budget Hotel,** City Road and Liverpool Street (P.O. Box 68–441), Auckland (tel. 09/392-801). Centrally located, it offers high-quality, inexpensive single and double rooms with tea and coffee facilities, but no private bath facilities—separate male and female bathrooms are provided on each floor. Most rooms have a good view of the harbor; all are attractively decorated, and there's one paraplegic unit. There's a guest lounge and a separate one for TV, as well as a good moderately priced restaurant that serves from 7 a.m. to 3 p.m. (they'll also provide picnic boxes with advance notice). Laundry service is available, and if your itinerary calls for it, you can arrange early check-in or late checkout. Rates are NZ$35 ($22) single, NZ$55 ($34.25) double, plus GST.

With the same owners as the Smart Budget Hotel (above), the **Park Towers Hotel,** 3 Scotia Pl., Auckland (tel. 09/392-800), is also centrally located, with many of the no-frills policies of its budget counterpart, but is a bit more upmarket. Of its 108 rooms, 28 have private facilities; there are several triple-occupancy rooms, and there's a lobby bar in addition to the restaurant and guest lounge. Rates run NZ$66 ($41.25) to NZ$126.50 ($79), including GST.

Offering a whole range of accommodation choices, the **Auckland Airport Skyway Lodge,** 30 Kirkbride Rd., Mangere (P.O. Box 73119), Auckland Airport (tel. 09/275-4443, or 15 on the courtesy phone at the airport), is far from the city center, but has a courtesy van as well as convenient bus transportation. It's an attractive modern building, with a TV lounge, pool table, sauna, spa pool, swimming pool, tea and coffee facilities, and ample guest parking. To begin at the lower end of the accommodation scale, although this is in no way a hostel, there are dormitories of four bunks each, with budget rates of NZ$25 ($15.50) per person. Then there are single, twin, and family serviced rooms that go for NZ$38 ($23.75) single and NZ$48 ($30) double. At the top of the scale are the two motel-flat units that sleep from two to seven, in two bedrooms with double and single beds. These come with fully equipped kitchens, private baths, and color TV, and rates are NZ$72 ($45) double, NZ$12 ($7.50) per additional adult. All rates include GST.

Motel Flats

Located on the direct airport route, the **Ranfurly Court Motel,** 285 Manukau Rd. (near Ranfurly Road), Auckland (tel. 09/689-059), is on the airport bus route and no more than a ten-minute bus ride from the city center. This two-story Best Western member has a pleasant setting of manicured lawn, roses, and hedges. There are 12 lovely one-bedroom flats, and each accommodates from two to four people.

Each unit has one full window wall, is nicely decorated, and comes equipped with telephone, radio, color TV, and electric blankets. And unlike most motel flats, these are serviced daily. There is a guest laundry, as well as car-wash facilities, on the premises, and a shopping center is just 100 yards away. Rates are NZ$70 ($43.75), single or double, and NZ$10 ($6.25) for each additional adult, plus GST. Five different breakfasts are available, ranging from NZ$3.50 ($2.20) for a croissant to NZ$8.50 ($5.30) for a cooked meal.

The **Barrycourt Motor Inn,** 10-20 Gladstone Rd. (off St. Stephens Avenue), Auckland (tel. 09/33-789), is a personal favorite of mine not only because of the quality of the units but also because the staff is unfailingly pleasant, friendly, and helpful—a reflection of owner Norm Barry's business philosophy. The original part of the motor inn consists of 22 units in a modern brick building: bed-sitters and one-bedroom and two-bedroom flats sleeping two to five people, with especially well-equipped kitchens and ample closets (both features throughout the Barrycourt). The Executive Block holds 80 units, most with terraces and harbor views. All units have tea- and coffee-making facilities, phones, color TVs, radios, and refrigerators; many also have complete kitchens, and two-bedroom suites have their own clothes washer and dryer—worth the NZ$126.50 ($73) splurge just to go home without dirty laundry! The best bets for budgeteers are five units in a lodge at the bottom of the property priced at NZ$75 ($47) for one or two people. Some have oak paneling, beamed ceilings, stained-glass panels, and leaded-glass windows. On-premises facilities include four spa pools, a laundry, and a Victorian building that houses the excellent Gladstone's restaurant (see "Where to Eat"); recent additions include a swimming pool, tanning salon, and a covered walkway connecting the reception area and restaurant. There's ample parking. The Barrycourt is conveniently located less than a mile from the CPO and within easy walking distance of Parnell Road's quaint shopping district. Rates range from NZ$75 ($47) to NZ$156 ($97.50), single or double, plus GST. The Portland Road bus stops right at the door. It's a Best Western, so ask about the Holiday Pass discount.

At the **Domain Motel,** 155 Park Rd., Grafton, Auckland (tel. 09/32-509), you'll find a location convenient to the city center along with a rare opportunity to do a good deed with your travel dollars. Beautifully situated overlooking the 200-acre Domain Park, it is owned by the Auckland Division of the Cancer Society (patients being treated at Auckland Hospital stay free), and superior accommodations are available to the public on an as-available basis. There are bed-sitter units with tea and coffee facilities, and one- and two-bedroom units with complete cooking facilities. Best of all, your room rent goes directly to help the society's good work. Rates for bed-sitters are NZ$65 ($40.75) single, NZ$75 ($47) double; for one or two bedrooms, NZ$75 ($47) single, NZ$85 ($53.25) double. Add GST to all.

If it's a quiet residential location you're after, the **Mt. Eden Motel,** 47 Balmoral Rd., Mount Eden, Auckland 3 (tel. 09/687-187), will certainly fill the bill. Only a short, pleasant walk from Mount Eden and Mount Eden Village shops, the 26-unit motel is set back from the road, eliminating traffic noise. In fact, with off-street parking just outside your unit you can forget driving into the city, since there's good bus service just a few minutes away. There are one- and two-bedroom units, as well as bed-sitters with double and twin beds, all with full kitchens, color TVs, telephones, radios, and private bathrooms. On the premises, you'll find an outdoor swimming pool, indoor Jacuzzi and two saunas, guest laundry, car wash, and barbecue area. Breakfasts are available, and there are restaurants nearby. Robyn and Jim Baker, the owner/operators, are both interested in and knowledgeable about helping with your sightseeing and ongoing itinerary. Rates are NZ$67 ($42) to NZ$70 ($43.75) single, NZ$74 ($46.25) to NZ84 ($52.50) double, NZ$12 ($7.50) per extra person, all plus GST.

Also in a tranquil location, yet handy to the city center, is the **Raceway Motor Lodge,** 67 St. Vincent Ave., Remuera, Auckland (tel. 09/480-7445), where Anne and Joe Powell are the friendly owners. Close to Ellerslie Racecourse and Alexandra Park, it is only a short walk from a good shopping center and licensed restaurants. All units have complete kitchens, color TVs, videos, radios, and telephones, and there's a guest laundry, as well as covered parking. Rates are NZ$65 ($40.75) single, NZ$75 ($47) double, plus GST. To reach the Raceway, take the Greenlane exit on the motorway toward Ellerslie Racecourse, and it's the second turn on the left.

The **Green Glade Motel,** 27 Ocean View Rd., Northcote, Auckland (tel. 09/ 480-7445), is five miles across the Harbour Bridge on the North Shore. Not to worry if you're not driving, however—owners Gill and Geoff Calvert will collect you from the Downtown Airline Terminal, and there's good bus transportation into the city. There are eight one- and two-bedroom units with complete kitchens, and five with tea and toast facilities. All have modern furnishings and bright, cheerful decor, and all come with color TV, radio, telephone, central heating, and electric blankets. This Best Western member has a swimming pool, heated spa pool, and a guest laundry. Continental or cooked breakfast is available for a small additional charge. A real bonus is the lovely, forested public reserve with stands of white pine just back of the motel, great for peaceful walks. Nearby are a licensed restaurant, golf course, beaches, and shopping centers. Rates, including GST, are NZ$71.50 ($44.75) single and NZ$77 ($48.25) double.

Farther from the city (21 km, a 25-minute drive), but in a gorgeous beachfront setting, the **Beach Court Motel,** 5 The Esplanade, Eastern Beach (tel. 09/534-5159), may tempt you to loiter a day or two to prepare for strenuous sightseeing ahead or to rest up at the end of your trip. There are marvelous views of Hauraki Gulf with its islands, and a very good swimming beach (safe for children) just across the road. The 17 units are exceptionally spacious, all with full kitchen, lounge, and one or two bedrooms. Ideal for families, with large public tennis courts immediately behind the motel and a five-acre municipal playground adjoining, units are brightly decorated (all will sleep four to six comfortably), have color TV and ironing board and iron, and there's a spa pool. The charge is NZ$75 ($47), single or double, GST included.

Out in the delightful Browns Bay section, the **Olive Tree Motel,** 24 Glencoe Rd., Browns Bay, Auckland 10 (tel. 09/478-7679), is an attractive, small (eight units) motel in a peaceful location near good beaches as well as restaurants and shops. Facilities include a pool, spa, and trampoline, and all units have a complete kitchen, telephone, and color TV. There's a honeymoon suite, and one luxurious two-bedroom executive suite. Seasonal rates are NZ$79 ($49.50) to NZ$83 ($52) for singles, NZ$86 ($53.75) to NZ$90 ($56.25) for doubles, with a NZ$11 ($6.90) charge for each additional person.

Mini-Splurges

While both of these two recommendations have rates in the upper register, neither is really so expensive as to qualify as a *big* splurge, and both are exceptional enough to consider spending the extra dollars. Both are located on Auckland's North Shore, about a 20-minute drive from the city center over the Harbour Bridge.

A mini-splurge with a unique setting is the **Mon Desir Hotel,** 144 Hurstmere Rd. (P.O. Box 331034), Takapuna, Auckland (tel. 09/495-139). Located on Auckland's North Shore, the Mon Desir has been a favorite of Kiwis for generations. Surrounded by ancient, giant pohutakawa trees and gardens filled with tropical flowering plants, on grounds that slope down to a lovely little private beach, the hotel exudes an air of serenity. Its guest rooms reflect casual comfort ("casual," however, does *not* mean "shabby" in this case!) rather than the slick elegance of more recent hostelries. Each has coffee and tea facilities and a fridge, and some have balconies. Continental or cooked breakfasts are available. There's a swimming pool, a spa, ample parking, and paraplegic access. The licensed Summerhouse Restaurant serves lunch and dinner on an à la carte basis (reasonable prices, with reductions for children under age 10), as well as an excellent buffet, and will gladly pack picnic lunches.

Prices at this atmospheric old hotel range from NZ$118.50 ($74) single to NZ$124 ($77.50) double, to NZ$169 ($106) for a large suite; ocean-view units start at NZ$130 ($81.25). All plus GST. Children free.

Just a short distance from the Mon Desir, the **Takapuna Beach Motel,** The Promenade, Takapuna Beach, Auckland (tel. 09/497-126), is a Best Western, so the rate discounts will reduce costs at one of the city's prettiest motels. Set back off the street in beautifully landscaped grounds, the 40 luxury suites, all with complete kitchens, are grouped around a heated pool and barbecue area, the focal point of convivial guest gatherings virtually every evening. Other on-premises facilities include spa pool, games room, guest laundry, and video. All suites will sleep two to six people, are nicely decorated, and have attractive modern furnishings, and there are a few with waterbeds. The beach (excellent swimming and windsurfing) is just a few steps away, and village shops and restaurants are quite close by (also, there's a charge-back arrangement for meals at the Mon Desir). All rates are for single or double occupancy (add GST to all). Standard suites are NZ$145 ($90.75); poolside suites are NZ$155 ($97) and NZ$165 ($103). Highly recommended.

Big Splurges

There was a time, not so long ago, when Auckland's luxury, big-splurge accommodations were so scarce as to be almost nonexistent. Not so today, however. As New Zealand has become more and more attractive to corporations as well as tourists, upscale hotels have sprung up to meet a growing demand, and Auckland, as the country's largest and most progressive city, now has several that are outstanding. Those listed below are, I believe, not only posh enough to provide every ounce of pampering your splurge dollars should buy, but offer the best value in every respect for those hard-earned dollars.

The **Hyatt Kingsgate Hotel,** 2 Princes St. (P.O. Box 3938), Auckland (tel. 09/366-1234, or toll free 800/228-9000 in the U.S.), sits on high ground just at the edge of the city center, overlooking adjacent Albert Park and affording terrific views of the harbor. Until early 1984 this was the Inter-Continental, always a favorite with Kiwis and international visitors. Since the Hyatt Kingsgate management took over, however, the hotel has been given a loving facelift, with everything from lobby and public rooms to guest rooms to restaurants renovated with quiet elegance. There are some 275 rooms, all of which have oversize beds, individually controlled heating and air conditioning, two direct-dial telephones, a mini-bar, fridge, and complimentary tea and coffee facilities. Each room has either a harbor or park view. If you want to splurge *all* the way, opt for the Regency Club, a "hotel within a hotel"—three floors that have been set aside to provide the services of a concierge, a private lounge, complimentary continental breakfast, evening cocktails and canapés, and such extras as cuddly bathrobes and deluxe toiletries. There are all sorts of shops, laundry and dry-cleaning services, babysitting, airport limousine service, and even a currency exchange. Other facilities include two cocktail lounges with music, a café for casual surroundings, and the gourmet Top of the Town restaurant that not only serves up some of the best food and service in town, but throws in a magnificent harbor view as well (see "Where to Eat"). Splurgy accommodations, without a doubt, with splurgy prices of NZ$200 ($125) to NZ$220 ($138), single or double, plus GST. For all those Regency Club extras, you'll pay NZ$240 ($150) to NZ$340 ($213), single or double, plus GST. *Note:* There are also Hyatt Kingsgate hotels in Rotorua and Queenstown; the central reservations telephone number is 09/391-818.

For luxury with a distinctly New Zealand flavor, it's the **Sheraton Auckland Hotel,** 83 Symonds St. (P.O. Box 2771), Auckland 1 (tel. 09/795-132, or toll free 800/325-3535 in the U.S.), in a setting that commands panoramic views of Auckland and its beautiful harbor. Native woods have been used throughout, and there are impressive Maori carvings and murals in all public rooms. The airy reception area has a glass dome and features a waterfall centerpiece. The 422 guest rooms are situated in three wings, and each has individual heating and air conditioning, direct-dial telephone, fridge, mini-bar, and in-room video movies. Just off the lobby, the sunken Rendezvous Lounge is a restful meeting place with marble floors and walls, touches of greenery, and a unique carved mural depicting Maori customs. The Steam Biscuit Factory (named for a mill that ground out flour for biscuits on this site from the colonial period right up to the 1950s) serves both light snacks and complete meals around the clock, while Partington's Restaurant offers more elegant dining. Governor Grey's Lounge becomes a sophisticated disco after dark. When you're not eating or drinking or dancing, there's a heated rooftop pool with poolside service (covered during cool months), exercise room, health club, and saunas. Other services include babysitters, dry cleaning and laundry, and a currency exchange. For the disabled, there are wheelchairs available. For all this luxury, you'll pay the same rates for single or double occupancy (twin and king-size beds are both available)—NZ$96 ($60) to NZ$260 ($163), depending on location.

For a super-splurge, there's the posh **Regent of Auckland,** centrally located on Albert Street, Auckland (tel. 09/398-882), where a double room goes for NZ$341 ($213) a night. The real splurge here is service; a staff of 500 fusses over guests in 332 rooms.

READERS' ACCOMMODATION SELECTIONS: "We were delighted with the **Siesta Motel,** 70 Great South Rd., Remuera, Auckland (tel. 09/502-106), and Royce and Helen Vogt, the owners. The location is right on the bus line to the center of the city and close to the race courses" (J. and E. Vick, Longmont, Colo.). . . . "The **Railton Travel Hotel,** 411 Queen St. (P.O. Box 68-241) (tel. 09/796-487), is very central, within walking distance of Queen Street shops. The hotel is run by the Salvation Army, the staff is friendly, and a lot of foreigners stay here. There is a laundry, ironing boards and irons, coffee- and tea-making facilities, and guest parking—good value" (G. Speed, Oslo, Norway). . . . "The **Tane Tourist Lodge,** 558 Great South Rd., Papatoetoe, Auckland (tel. 09/278-5725), was our 'find' of the trip, new and out toward the airport. We enjoyed a shiny, clean kitchen and the camaraderie of people from South Africa, England, and the U.S." (I. See, Long Creek, Ore.).

WHERE TO EAT

Eating out in Auckland can be just about anything you want it to be. There are scads of small, attractive, and inexpensive coffeeshop-type eateries, a wide range of cuisine at moderate prices, and an impressive array of posh restaurants serving international dishes. They're scattered all over the city, but there are interesting concentrations along Parnell and Ponsonby Roads (a large percentage along the latter fall into a high price range, which can only have a place in any budget vacation as a "big splurge"). You'll find examples of each in these pages, but you should also pick up a copy of the free *Auckland Dining Guide,* published quarterly and available at many hotels, as well as NZTP offices. Its listings are quite complete and there's a city map included showing restaurant locations. Remember: *GST of 12.5% must be added to all prices listed here.*

One of the most inexpensive ways to eat, of course, is to stop by a deli and pick up the makings of a meal in your motel flat—you'll be getting full value then from that lovely fridge, stove, pots and pans, dishes, etc. An alternative, especially on those days when you're absolutely pooped from sightseeing and don't want to face any sort of food preparation, is to order a delicious pizza and have it delivered piping hot right to your door. **Dial-A-Dino's Pizza** (tel. 781-103) delivers from 4:30 to 11 p.m. Sunday through Thursday and 4:30 p.m. to 1 p.m. on Friday and Saturday, and they have a wide variety of pizza toppings from which to choose: ham, salami, pepperoni, diced beef, mushrooms, onions, olives, prawns, smoked oysters, bacon, anchovies, capers . . . well, that's *part* of their list. They also offer crusty garlic bread and soft drinks, and delivery is usually within 30 minutes. Pizzas come in 6-, 8-, and 12-slice pies at prices of NZ$14.50 ($9.05) to NZ$30 ($18.75).

Those on dairy-free diets will be happy to know of the existence of **Badger's,** 47 High St. (no phone). Everything here is vegetarian, and much of it has no dairy content. Menu items include quiches, pastas, pies, pizzas, desserts, and fresh carrot juice, from NZ$1.50 (95¢) to NZ$7 ($4.40). It's no-smoking.

Nicholas Nickleby, 9 High St. (tel. 734-604), is a real find for budgeteers. It's a small, unpretentious, cozy, downstairs eatery where everything is home-made of the very freshest ingredients, and it's a great favorite with city center office workers (which means you'll do well to go earlier or later than regular office hours). The self-service counter always includes a nice variety of salads, small quiches, meat pies, meat rolls, soups, lasagne, and melt-in-your-mouth muffins and other pastries. Desserts, too, are exceptionally good. A cooked breakfast of bacon and eggs is also available in the morning. Best of all, a light meal will cost you no more than NZ$8 ($5). Open from 7:15 a.m. to 2:30 p.m. Monday through Friday.

The menu and prices at **The Hard to Find Café,** 47 High St. (tel. 734-681), make this an Auckland favorite. Helen and David Merton serve some of the best Mexican food I've had anywhere in the world (including my favorite New York City spot). Her marvelous tacos come with all kinds of fillings, including vegetarian, and the nachos are *really* crispy. Although the enchilada salad and sour cream alone makes a good lunch, for something even more filling, try the enchilada and taco with rice and salad. There's a daily fish dish, blackboard specials, a nice selection of desserts, and several special coffees. Prices? From NZ$4.95 ($3.10) to NZ$13.95 ($8.70)! No alcohol is served, but you're welcome to bring your own beer or wine. Hours are noon to 2 p.m. Monday through Friday for lunch, and 6 to 10 p.m. for dinner every day.

Dynasty, 28 Customs St. East (tel. 795-000), was the first licensed Chinese restaurant in Auckland when it opened in 1975, and since that time it has been a consistent favorite of locals. Food is Cantonese, with choices from Malaysia and Singapore as well, and the five chefs all trained in top Hong Kong restaurants. The pretty red-and-gold decor extends throughout all four levels of the restaurant, and specialties include all kinds of seafood as well as native lamb, venison, and beef. Prices are in the NZ$8 ($5) to NZ$12 ($7.50) range, and an especially good value is the Sunday Yum Char lunch at NZ$9 ($5.65). Hours are noon to 2:30 p.m. and 6 to 11 p.m. seven days a week.

Over on Parnell Road, **Fraser's Place,** 116 Parnell Rd. (tel. 774-080), is one of the special little places beloved by local residents and so seldom found by visitors. Ian Fraser left a successful business career to follow his heart into the kitchen of this sparkling deli-cum-restaurant. You enter through the deli, which displays such unexpected treasures as those melt-in-your-mouth Greek spinach-and-cheese pies for NZ$2 (80¢) and mini-quiches, to be eaten at the pine-stool counter just back of the shop or to take away (great to take home for that late-night snack when you don't want to go out). All sorts of sausages, cheeses, salads, and rolls as well. Upstairs, there are three distinctly different dining rooms: the Graffiti Room (you can leave your mark if you can find a spot on the wall), the Piaf Room, and the Conversation Room. The decor throughout is a treat, but it's the food that makes this place special. Ian was brought up in the East, and you'll find several spicy dishes on the menu like goulash, chili con carne, and mustard veal. Salad platters include smoked salmon, coppa and paw paw, shrimp and avocado, spanakopita Greek salad, and assorted cheese and fruit platters. Pâtés are homemade and out of this world. Be sure to include this stop in any Parnell Road wanderings. No wine license, but there are four special liqueur coffees, and you can bring your own wine along. Lunch can run NZ$6 ($3.75) to NZ$12.50 ($7.80). Hours are noon to 2:30 p.m. Monday through Saturday.

Also in Parnell, **Le Bouquet d'Or,** 305 Parnell Rd. (tel. 678-953), is cafeteria style yet stylish. It's a grand place for breakfast—you can sit and read the newspaper or plot the day's activities. The front porch is inviting, and it's handy for those in wheelchairs, who can just wheel right up. You can order everything from danish and coffee (or cappuccino) to fruit cups to meat-filled croissants to cheese pies. It's open from 7 a.m. to 5:30 p.m. on Sunday and Monday, later the rest of the week. You'll probably spend about NZ$5 ($3.15) here, no more than NZ$10 ($6.25) if you order lunch.

In the heart of downtown, the **Burlington Tea Rooms,** in the Bank of New Zealand building on Fort Street, just two doors from Queen Street (tel. 303-2727), features that most marvelous of inventions, the bottomless cup of coffee, and a full breakfast served all day long. Here that's weekdays only from 4:30 a.m. (for early birds) to 3:30 p.m. This place was founded in 1943 and continues to pride itself on quality, speedy service, and cleanliness. Better still, you'll spend next to nothing. Everything is made right here, and leftovers are given to the needy at the end of the day.

One of the most economical meals in town is the pub counter lunch at the small **Rugby Club,** 47-51 Fort St. (tel. 770-725), just a few blocks from Queen Street. Fish and chips or roast beef on rye will cost you NZ$5 ($3.15); oysters, prawns, or lasagne, NZ$4.50 ($2.80). An assortment of sandwiches and rolls is available for NZ$1.80 ($1.15). Rugby photos cover the walls. Lunch is served Monday to Saturday from noon to 2:30 p.m., and it's open until 10 p.m. (11 p.m. on Friday and Saturday). Licensed.

Café Picasso, 136 Grafton Rd. (tel. 390-558), set in stimulating art-school atmosphere, features a blackboard menu of snacks, salads, and hot dishes. There's outdoor seating for fine days, and owner/manager Ann Harvey serves a champagne breakfast on request. Breakfast starts at 6:30 a.m.; the place is open until 4:30 p.m. Monday through Friday for lunches and afternoon teas. BYO.

If it's pub grub you savor, head to the **Shakespeare Tavern,** 61 Albert St. (tel. 735-396), which has the distinction of being New Zealand's only in-house brewery. It makes lager, ale, stout, and even ginger beer (if you try them all, you leave with a certificate). The winsome publican, Peter Barraclough, has been here since 1975, and his friendly daughter, Karen, is often on duty in the lounge upstairs. Hathaway's, the restaurant located downstairs, is open from 11 a.m. to 7:45 p.m. Monday through Wednesday, until 9:45 p.m. on Thursday, until 10:45 p.m. on Friday and Saturday, and from noon to 9:45 p.m. on Sunday. Prices are moderate. The lounge closes at 7 p.m. Prices are moderate. You'll probably come away with a T-shirt or mug as a souvenir—it's that kind of place. Licensed.

The **Queen Street Brasserie,** at Queen and Customs Streets (tel. 778-920), on the ground floor of the Parkroyal Hotel, is a handy drop-in spot when you're shopping or sightseeing in the area. It's open from 6:30 a.m. to 11 p.m., with a wide variety of offerings, from snacks to light lunches to three-course meals, all at moderate prices. It's fully licensed, open seven days a week, and also serves counter lunches and take-aways from its delicatessen on the corner.

Rick's Café Américain, Victoria Park Market (tel. 399-074), doesn't look much like its *Casablanca* counterpart, but it's a terrific drop-in place for snacks, light lunches, and moderately priced dinners. The food is good and offerings range from potato skins with sour cream to chili to spareribs to fresh fish, at moderate prices that seldom exceed NZ$15 ($9.40) for a full meal, much less for lighter fare. It's open every day from 11:30 a.m. to midnight, and on Saturday and Sunday breakfast is served from 9 a.m. to noon. Licensed, of course, and sometimes there's live music.

For an exciting taste of Asia, climb the stairs to **Bananas,** 317 Parnell Rd. (tel. 799-360), where the atmosphere is intimate and the mix of foods from ten Asian countries tantalizing. Consider hot-and-sour soup (here they call it "tummy warmer"), Vietnamese spring roll, mien gay (cold Chinese noodles with shredded chicken and sesame dressing), and satay (grilled in the evenings). Grab a balcony seat on a nice day—actually, you'd best reserve it ahead of time. The restaurant is open for lunch from noon to 2:30 p.m. Tuesday through Sunday and for dinner nightly from 6:45 p.m. until late. Expect to pay NZ$10 ($6.25) to NZ$20 ($12.50) for a meal.

Harbourside, on the second floor of the Ferry Building (tel. 370-486), has an ideal location overlooking the harbor, and its seafood dishes have won their share of kudos. Oysters are NZ$8.50 ($5.30); the smoked seafood platter, NZ$15 ($9.40);

char-grilled snapper, NZ$16.90 ($10.50); and the salmon filet, $23.50 ($14.75). Brunch is served on Saturday, Sunday, and holidays and starts at NZ$20 ($12.50). Prices include GST. The restaurant is open daily from 10:30 a.m. to 10 p.m. Licensed.

Good, inexpensive Italian fare is the specialty at **La Trattoria,** 259 Parnell Rd. (tel. 795-358). It's a light, cheerful place filled with latticework and greenery, and there's an outdoor courtyard for fine days. For no more than NZ$15 ($9.40) you can stuff yourself with homemade spinach pasta, fettuccine, calamari, and a host of other Italian favorites, all of which come with garlic bread and a salad. Hours are 11 a.m. to 3 p.m. Monday through Friday, and 6 to 11 p.m. seven days a week. Fully licensed.

The small, intimate, **Topo GiGio Italian Restaurant,** 274-278 Dominion Rd., Mount Eden (tel. 688-823 or 687-539), is a perfect setting for its traditional cuisine. Serving everything from homemade pastas and gelato (Italian ice cream) to veal scaloppine to a wide selection of pizzas to a large selection of Italian wines, this pleasant eatery offers very good value for dollar. Prices for pizzas run about NZ$12 ($7.50), or NZ$11 ($6.90) delivered (cheaper!); pastas, NZ$9 ($5.65) for entrees, or NZ$14.90 ($9.30) main-dish size; scaloppine and other meat dishes, NZ$19.50 ($12.25). It's a relaxed, friendly place, with good service and Italian background music. Hours are 11:30 a.m. to 2:30 p.m. Monday through Friday, and 6 to 10 p.m. seven days. Fully licensed.

Cin Cin On Quay Brasserie and Bar, 99 Quay St. (tel. 376-966 or 376-967), is an eclectic, stylish waterfront focal point for ferrygoers, but more than that, for Aucklanders who know the credentials of its chef de cuisine Warwick Brown, winner of some 53 international medals in his 17-year career. He brings that expertise to this unusual eatery that features a wood-burning pizza oven, wood-fired grill with mesquite wood, and open kitchen, overseeing a menu that includes Italian, French, Chinese, and Japanese cuisine. The large bar serves drinks outside all day, specializing in imported beers and wines by the glass. Inside, marble floors add a touch of elegance to the large, casual dining area, and soft colors dominate the decor. Upstairs, there's mezzanine dining with a more formal ambience. Prices are surprisingly moderate, in the NZ$10 ($6.25) to NZ$16 ($10) range, and hours are 10 a.m. to 2 p.m. daily. Light meals and snacks of Italian pastries and the like are available.

For a more exotic dining experience, you'll like the **Baalbeck Lebanese Restaurant,** 58 Wellesley St., at Federal Street (tel. 734-693). The food is genuine Lebanese—lamb, beef, chicken, stuffed cabbage leaves, shish kebab, and the like—and dinner will run around NZ$20 ($12.50). The fun nights to go are Friday and Saturday, when belly dancers take to the floor. Open from 6 p.m. until late, Monday through Saturday. BYO.

The **High St. Cafe,** 51 High St. (tel. 799-067), is a bright, stylish place that serves food at virtually any hour you begin to feel hunger pangs. Monday through Friday, breakfast is served from 7 to 10 a.m. and lunch from 11:30 a.m. to 2:30 p.m., and every day of the week dinner is served from 6 to 11 p.m. and a late supper from 10 p.m. to 1 a.m. There's a long menu that includes such delicacies as smoked quail, médaillons of venison, smoked salmon quenelles, and lamb sweetbreads, as well as fish, pork, chicken, fettuccine, calves' liver, and a host of other dishes. Almost every dish can be ordered as an entree (small portion) or a main dish, and the moderate prices range from NZ$5 ($3.15) to NZ$16 ($10). A great favorite with Aucklanders.

If there's such a thing as casual elegance, that's what you'll find at **Andy's Seafood Brasserie,** 1 Teed St., Newmarket (tel. 504-273). This is quite possibly the freshest seafood to be found in the Auckland area, and it's no wonder, since Andy spent long years down on the waterfront and has fishermen friends who see that he gets the very best of the catch. And you can order those fresh fish pan-fried, deep-fried, grilled, broiled, or prepared in just about any other way you can imagine. Other specialties are crayfish mornay and deep-fried garlic-flavored king prawns. Portions are huge, so think twice before you order an entree *and* a main course, especially since a salad bar is included in the main-course price. Prices range from NZ$5 ($3.15) for entrees, to NZ$15 ($9.40) to NZ$20 ($12.50) for main courses. Children's portions are half price. Lunch is served from noon to 3 p.m. Monday through Friday; dinner is nightly beginning at 6 p.m. Fully licensed.

If just the thought of steak sets your mouth watering, then you should know about **Tony's**, 32 Lorne St. (tel. 732-138), one of Auckland's best steakhouses. In a setting of brick walls, rough beams, assorted antiques, high-backed booths, brass lamps, and velvet curtains, Tony's serves up such delights as reef and beef (steak with shrimp and scallops in cream sauce), steak béarnaise with tarragon and lemon-butter sauce, steak Italiano marinated in a soybean and garlic sauce, and . . . well, steak in just about any style you can imagine. The beef is always first-rate, and your steak arrives with either a salad or a side dish of hot vegetables. Other items on the menu include scallops, fresh fish, pasta, rack of lamb, and chicken. There's another Tony's just around the corner at 27 Wellesley St. (tel. 374-196), with similar decor and menu (it is, in fact, the original Tony's, which opened in 1968). Both are great local favorites, and you may encounter a short wait since they don't accept reservations. Steaks are in the NZ$13 ($8.15) to NZ$16 ($10) range, with other dishes slightly lower. Both locations are fully licensed, and hours are noon to 2:15 p.m. Monday through Friday, 5 to 10 p.m. Monday through Saturday, and 5 to 9:30 p.m. on Sunday.

A bright, airy place with lots of blond wood, greenery, a fountain, and pretty waitresses, **Cheers Café & Bar,** 12 Wyndham St. (tel. 398-779), just off Queen Street, is a licensed café that's open late (until 1 a.m.) seven days a week. The tempting and varied menu includes nachos, guacamole, calamari, oysters, mussels, smoked salmon, burgers, spareribs, salads, fish, fettuccine, satay, and steaks, at prices ranging from NZ$4.95 ($3.10) to NZ$14 ($8.75). Cheers is well known for its inventive cocktails, large range of beers, and assorted selection of freshly squeezed juices, teas, and cappuccinos.

It's unusual to mention a restaurant that is part of a hotel or motel in this section, but for sophisticated dining and attentive service at a reasonable price, you can't make a better choice than **Gladstone's,** in the Barrycourt Motor Inn, 10-20 Gladstone Rd., off St. Stephens Avenue, in Parnell (tel. 33-789). It's done up in turn-of-the-century motif with stained-glass panels, fabric wall coverings, and tables elegantly set with crystalware. The wine list is impressive, and the fare—all manner of fish and meat dishes—is excellent. Main courses range from NZ$15 ($9.40) to NZ$20 ($12.50), plus GST. Licensed. Hours are 11:30 a.m. to 1 a.m., but if you go along for the Cheers Hour (5 to 6 p.m.), all cocktails are half price.

Lovers of French cuisine will find a home at **Le Brie,** in St. Patrick's Square off Wyndham Street (tel. 733-935). This charming little bistro, with its blackboard menu and dark-green walls, serves up such goodies as rabbit casserole, a variety of terrines, escargots, and other traditional French dishes at surprisingly moderate prices. Dinner will run about NZ$30 ($18.75); it's licensed, but you can bring your own wine. Service here is a real delight. Hours are noon to 2 p.m. weekdays, 6 to 10 p.m. every night except Sunday.

The **Union Fish Company,** 16 Quay St. (tel. 796-745), recaptures early Auckland days. A marine-repair warehouse has been converted into a nautical environment that features a bar in the prow of a boat, a ship's figurehead, touches of brass, original maritime memorabilia, old maritime and early Auckland pictures, and a menu that calls itself a "bill of lading." Many Aucklanders consider this the best place in town for seafood Japanese style. Choose your own crayfish (lobster) from the tank, to be prepared any way you like, or select from such specialties as sashimi (raw fish with Wasabi mustard), Bluff oysters, Nelson salmon (fresh or smoked), scallops, green-lipped mussels, or a choice of fish from the daily menu. Dinner prices are in the NZ$21 ($13.25) neighborhood, including GST. Hours are noon to 2:30 p.m. Monday through Friday and 6 to 10:30 p.m. nightly. Reservations are a must.

Be sure to pay a visit to the **China Oriental Markets,** 2 Britomat Pl. (tel. 302-0678). It opened in late 1989, and you can't miss the lavender, blue, lime, and yellow façade. Inside there are 130 stalls featuring every type of food (and merchandise) imaginable. The complex is open seven days a week.

Dining in Devonport
If you visit Devonport, go into **The Left Bank,** 14 Victoria Rd. (tel. 452-615), and you'll discover a congenial, crowded café with a menu that includes tapas (everything from guacamole and corn chips to Thai marinated beef); avocado, bacon, and banana salad; fettuccine; fish of the day; and a sinful chocolate cake with chocolate sauce, almonds, and whipped cream. It's open from noon to 11 p.m. and is an easy walk from the ferry landing. Licensed.

There's nothing fishy about **Something Fishy,** 71 Victoria Rd. (tel. 454-263), except the specialties—mussels, prawns, squid, crayfish, and snapper, prepared simply and tastily. Main dishes cost NZ$14 ($8.75) to NZ$22 ($13.75). It opens at 5:30 p.m. Monday through Saturday. BYO.

Big Splurges
With Auckland's wealth of fine dining, it almost seems obligatory to indulge in at least one "big splurge" while you're there. The following are among those I consider worthy of that extra expenditure.

For sheer elegance, your splurge dollars simply couldn't be better spent than at the **Top of the Town** dining room on the 14th floor of the Hyatt Kingsgate Hotel, 2 Princes St. (tel. 797-220), which has won the coveted New Zealand Restaurant of the Year Award three times. Its window walls looking out to magnificent views of Waitemata Harbour and Albert Park would be justification enough for a meal here, but add to that a luxurious decor, service that is both polished and friendly, and a menu that features the best in New Zealand cuisine, and you'll find yourself yearning to indulge a second time. But if you plan just one visit, let me urge you to come in the evening, when soft candlelight inside is a perfect complement to the spectacular panorama of twinkling city lights outside. Dreamy! As for the food, it is superb no matter *when* you dine. Lunch specialties include smoked salmon, lamb chops with minted red-currant glaze, beef filet in cognac, a yeast pastry flan of whitebait and leeks, and a host of other delicacies. After dark, choose from such exotic dishes as crayfish rolled in nori over brandy with crab-cream sauce, a brace of stuffed quail with foie gras sauce, grilled filet of beef with raisin and cognac-pepper glaze, médaillons of venison in chartreuse, and . . . well, you get the idea. There's a good wine list, fabulous desserts and cheeses (imported and domestic) wind things up nicely, and special liqueur coffees concocted and flamed at your table add the final, sinfully indulgent touch. Prices? Every bit as indulgent as the decor, service, and food. "Lunch Over Auckland" will cost you NZ$33 ($20.75) for three courses, and at dinner, expect to pay NZ$40 ($25) to NZ$75 ($47), plus GST, depending on how high your resistance is to all those tempting à la carte goodies. Lunch hours are a leisurely noon to 4 or 5 p.m. Monday through Friday, and dinner is served from 7 to 11 p.m. Monday through Saturday. Need I add that reservations are a must?

For a water-level view of that beautiful harbor, head for **Sails,** The Anchorage, Westhaven Marina (tel. 789-890), nestled beside the approaches to the Auckland Harbour Bridge, off Fanshawe Street. This large, light, and airy restaurant is decorated in cool shades of green, white, and gray, but its most impressive decor is just outside a wall of windows, where hundreds of private sailboats are anchored. The most jaded soul is sure to respond to the sight of gently bobbing boats and sunlight sparkling off the harbor waters. The menu features—what else?—seafood, and I could make a meal just from the starters listed (a seafood terrine of scallops and crab, smoked fish with horseradish cream, oysters grilled with spinach and cheese or champagne and cream, fresh pasta with a garlicky tomato sauce, etc.). Main courses include orange roughy, seafood mornay, fresh crayfish, and nonseafood specialties of lamb, chicken, and pork. Desserts are excellent (I *dare* you to try the white-chocolate cups filled with boysenberry cream and served with chocolate-dipped strawberries—sinfully delicious!), and there's a good selection of cheeses. Sails is fully licensed. Coffee lovers will like to know that Twinings Grosvenor roast is served here. It's an à la carte menu, with main courses in the NZ$11 ($6.90) to NZ$15 ($9.40) range at lunch, NZ$15 ($9.40) to NZ$25 ($15.75) at dinner. Hours are noon to 2 p.m. Monday through Friday, and 6:30 to 10:30 p.m. every night. A delightful place and very popular, so be sure to book ahead. P.S. At dinner, ask for Austin or Brian (an expatriate American) as your waiter—another treat.

READERS' DINING SELECTIONS: "Of all the meals we ate in New Zealand and Australia, we remembered most fondly those at **Olivers,** 215 Parnell Rd. (tel. 795-176). I ordered a vegetarian plate, which didn't sound too exciting—you can envision steamed vegetables heaped on a plate. I was, however, served a number of vegetables, each prepared in a different way—no plain vegetables here! My husband had lamb, and it was also excellent. We returned the next night in disbelief, and it was just as good the second time around" (S. Butcher, Santa Barbara, Calif.). . . . "I want to share with you information about a wonderful Italian restaurant, **Valerio's,** Shop 12, 311 Parnell Rd. (tel. 375-217). It isn't cheap, but the food is wonderful and well worth the price. Valerio and Karen, his wife, run this restaurant, which is down a little shopping center. The atmosphere is warm, friendly, and relaxed, and was quite what we needed after a long day of traveling to Auckland" (S. Anderson, Cary, N.C.). . . . "We enjoyed dinners in two inexpensive restaurants in downtown Auckland. One was the small and quite cheap **Middle East,** at 23-A Wellesley Street, between Queen and Albert Streets. The other was a large, somewhat noisy, but quite acceptable place called **Ziggie's,** on Queen Street below Wellesley. It is something of a combination of cafeteria and restaurant" (J. Anderson, Pittsburgh, Pa.). . . . "For an excellent individual pizza, try **La Bella Napoli,** a tiny place at 401 Mount Eden Rd., only a half block from the Mount Eden Youth Hostel. Real mozzarella and a tender crust. A Mom-and-Pop operation and a neighborhood favorite for many years" (B. Crawford, Hollywood, Calif.).

THINGS TO SEE AND DO

If your time in Auckland is going to be limited and you can't quite figure out how you'll work in everything you'd like to see, the NZTP office will do their best to come up with an itinerary for you. Call them at 798-180 and tell them what you want to see and how much time you have.

The **Explorer bus** (tel. 866-335) stops at five major attractions around the city for NZ$5 ($3.15) and the ticket is good all day long. You may choose to take a city tour, since Auckland is New Zealand's most spread out city; in 1989 an outfit called **Daytrippers** (tel. 389-823) offered a full-day tour for NZ$7 ($4.40), plus GST, and a half-day tour for NZ$5 ($3.15). You can't get a better bargain than that (again, inquire at the NZTP office).

A visit to the **Auckland War Memorial Museum,** in the Auckland Domain (tel. 390-443), is a virtual necessity for a full appreciation of the Maori culture you'll be exposed to in other parts of the country. The imposing, gleaming-white museum, surrounded by sweeping lawns and flower gardens right in the city center, houses the world's largest collection of Maori artifacts, providing you with a rich background from which to understand the Maoris of today. Be sure to pick up a free guide map as you enter the museum.

In the Maori Court, the most impressive exhibit is probably the 82-foot war canoe chiseled from one enormous totara trunk and covered with intricate, symbolic carvings. You'll see that same artistic carving in the 85-foot meeting house, whose painted rafters and carved and painted wall panels are a wonder of red, black, and white scrollwork. The wall panels also feature tribal-motif carvings interspersed with traditional woven flax patterns. The meeting house sits between two storehouses raised on stilts to protect community goods from predators. Also in the museum are displays of gorgeous feather cloaks (each feather knotted in by hand) worn by high-ranking males, as well as a display of jade tikis. There's also a demonstration on the making of the *piu piu* (reed skirt) from flax. Look for the greenstone *mere* (war club), such a lordly weapon that it was reserved for the slaying of only the highest-ranking captives (who considered it an honor to meet their end with such a club). Look also for the Maori portraits, the life's work of famed New Zealand artist C. F. Goldie, a Pakeha who captured on canvas not only the ornate tattoos of chieftains and common folk, but their fierce tribal pride as well.

Elsewhere in the museum, there's a hall of South Pacific art, a hall of Asian art, a Pacific canoe hall, native bird displays (including that giant moa exhibit), and much, much more. Especially interesting is "Centennial Street," a reconstruction of an Auckland shopping street of 1866—equally interesting is a comparison of prices then and now! The Planetarium gives working demonstrations on Saturday beginning on the hour from 11 a.m. to 3 p.m. and on Sunday, also beginning on the hour, from noon to 4 p.m.

The shop near the entrance of the museum is worth a little browsing time for publications on Maori art and New Zealand flora and fauna, as well as reproductions and replicas of some of the exhibits—a good place to pick up mementos to carry home. There's also a coffee lounge (open from 10 a.m. to 3:45 p.m.), which serves sandwiches, salads, desserts, and beverages. Museum hours are 10 a.m. to 5 p.m. daily, and admission is free. You can reach it via the 635 bus from the Downtown Bus Terminal.

A nice ending to a museum visit is a call at the nearby **Winter Garden,** on the museum grounds, to view the impressive collection of tropical and subtropical plants. Hours are 10 a.m. to noon and 1 to 4 p.m. daily, and there's no admission charge.

And speaking of gardens, if it's rose-blooming time when you visit, plan a stop by the **Parnell Rose Gardens** on Gladstone Road (tel. 775-359). The Rose Garden Lounge serves lunches on weekdays. Bus 702 from the Downtown Bus Terminal will get you there.

The **Auckland City Art Gallery,** at the Kitchener and Wellesley Street intersection of Albert Park (tel. 377-700 for recorded information, or 390-831), is one of the most active art museums in the South Pacific. Its permanent collection ranges from European masters to contemporary international art, plus the most comprehensive collection of New Zealand fine art in the country. Works by New Zealand artists date from 1770 to the present and include a display of fine Maori portraits. A coffeeshop offers refreshment, and there's good browsing in the bookshop. On Sunday afternoons in winter the gallery features classical and jazz concerts; call for information. Hours are 10 a.m. to 4:30 p.m. daily (until 9 p.m. the last Thursday of each month), and there's no admission charge.

An outstanding example of 1880s architecture is the historical old **Auckland Customhouse** on Custom Street West. It's a massive, but rather graceful-looking building whose halls once rang with waterfront commerce. Today it has been beautifully restored and houses craft shops, two bookshops, Brandy's cocktail bar, and restaurants. Well worth a stop, both inside and out.

Parnell Village is actually a row of restored colonial houses along Parnell Road between St. Stephens Avenue and York Street in what is one of Auckland's oldest suburbs. Nowadays, those quaint old homes hold boutiques so fashionable they border on the trendy, art galleries, eateries, and pubs. But despite the bustle of shoppers, you'll get a real feeling of old Auckland just by ambling along the sidewalks and down tiny alleyways.

Kelly Tarlton's Underwater World, Orakei Wharf, 23 Tamaki Dr. (tel. 589-318), is the inspiration and last work of the late Kelly Tarlton, famed diver whose legacy to the country also includes the outstanding Museum of Shipwrecks in the Bay of Islands. His careful planning literally puts you inside an underwater environment by way of a moving walkway that passes through a clear tunnel surrounded by hundreds of native New Zealand fish swimming freely, apparently paying no mind at all to their gaping visitors. The experience is much the same as that of an actual

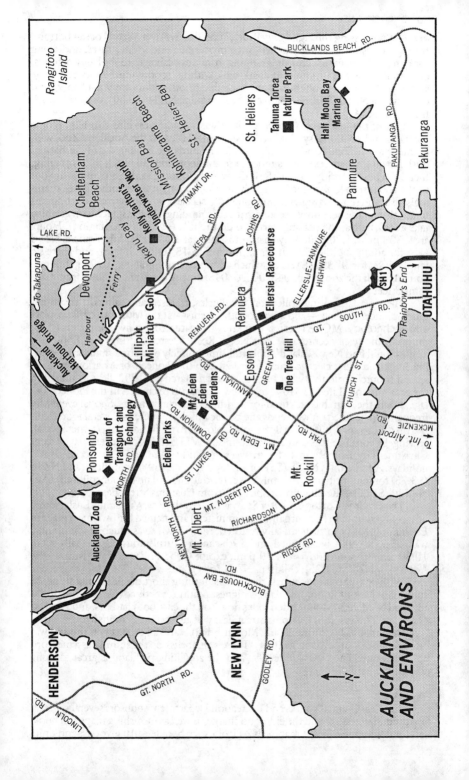

AUCKLAND
AND ENVIRONS

dive—after passing through heavy "surf," you'll move over a sandy ocean bottom, through forests of waving seaweed, into mysterious underwater caves, and along rocky reefs. Look for sea creatures ranging from tiny seahorses to the leggy octopus, and don't miss the magnificent shark tank with its toothy inhabitants and huge stingrays. Kelly's Café offers eats at reasonable prices. Hours are 9 a.m. to 9 p.m. daily, with a NZ$8 ($5) admission charge for adults, NZ$4 ($2.50) for ages 4 to 12, free for under-4s.

One of the few places to observe the kiwi, that flightless bird that has become New Zealand's national symbol, is the Nocturnal House at the **Auckland Zoo,** with entrance at Motions Road (tel. 787-487). The birds are exhibited daily in natural bush settings, which resemble a moonlit forest floor. You can watch them foraging, their long beaks seeking food in the leaf-covered ground. Don't plan a quick run out to the zoo just to look at the kiwis, however—more than 2,000 other birds, mammals, fish, and reptiles (representing some 200 species) will entice you from one area to another in the beautifully tended park surroundings. For instance, you can also take a look here at the tuatara, Earth's oldest reptile (see the Introduction). Hours are 9:30 a.m. to 5:30 p.m. daily (last admission is at 4:15 p.m.). Admission is NZ$8 ($5) for adults, NZ$4 ($2.50) for children 5 to 15 (under 5, free), and there's a family ticket for NZ$22 ($13.75), which admits two adults and up to four children. You can reach the zoo by bus 043, 044, or 045, leaving every ten minutes from Customs Street.

There's a fascinating collection of vehicles, trains, trams, aircraft, steam engines, pioneer artifacts—and a host of other items—at the **Museum of Transport and Technology.** MOTAT, as it is best known, is situated just five kilometers (three miles) from the city center on Great North Road, Western Springs (tel. 860-199). There, you'll find New Zealand's only full-time publicly operating tramway, including Auckland's first electric tram, circa 1902. In the Pioneers of Aviation Pavilion, special tribute is paid to Richard Pearse, who on March 31, 1902, flew an aircraft in the South Island. Life in 1840–1890 New Zealand is re-created in the Pioneer Village, where the church is still used for weddings and christenings. Special events are frequently scheduled on weekends and public holidays. There are several food facilities on the grounds, but the 110-year-old Colonial Arms Restaurant is rather special, serving Devonshire teas and à la carte meals. MOTAT is open every day, except Christmas Day, from 9 a.m. to 5 p.m. weekdays and 10 a.m. to 5 p.m. weekends and holidays. Admission is NZ$8 ($5) for adults, NZ$4 ($2.50) for children, and NZ$6 ($3.75) for senior citizens. A family ticket (two adults and up to four children) costs NZ$20 ($12.50). Reach it via city bus 145 from Customs Street East.

The **Ewelme Cottage,** 14 Ayr St., was built by the Rev. Vicesimus Lush (somehow, I find humor in that surname for a minister!) and named for Ewelme Village in England. It has been authentically restored, right down to as much of the original wallpaper as could be salvaged and 19th-century furnishings. Open daily from 10:30 a.m. to noon and 1 to 4:30 p.m., except Good Friday and Christmas Day. Adults pay NZ$2 ($1.25); children, NZ$1 (65¢).

With or without binoculars, the view is nothing short of spectacular from the summit of **Mount Eden,** Auckland's highest point. An extinct volcano, which was fortified by Maoris, Mount Eden looks down on the city, both harbors, and Hauraki Gulf. The 274 bus from Customs Street East will get you there, or it's a lovely drive.

One Tree Hill (Cornwall Park, Mount Eden) is also an extinct volcano and was also the site of a large Maori *pa* (fort). There's an obelisk on the summit as a memorial to that race. The views are terrific, and the adjoining parkland is great for long walks.

Walks

The City Council's Parks and Recreation Department sponsors several interesting **guided walks** around the city at no charge, as well as furnishing maps and booklets for do-it-yourselfers. Ask at the NZTP office for booklets that give days and times of walks that examine arts and crafts and specialty shops, current art exhibitions, historic spaces and places, marketplaces, the Auckland Domain, and a Domain nature walk. If you're a *real* walker, there's a self-guiding map for an interesting coast-to-coast walk across the 9-km (5½-mile) isthmus between the Pacific Ocean and the Tasman Sea. Allow about four hours, but since many parts of the track pass near bus routes and car parks, you don't have to do it all at once. Although, perforce, you must walk through industrialized sections, there are many wooded spots, archeological sites, parks, gardens, and panoramic views of the city and harbor which are ideal for a picnic.

Bush & Beach Ltd., 2/434 Glenfield Rd., Auckland 10 (tel. 378-209), are outdoor specialists offering a range of small-group (one- to eight-passenger) tours around the Auckland region. Led by experienced guides, the tours are flexible and focus on the unique aspects of each route. Among the offerings: a half-day (1 to 5 p.m.) Waitakere Range tour that visits surf beaches, rocky headlands, and a subtropical rain forest, with time to explore; a full-day (9 a.m. to 5 p.m.) west coast–east coast tour, passing through farmlands, vineyards, and orchards, with opportunities for walking; a half-day (9 a.m. to noon) tour to a mainland gannet colony that is one of only two in the world and 22 miles of black ironsand surf beach (September to April only); and a half-day (9 a.m. to noon) walk through native bush, combined with a visit to an extinct volcano and a beach (May through September only). Prices range from NZ$35 ($22) to NZ$75 ($47).

Sports

Golfers will find themselves welcomed at any of the many fine **golf** courses in the area. For details, call 276-6149 and ask for the name of the course nearest you and current greens fees. **Tennis** players are equally welcome at the Stanley Street Tennis Stadium, which has racquets and balls for hire. For bookings, call 733-623.

A Ferry Ride

One of the nicest ways I know to see Auckland is from the harbor ferry, which crosses to the North Shore. Usually you'll be aboard the zippy catamaran *Kea,* but from time to time the much-beloved and semi-retired steam ferry M.V. Kestrel, makes the journey. As the city recedes, you're treated to a focused look at big-city growth: the old red-brick ferry building with its clock tower stands in marked contrast to streamlined skyscrapers, and the stately white War Memorial looks down on it all with the dignity born of historical perspective. As you pass the naval base, it's perfectly permissible to raise your hand in salute to New Zealand's seafarers. Then, if you plan it right and return in the evening, the sparkling city lights turn big-city sprawl into diamond-studded magic. You catch the ferry at the Queen's Wharf terminal on Quay Street (its North Shore destination is Devonport), leaving every hour on the hour from 7 a.m. to 11 p.m., seven days a week. One-way fare is NZ$3 ($1.90) for adults, NZ$5 ($3.15) round trip.

The little suburb of **Devonport** is where the Maoris say their great ancestral canoe *Tainui* first touched land in this area, somewhere around the 14th century. You'll see a stone memorial to that event on the grassy strip along King Edward Parade foreshore—the bronze sculpture is an orb topped by a *korotangi* (weeping dove), one of the birds the Maoris brought with them from their homeland. There are four white-sand beaches in Devonport, as well as Mount Victoria, which sits near the business center and is now topped by a harbor signal station (great views from up there). You can also walk up to North Head and explore the old military fort with its tunnels and gun sites.

Stroll along King Edward Parade and look for no. 7, where one of New Zealand's most talented writers—he was also an artist and a poet—Rex Fairburn (1904–1957) once lived. A little farther along, you'll come to the **Masonic Hotel** at the corner of Church Street. It was built in 1866, and this is where you'll find the Masonic Tavern (see below). Just across the way, **The Works** is one of my favorite places in the country to watch craftspeople at work. In what was once the Duder Brothers' mercantile store, there's a potter, woodworker, toymaker, weaver, and a group of artists who work in watercolor as well as oil. It's open from 10 a.m. to 4 p.m. Tuesday through Sunday (tel. 453-212). Drop in on historian Paul Titchener at his **Book and Stationery Shop** at 9/11 Victoria Rd. (tel. 453-263) for a chat and to browse. Visit the **Devonport Museum and Gardens,** at 31-A Vauxhall Rd. (tel. 452-661), between 2 and 4 p.m. on weekends. Devonport is full of interesting houses that survive from the 1800s and early 1900s—no. 9 Mays St. is a marvel of cast-iron decoration, and virtually every house on Anne Street is a museum piece. The **Esplanade Hotel,** one of the first things you'll see as you debark from the ferry, dates from 1902.

There are an increasing number of good eateries in Devonport (see "Where to Eat") if you should decide to stay over for dinner. And if you're at all interested in an authentic workingman's pub, which dishes up massive helpings of good grub at inexpensive prices, stop in at the **Masonic Tavern** on King Edward Parade at Church Street. I first tasted paua fritters there, and they were delicious! Hot meals, as well as light snacks, all go for wee prices. Food is served from noon to 2 p.m. and 5:30 to 8 p.m. Monday through Wednesday, to 8:30 p.m. on Thursday, Friday, and Saturday.

Harbor Cruises

If the 20-minute ferry ride to Devonport just isn't enough time on the water for you, **Fuller's Captain Cook Cruises Ltd.,** Quay Street (tel. 394-901), offers a wide variety of cruises around the harbor. Sail out to Rangitoto Island or take shorter cruises concentrating on points of interest in the harbor itself. Call for current schedules and prices, then book through your motel or hotel, or buy tickets at the downtown waterfront ticket office opposite the Downtown Airline Terminal on Quay Street.

The **Auckland Harbour Cruise Co.,** near Quay and Albert Streets (tel. 734-557), offers a different type of harbor cruise aboard luxury *Pride of Auckland Harbour Challenge* yachts. Departing the Quayside Launch Landing, Quay Street, under full sail, you cruise the harbor for some two hours, relaxing on the large deck area or in the spacious saloon lounge. An informative commentary fills you in on points of interest, and there are even full sailing suits for those who wish to remain out on deck on cool or rainy days. There's also a bar and a full galley aboard. Schedules include a 10 a.m. morning-coffee cruise, 12:30 p.m. lunch cruise, 3 p.m. afternoon-coffee cruise, and a 6 to 9 p.m. dinner cruise. Fares are NZ$28 ($17.50) for the coffee and lunch cruises, plus NZ$12 ($7.50) for luncheon; the dinner-cruise fare of NZ$66 ($41.25) includes dinner. Seafood is the specialty, and all meals must be pre-ordered. Identify yourself as a Frommer reader and get a 15% discount. Highly recommended.

A Scenic Flight

If there's anything better than seeing Auckland and its harbor from the water, it must be to see it from the air. Well, **Sea Bee Air,** P.O. Box 1971, Auckland (tel. 774-406), has scenic flights that can give you that very special experience, and at prices that might stretch your budget, but certainly won't break it. Over at Mechanics Bay on the Auckland waterfront, you board the four-passenger seaplane on land, it then sort of waddles down to the shoreline and into the water, and the first thing you know, you're adrift. The motors rev up, you speed across the water, and lift off for an unforgettable flight over the inner city, the harbor bridge, Hauraki Gulf, the now-overgrown crater of the once-mighty Rangitoto volcano, a glimpse of other islands and the Coromandel Peninsula, then back to Mechanics Bay to settle down gently into the water once more and waddle back on to terra firma. It's a thrilling ten minutes that leaves Auckland and its surroundings indelibly stamped on your memory. The cost is about NZ$50 ($31.25). Rates for longer flights are slightly higher; helicopter flights are NZ$55 ($34.50) for ten minutes. In addition to scenic flights, Sea Bee Air also runs charter flights to almost anywhere, and regular service to the Bay of Islands and several other destinations.

Tours

Through the **New Zealand Tourist and Publicity Department (NZTP),** you can book several half- and full-day tours of the city and its environs. Half-day tours, morning or afternoon, cover sightseeing highlights, and an all-day tour includes eastern and western suburbs, the zoo, and a vineyard. Half-day tours run about NZ$26 ($16.25) for adults, half that for children, while the day-long tour will cost around NZ$50 ($31.25) for adults, half that for children. Contact the NZTP for current schedules and booking. They can also book one-, two-, and three-day tours to destinations like Waitomo, Rotorua, and the Bay of Islands.

Some of New Zealand's finest wineries are just west of Auckland, and **New Zealand Vineyard Tours,** P.O. Box 10–130, Balmoral, Auckland 4 (tel. 09/398-670), has tours of some of the best, operating from 10 a.m. to 3 p.m. every day of the week except Sunday. They'll pick you up at your hotel or motel, and the day will include visits to at least three vineyards, wine tastings, and a three-course lunch (with wine, of course). Call for schedule and price.

There are also several very good day tours from Auckland to sightseeing spots like Waitomo, as well as two- and three-day tours at very attractive prices to the Bay of Islands and Rotorua. Check current schedules and prices at the NZTP office.

Meet the Kiwis

One of Auckland's (and indeed, New Zealand's) very best attractions is offered by the **Auckland Tourist Hospitality Scheme,** and it doesn't cost a penny. Do this at the beginning of your trip if possible—it will give more meaning to every Kiwi contact you make thereafter. This group of enthusiastic volunteers will arrange for you to spend a morning, afternoon, or evening with an Auckland family for absolutely no other reason than to have an opportunity to talk on a one-to-one basis in the informal, relaxed atmosphere of a private home. It's a terrific chance to learn about New Zealand daily life firsthand and to exchange views from our different parts of the world. They'll try to match you by profession or hobby from among the 80 Auckland families who participate. They do *not* arrange overnight stays—just friendly visits. You can call them when you arrive, or better yet, write in advance to any of the following: Mrs. Polly Ring, 775 Riddell Rd., Glendowie, Auckland 5 (tel. 556-655); Mrs. Jean Mahon, 129 Taylors Rd., Mount Albert, Auckland (tel. 860-342); Mrs. Eve Swanson, 170 Cook St., Howick, Auckland (tel. 53-58098); Mr. Trevor Holloway, 126 Puhinui Rd., Papatoetoe (tel. 278-8434); and Mrs. Meryl Revell, 60 Prince Regent Dr., Half Moon Bay (tel. 53-55314).

Something for the Kids

Rainbow's End Adventure Park, Great South and Wiri Station Roads, Manukau City, Auckland (tel. 277-9870), is a leisure park with all sorts of action rides, video games, mini-golf, a roller coaster, and the Zim Zam Zoo (you'll have to *see* it!). There's an all-day Super Pass (which includes rides) at NZ$20 ($12.50) for adults, NZ$15 ($9.40) for ages 5 to 12; under 5, free. Or you can opt for the Fun Pass for NZ$4 ($2.50) that simply gives you entry to the park, and you pay for each ride. It's open seven days a week during summer months, but winter hours vary, so phone first. The kids'll love it—of any age!

READERS' SIGHTSEEING SUGGESTIONS: "How do you spend a cool, rainy day in Auckland? Take the Waiwera 895 bus one hour north to the **Waiwera Thermal Pools,** where both indoor and outdoor pools will soothe away the aches, pains, and frustrations" (B. Lushniak,

Chicago, Ill.). . . . "The **Civic Theatre** in downtown Auckland is a treasure. Currently it is used as a cinema, but the owner and ticket people, who are proud of the place, let us explore briefly" (M. Prolman, Anchorage, Alaska).

SHOPPING

Some of the best craft shops in Auckland are in the beautifully restored old **Customhouse,** 22 Custom St. West, which dates from 1888. You'll find pottery, quilts, hand-woven wall hangings, hand-knit sweaters, glasswear, porcelain, wood works, and a very good bookshop (which mails books home, saving you the GST). Stop in at the attractive Brandys cocktail bar and restaurant (there's music in the evenings Wednesday through Saturday) for lunch (from 11:30 a.m. to 2:30 p.m.), cocktails from 11 a.m. to 10 p.m., or at the Cellar Café for breakfast, lunch, or dinner from a moderately priced blackboard menu, or morning or afternoon tea. Shop hours are 9 a.m. to 5 p.m. Monday through Thursday, until 5:30 on Friday and Saturday, and noon to 5:30 p.m. on Sunday.

You can purchase preselected packs containing a variety of cuts of New Zealand lamb directly from the **Farm Produce Shop** (tel. 770-610), by the United Airlines check-in counter at the airport at the last minute, since these packs are already documented and ready to go. Hellaby's is open Monday through Friday from 8 a.m. to 4 p.m.

Plan to spend at least half a day shopping or just browsing or sightseeing in **Parnell Village.** That's the stretch of Parnell Road between York Street and St. Stephens Avenue. In restored colonial homes and stores, there are boutiques, art galleries, craft shops, antiques stores, restaurants, and pubs. It's great people-watching territory, and a place you just may pick up that one-of-a-kind souvenir. Most shops, restaurants, and pubs are open Monday through Saturday.

Victoria Park Market, Victoria Street West (tel. 396-140) is a lively gathering place for weavers, potters, leather workers, and other craftspeople, as well as a bustling fruit and vegetable market. It's open seven days a week from 9 a.m. to 7 p.m. (restaurants have later hours).

Some of the best souvenirs I've found in Auckland came from **Exclusively New Zealand,** 11 Customs St. East, opposite the Park Royal Hotel (tel. 395-642). It's a small shop with a huge stock of sheepskin rugs, hand-knit sweaters, woolens, Maori carvings and cassette tapes, greenstone tikis, carved keyrings, paua shell novelties, tea towels, T-shirts, and interesting items for the little folk like hand puppets and wooly lambs. The pleasant staff is especially helpful; they accept all major credit cards and will mail purchases overseas. Highly recommended.

The best place to buy that extra bag to take your gifts and souvenirs home in is **Modern Bags,** 7 East Customs St. (tel. 789-896). You'll find inexpensive, sturdy bags, and can also get your own bags repaired if they're popping at the seams. The shop is open weekdays only.

Among the exquisite items at **Mark West Suede & Leather,** 82 Queen St. (tel. 303-2790), are "buttery soft" jackets for men and women, and skirts and pants for women, as well as handbags and briefcases. They're open weekdays and Saturday mornings.

Leather Fashions Ltd., 530 Ellerslie Panmure Hwy. (tel. 574-789), has racks of leather, suede, and sheepskin apparel in classic as well as trendy designs. You can also have garments made to your own specifications in the color of your choice. Open weekdays and Saturday mornings; they accept major credit cards and ship overseas.

Wineworth's, at the Downtown Bus Terminal, is a good-value bottle shop.

AFTER DARK

You couldn't really call Auckland's nightlife "swinging." Still, there are enough things to do after dark to finish off a heavy day's sightseeing or shopping. In addition to the listings here, you'll find current goings-on in the *Tourist Times.*

Live music is on tap Wednesday through Saturday evenings at the **Queen's Head,** 404 Queen St. (tel. 302-0223), an exceptionally pretty pub that serves light, inexpensive meals. It's open from 11 a.m. to 10 p.m. Monday through Thursday, until 11 p.m. on Friday and Saturday. The original façade of a hotel dating from 1890 has been retained, a small architectural jewel that escaped the bulldozer.

Café Zira, in the DFC Building at 380 Queen St. (tel. 350-699), is a jazz club. (Jazz buffs will also be happy to know there are jazz cruises in summer.) **Governor Grey's,** in the Sheraton Auckland, 83 Symonds St. (tel. 795-132), is an elegant, so-phisticated nightspot that features an Irish night on Monday and jazz on Wednes-day, from 7 p.m. **Delmonico's,** at the Hotel De Brett, High and Shortlands Streets (tel. 375-100), often has live music Wednesday through Sunday.

In Parnell, the **Exchange** or the **Alexander** (the "Alex") provide engaging after-hours bar ambience.

For cultural offerings that include dance, concerts, and theater, check out what's happening at the new **Aotea Centre,** at Aotea Square on Queen Street. The **Auckland City Art Gallery,** at Kitchener and Wellesley Streets, has an "Open Late" program June through September that features music, live performances, films, videos, and lectures on the last Thursday of the month from 5 to 9 p.m. The **Mercury Theatre,** 9 France St. (tel. 303-3869), has resident companies, including op-era, that perform year round in everything from classics to musicals to modern plays, many of them by New Zealand playwrights. Ticket prices are in the NZ$12 ($7.50) to NZ$35 ($22) range.

---

2. A Side Trip to the Coromandel Peninsula

One of the most beloved holiday spots for Aucklanders is the Coromandel Pen-insula, where the Coromandel mountain range forms the spiky spine of this claw-like region that juts out between the Hauraki Gulf and the Pacific. For city dwellers, it's a haven of natural beauty that is a world apart from urban hassles, and for the visitor, it provides a capsule version of the North Island's history and glorious scen-ery.

The 1½-hour, 68-mile drive from Auckland is rewarded by dramatic land- and seascapes; wide sandy beaches; wild and rugged mountain peaks; quaint villages hugging both coastlines; relics of logging, gold mining, and gum fields; and studios of scores of talented artisans who have found an idyllic lifestyle on the peninsula. For travelers using public transport, InterCity buses run regular schedules to the entry town of Thames. Once a day an InterCity bus makes a round trip around the penin-sula, starting in Thames, and stopping 20 minutes at each destination along the way, for a fare of NZ$22 ($13.75). It's also possible to link up with a courier who makes the journey; inquire at the Brian Boru Hotel, which also operates a tour service for which you'll pay more, but you'll have more flexibility and time to linger.

While it is certainly possible to make a Coromandel Peninsula *day* trip from Auckland, let me urge you to spend at least one overnight in order to do the relaxed rambling your soul will begin to yearn for from the moment you arrive. At the end of your Auckland stay, try to plan two days on the peninsula before pressing on— you'll have explored a very special, little-known-to-outsiders, part of New Zealand, and you'll travel on exhilarated and refreshed by the experience.

USEFUL INFORMATION

Thames is the first town of any size as you reach the peninsula from Auckland. . . . **Information Centres** are on Queen Street, Thames (tel. 0843/87-284); Kapanga Road, Coromandel (tel. 0843/58-598); Albert Street, Whitianga (tel. 0843/65-555); Port Road, Whangamata (tel. 0843/58-340); Belmont Road,

Paeroa (tel. 0816/7042); and Whitaker Street, Te Aroha (0843/48-052). . . .
Driving time from Thames to Port Jackson at the tip of the peninsula is about three hours; to the town of Coromandel, one hour; to Whitianga on the Pacific coast, two hours.

WHERE TO STAY

The first thing that must be said about accommodations is that North Islanders flock to the Coromandels during December and January, so if you're coming then, be *sure* to book ahead. If you arrive during other months, you'll usually be able to find accommodations through the local Information Centres.

A Hostel

There's a delightful small **YHA Hostel** on Miro Street (P.O. Box 72), Te Aroha (tel. 0819/48-739). It's nestled in the foothills of Mount Te Aroha, and only ten minutes away from the famous hot spring baths of Te Aroha. Rates are NZ$8 ($5).

Campgrounds

Tent sites are available on a first-come, first-served basis in Conservation Lands and Farm Parks around the peninsula. Camping fees are NZ$10 ($6.25) per site. For details, contact the Department of Conservation, P.O. Box 78, Thames (tel. 0843/89-732).

The **Waiomu Bay Holiday Park,** P.O. Box 556, Thames (tel. 0843/78-777), has tent and caravan sites, bunkrooms, tourist cabins, and tourist flats in a wooded setting on the coast road, 13 km (7¾ miles) from Thames. Amenities include tennis courts, a swimming pool, barbecue area, and games hall. Tent sites are NZ$6 ($3.75) per adult; caravan sites, NZ$7 ($4.40) per adult; bunkrooms, NZ$8.50 ($5.30) per person; cabins, NZ$22.50 ($14) double; and tourist flats, NZ$40 ($25) double—all including GST.

Buffalo Beach Tourist Park, Eyre St. (P.O. Box 19), Whitianga (tel. 0843/65-854), is adjacent to the beachfront, within easy walking distance of six beaches, the wharf, and the shopping center. There are powered caravan sites, as well as tent sites, three on-site caravans, and a heated bunkroom. Owners Trudi and Alan Hopping even have a set of Clydesdale horses! Rates run NZ$8.50 ($5.30) per adult for tent and caravan sites, NZ$13 ($8.15) for the bunkroom, and NZ$34 ($21.25) double for on-site caravans, all without GST.

A Cottage

Here's an opportunity for a unique experience on a unique peninsula. **Jenny and David Shearer** rent out a cottage on their property at Oxford Terrace in Coromandel (tel. 0843/58-918). Just follow the sign that says "Potteries." The cottage sleeps four (two can take the double bed upstairs) and has a kitchen, showers, and washing machine; there's a "long drop" outside. The Shearers are as interesting as they are hospitable and talented. He used to be an engineer; she was a physical therapist; they have four grown daughters. They moved here to pursue their art, and their contentment shows in their work, their home, and their eyes. Be sure to visit their studio even if a "long drop" isn't for you. The cottage rents for a mere NZ$20 ($12.50) a day.

Bed-and-Breakfasts

Glenys and Russell Rutherford, Thames (tel. 0843/87-788), live one kilometer (half a mile) outside Thames, and their home overlooks the lovely Firth of

Thames. They know the area and some of the painters and potters who live here, and they're always glad to direct their guests to studios, as well as to historic and scenic points of interest. They have a double room with private facilities and two single rooms without. There's a games room cum lounge, as well as a swimming pool. Bed-and-breakfast rates are NZ$35 ($22) single, NZ$55 ($34.50) double, including GST, and they'll provide dinner with advance notice.

Magnolia, camelia, orange, rimu, and totara trees perfectly frame **Firlawn House,** on the main road in Coromandel (tel. 0843/58-947). The house, built in 1881, is filled throughout with Oriental appointments and touches; it has three guest rooms, one with a magnificent Chinese wedding bed, and an elegantly furnished TV lounge. The rooms do not have private facilities. There's a BYO restaurant on the premises, and the house has access for the disabled. A no-smoking rule applies. Rates are NZ$65 ($40.75) and NZ$85 ($53.25) double occupancy, plus GST. Breakfast includes tea and toast only.

A Licensed Hotel

The **Brian Boru Hotel,** Pollen and Richmond Streets, Thames (tel. 0843/86-523), is a marvelous two-story kauri building with a veranda. It dates back to 1874, and it's a focal point for locals, who love the bar and the fine dining room (which serves great seafood meals and good pub grub for moderate prices). There are 25 rooms in all, some with private baths, some without. Those without are NZ$30 ($18.75) single, NZ$55 ($34.50) double. For a single with shower and toilet, you'll pay NZ$55 ($34.50); for a double, NZ$75 ($47). Backpackers are given a break on off-peak periods, when they pay only NZ$15 ($9.40) per person sharing. Add GST to all rates, of course. Incidentally, Barbara Doyle, the managing director here, runs some lively "Agatha Christie–style Weekends" twice a month, and if you're in a sleuthing mood, you might check to see if one's scheduled during your visit—good fun.

Motels

If you blink when you drive into Thames, you might miss the **Best Western Crescent Motel,** at the corner of Fenton and Jellicoe Streets (P.O. Box 384), Thames (tel. 0843/86-506), and you'd be missing the special welcome that Bonnie and Peter Aldridge give guests who check into their small, eight-unit property. In the summer they host barbecues, and in the winter Bonnie's cheese muffins are a special treat. They'll provide a filling dinner for NZ$16 ($10) or homemade toasted sandwiches for NZ$6 ($3.75), each with only an hour's notice. Their breakfast menu has six different choices, ranging from NZ$6 ($3.75) to NZ$10 ($6.25). The units have a kitchen, TV, video, and separate bedroom, and sleep two to six people. Rates are NZ$58 ($36.25) single, NZ$64 ($40) double.

Just 11 km (6½ miles) north of Thames on the Coromandel Road, **Te Puru Park Motel,** West Crescent and Main Road, Puru Bay (mail address: P.O. Box 439, Thames; tel. 0843/78-686), has six attractive motel flats that sleep two to four people. There's a self-service laundry, a children's play area, and tennis courts next door. Rates are NZ$40 ($25) single, NZ$50 ($31.25) double, plus GST.

Also north of Thames, about 14 km (8½ miles), the **Seaspray Motel,** P.O. Box 203, Thames (tel. 0843/78-863), is also on the coast road, and has one- and two-bedroom flats. There's a self-service laundry on the premises, and Waiomu Bay is so close you feel you're sleeping on an ocean liner. There's a stately Norfolk pine and a picnic area in the backyard. Rates for singles are NZ$50 ($31.25), and for doubles, NZ$60 ($37.50), including GST.

The **Anglers Lodge & Motel,** Amodeo Bay, Coromandel (tel. 0843/58-584), is Joan and Alistair Thompson's pleasant beachfront complex about 16 kilometers (9½ miles) north of the town of Coromandel. There are one- and two-bedroom units, all with complete cooking facilities, and you can buy provisions from the small store right on the premises. Other amenities include a swimming pool, a spa pool in a glass geodesic dome, play area with trampoline, barbecue kiosk, lounge with billiard table, and boats for rent. Good bush and coastal walks are right at hand. Rates run NZ$61 ($38.25) single, NZ$75 ($47) double, including GST.

All units at **Coromandel Colonial Cottages,** Ring Road, Coromandel (tel. 0843/58-857), have two bedrooms and sleep up to six. Each has its own car port, and the restful rural setting holds such amenities as a spa pool, putting green, children's playground, and a barbecue area. Beaches, golf courses, and shops are close by, and there's a creek at the back of the property. Families are preferred. Rates are NZ$60 ($37.50) single, NZ$70 ($43.75) double, NZ$15 ($9.40) per additional adult, NZ$11 ($6.90) per child, plus GST.

In Whitianga, the **Mercury Bay Motor Lodge,** 111 Buffalo Beach Rd. North, Whitianga (tel. 0843/65-637), sits right on the edge of Buffalo Beach, with wonderful sea views and fully equipped units, a laundry with dryers, and a carwash. This is the only motel that is not separated from the beachfront by a road, giving you a delicious sense of having your own private beach just outside your door. There's a spa pool, games room, windsurfer, and sailing catamaran for your use. The folks here, Liz and Tom True, are especially helpful in arranging boat trips, fishing expeditions, and bush walks; she's a Kiwi, and he's a Floridian who gave up a career in the oil business for a more tranquil lifestyle. Rates run NZ$50 ($31.25) to NZ$72 ($45) for singles, NZ$60 ($37.50) to NZ$86 ($53.75) for doubles, plus GST. There are reductions at various seasons, so be sure to inquire.

WHERE TO EAT

You'll find small, local eateries in good supply around the peninsula, and your best bet is to look to the natives for pointers on the right choice. Failing that, look for hotel dining rooms, few though they are in number, to provide good, plain food at moderate prices. The first of the following is a marvelous old hotel, so evocative of the past that you get a trip back in time thrown in for free.

The **Brian Boru Hotel,** Pollen and Richmond Streets, Thames (tel. 0843/86-523) has a small bar that is one of the most attractive on the peninsula. Bistro lunches are served, and there's a Sunday-night smörgåsbord from 5 to 8 p.m. All three meals are served daily, and the à la carte menu features fresh local seafood at modest prices.

The **Coromandel Hotel,** Kaponga Road, Coromandel, is not quite atmospheric like the Brian Boru, but is a pleasant, understated, old-fashioned kind of a place, well worth a stop for a pint or a simple meal.

The **Whitianga Hotel,** Blacksmith Lane, is a modern replacement for a turn-of-the-century hotel that burned to the ground. In addition to all three meals in the dining room, bistro lunches are served in the lounge bar.

THINGS TO SEE AND DO

This is a rugged, wild region you've come to, and you should know right off that the only *easy* driving you can count on is the excellent sealed road that runs some 50 km (30 miles) from Thames to Coromandel. North of Coromandel, and on routes crossing the width of the peninsula, you'll find everything from partially sealed roads to graveled roadbeds that—in the words of one of my Auckland friends —are "little more than treks." That by no means implies that you should miss any of the spectacular forest and mountain scenery, only that you should drive with extreme caution, or that you should consider InterCity your personal chauffeur for this portion of your holiday.

Actually, "spectacular" isn't quite glorious enough to describe the peninsula's landscape—there's something so elemental about this old and historic point of land that it can be moving beyond words. Civilization has changed its face virtually not at all, and don't be surprised to find a sudden lump in your throat at vistas of open, curving beaches or beautiful old pohutukawa trees, New Zealand's famed "Christ-mas tree," clinging to cliff faces and lining those beaches, especially during December and January when they're a riot of crimson blooms.

In ancient times, Maori tribes recognized the spirituality of the place and declared its Mount Moehau area *tapu,* a sacred place. Modern man has not been untouched by the same spirit and continues to respect and protect those traditions. It isn't an exaggeration to say that you may well emerge from bush walks here feeling you've had something akin to a religious experience. You'll find good walks around Paeroa (near the Karangahake Gorge), Waihi, Whangamata, Tairua, Whitianga, Colville, Coromandel, and Thames. Headquarters for the **Coromandel State Forest Park** are at Kauaeranga, just southeast of Thames (tel. 0843/86-381 in Thames). They can provide walking guides, help for rockhounds (the peninsula is rich in gemstones), and information on camping within the park.

In Thames, you'll find historic mining areas well signposted, and there's an excellent **mineralogical museum** on the corner of Brown and Cochrane Streets. About halfway between Thames and Coromandel, stop at the little village of Tapu and ask directions to one of nature's oddities, a 2,500-year-old kauri whose trunk is a perfect square (the **"square kauri"** is out the Whitianga road, but it's best to ask before setting out to find it). Te Mata Beach, also at Tapu, is a good hunting ground for specimens of carnelian-agate gemstones.

There are good coast and bush walks all along the road from Thames to Coromandel, and a short detour to Te Kouma leads to a Maori pa site enclosed by stone walls. Coromandel is where gold was first discovered in New Zealand, in 1852, and the **School of Mines Museum** contains many relics of those early gold-fever days. Incidentally, the town, peninsula, and mountain range take their names from the timber-trading ship H.M.S. *Coromandel,* which called into this harbor for kauri spars in 1820. If you plan to drive to the northern tip of the peninsula, you'll find the last gasoline ("petrol") pumps at Colville, along with a good collection of arts and crafts studios. There's a pump at the Papa Aroha Motor Camp in Coromandel as well.

On the peninsula's east coast, **Whitianga** has an excellent historical museum, many arts and crafts studios, and is a major center for boating and charter fishing. Across the inlet at Ferry Landing is the country's oldest stone wharf. At Hot Water Beach, ask the time of the next low tide—that's when you can dig a hole in the beach, settle in and soon find yourself immersed in hot sea water, your own private spa pool!

While you're in the neighborhood, stop at the **Celeuso Orchard and Herb Garden Tearoom,** between Coroglen and Tairua and a five-minute drive from the Hot Water Beach. Orchard owners Ruth and Andy Pettit serve Devonshire tea, fresh juice, homemade scones and muffins with cream and jam, or soup and toast. You can eat on the porch or inside, where strains of classical music set just the right scene. The tea room, which has a tempting gift shop, is open daily from 10 a.m. to 6 p.m. (to 5 p.m. in winter).

READERS' SIGHTSEEING SUGGESTION: "The highlight of our two days in Coromandel was the **Driving Creek Railroad.** It's a don't-miss opportunity, and Barry Brickell is truly a man with a vision" (K. Reilly and J. Stein, Bayside, N.Y.). [*Author's Note:* For a donation, visitors may ride on engineer/conservationist Brickell's 1.8-mile narrow-gauge railway by appointment or daily at 5 p.m. in summer and learn about his native forest restoration program. Native plants and Brickell's pottery are for sale. Inquire at the Brian Boru Hotel in Thames.]

WHERE TO GO FROM HERE

North or south? From Auckland, *most* tourists head south to Waitomo and its glowworms and black-water rafting, then on to Rotorua and its concentration of

Maori culture. And rightly so. Nowhere else in the world will you find anything to compare with the mystical, silent glow of Waitomo's grotto. Nowhere else can you duplicate Rotorua's thermal steaminess or lakes, hills, and valleys alive with myth and legend, along with a Polynesian race who revere those tales of long ago and follow an ancient lifestyle while perfectly at home in the modern culture surrounding them. If push comes to shove and it comes down to north *or* south, then by all means opt for the southern route.

Ah, but if you can work in an extra two days, which will let you go north *then* south, you're in for one of this world's travel treats. Take the long route up and experience the shady "cathedral" created by centuries-old kauri forests; cut across the northern end of the North Island to Waitangi in the Bay of Islands and walk where the British negotiated with Maori chieftains to establish their first official New Zealand foothold; relive this country's history as you visit its first Christian mission, then the splendidly carved Maori meeting house; discover private beaches, some on uninhabited islands that account for the naming of this lovely spot; head out to the open sea for some of the finest deep-water fishing in the world, enjoy sunny days and balmy evenings, a friendly and hospitable local populace. You can *plan* on two days, but chances are you'll alter plans to extend your stay—or leave looking over your shoulder and wishing you had!

3. From Auckland to the Bay of Islands

In your trek north, then back south, you're going to have to come back through Auckland—luckily, however, *not* over the same route. There's a long route that wanders through 234 miles of New Zealand scenic splendor and history, and that will take a full day (count on at least seven or eight hours for the trip). Then there's the direct, 150-mile State Hwy. 1, which can take anywhere from three to four hours. Heed the voice of experience and take the *long* way up, the short route back. There's the distinct possibility that you'll stay over an extra day up north (that's what happened to me), and even if you don't, time pressures may begin to set in and you'll skip that long drive back, thus missing out on a part of New Zealand you really *shouldn't* miss.

Most of the longer route is over well-paved roads, but the most interesting part—the part that makes this whole day's drive worthwhile—will be along about 43 miles of gravel-surfaced, winding roads through the majestic Waiopua Kauri Forest. It's a good idea to pack picnic provisions, since you could well be miles from an eatery when your lunchtime alarm goes off, and besides, there's an idyllic picnic spot right in the forest. And be sure to get an early start—you'll need the whole day.

Leave Auckland via the Harbour Bridge (no toll) and take the East Coast Bays Road off Rte. 1 to pass through North Shore residential districts, superb beaches at pleasant seaside resort towns like **Orewa** and **Waipu** (resist the urge to stop for a swim—you can do that on your way back!), and as you turn inland, hills and farmland, which lead you into **Silverdale,** where you'll rejoin Hwy. 1. (If you strike Warkworth at morning tea time, try the **Dome Valley Tea Rooms,** just north of town.) Just above Kaiwaka, turn into Rte. 12 toward Dargaville.

This was a thriving timber and gum industry area during the late 1800s, and scene of some of the most devastating kauri-forest slaughters. Other trees were felled too—totara, rimu, and kaihikatea—but the kauri was the most sought-after because of its straight, firm trunk, which made it ideal for ship masts, and its beautifully mottled grain, much prized for making furniture. You'll see remains of numerous lumber mills along your way. Kauri gum was the source of many fortunes during those days, as well as the grinding poverty of gum diggers (Maoris and Yugoslav immigrants, mostly) who dug the gum from underneath peat for criminally low wages. The gum was scraped and washed for use as a base in paint and varnish, or polished to rich, clear amber, brown, or black to be used in the making of costume jewelry. You can relive those days of forest and labor exploitation if you stop at **Matakohe** to examine the photographs, gum displays—over 1,700 pieces, the largest collection in the world—and kauri furniture at the **Otamatea Kauri and Pioneer Museum** (tel. Paparoa 089/37-417—you'll have to call through the operator). The implements of the trade will bring it vividly alive: gum washing and digging equipment, a bush dam model and whim model, a bullock wagon and the 1929 tractor that replaced it, large kauri logs, and a bush hut. There's also a kauri house to visit, a tearoom, and a souvenir shop. The museum is open every day except Christmas from 9 a.m. to 5 p.m., and adults pay NZ$4.50 ($2.80); children, NZ$1.50 (95¢).

In **Dargaville**, stop by the **Northern Wairoa Museum**, newly moved to a 29-acre setting in Harding Park. The museum specializes in local Maori and maritime history. Together with many Maori artifacts, there's a comprehensive collection of relics recovered from some of the 110 recorded shipwrecks in this region. On a contemporary note, this is where you will find the masts from the Greenpeace ship *Rainbow Warrior,* which was sunk in 1985 by the French while moored in Auckland. The archives section has local newspapers dating back more than a century, as well as Kaipara Harbour log books. From the elevated concrete terrace out front, there's a marvelous panoramic view of the town and the northern Wairoa River as it winds its way up from Kaipara Harbour—you can see 40 miles of countryside in both directions. Picnic tables, barbecue pits, and toilets are situated on the grounds, and there's a restaurant. Admission is NZ$2.50 ($1.55) for adults, NZ$.50 (30¢) for children.

From Dargaville, it's only 30 miles north to the kauri forest (see below), the highlight of this drive. On the other side of the forest, you pass through seaside settlements of **Omapere** and **Opononi** before heading inland to **Ohaeawai** and Route 10, which will lead you to **Paihia** on the shore of the Bay of Islands.

READERS' BED-AND-BREAKFAST SELECTIONS: "We found the most wonderful bed-and-breakfast accommodation in Dargaville at the **Awakino Point Lodge** (P.O. Box 168; tel. 0884/7870), only minutes from town. The two-room suites with private bath are beautifully and comfortably furnished and very clean. The lodge is on a ten-acre farmlet, attractively landscaped with shrubs, flowers, and fruit trees. The hosts, Wally and June Birch, are warm and hospitable, and June is an excellent cook who will prepare dinner by prior arrangement. We had dinner, bed, and breakfast at a very reasonable rate. It was a great experience and we loved it" (N. Elias, Floral Park, N.Y.). . . . "We found the **Solitaire Guest House,** P.O. Box 51, Waimamaku, Hokianga (tel. Waimamaku 891), to be an excellent place to stay when we wanted to explore the kauri forest and coast tracks. The owners were the friendliest people we met in a land of friendly people. Their home is a beautifully restored kauri house, and for a very moderate price we had a room, dinner, and breakfast" (G. Brandenburg, San Diego, Calif.).

WAIPOUA KAURI FOREST

Within this 22,500-acre preserve, kauri stands account for some 9,000 acres! Tall and slender, with straight, firm trunks reaching up to branches that grow at the very top and arch into a dim, cool canopy, the kauri is such a commanding presence that you understand forthwith the Maoris' imparting of deity to the mighty tree. It is *lordly!* I don't even have to caution against rushing through this awesome abode of natural treasures—you won't! Be sure, however, to stop by the **Fire Lookout**, signposted to your left near the entrance—the 1,010-feet-above-sea-level observation post provides a breathtaking panorama of hills and forests and sea. Forest headquarters is at the next left turn, where you can inspect the **Maxwell Cottage,** which utilizes kauri wood in its construction and was the 1890s home of the first forest caretaker. A 15-minute walk off the road at the sign reading "Te Matua Ngahere" will bring you to the "Father of the Forest," a 98-foot-tall tree, 58 feet 10 inches around, whose exact age is shrouded in the mists of time. A short distance away stands the unique grouping of four trunks growing from one root, known as the Four Sisters. Farther north, just off the main road, the mundane sign stating "Big

Kauri Tree" hardly prepares you for **Tane Mahuta,** "God of the Forest." This immense tree soars to 169 feet, has a girth of 43 feet, and is estimated to be 1,200 years old! This is where you'll find that picnic spot I mentioned, set among tall punga ferns just across the road—a place to sit, absorb the silence and peace of the forest, and ponder the fact that once these giant trees were only a small part of thousands more.

4. The Bay of Islands

For New Zealanders, this is where it all began. "Civilization" in the guise of British culture, that is. But long before Capt. James Cook anchored the *Endeavour* off Motuarohia Island in 1769, civilization of the Maori sort existed in perfect harmony with the soft forces of nature, often at considerable *dis*harmony with their tribal neighbors. Maoris tell of the arrival of Kupe and Ngahu from Hawaiki, then of Whatonga and Toi, and later of the great chiefs Ruatara, Hongi Hika, and Tamati Waaka Nene. They point to the waterfront settlement at Kororareka, already well established when Captain Cook put in an appearance and gave the region its Pakeha name. Be that as it may, New Zealand's *modern* history also begins here in the Bay of Islands.

British settlers first set foot on New Zealand soil in 1804, and a whole litany of British "firsts" follows that date: 1814, the first Christian sermon (today, you'll find a large Celtic cross memorial planted on that very spot, a stretch of beach on the north side of Rangihoua Bay); 1820, the first plow introduced; 1831, the first European marriage; 1835, the first printing press; 1839, the first bank; and 1840, a whole slew of important "first" events—post office, Customs House, and official treaty between the British and Maori chieftains. After that, the British brand of civilization was in New Zealand to stay.

The Bay of Islands you will encounter is a happy blend of all that history—pride in those important happenings—and relaxed contentment in the natural attributes, which make this (as any resident will tell you) "the best spot in the country to live—or play." And play they do, for recreation is the chief industry up here. Setting and climate combine to create about as ideal a resort area as you could wish. Imagine a deeply indented coastline whose waters hold some 150 islands, most with sandy stretches of beach. Imagine waters so filled with sporting fish like the kingfish (yellowtail) that every world record for their capture has been set here. Imagine, too, a climate with *average* temperatures of 85°F (70°F is considered a cooler-than-usual winter day!), *maximum* humidity of 40%, and cool bay breezes every day of the year —imagine all that and you'll know what to expect in the Bay of Islands!

What you won't find is a local transportation system in any form other than the delightful little ferry that delivers schoolchildren, businesspeople, tourists, and freight from one shore to the other. Nor will you find any sort of wild nightlife. Toting up the "wills" and "won'ts," I'd have to say you come up with a balance in favor of a perfect place in which to soak up sun and sea and fresh air, and put the frenetic pleasures of big city life on hold.

ORIENTATION

There are three distinct resort areas in the Bay of Islands: Paihia (throw in adjacent Waitangi—it means "weeping water"), Russell, and Kerikeri. If you've come for the fishing, you'll want to be based in **Russell,** on the eastern shore and home of most charter boats; for almost every other activity, **Paihia,** across on the western shore, is the central location; and **Kerikeri** is the center of a thriving citrus-growing industry as well as a small, interesting "don't miss" sightseeing side trip.

Actually, no matter where you settle, you're going to come to know that neat little **ferry** intimately—unless you have your own boat, that's the only inexpensive way to get from one shore to another (well, there *is* a long-way-round drive, but it's much too time-consuming). Personally, I have a real fondness for that 15-minute voyage. For that little space of time, you're in close contact with the daily lives of the locals as you cross with women returning from a supermarket run, school kids as rambunctious on the after-school run as on schoolbuses the world over, and all sorts of daily-living goods being transported. It runs at hourly intervals beginning at 7 a.m. (from Russell) and ending at 6:30 p.m. (from Paihia). In summer, crossings are extended to 10:30 p.m., and on Sunday there's no 8:30 a.m. service. Fares are NZ$4.40 ($2.75) round trip for adults, NZ$2.20 ($1.40) for children 5 to 15. You'll soon have that schedule firmly fixed in your mind—it's important to be on the same side of the water as your bed when the service shuts down! If you should find yourself stranded, however, all is not lost—just considerably more expensive. The **Bays Water Taxi** (tel. 27-506, or prebook at Fullers) offers 24-hour service, and fares depend on the hour and number of passengers.

Three miles south of Paihia, at **Opua**, there's a flat-bottom **car-ferry** for drivers that crosses the narrow channel to Okiato Point, five miles from Russell. Crossings are 9 a.m. to 9 p.m., and the one-way fare for car and driver is NZ$6 ($3.75) plus NZ$1 (65¢) for each adult passenger.

Useful Information

You'll find the **Bay of Islands Information Centre**, P.O. Box 70, Paihia (tel. 0885/27-426), right on the waterfront in Paihia. The friendly staff, headed by Alan Oliver, arrange accommodations bookings throughout the entire Bay of Islands— bed-and-breakfast, motel flats, motor camp, or tent site—with no booking fee. They also keep up-to-the-minute information on all sightseeing and other activities. The office is staffed from 8 a.m. to 5 p.m. (to 4:30 p.m. in winter). . . . **A. E. Fullers Northland** (tel. 27-421 in Paihia, 37-866 in Russell), locally known simply as Fullers, handles all InterCity bookings, passenger and car-ferry bookings, and original Cream Trip and launch cruise bookings. Fullers Northland also operates coach tours to Cape Reinga, plus airline information and bookings (including international flights). All these services, plus all marine activity offices, are in the Maritime Building on the Paihia wharf. . . . There are daily Great Barrier and Mount Cook Airlines flights to and from Auckland. . . . For **taxi service,** call Paihia 27-506. . . . Three island taxis hire out for **fishing trips**—The Fizz (tel. 28-343), Think Pink (tel. 27-161), and Island Water Taxi (tel. 37-123). . . . The **telephone prefix** for Paihia and Russell is 0885.

A Special Event

Lucky you if your visit coincides with the February 6 celebration of **Waitangi Day!** It's like being in the United States on the Fourth of July. The center of activity is the Treaty House lawn, scene of the Waitangi Treaty signing, with a re-creation of that event, lots of Maori song and dance, and Pakeha officials in abundance, dressed to the nines in resplendent uniforms of yesteryear and today. The Royal New Zealand Navy is there in force, as are crowds of holidaying Kiwis. Book *way* ahead, then get set to join in the festivities.

WHERE TO STAY

The Bay of Islands is a budget traveler's dream: the area abounds in excellent inexpensive accommodations, and more are being built all the time. Most are of modest size, earning a modest-but-quite-adequate-thank-you income for couples or families who seem far more interested in their guests' having a good time than in charging "what the traffic will bear." Rates *do fluctuate according to season,* however, with a slight increase during holidays and a slightly higher jump during the peak summer months of December through February. Those are also the times it is absolutely essential to book *well in advance,* since the Bay of Islands is tops on just about every Kiwi family's holiday list, and many book from year to year. If you're planning a visit during any of these seasons, you can either write directly to one of the properties you see listed here, or write to the Public Relations Office and put yourself in their capable hands—no risk, I can assure you.

Hostels

The **Kerikeri Youth Hostel,** on the main road just north of the village (P.O. Box 62), Kerikeri (tel. 0887/79-391), is set in 2½ shaded acres, with river swimming just a five-minute walk from the hostel. There are 28 beds in six dormitory rooms, as well as a communal kitchen and laundry, a lounge and recreation/games room. Many of the area's historic sites are within easy walking distance. Seniors pay NZ$11.50 ($7.20); juniors, half price.

The **Centabay Backpackers Hostel,** on Selwyn Road, Pahia (tel. 0885/27-466), is the most centrally located hostel in town and quite appealing. It's run by the ever-helpful Gary and Kay Bathe, who arrange sailing, horseback riding, sea kayaking, fishing, and overnight camping trips to Cape Reinga. There are no rules or chores, and it is very clean, with dorm accommodations primarily, and some double rooms. Two lounges have a TV, and there are kitchens, a games room, and bike rental. The tariff is NZ$12 ($7.50) per bed per night, NZ$14 ($8.75) per person for the double rooms.

Out near the Museum of Shipwrecks and Treaty House, the **Mayfair Lodge,** on Puketona Road at the Kerikeri turnoff, Paihia (tel. 0885/27-471), has dormitory accommodation primarily, along with one double room and two twins. There is a games room with table tennis and a pool table, barbecue area, a TV lounge, in-house video, free spa pool, bicycle rental, and a laundry. They supply sheets and blankets, and will pick you up in Paihia (or ask the bus driver to drop you off). Rates are NZ$12 ($7.50) per person, NZ$13 ($8.15) per person for a double room.

Cabins/Campgrounds

Twin Pines Motor Camp, P.O. Box 168, Haruru Falls, Paihia (tel. 0885/27-322), has for 16 years been operated and upgraded by Gordon, John, and Mamie Putt, and it's one of the prettiest and best-run camps in these parts, steeped in history and boasting a turn-of-the-century tavern and restaurant on the premises. In a tree-shaded setting, with the falls as a backdrop, it's a restful and convenient location. The Putts, seasoned travelers themselves, provide low-cost accommodations in eight six-berth chalet-style cabins at NZ$13.20 ($8.25) for adults, NZ$6.60 ($4.15) for children; two four-berth tourist flats at NZ$39.60 ($24.75) double; nine on-site caravans with the same rates as cabins; a 25-bed lodge with facilities at the same rates as cabins; and a 12-bed dormitory at NZ$11 ($6.90) per person—all rates including GST. There's a kitchen, dining room, laundry, carwash, linen rental, color TV, and a barbecue. Fish-smoking facilities are available; river boat cruises and fishing charters can be arranged.

Right next door to the Twin Pines Motor Camp, the **Falls Motor Inn,** on Puketona Road (P.O. Box 14), Haruru Falls, Paihia (tel. 0885/27-816), has 14 one- and two-bedroom units, tent and caravan sites, a pool with a mesmerizing view of the Waitangi River, a small sandy beach, a dinghy, and an outdoor spa pool. You'll love the point with the flame tree on it (so do those winsome birds, the tuis, and campers); Room 10 affords a view of the falls. The activities board—and the helpfulness of hosts Graham and Joan Hodern—will keep you up-to-date on current happenings in the area. The Hoderns, long-transplanted from England, love the area and can point out nearby walks and other nature-oriented activities. Room rates are NZ$48 ($30) single, NZ$55 ($34.50) double, plus GST. The minimum site fee for the motor camp is NZ$18 ($11.25). Adults pay NZ$8 ($5) each.

The **Lily Pond Holiday Park,** Puketona Road, Paihia (tel. 0885/27-646), is midway between Puketona Junction and Paihia, and sits on park-like grounds right at the Waitangi River's edge. There are 250 sites, 100 caravan sites, four on-site caravans, and 11 cabins, all of a quality that has won a four-star grading by the Camp &

Cabin Association of New Zealand. You can rent linens, and there's a store on the grounds, a large, modern kitchen for campers, and a separate, fully equipped kitchen for the cabins. Rates are NZ$10 ($6.25) per adult for sites, NZ$12 ($7.50) per adult for caravan sites; and NZ$35 ($22) per couple for on-site caravans and cabins.

Bed-and-Breakfasts

I heard glowing remarks about the **Swiss Chalet Lodge Motel,** 3 Bayview Rd. (P.O. Box 106), Paihia (tel. 0885/27-615), long before I arrived in the Bay of Islands. Inge and Ed Amsler—she's Austrian; he's Swiss—have brought a bit of alpine charm to the South Pacific, and their attention to detail and comfort is scrupulous. You'll find nine spacious units, all with balcony, conversation area, writing table, video, kitchen, soft duvets on the beds, and a hairdryer in the bath (eight have tubs). The Swiss-style breakfast includes museli, fresh or canned fruit, yogurt, croissants, toast, cheese, and boiled eggs. Early-morning tea, cookies, and a newspaper are complimentary, and you'll find a Swiss chocolate on your pillow when you go to bed at night. This pretty property also features a jewelry shop with items from around the world, a barbecue, spa pool, wooden playground equipment handcrafted by Ed (who designed the lodge), and convenient covered parking. Windsurfing and motorboating are available for guests. Rates, including breakfast and GST, are NZ$40 ($25) single and NZ$65 ($40.75) double. Ask about their winter packages. Highly recommended.

For a farm-stay experience, **Mrs. Dorothy Bayly,** on Bayly Road (P.O. Box 36), Paihia (tel. 0885/27-379), near the golf course, offers bed, breakfast, and dinner in her two-story country home for NZ$65 ($40.75) per person. The three-course dinner includes wine and a before-dinner drink. There's a spa pool and tennis court on the property.

Motel Flats

IN RUSSELL Not *all* good New Zealand hosts are Kiwis, and that fact is borne out by Carole and Jim Hotchkiss, native Californians who picked up, bag and baggage, to become the owners/operators of the **Motel Russell,** Matuwhi Bay Road (P.O. Box 54), Russell (tel. 0885/37-854). Jim, an international airlines pilot, fell in love with the country during the course of frequent flights here and brought Carole over for an extended visit. She shared his enthusiasm, and now you'll find them happily ensconced in this pretty motel just a three-minute or so walk from the Russell waterfront. Helping to manage the property are Paddy and Lynda Powell, a young Kiwi couple eager to arrange game fishing, cruises, boat rental, and other water and fishing activities. Paddy, an expert angler and skipper, frequently escorts guests on fishing and sailing trips; Carole and Jim are more landlubbers and can offer advice to those who enjoy bushwalking. There are 13 units, all with complete kitchens, and Carole's good taste in decor and Jim's expertise in adding the little extras that mean so much to comfort. For example, there are two units with facilities for the disabled. Six have one bedroom and lounge (will sleep up to four), five with two bedrooms, and two double-bedded units, as well as three very pretty cabin-type units. The location is a wooded hillside, and Jim and Carole have landscaped it into a setting of real beauty, with a swimming pool fed by a picturesque waterfall. There's also a barbecue and a heated spa. I suppose the hospitality here is Kiwi/California style—however you label it, it's tops! Rates are NZ$55 ($34.50) single or double, with a slight increase during holidays and summer peak season. This is a Best Western member, so their discount rates apply.

The hospitality at **Wairoro Park,** P.O. Box 53, Russell (tel. 0885/37-255), could probably be labeled Kiwi-Dutch-English, since owner Jan Boerop is Dutch, his wife Beryl is English, and they're both now dyed-in-the-wool Kiwis. They've settled in on the Russell side of the Opua car-ferry (about a mile from the ferry, then a left turn up a hilly dirt road) in an absolutely idyllic setting of some 160 acres on the shores of a sheltered bay cove. They use a great many of those acres to run cattle and sheep, and in the midst of an orchard just steps away from the beach they have three two-story A-frame chalets. The first level of each holds a large lounge, fully equipped kitchen, shower, and separate toilet. Two bedrooms occupy the upstairs, and with the three divans in the lounge, the units accommodate up to eight. There's a covered carport and decks looking out to gorgeous views. The Boerops provide a dinghy or motorboat and a 12-foot catamaran at no charge for guests who want to fish. Regulars book from one holiday season to the next—which means, of course, that it's a good idea to write as far in advance as possible no matter when you're coming. Rates are NZ$66 ($41.25) double, NZ$12 ($7.50) per extra adult, NZ$6 ($3.75) per child. There's a Christmas holiday minimum charge of NZ$130 ($81.25) per chalet. Incidentally, there is an additional rustic, self-contained cabin that sleeps two and goes for NZ$45 ($28.25) year round. Rates include GST.

Linley and Bill Shatwell too came to Russell from other parts, although in their case it was only up from Auckland. Holidays in the Bay of Islands led them to buy the **Arcadia Lodge,** on Florence Avenue, Russell (tel. 0885/37-756), where they have four attractive, inexpensive units that are spotless and comfortable, and look out onto great views of the bay. Actually they're an extension of the main house. One, a self-contained unit with kitchen, bath, and toilet, sleeps six. Two will accommodate up to four, and another sleeps five. A fridge, stove, H&C, and electric heat are in all units. Rates for 1990 run NZ$18 ($11.25) single, NZ$35 ($22) to NZ$50 ($31.25) double, plus GST. This is a *very* popular place with budget travelers, both in New Zealand and among overseas travelers who've heard about it by word of mouth, so it's a good idea to book ahead if you can.

IN PAIHIA There are ten self-contained colonial-style cottages set in spacious grounds at the **Bay of Islands Motel,** 6 Tohitapu Rd., Te Haumi Bay (P.O. Box 131), Paihia (tel. 0885/27-348). Each cottage has a lounge, separate bedroom, full kitchen, and bath (shower and tub). Privacy is assured, since cottages are placed at angles to prevent the windows of one from facing those of another, and the whole effect is that of a charming mini-village. Other facilities include a swimming pool, spa pool, laundry, and a playground for the young fry, who will also enjoy nearby beaches (close enough to hoof it). Rates are NZ$55 ($34.50) single, NZ$63.80 ($40) double, including GST.

If you're looking for a secluded spot (the kind that travel writers are admonished not to put in their guides so that it stays secluded), **Hideaway Beach,** on a hilltop with a 180° view of the Bay of Islands and a bush walk to the beach, could be perfect. It has only three units, with kitchen, TV, and bath with shower, but no phone. There is a phone, just not in the room, along with a flower-covered boardwalk and patio and a laundry. It's located across the street and up the hill from the Paihia cemetery, and is owned by the nice folks at the Swiss Chalet. To make reservations, give them a call at 0885/27-615 (or write them: 3 Bayview Rd., P.O. Box 106, Paiha). The rate is NZ$65 ($40.75) double, plus GST.

The **Casa-Bella Motel,** McMurray Road, Paihia (tel. 0885/27-387), is a sparkling-white, red-tile-roofed, Spanish-style complex close to shops, restaurants, and the beach. There are a variety of nicely furnished units, all with full kitchen facilities, color TV, in-house video, and electric blanket. There are some waterbeds, and one very special honeymoon suite. On the premises there's both a heated swimming and a hot spa pool, as well as full laundry facilities. Picnic tables and benches shaded by umbrellas are set about on the landscaped grounds. Rates are NZ$59 ($37) to NZ$79 ($49.50), single or double, with a NZ$10 ($6.25) charge for each extra person. Add GST to all.

Chester and Louise Rendall are the proprietors of the **Bayswater Inn,** Marsden Road, Paihia (tel. 0885/27-444). Eight modern, spacious motel flats that sleep up to four each are in the rear of an 1884 house set back from the road behind a long, landscaped lawn. The old house is now one of Paihia's better restaurants (see

"Where to Eat," below), making this indeed a convenient place to stay. All seven units are nicely decorated, and each has its own outside deck, complete with chairs for sunning. There's a hot spa pool and a barbecue shed that is a companionable gathering spot for guests. The rate is NZ$90 ($56.25) double in summer, NZ$55 ($34.50) double in winter.

A Licensed Hotel

The **Duke of Marlborough Hotel,** The Strand, Russell (tel. 0885/37-829), is the Grand Old Man of the Bay of Islands, having watched the comings and goings of generations of residents and visitors from its waterfront perch since it opened as New Zealand's very first hotel. It has suffered major fires three times and three times been rebuilt. Grand it may be; stuffy it isn't. Just a few steps from the Russell wharf, its covered veranda is the natural gathering place for fishermen at the end of a day on the water in pursuit of those deep-sea fighters. The conversation tends to be lively, attracting locals as well as hotel guests. The Duke, in fact, could be called the social hub of Russell (if Russell could, in fact, be said to have a social hub!). Its public bar, across the street in the back, is also the center of community conviviality.

Regulars come back to the Duke year after year for its old-worldliness, and also for the homey comfort of its rooms. Beds have wicker headboards, floors are carpeted, walls are wood paneled, and tea- and coffee-making facilities and bathrooms are in each room. There's a fine dining room serving all meals (see "Where to Eat," below), a TV lounge, and a charming guest lounge with wicker furniture, a colonial-style bar, and a working fireplace. Year-round rates are NZ$50 ($31.25) to NZ$60 ($37.50) single, NZ$50 ($31.25) to NZ$90 ($56.25) double, including GST—a little above budget, but bargain prices for the likes of the Duke.

A Splurge

The **THC Waitangi Resort Hotel,** Private Bag, Paiha, Bay of Islands (tel. 0885/27-411), is actually set in the grounds of the Waitangi National Trust, affording superb land and water views and an enormous amount of tranquility. The property has 24-hour room service, piano music in the lounge on summer evenings, and a heated swimming pool. All rooms have mini-bars, tea and coffee facilities, and a small patio. It's a stone's throw from the Treaty House and the Maori war canoe. Standard rooms are NZ$84.40 ($52.75); larger, premium rooms run NZ$157.50 ($98.50).

In the Far North

Waitiki Landing, some 20 km (12 miles) southeast of Cape Reinga, is a tiny settlement on the banks of the Waitiki Stream and the site of a very special New Zealand holiday development. Set in the very heart of Te Paki Reserve's 56,800 acres of virgin wilderness, there's a complex of charming rustic log cabins that feature native woods and exposed beams combined with modern comforts. A first-class restaurant serves fresh seafood daily, and presents a Maori hangi dinner and cultural entertainment several times a week. Scenic tours by four-wheel-drive vehicles to nearby Cape Reinga/Ninety-Mile Beach, the North Cape, and other local attractions, as well as tramping, fishing, jet boating, and horse riding, and lodging are available.

WHERE TO EAT

As you would expect in such a popular resort area, the Bay of Islands has many good places to eat. Seafood tops the list of menu offerings (which should come as a surprise to no one), with fish coming to table just hours after they were swimming in the waters offshore.

In Russell

Freshness is something you can count on at the **Quarterdeck,** The Strand (tel. 37-761). In a setting of early Bay of Islands prints and photographs and high-backed booths, there's a terrific seafood platter, as well as snapper or whatever the latest catch has brought in, mixed grill, chicken, and light meals. There's a free salad bar with evening meals. Prices run NZ$8 ($5) to NZ$10 ($6.25) for the lighter fare, NZ$15 ($9.40) and up for full meals. Hours are 9:30 a.m. to 3:30 p.m. and 6 to 9 p.m. (with longer openings in high season) Monday through Saturday; closed Sunday. BYO.

The **Duke of Marlborough** (tel. 37-829) serves a pricier à la carte meal in its elegant dining room, daily from 6:30 to 9 p.m. They've added a salad bar and a dining deck overlooking the bay. Main courses are fresh seafood, roasts of lamb or sirloin, pork, and chicken. Meals are half price for children under 10. Breakfast is served from 7:30 to 9:30 a.m.; lunch, from noon to 1:30 p.m. Fully licensed, with an excellent wine cellar.

The **Reef Bar Bistro,** located in the Duke Tavern behind the Duke of Marlborough (tel. 37-831), serves delicious bistro meals in its family and garden bar. Fresh fish (caught daily by local boats) oysters, scallops, shrimp (*tons* of shrimp in the shrimp cocktail!), steaks, and light snacks are all at low, family prices—in the NZ$8 ($5) to NZ$13 ($8.25) range. It's closed on Sunday, open other days from noon to 2 p.m. and 5:30 to 8:30 p.m. Fully licensed, of course.

For a splurgy dinner, head for **The Gables,** on the Strand facing the waterfront (tel. 37-618). This was one of the first buildings on the waterfront, built in 1850, and was a riotous brothel in the days of the whalers. Its construction is pit-sawn kauri on whalebone foundations (in fact, there's a huge piece of whale vertebrae, discovered during the renovation, now on display in the small bar). Decor is early colonial, with a kauri-paneled ceiling in the bar, kauri tables, prints, maps, photographs of early New Zealand, and the cheerful warmth of open fires. The menu changes seasonally, but seafood, beef, lamb, game, and fresh vegetables and fruits are a mainstay. Main courses on the à la carte menu are in the NZ$19 ($12) to NZ$24 ($15) range, and the Gables is fully licensed, with a respectable wine list, or BYO. It's open daily in summer from 7 to 11 p.m. (also serves lunch December through February, from noon to 2 p.m.). Open Tuesday through Saturday in other seasons (it sometimes closes from the end of May through July, so be sure to check). Bay of Islanders love this place, so book early; there's a minimum NZ$18.50 ($11.50) per person.

On the Paihia Side

Bistro 40, in the Bayswater Inn, Marsden Road (tel. 27-444), is in a charming house that dates back to 1884 and overlooks the bay. Meals are served in a bright sunny front room, with red-checked tablecloths adding a homey touch. From mid-December through March there's also service on a small terrace shaded by a passionfruit-vine-laden trellis. Typical main courses of fish and meats cost NZ$15 ($9.40) to NZ$25 ($15.75). Hours are from 6 p.m. every evening December through April; closed Tuesday in winter. It's BYO, and reservations are essential.

The tiny **Leroy's,** on Kings Road (tel. 27-783), is the constant subject of letters from readers, all writing to say how much they've enjoyed the Cape Cod atmosphere of this place, the friendliness of owners and staff, and most of all, the food. Its popularity is well deserved: lightly battered, really fresh seafood comes from the kitchen deep-fried and crisp, accompanied by tartar sauce, fresh vegetables, a salad bowl, and tons of chips, plus bread and butter. But if you're a devotee of the broiler, all you have to do is ask, and yours will arrive broiled to perfection. There are all sorts of seafood offered—the fish of the day, oysters, scallops, shrimp, etc.—and a heaping combination platter. Steaks are on the menu as well. Prices are in the NZ$10 ($6.25) to NZ$18 ($11.25) range, with children's servings about half price. During the summer, hours are 5 to 10 p.m.; in winter it closes earlier. There's also a take-away service for fish and chips and full meals. BYO.

Also very popular with both residents and visitors is the **Bella Vista,** on the waterfront at Waitangi Bay (tel. 27-451). Its big front windows look out to bay views, which somehow make the food taste better (and cocktails here at the sunset hour are really something special!). Upstairs, elegance holds sway in the lounge as well as in the dining room. Such delicacies as hapuka and lobster are specialties, and steak is a staple. Fresh fruits, such as boysenberries or kiwi fruit, come with globs of fresh whipped cream and confectioners' sugar. Prices run NZ$12 ($7.50) to NZ$21 ($13.25), which includes fresh vegetables or salad with your main course. Hours are 6 to 10 p.m., later in summer. Fully licensed, and reservations are usually necessary upstairs.

Lunch will undoubtedly be your main meal on Sunday if you go by the **THC Waitangi Hotel** (tel. 27-411) for the poolside barbecue, which features live jazz. For NZ$17 ($10.75) you can eat as much as you want of steak, lamb, bangers, and salads. Children under 15 pay half. Hours are 12:30 to 2 p.m., and it's a good idea to make reservations. On Sunday evenings in summer, the hotel features a carvery buffet, with fresh bay seafood, salads, and vegetables; cold cuts, hot entrees, and a hot carved roast; and a table full of desserts. The cost is NZ$24.20 ($15.25). Over at the Waitangi's **Anchorage Bar,** in a plainer but very pleasant setting, dinner (everything from salads to fish and chips to seafood to roast beef) ranges from NZ$4.50 ($2.80) to NZ$9.95 ($6.25). Both are fully licensed, of course.

Jane's Restaurant, on State Hwy. 10 between Paihia and Kerikeri (tel. 78-664), looks like a roadhouse on the outside, an Olde English restaurant on the inside. The low-beamed ceiling, fireplaces, ornaments, and paintings make this a cozy, relaxed setting for the superb food that comes to the table. It's a far-ranging menu, with average lunch prices of NZ$9 ($5.65), and dinner for about NZ$18 ($11.25). It's essential to reserve ahead during the season and on weekends. Hours are noon to 2 p.m. and 6:30 p.m. until late daily. Fully licensed, with a good selection of wines.

Named after its consummate hostess, **Esmae's,** at 41 Williams Rd. (tel. 28-400), features home-style New Zealand cooking and the menu even tells you where the fish or meat comes from. Esmae Dally will meet, greet, and seat you. If you take advantage of the Budget Corner meal—a meat, chicken, or fish dish with salad and fries—you'll pay only NZ$12 ($7.50); otherwise, expect to pay about NZ$25 ($15.75). It's open nightly from 5:30 p.m. BYO.

Upstairs in the Selwyn Road Shopping Center, **La Scala Restaurant** (tel. 27-031) has a pretty garden atmosphere, with window walls, green carpet, light-wood tables, cane-back chairs, and greenery everywhere. The freshest of seafood is the specialty, as are New Zealand steaks. In addition to the fish of the day, scallops, oysters, and crayfish, there are such items as honey prawns (shrimp battered, dipped in honey, and sprinkled with sesame seeds). Prices are in the upper ranges—NZ$15 ($9) to NZ$30 ($18.75)—and there's a children's menu for under NZ$10 ($6.25). Fully licensed. Open for dinner only, 6 to 10 p.m.; closed Monday. Reservations are a must.

If you love diners, the Bay of Islands won't disappoint. The **Blue Marlin Diner,** across from the Information Centre (tel. 27-590), is open for breakfast from 7 a.m. to 3 p.m. and for short-order snacks and suppers from 5:30 to 8 p.m.

If you can't muster the energy to go out at the end of the day, there's always **Dial-a-Pizza** (tel. 27-536).

THINGS TO SEE AND DO

Again, I'll issue my standard Bay of Islands caution: There's so much to see and do up here that you're going to be sorely tempted to stay over an extra day or so. For example, with just two days, you'll barely have time to take one of the cruises (which you should do if you have to skip everything else!) and do a little sightseeing, the other to see the rest of the historical sights. But then there's the day-long trip to Cape Reinga, swimming, fishing, boating, diving, etc., for which you'll have no time. So I suppose it comes down to assigning priorities to fit the length of your stay.

The very first thing on your agenda should be to go by the Bay of Islands Information Centre and pick up brochures outlining the various bay cruises and setting out schedules and prices for each. In fact, they can furnish specific information on just about any of the activities listed in this section, although you'll have to make the reservations yourself.

Fullers Northland (tel. 27-421 in Paihia, 37-866 in Russell), known simply as Fullers, and the largest and most visible tour operator in the Bay of Islands, offers half a dozen cruises and outings, among the most popular the Cape Brett–Hole in the Rock cruise aboard the fully licensed catamaran *Tiger Lily III;* there is also the Cream Trip bay cruise with an island stopover at lunchtime, a day-long trip to Cape Reinga via Ninety-Mile Beach, and the Tu-Tu (in Maori it means "to play around") Fun Bus adventure in a 40-seater, six-wheel-drive dune buggy (for more information, see "Sightseeing").

Kirky's Cruises (tel. 27-221 in Paihia) has gotten rave reviews from travelers who prefer to explore the bay in a smaller boat that holds no more than 20 people and goes into places the bigger boats have to pass by. The company's 3½-hour Supercruise gets you around the bay and out to Cape Brett and the "Hole in the Rock," and it also takes you right into the dramatic rock formation called Cathedral Cave. Kirky's also offers jet-boating and a twilight cruise with an island stopover for a barbecue.

Another small operator, **King's Adventure Tours** (tel. 28-171), offers an exceedingly popular day tour to Cape Reinga via Ninety-Mile Beach; a half-day tour called Bay Wonder, which incorporates Kerikeri, Waimate, and the kauri forest; and an evening tour with some unusual bedfellows—Ninety-Mile Beach, kauri trees, and glowworms.

Sporting Activities

There are beaches galore for good **swimming** from November through March. They're lined up all along the town waterfronts, and delightful little coves with curving strands are just awaiting your discovery down almost any side road along State Hwy. 10 headed north—if you pass through privately owned land to reach the water, you may be asked to pay a small fee, something like NZ$1 (65¢).

You can arrange to play **golf** at the beautiful 18-hole waterfront course at Waitangi Golf Course, where clubs are for hire (call 27-713).

Deep-sea fishing is at its best up here. In fact, world records for yellowtail, marlin, shark, and tuna have been set in these waters. There are a couple dozen big-game fishing charter boats operating out of Russell, but I might as well warn you that it can be an expensive proposition unless you can form your own group (or fall in with a group that has a vacancy) to share the NZ$700 ($438) to NZ$800 ($500) cost for ten hours' fishing. With a party of four (the maximum), the per-person cost becomes a more manageable, but still hefty $109 (U.S.). If the fact that some 600 striped, blue, and black marlin were landed in these waters makes this an irresistible expense, **Game Fishing Charters,** in the Maritime Building in Paihia (tel. 27-311), may be able to help you line something up.

Light-line fishing is much more affordable, and **Bay Water Taxi** (tel. 27-506) charges NZ$75 ($47) per hour for a party of four. They supply rods and bait. There are also a number of charter boats available, and two very good ones are the M.V. *Waimarie* and M.V. *Arline.* For a party of four, it's NZ$33 ($20.75) per person for five hours of fishing, with line and bait provided. Tea is provided too, but you bring your own lunch.

If the idea of a couple of days of **sailing** aboard a fully equipped yacht appeals to you, get in touch with the people at **Rainbow Yacht Charters,** on the wharf (P.O. Opua), Pahia (tel. 27-821). You get to be the skipper, your family or friends the crew. The yachts accommodate six to eight people and may be chartered for a minimum of two days, at prices *starting* at NZ$420 ($262) in peak season, NZ$260 ($163) in low season. If you're not ready to venture out on your own, sign up for a Cruise and Learn course that lasts three or four days; you rent the yacht or launch at the usual rate and pay an additional NZ$320 ($200) for instruction. The boats are a dream, and having been a closet "boatie" all my life, this is another New Zealand treat I'm definitely budgeting time for next trip. For full details, contact the company in the States at 2618 Newport Blvd., Newport Beach, CA 92663 (tel. 714/675-2250 or toll free 800/231-1468 outside California).

There's good **scuba-diving** in these waters, and **Paihia Dive, Hire and Charters Ltd.,** on Williams Road (tel. 27-551), can provide all equipment and arrange dives.

The Bay of Islands is rich in excellent **scenic and historic walks,** and the park rangers at the following addresses can furnish details of all trails, as well as a very good booklet called *Walking in the Bay of Islands Maritime and Historic Park.* Go by Park Headquarters in Russell (P.O. Box 134; tel. 37-685) or the Ranger Station in Kerikeri (P.O. Box 128; tel. 78-474) for their friendly assistance. There are also beautiful camping sites, some of them on uninhabited islands in the bay, with nominal per-night fees. You must reserve with the park rangers at Russell—you might write ahead and ask for their useful booklet *Huts and Camping.* Send $1 U.S. for each booklet.

Sightseeing

There's a wealth of sightseeing to be done on land in the Bay of Islands, but nothing compares with the bay itself. All those islands are set in a bay which is so sheltered it is known to mariners as one of the best hurricane anchorages in the South Pacific—literally, one of Mother Nature's jewels. And if you do no other sightseeing during your stay, you should take one of the **bay cruises** that circumnavigate these islands. There's the three-hour Cape Brett cruise, with its breathtaking passage through the "Hole in the Rock" when the weather is right; the price is NZ$39 ($24.50). Then there's the longer (four-hour) Cream Trip, which retraces the route used in years gone by to collect cream for market from the islands and inlets around the bay. Along this route, your knowledgeable skipper will point out Captain Cook's first anchorage in 1769; the spot where Dr. Samuel Marston preached the first Christian sermon on the beach; island locales of violence, murder, and cannibalism; and Otehei Bay, on Urupukapuka Island, which was the site of Zane Grey's camp so well written of in his *The Angler's Eldorado.* The price of the Cream Trip is also NZ$39 ($24.50).

If time permits (it will take an entire day) I heartily recommend the trip to **Cape Reinga.** There's something intriguing about being at the very top of New Zealand (and if you visit Stewart Island down south, you'll have seen the country from stem to stern!). And besides, there's a mystical aura about the cape, since the Maoris believed that it was from a gnarled pohutukawa tree in the cliffs here that souls jumped off for the return to their Hawaiki homeland after death. Then there's the drive along hard-packed golden sands of the **Ninety-Mile Beach** (which measures a literal 52 miles!) at low tide. King's tour leaves Paihia at 8 a.m., returns at 6:45 p.m., and costs NZ$40 ($25). Fullers' tour leaves Paihia at 7:30 a.m. and returns at 6 p.m., for NZ$45 ($28.25).

On land, your sightseeing will be divided between Russell and Waitangi. At the top of your "must see" list should be the **Treaty House** in Waitangi, where the British Crown succeeded in having its first treaty with the Maoris ratified by enough chieftains to assure its acceptance by major Maori leaders throughout the country. It's the birthplace of modern New Zealand.

The Georgian-style house was the home of James Busby from 1832 to 1880, and its broad lawn was the scene of the colorful meeting of Pakeha and Maori during those treaty negotiations 150 years ago on February 6, 1840. Inside, there's a museum display of a facsimile of the treaty written in Maori, other mementos of those early days, and rooms with period furnishings. An audio-visual presentation of the treaty's history may be seen at the Visitors Centre. On the grounds stands one of the most magnificent *whare runangas* (meeting houses) in the country, constructed for the 1940 centennial celebration, containing elaborately carved panels from all the Maori tribes in New Zealand. Just below the sweeping lawn, on Hobson's Beach, there's an impressive 117-foot-long Maori war canoe, also made for the centennial, from three giant kauri trees. The Treaty House and its grounds are open daily from 9 a.m. to 5 p.m. Adults pay NZ$3.50 ($2.20) admission; children are free.

If you've an ounce of romance in your soul, you won't want to miss the **Museum of Shipwrecks,** a three-masted barque, the *Tui,* moored near the Waitangi–Paihia bridge. The late Kelly Tarlton, a professional diver, made this the focus of his life's work, excavating treasure from more than 1,800 ships that have perished in the waters off New Zealand. Beside each display of treasure he brought up from the deep, there's a photograph of the ship from which it was recovered. There's a continuous slide show depicting Kelly going about his work underwater, and realistic sound effects of storms, the creaking of timbers, and the muffled chant of sea shanties. Well worth the NZ$4 ($2.50) admission; children pay NZ$2 ($1.25). Open 9 a.m. to 5 p.m. daily except Christmas Day.

Russell is a veritable concentration of historical sites. It was there that the great Maori leader Hone Heke burned everything except mission property at a time when most of what was there *should* have been burned in the interest of morality and environmental beauty, since the town seethed with all sorts of European vices, diseases, and injustices against the indigenous people (see the Introduction). The old Anglican church and headstones of sailors buried in its graveyard bear to this day bullet holes from that long-ago battle.

Make your first stop the **Bay of Islands Maritime Park Headquarters and Visitors Centre** to watch the 15-minute audio-visual presentation *The Land Is Enduring* and get a grasp of the Maori and English history of this area. The center has camping information and maps, and sells a variety of books, prints, cards, T-shirts, and sweatshirts. It's open daily from 8:30 a.m. to 5 p.m. (until 4:30 p.m. in winter).

Right on the waterfront, **Pompallier House** was built in 1841 by the French Bishop Pompallier for the Roman Catholic printing press used from 1842 to 1849 to print religious documents in the Maori language. You can see that press here today. There's also a collection of carved whale ivory and various other artifacts of the times. It's open every day, except Good Friday and Christmas Day (and Thursday and Friday from June 1 to August 9), from 10:30 a.m. to 12:30 p.m. and 1:30 to 4:30 p.m. Adults pay NZ$3 ($1.90); children, NZ$.50 (30¢).

On the highest elevation in Russell stands the flagstaff Hone Heke chopped down in defiance of British rule. It is reached by auto or on foot, and the lookout up there affords one of the best views of the bay.

You really should take time to make the 20-minute drive to **Kerikeri,** a small town that figured prominently in the country's early history. It holds the oldest European building in New Zealand, the **Kemp House,** built between 1832 and 1835 as a mission supply center, which is now a museum and general store. Kerikeri is also an arts and crafts center, and you can watch many of the artisans at their work in small shops. A direct descendant of Hone Heke constructed the replica Maori village of **Keri Park** without hammer or nails, as his ancestors built their own dwellings. Another authentic reconstruction of a pre-European Maori settlement is **Rewa's Village.**

SHOPPING

Do take time from all the other activities in the Bay of Islands to browse around the several very good shops in the area. I have lugged home some of my best New Zealand handcrafts from up here, including a gorgeous natural-wool, hand-knit sweater from the **House of Gifts,** The Strand, Russell, where Aline and Jim Ryan keep an assortment of good-quality gifts and souvenirs at reasonable prices. Over on the Paihia side, **Classique Souvenirs** is a good bet for good buys; you'll find exceptional craft items at **Katoa Crafts** (pottery, weaving, woodwork, paintings, etc.); and a very good selection is at **Waitangi Crafts and Souvenirs** on Mardsden Road. Shop for sweaters at the **THC Waitangi Resort Hotel.** Prices, far from being resort-area-inflated, are competitive with city shops and in many cases lower—and it's fun to shop with the friendly Bay of Islands proprietors, who take a personal interest in seeing that you find what you want. Most are open daily during peak season, and weekdays plus Saturday mornings at other times.

AFTER DARK

Pub pickings are limited to the **Duke** in Russell (where conversation is likely to center around fishing), the **THC Waitangi pub** and **Anchorage Bar** (where you'll bend an elbow with residents of the Paihia side of the bay, including a Maori or two, and holidaying visitors), and the **Twin Pines Tavern** at the Twin Pines Motor Camp (where campers are joined by neighborhood residents). Other possibilities include the **Lighthouse Tavern,** upstairs in the Selwyn Mall in Paihia; the **Roadrunner Tavern,** 2½ miles south of town; and the **Terrace Nightclub,** on Kawakawa Road in Opua, open nightly from 10 p.m. until late.

---

5. From Auckland to Waitomo

If you're going from the Bay of Islands directly to Waitomo, count on a long day's drive, shortened considerably if you return to Auckland via Hwy. 1 (about a four-hour drive). Along the way, you might stop by the **Waitomo limestone caves,** three kilometers (two miles) south of Kawakawa—they're about half a kilometer up a dirt road to the left of Hwy. 1, and guided tours are at 10 and 11 a.m., and 1, 2, and 3 p.m. Farther south, the town of **Warkworth** was once the center of extensive sawmilling of kauri spars to furnish masts for the Royal Navy, and there are the remains of several Maori *pas* (fortified villages) in the area. About seven kilometers (four miles) away, at the coastal town of **Sandspit,** you can take a launch to Kawau Island to visit **Mansion House,** the restored home of Gov. George Grey. Then there are those beautiful beaches nearer Auckland at **Waiwera** and **Orewa.**

These are all possibilities en route, but on a one-day drive to Waitomo, you'll have to keep an eye on the clock. If you leave the Bay of Islands around 8 a.m., driving at a steady pace (with a lunch break) will get you to Waitomo not much before about 5 p.m. An alternative is a leisurely drive back to Auckland or some other intermediate spot for an overnight stop, and an early-morning start to go on to Waitomo the following day.

If you're traveling by bus, there's excellent InterCity transportation from the Bay of Islands to Auckland, and service leaving Auckland at about 9 a.m. for Waitomo, which stops for a tour of the caves, then goes on to Rotorua. You can, of course, break the journey with an overnight stay at Waitomo and continue on to Rotorua the next afternoon.

From Auckland, the 125-mile drive to Waitomo passes through rich farm country and horse and cattle farms. A good lunch stop is the Victorian **1870 Restaurant,** Main Highway, at Ngaruawahia (tel. 07124/8121). This is an old clapboard house, built in 1869, which has been in its day a police station, post office, and courthouse, and its atmosphere is still very much of the 19th century, with interesting antiques in the licensed dining room. The fare is simple, good, and moderately priced. Hours vary, so call ahead to check. Closed Monday.

Hamilton is New Zealand's largest inland city and the commercial and industrial center of this agricultural area, as well as the site of the University of Waikato. Several major religions are centered here: it's the see city for the Anglican Diocese of Waikato; the Mormons have their magnificent South Pacific temple headquarters at Temple View, high on a hill at Tuhikaramea southwest of the city center; and there's a Sikh temple on the northern outskirts of town at Horotiu. Throughout the city, you'll see lovely gardens both in city parks and private lawns.

A scant ten miles before you reach Waitomo and the caves, there's a **Kiwi House** at Otorohanga, as well as an excellent youth hostel, which is open only from December 17 to January 25. The remaining distance to Waitomo runs through more roll-ing farmland.

A FARM STAY FOR CAMPERVANS EN ROUTE

On State Hwy. 3, about halfway between Hamilton and Waitomo, the **Park-lands Dairy Farm,** Kio Kio, R.D. 4, Otorohanga (tel. 08226/818), is run by Owen Rountree and family, whose hospitality goes far beyond that of most owners. That is undoubtedly because this is their *home,* and what they're offering—in addition to power points at campervan sites, showers, toilets, and a barbecue—is a real "down home" farm welcome. Guests are invited in for a cuppa in the evening, and when it's farm-chore time, guests often go right along and become an honorary New Zealand dairy farmer by milking a cow or feeding a calf—and the Rountrees present them with a certificate in honor of their accomplishment! This really is a motor camp with a difference, and it's a convenient base for Waitomo Caves sightseeing. Rates are NZ$12 ($7.50) double, NZ$6 ($3.75) for each additional adult, NZ$4 ($2.50) for each additional child, all plus GST. The family will provide a cooked farm breakfast for an extra charge, and dinner with advance notice.

6. Waitomo Caves

Waitomo Village owes its existence to the more than 200,000 visitors who come annually to visit three remarkable limestone caves, and its main street holds a general store, post office, and tavern (which sells tickets to the caves as well as souve-nirs, and has the usual bottle store, public bar, and bistro restaurant). At the top of a gracefully winding driveway stands the THC Waitomo Hotel (with not a budget-priced room under its roof). Across from the general store, a large open field is called The Domain, where cabins may be rented. Waitomo Cave, with its splendid Glow-worm Grotto, is some 400 yards beyond the tavern, and about 2½ miles away are Ruakuri and Aranui Caves, both of which rival Waitomo as sightseeing attractions.

WHERE TO STAY

A Hostel

It's the closest thing Waitomo has to a youth hostel, and hostelers, backpackers, or cavers will find the **Hamilton Tomo Group Lodge,** about half a mile past the Waitomo Cave on the main road (P.O. Box 12), Waitomo Caves (tel. 0813/87-442), quite adequate. The bunkhouse will sleep 30 (but has been known to accom-modate more in a pinch) on wooden bunks that have rubber mattresses. House rules are basic: no alcohol, guests must tidy up, and lights go out at midnight. Reserva-tions? You don't need them—you simply go to the lodge, drop NZ$8 ($5) plus GST, in the Honesty Box, and claim your bunk space. There's not likely to be much space on a weekend, since that's when there's an invasion of great numbers of tramp-ers and cavers who are members of the Hamilton Tomo Group, but you'll be fitted in if possible. Equipment in the lodge includes light, heat, hot water, showers, electric stove (plus all cooking and eating utensils), refrigerator, washing machine, drying room, and radio. There's an interesting caving display, and lots of club photos. You'll need to bring in food from the general store, since there's none closer.

Motor Camps

The **Waitomo Caravan Park,** P.O. Box 14, Waitomo Caves (tel. 08133/87-639), has a total of ten cabins located in two blocks. Each will sleep four in two bunk beds. Furnishings are simple: cold-water sink, table, chairs, and a small hotplate. Cooking and eating utensils are not supplied, but may be rented for a small fee. Also on the premises are communal showers, laundry, and kitchen. There are also powered caravan and tent sites. You'll find the busy owners, Tony and Patty Doull, at the Mobil gas station, tea room, or general store, all of which they also run. If you've arrived without a reservation, check in at the general store. Rates (exclusive of GST) are NZ$6 ($3.75) per person.

In Otorohanga, 16 km (10 miles) from Waitomo Caves, the **Otorohanga Motor Camp,** c/o Otorohanga Taxis, Wahanui Crescent, Otorohanga (tel. 08133/ 8214), is on Domain Drive right next to the Kiwi House and swimming pool. Just help yourself to any unoccupied or unreserved site and the nonresident caretaker calls in the mornings and evenings to collect your fees. There's a kitchen with an electric range, hot- and cold-water sinks, refrigerator, and freezer. Other amenities include toilets, showers, a laundry, a barbecue area, and a play area. Tent sites cost NZ$10.50 ($6.55) for two people; an extra person is NZ$5.50 ($3.45); children 5 to 16, NZ$3.50 ($2.20); and children under 5, free. Caravan sites are NZ$12 ($7.50) for two people and NZ$6 ($3.75) for an extra person, and children are charged the same as above. On-site caravans cost NZ$12 ($7.50), plus camp charges. All prices include GST.

Motel Flats

You'll find the **Waitomo Country Lodge,** near the corner of Waitomo Caves Road and Hwy. 3 (P.O. Box 343), Otorohanga (tel. 08133/8109). Bryan and Faye Cooke, owners of this Best Western motel, are always happy to give expert sightseeing advice. There are 17 serviced units (one with a waterbed), and all have tea and coffee makings, fridge, TV, telephone, and electric heat. There's a spa pool, bar, and licensed restaurant on the premises. Rates are NZ$48 ($30) single, NZ$60 ($37.50) double, including GST.

A Licensed Hotel

In Otorohanga, 16 km (10 miles) north of the caves, the **Royal Hotel,** on Te Kanawa Street off Maniapoto Street (tel. 08133/8129), has charming, immaculate rooms with flowered carpets, white bedspreads, and lace curtains. All have H&C, and bath and shower facilities are in the hall. The communal kitchen has tea-making facilities and a laundry. There's a swimming pool, and the Rangatira Room restaurant serves all meals every day (see "Where to Eat," below). The reasonable rates are NZ$33 ($20.75) single, NZ$55 ($34.50) double without facilities or NZ$71 ($44.50) with them, including GST.

WHERE TO EAT

Picnics can be a pleasure, either at the outdoor umbrella tables at the **general store** or the facilities on the Domain. You can also buy hot and cold snacks and light meals at the general store's tea room.

There's a sort of Victorian pub air about the **Otorohanga Royal Hotel's Rangatira Room.** Dark-wood paneling, padded captain's chairs, wide booths, and fringed lampshades make it cozy. A nice touch is the series of Maori chieftain portraits on restaurant and lounge walls. All three meals are served seven days a week; the food is good, and prices are reasonable.

The **THC Waitomo Hotel** offers a variety of eating possibilities, all pretty pricey (but families get a break in their "half price for children" policy). Costs for grownups' breakfast run about NZ$9 ($5.65) or NZ$15 ($9.40), and it's served from 7:30 to 9 a.m. There's a barbecue or grilled lunch for NZ$13 ($8.15), plus GST.

There's the licensed restaurant at Waitomo Country Lodge, bistro meals at the

Tavern, and in Otorohanga, Maniapoto Street has several good, inexpensive restaurants from which to choose.

THINGS TO SEE AND DO

The caves are *the* attraction at Waitomo, chief among them the Waitomo Cave with its Glowworm Grotto. But you should include the Ruakuri and Aranui caves in your sightseeing—each has its own delights, the cost is low, and they're all worth the time.

The Caves

Forty-five-minute guided tours are run on regular schedules at all three caves—tickets and tour times are available at the Tavern and at the THC Waitomo Hotel. There's a two-cave combination ticket at NZ$15 ($9.40) for adults; one cave costs NZ$9.60 ($6). Children pay half price. Be sure to wear good walking shoes and carry a sweater if the weather is a bit cool—it'll be cooler underground.

For me, the most wonderful (and I *mean* wonder-full) time to visit the **Glowworm Grotto** in Waitomo Cave is in the evening. Crowds are smaller, for one thing, and somehow the experience just seems to be one for after dark. Sheer delight.

About 400 yards from the THC Hotel, a guide greets you at Waitomo's entrance to escort you through large antechambers, pointing out limestone formations with names like "The Organ," 8 feet high with a 24-foot base.

Largest cavern in any of the caves is "The Cathedral," which rises 47 feet and is an acoustically perfect auditorium that has seen performances by such recording artists as the Vienna Boys' Choir and Dame Nellie Melba.

Then it's on to a small grotto festooned with glowworms, where your guide fills you in on the glowworm's life and death cycle. Fascinating! A very *short* cycle it is, for the adult fly lives exactly four days, just long enough to produce the next generation. Having done that, it simply dies and becomes food for the next batch of glowworms.

The whole process begins with a tiny egg, which has a 21-day incubation period, then hatches into an inch-long grub. The grub then cloaks itself in a hollow mucous tube-like nest, which is pinned to the grotto roof with a multitude of slender threads, each holding minute drops of acid and suspended like fishing lines down from the roof. The bait for those lines is the hypnotic blue-green light that comes from the larva's light organs (and that, of course, is what you see as you pass through the grotto) to attract a night-flying midge, which is "caught" by the threads, paralyzed by the acid, and reeled up and eaten by the larva. After about six months, the larva pupates for about two weeks in a hard, brown cocoon about half an inch long and suspended by a circle of those slender threads. The pupa's flirtatious light show attracts several males, which proceed to help the fly escape her cocoon. Four days of egg laying, then it's time to end it all by diving into the lines cast by new larvae as a main course along with the midges.

Now that you understand how and why the glowworms glow, your guide is ready to take you on an unforgettable boat ride down the underground river, which flows through the 100-foot-long, 40-foot-high, 50-foot-wide Glowworm Grotto. As you board the large, flat-bottomed boat, he will caution you that absolute silence is required, since the glowworms will extinguish their lights at the slightest noise. I must say that the warning is probably unnecessary, since the spectacle of more than 10,000 of those tiny pinpricks of light leaves one awed beyond words, and silence seems the only fitting way in which to view them. The boat glides slowly along what is called the "Milky Way," then returns to the dock, where you climb back up through the cave and are given an opportunity to question your guide on any of the things you have seen. It's a unique experience, and one that is sure to live in your memory.

Ask at the THC Hotel desk if you need transportation to the other two caves, which are some 2½ miles away. Dramatic Ruakuri, with its labyrinth of caverns alive with the sound of an underground waterfall and its river, which flashes in and out of sight, is the largest of the three. The smallest is Aranui, and many people think it's the loveliest. There's an unusual delicacy about its limestone formations and ivory-colored, translucent stalactites. Light refreshments are available near these two caves.

Kiwi House

While in this area, stop by the **Otorohanga Nocturnal Kiwi House** on Alex Telfer Drive, off Kakamutu Road (tel. 08133/7391). The Otorohanga Zoological Society always has one pair of the national bird awake and on view, and there's always a knowledgeable person on hand to tell you about them and answer any questions you may have. There's also a large aviary on the grounds, which has an interesting collection of waterfowl. Hours are 10 a.m. to 5 p.m. in summer, 4 p.m. other months. Admission is NZ$5 ($3.15) for adults, NZ$1.50 (95¢) for children; under-7s, free.

ON TO ROTORUA

It's an easy, three-hours-or-less drive from Waitomo to Rotorua, through rolling farmland and long stretches of bush. Approaching that steamy thermal town, you'll catch glimpses of its gleaming lakes and volcanic peaks. There's an "other world" aspect about Rotorua and its environs, which will begin to capture your imagination even before you roll into town.

ROTORUA

The first tourists to arrive in Rotorua were Maoris, members of the Arawa tribe whose seagoing canoe reached the shores of the Bay of Plenty sometime during the 14th century. Pushing inland to Lake Rotorua, they stayed on to become settlers. Today's tourist will find some 5,000 of their descendants happily following much of the traditional tribal lifestyle in the largest area in New Zealand that is both preserved and promoted as a showcase for pre-European culture.

Those early arrivals found the area ideally suited to settlement. Nature supplied not only everything they needed for survival, but threw in mysterious volcanic cones, large, deep lakes, and all those steaming thermal pools as natural habitats for innumerable Maori spirit gods who, of course, were unseen passengers in the Arawa canoe as it crossed the Pacific. There's a Maori legend centered on the antics of the gods to be told about almost every one of the natural wonders you'll see in Rotorua.

The Arawas are quick to tell you the one that explains in Maori terms the awesome thermal activity around Rotorua. It seems the great navigator-priest Ngatoroirangi, having reached the summit of Mount Tongariro, suffered greatly from the cold and implored his goddess sisters back in Hawaiki to send along some of their native warmth to this frigid, windswept place. Their response was a generous one—they pitched their gobs of fire across the water, which hopped, skipped, and jumped over the land, touching down at White Island, Rotorua, Wairankei, Taupo, Tokaanu, Ketetahi, finally reaching the freezing Ngatoroirangi at Mount Tongariro. Geologists, on the other hand, simply say that underground lava or superheated rock heats and pressurizes underground water, sending it spouting up via any escape route it can find—natural fissures, porous rock, etc. Personally, I think the Maoris have the better story!

Whatever the explanation for the North Island's giant (150-mile-long, 20-mile-wide) thermal region, Rotorua sits right in the middle of the most intense activity (that explains the strong smell of sulfur here). The overheated water will bubble up all around you in the form of geysers, mud pools, or steam bores. You'll bathe in it, see the locals cooking with it, stay in guesthouses that are heated with it, or simply walk carefully around the boiling mud pools watching this performance—of whatever gods—in sheer fascination.

Just as fascinating is the vast gallery of Maori culture through which you will wander. Through song and dance you'll hear some of those legends firsthand; at a hangi feast you'll taste food cooked in a centuries-old manner; in a model Maori village you'll watch the younger generation learning from their elders such age-old skills as carving and weaving. In craft shops you'll find a splendid array of "just the right gift" items.

---

1. The City and Surroundings

Rotorua sits in the curve of Lake Rotorua's southwestern shore, spreading inland in a neat pattern, which will have you oriented in a matter of hours. The center of town is not large: a good ten-minute walk will take you from the southside bus and rail depot (named the **Travel Centre**) northward past those two tourist landmarks, the **post office** and **NZTP office,** to the lovely **Government Gardens.** Older, downtown hotels are also along this route, while more modern hotels are more or less concentrated along the southern end of **Fenton Street,** which is the main street, running from the lake for two miles south to Whakarewarewa (never mind, just call it "Whaka," as the locals do), a thermal reserve owned by Maoris. There are city and suburban buses, but they are infrequent (about one an hour) during weekdays and nonexistent on weekends. Unless you're driving, best reserve an in-town room and use coach tours to reach those sights out of walking distance. Tours are numerous, well planned, and not too expensive—this is, after all, perhaps the North Island's major tourist town, and you may be sure that whatever you want to do or see, someone will have devised an easy, inexpensive way for you to do it.

USEFUL INFORMATION

The center of tourist information in Rotorua is the **NZTP office** at 67 Fenton St. on the corner of Haupapa Street (tel. 073/485-179); hours are 8:30 a.m. to 5 p.m. daily. It is loaded with tourist information and has a helpful staff who will make bookings. . . . Look for *Thermalair* and *Rotorua Magic,* free publications listing current goings-on, which you'll find in many hotels and in the tourist offices, and check the evening newspaper, the *Daily Post,* for day-to-day events. . . . The **Travel Centre** (arrival and departure point for InterCity coaches, trains, and most sightseeing tours) is on Amohau Street (tel. 481-039). . . . **Air New Zealand** has a ticket terminal on Amohau Street, just off Fenton Street (tel. 487-159). . . . **Newmans** office is at 113 Fenton St. (tel. 70-599). . . . You'll find **taxi ranks** at the Travel Centre, and on Fenton Street near the Ansett office, or you can call a cab at 485-079. . . . The **Chief Post Office (CPO),** on the corner of Tutanekai and Hinemoa Streets, is open from 8:30 a.m. to 5 p.m. Monday through Thursday, until 8 p.m. on Friday. . . . The **telephone prefix** is 073.

WHERE TO STAY

Rotorua is replete with accommodations, and they come in all shapes, sizes, and price ranges. In addition to nine major hotels, there are more than 100 motels and 15 motor camps. Those in the budget range are among the best you'll find in this category anywhere in the country. Indeed, don't expect Rotorua to conform to the usual popular resort image of "charging what the traffic will bear for the least service we can get away with"—this is a resort of a different stripe, one where prices are moderate, service friendly and efficient, and accommodation standards exceptionally high.

Hostels

Just about the best buy in Rotorua is the **YHA Hostel,** at the corner of Eruera and Hinemaru Streets, Rotorua (tel. 073/476-810). It's a large, comfortable building, accommodating 68 in 18 rooms, and there are family rooms. There's a well-equipped kitchen as well as steam ovens, a provisions shop, laundry facilities and irons, a recreation room, and bicycles for rent. It's open during the day and closes at 11 p.m. Situated right in town, it's only about two minutes from the bus station. The nightly rate is NZ$14 ($8.75).

Budget, hostel-type accommodations are also available at the **Ivanhoe Tourist Lodge,** 54 Haupapa St., Rotorua (tel. 073/486-985), just off Tutanekai Street. There are single, twin, and double cabins, all heated, and single, twin, and double serviced rooms. Linen and blankets are available for a small fee. All cabins and rooms are carpeted, and each has mirrors and dressers. Facilities are all communal: a fully equipped, modern kitchen; large dining or common room (with a brilliant mural of the area); hot thermal pool; TV lounge; and games room. Rates run from NZ$14 ($8.75) for small dormitories to NZ$20 ($12.50) for serviced rooms, all plus GST.

Cabins/Campgrounds

Holdens Bay Holiday Park, 21 Robinson Ave., Holdens Bay (P.O. Box 9), Rotorua (tel. 073/459-925), only 6 km (3½ miles) from Rotorua, has a pretty setting very near Lake Rotorua. On the extensive grounds, there are tent and caravan sites, tourist cabins (bring your own linens and blankets), and modern tourist flats (just bring yourself), as well as a swimming pool, hot spa pools, a store, childrens' play area, laundry, TVs for rent, a barbecue, car wash, and games room. Rates are NZ$8 ($5) per person for tent and caravan sites, NZ$30 ($18.75) double for cabins, and NZ$45 ($28.25) double for tourist flats, all including GST.

Set in wooded grounds through which an excellent trout stream meanders under drooping willow trees, the **Waiteti Holiday Park,** 14 Okona Crescent, Ngongotaha, Rotorua (tel. 073/74-749), has tent sites down near the riverbank, 28 power sites for caravans, three on-site caravans that sleep up to eight, a bunkhouse that accommodates 48, tourist cabins that will sleep four to six people, and motel and tourist flats that sleep five. The management can help with any sightseeing arrangements. You supply linens in all except the motel flats, but they may be rented for a small fee. There's a community kitchen (fully equipped), showers, toilets, laundry, TV lounge, barbecue area, children's swings, a games room, and indoor swimming pool. This is a convenient, attractive, and very friendly motor camp, which gets my highest recommendation. Rates range from NZ$6.50 ($4.05) for tent sites, to NZ$25 ($15.75) double for cabins, to NZ$38 ($23.75) double for tourist flats, and NZ$45 ($28.25) double for motel flats, all plus GST.

Besides being secluded, right on the lake and only a little over a mile from downtown Rotorua, **Lakeside Motor Camp,** 54 Whittaker Rd., Rotorua (tel. 073/481-693), has an abundance of trees, swings and a trampoline, a games and TV room, pool, showers, laundry, communal kitchen, car wash, and camp store. Swimming, boating, fishing, and waterskiing are all at your doorstep. Tent sites are NZ$7.50 ($4.70) per person; van sites, NZ$16 ($10) for two people; on-site caravans, NZ$25 ($15.75) for two; cabins, NZ$33 ($20.75) double; tourist flats (they aren't serviced and do not have bedding or tea and coffee facilities), NZ$43 ($27) double; and chalets, NZ$48 ($30) double. The gate to the property closes at 11 p.m., so you can't stay out too late.

Bed-and-Breakfasts

Doreen and Leon Maitland own and operate the **Tresco International Guest House,** 3 Toko St., Rotorua (tel. 073/489-611), with seven attractive rooms. They are sparkling clean, with H&C and tea- and coffee-making facilities, and there's a homey, happy air about this place. In addition to off-street parking, there's a guest laundry, TV lounge with video, and a mineral plunge pool. The guesthouse is only one block from the city center. Rates for bed-and-breakfast (it's a four-course cooked meal) are NZ$36 ($22.50) single, NZ$55 ($34.50) double, and NZ$66 ($41.25) triple, all including GST.

There's a warm, homey air about **Eaton Hall,** 39 Hinemaru St., Rotorua (tel.

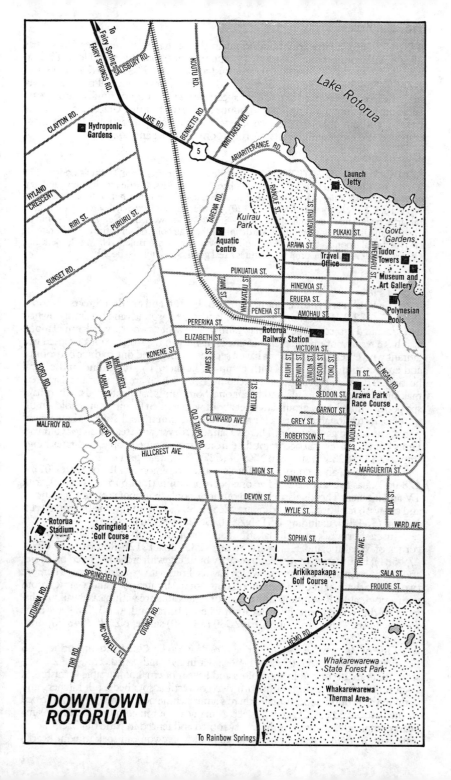

DOWNTOWN ROTORUA

073/470-366), a two-story house right in the center of town. Grace Dorset has filled it with comfortable furnishings (some antiques), old china, and lots of bric-a-brac. There's a cozy TV lounge, and the budget rates of NZ$34 ($21.25) single and NZ$55 ($34.50) double include GST and a cooked or continental breakfast. Evening meals can be booked and feature specialties reminiscent of English inns (roast beef and Yorkshire pudding, etc.). A bonus here is the fact that Grace, as a bona-fide ticket agent, can organize and *issue tickets* for sightseeing attractions, fishing trips, concerts, and sightseeing flights. Corner room 3 is quiet and cozy.

READERS' B&B SELECTIONS: "There's a lovely warm feeling at **Traguair Lodge,** 126 Ranolf St., Rotorua (tel. 073/486-149), where Mr. and Mrs. Currie are charming and gracious hosts" (M. Faley, Denver, Colo.). . . . "We stayed with **Heather and Brian Oberer,** Ngakuru, R.D. 1, Rotorua (tel. 073/32-720), for four days and were enchanted by the beautiful farm, by Heather's magnificent cooking—the best food we had in New Zealand—and by Heather and Brian themselves. This was definitely the high point of our entire trip. The rate for two beautiful rooms, breakfast, and dinner was very reasonable" (N. Ward, Berkeley, Calif.)[*Author's Note:* The property features a real geothermal mineral pool.]

Motel Flats

The **Boulevard Motel,** on the corner of Fenton and Seddon Streets, Rotorua (tel. 073/482-074), is set on two acres of landscaped grounds and is a family-owned and -operated project of the Bradshaw family. The white, two-story, balconied motel also has a restaurant on the premises and is just down the street from a licensed restaurant with entertainment. Flats have a separate lounge and one to three bedrooms, and are beautifully furnished, with complete kitchen, TV, telephone, and central heating. There are serviced units (sleeping two), which are smaller and have tea-making facilities, fridge, TV, and telephone. Some units have waterbeds; others have spa pools. Those lovely grounds are set about with garden furniture and hold a multitude of recreational facilities: a putting green, swimming pool, four spa baths, swirl pools, sauna, and games room. There's a laundry, dryer, and steam iron for your use. Units come in sizes that accommodate from three to nine people, and rates range from NZ$38 ($23.75) single to NZ$44 ($27.50) double, plus GST.

Tidy, quiet, and economical, **Tom's Motel,** 6 Union St., Rotorua (tel. 073/478-062), has five studios and five one-bedroom units (for up to five people), with TV and kitchen. There's also a heated outdoor pool, an indoor spa pool, a laundry, and car-wash facilities. The studios are NZ$49.50 ($31) and the one-bedrooms run NZ$55 ($34.50), including GST; NZ$10 ($6.25) per extra person.

Just a short walk from the lakefront and town, the **Ambassador Motel,** on the corner of Whakaue and Hinemaru Streets (P.O. Box 1212), Rotorua (tel. 073/479-581), is an attractive white, three-story building with arched covered balconies and self-contained units, some of which have ceilings with exposed beams. There are two private thermal pools, a swirl pool, outdoor freshwater pool, and a games room with a pool table. Restaurants and a host of attractions are within easy walking distance in this central, but quiet, location where Murray and Ann Whitaker are the friendly hosts. Year-round rates are NZ$60 ($37.50) single, NZ$70 ($43.75) double, plus GST.

One of Rotorua's most attractive motels is **Wylie Court Motor Lodge,** 345 Fenton St., Rotorua (tel. 073/461-494). Set in 2½ landscaped acres, the 27 two-story units are decorated in soft colors and have modern, comfortable furnishings. Each unit has a full living room with two convertible sofa beds, full kitchen, and bath on the ground floor; upstairs there's a mezzanine bedroom with a double bed (some have waterbeds). Each will sleep as many as four in comfort. What wins my heart completely, however, is the pretty roofed and fenced-in patio out back of each unit, with its own private heated plunge pool where you can soak to your heart's content whether or not there's a bathing suit in your luggage—sheer luxury! Barry and Glen Johnston, their son, Tony, and his wife, Sharon, have provided loads of amenities: a heated swimming pool, children's playground, thermal pool, guest laundry, in-room video, the daily newspaper delivered to your door, and a cooked or continental breakfast at a small additional charge. They also provide a courtesy car to and from the airport. Rates are NZ$69 ($43.25) single, NZ$85 ($53.25) double, plus GST. It's a Best Western, so discounts apply. Highly recommended, both for its facilities and its genial hosts.

At the **Motel Sulphur City,** 241 Fenton St., Rotorua (tel. 073/486-513 or 477-400), owners/operators Tom and Margaret Harrison offer special budget rates for standard units with full kitchen and adjoining lounge, as well as one- and two-bedroom units. You can stay one night for NZ$50 ($31.25), two or three nights for NZ$45 ($28.25) per night, four or five nights at NZ$40 ($25) per night, and six or seven nights at NZ$38 ($23.75) per night—all plus GST. Light breakfast is available. The Harrisons will pick up guests at the bus station.

The economy-priced **Studio Motel,** 315-A Fenton St., Rotorua (tel. 073/470-360), has attractive one- and two-bedroom units that can sleep up to five persons, as well as a spa pool. A bonus comes in the form of pottery made by owner Barry Ball, who has had many exhibitions in New Zealand. His studio is on the premises, and his pottery is for sale in the reception room. Prices begin at NZ$44 ($27.50) double and go up to NZ$70 ($43.75) for up to five. It's a good idea to reserve ahead.

At the pretty **Acacia Lodge Best Western Motel,** 40 Victoria St., Rotorua (tel. 073/487-089), Louise and David McCliskie have 18 brick units with colorful flower boxes outside large picture windows in each unit. Each has full kitchen facilities, color TV, radio, telephone, and central heat. Some have waterbeds, and there are some family units. Other amenities include a sauna, mineral pools, a nice play area, and laundry facilities. The quiet, peaceful location is close to the city center and sightseeing attractions, and there's courtesy-car service to the airport and bus station. Rates (all plus GST) are NZ$57 ($35.75) single, NZ$67 ($42) double; Best Western discounts apply.

One reader praises the humor and helpfulness of Doreen and Ivan Durr, the owners of the **Hylton Motel,** 287 Fenton St., Rotorua (tel. 073/485-056), which feels more like a private house. They offer three two-bedroom units with kitchen, which they will rent to two people for NZ$70 ($43.75) and to four for NZ$100 ($62.50). Each room has a TV, and there is a pool. The Burrs will supply a continental or cooked breakfast on request.

A reader from Australia wrote to tell me about the **Bel Aire Motel,** 257 Fenton St., Rotorua (tel. 073/486-076), and his recommendation certainly stood the test of close inspection. This small (eight units), centrally located motel offers spotless one- and two-bedroom units that sleep two to seven people, each with a full kitchen, geothermal heating, radio, TV and video, and telephone. There's a hot mineral pool, as well as a guest laundry, drying room, and the owner/operators, Joan and Mike de Latour, can furnish breakfast on request. They'll also pick up and deliver guests to the airport or bus terminal. Rates are NZ$54 ($33.75), single or double.

READER'S MOTEL SELECTION: "We found clean, comfortable, and inexpensive accommodations at **Motel Six,** 251 Fenton St. (tel. 073/481-029)" (S. Murdoch, Norfolk, Va.).

A Mini-Splurge

You could walk right by **Ledwich Lodge,** at 12-14 Lake Rd. (P.O. Box 769), Rotorua (tel. 073/470-049), which is actually a motel, without giving it a second glance. It's small, with a façade that doesn't draw attention to itself, and it has no grounds. But look again—the lake is its front yard and it's within walking distance of everything in town. It also has exceptionally pretty units with a bay window, bright tropical-print curtains, a large bath with spa pool, a queen-size bed covered with a feather duvet, a full kitchen, thermal heating (this old-fashioned system that is being phased out in Rotorua), lots of wood trim, TV, and in-house video. In addition, there is a small, thermally heated pool and picnic area, and guests have access to a steam box for hangi-style cooking; breakfast is available. But I've saved the best for last: the managers, Colin and Valerie Hooper, who can only be described as real sweethearts. No wonder travelers come back again and again. Rates start at NZ$88 ($55) double, plus GST; NZ$11 ($6.90) for one extra person. There are larger units, as well as two units for the disabled.

A Licensed Hotel

This listing is—I admit it—a little sneaky. It has absolutely no place in a budget travel book. Still, if you're particularly flush when you hit Rotorua (or you're hypnotized by the thermal goings-on hereabouts), you may want to throw the budget out the window and stay at **Geyserland Resort,** Whaka Road, Rotorua (tel. 073/482-039). What makes it so special is its panoramic view of the Whaka Thermal Reserve, just outside the windows of most of its 75 rooms. From your room with a window wall facing the reserve, you can watch the Pohutu Geyser shoot up as high as 50 feet in the air, and those steaming, bubbling mud pools will keep you posted at the window. The hotel itself has the usual luxury hotel trappings, with pretty and comfortable rooms, spa pools, a swimming pool, and a first-class restaurant. If you lean toward luxury hotels, this one is as good as any; but as I said, it's all that steam out there that makes it warrant space in a budget guide, so if you reserve, be sure to specify that you want a room overlooking the thermal reserve, *not* a poolside room. Rates including GST are NZ$115.50 ($72.25) single, NZ$126.50 ($79) double; children under 12 stay free in their parents' room. *Note:* From May 1 through the end of September they frequently run two-day special or weekend rates at substantial reductions—be sure to inquire. Just thought you'd want to know!

Big Splurges

The **THC Rotorua International Hotel,** Froude St., Rotorua (tel. 073/481-189), overlooks the fascinating thermal activity of legendary Whakarewarewa. It is also the setting of Rotorua's most authentic Maori hangi and concert each night, the only one in town that invites guests to witness the actual lifting of the hangi from its earthen oven. Guest rooms are all air-conditioned, and have private facilities, tea- and coffee-making facilities, fridges, mini-bars, color TVs, and telephones. There are two bars, and two excellent restaurants, as well as two heated swimming pools, hot tubs, guest laundry, and a tour desk. While regular rates range from NZ$90 ($56.25) to NZ$150 ($93.75), plus GST, single or double, there are frequent special offers, such two nights and two cooked breakfasts for NZ$99 ($62) per person. Even without a reduction, however, this definitely rates as a big splurge that offers good value for dollar.

The **Hyatt Kingsgate Rotorua,** Eruera Street (P.O. Box 1044), Rotorua (tel. 073/472-234), is Rotorua's only luxury hotel right in the heart of town. It also holds the country's only retractable glass-domed swimming pool (open to the elements in good weather, protected from them in bad). The lobby features a magnificent Maori carving that depicts Tanemahuta attempting to push his father, Ranginui (Great Sky), and his mother, Papatuanuku (Earth), apart, with symbolic falling rain and rising mist symbolizing the perpetual grief of the parents at their separation. Rooms are top-quality, both in furnishings and decor, and two floors are set aside for the deluxe Regency Club rooms for a *really* big splurge (lots of extra services). All rooms have private facilities, tea- and coffee-making facilities, fridges, mini-bars, color TVs, and videos. Of special note, there's wheelchair access to all public areas and guestrooms. In addition to two bars, there are two very good restaurants, six spa rooms, guest laundry, and a fitness center complex. Rates run from

NZ$150 ($93.75) plus GST, single or double. Children under 18 share rooms with parents at no charge, and a special family package costs NZ$79 ($49.50) per night, depending on availability.

WHERE TO EAT

For those times when eating in is a good idea either for budget or energy (at the end of a long sightseeing day) reasons, you have two good Rotorua alternatives. If you've a yen for fresh New Zealand specialties like marinated mussels, oysters, clams, or cooked lamb, hie yourself over to **Fenwick's Delicatessen,** next to the hospital at 38 Hinemoa St. (tel. 470-777). It's chock-full of ready-to-eat goodies, as well as a wide selection of cheeses, hot barbecued rôtisserie chicken, salads, sweets, and a host of specialty goods, all at very good prices. Hours are 8 a.m. to 5:30 p.m. Monday through Friday, until noon on Saturday; closed Sunday.

You'll have trouble passing the window at **Chez Suzanne Pâtisserie,** 61 Hinemoa St., next to the *Daily Post* building (tel. 486-495), without going in. The selection of pastries and sandwiches may be small but they are exceedingly fresh. It's a small place, with a few booths, a counter, and a few wooden tables with fresh flowers on them. Filled croissants are NZ$2.40 ($1.50) and sandwiches run NZ$.90 (55¢) to NZ$2.50 ($1.55). It's open weekdays from 8:30 a.m. to 5 p.m. (sometimes 6 p.m.) and on Saturday from 8:30 a.m. to 2 p.m.

For a filling breakfast in a delightful setting, drop by **Eaton Hall,** a bed-and-breakfast at 39 Hinemaru St., across from the Hyatt, which invites the public to drop by for the first meal of the day. Cooked breakfast costs NZ$4.70 ($3.90) to NZ$6.50 ($4.05); a combination cooked and continental breakfast is NZ$8.50 ($5.30). There are only four tables, covered with lace tablecloths, so you may have to wait your turn for this good value. Come between 7 and 9:30 a.m.

You'll find **Cobb & Co.,** with the usual colonial decor and moderately priced food, in the Grand Hotel on Hinemoa Street (tel. 482-089). It's fully licensed and serves a good selection of grills, seafoods, and light meals. There's a children's menu and half portions of some items. There is continuous service every day of the week from 7 a.m. to 10 p.m.

A local favorite (and likely to become one of yours, as well) is the **Lake View Restaurant** on Lake Road (tel. 485-585), in a century-old building overlooking the lake and Ohinemutu village. In its younger days it served as a leading hotel, but now it's content to meet the eating and imbibing needs of its clientele. The dining room has wood booths with high backs and gold velvet seats, red carpeting and drapes, and impressive Maori portraits in the bar. The large bar and lounge is fitted out with comfortable divans and easy chairs facing large windows looking out onto the lake. Seasonal menus feature steak, chicken, seafood, and vegetarian dishes. Main-course prices are in the NZ$8 ($5) to NZ$12 ($7.50) range (including salad and vegetables). Lunch hours Monday through Saturday are noon to 2 p.m.; dinner is Monday through Thursday from 6 to 9 p.m., to 10 p.m. on Friday and Saturday. Bar hours are 11 a.m. to 10 p.m. (11 p.m. on Friday and Saturday). Although the dining room is fairly large, reservations are usually in order. Fully licensed, of course.

Surprisingly, one of the best value-for-dollar lunches is to be found at the posh **Hyatt Kingsgate Rotorua,** Eruera Street (tel. 477-677), where an all-you-can-eat theme buffet (Chinese or Italian, for instance) is served poolside for just NZ$7 ($3.30). Don't confuse it with the downstairs Brasserie (also poolside), where light lunches of sandwiches and salads start at NZ$10 ($6.25); the Brasserie's buffet lunch is NZ$16.90 ($10.50), and its buffet dinner runs NZ$21.80 ($13.75). Both are fully licensed.

For moderately priced food, well prepared and served in a casual atmosphere, it's hard to beat **Floyd's Cafe,** 48 Haupapa St. (tel. 470-024). The seafood crêpe is a standout, as is their spaghetti bolognese, and you can eat well for about NZ$10 ($6.25). Open from 11 a.m. to 11 p.m. Monday through Friday, and 6 to 11 p.m. on Saturday. BYO.

The **Gazebo,** 45 Pukuatua St. (tel. 481-911) is a casual, cozy spot with a black-board menu, lots of greenery (as befits its name), and specialties such as terakihi meunière, whole baby salmon in lemon cream, chicken breast champagne, and lamb. Main courses at lunch will run between NZ$8 ($5) and NZ$13 ($8.25); at dinner, about NZ$18 ($11.25). Hours are noon to 2 p.m. Tuesday through Friday and 6 to 10 p.m. Tuesday through Saturday. BYO.

Zanelli's Italian Café, 23 Amohia St. (tel. 484-908), serves generous portions, and you can easily make do with an entree and salad. Entrees are NZ$7.50 ($4.70) and main dishes go for NZ$13 ($8.15). There's a whole blackboard devoted to desserts. The atmosphere is lively, and the only drawback is that it gets smokey. Hours are 6 to 9:30 p.m. weekdays, to 10 p.m. weekends.

Lunch will most assuredly be your main meal of the day if you book for the elaborate seafood buffet at the **THC Rotorua International Hotel,** Froude Street (tel. 481-189). Be sure to reserve early, for this endless supply of the freshest of seasonal seafoods is a great favorite with locals and other visitors alike. You'll pay NZ$16.50 ($10.25) and leave knowing you've found real value for your dollars. Licensed.

READER'S DINING SELECTION: "**Lewisham's,** 115 Tetaneka St. (tel. 481-786), is like a pretty little cottage in the middle of a city, and the food is Austrian, heavy on meat dishes" (J. Abrams, Brooklyn, N.Y.).

Fast-Food Notes

On the theory that you can drop in for a Big Mac almost anywhere in the world, I don't normally send readers to **McDonald's.** In Rotorua, however, I emphatically recommend that you go by the one on the corner of Fenton and Amohau Streets to view the exquisite wall-size carvings done by the Maori Arts and Crafts Institute. Best of all, they give you a free booklet beautifully illustrated with photos and Maori legends. Kudos to McDonald's for this recognition of indigenous culture.

Floyd's Express, 113 Tutanekai St., at Whakane Street, near the lake (tel. 460-976), offers take-away or counter snacks and has daily lunch specials for NZ$4.90 ($3.05). You can get short orders such as salads, curry, chowder, soup, fries, and potato skins. It's open from 11 a.m. to 8:30 p.m. daily.

The best burgers in Rotorua, I'm told by someone who's sampled many a one, come from **Chez Bleu,** 160 Fenton St. (tel. 481-828), and there are 30 to choose from, plus full meals and ice cream. Burger prices range from NZ$2.70 ($1.70) to NZ$9.20 ($5.75), and you can't beat the hours: 7 a.m. to 11:30 p.m. Sunday through Wednesday, until 3 a.m. on Thursday, and until 4 a.m. on Friday and Saturday. There's delivery service too.

Big Splurges

I could recommend the **Aorangi Peak Restaurant** on Mountain Road (tel. 70-046) for the view alone—its mountaintop perch looks down on a dazzling array of lakes and forests and the city—but when you add the elegant octagonal split-level dining room and upstairs lookout lounge and cocktail bar, plus meals of gourmet quality, this is *the* place to splurge! (If you're into justifying splurges, just count a part of your dinner check as a sightseeing charge.) Personal service and quality are equally important here, so you'll get a bit of pampering. The menu is designed to present the best of New Zealand produce in interesting and innovative ways, complemented by a noteworthy wine list. A meal will run around NZ$45 ($28.25). Reservations essential.

Your big-splurge dollars will be well spent at **Caesar's,** 83 Arawa St. (tel. 470-984). The setting is just this side of elegant, the table settings go all the way, and there are innovative dishes of New Zealand foods on the menu. The lamb dishes are award winners, and the smoked chicken and smoked eel with horseradish is outstanding. Service is especially friendly, and your dinner bill will run around NZ$35 ($22). Open every evening. Licensed and BYO.

A favorite with locals as well as tourists is **Rumours,** 81 Pukuatua St. (tel. 477-277). It's on the small side, so best book when you first get into town. Decor is modern, and there's a menu featuring seasonal specialties, from seafoods to game dishes, all prepared in sophisticated style that probably falls into the continental category. Dinner will run about NZ$30 ($18.75), and hours are 6 to 11 p.m. Tuesday through Saturday. BYO.

Maori Concerts and Hangi Feasts

You'll find some show-stopper Maori concerts in the big hotels (see below), but for authenticity and insight into the Maori musical heritage you can't beat the nightly 8 p.m. concert at the Tametekapua meeting house in Ohinemutu. The surroundings, for one thing, are authentic in this meeting house of the Arawa tribe, which opens to the public only at night. The singing group was founded by the elders of the tribe to help their young people learn to sing and perform the traditional songs. The performers are mostly 13 to 18 years old; the younger ones stand at the back and work their way forward over the years. Tickets are NZ$10 ($6.25) for adults, NZ$4 ($2.50) for children, and the money goes for the upkeep of St. Faith's Church and the meeting house, and to transport the youth abroad for singing engagements. In 1989 they performed in North Carolina and the Netherlands.

Hangi ("earth oven") cooking is traditional with the Maoris in preparing their communal meal. A large pit is filled with a wood fire topped by stones; then when the stones are heated through, baskets of food are placed on top and covered with damp cloths. Earth is then shoveled over all to create a natural steam oven. After about three hours, dinner is unveiled, with intermingling flavors of the various foods lightly touched by wood smoke.

There's a hangi feast every night of the year at the **THC International Hotel** on Froude Street, on the edge of the Whaka Reserve (tel. 481-189). The NZ$34 ($21.25) tab would put this in the splurge category were it not for the fact that it includes an hour-long Maori concert featuring first-class performers. Tickets for the concert only cost NZ$12 ($7.50).

Hangi preparations begin long before your scheduled arrival at 6 p.m. By 3 p.m. the ngawha (natural Maori rock steamer) is being filled: meats like wild pork, lamb, chicken, and venison go in first for longer cooking; vegetables such as pumpkin, kumara, potatoes, and watercress are placed on top. Don't show up any later than 6:15 p.m. or you'll miss the opening of the ngawha, when a costumed Maori maiden lifts the food out with all due ceremony and leads a procession of food-bearing followers into the dining room, where it is spread on a buffet table. Accompaniments like marinated mussels, smoked eel, raw marinated fish, salads, Maori bread, and tamarillos (tree tomatoes) with fresh cream complete the eat-as-much-as-you-can-hold feast. The traditional hangi would never include desserts, but the International provides sweets and Pakeha beverages (tea, coffee, and wine). By 7 p.m., all is ready for you to dig in. Enjoy!

At 8 o'clock, an outstanding troupe of Maori singers and dancers will begin an hour-long concert of Polynesian dances, action songs, and pois. By any standards, this is a "money's worth" splurge.

A reader wrote to say that of all the hangi and concert offerings in Rotorua, his favorite was at the **Sheraton Rotorua Hotel,** on Fenton Street (tel. 487-139), and I have to admit that it's polished and fun-filled, with emphasis on audience involvement and enjoyment. The banquet room is warm and inviting, the buffet-style meal elegantly presented, and the tables graced with fresh flowers. The performers have great fun with the music, the dancing, and most of all, the audience. A highlight, especially for children, is singing "Hokey Pokey" using the Maori words for names of body parts. The show ends with audience and performers linking hands and singing together—really quite moving. I asked one of the dancers what the significance of her quivering hands was, and she told me "Life." The meal starts at 7 p.m., the concert at 8:15 p.m. The cost of the hangi and concert is NZ$35 ($22); the concert alone, NZ$22 ($13.75).

THINGS TO SEE AND DO

While "budget" usually translates as "do it yourself," there are two exceptionally good **tours** in Rotorua that will save you time and inconvenience, which in the long run can mean a dollar savings. One is the City Tour, the other a full-day Waimangu Round Trip, which has been one of the area's most popular tours since it began in 1902.

InterCity operates a wide variety of half- and full-day excursions. If you're here for a short stay, I'd say a half-day tour is a must. Coaches depart from the Travel Centre at 8:45 a.m. and 1:45 p.m. daily; from the NZTP Travel Office, at 9 a.m. and 2 p.m. The informative tour of Rainbow and Fairy Springs is only given to bus groups, a decided plus. And at the Whaka Thermal Reserve, bus tours are met by a Maori guide and taken right through, whereas individuals have to wait for a group to form. InterCity tour fares range from NZ$21 ($13.25) to NZ$54 ($33.75) for adults and NZ$10 ($6.25) to NZ$26 ($16.25) for children.

The following are some of the major attractions offered on the tours, and you can, of course, visit them on your own, especially those in downtown Rotorua such as Tudor Towers, the Government Gardens, and Ohinemutu. Narrowing down your choices of which places to visit is difficult, and it really helps to go to the NZTP Travel Office or the Travel Centre and look at their short videos of 15 different attractions to get a vivid idea of what each is like. If you just don't have time to get out to the major thermal sites, you can easily view a few on a small scale locally—look for one at the lakeshore behind the Hyatt Hotel; walk around behind the golf course from Tudor Towers, hugging the lakeshore and you should see another on the left; from the parking lot at Geyserland Hotel, you can gaze out over all of the thermal valley. Heavy rainfall increases geothermal activity, so showers won't necessarily dampen your sightseeing here.

The Government Gardens

Stately **Tudor Towers** (one of New Zealand's oldest buildings) reigns over this downtown city park. The gardens themselves are a lovely mix of rose gardens (which are lit at night), croquet and bowling lawns, and steaming thermal pools. They're a delightful in-town resting spot, and the Tudor Towers provide worthwhile sightseeing. Inside, you'll find the **Rotorua Art Gallery,** displaying paintings of both native and international artists as well as the small but interesting **City of Rotorua Museum,** which focuses on a significant collection of Maori carvings and artifacts and the unique history of the volcanic plateau. Admission to both is free. Built as a fashionable bathhouse, the largest in the country, along European spa lines, the Tudor Towers also houses a licensed restaurant.

The chief attraction at the gardens, however, is the **Polynesian Pools** (tel. 481-328) overlooking the lake. Here, for a mere pittance, you can experience the mineral pools at your leisure, for as long as you choose, and you can rent a swimsuit and towel, if necessary. There are pools open to the sky, enclosed pools, and private pools. The soft alkaline water in the large pool maintains a constant temperature of about 100°F, while the smaller pools (reached along wooden walkways) contain water high in sulfur and magnesium—very good for sore muscles—at temperatures of 80° to 100°F. Private pools and a sauna are available for NZ$6 ($3.75), as well as gentle water massage for NZ$30 ($18.75) for half an hour. There's an ice-cream parlor and a well-stocked souvenir shop. Admission is NZ$5 ($3.15) for adults, NZ$2 ($1.25). You can rent a swimsuit and towel for NZ$2 ($1.25) and a locker for NZ$1

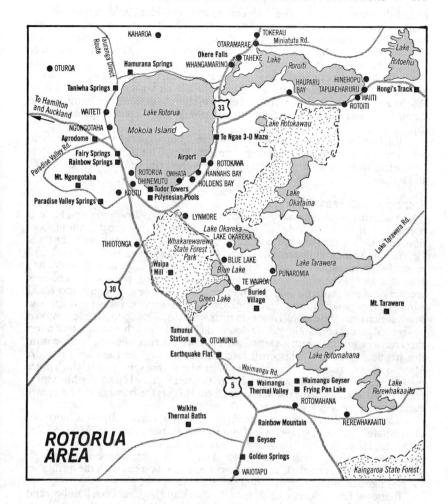

ROTORUA AREA

(65¢). Hours are 9 a.m. to 10 p.m. daily. Just beyond the reception area, be sure to take a look at the excellent mural of the migration of Polynesians from Hawaiki.

Ohinemutu

This is the suburb, along the lake about half a mile north of the city, where the largest Arawa subtribe, the Ngati-whakaue, dwells. Although the residences are very much in the Pakeha style—small, everyday bungalows—the lifestyle holds to tribal custom. On a *marae* (open courtyard, or clearing) stands the beautifully hand-carved Tamatekapua meeting house. This is where most tribal matters are discussed and important decisions taken; concerts are also held here every night. Homes are thermally heated, and in every backyard you'll see the steam ovens where much of the family cooking is done.

Perhaps the most outstanding structure you'll see in Ohinemutu is **St. Faith's Anglican Church,** a remarkable representation of the Pakeha Christian faith as interpreted through Maori art. The Tudor-style church building holds a revelation of Maori color, intricate carving, exquisite scrollwork, and even an integration of ancient Maori religions, as represented by the figures of mythical demi-gods and their primitive subjects, which are carved in the base of the pulpit. There's a lovely, truly spiritual, blending of the two cultures in a magnificent plate-glass window looking out to the lake whose full-size figure of Christ is haloed, but clad in a Maori cloak of kiwi feathers, and appears to be walking on the lake. It was sandblasted by a local Pakeha artist, Mr. Mowbray, and in the figure's stance he captured the unmistakable dignity and grace of Maori chieftains. A visit to St. Faith's is a touching, memorable experience.

Tombs of Maori tribal leaders are outside the church, all above ground and safe from the restless rumblings of all that thermal activity. Take time to explore the settlement, as there are other examples of Maori carving and decoration in buildings and statues.

Rainbow and Fairy Springs

A sanctuary—that's what you'll find at Rainbow and Fairy Springs on Hwy. 5 north of town. For the world-famous rainbow trout, which grow to gigantic proportions in complete safety from the angler's hook in these protected waters; for birds (several rare species); for trees and plants (some 135 varieties of fern alone); and most of all, perhaps, for mankind. As you follow the map (pick it up at the entrance) around a 350-yard path—meandering through deep bush thick with lush, dark greenery and alive with birdsong from those soaring free or resting in treetops and joined by those in the small aviary; stop to watch the antics of brown and rainbow trout, which push and butt each other in their haste to gobble up food pellets thrown by visitors; gaze at peacefully grazing deer in their paddock—there's an ease of mind that creeps in, bringing with it a sense of the harmony between humanity and nature that has been achieved in this small patch of earth. Along the Fairy Springs walk, Maori myth takes on a little more reality when you see the spring from which more than five million gallons of water per day well up through the black and white sands. It isn't hard at all to credit the Maori belief that here is the home of the legendary Patupaiarehe, the fairy folk.

Rainbow and Fairy Springs are about 2½ miles from Rotorua, north of Ohinemutu. They're open every day from 8 a.m. to 5 p.m., and cost NZ$6 ($3.75) for adults, NZ$2 ($1.25) for children. There's a good souvenir shop, a cafeteria for light snacks, and an attractive licensed restaurant for light, inexpensive meals. If you're not driving or on the City Tour described above, you can reach the springs via the Ngongotaha bus that departs the Travel Centre.

Rainbow Farm, directly across the main Auckland highway from Rainbow and Fairy Springs, features the entire range of farm animals: horses, cows, goats, sheep, pigs, ducks, dogs, and genuine gumboot farmers. Shows are conducted by two showmen and take place against a backdrop of a 1930s farm scene viewed through stage-wide opening doors. The showmen give a lively commentary of a busy day on a farm and combine working animals with an entertaining, educational and rather nostalgic view of Kiwi farm life. Regular shows are staged at 10:30 a.m., 1 p.m., and 2:30 p.m., but you're welcome to stroll around the farm any time before or between shows. No admission charge for the farm; prices for the show are NZ$5 ($3.15) for adults, NZ$2 ($1.25) for children, NZ$14 ($8.75) for a family ticket.

New Zealand Maori Arts and Crafts Institute

On Rotorua's southern edge, just at the Whaka Reserve entrance, the New Zealand Maori Arts and Crafts Institute exists for the sole purpose of keeping alive the ancient skills of Maori tribes. Youngsters are selected from all over the country to come here as apprentices to master artisans. Here, boys study carving for a minimum of three years, after which they may take their newly acquired skills back to their own tribes or stay on to become teachers at the institute. Girls learn to weave traditional cloaks and make the distinctive flax skirts and intricately patterned bodices. As a visitor, you are very welcome as an observer, and it's impossible not to respond to this perfect blending of beauty, myth, and spiritual symbolism as one generation passes a living heritage on to the next. Take away a lasting memento in the form of products made here and on sale in the attached shop. The institute is open every day from 8:30 a.m. to 5 p.m., with the exception of the carving school, which closes on Saturday, Sunday, and three weeks at Christmas.

Whakarewarewa Thermal Reserve

To walk through the Whaka Thermal Reserve (one entrance is across from the institute) is to view the most dramatic concentration of Rotorua's thermal wonders. It is the home of many members of the Tuhourangi Ngati Wahiao subtribe of the Arawas, and they will furnish a free Maori guide to show you through on the hour, every hour from 9 a.m. to 4 p.m. While you're free to wander on your own, I don't advise it for many reasons (you'll miss a *lot* of information, and you could just miss your footing and land in one of those boiling mud pools). Besides, who but a Maori who knows, understands, and respects this unique landscape could tell you the legends that interpret its many moods? If you must go alone, be sure to stay on the marked paths.

Inside the reserve, there's a model village patterned after Rotowhio, a pre-European village whose layout and construction has been faithfully reproduced. There are eight active geysers, which may perform for you if your timing is right (they don't operate on a fixed schedule, so it's a matter of luck). Adjoining **Prince of Wales Feathers Geyser** and **Pohutu Geyser** are particularly impressive and seems to have worked out an act that showcases them both. The Prince gets things started with a jet, which works up to 30 feet, at which time Pohutu goes into action, erupting to as much as 60 feet, with little offshoot eruptions, which sometimes more than double that height. They are, as I said, unpredictable—eruptions have been clocked as little as two and as many as nine in a 24-hour period and lasting sometimes 20 minutes, sometimes only 5. Whaka is open from 8:30 a.m. to 5 p.m. every day, and admission is NZ$4.50 ($2.80) for adults, NZ$2 ($1.25) for children. If you're lucky, there'll be a noontime concert (usually Labor Day to Easter, and school holidays).

At the Tryon Street entrance to Whaka Reserve (on the northern edge), you'll find the **Little Village,** which is, I suppose, a Pakeha answer to Whaka's Maori *pa*— it's a model of a European village of the 19th century. Around the village green are clustered colonial-style shops: a weaver's cottage, newspaper office, gemstone shop, potter, and such. It's open daily.

Full-Day Waimangu Round Trip

This tour has my wholehearted recommendation. And even though it entails a three-mile walk through steamy Waimangu Valley, unless you're really infirm it shouldn't be too strenuous. Just be sure to wear comfortable walking shoes. Bus departure is from the **New Zealand Tourist and Publicity (NZTP)** office, 67 Fenton St. (tel. 485-179) at 9 a.m., and you'll return at 4:45 p.m. There are morning and afternoon tea stops, and you can bring your own lunch or purchase one from the tour operators for NZ$6 ($3.75). The fare is a hefty NZ$54 ($33.75) for adults, NZ$26 ($16.25) for children, but you'll cover 42 miles and the better portion of Rotorua's history. Tours operate daily from December 26 to Easter; on Tuesday, Thursday, Saturday, and Sunday other months.

Heading south past Whaka, you pass **Earthquake Flat** and a crater lake, which changes hue from green to blue every 36 hours, en route to **Waimangu Geyser.** Stilled now, it erupted regularly during the first four years of this century, spewing rocks and earth as far as 1,500 feet and claiming four lives before it fell silent. Its crater gave one gigantic, three-day-long last gasp in 1917, exploding with a violence, which flung debris as far as 1,000 feet. Two weeks later the crater began to fill with water, and in a short time a six-acre boiling lake was formed, which has been aptly named **Frying Pan Lake.** Temperatures of the water from subterranean springs that feed it average 210°F at the surface, 315°F in the depths.

From the lake you strike out on foot for 2½ miles to **Mount Tarawera,** which erupted in 1886 to destroy the famous pink and white silica terraces that had been a popular tourist attraction. Six European visitors lost their lives, and the 800-foot-deep hot Rotomahana Lake was formed. A launch takes you out on the lake, past steaming cliffs, which are stratified with brilliant color—an incredible sight! At the end of the launch cruise, there's another half-mile walk to **Lake Tarawera,** one of the largest in the area and famed for its fishing. After a seven-mile cruise across the lake, with clear views of Mount Tarawera's blasted summit, you're met by coach to travel on to the nearby **Buried Village of Te Wairoa,** which perished in the Mount Tarawera eruption and has been excavated and well preserved. You'll also see the **Wairere Falls,** which descend 150 feet in three stages. The drive back to Rotorua passes both the **Green** and **Blue Lakes** and the **Redwood Grove Forest.** One suggestion: Those soothing, hot Polynesian pools may be the perfect end to a full and satisfying day!

Not as well known perhaps as Waimangu—and I'm definitely tooting its horn—the **Waiotapu Thermal Wonderland,** 4 km (2½ miles) beyond Waimangu on Hwy. 5, is the most colorful of all the thermal areas, lavished with hues of yellow, gold, ochre, salmon, orange, and green. It also claims the largest mud pool in the southern hemisphere (you only see about a third of it) and the **Lady Knox Geyser,** which spouts off at 10:15 a.m. every day. Some of my favorite spots include the Champagne Pool, complete with bubbles and fizz; the Artist's Palette, which changes constantly; the Opal Pool, which has a vibrant color; the Terraces, where you'll feel as if you're walking on water; and the Maori Sacred Track—all well marked on the map you're given. This thermal preserve has been a family business since 1931 (though not always the same family); the Sewell family is in charge now and runs a top operation, including the souvenir shop, which is large, well stocked, and well priced. There's something spiritual about this place—allow time to enjoy it. You can get a local bus to Waiotapu, but it's a bit of a hike into the thermal park. Hours are 8:30 a.m. to 7:30 p.m. (5 p.m. in winter), but the Sewells are flexible "because we live here." Admission is NZ$5 ($3.15).

The Agrodome

Maybe it's because the shearing of sheep has been a romantic thing for me since I saw Robert Mitchum in *The Sundowners* years ago that I found the Agrodome performance so intriguing I went back for a second show! Whatever the reason, it *is* a highlight of any Rotorua visit, and I expect to be in the audience any time I'm in the neighborhood. Located four miles north of Rotorua, the Agrodome, Riverdale Park (tel. 74-350), is a huge (7,000 square feet) octagonal building in a 200-acre pastureland, which displays rams of 19 different breeds of sheep in a 60-minute show that packs into an entertaining and delightful commentary more information on the engaging creatures than you probably thought existed. Each ram is released from its paddock to climb onto a pedestal while the recorded voice of champion shearer Godfrey Bowen tells you about its breed—its origins, primary uses of the wool or meat, its importance in New Zealand's sheep industry, etc. When all 19 are in place on the platform, a master shearer explains the tricks of his trade and proceeds to demonstrate his skill on a sheep you'd swear was luxuriating in the whole thing if you hadn't just been told that its relaxation is the result of one of those tricks. The shearer then whistles in his sheep dog and puts him through a few paces before inviting you to come down front, meet the dog and rams personally, and snap any photos you'd like before the entire audience adjourns outside to witness a fascinating demonstration of the dog's response to a series of a few simple commands. New facilities include a farmyard nursery and dairy display, a horse ride over 300 acres of prime farmland, and a model railway exhibition. Agrodome performances are at

9:15 and 11 a.m. and 2:30 p.m. every day (with additional shows during heavy tourist seasons), with admissions of NZ$4.84 ($3.05) for adults and NZ$2.20 ($1.40) for children, including GST. Incidentally, the shop at the Agrodome has been the source of two of my most prized New Zealand purchases—both the selection and the prices are excellent. There's also a coffeeshop serving teas and light lunches, and Doogie's licensed café/restaurant.

Whakarewarewa Forest Park

This popular forest (tel. 475-555) has an entrance right on the outskirts of town, a refreshing walk into many different types of trees and lush bush. You'll see majestic redwood trees dedicated to the men of New Zealand's Forest Service who gave their lives in both World Wars. Look for the network of color-coded walking tracks throughout, all starting from the Visitors Centre on Long Mile Road, just off Tarawera Road. Inside, the Visitors Centre has a helpful staff, interesting displays, refreshments, a film on the history and management of the country's forests, and a variety of woodcrafts for gifts and souvenirs. The park is open from 9 a.m. to 5 p.m. daily.

Other Activities

For a breathtaking view of Rotorua, the lakes, and the entire steamy landscape that surrounds them, take the **Skyline Skyride,** Fairy Spring Road (tel. 70-027). You ascend some 2,975 feet in a glass-enclosed gondola, and it's well worth the NZ$5 ($3.15) charge for adults, NZ$1.50 (95¢) for children.

If you're intrigued by mazes, there's a terrific one about ten minutes from the city on Hwy. 30 (tel. 59-565), three kilometers (two miles) past the airport on Te Ngae Road. It's the **3D Maze**—some 1.7 km (about a mile) of pathways, and it's even accessible to wheelchairs. Great fun, and admission is a mere NZ$2 ($1.25) for adults, NZ$1 (65¢) for children.

Golfers will find a warm welcome at the nine-hole **Government Gardens Golf Course** (tel. 489-126; after hours, 480-882). Located at the Gardens, right on the shores of Lake Rotorua, it's within easy walking distance from the city center, and for *real* golf buffs, there's a ten-game price concession. Not to worry if you didn't bring clubs, as they're available for rent. There's a snack shop on the premises, and, if you're too far away to walk to the course, they'll arrange transportation. The **Lakeview Golf Course,** a ten-minute drive from Rotorua on the Hamilton Hwy. (tel. 74-675), has 18 holes blessed with a panoramic view of the city. There are clubs and "trundlers" for rent.

If you've the urge to do as the black swans do and get out on Lake Rotorua, hop aboard the **Lakeland Queen,** which offers morning or afternoon tea, lunch, and dinner cruises. The paddlewheeler is fully licensed, and all but the dinner cruise bring you close to Mokoia Island, where legendary lovers Hinemoa and Tutanekai met. The booking office is at the lakefront (tel. 486-634 or 471-766). Prices start at NZ$13 ($8.15) for adults and NZ$3 ($1.90) for children.

You can see the lake in other ways too—consider from a helicopter, float plane, small airplane, or fishing boat. It's a splurge, for sure, but to find out more, inquire at the NZTP Tourist Office, the Travel Centre, or at the waterfront.

Fisherfolk who long to try their luck in Rotorua's rich fishing grounds should contact Roger Forrester, a member of the New Zealand Professional Fishing Guides Association (tel. 479-299). During summer months, Roger can furnish licenses and tackle, and he'll take you out on his cabin cruiser for three hours for a charge of NZ$60 ($37.50) per person. I can't swear to what kind of catch you'll bring home, but Roger is considered tops by the locals, and if there's fish biting, I'm certain he'll get you to them.

Bikes are for rent from **Lady Jane's Ice Cream Park,** at the corner of Whakane and Tutanahai Streets, for NZ$5 ($3.15) a day; scooters are NZ$7 ($4.40) a day and require a NZ$40 ($25) deposit.

SHOPPING

I've already mentioned the excellent shop out at the Agrodome, and you'll find other good shops galore in Rotorua. One, however, is unique—it's the only "straight out" rugby store in New Zealand. It's **Sportsmaker,** 16 Eruera St. (tel. 479-670), where Sel and Elaine Howse have assembled what amounts to a small rugby museum as well as a commercial venture. If you've become a fan, even if only in fantasy, you'll love this place, with its All Black jerseys, T-shirts, pennants, banners, hats, etc. Of course, the All Blacks are not the *only* rugby team listed—you'll find plenty of souvenirs of other world-famous teams within its walls. Hours are 8:30 a.m. to 5 p.m. Monday through Friday and 9 a.m. to noon on Saturday.

Penney's Souvenirs, 32 Hinemoa St., at Hinewanu Street (tel. 485-787), opposite the Hyatt, has a marvelous selection of carvings, greenstone and paua items, sheepskins, and general souvenirs, as well as T-shirts. Owner Reg Durrant will open after hours for a group (call him at 489-717 after hours), a great convenience if you just can't fit shopping into a day of sightseeing. Open daily until 7 p.m. You'll have a unique opportunity to watch your New Zealand souvenir in the process of being created if you pay a visit to **Ruihana Carvings,** 35 Lake Rd. (tel. 477-174; after hours, 486-516). Master carver Louis Ruihana Phillips carries on the traditions of his Maori ancestors, and both he and his wife, Mere, will carefully explain the significance of the carvings. They're open seven days a week from 8 a.m. to 5:30 p.m., but they'll open after hours if you call for an appointment. The shop also carries traditional Maori skirts, headbands, and other items, as well as leatherwork.

For general browsing, try the **Tutanekai Mall,** a pedestrian shopping area between Arawa and Pukaki Streets. The most popular **bottle shop** is on Ti Street, off Fenton Street (on the left as you drive out Fenton from downtown).

AFTER DARK

Check *Thermalair* for dine-and-dance venues or special events. Or just skip the rest and plan on a Maori concert. You won't be sorry. The Sheraton Hotel Bar is a popular gathering spot.

READER'S MAORI CONCERT SUGGESTION: "The Maori Arts and Crafts Institute holds a Maori concert in the meeting house at 12:15 p.m. each workday that lasts 45 minutes and is excellent. I would highly recommend it for those interested in Maori culture but not 'pigging out' at an elaborate feast. The meeting house setting contributed to the richness of the atmosphere" (E. Angeletti, Greenville, S.C.). [*Author's Note:* These concerts are available only during summer and school holidays.]

WHERE TO GO FROM HERE

Limited time will point you from Rotorua to Taupo, the Tongariro National Park, and Wanganui. For those who can spare a few days, however, there is a glorious drive awaiting around what is called New Zealand's **Eastland–Sunrise Coast,** since it is the place where the sun is first seen each morning. Magnificent seascapes (some of the most exciting in the country), secluded coves and bays, deserted beaches, tiny Maori settlements, and finally the Poverty Bay town of **Gisborne** and Hawke's Bay's crowning jewel, **Napier.** It's an area alive with history, both Maori and Pakeha. You'll see where the Arawa canoe made landfall; where Capt. James Cook first saw the New Zealand mainland and where he stopped on his second voyage; where ferocious, decisive battles between Maori and Europeans were fought; and along the way there are some of the finest examples of Maori carvings in New Zealand.

This swing around the Sunrise Coast is an off-the-beaten-track digression that I strongly urge you to take if you can fit it into your timetable. It's a bit of New Zealand far too many visitors miss. But if you just don't have the time, skip this section and proceed to **Taupo.**

The drive to Taupo is a short 52 miles over excellent roads. Five miles before you reach Taupo, look for the steamy **Wairakei Geothermal Project,** which harnesses all that underground energy to furnish electrical power. More about that in Chapter V.

2. The Bay of Plenty/Eastland

There are two ways of commencing the splendid East Cape drive from Rotorua: head northeast on Hwy. 30 for Whakatane in the Bay of Plenty, a 57-mile drive; or drive due north for 55 miles to Tauranga, then turn east on Hwy. 2 for the 62-mile stretch to Whakatane. I'd say that decision rests on where your own interests lie.

NORTH TO TAURANGA

Tauranga, and its adjacent beach resort/port of Mount Maunganui, is now a peaceful center of citrus fruit farming, but its history is one of fierce battles, both in intertribal Maori wars and between the British and Maoris. The **Public Relations Office,** on The Strand (tel. 075/88-103), can direct you to several interesting historical spots.

The gardens of the **Elms Mission House,** on Mission Street, built by an early missionary and one of the finest examples of colonial architecture of its time (1847), are open to the public from 9 a.m. to 6 p.m. daily except Sunday. The library dates from 1837 and is probably the oldest in the country. On the carefully tended grounds, you'll see kauri, rimu, and orange trees, along with kiwifruit orchards, a special treat if you haven't gotten to see any before now. It's highly recommended, and there's no admission charge.

If you like poking around old cemeteries, as I confess I do, **Otamataha Pa** will be of interest. It was the burial ground for the Church Mission Society from 1835 to 1881, as well as for soldiers and sailors who died in the Land War in 1864–1865. It's near the Mission House and just up the hill from **Robbins Park Rose Garden** and picnic area on Cliff Road.

Tauranga Historic Village, on 17th Avenue West (tel. 81-301), bows to the past with 14 acres of a re-created colonial village, with cobblestone streets, a blacksmith's shop, a military barracks, a Maori village, and much more. Rides by train, double-decker bus, or horse-drawn cart give another perspective. You'll find a tea room and a licensed restaurant in the village—old-fashioned, of course. It's open daily from 10 a.m. to 4 p.m.

Mount Maunganui, a leading port 12½ miles from Tauranga, is best known and loved by thousands of Kiwis for its **Ocean Beach,** a stretch of golden sand along what is called the best surfing beach in New Zealand. (**Papamoa Beach,** on the other hand, is quiet, and there's a take-away restaurant.) The **walking track** around the mountain takes about an hour. You can also climb to the top of the mountain, for which you should allow a couple of hours. At the base of the mountain, on Adams Avenue, are **hot saltwater pools** where, for a small admission fee, you can ease your aches away; there's swimsuit and towel rental for those who arrive unprepared. The water in the pools is not recycled, and there is a fresh supply every three hours; hours are 8 a.m. to 10 p.m. daily.

Tauranga has 45,000 inhabitants; Mount Maunganui, only 14,000. This area is second only to Auckland in popularity among vacationing Kiwis, some 500,000 of whom come here every year, compared to 41,000 international visitors. In summer **shopping hours** are longer on weekends than most anywhere else in New Zealand: until 4 p.m. on Saturday and, in Mount Maunganui, until 4 p.m. on Sunday as well. A car comes in very handy here, but if you're hoofing it and need a **taxi,** call 486-086. **Fishing trips** can be organized easily from the wharf on the Strand.

You can get a three-course meal at **Charlie Brown's,** 194 Cameron Rd. in

Tauranga (tel. 85-520), for about NZ$16 ($10). There's a children's menu. It's open daily except Sunday from 5:30 p.m. Licensed.

About 20 miles north of Tauranga on the road to Thames (see Chapter III) is a place you won't want to miss if meals are a big event in your life: the **Vineyard Restaurant** (tel. 442-760 or 20-620), part of Morton Estates winery. There are free tastings and a prix-fixe dinner is offered for NZ$28 ($17.50) per person, plus GST. Lunch, served from 11:30 a.m. daily, may be ordered from a blackboard menu, and main dishes run about NZ$12.50 ($7.80). On weekends there is often a jazz brunch from 11:30 a.m. to 3 p.m., with a NZ$2.50 ($1.55) music cover. There are three dining rooms with fireplaces and fresh flowers, as well as a patio. If you go, you can expect a memorable meal and commendable service and presentation; it's worth the drive.

In Katikati, a little north of Morton Estates on the Thames highway, do as the locals do and drop by the **Katikati Tavern** for fish and chips from noon to 2 p.m.

About 19 miles south of Tauranga lies **Te Puke**, the "Kiwifruit Capital of the World," and **Kiwifruit Country,** a popular attraction that you'll recognize by the giant slice of fruit (a camouflaged observation tower) out front. Stop by; there's no admission charge to look around, and you can wander through the grounds and theme orchard, which features 60 different fruits and nuts, from macadamias to feijoas (try this local fruit if you can) to pomegranates. There's also an audio-video show and children's playground. For a fee, you can take a half-hour tour of the working orchard and listen to a taped commentary; the cost is NZ$7 ($4.40) for adults, NZ$5.50 ($3.45) for senior citizens, and NZ$3.50 ($2.20) for kids. The fruit is harvested in May and June. Kiwifruit Country also has a children's playground; gift shop featuring kiwifruit products; complimentary tasting of kiwifruit wines, liqueur, and apéritif; and a café featuring kiwi burgers and kiwifruit parfait.

NORTHEAST TO WHAKATANE

It is from Hwy. 2 (a little over 27 miles east of Tauranga) on the drive to Whakatane that you can take a short detour to the little settlement of **Maketu** and see the cairn that marks the Arawa canoe landing place, and also the Te Awhi-o-te-rangi meeting house, a beautiful example of Maori carvings. Tauranga makes an interesting prelude to the East Cape Drive if time permits. At Whakatane, stop by the **Public Relations Office** on Boon Street (tel. 076/860-58) for details on some of the more interesting sights in the town and nearby. This is the legendary settling place of Toi (see the Introduction) on his search for his grandson, Whatonga, and the earthworks out on the road to Ohope are traditionally held to be those of his *pa*. It is also the landing place of the great Mataatua canoe, part of the Hawaiki migration fleet. A model of that canoe can be seen next to the imposing rock arch known as **Pohaturoa Rock** (once part of a sacred Maori cave and now a memorial to those who died in World War I). On Mataatua Street, right in the center of town, you'll see the beautiful **Wairere Waterfall.**

Some 37 miles east of Whakatane, Hwy. 2 brings you to Opotiki and State Rd. 35, known as the **East Cape Road,** which hugs the coastline for most of its 213-mile route up around New Zealand's most easterly point and down to Gisborne on Poverty Bay. The drive—breathtaking in any season—is a heart-stopper during the Christmas season, when hundreds of pohutukawa trees burst into brilliant scarlet blooms along the cliffs overlooking the sea. All along, you'll find lovely deserted beaches, sea views, and native bush, which combine to make this one of New Zealand's finest scenic drives. This, as you might suspect, is an area with a heavy Maori population, and most of the small villages and towns you'll pass through either still are, or once were, Maori centers. Sadly, some of the most exquisite Maori carvings from the area have been removed: the Auckland War Museum's Te Toki-a-Tapiri war canoe and Wellington's National Museum's Te Hau-ki-Turanga meeting house and Nuku te Whatewha storehouse all came from this region. There are, however, still outstanding examples of the art to be seen along the drive.

Many people decide to break the long drive (about eight hours if you stay behind the wheel) with an overnight stop, and below I'll tell you about accommodations possibilities. Campers will find ample facilities along the way.

Opotiki was once a large Maori settlement, but today is best known for its **Church of St. Stephen the Martyr,** scene of the particularly brutal murder of German Lutheran missionary Carl Sylvius Volkner in 1865. Blood-stained relics of that grim event are on exhibit in the church. At **Te Kaha,** Tu Kaihi meeting house in the *marae* has an elaborately carved lintel you'll be welcome to view if you ask permission before entering the *marae.* A little farther along, **Waihau Bay** has good views across Cape Runaway (so named by Captain Cook as he watched Maori canoes "run away" when shots were fired over their heads), as well as very good beaches. **Whangaparaoa** is where the great migration canoe *Tainui* landed—its captain's wife is credited with bringing the kumara to New Zealand. One of the many turnoffs that will tempt you is that at **Lottin Point** (it's signposted), where a 2½-mile drive through farmland leads to the coast and grasslands growing right to the water's edge.

Hicks Bay could well be your overnight stop. It's not quite midway, but has marvelous views, a modern motel, and one of the finest carved meeting houses on the East Cape. Its name comes from one of Captain Cook's officers, who first sighted it, and it was the site of a tragic Maori massacre in which one European was killed and eaten on his wedding night (after which complaints were registered that he was too tough and stringy to be tasty!). Turn left at the general store to reach the **Tuwhakairiora meeting house,** whose carvings were done in 1872. It is dedicated to local members of the Ngati Porou tribe who died in overseas wars, and its unique rafter design (found only in this region) is symbolic of the honor of death in battle for the warrior.

A little farther along, the road descends to sea level to follow the narrow bay to where the little town of **Te Araroa** nestles under the cliffs. Thirteen miles east of Te Araroa, along an all-weather road, stands the East Cape Lighthouse, in an isolated location. There's been a light here since 1906. The track to the lighthouse must be covered by foot, and it leads up some 600 steps—perhaps a look from afar will suffice. Sunrise is lovely here.

One of New Zealand's most ornate Maori churches is the **Tikitiki Church,** a memorial to Maori soldiers who died in World War I. The carved panels and rafter patterns depict Ngati Porou tribal history, and two war hero brothers are featured in the east window. Closer to Gisborne, you can view another beautifully carved modern meeting house near the wharf at **Tokomaru Bay.** This is where a brave band of women, two warriors, and three whalers successfully defended a headland *pa* from attack by a large enemy force. **Anaura Bay,** just 43 miles from Gisborne, was Captain Cook's landing place on his second New Zealand voyage. The *Endeavour* hung around for two days trying to get watercasks beyond the surf before heading south for a better watering place. **Whangara,** 17 miles away from Gisborne, is a good spot to fill up the gas tank (petrol stations are few and far between in these parts). And Gisborne, of course, was the place Captain Cook *first* sighted the New Zealand mainland (more about that later).

It must be said that for those who simply wish to reach Gisborne from the Bay of Plenty, there's a shorter, faster way to get there than around the East Cape. Highway 2 is a pleasant, three-hour drive on a winding road through green farmlands, native bush, along rushing mountain rivers, and through **Waioeka Gorge**—not a bad drive, mind you, but nothing to compare with the East Cape.

WHERE TO STAY EN ROUTE

You won't get a more pleasant welcome in Tauranga than at the **Ambassador Motor Lodge,** south of downtown at 9 15th Ave., Tauranga (tel. 075/85-665 or 85-226). The small property is co-owned by a parents/children team, Robert and Janet Wilberfoss and their daughter and her husband, Jane and Alistair

Bowden. Amenities include plenty of flowers and gardens, an outdoor pool, a spa pool, trampoline, swings, laundry, portable barbecue, and three studios and five larger units, all quite comfortable with TV, coffee and tea facilities, and nice, hard mattresses. This is a Best Western property, so the discounts apply. Rates are NZ$50 ($31.25) single and NZ$60 ($37.50) double, plus GST. Breakfast is available daily, and dinner during the week, which is nice if you arrive late and don't want to go into town.

Tiny Waihau Bay is where you'll find recommended accommodations in the **Waihau Bay Lodge,** East Coast Hwy. (Private Bay), Opotiki (tel. 07653/804). It's been a guesthouse since 1914, has a licensed restaurant, and is close to a fine beach and good fishing. Rates are NZ$52 ($32.50), plus GST, per person for the eight rooms (one single, four doubles, and three triples), and the rate includes dinner, bed, and breakfast.

Be sure to reserve ahead at the **Hicks Bay Motor Lodge,** Private Bag, Te Araroa (tel. 07944/880). They have self-contained kitchen units, as well as serviced rooms with tea-making facilities, a tourist-licensed restaurant and house bar, and a shop on the premises. Rates run NZ$70 ($43.75) to NZ$99 ($62), plus GST for one or two people, NZ$12 ($7.50) per extra person. (There's a surcharge for a one-night stay). Across from the motel there's an interesting bush walk, and there's also a glowworm grotto in back.

At Te Araroa, you will find the country's most easterly hostelry, the **Kawakawa Hotel,** P.O. Box 64, Te Araroa (tel. 07944/809). It is licensed and is known for its restaurant. Rooms are simple, with either baths or showers, and rates are NZ$35 ($22) single, NZ$50 ($31.25) double, plus GST.

---

3. Gisborne

Because of its closeness to the International Date Line, Gisborne is judged to be the most easterly city in the world and the first to see the sun's rays each morning. It's also the place where New Zealand's European history began. Capt. James Cook's *Endeavour* entered these waters in early October 1769, and it fell to the lot of the 12-year-old surgeon's boy, Nicholas Young, to be the first to sight land—a fact that must have caused some consternation among the rest of the crew, since the good captain had promised a gallon of rum as a reward, two if the sighting should be at night! True to another promise, Captain Cook named the white bluffs the boy had seen at the southern end of the bay's wide entrance "Young Nick's Head." As for Young Nick, he is also celebrated by a statue at the mouth of the Turanganus River at Waikanae Beach. It was two days later, on October 9, 1769, that a party ventured forth from the ship, and after a series of misunderstandings with Maoris over the next two days (during which one Maori was killed when the English thought he was trying to steal a beached longboat, another when he reached toward a sword, and four more when they resisted being taken aboard the *Endeavour* from their canoe), Cook found it impossible to gain Maori cooperation in gathering the fresh water and provisions he needed. Small wonder! At any rate, he left in disgust, writing in his journal that he was sailing "out of the bay, which I have named *Poverty Bay* because it afforded us not one thing we wanted."

One thing is a virtual certainty: had Captain Cook gotten off on the right foot with the indigenous people, a name incorporating the word "poverty" would never have occurred to him! Gisborne is in fact the very center of one of New Zealand's most fertile areas, with a balmy climate that sees more than 2,215 hours of bright sunshine annually. It's a gardenland of vegetable farms and orchards bearing citrus fruits, grapes, and kiwifruit. Dairy and sheep farms prosper. That sunny climate, combined with beaches that offer ideal swimming, surfing, and fishing conditions, also make it a holiday resort that is becoming increasingly popular with Kiwis from all over the North Island.

ORIENTATION

Gisborne is situated on the northern shore of Poverty Bay where the Waimata and Taruheru Rivers come together to form the Turanganui. Riverside park areas abound, and most bridges were built for pedestrian as well as vehicular traffic. The city center is compact, with Gladstone Road a main thoroughfare.

Useful Information

The **Eastland Information Centre** is located at 209 Grey St. (tel. 079/86-139), where the friendly staff offers enthusiastic assistance to visitors from 8:30 a.m. to 5 p.m. Monday through Friday, weekends and holidays until 2 p.m. . . . For information on **bus and train services,** phone 486-199; **air services,** 79-490 for Air New Zealand and 81-608 for Eagle Air between the hours of 8 a.m. and 5 p.m. . . . A public ladies' **rest room** with a changing room for infants and a child-care center is open from 9:30 a.m. to 5 p.m. Monday through Friday, at the Peel Street end of Palmerston Road. . . . Gisborne is served by InterCity and Dominion coaches, and Air New Zealand flights. . . . The **telephone prefix** is 079.

WHERE TO STAY

A Hostel

The **Gisborne YHA Hostel,** 32 Harris St. (on the corner of Wainui Road), Gisborne (tel. 079/83-269), is in a relaxed urban setting close to beaches and major sightseeing. There are 38 beds in five rooms, communal showers, and kitchen. Across the street there's a food shop open seven days a week. Seniors pay NZ$11 ($6.90), and juniors, NZ$5.50 ($3.45), plus GST.

Cabins/Campgrounds

Gisborne has an excellent motor camp run by the City Council. It's handy to good swimming and surfing beaches, spotless, and provides above-average facilities. During high season (summer months), advance reservations are absolutely necessary, as it is extremely popular with Kiwis.

The **Waikanae Beach Motor Camp,** at the beach end of Grey Street, Gisborne (tel. 079/75-634), has brown-wood blocks of cabins arranged U-shape around a grassy courtyard with attractive plantings. There are tourist cabins, which sleep four in two twin-bedded rooms and have private toilet and shower, refrigerator, gas range, crockery, cutlery, and cooking utensils; you supply linen and blankets. Charges range from NZ$10 ($6.25) for two people for tent sites to NZ$12 ($7.50) for two for power sites to NZ$42 ($26.25) double for tourist cabins—all plus GST. On the premises is a large laundry, kitchen, showers, children's play area, and tennis courts. The beautiful and safe Waikanae Beach is just across the road, and the city center is an easy walk away. The Olympic Pool complex and mini-golf are nearby.

A Bed-and-Breakfast

My favorite New Zealand bed-and-breakfast is probably **Greengables Travel Hotel,** 31 Rawiri St., Gisborne (tel. 079/75-872), run by Hilton and Elizabeth Croskery. Greengables is an old house, set in shaded grounds and approached by a rose-bordered walk, which has been renovated (without losing one bit of its original charm). There are nine spacious rooms (two of them singles, for you loners), all with H&C and nicely furnished, which share four showers. My own favorite is on the ground floor and has a pretty bay window. The old-fashioned lounge has a fireplace, and the attractive dining room looks out onto the lawn. This is a friendly, helpful family who provide Kiwi hospitality at its best—and one of the best breakfasts you'll find in Kiwiland. Rates are NZ$40 ($25) single and NZ$65 ($40.75) double, including breakfast and GST.

Motel Flats

My top motel recommendation in town goes to the **Gisborne Motel,** 509 Gladstone Rd., Gisborne (tel. 079/88-899). Its spacious units all have glass window walls to let in that gorgeous sunshine, and all are nicely furnished. There's a guest laundry, heated spa pool, video, and car wash. All units have full kitchens, but cooked and continental breakfasts are also available. Beverley and Alan Staunton (he's an ex-service man) have traveled extensively and enjoy meeting their guests with friendly hospitality. The location is a short drive (longish walk) into the city center. Rates here are NZ$52 ($32.50) to NZ$58 ($36.25) single, NZ$62 ($38.75) to NZ$68 ($42.50) double, including GST.

The **Teal Motor Lodge,** 479 Gladstone Rd., Gisborne (tel. 079/84-019), is something a little different—it's a New Zealand motel with a decidedly Oriental flavor, run by Valmai and John Haynes since 1979. Set on almost two acres of shaded and landscaped lawns, only a short walk to the city center, the spacious rooms have an airy look, with exposed beams and stained timber exteriors, and exciting color combinations in decor throughout. There's a restful air about the place, not to mention a saltwater swimming pool and a location that makes walking into town easy. There are 18 flats with one or two bedrooms and full kitchens, and three serviced rooms with tea-making facilities. Units sleep two to six. Rates for serviced rooms are NZ$54 ($33.75) to NZ$64 ($40); flats run NZ$64 ($40) to NZ$74 ($46.25) for two people—all plus GST.

A Self-Catering Flat

Alison and Eric Thompson have a lovely old home, high on a hill in the Whautopoka section overlooking the city and Poverty Bay, with a self-contained flat on one side of the ground floor. It has a separate entrance, one bedroom, lounge, and kitchen—perfect for a couple or two friends. Sheep graze peacefully on the hills out back, and there are great nature walks close by. All reservations *must* be made well in advance: contact Alison at 22 Hill Rd., Gisborne (tel. 079/89-795). The rate is NZ$55 ($34.50), plus GST, double.

WHERE TO EAT

For eating on the fly, you have several choices for basic budget fare: **Captain Morgan's,** at 285 Grey St. (tel. 87-821); the **Cook's Galley,** in the Royal Hotel, 279 Gladstone Rd. (tel. 89-299); and **Robert Harris,** Treble Court (tel. 80-661).

There are two restaurants in the **Sandown Park Motor Hotel,** on Childers Road (tel. 84-134). **Longjohn's** is a fun sort of place, with a large longboat filled with seats running down the center, a bricked barbecue grill over on one side (you select your own meat and can cook it yourself if you wish), a bar on the other, and entertainment every night except Sunday. Prices, which include a salad bar with unlimited servings, run NZ$11 ($6.90) to NZ$14 ($8.75) for lamb, chicken, fish, and ham; NZ$10 ($6.25) to NZ$15 ($9.40) for choice steaks. Hours are noon to 2 p.m. and 5 to 9 p.m. every day except Sunday.

For more elegant dining at the Sandown, try the **Gazebo,** a pretty garden-style restaurant with a window wall overlooking the hotel's landscaped grounds. It's a warm, relaxed room, and the food is first rate. Main courses include a nice selection of seafood, beef, lamb, chicken, and veal at prices of NZ$17 ($10.75) to NZ$23 ($14.50). On Sunday night there's a family-night buffet from 6 to 8 p.m., and during the summer an outdoor barbecue on Sunday from 5:30 p.m.

READERS' DINING SELECTIONS: "For good home-cooking, go to **The Mill** family restaurant at the southwest end of town, at the corner of Mill and Gladstone Roads (tel. 83-540). The little diner is immaculate, with moderate prices for eat-in, take-away, or grocery-store goods"

(J. and P. Conrad, San Jose, Calif.). . . . "We stayed in Gisborne a few days and ran across some 'finds': **Marina,** at Marina Park, Vogel Street (tel. 85-919), and **Pinehurst Manor,** 4 Clifford St. (tel. 86-771), both outstanding and not too big a splurge; and for good value, **Pete's on the Beach,** at Midway Beach (tel. 75-861)" (S. and T. Hazen, Boulder, Colo.). . . . "It was a treat to run across Chinese take-out at **China Palace Restaurant Café,** at the corner of Gladstone and Peel Streets (tel. 75-037)" (L. Harris, Baltimore, Md.). . . . "We warmly recommend **Bread & Roses,** at the corner of Lowe Street and Reads Quay (tel. 86-697). This is a small restaurant, with a friendly, cozy atmosphere. The service was very good, and the food was excellent" (G. Speed, Oslo, Norway).

THINGS TO SEE AND DO

To get a panoramic view of Poverty Bay, the city, its harbors and rivers, head for **Kaiti Hill Lookout.** It is signposted at the northern end of Gladstone Bridge, and you can drive most of the way, walking the last little bit to a brick semicircular lookout point at the very edge of the hill. There's a statue of Captain Cook there that looks suspiciously like Napoleon (notice the hand in the jacket, so characteristic of "The Little Emperor") looking out toward Young Nick's Head on the opposite side of the bay.

At the foot of Kaiti Hill, you'll pass one of New Zealand's largest Maori meeting houses, **Poho-o-rawiri.** It's so large that the traditional construction of a single ridgepole supported by pillars had to be abandoned in favor of more modern methods. All its carvings (which are splendid) were done in Rotorua. You'll usually find the side door open; if not, look up the caretaker, who lives just next door.

Also at the bottom of Kaiti Hill, on Kaiti Beach Road, there's a memorial on what is thought to be the spot on which Captain Cook landed, as well as a cannon, which may or may not have been salvaged from the wreck of the *Endeavour* (seems there's some dispute because it's made of iron, while Captain Cook's ship supposedly carried brass cannons).

Canadians will want to go by **Alfred Cox Park** on Grey Street to see the giant totem pole, which the Canadian government presented to New Zealand in 1969 to mark the Cook Bicentenary and to acknowledge the debt both countries owe that great explorer. It's adjacent to the Eastland Information Centre.

This area is filled with historic *pa* sites in the hills behind Poverty Bay Flats—ask at the Information Centre if any meeting houses are open to the public. There are also some excellent walkways in the area, and the Information Centre can furnish detailed trail booklets.

Swimmers will want to take advantage of the superb surf at both **Waikanae and Midway Beaches.** Surfers prefer **Wainui and Makarori Beaches.** Smallfry (as well as the young at heart) will enjoy the **Adventure Park** and Young Nick's Playground.

There is excellent **fishing** in these waters, both offshore and in the rivers. You can arrange charter boats and guides through the Information Centre. Anglers will want to ask for the *Guide to Trout Fishing in the Gisborne Area,* compiled by the Gisborne Anglers Club.

The **Gisborne Museum & Arts Centre,** 18-22 Stout St. (tel. 83-832), has displays depicting Maori and European history along the East Coast, as well as geological and natural exhibits. The Art Gallery hosts traveling New Zealand exhibitions as well as those of local artists and craftspeople. It's open from 10 a.m. to 4:30 p.m. Tuesday through Friday, and 2 to 4:30 p.m. on Saturday, Sunday, and holidays; closed Monday (but open on Monday from 10 a.m. to 4:30 p.m. from late December to the end of January). Adults pay NZ$2 ($1.25); children and students, NZ$1 (65¢).

Next door to the museum are **Wyllie Cottage,** built in 1872, and the **Star of Canada Maritime Museum.** The ill-fated *Star of Canada* struck rocks at Kaiti Beach in 1912.

Spectacular scenic flights of the area are provided by **Air Gisborne Ltd.** at the Gisborne Airport (tel. 746-84), including a 15-minute "Town and Around" flight and the "Captain Cook Special," a 45-minute flight, which flies over all prominent historic and sightseeing spots as well as East Coast cattle and sheep stations. There are flights to Lake Waikaremoana and White Island, plus day trips to Rotorua and Lake Taupo. A minimum requirement of two adults is necessary.

There are four one-hour **walks** (one is actually one to three hours) in Gisborne, all easily mapped out in the brochure *Gisborne Walking Tours,* available through the Information Centre, which can also give you information on four longer walks (2 to 5½ hours) in the Eastland area, in Wharerata, Cook's Cove, Anaura Bay, and Otoko.

The **Eastwoodhill Arboretum,** 35 km (22 miles) due west of Gisborne (tel. 39-800), is the largest collection in the southern hemisphere of trees and plants native to the northern hemisphere. If you're partial to daffodils, you'll find 2½ acres of them in yellow profusion here in spring, and in fall the oaks, maples, and ash put on a show. Open from August through May; by arrangement other times.

Most of New Zealand's white-wine grapes are grown near Gisborne, so if you are a wine connoisseur, have the Information Centre direct you to a couple of outstanding **wineries** just outside Gisborne: **Millton,** on Papatu Road (tel. 28-680), and **Honey Wood,** on Shelley Road (tel. 74-223 or 82-708). Fruit and honey wines are produced at the latter, where you can also buy local honey, local pottery, and handmade gift items. Call ahead to make sure they are open to visitors.

ON TO NAPIER

The 146-mile drive along Hwy. 2 from Gisborne to Napier passes through some of the most picturesque natural scenery in the country. Rugged hill-country sheep stations, lush native bush, Lake Tutira, and a breathtaking view of Poverty Bay Flats from the top of the Wharerata Hills some 23 miles outside the city. **Morere Springs Scenic Reserve,** between Poverty and Hawke's Bays (you'll see the sign along the highway), is a nice stopoff point for forest walks (there are four tracks, from half an hour to three hours, from which to choose), picnicking, or soaking in thermal pools. Incidentally, if you're traveling by public transport, opt for rail on this segment of your trip—the train hugs the coastline for long stretches, giving magnificent sea views not visible from the highway farther inland.

---

4. Napier

Hawke's Bay has been called the "Greenhouse of New Zealand" because of its sunny climate and ideal growing conditions for all kinds of vegetables, citrus fruits, and grapes. Indeed, when you see the expanse of vineyards, you may well think of it as the "Winery of New Zealand." Its high-spirited resort center is Napier (pop. 58,000), one of the country's most delightful holiday spots. Spread around the wedge of Bluff Hill (which was virtually an island when Captain Cook described it on his voyage south from Poverty Bay), Napier was founded by whalers in the mid-1800s. You won't find any trace of those early settlers in today's city, however: In 1931 an earthquake of such violence that it was recorded as far away as Cairo and Calcutta demolished the entire city and nearby Hastings, killing hundreds of people. In its aftermath, not only did a completely new city arise, but it arose on *new ground,* for the quake had lifted the inner harbor floor, creating 10,000 acres of dry land—the site of the present airport, for instance, was under water prior to 1931.

ORIENTATION

The pride—and showplace—of Napier is its **Marine Parade,** a beautiful stretch of waterfront lined with stately Norfolk pines. Many visitor activities center around the Marine Parade, which holds a wide variety of attractions. **Kennedy Road,** the principal thoroughfare, diagonally bisects the town. The best beach in the area is **Westshore Beach,** located in Westshore Domain, part of the new-land legacy of the 1931 disaster.

Useful Information

You'll find the **Visitors Information Centre** at the northern end of the Marine Parade (tel. 070/357-182 or 354-949). Hours are 8:30 a.m. to 5 p.m. weekdays, 9 a.m. to 5 p.m. weekends and public holidays; closed only on Christmas Day. Racks are filled with helpful brochures, maps (including a scenic drive), and visitor guides. Noreen Young and her staff can help with accommodations and book fishing trips, golf, and sightseeing tours. . . . **Mount Cook Line** (tel. 435-919) has coach service to Taupo (both directions) twice daily. . . . **Newmans Coach Lines** depot is located on Dickens Street (tel. 352-009). . . . There is rail service to Wellington; the **railway station** is being relocated at this writing. . . . **Air New Zealand** has service to Auckland, Wellington, Gisborne, and Christchurch; its office is at the corner of Hastings and Station Streets (tel. 355-588). . . . There's no airport bus into town: taxi fare is about NZ$12 ($7.50). . . . The **Chief Post Office (CPO)** is on Dickens Street. . . . **InterCity buses** leave from Dickens Street (long-distance buses may leave from the railroad station). . . . **Taxi ranks** are at Clive Square and sometimes at the corner of Emerson and Hastings Streets by the Bank of New Zealand (tel. 357-777). . . . The **telephone prefix** is 070.

WHERE TO STAY

A Hostel

Napier's **YHA Hostel** couldn't have a better location—it's right on the beachfront, across the street from Marineland, at 47 Marine Parade, Napier (tel. 070/357-039). The former guesthouse has 45 beds in 22 rooms, it's closed from 10 a.m. to 5 p.m. Front rooms overlook the bay; there's a pleasant kitchen and dining room with a piano, a smoking lounge, laundry facilities, and bike rental. Seniors pay NZ$12 ($7.50), and juniors, NZ$6 ($3.75), including GST.

Cabins

It's hard to find superlatives strong enough for Napier's **Kennedy Park Motor Camp** on Storkey Street, off Kennedy Road, Napier (tel. 070/439-126). If you've been impressed with Kiwi motor camps in general, just *wait* until you see this one! Set in 17 acres of trees, grass, and colorful flowers (including an acre and a half of roses!), with top-grade accommodations, this has to be the "Ritz" of New Zealand camps. Those accommodations run the gamut from tent sites to ungraded cabins to graded (two-star) cabins to tourist flats and motel units. The 110 sites with no power run NZ$7 ($4.40) per person when there's more than one; those with power, just pennies more. Ungraded cabins come with beds, tables, and chairs, and you supply cooking and eating utensils, linen and blankets, and use the communal toilet and shower facilities. Rates are NZ$21 ($13.25) for two. The 16 graded cabins sleep four (plus rollaway bed if needed), have easy chairs, and are furnished with H&C sinks, fridge, range, electric jug, toaster, crockery, cutlery, frying pan, pots, and utensils. You supply linen and blanket, and use the communal toilet and shower facilities. Doubles pay NZ$27 ($17). Tourist flats fill that gap between cabins and motel units—they're actually of motel quality, but lack such extras as a TV and telephone, and they're not serviced. You supply linen and blankets (which can be rented from the camp *for this type accommodation only*). These 20 units cost NZ$39 ($24.50) for two. Finally, motel units come in varying sizes: bed-sitters, one- and two-bedrooms. Many have peaked, pine-beamed ceilings, a window wall and stucco and wood-paneled walls. All are of superior quality, and well-chosen furnishings, look out over lawn and gardens, and run from NZ$48 ($30) to NZ$54 ($33.75) double. Add GST to all rates.

A Bed-and-Breakfast

The **Pinehaven Travel Hotel,** 42 Marine Parade, Napier (tel. 070/355-575), is just down the street from the YHA Hostel and across the road from Marineland. Judith Butt and her family have hosted guests from all over the world off and on for ten years. Pinehaven has three family rooms, four twins, and one double, all with H&C and comfortably furnished. Although the bedrooms are not heated, they all have electric blankets. Downstairs there's a TV lounge with tea- and coffee-making facilities. Rates are NZ$33 ($20.75) single, NZ$45 ($28.25) double, plus GST. Continental or cooked breakfast is optional and extra.

Motel Flats

Some of the best motel flats are at Kennedy Park Motor Camp, described above.

You park outside your own unit at the **Snowgoose Lodge Motel,** 376 Kennedy Rd., Napier (tel. 070/436-083). Ray and Pierrine Cooper keep things shining at the Snowgoose, outside as well as in, and the front lawn has even won an award for the best motel garden in Napier. The one- and two-bedroom units are all nicely furnished and have TV, phone, radio, and electric blankets. Most also are brightened with one or two of Pierrine's growing plants. There's a newer block of executive suites that have their own spa bath (sheer luxury, that!). On-premises facilities include a laundry, car wash, children's play area, games room, outdoor swimming pool, and private spa pool—no charge for the use of any. Shops are nearby, and the Coopers can arrange babysitting. Rates at this Best Western (where your Holiday Pass discount applies): NZ$52 ($32.50) single and NZ$64 ($40) double for bed-sitters; NZ$59 ($37) single and NZ$71 ($44.50) double for full-kitchen units, and NZ$67 ($42) single and NZ$79 ($49.50) double for executive units with spa bath and/or waterbed.

The **Marewa Lodge,** 42 Taradale Rd., Napier (tel. 070/435-839), has 20 attractive units arranged in an L-shape around a large lawn and children's playground. All are equipped with TV, phone, radio, electric blanket, and electric heater. Each unit opens up to a terrace furnished with garden chairs for sunbathing. Bed-sitters have rangettes for cooking; other units have full stoves and ovens. There's plenty of parking space, a spa pool, car wash, and laundry facilities. Babysitters are available, and there's a shopping area close by. Rates are NZ$54 ($33.75) single and NZ$64 ($40) double, plus GST.

At the **Reef Motel,** 33 Meeanee Quay, Westshore, Napier (tel. 070/54-108), Norma and Malcolm Smith are among the friendliest and most helpful hosts in Napier. They know and love the area and thrive on helping visitors to do the same. The motel's seven units each sleep two to six, with separate bedrooms, a living room that opens into a kitchen, bath, phone, and color TV. Upstairs units have great views. There's a spa pool and laundry facilities on the premises. Both cooked and continental breakfasts are available, and the Smiths run a courtesy car to rail, bus, and air terminals. Rates (add GST) are NZ$49 ($30.75) single, NZ$59 ($37) double, and since this is a Best Western, the Holiday Pass discounts apply. Highly recommended.

The **Blue Dolphin Motel,** 371-373 Kennedy Rd., Napier (tel. 070/439-129), is owned by Paul and Jenny Guest, Napier residents for over 30 years. There are nine self-contained units with full kitchen facilities and separate bedrooms that sleep two to five people. All have phone, radio, TV, and video, and are serviced daily. There's a games room, heated outdoor spa pool, and a fully automatic guest laundry. Cooked or continental breakfasts are available. Rates run NZ$55 ($34.50) single, NZ$65 ($40.75) double, and the Guests will give a 10% discount to readers who present this book. All rates are plus GST.

The **Spanish Lady Motel,** 348 Kennedy Rd., Napier (tel. 070/439-188), a small property with an unassuming exterior hides the amenities hard to find in most New Zealand lodgings: washcloths in the bath and a sink with one faucet for hot and cold water (instead of the inconvenient two). Add to that good lighting and a firm mattress—heaven! There are also jelly beans on the tea tray for the kids, a pool, spa pool, playground, ice machine, and cactus garden. Owners Janice and Don McJorrow have been here since 1979 and their attention to detail shows. Of the 11 one- and two-bedroom units, Rooms 4 through 7 have been recently refurbished and are especially comfortable. Rates are NZ$57 ($35.75) single and NZ$67 ($42) double, plus GST. Ask Don about his golf package. This is a Best Western property and the usual discounts apply.

The big draw of the **Edgewater Motor Lodge,** ideally situated overlooking Hawke's Bay on Marine Parade, Napier (tel. 070/331-148), is that every unit has a balcony facing the bay with no buildings obstructing the view—just trees, plants, and a children's playground. Let me say up front that the smaller units don't have kitchens, but they do have tea and coffee facilities. All the units have good lighting (always a plus), in-house videos, and other videos that can be rented out to the room. You'll also find a game room, laundry, saltwater plunge pool, and two spa pools. The 19 units range from studios to two-bedroom, and include a unit for the disabled. Room 20 is especially pretty and features a waterbed (if you don't want to slosh when you sleep, choose Room 19). Rates are NZ$76 ($47.50) for a studio (with double bed) and NZ$95 ($59.50) double. The 10% Motor Lodge discount applies.

A Licensed Hotel

Besides being noteworthy for its architectural beauty, the **Masonic Hotel,** a landmark building on Marine Parade, Napier (tel. 070/358-689), has quite a past. It was built in 1861, destroyed by fire in 1896, rebuilt in the next year, destroyed by the earthquake and fire in 1931, and rebuilt again the following year. The hotel has an old-fashioned lobby with a grandfather clock, a graceful curving stairway, and a games room for small children. The 50 rooms here go fast, so you'd best reserve ahead. Nine of the rooms do not have private bath; the others have showers, H&C, and tea and coffee facilities. The price is NZ$50 ($31.25), single or double.

WHERE TO EAT

A favorite of Napier citizens is **Juices & Ices,** on Emerson Street at Clive Square (tel. 35-994), where the specialty is ice cream, with a dozen flavors from which to choose. You can also order toasted sandwiches, soup, and fresh fruit juices. Juices & Ices has a cheerful ice-cream-parlor ambience; hours are 8:30 a.m. to 5 p.m. weekdays and 10 a.m. to 1 p.m. on Saturday.

Everything is fresh, homemade, and inexpensive, too, at the **Napier Cafeteria,** on Hastings Street just off Tennyson Street (tel. 356-800). Whether you go for breakfast or a hot lunch of a roast, shepherd's pie, meat pie, savory, or whatnot, you can count on quality food served in cheerful surroundings at budget prices. Hours are 7:30 a.m. to 4 p.m.

There's a **Cobb & Co.** in the Masonic Hotel on Tennyson Street (tel. 358-689), with its usual family fare. There are daily specials, as well as the steak, fish, lasagne, and other menu offerings you can expect in this excellent chain. It's licensed and open seven days a week from 7:30 a.m. to 10 p.m. Nice colonial decor.

Early risers will appreciate **Mabel's Restaurant,** 204 Hastings St. (tel. 355-655), where morning tea is featured weekdays from 7 to 9:30 a.m. You can also get a light, reasonably priced meal of soup, quiche, or salad. Just check the blackboard selections. Closing time is 3 p.m.; open weekdays only.

Tops for good value is the roast of the day for NZ$11 ($6.90) at the **Victoria Restaurant,** in the Victoria Hotel on Marine Parade (tel. 353-149). The menu features lamb, fish, chicken, steak, and pork. It's a pretty place with lace curtains at the windows; dinner is served nightly from 6 p.m., and reservations are required. Licensed.

An intimate place to dine is **The Old Flame,** in a single-story house on Tennyson Street across from the Municipal Theatre (tel. 356-829). It's strictly smörgåsbord, with heaving tables of tempting New Zealand dishes. The place has a medieval look, rather than deco, for a change. Lunch is served from noon to 2 p.m. and costs NZ$12 ($7.50); dinner, from 6 to 9 p.m., costs NZ$23 ($14.50). Reserve, especially on weekends. BYO.

You'll find **Beaches Restaurant** in the War Memorial Building, Marine Parade (tel. 58-180), just behind the floral clock. From its windows at the water's edge, there's an expansive view of Hawke's Bay from Mahia Peninsula to Cape Kidnappers. Seafood is the specialty here, with crayfish, oysters, mussels, paua, calamari, prawns, shrimps, scallops, and fresh fish available. The menu also features lamb, beef, and poultry; vegetarian dishes can be prepared if requested when you make your reservation. There's an extensive all–New Zealand wine list, with selections from most local vineyards. Lunch prices begin at NZ$8 ($5) for main courses; at dinner, main courses start at NZ$18 ($11.25). Lunch hours are noon to 2:30 p.m. on Wednesday, Thursday, and Friday; dinner, from 6 p.m. Monday through Saturday; closed Sunday. It's a good idea to reserve, and essential if you want a table by the window.

Special Note: I'm not sure this entry belongs under "Where to Eat," but because New Zealand budget travel is so closely tied to those wonderful motel flats and their kitchens, I thought you should know about **Chantal Wholefoods,** 11 Hastings St. (tel. 58-036). Even if you're not a strict vegetarian, I think you'll love this store—all sorts of natural foods, dried fruits, nuts, tofu, and in addition, marvelous wholegrain breads to make any sandwich taste its best. Chantal's is very much like an old-fashioned grocery store. The foods are all in open drums and you package them yourself—it's lots of fun, and prices come out cheaper than those in supermarkets.

THINGS TO SEE AND DO

Plan to spend most of your time along the **Marine Parade's Golden Mile.** Down at the southern end, there's the **Aquarium** (tel. 357-579), one of New Zealand's best. Stop for a moment to view the bronze sculpture showing two trawler fishermen hauling a net full of fish. It's so masterfully executed that fishermen have been known to stand and point out each species of fish in the net. The Aquarium's central feature is a huge saltwater oceanarium, which holds over 25 species of ocean-dwelling fish, ranging in size from crayfish to sharks. Feeding time is 3:15 p.m., which can get pretty exciting. You'll also get to see a crocodile, turtles, vividly colored tropical fish, seahorses, the lethal piranha, and octopi. The Vivarium, on the top floor, holds the tuatara, a living fossil unique to New Zealand, and also aquatic reptiles like water dragons, turtles, and frogs. The Aquarium is open every day except Christmas from 9 a.m. to 5 p.m. (until 9 p.m. from December 26 through January). Adults pay NZ$6 ($3.75); children, NZ$3 ($1.90).

Walking north, you'll come to the **Boating Lake,** with paddleboats for children and adult-size bumper boats, as well as small racing cars, which are open from 10 a.m. to 9:30 p.m. every day.

Next comes **Marineland** (tel. 357-599), where a 45-minute show puts dolphins, leopard seals, and sea lions through their paces in sports competitions and other antics much like those we see in the States. Also on hand are blue penguins, fur seals, otters, and gannets. Marineland is open daily from 10 a.m. to 4:30 p.m., and show times are 10:30 a.m. and 2 p.m., with an additional 4 p.m. performance from December 26 through January. Admissions: NZ$6 ($3.75) for adults, NZ$3 ($1.90) for children. Marineland now houses **Lilliput,** an animated village and model railway with authentic New Zealand rolling stock and locomotives. Admission is NZ$2 ($1.25) for adults, NZ$1 (65¢) for children.

The **Stables Colonial Museum and Waxworks,** opposite Marineland (tel. 351-937), re-creates the past with rooms from another era; my favorites depict a man in an outhouse, a doctor taking the blood pressure of a wicker-chair-bound patient, and a prostitute's quarters (this one provokes a bit of speculation about what *exactly* is going on). But the pièce de résistance of the museum is *Earthquake 31,* a documentary about the infamous earthquake; try to see it at the beginning of your sight-seeing to best understand the unique history of this place. The 23-minute film includes actual footage of Napier before and after the earthquake and an interview with older citizens who lived through it, two of them teachers. Outside the movie theater, which has a floor that actually moves during footage of the quake, there is a dramatic replica of the collapse of the local nurses' home and the rescue performed by sailors and firefighters. Admission to the museum and the film is NZ$4 ($2.50), or NZ$2.50 ($1.55) each. (If you have to choose one, pick the film.) It's the brain-child of owner Keven Percy, who runs the place with his wife, Judy. It's open daily from 9 a.m. to 5 p.m.

Other amusements in Napier include children's bumper boats, radio boats, putt-putt golf, and roller skating. Stop for a while and soak in the beauty of the **Sunken Gardens,** with their waterwheel and floating white lotus sculpture. Then, on past the PRO, there's the **Sound Shell,** which is used on summer weekends for an arts and crafts market.

Next, there's the **Hawke's Bay Art Gallery and Museum** (tel. 357-781) with a wide range of exhibits, many of which are related to the art and history of the region. A Tourism Design Award–winning exhibition, "Nga Tukemata" ("The Awakening"), presents the art of the local Ngati Kahungunu tribe and an audio-visual presentation tells the story of the disastrous Hawke's Bay earthquake of 1931. The "Newest City on the Globe" exhibition shows the rebuilding of Napier in the early 1930s in its famed art deco style. Paintings and the decorative arts from this period are also featured. Hours are 10 a.m. to 4:30 p.m. weekdays, 1 to 5 p.m. weekends. It's closed Monday except on school holidays. There's a small admission charge.

The **Kiwi House,** at the end of the Golden Mile (tel. 357-553), is where you are guaranteed to see kiwi birds. Also on view are owls, night herons, sugar gliders, whistling frogs, and many others. There's a sheepskin shop in the main entrance. Hours are 11 a.m. to 3 p.m. daily. Admission is NZ$2.50 ($1.55) for adults, NZ$1 (65¢) for children.

Finally, there's the city of Napier itself, virtually an open-air museum of art deco and Spanish architecture as a result of massive reconstruction between 1931 and 1933. Half a century later, the buildings are remarkably unchanged and no doubt represent one of the world's most concentrated collections of buildings from this period. Historic **Clive Square,** on Monroe Street between Emerson and Dickens Streets, was the village green from the 1860s to the mid-1880s, when it became a public gardens. After the earthquake, it was the site of "Tin Town," a temporary shopping area.

A map outlining a self-guided walk through the downtown deco area and another showing a more extensive scenic drive are available from the Information Centre for NZ$1 (65¢). Guided walks leave the Hawke's Bay Art Gallery and Museum every Sunday at 2 p.m. and include slide and video presentations and refreshments. They are conducted by the Art Deco Trust, which promotes the city's architecture and can be contacted at P.O. Box 429, Napier.

Swimming

Westshore Domain is Napier's most popular swimming beach, about a mile and a half of gray sand and pebbles. Surf at the **Marine Parade** beach is a bit too rough for good swimming, but it's a good place to get a little sun. There is, however, a saltwater pool at Marine Parade featuring the "Wild Rampage Ride." **Onekawa Park** at Maadi Road and Flanders Avenue has two Olympic-size pools, one indoor, the other outdoor. Small fee.

Gannets

This is the only place in New Zealand where gannets are known to nest on the mainland (they are commonly found on offshore islands). There's a colony of some 6,000 out at **Cape Kidnappers,** that dramatic line of cliffs that forms Hawke's Bay's southern end some 17 miles south of Napier. The gannet sanctuary is open to the public from late October to June, and the graceful, colorful birds are worth a visit. To reach them, drive 13 miles south to Clifton Domain; then it's a little less than a two-hour walk along four or five miles of sandy beach. That walk *must* be made at low tide, since high tides come right up to the base of the steep cliffs, which is why private vehicles may not be taken out to the sanctuary. Be sure to check with the Visitors Information Centre in Napier (tel. 357-182) or Hastings (tel. 60-205), or the Department of Conservation in Napier (tel. 350-415), about the tides or taking a tour there. The best time to view the birds is from early November to late February; migration begins in March.

There are two options to going on your own: **Burden's Motor Camp** in Te Awanga (tel. 750-400 or 750-334 in Hastings) runs organized trips at moderate prices; and there's a Land Rover trip operated by **Gannet Safaris** (tel. 777-597 in Hastings) at considerably higher prices, but which also include a farm visit. The trips are 4 and 3½ hours long, respectively; take along a sweater and some snacks.

Other Activities

There are two important **wineries** you can visit in the Napier vicinity, the Mission Vineyards and Brookfields Winery. Ask at the Information Centre for brochures about tours and directions for reaching them. Also, Napier is where you can see how all those sheep get transformed into car seatcovers, rugs, and more. You can take a free 25-minute tour through the **Classic Sheepskin Tannery** on Thames Street off Pandora Road (tel. 359-662), seven days a week at 11 a.m. and 2 p.m. The shop there sells sheepskin products at factory prices, and they have a fully insured, worldwide mailing service. There's also a courtesy car available on weekdays.

AFTER DARK

You'll always find folks congregating in the **Masonic Hotel.** The younger crowd goes to the **Med Bar,** where there is live music Thursday through Saturday from 8 p.m. The older crowd, often with kids in tow, heads for the **Cobb Bar** (many are actually waiting for a table in the restaurant, but the bar is invitingly congenial).

Ego's Night Club, in a small art deco building on Hastings Street (tel. 357-030), is open Wednesday through Saturday from 8 p.m. until 3 a.m. Take in a movie at the art deco **Odeon Theatre** on Hastings Street, or the **State Theatre,** deco even more so, on Dickens Street; or see a show or concert (very inexpensive) at the **Municipal Theatre** on Tennyson Street (if nothing else, try to see the auditorium).

HASTINGS

Just 12 miles from Napier on Hwy. 2, Hastings is a town of lovely parks and gardens and Spanish Mission–style as well as art deco architecture—most definitely worth a visit. If you're not driving, there is regular bus service between the two towns. Stop by the **Visitor Information Centre,** on Russell Street North (mailing address: Private Bag, Hastings; tel. 60-205), for brochures, information, a Spanish Mission Tour map, and a scenic drive guide. Hours are 8:30 a.m. to 5 p.m. weekdays, to 1 p.m. on weekends and holidays. Inquire at the Information Centre about tours in a taxi, as well. No matter how you get around, the **scenic drive** is one you really shouldn't miss.

Pick up the *Taste Our Tradition* brochure from the Information Centre for directions on visiting the local wineries. One of the best is the **Vidal Winery,** 913 St. Aubyn St. East, near Sylvan Road (tel. 87-605). Vidal has a lot to offer, including the Vineyard Bar and Barrel Room Restaurant right on the premises. They have a rustic, wine-cellar setting, with beamed ceiling, old oak casks lining the walls, and candlelight. There's also a barbecue area outside with umbrella trees and a grape arbor. The menu on Saturday night, November through February, includes delicious homemade soup, quiche, baked potato and salad, honeyed chicken, and a variety of steaks. A basket of hot bread and butter accompanies all meals, and need I say you can order wine? Prices are in the NZ$7 ($4.40) to NZ$18 ($11.25) range. The Vineyard Bar is open from 10 a.m. to 9 p.m. Monday through Saturday; the Barrel Room, from noon to 2 p.m. and 6 to 9 p.m. Monday through Saturday; drinks and light snacks are available in the Vineyard Bar.

Be sure to drive up to **Te Mata Peak,** about seven miles from the Hastings Information Centre. The view is spectacular, and ask locals or the center about the lovely Maori legend that gave it its name. Take Havelock Road to Te Mata Road to Simla Avenue to Te Mata Peak Road and ascend the 1,310-foot-high peak for a stunning 360° panoramic view.

Within the eight acres that make up **Fantasyland,** in Windsor Park, entered via Grove Road (tel. 69-856), are enough assorted attractions and amusements to delight any child and all but the most hardened of his or her elders. Each time I go there are new additions, all elaborately but tastefully executed. Who wouldn't be intrigued by a pirate ship complete with cannons, a turreted castle, and a spaceship parked on its moon base! The tree house (open to any and all climbers) draws me every time, as does the little village with its firehouse, jail, and stores. A terrific array of playground equipment, go-karts, bumper boats, battery-operated cars and tricycles are available for active youngsters, and for those of us not so active, there's a miniature train ride around the park, along with miniature golf. Canoes and rowboats compete with swans and ducks on the pretty pond, and the shady, landscaped grounds invite an extended spell of just plain loafing—spreading a picnic on the handy tables set about (easily arranged with food from the take-away bar). The tea shop is a refreshment alternative. Adults pay NZ$2 ($1.25), and children under 12 go in free (some of the rides charge a minimal fare). Open daily from 9 a.m. to 5 p.m.

READERS' MOTEL SELECTIONS: "We discovered a reasonable, quiet, peaceful, sparkling-clean motel in Hastings that is situated next to Ebbet Park a few blocks from the center of town. It's the **Ebbet Park Lodge,** 614 Gordon Rd., Hastings (tel. 070/68-086). The owners [Nola and Rex McLean] personally served us piping-hot bacon, eggs, tomatoes, and toast each morning for breakfast" (P. McGilvray, Sacramento, Calif.). . . . "The **Windsor Park Motor Camp** in Hastings is in a corner of a park and couldn't be a more restful place to lay your head—or sleeping bag. We camped, but there are tourist flats, cabins, and caravan sites too, and the park has a swimming pool and water slide" (J. Kelly, Phoenix, Ariz.).

5. Napier to Taupo

Your drive from Napier to Taupo via Hwy. 5 will take two hours, but there was a time when it took two days. That was when stagecoach service was first initiated over a route that had been used by Maoris in pre-European days on forages to collect seafood from Hawke's Bay.

The landscape you'll be passing through changes from lush vineyards to cultivated farm fields to rugged mountain ranges—it doesn't take much imagination to know why in the early days the journey was so arduous. About 3½ miles before you reach Taupo, look for the lonely peak of **Mount Tauhara,** an extinct volcanic cone rising from the plains.

V

LAKE TAUPO AND BEYOND

Whether you come into Taupo from Rotorua past Wairakei's steamy thermal power complex or from Napier under the lonely eye of Mount Tauhara, it is the lake on whose shores the town sits that will draw you like a magnet. Lake Taupo, New Zealand's largest (238 square miles), opens before you in a broad, shimmering expanse, with its far shores a misty suggestion of cliffs, coves, and wooded hills. There's a bit of magic at work in Taupo—and it's easy to see its immediate attraction to descendants of the *Arawa* canoe. Perhaps that's because the great lake was created, present-day Maoris will tell you, by the magic of Ngatoroirangi, the legendary navigator of that migrating canoe, when he stood on Mount Tauhara and flung a gigantic tree from its summit, which landed here, leaving a vast trough as it plowed through the earth. When water welled up to fill the trough, Lake Taupo was born. Its very name is linked to legend—the Maoris called it Taupo-nui-a-Tia, or "the great cloak of Tia," after one of the *Arawa* chiefs who explored much of this region, naming and claiming choice spots for his tribe. If you're not a believer in magic, you'll accept the Pakeha explanation of its origin: that it lies in a series of volcanic craters created in the aftermath of some of the most violent eruptions in the country's history.

1. Taupo

What you'll find today is a pleasant, medium-size town of 16,500 people. What's appealing about Taupo is that it comes across as a *real* place, not just a tourist draw, probably because travelers often rush past it on their way to Rotorua. While you'll certainly find that it welcomes visitors, you'll also see plenty of people just going about their daily lives, going to work or school, congregating with friends in local cafés, or indulging in an ice-cream cone (there are half a dozen parlors here that encourage just that).

For locals and visitors alike, the lake itself is as much the central attraction today as it was in those far-off times, although there is an abundant supply of land-based attractions as well. Waterskiing has gained such popularity that there are now specified ski lanes along the shoreline. Pleasure boating is a never-ending diversion in these parts. And the fishing on which the Maori settlers so depended has changed only in the addition of two imported trout species to enhance the native fish population. It was in 1868 that brown trout eggs were introduced from Tasmania, followed by California rainbow trout in 1884. Lake Taupo rainbows are now considered a totally self-supporting wild population. It is the trout that draw anglers here in such numbers that those on shore have been so tightly packed as to be likened to a human picket fence. And there is seldom a time when the lake's surface is not alive with boats trolling lines in their wake. Landlubbers have been coming in nearly equal numbers since the late 1870s to visit the thermal pools and view the natural wonders of the lake's environs.

ORIENTATION

Taupo is spread along the northeastern tip of the lake, just where the Waikato River, New Zealand's longest, flows out of Lake Taupo's Tapuaeharuru Bay. Its main street is **Tongariro Street,** named after the largest river flowing into the lake. Perpendicular to Tongariro is another important street, named **Heu Heu** (the Maoris pronounce it "hue-hue"; the Pakehas, "who-who"). The small settlements of **Acacia Bay** and **Jerusalem Bay** are just across on the western shore of the bay. Highway 1 leads south along the lake's eastern shore.

Useful Information

The rainbow-striped **Public Relations Office (PRO)** is just off the lakefront on Tongariro Street (tel. 074/89-002) and can book accommodations, tours, and other activities, as well as provide a wide range of informative brochures on area attractions. Hours are 8:30 a.m. to 5 p.m. daily. . . . A couple of places a stone's throw from the PRO on Heu Heu Street have **one-hour film developing.** . . . The striking purple-and-salmon-colored **post office** is at the corner of Ruapehu and Horomatangi Streets, and is open weekdays from 8:30 a.m. to 4:30 p.m. . . . **Fishing licenses** and information can be obtained from the PRO. . . . **Fishing guides** may be booked through the PRO. . . . There is regular **bus service** to Taupo from Napier and Rotorua. . . . The **telephone prefix** is 074.

WHERE TO STAY

Only during the holiday season should it be necessary to reserve very far in advance, since there are over 3,000 beds available in the immediate vicinity. The efficient, well-run PRO can furnish a list of area accommodations, complete with current prices.

Hostels

As its name implies, the **Taupo Summer Hostel,** Taupo Nui-a Tia College, Spa Road, Taupo (no telephone), is open during *summer months only*. It's a hospitable place that occupies the College Home Science building, and there's a barbecue area as well as tennis courts (racquets available for a small charge). The overnight rate is NZ$12 ($7.50) for adults, half that for children, including GST.

The **Rainbow Lodge Travellers Hostel,** 99 Titraupenga St., Taupo (tel. 074/ 85-754), is just off Spa Road and only a short distance from main highways, shops, the bus depot, and the lake. There are dormitory rooms and double rooms. Most guests supply their own linens, but they are available for rent. Communal facilities include toilets, bathrooms, kitchen, dining room, lounge, laundry, games area, and a sauna. They'll help you arrange all sorts of activities (fishing, tramping, canoe trips). Per-person rates begin at NZ$12.50 ($7.80), plus GST.

The **Blue Horizon,** 7 Tuwharetoa St., Taupo (tel. 074/87-337), primarily offers motel flats, but it does have three beds available for backpackers, who have their own bath and access to a laundry; linens can be rented. The rate is NZ$15 ($9.40) per person.

Cabins

Taupo Cabins are conveniently located near the thermal baths and other attractions at 50 Tonga St. (P.O. Box 795), Taupo (tel. 074/84-346), and offer one of the best accommodations bargains in the area. There are two-, four-, and five-berth cabins furnished with two-tier bunks (you supply linen, blankets, crockery, cutlery, cooking utensils, and use the communal kitchen); two- and four-berth "flatettes" with H&C, cooking facilities, and utensils (you supply linen, blankets, and cutlery); four-berth tourist flats with cooking facilities plus toilet and shower (you supply or rent only linen and blankets). There's a large community kitchen, communal showers and toilets, and a laundry with iron and ironing board (metered for a small fee). Should you arrive without linens, blankets, or cutlery, they are available for rent. Rates run NZ$12 ($7.50) to NZ$20.50 ($12.75), including GST per person, depending on type of accommodation.

In a quiet rural setting overlooking the lake, **Acacia Holiday Park,** Acacia Bay Road (P.O. Box 171), Taupo (tel. 074/85-159), offers tent and caravan sites, cabins, and self-contained tourist flats. On the premises there's a hot spa pool and recreation room with a pool table. Best of all, the friendly owners take much pleasure in providing visitors with information, maps, and brochures on local attractions. Rates are NZ$15 ($9.40) per couple for tent and caravan sites; NZ$24 ($15) double for cabins, and NZ$42 ($26.25) double for tourist flats, including GST.

There's a **free campground** across from Huka Village Estate and very near Huka Falls. It's popular and quite idyllic, but be forewarned that there are no facilities and you always have to boil your water. Still, you'll have the same view as your neighbors at Huka Village Estate, who are paying NZ$517 ($323) per night for a double room!

Bed-and-Breakfasts

The friendly graciousness of **Bradshaw's Guest House,** 130 Heu Heu St., Taupo (tel. 074/88-288), has elicited scores of letters from readers, and on one of my research trips for this book I ran into enthusiastic budgeteers singing its praises long before I reached Taupo. Bradshaw's is a homey, white house set on a quiet residential street very close to the center of town. Rooms are nicely done up, with attractive furnishings and lots of wood paneling. There's a cozy TV lounge (with books for non–tube addicts), a tea and coffee room, laundry, a dining room that faces the lake, and 12 bedrooms, 3 of them singles. A few have private baths (with tub), and three have TV. Bed-and-breakfast rates, which include GST, are NZ$27 ($17) single without private facilities, NZ$31 ($19.50) single with private facilities, NZ$54 ($33.75) double with private facilities. The evening meal costs NZ$12 ($7.50).

It's a little hard to find **Margaret and Howard Kidd,** Tuhingamata Road, Taupo (tel. 074/48-321), and they suggest that you call for directions before heading for their comfortable country home set on some 64 acres of farmland. What you'll find when you reach them is a large house with a solar-heated swimming pool and heated spa pool, as well as a guest lounge with billiards and table tennis. Bedrooms each have one single and one double bed and private facilities. The Kidds and their teenage daughter are health-food devotees, so breakfast (and dinner if you order in advance) is sure to be nutritious as well as appetizing. They have a yacht, skiboat, and two autos for guests' use (additional charge), and they are knowledgeable about almost anything you will want to do in Taupo. Bed-and-breakfast rates are NZ$50 ($31.25) single, NZ$75 ($47) double, plus GST.

Motel Flats

On the corner of Kaimanawa and Heu Heu Streets you'll find the attractive **Adelphi Motel,** P.O. Box 1091, Taupo (tel. 074/87-594), presided over by Fay and Gordon Clark. The ten units include one on the top floor (the only second-floor unit) with marvelous views of the lake and mountains, and one especially designed for the disabled. There are one- and two-bedroom units, sleeping two to six, all with fully equipped kitchen, TV, radio, and electric blanket. There are two private spa pools on the premises as well as a laundry, car-washing facilities, and a trampoline. Breakfast is available for a small charge, dinner on request, and Best Western discounts apply for the rates of NZ$58 ($36.25) single, NZ$70 ($43.75) double, plus GST, at this member of the chain. Rates increase during holiday periods.

Dunrovin Motel, 140 Heu Heu St. (P.O. Box 647), Taupo (tel. 074/87-384), is right next door to Bradshaw's on the same quiet street, yet very central to the town. Peter and Virginia Webb offer one- and two-bedroom units, with twin and double beds, sleeping two to eight. All have complete kitchen, radio, and TV. A children's play area is on the premises, and cooked or continental breakfasts are available for an additional charge. Rates are NZ$47 ($29.50) single, NZ$60 ($37.50) double, including GST.

Cedar Park Motor Lodge, at Two Mile Bay (P.O. Box 852), Taupo (tel. 074/86-325), is across Hwy. 1 from the lakefront, just 4 km (2½ miles) from the center of town. It's one of the most attractive accommodations in Taupo, with some two-story units, which feature peaked ceilings and picture windows looking out over the lake. Each unit has a separate lounge, two bedrooms, complete kitchen, TV, video, radio, telephone, and electric blankets. There's a heated swimming pool, hot spa pools, children's play area, barbecue, laundry, and car-wash facilities. Also, a very good BYO restaurant right on the premises (patronized by the locals as well as guests). Rates are NZ$55 ($34.50) single, NZ$77 ($48.25) double, plus GST (except during holiday periods when charges are higher).

Just across from the lakefront, **Tui Oaks Motor Inn,** Lake Terrace and Tui Street (P.O. Box 31), Taupo (tel. 074/88-305), is a convenient place to stay, since on-premises facilities include a house bar, licensed restaurant with lake view open daily, a swimming pool, spa pool, barbecue, laundry room, and a tour desk. Guest units include some serviced motel rooms, some that have complete kitchens, TVs, and radios (there's one waterbed). Top-floor units have high ceilings and skylights. Rates begin at NZ$60 ($37.50) single and go all the way up to NZ$85 ($53.25) double, including GST. Rates are higher on holidays.

You can't miss the **Suncourt Motor Hotel,** on Northcrost Street (P.O. Box 837), Taupo (tel. 074/88-265). It's a large property set back from the road on an expansive lawn. The majority of its rooms are singles and doubles, along with 13 family units for up to seven people. The rooms are large, with TV, radio, refrigerator, and bathtub. There's a restaurant, a couple of bar/discos, an inviting outdoor pool lined with deck chairs, a spa pool, children's playground, laundry, and plenty of off-street parking. This is a good place for families: children under 12 stay for free, and it's an easy walk into town. Rates are NZ$78 ($48.75) single and NZ$83 ($52) double; the family units are NZ$93 ($58.25).

The **Lakeview Terrace Motel,** at 90 Lake Terrace, Taupo (tel. 074/87-842), is within easy walking distance of downtown. The units look and feel like cabins; those upstairs feature lake views and balconies, while the ones downstairs have patios with plants, picnic tables, and umbrellas. All have TV, kitchen, H&C, and tea and coffee facilities. The grounds overflow with lush plants. Two-bedroom units accommodate up to six people. Off-season rates are NZ$55 ($34.50) single and NZ$60 ($37.50) double; units start at NZ$80 ($50) in season. All rates include GST.

The **Blue Horizon,** 7 Tuwharetoa St., Taupo (tel. 074/87-337), is situated right in the heart of town, across from the PRO. It has 22 rooms, all with TV, private bath, heater, and tea and coffee facilities; half have refrigerators. There is a laundry, and continental breakfast is available. The rate for a single is NZ$30 ($18.75) and a double goes for NZ$48 ($30); two adults with two kids pay NZ$62 ($38.75)—all plus GST.

A Mini-Splurge

The prettiest lodging in town is the **Cottage Mews,** right beside the lake on Lake Terrace, Taupo (tel. 074/83-004), a colonial-style motel with gray wood siding and white trim (a bit of New England in the South Pacific); a wheelbarrow filled with bright posies sits at the entrance. Impressive split-level units have a balcony, toilets both upstairs and down, a large spa bath, and striking wood trim throughout. Some units have lake views, private patios, a waterbed or a queen-size bed. Breakfast is available at an additional charge. Rates start at NZ$80 ($50); for split-level units you pay NZ$5 ($3.15) more, and for my favorite, the lake-view accommodation, NZ$10 ($6.25) more. You couldn't make a lovelier choice.

Big Splurges

For an elegant lakeside stay, **Manuels Motor Inn,** on Lake Terrace, Taupo (tel. 074/85-110), mirrors its owner's love of the Mediterranean. The lobby is welcoming, with a chandelier and giant mirror, and fresh flowers. The 18 standard rooms have either a balcony or patio; all have sofa beds along with a double bed. There are seven suites with a mini-bar and coffee and tea facilities. A few of the rooms have bathtubs (a favorite feature of mine). The swimming pool is thermally heated, and the grotto spa pool, complete with glowworms, is Disney-inspired. A lounge with overstuffed chairs overlooks the lake, and wrought-iron tables and chairs on the patio at the lakeshore are conducive to sipping the brandy Alexanders or piña coladas available from the bar. The hotel's Edgewater restaurant (see "Where to Eat," below) is one of New Zealand's finest. Room rates start at NZ$125 ($78.25), suites at NZ$160 ($100).

The **THC Wairakei Resort Hotel,** Private Bag, Taupo (tel. 074/48-021), is about a 15-minute drive from Taupo. All 60 guest rooms have private facilities, tea and coffee facilities, fridge, and mini-bars. In addition, there are 15 luxury villa suites. The Graham Room Restaurant features local fish on its à la carte menu and serves an excellent buffet at breakfast. There's also Robert's Bistro, a casual eatery serving lunch and dinner every day. Other amenities include lighted tennis courts, two heated pools, spa pools, a games room, children's playground, guest laundry, and dry-cleaning service. Golfers will love this THC, since there's an 18-hole championship golf course right at hand, and a 9-hole family golf course on the grounds. Guest room rates begin at NZ$70 ($43.75), single or double, for standard rooms and rise to NZ$150 ($93.75), single or double, for those deluxe suites, all plus GST. As with all THCs, however, there are often special package rates on offer, so be sure to inquire before booking.

WHERE TO EAT

There's a **Cobb & Co.** in the Lake Establishment Hotel on the corner of Tongariro and Tuwharetoa Streets (tel. 86-165), just across the street from the PRO. In addition to the standard fare of the chain, the Taupo Cobb & Co. adds local specials daily on a blackboard menu. Another special feature here: the chef will cook that trout you caught in the lake—talk about fresh! Hours, as usual, are 7:30 a.m. to 10 p.m. seven days a week. It's fully licensed, and main courses average about NZ$10 ($6.25).

A very special place for lunch is the **Huka Homestead** at the Historic Village (a sightseeing must) on Huka Falls Road (tel. 82-245). You'll love the farmhouse atmosphere, and the smörgåsbord table offers a wealth of homemade breads, scones, soups, salads, cheeses, meats, and desserts. You can lunch exceedingly well for about NZ$12 ($7.50) and get in some of the best sightseeing hereabouts at the same time. Hours are 10 a.m. to 4 p.m. seven days a week.

Margarita's Bar and Restaurant, located above the Real Estate House at 63 Heu Heu St. (tel. 89-909), specializes in Mexican and not-so-Mexican food, creative cocktails, inviting atmosphere, and reasonable prices. Open daily from 5 p.m. to 1 a.m. The average price of a meal is NZ$10 ($6.25) to NZ$15 ($9.40). It's fully licensed, but BYO bottled wines are acceptable.

Echo Cliff, 5 Tongariro St. (tel. 88-539), is right at the lake, upstairs over Sullivan's Sports. Good value here, with a menu that includes all the New Zealand standards (seafood, lamb, veal, chicken, beef, etc.), plus Dutch Indonesian and continental dishes, all at prices that let you dine very well on three courses for around NZ$25 ($15.75). Fully licensed. Dinner from 5:30 p.m. to 9 p.m.; closed Tuesday.

The **Lakeside Café,** 3 Tongariro St. (tel. 86-894), is right on the corner overlooking the lake. Open seven days a week, their specialty is breakfasts—American (hash browns, pancakes, etc.), English, or continental, plus freshly squeezed fruit juice, homemade pastries, and delicious coffee. Also good for lunch. Everything here is homemade and moderately priced.

Craig's, 38-40 Tuwharetoa St. (tel. 85-276), is a casual, modern place with linen tablecloths and flowers on the table, an interesting menu, and friendly service. Among the dishes featured are steak, pheasant, venison, and several other game main courses. Lunch, served daily except Sunday, costs NZ$8.95 ($5.60) and includes a complimentary glass of wine, juice, or soft drink. Expect to pay around NZ$25 ($15.75) for dinner. Opens for dinner at 6 p.m. Tuesday through Saturday. BYO.

It's easy to overlook the **Cat's Whiskers Café,** tucked between Heu Heu and Horomatangi Streets in 4 Marama Arcade (tel. 86-152). This well-kept little secret has sandwiches that you mix from fresh ingredients, quiches, cookies, daily blackboard specials, muffins, and herbal tea (hard to find in this part of the world). It's open from 9 a.m. to 4 p.m. Monday through Friday, until 2 p.m. on Saturday.

The **Potato Palace,** where Lakeside Terrace meets Tongariro Street (tel. 81-139), serves only two items: filled potatoes and ice cream, and the prices are as low as you'll find. It's open Monday through Wednesday from 11 a.m. to 6 p.m., until 7 p.m. Thursday through Sunday.

The **Pioneer Café,** on Paorahape Street right around the corner from the bus station, is a down-home place with lace curtains and tablecloths, booths, a pot-bellied stove, vintage photos of Taupo, and friendly service. Tables and umbrellas are set up outside in good weather. The sign over the kitchen door attests "Welcome, fishermen, to Taupo. Good fishing." Cafeteria-style selections include sandwiches on whole-wheat bread, mince pies, chicken kebabs, soup, burgers, macaroni and cheese, fish and chips, and beef Stroganoff. Owners Judi and Peter Lee make you feel welcome. The café opens early, at 6 a.m., for the anglers, and closes at 5 p.m. (3 p.m. in midwinter).

For the evening meal, **Brookes,** 22 Tuwharetoa St. (tel. 85-919), comes up with hearty dishes at moderate prices: dinner will run about NZ$18 ($11.25), and there are children's plates for half price. Grilled filet, hapuka steak, pan-fried turkey, and some seafood dishes are featured on the menu, and doors open at 6 p.m. seven days a week. BYO.

A Big Splurge

One of the best and most beautifully prepared meals I've had in New Zealand was in the award-winning **Edgewater** restaurant in Manuels Motor Inn, on Lake Terrace (tel. 85-110). My avocado appetizer with fresh salsa verde and lamb dish with wild mushrooms and wild-rice crêpe were so beautifully presented I barely had the heart to disturb them with my fork. They were deliciously memorable, as was my window-seat view of the lake and the moon rising above it. Expect to pay NZ$45 ($28) for a three-course meal with a couple of glasses of wine. The restaurant, richly decorated in deep green and mauve, is open nightly from 6:30 p.m.; reserve ahead.

THINGS TO SEE AND DO

Well, there's **fishing.** And even if you've never cast a line, this may be the very time to join that "picket fence" and experience the singular thrill of feeling a nibble and pulling in a big one. And they do grow big in Lake Taupo—the *average* trout size is 4½ pounds, with 8 and 10 pounds not unheard of. Just remember that there's a limit of eight rainbow trout and five brook trout per person per day.

Most restaurants are happy to cook up your catch of the day; they aren't allowed to offer it on their menu (which is probably why so many trout live to grow so big). The PRO can fix you up with a license (you can get one for just one day if you like) and fill you in on rules and regulations, as well as help you find a guide if you'd just rather not be a "picket." Brian Leverell at **Taupo River Guides,** 39 Ngamoto Rd. (tel. 074/84-519), is one of the best in the area and charges about NZ$40 ($25) an hour, which includes transport, all fishing equipment, and lunch if you're fishing when that time rolls around.

There are **lake cruises** aboard the steamer *Ernest Kemp* every morning and afternoon, seven days a week. It's a 2¼-hour sail, well worth the fare of NZ$18 ($11.25) per person (there are special family prices on holidays)—a great way to experience the lake itself and get a very different look at its shoreline. Check at the PRO for exact sailing times and booking, or go along to the Boat Harbour.

The *Taupo Cat* glides all around the lake from 9 a.m. to 3 p.m., serving morning tea, a large buffet lunch, and afternoon tea along its route. The inclusive price of this outing is NZ$55 ($34.50); there is also a sunset cruise. The catamaran departs from Pier 87, an easy walk from the PRO; make reservations and double-check the schedule at the PRO or call 86-052.

Truly thrilling **scenic flights** leave the lakefront by Taupo Boat Harbour, ranging from a ten-minute flight over Wairakei's steaming valley, Huka Falls, and Taupo, to one-hour forays as far away as Tongariro National Park, to a two-hour excursion that takes you even farther afield. Prices begin at NZ$20 ($12.50) to NZ$96 ($60) —children pay half. You'll find the **Float Plane Office** (ARK Aviation Limited, P.O. Box 238) at the Boat Harbour (tel. 87-500 or 89-441).

The PRO puts out an excellent booklet, *Walking Trails,* outlining city and near-city **walks** as well as tramping trails in the area. There are long walks and short walks, walks close to town and others as far away as Tongariro National Park. What a peaceful interlude to take the 45-minute forest walk, and for sheer scenery excitement there's the contrast of thrilling thermal activity and serene pine plantations along the Craters of the Moon track. The booklet gives clear, concise directions (with maps for most tracks), as well as estimated times and such helpful information as the fact that all of Mount Tauhara is a Maori Reserve and I trust you will treat it with proper respect, leaving only footprints (and perhaps a bit of your heart). A terrific idea is to intersperse sightseeing or other sports activities with a walk into the very soul and being of New Zealand, its forests, mountains, and rivers.

To see firsthand the awesome power of all that steam you've only glimpsed in Rotorua, take the five-mile drive out to the **Wairakei Geothermal Project** (tel. 48-216). When work began in 1950 to harness all that power, this was the second-largest such project in the world and the first to use wet steam. Scientists from around the globe came to observe. Using some 60 bores and over 12 miles of pipeline, the project now supplies a great deal of the North Island's electricity requirements. Stop by the Information Centre (on the left as you drive into the valley), which is open from 9 a.m. to noon and 1 to 4:30 p.m. every day of the year, including holidays. The display and audio-visual show give a compelling overview of local geothermal activity and furnish answers to all the obvious questions that spring to mind (ask for the sheet titled "Questions Often Asked"). Study the excellent borefield model and drilling-process diagram, then leave the center and follow the marked road, which crosses the borefield itself, to a lookout from which you can view the entire site. You can also visit the power station itself during the hours listed above.

The **Wairakei International Golf Course,** at the THC Wairakei (tel. 48-152), is challenging, not to mention dramatic, with thermal vapors rising in the background. Visitors are welcome and rental equipment is available; call ahead.

Just in front of the De Brett Thermal Hotel, a short way out of town on Hwy. 5, a cut has been made through the pumice on the south side of the road and pumice strata has been marked and dated showing **volcanic debris** dating as far back as 1480 B.C. and as "recently" as A.D. 131. It's an eerie feeling to gaze on physical evidence of the earth's history! The De Brett, itself, is worth a short visit, since its grounds incorporate the fabulous **Onekeneke Valley of Hot Pools.**

Be sure to visit **Huka Homestead,** a replica pioneer village in which authentic buildings from New Zealand's days of early European settlement have been restored and brought back to life with working exhibits of village life as it was then. One cottage holds a shop stocked with handcrafts. There are picnic facilities in this lovely, shaded site, but I strongly recommend that you time your visit to include lunch at the pioneer tea and lunch room (see "Where to Eat," above). The village is out the Huka Falls Road about a mile and a half from the center of town. There is free transportation at 10:30 a.m. and noon from the PRO, but you have to reserve in advance.

Huka Falls themselves aren't huge but are impressive for the speed at which the water moves over the 35-foot drop—62,000 gallons per second. The word "huka" means "foaming" in Maori, and the water does resemble the agitation cycle of a washing machine. If you're in the mood to walk, follow the walkway from town; it should take about an hour. If you feel like walking farther, from here you can walk to **Aratiatia Rapids,** but allow two hours to get there. Time your arrival for 10 a.m. or 2:30 p.m., when water is released from the dam, creating quite a difference in water level.

If you find geothermal areas compelling—especially if you didn't see any around Rotorua—visit **Craters of the Moon,** on a mile of unpaved road off Hwy. 1 between the Wairakei Geothermal Power Station and Taupo (watch for the sign). The area looks like the aftermath of a fire, quite eerie, especially with the gurgling sounds the bubbling mud makes. Get out of your car to experience it fully, but be sure to stay on the marked paths. There's no admission charge, whereas you pay NZ$4 ($2.50) at the nearby **Wairakei Thermal Valley.**

Minibus tours of the region around Lake Taupo are given daily by **Paradise Tours** and led by knowledgeable and affable guide Sue King. Book through the PRO or call Sue after hours at 89-955. The tours, given every morning and afternoon, last 2½ hours.

For getting around Taupo by bicycle, contact **Roy's Cycle World,** on Ruapehu Street (tel. 86-117; after hours, 84-402).

AFTER DARK

Nightlife is low-key at best in Taupo. Most of it is on Northcrost Street at the Suncourt Motor Hotel in **Gulliver's Bar,** where there's a disco on Thursday night, and in **Swift's,** where there's another disco on Friday and Saturday nights. You can also stop for a drink at the **Red Barrel Wine Bar,** where Lakeside Terrace and Tongariro Street meet. If you've been fishing for trout on Lake Taupo all day, you'll be ready for bed by nightfall anyway.

READER'S SHOPPING SUGGESTION: "I found Taupo to have a small but nice selection of clothing stores with good prices, and **The Pottery,** at 87 Tongariro St. (tel. 83-921), had the best prices for pottery I saw in New Zealand. Wayne Porteous's work—everything from cups to tiles to plates—is wonderful" (S. Craft, Boston, Mass.).

READER'S FISHING SUGGESTION: "My wife is a wheelchair person, and most of the time when I went fishing, she stayed in the motel alone. However, at Lake Taupo, Roger Jones, of **Taupo Lakeside Services** (tel. 85-596), insisted that she always come along, and the fact that she was in a wheelchair made no difference. He lifted her, chair and all, into the boat and she had a glorious time on the water, all because of Roger's thoughtfulness" (C. Blacharsh, West Hempstead, N.Y.).

2. Taupo to Tongariro

The 58-mile drive from Taupo to Tongariro National Park is an easy one—good roads with changing scenery as you follow Hwy. 1 along the eastern shore of Lake Taupo through small towns and fishing settlements, around charming bays, always with that vast lake on your right. Look for **Motutaiko Island** (the only one in the lake) as you approach Hatepe. As you near the southern end of the lake, you'll begin to catch glimpses of volcanic cones, which are at the heart of the park. Highway 47 cuts off from Hwy. 1 to lead you through plateau-like tussocklands across to Hwy. 48 and the entrance to park headquarters and the elegant Château. It's clearly signposted, and as you leave Lake Taupo behind, the volcanic nature of this terrain begins to dominate the landscape. By the time you reach the Château, you've entered another world from that of the lakeside you've just left.

READERS' DRIVING SUGGESTION: "We felt that the drive up to **Turoa skifield on Mount Ruapehu** was a prettier drive than the one to the Château and you got much more the feeling of being on a volcano. There are several waterfalls to stop off and walk to" (J. and P. Conrad, San Jose, Calif.).

READER'S SHOPPING SUGGESTION: "I highly recommend the **Sporting Life Sport Shop**, in Turangi at no. 70 Turangi Mall, for accurate, very friendly, and reliable service. The selection of fishing supplies to rent and for sale is excellent, and if the owner, Graham, doesn't know, it's not worth knowing" (S. Martin, Portland, Ore.).

WHERE TO STAY EN ROUTE

At the southern end of Lake Taupo, the **Settlers Motel,** State Hwy. 1 and Arahori Street (P.O. Box 30), Turangi (tel. 0746/7745), is a Best Western. The eight serviced kitchen units all have telephones, radios, and heaters, and there's a guest laundry. They can provide fishing guides, and they've even included fish-cleaning facilities so you can catch your dinner, then cook it up in your unit. Licensed restaurants and shops are a short walk away. Rates range from NZ$50 ($31.25) single, NZ$60 ($37.50) double, for studios, to NZ$56 ($35) and NZ$66 ($41.25) for one-bedroom units, all plus GST. There are also two-bedroom units, and one with a waterbed. Best Western discounts apply, of course.

The **Bridge Fishing Lodge Motor Inn,** State Hwy. 1 (P.O. Box 42), Turangi (tel. 0746/8804), has 34 rooms for single or double occupancy, 7 with fully equipped kitchens. Rooms have tea and coffee facilities, fridges, private baths, telephones, TVs, videos, radios, and heaters. There's a licensed restaurant, bar, guest lounge, sauna, barbecue, laundry, and a tour desk at this Motor Lodges member. They'll also rent you fishing tackle and waders if the fish in the lake and river prove too great a temptation. Rates range from NZ$70 ($43.75), single or double, to NZ$100 ($62.50) for a family suite that will sleep six, all plus GST.

3. Tongariro National Park

This was New Zealand's first national park (the world's second, after Yellowstone), and the original 1887 deed from Te Heuheu Tukino IV and other Tuwharetoa tribal chiefs transferred only some 6,500 acres (all the land within a one-mile radius of the volcanic peaks), an area that has now been expanded to 30,453 acres. It's a dramatic landscape, dominated by the three active volcanoes that rise with stark beauty from health-like plains. Drama-loving Maoris considered the volcanoes to be sacred (*tapu*), found mythical explanations for their origins, and chose caves on their slopes as burial sites for their chiefs.

Ruapehu, with its 9,175-foot snow-capped summit, is the highest mountain on the North Island and provides its principal skiing facilities while holding in its basin the simmering, ice-ringed Crater Lake. Its most recent eruption was in 1971. **Ngauruhoe,** rising 7,515 feet, smolders constantly and from time to time sends showers of ash and lava spilling from its crater (the last in 1954) to alter its shape once again. **Tongariro,** lowest of the three (6,458 feet), is also the most northerly and the center of an engaging Maori legend. There were once, so the story goes, many mountains in the North Island's center, all male with the exception of Pihanga, who was wed to Tongariro and was the object of the other mountains' lustful fantasies. According to one version of the legend, Pihanga's heart belonged only to Tongariro, who defeated the other mountains and exiled them from the region. Another version has Pihanga discovered by Tongariro dallying with Taranaki, which resulted in a fierce fight that ended with a swift, hard kick to Taranaki's backside and his hasty retreat to the west coast, where he stands in solitary splendor today as Mount Egmont, an almost perfect replica of Japan's Mount Fuji. You can follow his trail, which became the Wanganui River, and still see the enormous depression under Mount Egmont's Fantham's Peak put there by Tongariro's kick. When mists surround Egmont today, Maoris will tell you he is weeping for his lost love.

For non-legend-believers, there is the nonlegendary fact that these are at the end of a volcanic chain that extends all the way to the islands of Tonga, 1,000 miles away. Their origin is fairly recent, as these things go, dating back only about two million years.

ORIENTATION

You'll find the **THC Château Tongariro** and the **National Park Headquarters** in the little village of **Whakapapa** at the end of Hwy. 48. The Château is the center of visitor activities such as booking ski and tour trips, dining, and drinking; the Visitors' Centre of the park headquarters is the center of information and assistance in planning tramps through the park. They keep up-to-date weather-conditions data, and provide detailed maps, guiding services, camping permission, and hunting permits. The popular ski fields (used by as many as 6,000 visitors per day during season) are 4½ miles above the village.

WHERE TO STAY

Accommodations are as scarce as the proverbial hen's teeth! There is, of course, the elegant **THC Château Tongariro,** Mount Ruapehu, Tongariro National Park (tel. 0812-23/809), and if this is a big stop on your itinerary, you might consider a night or two at big-splurge prices, ranging seasonally from NZ$83 ($52) to NZ$115 ($72), single or double, plus GST. It's a grand hotel in the manner of years gone by, but with a 1930s deco-style lounge. Rooms and suites are elegant, and there are such additional comforts as a heated pool and sauna. The Château justifies its listing in a budget travel guide on two counts: it's an outstanding hotel, internationally famous; and it's one of those scarce hen's teeth in this neighborhood!

Now, on to accommodations more in our budget range, few though they may be. Need I say that *early* bookings are absolutely necessary during the skiing season? Actually, it's a good idea to reserve as far in advance as possible in any season, what with accommodations being so scanty. You might also consider a Turangi base, only a short drive from the park (see above).

Cabins

Whakapapa Motor Camp, c/o Department of Conservation, Private Bag, Mount Ruapehu (tel. 0812-22/3897), is down the first right turn after you pass park headquarters. Set on the banks of Whakapapanui Stream, it's surrounded by lush bushland. There are tent and caravan sites (all nicely screened by foliage), four six-berth cabins, and two four-berth cabins. Cabins come with two-tier bunks, table and chairs, and electric heating. On the premises are toilets and showers, electric stoves, a laundry with drying room, and a small camp store. Rates: NZ$6 ($3.75) for tent sites, NZ$8 ($5) for caravan sites, and NZ$9 ($5.65) per person, NZ$28 ($17.50) minimum, for cabins. Tourist flats are available for NZ$12 ($7.50) per person, NZ$38 ($23.75) minimum, and bunk-room accommodation is available from November to the end of June for NZ$10 ($6.25) per person per night.

Trampers on the mountain slopes can arrange through the park headquarters rangers to use rustic, strategically placed **huts**, which are equipped with bunks and coal stoves, and cost a mere NZ$8 ($5) per person. Tickets are available at the Taupo Information Centre.

Lodges

The rustic **Ruapehu Skotel** (mailing address: c/o Mount Ruapehu Post Office; tel. 0812-22/3719), located on the lower slopes of Mount Ruapehu above the Château, offers both self-contained chalets and lodge accommodations. The attractive, paneled, slant-roofed lodge rooms can accommodate two, three, or four; most have H&C and many have shower and toilet. There's a large, bright guest kitchen with individual food lockers, stoves, and fridge. Also on the premises are a laundry with washers and dryers, a sauna, private spas, a gym, and a large game room. The lounge invites conviviality, and there's a restaurant and bar. Chalets sleep six (four bunks and two single beds); kitchens are completely equipped, and there's a TV. Outside, views of Ngauruhoe's cone are spectacular. All buildings are centrally heated and have piped-in music. This is a lively place, with movies, hikes, fishing, and botany expeditions. Summer rates begin at NZ$36 ($22.50) double with H&C, NZ$65 ($40.75) double with private facilities, NZ$82 ($51.25) double in a chalet, and NZ$7 ($4.40) per extra person. Rates include GST, but expect them to be higher during ski season.

There is also a combination of facilities at **Mountain Heights**, on Hwy. 4 (P.O. Box 7), Tongariro National Park (tel. 0812-22/833). The 14 lodge rooms sleep up to seven and are comfortably furnished. Six self-contained units have complete kitchens and one bedroom that sleeps four. In each, there's electric heating, electric blankets, TV, and toilet and shower. No kitchen facilities for lodge rooms, but the dining room serves breakfast and dinner. There is a laundry and drying room, and ski rental is available. Lodge rates start at NZ$40 ($25) for a double room.

A Motel with Meals

The **Buttercup Alpine Motel**, P.O. Box 45, Tongariro National Park (tel. 0812-22/702), sits at the junction of Hwys. 4 and 47 at National Park township. This friendly place provides a host of planned activities such as white-water rafting, skiing, and hiking expeditions, as well as a nice selection of accommodations. There are eight Red Pool Lodge units sleeping up to four, with private plumbing, tea and coffee facilities, TV, and piped-in music; bathrooms are shared. The Long Lodge, for singles or couples, has bedrooms with a double bed, wash basin, and TV; again, baths are shared. Both lodges are surrounded by native trees and fern gardens. The attractive Butternut Farmhouse Restaurant and Den has a pot-bellied stove, with musical performances through dinner and sing-alongs around the fire afterward. Hot gluhwein is served, and sometimes there are fancy-dress parties. Rates are NZ$60 ($37.50) per person, NZ$40 ($25) for children under 13; babies are free. The tariff includes dinner, bed, and breakfast, so this is a great value.

WHERE TO EAT

You can eat at any price range at the **Château.** For the truly budget-minded, there's the paneled, no-frills **Cafeteria,** open every day from 8 a.m. to 5 p.m., where you'll find meat pies, sandwiches, salads, and such at low prices. The cozy, pub-like **Carvery** serves a quite nice NZ$20 ($12.50) evening meal with a choice of roasts, fish, grills, and salads. For an elegant—and expensive—dinner, it's the high-ceilinged, chandeliered **Ruapehu Room,** from 6:30 to 9 p.m. The à la carte menu features New Zealand specialties, as well as many exotic dishes, which are prepared or flamed at your table.

The Château can also supply you with box lunches for a day on the slopes, and during ski season there are kiosks and snackbars open at the ski fields.

THINGS TO SEE AND DO

Skiing is *the* activity during the season, which normally lasts from June 15 to the end of October, with three well-developed fields inside the park. The most popular is Whakapapa Skifield, on the northwestern side of Mount Ruapehu just 4½ miles beyond the Château. For snow and ski information, call 0658/58-255. The Château can also rent you ski equipment, provide instruction and a current brochure detailing all charges. If you have your own equipment with you, expect to spend about NZ$40 ($25) for lifts and tows for a full day. All facilities operate from 8:30 a.m. to 4:30 p.m. unless weather conditions interfere, and there's public transportation via coach to the ski field from the Château, which I heartily recommend that you use, since driving and parking can be a real problem.

In any other season, there are fascinating **walks** to view more than 500 plant species, the giant rimu trees (some well over 600 years old), and 30 bird species within the park's boundaries. Then there's that hot **Crater Lake** on Mount Ruapehu, the **Ketetahi Hot Springs,** and a pleasant, 20-minute **Ridge Track.** Ambitious trackers can take a whack at climbing all three volcanoes in one day—but believe me, it takes a *lot* of ambition, with a healthy dose of stamina thrown in! Check with the park headquarters for details on all park possibilities.

---

4. Tongariro to Wanganui

The 89 miles from Tongariro National Park to Wanganui pass through some of the most scenic countryside in the North Island. Indeed, the 32 miles of winding road between Raetihi and Wanganui pass through what has been labeled the "Valley of a Thousand Hills." These are the **Parapara Hills,** formed from volcanic ash, with shellrock seams and great walls of "papa" rock (a blue clay), which can, incidentally, be quite slippery when landslides put it across the highway. This entire drive, however, is one to be done at a leisurely pace (with an eye out, especially in winter, for patches of that clay across the road) so as to enjoy the spectacular scenery. Sheep farms line your way, with at least one deer farm visible from the highway. There are numerous rest areas en route, offering delightful panoramic views, and in autumn, silver birches dot the landscape with brilliant golds and oranges.

You'll pass the beautiful **Raukawa Falls,** skirt three small lakes whose waters shade from green into red into black over the course of the year and are held sacred by the Maoris, then cross the Wanganui River over the Dublin Street Bridge to enter Wanganui.

READERS' DRIVING SUGGESTION: "An area that deserves a look is known as **Taranaki,** the area from Tongariro to New Plymouth, a lovely town with gardens and parks that were the nicest we found on the North Island. The circle drive with three good roads into Mount Egmont are all worth taking. And Mount Egmont itself is superb, just like a volcano cone; it's quite impressive to stand on the beach and look 8,400 feet up the mount. The Whitecliff drive and hike are also super" (J. and P. Conrad, San Jose, Calif.).

5. Wanganui

Wanganui is one of New Zealand's oldest cities and was settled amid much controversy over just how title to the land was obtained by Col. William Wakefield on behalf of the New Zealand Company in 1840. It seems he took ashore an assortment of mirrors, blankets, pipes, and other trinkets and piled them on the site of the present-day Moutoa Gardens. With this offering, he "bought" some 40,000 acres of Maori land. The Maoris, however, replaced Wakefield's gifts with 30 pigs and nearly ten tons of potatoes—their customary "gift for gift"—and had no idea they had transferred title to their lands. Despite the dispute, settlers began arriving and the town prospered, even though constantly caught up in Maori-Pakeha conflicts, some of which were quite violent. It wasn't until 1848 that land problems were laid to rest with the payment of £1,000 for about 80,000 acres clearly defined in a bill of sale from the Maoris, which ended with the words "Now all the land contained within these boundaries . . . we have wept and sighed over, bid farewell to and delivered up forever to the Europeans."

It was, of course, the Wanganui River (whose riverbed was carved out by Taranaki in his wild flight from Tongariro's wrath) that made this site such a desirable one for the Europeans. It had long served as an important waterway to the interior, as well as affording an excellent coastal harbor. It was said by the Maoris that the great explorer Kupe sailed the river. Pakehas soon established regular steamer service between the town and Taumarunui, and because of the magnificent scenery along the riverbank, the three-day journey quickly became an important sightseeing trip for tourists from all over the world. The steamer plied the river until 1934, and it's a pity that fire destroyed the wonderful old hotel and houseboat that provided overnight accommodations to those travelers. A large portion of the Wanganui River is part of a national park.

ORIENTATION

Today's Wanganui has every bit as much friendly hospitality as it has age and history. Indeed, its slogan is "The Friendly City," and **Hospitality Wanganui** (a volunteer group of enthusiastic residents) operates a Host Panel to squire overseas visitors around. They provide a personal guide who will devote as much time as necessary to seeing that you get to see and do everything there is to see and do in Wanganui. There's never a charge. You'll find the **Information Office** in the forecourt of the Municipal Chambers at 100 Guyton St. (tel. 064/53-286) and they'll assign you a personal host or hostess. Your guide will furnish transportation and often steer you to special events you might not have known about otherwise. Every volunteer is knowledgeable about the area, so if you have a special interest (history, archeology, botany), they'll happily take you to spots most likely to appeal to that interest.

The Information Office can also furnish useful brochures, book river tours, and provide maps.

WHERE TO STAY

That famed Wanganui hospitality extends to virtually every owner or manager of accommodations I have met, and you can be sure of a friendly reception no matter where you end up staying. There are good digs both in town and in the Castlecliff seaside suburb.

The Y

A big old gracious house right in the city center serves as Wanganui's **YWCA,** 232 Wicksteed St. (parallel to Victoria Avenue), Wanganui (tel. 064/57-480). There are only nine rooms available, with one bed per room, and it's necessary to write or call as far in advance as possible. Rooms are simple, but homey and comfortable. Those on the top story have marvelous views. There is a guest kitchen, laundry, and TV lounge. There's no age limit, and the rate is NZ$9 ($5.63) per person.

Cabins

The **Alwyn Motor Court and Motel Flats,** 65 Karaka St., Castlecliff, Wanganui (tel. 064/44-500), offers excellent value-for-money under the auspices of Joyce and N. J. Fiddes, who bought this business because they love to meet people from overseas. Just four miles from the city center, and close to a city bus line, the Alwyn is only a short walk through the bush from Castlecliff Beach. All units face a concrete courtyard and swimming pool, and all are bright, with two-tier bunks, and communal shower and toilet. Rates for these units are NZ$22 ($13.75) double, NZ$7 ($4.40) per extra adult, NZ$4.50 ($2.80) per extra child. Three have shower and toilet as well as a stove, and cost NZ$30 ($18.75) double. All cabins have electric heaters, fridge, cooking pots, toasters, dishes, and cutlery. You must supply linen and blankets, but the Fiddeses have them for rent at a small charge. Off the courtyard there's a laundry and TV-games room, with table tennis and a pool table. In addition to the cabins, there are four lovely two-bedroom motel flats, nicely decorated. All have full kitchens, showers, TVs, and all bedding. The one on the top floor has a marvelous sea view. These rent for NZ$46 ($28.75) double, NZ$11 ($6.90) per extra adult, NZ$7 ($4.40) for children under 12. The Fiddeses are friendly and extremely cooperative when it comes to working out weekly and off-season rates, and all rates include GST.

Four miles east of town, on the city side of the river, the **Aramoho Honday Park** (write c/o Camp Manager), 460 Somme Parade, Wanganui (tel. 064/38-402) has spacious, shady grounds. There are bunk cabins, each with four bunks; graded cabins that sleep two to six people, with H&C, small electric stoves, cooking utensils, and heaters; and tourist flats and chalets that sleep up to seven people, with complete kitchen, china, cutlery, pots, toaster, electric jug, and private toilet and shower. One chalet sleeps nine and is equipped for paraplegics. You can rent linen, blankets, and irons. The communal kitchen has gas stoves and fridge, the laundry includes dryers and an ironing board, and toilets and showers are stainless steel and Formica. Very near the river is a family barbecue, and there's a seven-day grocery store just across the road. Tent and caravan sites are also available in tree-shaded spots. Rates run NZ$7 ($4.40) per person for tent sites, NZ$10 ($6.25) single for bunks, NZ$30 ($18.75) double for cabins, and NZ$45 ($28.25) double for chalets. Rates all include GST.

See also the caravan and camping facilities at both the Lake Wiritoa and Avro Motels (see "Motel Flats," below).

A Bed-and-Breakfast

It is seldom that I run across an inn in the old-fashioned sense of the word, but the **Riverside Inn,** 2 Plymouth St., Wanganui (tel. 064/32-529), fits that category admirably. Set back from the street in a flower garden, the rambling wooden house, which dates from the early 1900s, has been lovingly brought up-to-date through renovation, with due respect for its age and character. Its convenient location is just a short walk from the center of town. Accommodations consist of ten rooms, only one with private shower and toilet, and the decor features lace curtains at windows, fringed lampshades, and potted plants. The parlor is furnished in wicker and cane, and there is a TV lounge and breakfast room with tea and coffee facilities. In summer, owners Maree and Don Adams serve tea or barbecues in the garden. Don also runs Rivercity Tours and is a whiz at helping you find just the right activity, be it sightseeing, hiking, or canoeing for one to five days. Inn rates, including continental breakfast and GST, are NZ$32 ($20) single, NZ$43.50 ($27.25) double. Cooked breakfast and dinner are available for an extra charge. Those on a tighter budget may pay NZ$11 ($6.90) per person for bunk space in cabins; breakfast or dinner, if desired, is extra.

Motel Flats

There's much to choose from at the **Avro Motel,** 36 Alma Rd., Wanganui (tel. 064/55-279). The garden-like grounds hold bed-sitters and one-, two-, and three-bedroom units, all with wide windows overlooking the lawns, TV, and telephone. There's an outdoor swimming pool, two spa pools, a children's play area, and a laundry. Alison and Graham Shaw are the hosts at this nice motel, just about a mile from the city center and on a city bus line. Rates start at NZ$60 ($37.50) single, NZ$70 ($43.75) double. During the winter months, weekly rates can be arranged. Incidentally, the Avro has marvelous caravan facilities: 14 hookups, each with a small cabin enclosing a shower, toilet, and dressing room. Caravan guests may also use the laundry, and there's a nine-hole golf course nearby. Rates are NZ$20 ($12.50) double. All prices include GST.

One of Wanganui's prettiest motels is the **Acacia Park Motel,** 140 Anzac Parade, Wanganui East (tel. 064/39-093), set in two acres of parkland overlooking the river, with units spread among magnificent old trees. The attractive brown wooden units have TV, radio, electric blanket, electric heating, and telephone. Eight are fully self-contained, sleeping four to six, with shower, toilet, fridge, electric range, and full kitchen. Five serviced units sleep up to three and have a fridge, tea and coffee facilities, toaster, and electric fry pan. There's a guest laundry with dryer and drying room, a spa pool, games room with a pool table, children's play area, and a trampoline. Rates begin at NZ$50 ($31.25) single, NZ$60 ($37.50) double, for serviced units; and NZ$65 ($40.75) double for kitchen units—all plus GST. The Acacia is about a mile from the city center, on a bus line and directly across the road from the Wanganui River Jet Boat Tours and paddleboat jetty.

Another motel with an especially attractive setting is the **River City Motel,** 59 Halswell St., Wanganui (tel. 064/39-107), just across from the Peat Park Deer Reserve. The grounds are planted with flowering bushes and trees, with views of wooded hills and fields filled with grazing sheep. This rural-type setting is just one mile from the center of town, and about a two-minute walk from a city bus stop. The eight two-bedroom units can sleep up to six (one will accommodate eight), and they come with a full kitchen, electric heater, electric blanket, phone, radio, and TV. On the premises are a swimming pool, spa pool, putting green, trampoline, children's swings, and a barbecue, as well as a laundry and car-wash facilities. Rates are NZ$56 ($35) single, NZ$77 ($48.25) double, including GST.

One of Wanganui's newest and prettiest motels is a Best Western. The **Gateway Motor Lodge,** on the corner of the Southern Motorway and Heads Road (P.O. Box 970), Wanganui (tel. 064/58-164), has attractive units with vaulted, beamed ceilings. Serviced units have satellite TV, radio, telephone, and tea- and coffee making facilities. Two-bedroom family units add a full kitchen. Rates are NZ$60 ($37.50) single, NZ$67 ($42) double, for serviced units; NZ$90 ($56.25) double, NZ$12 ($7.50) per extra person, for family units, plus GST.

A Licensed Hotel

You should know right up front that what follows is the exact opposite of an objective viewpoint: it is an unabashedly subjective, totally in-love-with report from yours truly of one of those great old hotels, which has managed to survive with all the spirit and character of the "grand" hotels of yesteryear. **Hurley's Grand Hotel,** on the corner of Guyton and St. Hill Streets (P.O. Box 364), Wanganui (tel. 064/ 50-955), was owned and operated by Tim Hurley's father for many years before Tim took over; guests still receive all the care and attention of friends who have come for a family visit. Modernization has been limited strictly to facilities and furnishings, with such lovely holdovers from its beginnings as dark-wood paneling and fireplaces in the spacious public rooms, oil paintings in gold-leafed frames, the marvelous old carved-wood staircase, and a bar crammed full of excellent carvings by local Maoris. Modern the furniture may be (like huge, comfortable chairs grouped around low tables in the lounge), yet the decor (upholstering, draperies, etc.) retains a period look in keeping with Hurley's origins. The 60 guest rooms range in size from those accommodating just one to those sleeping up to five comfortably. Each is individually decorated, a nice departure from the standardized look of most present-day hotel rooms. A two-family suite features two bedrooms, one on each side of the central lounge (at just NZ$10, or $6.25 U.S., per person above the regular rate), and one luxurious suite is furnished entirely with antiques. Rates range from NZ$70 ($43.75) to NZ$165 ($103), plus GST. In addition to the Bird Cage Bar (a great local favorite), there's a beautiful restaurant.

READERS' FARMSTAY SELECTION: "We loved staying with **Jill and Gerald Hare,** Te Rama, Nukumaru Road, Waitotara (tel. 064/23-837). They're a charming young couple who seem to enjoy meeting people from other countries, and they made us feel right at home. Their sheep and beef farm is about 30 km (18 miles, about 20 minutes' driving time) from Wanganui, and there's a lovely, casual, family feeling to their place. They can accommodate four adults or two adults and two children (no objection to children here)" (L. Cowley, Surrey, B.C., Canada). [*Author's Note:* Guests have their own bathroom and laundry privileges, and the rate of NZ$50 ($31.25) per person includes dinner, bed, and breakfast.]

WHERE TO EAT

My favorite small, inexpensive eatery in Wanganui is the **Top-o-Town Coffee Shop,** 198 Victoria Ave. (tel. 58-400), where everything is fresh and homemade. It's a cozy place with friendly people behind the self-service counter. They serve morning and afternoon teas and light meals. There are savouries, meat pies, sandwiches, pies, and some of the best homemade cakes and pastries you're likely to find anywhere, which range from NZ$3 ($1.90) to NZ$8 ($5). Open from 8 a.m. to 4 p.m. Monday through Friday and 9 a.m. to noon on Saturday, except on long weekends.

Hurley's Grand Hotel, at corner of Guyton and St. Hill Streets (tel. 50-955), merits a rave in the food department as well as for its superb accommodations (see above). No matter what your price or appetite range, that grand old hotel comes up with just the right place to eat. For inexpensive hot meals or bar snacks, there's **The Strand,** a bistro-bar combining the same rich dark woods as other hotel public rooms with a friendly, relaxed pub atmosphere. The same menu is served for lunch (11:30 a.m. to 2 p.m.) and dinner (5:30 to 8 p.m.), and features steaks, fish, chicken, and roasts for prices of NZ$6 ($3.75) to NZ$15 ($9.40). The Strand is open every day except Sunday. The **Bird Cage Restaurant,** on the other hand, can only be described as elegant, with lovely old chandeliers, flocked wallpaper, and a beautiful embossed ceiling, which will draw your eyes upward throughout any meal. Breakfast, lunch, and dinner are all served, but it's dinner that deserves special mention. Both the menu and service match the elegance of the room, yet there's not the slightest hint of stuffiness (which so often afflicts elegant restaurants). Dishes such as beef, fish, and a variety of roasts are reasonably priced from NZ$10 ($6.25) to NZ$20 ($12.50) on the à la carte menu. An excellent wine list complements your choice of entree. Open seven days a week and dinner is served from 6 to 9:30 p.m. On weekends, best reserve.

The **Garden Bistro Family Restaurant and Bar,** 33 Somme Parade (tel. 38-800), is a licensed restaurant set on the riverbank. You can order fish, steaks, roasts, and salad plates. But no matter what you choose, it will come in *huge* portions. The price, however, is anything but huge—an average meal will run about NZ$10 ($6.25). There's a special Kid's Menu for even less. Hours are noon to 2 p.m. and 5:30 to 9 p.m. daily except Sunday. After dinner, go next door to **Dali's** to listen to rock 'n' roll.

Note: There's an excellent deli and bottle store next door to the Garden Bistro, the **Riverside Cellars,** with all sorts of cheeses, cold cuts, salads, frozen meals, and other deli items for eating in your motel flat.

Meals are home-cooked, very nearly gourmet, and easy on the budget at the **Shangri-La** on St. John's Hill (tel. 53-654). And they're served in a lovely setting, with a window wall overlooking Virginia Lake and the winter gardens. Maurice Vige, the French owner-chef, took his training in Paris and is quite meticulous in the preparation of all the food appearing on his tables. As a result, everything from European specialties to basic Kiwi dishes to homemade pies to burgers and fries is culinary perfection. The morning and afternoon Devonshire teas (served from 9 a.m. to 5 p.m.) are a real treat—under NZ$4 ($2.50). Lunch is served from 11:30 a.m. to 2 p.m. BYO. Open seven days a week.

I'd list **Liffiton Castle,** 26 Liffiton St. (tel. 57-864), under a "Big Splurge" heading, except that prices aren't really *that* astronomical—so let's just call it a "Big Treat." This is a century-old house, which over the last five years has been renovated with loving care spiced up with a dollop of humor. You enter over a moat into a bar whose centerpiece is the bar itself, a renovated theater box from the old Majestic Theatre—notice the three jesters behind the bar (no, *not* the bartenders!), also from the Majestic. There are pressed-tin ceilings from the Wangani Girls College; a dance floor from the Boys Technical College; a handsome, hand-carved 17th-century mantel; arched windows from a local church; an antique English sideboard; and an Armoury Room. All that (plus a good bit more) creates an interesting, warm, inviting —and fun—atmosphere. And there's music for dancing most evenings. The food? Superb! Steaks are a specialty, all of superior grades and beautifully cooked. Seafood, chicken, wienerschnitzel, and roast beef are also on the menu, and there's a good wine list, reasonably priced. Main dinner courses are in the NZ$15 ($9.40) to NZ$20 ($12.50) range. Hours are 6 to 10 p.m. every day except Sunday, and it's a good idea to reserve, especially on weekends—the locals love this place!

THINGS TO SEE AND DO

To put first things first, take a look at Wanganui and its environs, which will bring everything else you see into perspective—it's the look you get from **Durie Hill,** at the south end of the Wanganui Bridge at Victoria Avenue. Pick up the souvenir booklet that tells you the history of this place, then go through a 672-foot tunnel to reach a unique elevator, which takes you to the summit, 216 feet up. From the platform at the top, Wanganui is spread before you: the historic river's winding path is clear; to the west stretches the Tasman Sea; and to the north rises Mount Egmont (that unlucky lover, Taranaki). Of course, if you're game to walk up 176 steps, the top of the nearby **War Memorial** will give you a view that extends from Mount Ruapehu all the way to the South Island (you'll have to take that on faith—as yet, I haven't summoned up the stamina to make the climb!). Even from the ground, the War Memorial is worth a few minutes of your time. It's constructed of shell rock from the riverbanks, which holds two-million-year-old fossils that prove conclusively Wanganui was once a part of the sea.

There are delightful **walks** in and around Wanganui. The *Scenic Walks* brochure you can get at the Information Office guides you around six, which are short and easy and cover most of the things you'll want to visit. Another, the **Atene Skyline Walk,** takes a full day (about eight hours), but rewards you with stunning views of the area and a "meander" around what was once seabed.

Children will enjoy the romp, grownups the respite, at the **Kowhai Park Playground** on Anzac Parade near the Dublin Street Bridge. The Jaycees of Wanganui built it, and its four acres now hold a Tot Town Railway (complete with station, tunnel, and overhead bridge), a huge whale, brontosaurus, clock tower, sea-serpent swings, all sorts of storybook characters, and even a mini-volcano to explore. And speaking of parks, save time for a leisurely stroll through the one at **Virginia Lake** (adjacent to Great North Road and St. John's Hill), whose grounds are a serene haven of trees, flowers, water lilies, ducks, swans, an aviary, and beautiful winter gardens.

You won't want to miss the **Wanganui Regional Museum,** in the Civic Center one block east of Victoria Avenue at the end of Maria Place. There's a large Maori collection, a settler's cottage, natural history exhibits, and a 75-foot war canoe built in 1810, which is one of the largest in the country and still has bullets from the Maori wars imbedded in its hull.

The riverside **Moutoa Gardens** historic reserve is where Maori-Pakeha contact was first made and the first controversial "purchase" of Maori land was transacted. There are memorials to Maori war dead, statues, and the city courthouse there now. It's down at Taupo Quay, off Victoria Quay (beside the huge computer center, a vivid contrast between yesterday and today).

Not quite—but almost—a sightseeing spot is **Victoria Court,** a new shopping courtyard off Victoria Avenue near Guyton Street. Interesting crafts and antiques are in the shop, and there's a very good art gallery featuring the works of New Zealand artists. About a mile from the city center, on Tawa Street, **Gonville Cottage Industries** holds a Craft Market the first Saturday of each month from March to December, with stalls held by local craftspeople.

The suburb of Putiki is the setting for **St. Paul's Anglican Memorial Church,** built in 1936 by Maoris and Pakehas working together. The stained-glass Williams Memorial Window features the figure of Christ wearing robes with a Maori-design border, and there is fine carving in the church's interior. It's open every day from 9 a.m. to 6 p.m.

Plan to spend an hour or two at **Holly Lodge Estate Winery,** Papaiti Road, Upper Aramoho, Wanganui (tel. 39-344). Drive out or take The Wine Trip paddlewheeler from the city marina at the foot of Victoria Avenue. Owners Norman and Alza Garrett will show you around the vineyards and outbuildings where wines are produced, explaining every step of the process as you go. The Wine Shop and Tasting Bar give you a chance to test several of the wines and buy at wholesale prices. Be sure to step into the small craft shop, where most items have been made locally, and the interesting Antique Porcelain Doll Emporium, to see how dolls are made entirely on the premises, from the pouring of porcelain clay to the sewing of their lovely period clothing (they go to retail outlets all over the country, but can be bought here at very reasonable prices). Another "don't miss" is Geraldo's, a small museum of memorabilia of early Wanganui assembled by Gerald Weekes, a former information officer (and, of course, named for him). The Garretts also run a very good jet-boat river trip (see below) from their wharf across the road from the vineyards.

Just about a mile past Holly Lodge, you'll find the **Waireka Estate,** Papaiti Road, Upper Aramoho, Wanganui (tel. 064/25-729). This is a charming privately run museum set in a 1912 single-story villa surrounded by extensive gardens. The museum collection (amassed by generations of the Robertson family) includes Maori artifacts and weaponry, European and military artifacts, antiques, Victoriana, African hunting trophies, and all sorts of odds and ends. One of the nicest features of a half-hour tour here is the "hands on" policy of the owners—you actually get to hold those Maori weapons. Devonshire teas are served on fine Royal Grafton bone china, outside on the lawn in fine weather, inside by the fire when things turn chilly. There are train rides around the gardens, croquet, and mini-golf. The charge for the tour is NZ$4 ($2.50); for the Devonshire tea, NZ$4.50 ($2.80). The estate is open daily from December 26 to the end of January; the remainder of the year, by prior arrangement only (a phone call will suffice). Visitors may reach the property aboard the M.V. *Waireka* riverboat, which departs from Moutoa Gardens in Wanganui at 10 a.m. and 2 p.m. daily during holiday periods; the trip costs NZ$11 ($6.90).

Two nearby scenic reserves warrant a visit. **Bushy Park** is 15 miles north of Wanganui (turn off Hwy. 3 at Kai Iwi and drive five miles to the park), and was originally the homestead of James Moore, who came to Wanganui in the mid-1860s. The fine old home was occupied by his descendants until 1962. It stands in spacious lawns and gardens planted with a large variety of native plants, with a backdrop of some 220 acres of native bush. The park is open every day, and admission is NZ$4 ($2.50) for adults, half that for children. There is accommodation for 16 in six bedrooms in the homestead for NZ$40 ($25) single; guests bring their own food and use a well-equipped kitchen. There are two caravan power connections, and a new bunkhouse accommodates groups of 12 for NZ$10 ($6.25) each. Write or call: The Manager, Bushy Park, Kai Iwi, RD 8, Wanganui (tel. 064/29-879).

The **Bason Botanical Reserve** is on Rapanui Road, and its Homestead Garden is a delightful place for a stroll among more than 100 camellias and a wide assortment of shrubs, vines, annuals, bulbs, and perennials. The ultramodern conservatory holds the interesting display center and tropical plant house. Open daily from 9:30 a.m. until dusk (conservatory hours are 10 a.m. to 4 p.m. weekdays, 2 to 4 p.m. weekends and holidays).

Exploring the River

Exploring the river by jet boat takes top priority for most visitors to Wanganui, and there are several options for doing it. But let me suggest that before you set out, drop by the Information Office and purchase the excellent Wanganui River map published by the Department of Lands & Survey (be sure you get #NZMS 258, Edition 2)—it's an excellent investment, showing the river and its banks in detail, with historical notes on each point of interest. I further suggest that you study the map *before* you book your river trip—while there is certainly no *un*interesting part of the river, there may be some portion you'd particularly like to see, and you'll want to be certain you choose a jet boat that will take you there. The Information Office can also give you current details on which jet-boat tours are operating, departure and return times, and prices in effect at the time of your visit (I try, but you know what can happen to prices!).

Te Awa Jet Boat Tours (tel. 27-769 or 25-758) has its terminal on Anzac Parade and offers a variety of good river tours. There are two all-day trips: one to the intriguing "Bridge to Nowhere" (240 km, or 145 miles; fare: NZ$95, or $59.50 U.S.) and one to Pipiriki and the "Drop Scene" (210 km, or 125 miles; fare: NZ$85, or $53.25). Shorter trips at lower prices range from a 35-minute boating tour around the bridges to a 1½-hour, 52-km (31-mile) ride, to the 4-hour, 120-km (72-mile) ride to Koroniti Marae. You'll be treated to a first-rate narrative all the way on points along the river, and the scenery is breathtaking, as are some of the rapids encountered (and easily overcome by your expert guides). They supply protective wet-weather gear, and on the longer trips, hot drinks and tea and coffee are furnished—you're asked to bring a packed lunch on the all-day jaunts. *Note:* You should carry a light sweater no matter what the weather, and be sure to wear comfortable clothing and shoes.

There's a lovely two-hour jet-boat tour from the terminal at Holly Lodge Estate Winery (see above), which takes you out to Hipango Park, with a tea, coffee, or sherry stop before returning. Your guide is not only informative but entertaining as well, with interesting anecdotes about the river and the country through which you are passing.

Another excellent way to explore the river is with **Rivercity Tours** (tel. 32-529 or 56-635). As either a substitute for or supplement to the jet-boat tours, these minibus road tours are highly recommended. The company also offers one-day boat trips on the river, as well as one- to five-day canoe adventures, suitable for people of all ages and experience. Call for schedules and prices.

READERS' DRIVING SUGGESTION: "If you've got the time, the drive from Wanganui up the Wanganui River to Pipiriki over to Raetiki and back down to Wanganui is breathtaking, with deep gorges, interesting Maori villages, oyster shells imbedded in limestone, but about 36 miles of road that was probably the worst we were on" (J. and P. Conrad, San Jose, Calif.).

READER'S SHOPPING SUGGESTIONS: "We arranged a private tour of **Woolen Mill Ltd.** on Kelvin Street, and we bought two 'rally rugs' (like stadium blankets). We also went to the **Sovereign Woodware,** 79 Tawa St. (tel. 42-558), where we bought three beautiful inlaid wooden pieces; they were seconds, but the flaws were so slight they didn't detract from their beauty at all. The savings were great" (C. Cluff, Tucson, Ariz.).

---

6. Wanganui to Wellington

Following Hwy. 3 south from Wanganui until it joins Hwy. 1, you're in for an easy three-hour, 122-mile drive along excellent roads: pastoral scenes of grazing sheep and cultivated fields at first, smashing sea views later, then a four-lane expressway leading into the beautiful harbor and splendid hills of wonderful, windy Wellington.

READER'S SIGHTSEEING SUGGESTION: "If you go from Wanganui to Wellington via Palmerston North over Rte. 2, about 28 km (17 miles) north of Masterton is the **Mount Bruce National Wildlife Centre,** well worth a stop. The center is a part of New Zealand's conservation efforts to make certain the nation's wildlife heritage is passed on to future generations, and there are numerous rare and endangered species of birds and lizards, many of which can be seen nowhere else in captivity. It's an enjoyable and educational stop, and you should allow one or two hours" (J. Long, Media, Pa.). [*Author's Note:* Other readers ditto this.]

READERS' DINING SUGGESTION: "Taking the scenic route to Wellington, you'll go through **Sanson,** where on the north edge of town is the **Brooklyne Teahouse.** It has delicious, very inexpensive homemade food, sweets that melt in your mouth, beautiful gardens, and even a children's play area" (J. and P. Conrad, San Jose, Calif.).

VI

WELLINGTON

1. THE CITY AND SURROUNDINGS
2. ACROSS TO THE SOUTH ISLAND

"**W**onderful, windy Wellington" it is called—with derision by Kiwis who don't live here, with affection by those who do. Well, there's no denying that it *is* windy: 60-mph winds sweep through what is the only substantial gap in New Zealand's mountain chain on an average of 40 days each year. Winds notwithstanding, however, Wellington is easily New Zealand's cultural center and one of its most beautiful cities. Indeed, its magnificent harbor rivals any in the world. Your first view of that harbor, with the city curved around its western and southwestern shoreline and surrounding hills abloom with what appear from a distance to be tiny dollhouses spilling down their sides, is likely to make you catch your breath, even if that view should happen to be in the rain (which is a distinct possibility!). On a fine day, there are few city views anywhere to equal it.

This gorgeous place was discovered in A.D. 950 by Kupe, the great Polynesian explorer, and by the time Captain Cook stopped by (but didn't land) in 1773, the harbor was lined with Maori settlements. When New Zealand Company representative Col. William Wakefield's good ship *Tory* arrived on the scene in September 1839, warring between the Maori tribes had become so fierce, and the local tribes were so fearful of their more powerful enemies, that (after a bit of negotiating back and forth, and a few of the usual misunderstandings about land transfers, etc.), they accepted the Pakeha as the lesser of two evils. By January 1840 settlers began coming in goodly numbers, and after a rather rowdy beginning (when, according to contemporary reports, meetings were held to try to determine how the citizenry could protect themselves from the lawless police force!), the town began a growth that has never really stopped. A tug-of-war with Auckland finally resulted in Wellington's being named the colony's capital on the basis of its central location and the belief that the "middle island" (that's the South Island's claim to being the "mainland," one you'll hear often after crossing Cook Strait) might well pull out and establish a separate colony altogether if it were not afforded better access to the capital than far-away Auckland provided.

Wellington today, while peopled mainly by civil servants, diplomats, and corporate home-office staffs, maintains a conservative—but far from stuffy—air. There is perhaps more sheer diversity here than in any other of New Zealand's cities: narrow streets and Edwardian buildings nudge modern edifices of concrete and glass; massive office buildings embrace continental-style restaurants; fashionable boutiques are housed in psuedo-colonial-style complexes while craft shops hold sway in avant-garde structures; and the after-dark scene is definitely Kiwiland's liveliest. The last few years, in fact, have seen even more diversity with the approach of a 1990 legislative deadline for bringing all major buildings up to earthquake-resistant standards. Those requirements have resulted in massive demolition of older buildings and the erection of even more modern high-rise structures. Indeed, it is estimated that within the next few years as many as half the office and commercial spaces in the city center will be replaced. The times they are *truly* a-changing in wonderful, windy Wellington!

What is not likely to change—and it's important to us as visitors—is the ebb and flow of the city's population as government workers depart on weekends for visits home, then flood back into town on Monday. That means an abundance of accommodations are available over weekends, very few during the week (more about that later under the "Where to Stay" heading).

In short, Wellington has from the first been a *cosmopolitan* city, and it's growing more so all the time.

It's also your port of embarkation for the South Island's wonders—but pray don't embark until you've explored this hub around which New Zealand's government revolves. And from a practical point of view, plan your explorations for a weekend when rooms are easier to come by, and special rates are offered to fill rooms vacated by that disappearing weekday population.

1. The City and Surroundings

ORIENTATION

The main point of reference in the city is, of course, the harbor. **Willis Street** is the main street; for shopping, try Lambton Quay, Manners Street, Cuba Street, and Courtenay Place. There is good city bus service, with most lines beginning at the railway station or **Courtenay Place.** Newsstands give away a good timetable with a small map, or you can call 859-955 from 7 a.m. to about 11 p.m. for route information. Fares are based on distance traveled, and you can purchase ten-trip concession tickets. InterCity runs commuter trains to suburbs on fairly frequent schedules; phone 725-399 for timetable information. If you're driving, avoid downtown Wellington traffic by parking in one of the center-city parking lots. They're on Clifton Terrace, in the Lombard Parking Building on Bond Street near Victoria Street, at James Smith's Council Car Park behind the Opera House (entrance on Wakefield Street), and at the Michael Fowler Centre on Wakefield Street (four-hour maximum stay); prices start at NZ$1 (65¢) for up to two hours and go to NZ$10 ($6.25) for more than six hours. Additional off-street parking is available in the Plimmer Building off Boulcott Street, evenings only for NZ$1 (65¢) per hour, free on weekends, and in the Renouf Building on Willis Street on weekends only for NZ$2 ($1.25) per visit. Ask for a copy of the *Wellington Parking Guide,* with handy maps from the PRO (address below). The best lookout for a panoramic view of the city is 648-foot **Mount Victoria** in the southern end of the city (hop the no. 20 bus for the 15-minute ride); the easiest lookout to reach is **Kelburn,** with its cable car from Lambton Quay.

Useful Information

The **New Zealand Tourist and Publicity (NZTP)** office is at 25-27 Mercer St. (tel. 04/739-269), just one block away from the Town Hall. Hours are 8:30 a.m. to 5 p.m. Monday through Thursday, to 8 p.m. on Friday, and 9:30 a.m. to 12:30 p.m. on Saturday. . . . You'll find the **PRO Visitors' Centre** in the Town Hall, Wakefield

Street, Civic Centre (tel. 04/735-063), open from 9 a.m. to 5 p.m. every day except Christmas; ask for the monthly "What's On," as well as "Greater Wellington" and other brochures, which are plentiful. . . . The free *Capital Times* is published weekly, giving information on current activities. It's distributed in most hotels as well as by the NZTP office and PRO.

Wellington Railway Station is on Waterloo Quay, and long-distance buses (except Newmans) depart that station (tel. 725-399 for long-distance bus and rail information). . . . For **city bus** information, call 859-955. . . . **Newmans buses** leave from 260 Taranaki St. . . . The **Air New Zealand** office for domestic and international reservations and information is at 179 Fetherston St. (tel. 859-911). . . . For information on the **Wellington–Picton Ferry,** call 725-399. . . . **Taxi ranks** are in front of the railway station, in the Lambton Quay shopping area between Grey and Hunter Streets; on Bond Street, just off Willis Street; on Dixon Street between Cuba and Victoria Streets; and on Cambridge Terrace near Courtenay Place. There's a NZ$1 (65¢) surcharge if you telephone for a taxi (tel. 859-900, 859-888, or 848-022), and on weekends and holidays.

The **Central Post Office (CPO)** is on Waterloo Quay, open from 8 a.m. to 5 p.m. Monday through Friday, with a philatelic bureau on the premises for stamp collectors. . . . For a 24-hour gas (petrol) station, try **Central Service Station Ltd.** on Jervois Quay, **BP Supershop** on Taranaki Street, or **Multifuels** at 221 Wakefield St. . . . Wellington's **telephone area code** is 04.

Wellington Airport

Vickers Coachlines (tel. 872-018) runs a coach service every 20 minutes on weekdays, 30 minutes on weekends, from 6 a.m. to 9:20 p.m. to the Wellington Airport, which is six miles south of the city center. Coaches depart from Bunny Street (close to the railway station), and there are several pickup points in the city. Airport bus stops have white signs with a red, white, and blue "V"; fares are NZ$4.50 ($2.80) for adults, NZ$2.30 ($1.45) for children. Domestic flights and flights between New Zealand and Australia arrive and depart at the airport.

The **information office** in the domestic terminal is staffed from 7:30 a.m. to 8:30 p.m. on weekdays, 8 a.m. to 8 p.m. on Saturday, and 9 a.m. to 8 p.m. on Sunday. The information desk in the international terminal is not always staffed but has a selection of brochures for the taking.

There's a good medium-priced restaurant at the airport, which serves generous portions from 10 a.m. to 8 p.m. every day, and a modern cafeteria serving light meals and snacks, open from 6 a.m. to 9 p.m. every day. Also, a bar, post office, nursery, bank, small duty-free shop, and car-rental desks. The bank is open one hour before any overseas departure and for each overseas arrival. There are ample luggage carts provided at no charge.

WHERE TO STAY

There are two things that must be said right up front about accommodations in Wellington: you should reserve as far in advance as possible; and you'll stand a much better chance of finding budget accommodations on weekends than during the week. It all has to do with the city's resident population tide—in on Monday, out on Friday evening. It is true that there are a lot of bed-and-breakfast listings, but the majority cater to their permanent guests and few are interested in transients like you and me. That tidal flow does, however, create one unique situation in the capital city: many superior hotels and motels cut prices drastically over the weekends when they have a surplus of rooms, and that means a little shopping around may well net you a budget price in a "splurge" location. More and more restaurants, shops, and sightseeing attractions are remaining open for the weekend, making it quite possible to take advantage of those special rates without sacrificing your usual holiday activities.

Hostels

The **YHA Hostel** is at 40 Tinakori Rd., Wellington (tel. 04/736-271), only about a ten-minute walk from the railway station and the Picton ferry terminal. Eight rooms hold 48 beds; there are two twin rooms. Advance reservations are especially advisable from December to February. Sightseeing attractions such as the Parliament buildings, Dominion Museum, and cable car are all handy to the hostel. Seniors pay NZ$14 ($8.75), and juniors, NZ$7 ($4.40), including GST.

The **Ivanhoe Inn,** 52 Ellice St., Mount Victoria, Wellington (tel. 04/842-264), is perched on one of Wellington's picturesque hillsides in a row of small colonial houses. The red-and-white wooden house has been recently renovated, and most rooms are quite spacious. There are singles, twins, and doubles, all with H&C, and a dormitory. Other facilities include a fully equipped kitchen, dining room, and TV lounge. Breakfast is available at a small charge. Rates start at NZ$13.20 ($8.25) for the dormitory and NZ$22 ($13.75) single, including GST.

The **Rowena Budget Travel Hotel,** 115 Brougham St., Mount Victoria, Wellington (tel. 04/857-872), has a variety of accommodations: dormitories, singles, doubles, twins, and triples. In addition to the three guest lounges, there's a dining room (cooked or continental breakfasts are available at a small charge), separate cookhouse, barbecue, and picnic area. It's on four city bus routes, and drivers will appreciate the off-street parking. Rates begin at NZ$13.20 ($8.25) for a dormitory bed, NZ$16.50 ($10.25) for a single, including GST.

The **Trekkers Hotel Motel,** on Dunlop Terrace, Wellington (tel. 04/852-153), off Vivian Street, has bunks for NZ$20 ($12.50) a night, along with higher-priced hotel and motel units. It's been around since 1908, when it offered budget accommodation under the monniker People's Palace. It was refurbished in 1987 and has three licensed restaurants, a sauna, and a spa pool.

The **Rosemere Private Hotel,** 6 MacDonald Crescent, Wellington (tel. 04/843-041), perches at the top of one of Wellington's steep hills at the end of Dixon Street, across Willis. New managers, Roger and Pamela Munn, are upgrading the bed-and-breakfast facilities, but at this time I only suggest it as lodging for backpackers, for whom two rooms are allocated at rates of NZ$14 ($8.75) per bunk. There is a library of international magazines and newspapers and a book exchange for foreign guests. Call for courtesy pickup from the ferry terminal.

The Y

Unfortunately, there is neither a YMCA nor YWCA in operation in Wellington at present.

Cabins

Since the Lower Hutt City Council took over operation of the **Hutt Park Motor Camp** at 95 Hutt Park Rd., Moera, Lower Hutt (tel. 04/685-913), some nine miles northeast of the city, great improvements have been made to both grounds and cabins. The only motor camp in the Wellington/Lower Hutt area, it is a large, shaded camp with some 58 cabins, many of which are equipped for wheelchairs. They range in size from a two-berth cabin with only basic furnishings to a three-bedroom cottage with private bath and cooking facilities. You must supply linen, blankets, and cutlery, none of which is available for rent. There's a nine-hole golf course on the 92-acre premises, which is available to guests at half price. Other facilities include two laundries (coin-operated), kitchens, dining rooms, shower rooms, TV lounge, and children's play area. There are grocery stores nearby, as well as a racetrack for trotters. Tourist cabins with kitchen and bathroom are NZ$42 ($26.25) for two, plus NZ$8 ($5) per extra person; without bath, NZ$30 ($18.75) for two. Basic cabins (using camp facilities) are NZ$22 ($13.75) for two. Powered caravan sites for two cost NZ$18 ($11.25), plus NZ$8 ($5) per extra person, or

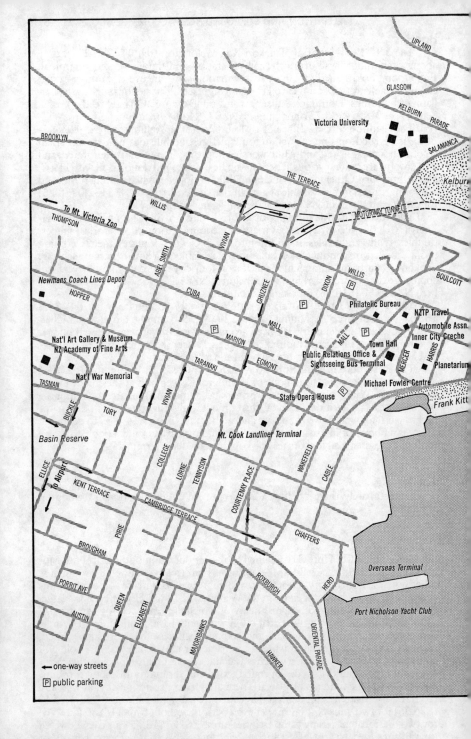

UPLAND

GLASGOW

KELBURN PARADE

Victoria University

SALAMANCA

Kelburn

BROOKLYN

THE TERRACE

WILLIS

To Mt. Victoria Zoo
THOMPSON

MOTORWAY TUNNEL

VIVIAN

ABEL SMITH

WILLIS

BOULCOTT

Newmans Coach Lines Depot
HOPPER

CUBA

GHUZNEE

DIXON

P

Philatelic Bureau

NZTP Travel

P

Automobile Assn.
Inner City Creche

MALL

P

Nat'l Art Gallery & Museum
NZ Academy of Fine Arts

MARION

MALL

P

Town Hall

MERCER

HARRIS

Planetarium

TARANAKI

EGMONT

Public Relations Office &
Sightseeing Bus Terminal

Michael Fowler Centre

TASMAN

Nat'l War Memorial

BUCKLE

TORY

VIVIAN

P

State Opera House

Frank Kitt

Basin Reserve

ELLICE

To Airport

KENT TERRACE

COLLEGE

LORNE

TENNYSON

Mt. Cook Landliner Terminal

COURTENAY PLACE

WAKEFIELD

CABLE

CAMBRIDGE TERRACE

PIRIE

CHAFFERS

HERD

Overseas Terminal

BROUGHAM

PORRIT AVE

QUEEN

ELIZABETH

MAORIBANKS

ROXBURGH

ORIENTAL PARADE

Port Nicholson Yacht Club

AUSTIN

HAWKER

one-way streets

P public parking

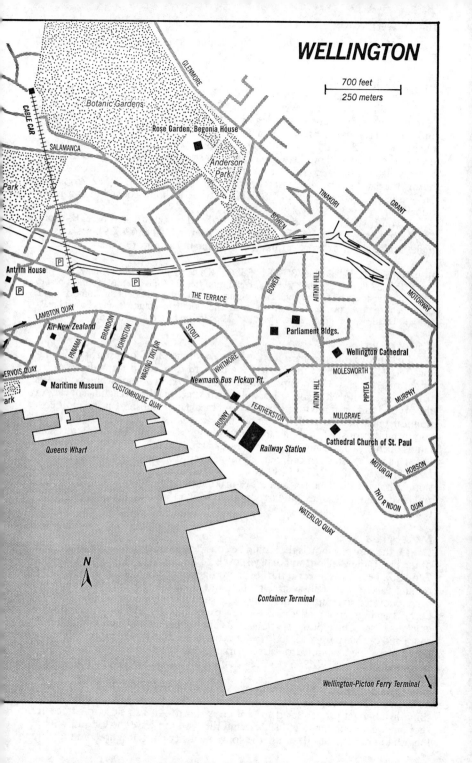

WELLINGTON

700 feet
250 meters

Botanic Gardens

Rose Garden; Begonia House

GLENMORE

CABLE CAR

SALAMANCA

Anderson Park

Park

BOWEN

TINAKORI

GRANT

MOTORWAY

AITKIN HILL

THE TERRACE

Antrim House

LAMBTON QUAY

Air New Zealand

PINAMA

BRANDON

JOHNSTON

WARING TAYLOR

STOUT

Parliament Bldgs.

Wellington Cathedral

WHITMORE

MOLESWORTH

AITKIN HILL

PIPITEA

MURPHY

JERVOIS QUAY

Maritime Museum

CUSTOMHOUSE QUAY

Newmans Bus Pickup Pt.

BUNNY

FEATHERSTON

MULGRAVE

Cathedral Church of St. Paul

ark

Queens Wharf

Railway Station

MOTUROA

THORNDON

HOBSON

QUAY

WATERLOO QUAY

N

Container Terminal

Wellington-Picton Ferry Terminal

NZ$27 ($17) for families. There's frequent bus service into Wellington via the Eastbourne bus.

Bed-and-Breakfasts

Tinakori Lodge, 182 Tinakori Rd., Wellington (tel. 04/733-478), is a century-old home presided over by Gloria (she's an American who has lived many years in New Zealand) and Jack (he's a Kiwi) Hastings and their hospitable cat, Alexander. Guest rooms here are fresh and bright, comfortably furnished, retain much of the character of the old home, and each has H&C, color TV, electric blankets, and heater. The substantial breakfast is served buffet style, and an attractive feature here is the availability of tea, coffee, hot chocolate, soup, cheese, crackers, and cookies all during the day. Bed-and-breakfast rates (add GST to all) are NZ$50 ($31.25) single, NZ$66 ($41.25) double, and NZ$88 ($55) triple. A home-cooked dinner is optional.

If you have difficulty booking into a bed-and-breakfast listed here, **Harbour City Home Stays,** P.O. Box 14–345, Wellington (tel. 04/862-339), has a list of high standard homes that offer this type of hospitality at quite reasonable rates.

READER'S BED-AND-BREAKFAST SELECTION: "The **Victoria,** a new bed-and-breakfast at 58 Pirie St., Mount Victoria, Wellington (tel. 04/858-512), is a spotless beauty undergoing restoration. Ornamental cast-iron lace decorates the exterior of this home on a hill, convenient to downtown and Mount Victoria. The room rate includes a fine cooked breakfast" (P. Dienhelt, Ashippun, Wisc.). [*Author's Note:* It's on bus routes 2 and 5.]

A Motor Inn

I fell in love with the charming **Carillon Motor Inn,** 33 Thompson St., Wellington (tel. 04/848-795), although it was a bit hard to find—down a driveway between nos. 29 and 35 Thompson St. The rambling, two-story white house sits halfway up one of Wellington's hills, well off the street, and has a magnificent view of the city and harbor. It was formerly a bed-and-breakfast establishment and more economical, but inside, the rooms, most of which are quite spacious, are attractively and comfortably furnished, and the large guest lounge is inviting. The licensed restaurant is open breakfast daily; continental breakfast costs NZ$7 ($4.40), and cooked, NZ$10 ($6.25). You can order an evening meal Monday through Thursday for NZ$12.50 ($7.80) to NZ$15 ($9.40). All rooms have their own bathroom, television, in-house video, and tea- and coffee-making facilities. Two motel flats sleep six and have cooking facilities. Single rooms are NZ$65 ($40.75); doubles are NZ$85 ($53.25).

Motel Flats

Of the very few motels that could be considered "budget" in Wellington, one of the best is the **Wellington Luxury Motel,** 14 Hobson St., Wellington (tel. 04/726-825), near Davis Street at the northern edge of the city center and about a five-minute walk from the railway station. It's a large house built back in 1912, which has been renovated to create five nice units with such charming extras as bay windows, beamed ceilings, and small leaded window panes. Noeleen and Ron Archer are the gracious hosts. Three of the spacious units are bed-sitters, and two have one bedroom and can sleep up to six. All are attractively furnished and have color TV and telephones. There's limited off-street parking, and city bus transportation half a block away. Rates are NZ$66 ($41.25) double, NZ$10 ($6.25) for each additional person, plus GST.

The **Apollo Lodge,** 49 Majoribanks St., Wellington (tel. 04/851-849), would be a real find even if it weren't the most convenient location in Wellington at anything like budget prices. But that location is superb—it's so close to city center shopping, entertainment, and sightseeing that you can leave the car and walk (a longish but pleasant stroll) or use the convenient city bus transport, and there are several first-rate restaurants right in the neighborhood. I found the staff here extremely friendly and helpful, always a plus. The 33 attractive units are set in off the street, and eight have separate bedrooms. You have a choice of full kitchen facilities or of serviced units with jug, toaster, and fridge. All are fully carpeted and come with TV, radio, telephone, electric blankets, and heaters. Cooked or continental breakfasts are available, and there's a full-service laundry as well as highchairs and a play area for children. Rates for motel units are NZ$88 ($55), single or double, including GST. If you're traveling with a large party, you might want to book the three-bedroom (sleeps seven) bungalow also on the grounds that goes for the same rate as a motel unit. *Note:* The Apollo is very, very popular with regular Kiwi visitors to Wellington, and your best bet here is weekends (as I seem to keep saying!).

An American from Washington, D.C., greeted me with an unsolicited recommendation—"This place is fantastic, not only for the facilities and comfort, but for the friendliness of the owner"—when I arrived at the **Majoribanks Apartments,** 38 Majoribanks St., Wellington (tel. 04/857-305 or 858-879). My encounter with owner John Floratos certainly confirmed the traveler's comments, but in addition, I was much impressed with the 14 bright, nicely decorated apartments in this property just across the street from the Apollo. All have fully equipped kitchen, TV, radio, and telephone. There are one- and two-bedroom units, and there's good off-street parking. The rate is NZ$88 ($55), single or double; each additional adult is NZ$13.20 ($8.25), and children, NZ$8.80 ($5.50). Rates include GST.

Licensed Hotels

Trekkers Hotel, Dunlop Terrace (P.O. Box 27–125), Wellington 1 (tel. 04/852-153), is very central and offers a variety of accommodations. Its 120 rooms include small dormitories (two or four bunk beds), singles, and doubles, both with and without private facilities (H&C in those without), six rooms with facilities for the disabled, and six motel units in a separate block. They vary in style from new and modern to older and recently renovated, and the reception areas and guest lounge all have a bright, modern look. There's a guest laundry, sauna, spa pool, restaurant, and café. Rates are just as varied, beginning at NZ$20 ($12.50) per person for dormitory beds and climbing to NZ$120 ($75) for motel units that will sleep four, with a rather wide spread between those for singles and doubles with or without private facilities. Plus GST, of course.

It isn't often that I can recommend a luxury hotel to budget travelers without giving it a "Big Splurge" heading. That isn't necessary, however, in the case of the **West Plaza Hotel,** 110-116 Wakefield St. (P.O. Box 11648), Wellington (tel. 04/731-440)—it's one of Wellington's newer (mid-1985) posh hotels, smack in the middle of the city center, with quite affordable rates. Now, frankly, after taking a look at the beautiful, two-level marble lobby done in soft shades of cream and rose, with lots of brass and greenery, and the terrific guest rooms, I'm not at all certain that the folks here will be able to resist raising those rates (although they *swear* their motto is "Our service reflects international standards—our rates don't"). However, if they hold to their standards without a price increase, travelers with an eye on the purse strings will be able to afford superior accommodations, a lovely off-foyer coffeeshop that serves from 7 a.m. to midnight, and one of the most restful cocktail lounges and bars in the city (worth a visit even if you aren't a guest). Rates? They begin at NZ$176 ($110) *for one to three people.* Put that on a per-person basis, and you have real value for dollar. And, as I said, it's right in the center of town, just across from the PRO, and almost facing the new Michael Fowler Centre.

Tucked off Lambton Quay and up the Plimmer steps near Willis Street is **Plimmer Towers** (tel. 04/733-750), with rooms so comfortable and relaxing and views so compelling that you'll have trouble going outside to explore Wellington. The artwork and curtains reflect New Zealand's majestic mountains. The hotel has a licensed restaurant and a gym, and its location is ideal for walking and convenient to restaurants and entertainment. The units with the best views—Suites 201, 211, and

221—are far beyond budget at NZ$225 ($141) plus GST, but you can get what they call a small bureau room for NZ$140 ($87.50) or a large bureau room for NZ$168 ($105), plus GST.

A Big Splurge

With what has to be the best location in town, the **THC James Cook,** The Terrace, Wellington (tel. 04/725-865), is a "big splurge" well worth considering. It's in the very heart of the city center, and its 260 rooms all come with private baths, tea- and coffee-making facilities, fridges, mini-bars, color TV, in-house video, and telephone. There's same-day laundry and dry-cleaning service (except Sunday), business facilities that include secretarial service and copy machines, a first-class restaurant (see "Where to Eat"), and an inexpensive coffeeshop. It is also just steps away from shopping, sightseeing, dining, and entertainment. The normal rate of NZ$195 ($122), plus GST, single or double, is lowered dramatically for weekend specials. Highly recommended.

Out of Town in Foxton

Some three miles from Foxton Beach (and a little over an hour's drive to Wellington), the **Constellation Motel,** State Hwy. 1, Foxton (tel. 069/38-863), is a quiet, peaceful base from which to explore Wellington. The motel has ten kitchen units that are nicely decorated, and there's a spa pool, children's playground, and pool table for guests. Rates begin at NZ$48 ($30) single, NZ$58 ($36.25) double, plus GST.

WHERE TO EAT

You'll find good, inexpensive places to eat along almost any Wellington street. And there's an interesting diversity of cuisine offered in the city's restaurants—350 of them. Space limitations necessarily mean that my listings will omit many that are worthy of note. Drop me a line if you find that special eatery you think other budgeteers should know about, and I'll include as many as possible in future editions.

For a quick bite during a day of sightseeing downtown, stop by **Incredible Edibles,** upstairs in Gresham Plaza on Lambton Quay. You'll find all manner of sandwiches, filled pies, soups, and desserts served cafeteria style. A lot of folks who work in this area drop in at lunchtime. It's quick and inexpensive.

With its tile floor and bohemian ambience, **City Limits Café,** 122 Wakefield St. (tel. 726-468), features lunch from NZ$2.50 ($1.55), with main courses set at NZ$9 ($5.65), and dinner for NZ$6.50 ($4.05) to NZ$16.50 ($10.25). A light breakfast is available from 8 a.m.; lunch is served from 11:30 a.m. to 2:30 p.m., and dinner, from 6 p.m. until late. The walls are filled with posters of the latest theatrical and musical events around town.

Glossops, 149 Willis St. (tel. 849-091), is a cozy little place with green-and-white tablecloths, and a blackboard menu featuring all home-cooked meals and fresh New Zealand produce. And they are delicious! Salad plates, sandwiches (they're open and hearty-appetite size), seafood, savory croissants, beef, pork, and chicken are featured, and the waist-expanding desserts include homemade ice cream and chocolate-fudge torte. All entrees are NZ$6.25 ($3.90); all main courses, NZ$13 ($8.15)—slightly less at lunch. Not licensed, but you're welcome to BYO. Hours are 11:30 a.m. to 2:30 p.m. and 6 to 9:30 p.m. Sunday through Thursday, to 10 p.m. on Friday and Saturday.

For good Italian food, excellent service, and just plain fun people-watching, I heartily recommend at least one meal at **Mangiare,** 35 Dixon St. (tel. 844-343). This upstairs restaurant is bright with draped, striped awnings, clusters of wine bottles hanging about on the walls, and a small front room whose windows overlook the busy street below. It's a favorite of locals, and at lunch there's the happy buzz of office workers from nearby, while candlelit tables at night are likely to be filled by many of the same who've returned for a more relaxed meal. Specialties are—what else?—spaghetti, cannelloni, pastitsio, ravioli, and calamari, with dessert surprises that include baklava (it used to be a Greek restaurant, and this favorite, as did pastitsio, just stayed on). Service is friendly as well as efficient, and pasta dishes are all NZ$9.50 ($5.95). Dinner is served seven days a week beginning at 5:30 p.m. BYO and licensed.

The kid brother to Mangiare, **La Casa Pasta** has opened across the street, at 33 Dixon (tel. 859-057), and serves home-style Italian cooking, including lasagne, fettuccine, canelloni, and spinach pie. All dishes are NZ$9.50 ($5.95). Open for lunch Monday through Friday from noon to 2 p.m., and for dinner nightly from 5:30 to 10 p.m. Licensed and BYO.

Anyone tempted by the offer of "two meals for the price of one" should head over to **Chevys**, at 97 Dixon St. (tel. 842-723), after 5 p.m. on Monday and Tuesday. You'll see the neon cowboy and his wiggling lasso a few blocks before you arrive at the door. The casual, congenial place has decidedly American fare: BLTs, chicken wings, nachos, barbecued spareribs, Philadelphia steak sandwiches, omelets, seven kinds of burgers, potato skins, and even banana splits. Depending on your appetite, you might spend NZ$10 ($6.25) to NZ$20 ($12.50). Open from 11:30 a.m. to 11 p.m. Monday through Thursday, until midnight on Friday and Saturday. Licensed.

A local favorite, **Kloster Keller,** 49 Manners Mall (tel. 735-222), features Austrian cuisine—bratwurst, wienerschnitzel, frankfurters, and potato salad, with a little Hungarian goulash thrown in for good measure—all for about NZ$10 ($6.25) per dish. Place your order at the counter and wait for your number to be called. This small place is chock-a-block with booths and tables. It's open from noon to 10 p.m. Monday through Thursday, until 11 p.m. on Friday, and 6 to 11 p.m. on Saturday.

For someplace a little more sophisticated in both menu and decor, try **Kasey's,** at 8 Edward St. (tel. 857-043). Menu selections include spaghetti in saffron cream with mussels and tomato stew, vegetarian spicy samosa, tandoori spiced chicken, along with fish, lamb, and beef dishes. There is also a large selection of wines by the glass. The prices are straightforward: NZ$7 ($4.40) for appetizers, entrees, and desserts, and NZ$16 ($10) for main courses. Open for lunch and dinner daily, from noon to 3 p.m. and 5:30 to 11 p.m. or midnight. A jazz band is on hand on Thursday and Saturday from 7:30 to 10:30 p.m.

If you're driving, or happen to find yourself out in the lovely Evans Bay area, plan on one meal at the **Greta Point Tavern,** 467 Evans Bay Parade (tel. 861-066). Actually, the two-mile walk from downtown along Oriental Bay, Roseneath, and Evans Bay Parade to the tavern is picturesque and well worth doing. The large black building with rose trim sits right on the waterfront, and has windows the entire length of its south side, looking out to sweeping views of the bay (often filled with sailboats) and a nearby marina with its forest of masts. The large, high-ceilinged room, which once housed a commercial laundry, now has a wooden lifeboat suspended from the overhead pipes. There's a nice upstairs Promenade Deck bar, and downstairs you'll find the Anchorage Lounge Bar, as well as the Galley Restaurant, featuring fresh seafoods. The restaurant is self-service and fully licensed, and the long counter will have you drooling while trying to decide between Bluff oysters, roast baron of beef, marinated mussels, baked leg of lamb, and a host of other tempting dishes on display. All main courses come with vegetables or a salad, and prices are in the NZ$8 ($5) to NZ$14 ($8.75) range. It's open for lunch Monday through Saturday from noon to 2:30 p.m. and on Sunday from 11:30 a.m. to 2:30 p.m.; for dinner, Monday through Saturday from 5:30 to 9:30 p.m., until 9 p.m. on Sunday.

The **Mexican Cantina,** 19 Edward St. (tel. 859-711), is set in a former warehouse, and it's such a favorite with locals that you may find yourself waiting in line at lunch. The atmosphere is casual; the decor is south of the border; the menu features all those beans, tacos, and tostados you'd expect, and prices are in the NZ$8 ($5) range at lunch, under NZ$15 ($9.40) for dinner. Open from noon to 2 p.m. Monday through Friday and 5:30 to 9:30 p.m. daily. BYO.

Rinascimento, 4 Roxburgh St. (tel. 858-340), is a casual, rather rustic restaurant serving up really good Italian dishes (pasta, stuffed squid, mussels in white wine sauce, veal in various forms, etc.) at prices that average NZ$19 ($12) for a complete dinner from the à la carte menu. It's BYO, and hours are 6 to 9 p.m. Monday through Thursday, 6 to 9:30 p.m. on Friday and Saturday.

The Burmese restaurant **Monsoon,** 124 Cuba St. (tel. 842-827), specializes in such Burmese and Asian dishes as chicken with ginger and spring onion, Singapore chow mein, beef with green pepper and black-bean sauce, and a host of curries. It's a small, cozy place, and reservations are a good idea for dinner. Main courses range from NZ$11 ($6.90) to NZ$15 ($9.40), and hours are noon to 2 p.m. and 6 to 10 p.m. every day except Sunday. BYO.

The **Middle East,** Regent Centre, Manners Mall (tel. 724-538), is exotic in decor as well as cuisine, with lots of brass, tapestries, Israeli lithographs, and Mediterranean-style tables and chairs. It's upstairs in the Regent Centre, and as for the menu, selections include souvlaki, shish kebab, stuffed grapevine leaves, capsicums, and . . . well, there are dishes from Greece, Turkey, Israel, Lebanon, Syria, and Yemen, and you'll dine to the strains of taped music from all those countries. On Thursday and Sunday nights, belly dancers complete the scene. Main courses are modest in price, ranging from NZ$5 ($3.15) to NZ$12 ($7.50); hours are noon to 2:30 p.m. Monday through Friday and 6 p.m. to after midnight every night. Fully licensed.

Mykonos, 23 Coutts St., Kilbirnie (tel. 877-040), is a lively spot, the walls adorned with pictures of the Greek owner's homeland and wine bottles, with bits of greenery spotted around the room. Menu specialties are lamb, spanakopita, seafoods prepared in the Greek fashion, and that great Greek dessert, baklava. Your dinner tab will run around NZ$25 ($15.75); it's BYO, and hours are from 6 p.m. Tuesday through Saturday.

A Final Note: If you'd like to have dinner with a Wellington family, **Harbour City Home Stays,** P.O. Box 14–345, Wellington (tel. 04/862-339), can arrange a home-cooked New Zealand dinner for about NZ$40 ($25) a person, plus GST—but be sure to give them sufficient advance notice.

Slightly Big Splurges

Wellington has several *really* "big splurge" restaurants that would hold their own anywhere in the world. The following, however, is a *moderately* "big splurge" about which you could say the very same thing.

Roxburgh Restaurant, 18 Majoribanks St. (tel. 857-577), is another very pleasant, attractive place to eat. It's in an old, two-story house just off Cambridge Place, and the cuisine here is mostly German, with traditional specialties such as Rheinischer sauerbraten, venison and other game, and lamb, along with New Zealand seafood. Friendly service, pink linen napkins, fresh flowers at each table, complimentary sherry, and an open fireplace on cool evenings add the pampered feeling that makes an average dinner tab of NZ$25 ($15.75) seem more than a bargain. Hours are 6 to 10 p.m., and you *must* reserve. BYO.

A Big Splurge

Whitby's Restaurant, at the THC James Cook, The Terrace (tel. 725-865), is an elegant room on the second floor of the hotel that serves up terrific breakfast and lunch buffets, for around NZ$20 ($12.50), but it is at dinner that the chef really shines. Chef Albert Hutching, in fact, holds the coveted Lamb Cuisine Award. And if you order his lamb Whitby (a loin of lamb stuffed with white veal liver, served with smoked sweetbreads and a spinach-and-pine-nuts combination in filo pastry with a tamarillo sabayon), you'll most certainly want to give him your own personal gourmet award—it's luscious. Other New Zealand specialties, such as smoked venison, quail, pheasant, hare, salmon, Bluff oysters, and filet of beef are on the extensive menu, along with roasts of beef, pork, and lamb. Desserts are fabulous. The room itself is romantic by candlelight, and on Saturday and Sunday nights the Haydn Quartet plays classical music. Main courses are in the NZ$19 ($12) to NZ$25 ($15.75) range on the à la carte menu, and dinner hours are from 6 p.m. seven days a week. Reservations are essential on weekends,when Wellingtonians favor Whitby's for dining out, and a good idea other nights. The breakfast buffet is served from 7 to 9 a.m.; lunch, from noon to 2 p.m. Licensed. Highly recommended.

READERS' DINING SELECTIONS: "The **Mount Cook Café**, 75 Wallace St., is one of the best restaurants in the city. While it's certainly not cheap, the food is first-rate, the service is good, and the atmosphere is terrific—a highly recommended splurge. The **As You Like It Café** in Newtown is similar to the Mount Cook Café and has an excellent reputation" (C. Adair, Los Angeles, Calif.). . . . "When it comes time for junk food, **Capital City Fish Supply**, at 9 Courtenay Pl., serves the best fish and chips in town. Ask Helen to teach you how to eat them Kiwi style" (C. Thomas, Washington, D.C.). . . . "The best spot for lunch is the **Great New Zealand Soup Kitchen**, on Waring Taylor Street across from the Central Police Station; it has the best soup in town" (D. Brown, Toronto, Ont., Canada).

THINGS TO SEE AND DO

For the fullest appreciation of Wellington's spectacular setting, take the **cable car** at Lambton Quay opposite Grey Street. It's a marvelous 4½-minute ride in sleek red cars, which climb to an elevation of 400 feet. Fares are NZ$.80 (50¢) for adults, half that for children. The beautiful harbor lies at your feet, and it's a great loitering spot to drink in the beauty of that curving shoreline backed by jagged hills. The cable car runs from 7 a.m. to 10 p.m. Monday through Friday, 9:20 a.m. to 6 p.m. on Saturday, and 10:30 a.m. to 6 p.m. on Sunday and public holidays. If you should be there on a Tuesday night from March to October between 7:30 and 9:30 p.m., you can visit the **Carter Observatory** (tel. 728-167) and take a telescopic look at the heavens above for a small charge—there is talk that this will not be available in the future, but do check. The **Botanic Gardens** entrance is also at the top of the cable-car ride, open from dawn to dusk. Stop by the Interpretive Centre for brochures and a full briefing on the gardens. Your downhill stroll through lush greenery can be broken by a stop at the Begonia House and its Tea House in the Lady Norwood Rose Gardens (open from 10 a.m. to 4 p.m.) for a look at hundreds of begonias, bush foliage, and ferns. From the foot of the gardens, you can get back to the city on a no. 12 bus.

The best possible way to get an in-depth look at the city itself and its immediate environs is to take the escorted **bus tour,** which leaves from the PRO building on Wakefield Street every day at 2 p.m. and also at 10 a.m. in summer. For the bargain price of NZ$17 ($10.75) for adults (children ride for half price), you'll be driven some 30 miles, with 2½ hours of informative narrative as you see the financial and commercial center, take a look at government buildings and Parliament's unique Beehive building, visit the lookout on Mount Victoria (with a stop for picture tak-ing), skirt the bays, stop for afternoon tea, then reenter the city via View Road, a scenic drive, which does full justice to Wellington's headlands, hills, bays, and beaches. For information and reservations, telephone 735-063. The PRO can also furnish details on a wide variety of other city and area tours available.

If you prefer a do-it-yourself tour of much the same territory, pick up the PRO's *Scenic Drive* booklet and map. Three routes are outlined, and they're color coordi-nated with discs on lampposts along each route so you won't go astray. They cover Wellington from top to bottom, traveling southeast on one route, west on another, and north on the third.

You can tour **Parliament** any weekday free of charge. Just telephone 719-457 for tour times. And if by this time you're hooked on New Zealand history and cul-ture, spend some time at the **National Library of New Zealand**, which is across the road from Parliament, at 70 Molesworth St. You can browse in the National Library Gallery, bookshop, and the New Zealand collection of books, all on the ground floor. The **Alexander Turnbull Library,** in the same building, is the research wing of the National Library, specializing in New Zealand and the Pacific. On the second floor, you can peruse files of photographs; books, newspapers, drawings, paintings, and maps are available for research. Hours are 9 a.m. to 5 p.m. weekdays and 9 a.m. to 1 p.m. on Saturday. There are free public tours of the building at 2 p.m. on Monday, Wednesday, and Friday.

And speaking of Kiwi history, keep an eye out for **12 shoreline plaques,** which have been embedded in footpaths to show the sites of early Wellington: you'll find them at Pipitea Point, on the south side of Davis Street and Thorndon Quay; at the top of the steps leading to Rutherford House; in Mason's Lane, on the north side; on Lambton Quay, north of Woodward Street; on the Lambton Quay footpath near Cable Car Lane; at Steward Dawson's, on the west side of the Lambton Quay corner; at Chews Lane, on the east side of the Willis Street footpath; on Mercer Street, outside George Harrison Ltd. on the Willis Street corner; on Farrish Street, on the southeast side of Farrish and Lombard Streets; on Cuba Street outside Smith and Smith Ltd., on Taranaki Street outside the Caltex Service Station; and on Wakefield Street next to the Schaffer Street bus stop.

Antrim House, 63 Boulcott St. (tel. 724-341), is headquarters of the New Zealand Historic Places Trust, and its information room has displays of its properties and the organization's work. Open Monday through Friday from 8:30 a.m. to 5 p.m. The birthplace of New Zealand-born short-story writer, poet, and essayist **Katherine Mansfield,** 25 Tinakori Rd. (tel. 737-268), is open Tuesday through Sunday from 10 a.m. to 4 p.m.

The **National Art Gallery** and adjoining **National Museum** are on Buckle Street. The art gallery emphasizes both New Zealand and international art, and on most Sundays at 2:30 p.m. there's a free music recital, theatrical performance, film, or lecture. Artifacts of South Pacific, New Zealand, and Maori history are featured at the museum. No admission charges at either, and hours are 10 a.m. to 4:45 p.m. daily. Closed Christmas Day and Good Friday. Bus 11 stops at Buckle Street; buses 1 and 3 run to Basin Reserve, about a five-minute walk.

Those interested in things of the sea will want to visit the **Maritime Museum** on Queens Wharf, where Wellington's close association with seafarers and their vessels is well documented. No admission charge, and hours are 10 a.m. to 4 p.m. on weekdays, 1 to 4 p.m. on Saturday and Sunday.

The **Wellington Zoo,** at Newtown (tel. 898-130), dates back to 1906 and its collection includes kangaroos, wallabies, monkeys, and flightless birds (there's a nocturnal **Kiwi House** open from 10 a.m. to 4 p.m.). In fine weather on weekends and holidays there are miniature railway rides from noon to 4 p.m., for minimal charges. You can watch them feed the tigers at 2 p.m., lions at 3:20 p.m. (except on Monday and Friday). Zoo hours are 8:30 a.m. to 4:30 p.m., and you can get there on the New Town Park bus (no. 11) from the railway station. Buses to Houghton Bay, View Road, and Melrose also pass the zoo. Admission is NZ$4.50 ($2.80) for adults, NZ$2 ($1.25) for children.

READERS' SIGHTSEEING SUGGESTIONS: "From Old St. Paul's in Mulgrave Street you can get a map for the **Town and Gown Walk,** which starts near the Skyline and ends near 12 Boulcott St." (P. Adams, Denver, Colo.). . . . "Len Southward (Main Road North, Paraparaumu) near Wellington has built what is now known as the largest and most complete **Antique Car Museum** in the southern hemisphere, and you can bus up there, drive, or go by train. The museum includes a gift shop, restaurant, and theater" (B. Huxtable, Lansing, Mich.). . . . "I'd like to put in a plug for some tourist attractions in the Wellington area. **Kapiti Island:** the Forest and Bird Society runs irregular trips; write them in advance at their Wellington office, or get a permit from the Department of Internal Affairs and find a boat owner in Plimmerton, Titahi Bay, or Paraparaumu to take you across. It's a slice of New Zealand before the Pakeha arrived—primeval bush and tame birds. Most spectacular are the wekas (flightless rails) and kakas (arboreal cousins of keas), both quite unashamed about sharing your lunch! The boat trip will cost a few dollars only. There's a spectacular beach at **Castlepoint,** east of

Masterton. The cliffs here are made entirely of fossil shells cemented together, and the presence of a lighthouse adds to the grandeur" (R. Goldie, Toronto, Ont., Canada).

Excursions by Bus

The **Downtowner** bus costs NZ$2.20 ($1.40) for five rides in the downtown area or on the cable car during off-peak hours (9 a.m. to 3 p.m.). The **Daytripper** allows one adult and two children under age 15 to ride all day for NZ$5.50 ($3.45). This is a fine way to see the city: jump on any bus, leap off when you see something interesting; go to the beach (take the Lyall Bay, Island Bay, or Seatoun bus from Willis Street) and stay all day or catch the next bus back. Take bus 12 or 14 to one of the hill suburbs, have a cup of coffee in a local café, then catch a bus back and enjoy the views all along the way. You can even use the same bus ticket after dinner for after-hours exploring.

Harbor Cruises

The bargain way to see the water is the **East by West ferry** (tel. 499-1273 for timetable information), which crosses the harbor from Queen's Wharf in Wellington to Days Bay. The 25-minute ride on the *Government Print I* costs NZ$5 ($3.15) each way, NZ$4 ($2.50) for senior citizens, and NZ$2.50 ($1.55) for children. The ferry has a full bar and also serves coffee. At Days Bay, you can enjoy the park, have afternoon tea in the pavilion, or walk around to Eastbourne for galleries, gift shops, and a restaurant or tavern.

Other, more costly cruises are offered by **Harbour City Cruises** (tel. 852-466) and **Bluefin Launches** (tel. 698-203); both offer day and nighttime cruises, with or without food and beverage.

Walks

Wellington is conveniently central to many hiking areas, some that afford prime views of the city and harbor. Ask at the PRO for the *Bus & Walk* brochure, which outlines 16 walks and gives information on getting to them from Wellington and back into town by bus. An easy, educational choice is a visit to the **Otari Open Air Native Plant Museum** (tel. 753-245), which offers four hikes of half an hour to an hour, some through 198 acres of native bush and five acres of cultivated gardens; take the no. 14 Wilton Route bus to the entrance on Wilton Road. The bus trip takes 20 minutes.

Sports

Many of the city's **gymnasiums** welcome drop-in guests. An aerobics or stretching class or a weightlifting session costs NZ$6 ($3.75) or NZ$7 ($4.40). The PRO can provide details. The **Wellington Regional Aquatic Center,** in the suburb of Kilbirnie (tel. 724-599), has four heated pools: a lap pool, learners' pool, and adjoining junior and toddlers' pools with an access ramp for the disabled. There are also diving facilities, spa pools, saunas, a sundeck, café, and YMCA fitness center. You can rent swimsuits and towels; goggles are for sale. The no. 2 bus to Miramar takes you to the door.

The **Wellington Renouf Tennis Centre,** on Brooklyn Road at Central Park (tel. 846-294), has 14 outdoor and 4 indoor courts available for rent at about NZ$28 ($17.50) an hour. It's open from 6 a.m. to 11 p.m. Monday through Friday and 8 a.m. to 11 p.m. on Saturday and Sunday. Practice or hitting partners can be arranged on short notice, and there's a café on the premises.

SHOPPING

The prices at the **Robbie Burns Bottle Shop,** at 75 Kent Terrace, are substantially below others in the city; for instance, Mac's beer sells here for several New Zealand dollars less than elsewhere. **John Bull & Co. Ltd.,** 8 Bond St. (near Town Hall), and **Rumble's Wine Cellar,** 32 Waring Taylor St., have good New Zealand wines.

For window-shopping and browsing, stroll the **Manners and Cuba pedestrian malls,** which are particularly fun on Friday night when the buskers are out. You'll find crafts and secondhand shops on **Cuba Street** near Ghuznee Street.

The **Wakefield Market** is held on Friday, Saturday, and Sunday, and is filled with clothing, leather goods, and jewelry. Antiqueskshops are in the suburb of Brooklyn.

Aki, on Victoria Street, is a good souvenir shop. For splurge shopping, head to **Vibrant Handknits** on Kent Terrace. **Leitch Gallery,** in Regent Centre off Manners Mall, sells prints of Wellington that make fine souvenirs.

The **duty-free shop** in central Wellington is at the DFC Centre, on Grey Street, with a branch out at the airport.

One item to look for in Wellington may well become your most treasured souvenir—the whimsical Tidy Kiwi poster. That egg-shaped national bird is shown using its long, pointed bill to pick up papers and put them into a litter bag. It will cost you only NZ$2.20 ($1.40) and will serve to remind you (and any *un*tidy little birds of your own back home) just how clean and tidy is this very civilized country. You can pick one up at the offices of **Keep New Zealand Beautiful, Inc.,** on the 13th floor or, Boulcott House, 47 Boulcott St. (tel. 738-205). If you can't manage a visit, drop them a line and they'll mail the poster.

AFTER DARK

Check the current issue of the *Capital Times* and the PRO's monthly publication *What's On* for entertainment, as well as the following: the **THC James Cook** has a piano bar nightly, classical string quartet on Saturday and Sunday; **Paisley Park,** upstairs at 24 Taranaki St., is open seven nights a week from 7 p.m. to 1 a.m. for live music (the cover charge varies) or for recorded music, along with Dutch-style food, drinks, and an inviting atmosphere; and the **Blues Bar,** on the top (ninth) floor of the Plaza International Hotel, features blues and live jazz Tuesday through Saturday nights.

The **Downstage Theatre,** in the Hannah Playhouse on Cambridge Terrace (tel. 849-639), presents first-rate theater in an exciting theater structure that provides for flexibility in staging in the main auditorium and a smaller cabaret in the bar. The Downstage is a year-round enterprise, staging classics and contemporary drama, musicals, and comedies, and works of New Zealand playwrights. Check the newspapers for current showings. Reserve as far in advance as you possibly can, however, for Downstage productions are very popular. Ticket prices are NZ$23 ($14.50) for the auditorium and NZ$18 ($11.25) for the gallery. Students, senior citizens, and groups of ten receive a NZ$5 ($3.15) reduction. **Bats Theatre,** on Kent Terrace, presents plays that attract a young audience, as well as folks who are not traditional theater-goers.

Check the newspapers to see what's doing at the new **Michael Fowler Centre,** an exciting contemporary structure that has been added to Wellington's old Town Hall to enlarge auditorium space. There are concerts and other events scheduled there throughout the year.

2. Across to the South Island

A special tip to those who won't be going on to the South Island (poor souls!): A marvelous day trip is the round trip on the ferry. You can take either of the morning departures, enjoy a sea voyage, and have five full hours in Picton before returning on the 6:40 p.m. ferry from Picton. I highly recommend it.

From Wellington's Aotea Quay (north of the city center), the Cook Strait ferries depart several times daily for Picton, across on the South Island. Earliest sailing is 8 a.m.; the latest, 6:40 p.m. Be *sure,* however, to check current sailing times by calling 725-399. City buses for the terminal leave from Platform 9 at the railway station 35 minutes before sailing time and meet arriving vessels. Also, since crossings can become quite crowded during summer months and holiday periods, it's a good idea to make your reservations as early as possible (perhaps through InterCity offices at your point of arrival). Fares for the 3⅓-hour, 52-nautical-mile trip are NZ$30 ($18.75) for adults, NZ$15 ($9.40) for children, plus GST. If you're going on to Christchurch, an express train leaves for Christchurch at 2:10 p.m. (connects with the 10 a.m. sailing from Wellington), and for a small charge your luggage can be through-checked at the luggage office at the Wellington Railway Station. Also, buses to and from Blenheim, Nelson, and Christchurch connect with some ferry arrivals and departures.

You'll travel on the Interisland Line on either the refurbished *Arahanga, Arahura,* or *Aratika,* each of which has a licensed bar, cafeteria, television lounge, information bureau, and shop. The *Arahura* and *Aratika* also have a family lounge with toys to keep young children amused during the voyage, video and movie theaters, a recliner lounge, and a work room. Crossings generally take on a jovial air, with passengers strolling the decks (whatever you do, don't go inside until you've viewed the departure from Wellington's lovely harbor from the rail—a sight you'll long remember) or congregating happily in the lounges, passing the time over friendly conversation and mugs of beer. *Warning:* Someone once spoke of Cook Strait's "vexed waters," and in truth the swells can be a little unsettling. If you're subject to a queasy stomach at sea, best pick up something from the pharmacy before embarking. *Another tip:* If you don't want to miss one minute of the magnificent views or the company of friendly schools of dolphins, take along a picnic lunch to eat outside under the sky and the curious glances of seagulls wheeling overhead.

As you approach the Marlborough Sound, its green waters lap shorelines (more than 600 miles in all) of wooded hills, sheer cliffs, sandy beaches in sheltered coves, and tidy little hideaway cottages, some of which may only be approached by water. Most of the islands and native bush reserves are a part of the Marlborough Sound Maritime Park, and there are picnic grounds, lookouts, and forest walks, as well as scenic roads, scattered throughout. The Maoris knew these waters as rich fishing grounds, and today they are still fished for blue cod, snapper, terakihi, grouper, kingfish, and butterfish. Protected sea fish like dolphins (and the occasional seal) romp playfully around the ferries. If you're crossing in the summer, you'll pass scores of pleasure and fishing launches and wave to happy bathers on the beaches.

Picton, your South Island debarkation point, actually lies *north* of Wellington, so you'll be sailing north to reach the South Island. Curious. Situated at the head of Queen Charlotte South, it was named by Captain Cook in 1770 for King George III's wife. He found it "a very safe and convenient cove," and indeed used it as an anchorage for much of his later Pacific exploration. He can also be credited for bringing the first sheep to New Zealand, when he put ashore a ram and a ewe in 1773—prophetic, even though that particular pair survived only a few days, and thus the good captain cannot lay claim to having furnished the fountainhead of today's millions of wooly creatures.

Most travelers scurry from ferry to train, bus, or rental car and are then off to explore an island so different from the one they've just left that there have been times in the past when there was great agitation for its independence as a separate colony. However, if time permits and the Marlborough Sound tempts you beyond resistance, you might consider staying over for some time on the water aboard one of the several launches that offer several-hours-long or day-long cruises. You'll find a cluster of launch operators at the corner of London Quay and Wellington Street near the marina in Picton. The cozy **Seaspray Tearooms Café,** on London Quay, is a good spot to get a quick bite to eat or cup of tea.

Note: If you're making this crossing south to north and weather should cause a cancellation or delay in your scheduled voyage (as has been known to happen in these fickle waters), you could be looking for a place to spend the night. There are two motels on High Street, just a five-minute walk from the ferry landing, and others are nearby. The **Picton Backpackers,** on Auckland Street (tel. 057/36-596), is in an inviting white house with wrought-iron trim an easy walk from the ferry. Accommodation in the four dormitories starts at NZ$15 ($9.40), and there are three double rooms for NZ$30 ($18.75) each. The hostel also has a lounge, laundry, kitchen, and large back lawn. And there's a good Best Western motel, the **Koromiko Park,** P.O. Box 86, Picton (tel. 057/37-350), 6 km (3½ miles) from the ferry on Hwy. 1, with rates of NZ$55 ($34.50) single and NZ$58 ($36.25) double, plus GST.

READER'S ACCOMMODATION SELECTION: "We stayed at the **Harbour View Motel,** 30 Waikawa Rd., Picton, run by Jim and Jill Reid. The beautiful room with balcony and kitchen overlooking the twinkling lights of tiny Picton was clean and convenient. Jim provided a laundry and drying room, and a morning paper, and drove us to the Newmans bus station" (P. Dienhelt, Ashippun, Wisc.).

NELSON AND THE WEST COAST

Crossing the Cook Strait is something akin to crossing an international boundary, so different are New Zealand's two islands. That's not really surprising, because both geography and history are quite different on the two sides of that stretch of water.

It is in the South Island that the majestic Southern Alps raise their snowy heads along the diagonal Alpine Fault that forms its craggy backbone. Along its West Coast are the lush, mysterious rain forests, while to the east of the Alps the broad Canterbury plains stretch to the sea. It was on those plains that prehistoric moa hunters lived in the greatest numbers, roaming the tussocklands in search of the giant birds that grazed there. When waves of Maoris began arriving, it was to the North Island that they gravitated, since its climate was more suitable for the growing of *kumara* and to their agrarian lifestyle. Thus, there were relatively few Polynesian settlements along the fringes of the South Island. It was the waters of the South Island that first lured sealers and whalers, although whalers found the northern Bay of Islands a more hospitable base for their land operations. Then when Europeans began arriving in great numbers and fierce land wars raged in the more populated North Island, South Island Maoris faced those conflicts only when tribes pushed from their lands in the north crossed the strait to battle southern tribes for territory. Because one tribe after another obliterated those who came before them, little evidence was left of South Island Maori culture, legend, and tradition.

The discovery of gold in Central Otago and on the West Coast finally brought whites pouring into the South Island in vast numbers. They came from Australia, from Europe, and from the goldfields of California to this new "promised land," and the South Island's tranquility and isolation gave way to a booming economy, which for a time saw it leading the country in terms of both population and prosperity. Inevitably, the goldfields were mined beyond profitability, but then came the advent of refrigeration, which meant that meat could be exported on a large scale. The South Island's grasslands became gold mines of a different sort, and it is on this side of the strait that you'll see the most of these wooly four-legged nuggets busily eating their way to the butcher. As a tourist, you can give them a tip of the hat as you pass, for it is their need for widespread grazing land that accounts for the fact that today only a little more than one-quarter of New Zealand's population lives on the South Island. This means that you'll find uncrowded roadways, unhurried city lifestyles, and unspoiled scenic grandeur.

Newmans coaches meet all daylight ferries in Picton, and they'll have you off to Nelson to begin your South Island odyssey for a fare of NZ$20 ($12.50). It's a two-hour trip—70 miles along Rte. 6—filled with clifftop views, seascapes glimpsed from bush-lined stretches of the road, and rolling farmlands: a pleasant, picturesque journey you may want to break with a stop by the giant totara tree in picnic grounds near Pelorus Bridge (Newmans coaches also stop at the tea room here).

1. Nelson

Nelson sits on the shores of Nelson Haven, sheltered by the unique seven-mile natural wall of Boulder Bank. Its 2,500 hours of annual sunshine, its tranquil waters, and its golden sand beaches make it perhaps the South Island's most popular summer resort. That wonderful climate, combined with the fertile land hereabouts, also makes it an important center of fruit, grapes, hops, and tobacco growing. And maybe all that sunshine has something to do with an easy-going, tolerant outlook that makes it a haven for those of an artistic bent. Potters are here in abundance, drawn by a plentiful supply of fine clay and the minerals needed for glazing; weavers raise sheep and create natural-wool works of art; artists spend hours on end trying to capture on canvas the splendors of a Nelson sunset or the shifting light on sparkling water.

Col. William Wakefield hoisted the New Zealand Company flag on Britannia Heights in December 1841 and placed a nine-pound cannon there as a signal gun (it's there today for you to see), and settlers began arriving on February 1, 1842, a day still celebrated annually in Nelson. They named the new town Nelson to honor that great British seafaring hero, since the company's first New Zealand settlement, Wellington, had been named for Britain's most famous soldier. Lord Nelson's victories, ships, and fellow admirals are commemorated in street names like Trafalgar, Vanguard, and Collingwood. Graves of some of those early settlers lie under the trees at Fairfield Park (at the corner of Trafalgar Street South and Brougham Street), and many of the gabled wooden houses they built still cling to Nelson's hillsides and nestle among more modern structures on midtown streets. Some have become the homes and studios of the artistic community.

Nelson has two distinctions of which it is equally proud: it is known as the "cradle of rugby" in New Zealand, first played here in 1870 (although Christchurch's Football Club is older than Nelson's, it didn't adopt the national sport until some five years after its introduction at Nelson's Botanical Reserve); and a native son, Baron Rutherford, has been called the "father of nuclear physics" because it was he who first discovered the secret of splitting the atom (along with other scientific achievements, which brought him international renown), and his name is perpetuated in place names like Rutherford Park, Street, and Hotel.

Come harvest time, as many as 3,000 workers—many of them students—come trouping into town to stay until the millions of apples, pears, hops, and tobacco leaves have been brought in from the surrounding fields. With its characteristic openness of spirit, Nelson assimilates them as quickly and easily as it does the hordes of tourists who descend on its beaches year after year. There's a refreshing brand of hospitality afoot in this town, which makes it a fitting introduction to the South Island.

ORIENTATION

Two landmarks will keep you oriented in Nelson: its main street, **Trafalgar Street,** and **Church Hill,** crowned by Christ Church Cathedral and surrounded by lush lawns and plantings that are a local gathering point.

Useful Information

You'll find the **Nelson Regional Promotion Office (RPO) Information Centre** on the corner of Trafalgar and Halifax Streets (P.O. Box 194), Nelson (tel. 054/82-304). Hours are 8:30 a.m. to 5 p.m. Monday through Friday. . . . The *Tourist Times,* published monthly, and the *Nelson Visitors' Guide* give you an update on what to do and see; they are available from the RPO and local hotels and motels. . . . **Newmans Coach Line** (tel. 88-369) is conveniently housed in the same building as the RPO, and coaches arrive and depart from here. . . . The **airport shuttle van** (tel. 82-304) operates regularly and costs only NZ$2 ($1.25). . . . **Taxis** pick up riders outside the Majestic Theatre on Trafalgar Street and on Bridge Street opposite Suburban Bus Company (tel. 88-225). . . . The **telephone prefix** for Nelson is 054.

WHERE TO STAY

It is true of Nelson, as of most beach resorts, that accommodations are hard to come by during summer months (December through January), and many Kiwi families book here from year to year. While it's not impossible to arrive roomless and find a place to lay your head, it is very, very chancey. Book early. Or plan to come in late fall (April and May) or early spring (September or October) when things are not so crowded and the weather is still fine.

As is also true of most resorts, Nelson has a wide variety of accommodations. You'll find them in the city proper and at the beachside suburb of **Tahunanui,** which is four miles away, but served by city buses. The RPO is not set up to handle reservations, but will refer you to the **Nelson District Motel Association,** where members serve on a rotating basis as a central booking agency for all members. They are very accommodating and will do their best to find a vacancy for you in the price range you require. If you come into town when the Regional Promotion Office is not open, there will be a sign posted in their window giving the name, address, and telephone number of the "on duty" motel.

Free Room and Board

Well, it isn't exactly "free"—it's room and board in exchange for daily farm and domestic work averaging four or more hours a day. For that, you'll be getting three healthy meals, rather basic accommodations, and a rich learning experience in the practice of conservation. If that has an appealing ring, read on.

Todd's Valley Farm, c/o G. R. Roberts, R.D. 1, Nelson (tel. 054/520-553), is the home, farm, dream, and ecological laboratory of G. R. (Dick) Roberts, a graduate of Cambridge University, teacher of biology and geography, and documentary photographer. After some few years of teaching, Dick decided in 1969 that the time had come to translate ideas into action, and he bought a beautiful, but uneconomical, 250-acre valley farm six miles north of Nelson. Only about 15 acres are flat land—the rest rise as high as 1,400 feet above the valley floor. Dick does not claim to be 100% "organic" in his farming methods, but he has nurtured the flourishing vegetable garden with none of the dubious benefits of insecticides. On the slopes, he is working out an integrated approach to biological control by mixing many species of fruit and nut trees according to microclimates. Rough hill pastures are grazed by about 300 sheep.

Dick welcomes visitors who are genuinely interested in conservation, willing to work at it, and ready to take instruction and suggestion. Although the farm is not by any means a commune, he believes that the cooperative efforts of like-minded people contributing toward a constructive alternative way of life provide an important contribution to society as a whole. "Dropouts, unproductive people, and those not willing to accept responsibility," he says, "are not part of that plan." Please do not apply unless you can stay a minimum of two weeks (brief visits may be arranged, however, for those with an avid interest in ecological land use). At Todd's Valley, conservation is a way of life: you are expected to recycle all wastes, and to refrain from smoking in the house or using drugs. You are heartily invited, however, to enjoy the warm, sunny valley two miles from the sea in all its natural beauty, gorge yourself on the fresh vegetables, and become intimately involved with the land and its problems. When you've contributed what you can and are ready to move on, Dick may be able to put you in touch with others with similar concerns in New Zealand—an entree into a circle of involved, concerned, vitally interesting people.

If you'd like to stay at Todd's Valley, write or telephone Dick in advance. He can only give beds to a few people at a time, although those who wish to camp are also welcome. *Note:* Occasionally, the farm is closed to visitors.

Hostels

The **YHA Hostel** at 42 Weka St., Nelson (tel. 054/88-817), is an inviting yellow house with a green tin roof and a huge front yard. It has 32 beds in eight rooms, hot showers, and a kitchen. All facilities are open all day. Rates for seniors are NZ$12 ($7.50); for juniors, NZ$6 ($3.75)—plus GST.

It looks like a ski lodge, but **Tasman Towers,** 10 Weka St., Nelson (tel. 054/87-950), is indeed a hostel. Its modern lounge is a natural congregating place, and the posted map of Nelson is the easiest to read you'll find. There are 17 rooms, mostly doubles and twins, a kitchen, laundry, and luggage storage. A no-smoking rule is enforced. The rate is NZ$13 ($8.15) per person.

All nine rooms in **Bumbles,** downtown at 8 Bridge St., Nelson (tel. 054/82-771), have their own sink with H&C, carpeting, and colorful duvets on the beds. There is also a dormitory with ten beds. The annex has another 11 units, each with private bath, heater, and tea- and coffee-making facilities. All rooms are no-smoking. There is a vegetarian/seafood restaurant open for lunch and dinner, as well as a kitchen, laundry, and baggage storage for guests' use. The owners, John and Joanne McTavish, have put their hotel and restaurant experience to good use here. Rates are NZ$10 ($6.25) per person for the bunkroom, NZ$18 ($11.25) per person for rooms for two to four people (price includes linens and duvet), and NZ$50 ($31.25) double for rooms with private bath.

READERS' HOSTEL SELECTIONS: "All hostelers traveling in Nelson should check out **Pavlova House,** 328 Brook St. (tel. 054/89-906), an excellent and homey private hostel. On arrival we were treated to a 'cuppa' and a piece of Pavlova (hence the name) by our hosts, Cedric and Isabel Hockey. This is how every lucky arrival is greeted. The Hockeys also pick up all new arrivals at any time and run a twice-daily shuttle service for guests. The house is spotless, well equipped, and well furnished. There's an informative notice board, free bicycle, plenty of books and games, a large veranda, and even a couple of hammocks. We had a 'luverly' time and have never stayed in a better hostel" (H. and R. Waines, Essex, U.K.). [*Author's Note:* Another reader, T. Erickson, of Cloquet, Minn., echoes these sentiments.] . . . **"Peter and Pat King** operate a farm in Eves Valley, 20 minutes south of Nelson (tel. 054/23-781), and they have an old house on the property where visitors can bunk for very little money per night. The time I spent here was one of the highlights of my New Zealand trip; the hosts and the setting are great, and if you call a few days ahead, they might pick you up in Nelson" (N. Di Palermo, Vancouver, B.C., Canada).

Cabins/Campgrounds

The **Tahuna Beach Holiday Park,** Beach Road (Private Bag), Tahunanui, Nelson (tel. 054/85-159), is one of the largest motor camps in New Zealand, regularly handling as many as 4,500 travelers per night during summer months and even more at Christmas. Spread over 55 acres, the camp is a short three-minute walk to the beach, and local bus service is at the corner; shuttle service is also available. The well-kept grounds hold a large selection of vacation accommodations as well as tent and trailer sites. If you're not traveling with your own linens, they may be rented for a small charge. Amenities include seven shower and toilet blocks, six kitchens and laundries, ironing boards, car wash, TV lounge, children's adventure playgrounds, and miniature golf. A large food shop on the grounds is open every day. This is a beautifully maintained place, with all accommodations kept freshly painted, carpeted, and comfortably furnished. Vacation units are "star graded" for quality and price: top-quality, fully self-contained, four-star units at NZ$64 ($40); self-contained, three-plus-star units at NZ$38 ($23.75); semi-self-contained, three-star units at NZ$33 ($20.75); two-star and two-plus-star units at NZ$22 ($13.75) and NZ$27 ($17). Sites are NZ$14 ($8.75). All rates are for double occupancy, including GST. On all units, there's a surcharge for one-night stays.

Bed-and-Breakfasts

The lovely **Willow Bank** guesthouse, 71 Golf Rd., Tahunanui, Nelson (tel. 054/85-041), is a gracious, two-story house set back from the road on shaded lawns and just a short walk from the beach. There's a pretty outdoor swimming pool, a spacious TV lounge with pool table, laundry facilities, off-street parking, and a courtesy car to all terminals. Rooms are attractively done up, comfortable, and have H&C, electric blankets, and thermostatic heaters. You can have a full, cooked breakfast or continental breakfast in the spacious dining room. Rates for bed-and-breakfast are NZ$44 ($27.50) single, NZ$66 ($41.25) double. Add GST.

You'll know the **Palm Grove Guest House,** 52 Cambria St., Nelson (tel. 054/84-645), by the two gigantic palms that tower above the two-story white house. And you'll remember it for the friendly hospitality of Mrs. Devlin, your hostess. The house is bright, cheerful, and sunny throughout, with comfortably furnished rooms, some of which look out to nice mountain views. There's a tea and coffee room off the guest lounge, and a light and airy dining room. Only four of the six rooms have H&C, but all are convenient to baths. There are two singles, two with twin beds, one with three single beds, and one family room with one double bed and one single. Bed-and-breakfast rates are NZ$25 ($15.75) per person, and include GST. Highly recommended.

Trafalgar Autolodge, 46 Trafalgar St., Nelson (tel. 054/83-980), is another old two-story home, which has been restored with loving care. There's an attractive dining room and lounge with TV and radio, tea- and coffee-making facilities, laundry facilities, and off-street parking. All rooms have H&C, are fully carpeted, and are nicely furnished. Bed-and-breakfast rates are NZ$33 ($20.75) single, NZ$50 ($31.25) double, including GST. Hosts Bill and Aida Verberne provide a homey, friendly place to stay only a one-minute walk from the city center. There are also six motel units (see below), which are quite nice.

A reader wrote that his experience at the **California House,** at 29 Collingwood St., Nelson (tel. 054/84-173), had caused him to triple his stay in Nelson. Moreover, proprietor Carol Glen (who closes the doors in winter and goes to California) always made sherry, tea, coffee, and cookies available and prepared excellent, varied breakfasts. The charming yellow house has a flower-trimmed walkway, a wide, wraparound porch, leaded-glass trim, a study complete with Scrabble and Trivial Pursuit, a country kitchen, and delightful rooms. That reader was right: you'll definitely want to extend your stay. Strict no-smoking and no-children rules are enforced. Rates range from NZ$60 ($37.50) single, NZ$80 ($50) to NZ$110 ($68.75) double. Add GST.

Motel Flats

Those motel flats at the **Trafalgar Autolodge** (see above) sleep four, are bright, clean, and attractively furnished, and have fully equipped kitchens, TV, radio, telephone, electric blankets, and private shower and bath. Off-street parking, and laundry facilities are available. Rates are NZ$50 ($31.25) single, NZ$60.50 ($37.75) double, including GST.

One of my favorite Best Western motels in New Zealand is the **Courtesy Court Motel,** 30 Golf Rd., Tahunanui, Nelson (tel. 054/85-114). That's partly because of its proximity to the beach (a short walk), pretty grounds (with well-tended, colorful flowerbeds), and comfortable accommodations, but mostly because of Doris and Wally Cheesman, who have owned and operated the place since 1968. Friendlier, more helpful hosts you just won't find anywhere. And I like the arrangements of the units around an inner court away from street noises and facing the attractive heated swimming pool. There are bed-sitters, one-bedroom units that sleep as many as four, and two-bedroom units that will sleep six; all have complete kitchen, soft carpets, electric blankets and heaters, color TV, radio, telephone, a drying rack for hand wash, wash cloths, and a complimentary morning paper; one "honeymoon" unit has a waterbed and spa bath. A luxury "executive suite" is also available, with space for six. A guest laundry, spa pool, and children's play area are additional conveniences. Doris and Wally welcome children and will gladly provide a cot and highchair as well as arrange for babysitters. Rates (which are, of course, subject to Best Western discounts) are NZ$60 ($37.50) single, NZ$70 ($43.75) double, plus GST. The entrance to Golf Road is at Kentucky Fried Chicken in the Tahunanui shopping area.

"Cozy, quiet, and convenient," says Des Puklowski, who with his wife, Sue, runs the **Mid-City Motor Lodge,** 218 Trafalgar St., Nelson (tel. 054/83-595 or 69-063), right smack in the center of the city center. Well, I have to agree with him, and I have to add that you might walk right past it without realizing that it is a motel. You see, this one is located on the first, second, and third floors of a modern five-story office building! Each unit is smartly done up, fully serviced, and has TV, phone, large shower room, and cooking facilities. There's a laundry room and off-street parking. There are 15 units on the three floors and a family unit up on the rooftop. Mr. and Mrs. Puklowski are warm, friendly hosts who are especially fond of American guests—in fact, they'll give a NZ$5 ($3.15) discount to anyone who arrives clutching this book. Rates begin at NZ$60 ($37.50) single, NZ$66 ($41.25) double, and these rates include GST. There are also five two- and four-bedroom luxury units for NZ$70 ($43.75). Continental or cooked breakfast is available.

What I particularly like about the small **Waimarie Motel,** 45 Collingwood St., Nelson (tel. 054/89-415), is its setting on the bank of the Maitai River. There are only five units, but each has a separate bedroom, fully equipped kitchen, TV, and video. The units are spacious, and there's a garage for parking. From here, you're only a few minutes' walk from downtown. Continental breakfast is available. Rates are NZ$61 ($38.25) single and NZ$71 ($44.50) double.

The **Blue Waters Motel,** 66 Golf Rd., Tahunanui, Nelson (tel. 054/85-080), is another very good Best Western. Units are centered around a pretty landscaped lawn (with a lovely lemon tree) and heated swimming pool. The well-appointed one- and two-bedroom units have TVs with video, telephones, and electric blankets, and one has a waterbed. Amenities include a hot spa, trampoline, and guest laundry, and cooked or continental breakfasts are available. Rates are NZ$64 ($40) single, NZ$74 ($46.25) double, plus GST, and Best Western discounts apply. Pat and Duncan Fuller are the congenial hosts.

Mini-Splurges

You can't miss the striking **Beachcomber Motor Inn,** at 23 Beach Rd., Nelson (tel. 054/85-985), with its red-tile, pagoda-style roof. It has 28 rooms, including three waterbed suites, some with interlocking doors to expand to family units. All have H&C, tea- and coffee-making facilities, towel-warming racks in the bath, TV, and in-house videos (two a night!). Upstairs units have spa pools for a private soak. There is also a licensed restaurant that serves European and Chinese dishes, and a pool. Rates are NZ$81 ($50.75) single, NZ$94.50 ($59) double,

NZ$105.75 ($66) triple, NZ$112.50 ($70.25) for waterbed suites, and NZ$144 ($90) for family units. All rates include GST.

The **Quality Inn,** P.O. Box 248, Nelson (tel. 054/82-299), has an ideal location at Trafalgar Square opposite the cathedral. There are nine floors of double and twin rooms and suites. The baths come with a large tub, and there's 24-hour room service (to me, that's happiness), not to mention a brasserie, pool, spa pool, sauna, workout room, and a large lobby filled with leather chairs. Standard rooms are NZ$80 ($50), single or double, though there is one floor of rooms at NZ$66 ($41.25), a very good value; superior rooms cost NZ$93.50 ($58.50); and suites, NZ$132 ($82.50)—all including GST.

WHERE TO EAT

One of my favorite places in Nelson for good, home cooked light meals in pleasant surroundings is the **Manhattan Coffee Lounge,** 206 Trafalgar St. (tel. 84-475), between Hardy and Bridge Streets. Framed art prints line the walls, owner G. L. Hobbs and the staff behind the self-service counter are friendly and helpful, and all baking is done right on the premises. A full cooked breakfast runs NZ$4.50 ($2.80), and light, inexpensive fare—savouries, pies, sandwiches—is served throughout the day. Hours are 7:30 a.m. to 5 p.m. Monday through Thursday, until 9 p.m. on Friday, and until 1 p.m. on Saturday.

More than just an eating place, **Chez Eelco Coffee House,** 296 Trafalgar St. (tel. 87-595), is just about the most popular meeting place in town for students, artists, craftspeople, townspeople, and tourists. In fine weather there are bright umbrella tables on the sidewalk out front. Inside, there are red-and-white café curtains, matching ruffled lampshades, and candles in wine bottles after dark. Eelco Boswijk (a Dutchman who came to New Zealand over 30 years ago) has owned the high-ceilinged, cavernous place since 1961, and has always run it much like one of New York City's Greenwich Village coffeehouses. There's the buzz of contented conversation, table-hopping regulars, a backroom whose walls are a virtual art gallery, a piano for the occasional pianist, and paper placemats that give names and addresses of local artists. The extensive menu includes toasted sandwiches, hamburgers, scones, omelets, yogurt, salad plates, steaks, chicken, Marlborough mussels, Nelson scallops, native cheeses, and sweets that include fresh cream cakes. In short, it's a place to drop in for coffee or tea and a snack, enjoy a light meal, or order your main meal of the day. Then sit back and dine at your leisure. Popular specialties are mussel chowder and salad bowl with hot roll, both at NZ$5 ($3.15). Prices run NZ$1 (65¢) to NZ$18 ($11.25) for a filet steak, the most expensive item on the menu. Open daily from 7 a.m. to 11 p.m. Breakfast is available.

The **Hitching Post,** 145 Bridge St. (tel. 87-374), sports an old hitching ring on its front door and a pot-bellied iron stove inside. Pizzas, salads, and steaks share the menu here in a price range of NZ$8 ($5) to NZ$20 ($12.50). Try the large milkshakes for NZ$1.30 (80¢). The dining room is rustic and cozy, but I must confess to a weakness for the courtyard out back, where a brick barbecue is provided for those who want to cook their own steak or ham. In a setting of Kiwi vines and other native plantings, you dine on white garden-type furniture, and for before- or after-meal entertainment, a giant backgammon board adorns the cement tile floor (even if you don't play, it's fun to watch others while you dine). You can reach the courtyard either through the main dining room or by way of a small wooden door out front, which opens to a narrow pathway leading to the back. The Hitching Post is a good dropping-in place, since service is continuous from 8 a.m. to 9 p.m. Monday through Friday, 5 to 9:30 p.m. on Saturday, and 5 to 9 p.m. on Sunday in summer.

One of the most fun places to eat (and drink) in Nelson is actually in Stoke, at **Robinson's,** on the grounds of Robinson Brothers, on the Main Road (tel. 77-477), producers of natural fruit juices and fruit wines. The menu is simple and hearty, and it changes with the seasons. The smell of apples and the sound of birds permeate the place. The drinks list even includes apple wine. Entrees cost about NZ$5.50

($3.45), and the main courses, NZ$13 ($8.15). A filling open-face sandwich will cost you NZ$9 ($5.65). Open daily for lunch from 11 a.m. to 4 p.m. (until 3 p.m. in winter) and for dinner from 6 to 10 p.m. Licensed.

Figpecker's, 135 Bridge St. (tel. 89-891), is a casual sort of eatery that offers extremely good value for your dollar. The extensive menu ranges all over the map, with ethnic dishes that range from Chinese to German to Italian, and the beauty of it is that most are above average in preparation and below average in cost. There's a NZ$10 ($6.25) lunch special weekdays, and a NZ$15 ($9.40) four-course dinner offered Monday through Saturday. Open every night but Sunday from 6 p.m., with live music on some summer weekends. Licensed.

If you like sunsets and seafood, combine the two at the **Fisherman's Table,** Wakefield Quay (tel. 83-319), where you can get an outside table and enjoy the sea breeze. Seafood chowder costs NZ$6.50 ($4.05), and seafood main dishes start at NZ$14.50 ($9.05). Breakfast fare includes pancakes from NZ$3 ($1.90) to NZ$5 ($3.15) and omelets from NZ$6 ($3.75) to NZ$8 ($5). Open weekdays from 7 a.m. to 3 p.m. (breakfast ends at 11:30 a.m.) and 5:30 to 10 p.m. for dinner (from 8 a.m. on weekends). Licensed.

Popular with locals and visitors alike, **City Lights,** 142 Hardy St. (tel. 88-999), with its pink façade, has a lively atmosphere. Main dishes cost NZ$16 ($10) to NZ$20 ($12.50) and feature meat and fish dishes served with hot vegetables. There are daily blackboard specials and a vegetarian dish. Chilled strawberry soup is a favorite. The owners are Ben Van Dyke, from California, and his wife, Miranda, from New Zealand. Open from 5:30 p.m. to late, October through April. BYO.

Ribbetts, 20 Tahunanui Dr. (tel. 86-911), is in a former butcher shop with café curtains and a black-and-white tile floor. It serves outstanding Indian, Italian, and European dishes (including frogs' legs). Dinner prices are in the NZ$25 ($15.75) to NZ$30 ($18.75) range, and hours are 6 to 10 p.m. daily except Tuesday. BYO.

A Splurge

The house that is now home to **Juniper's,** 144 Collingwood St. (tel. 88-832), was built for a vicar, then inhabited by a commune. Today it's home to Nelson's top restaurant, which has soft pink walls, black tablecloths, and fresh flowers and candles on all the tables. There's a small bar with a fireplace. Entrees include garlic mussels and duck dim sum, and main dishes feature apricot chicken, venison medallions, quail chartreuse, and rack of lamb. Need I say more? Hosts Christine and Pradeep Kumar are most welcoming. Figure on spending NZ$30 ($18.75) to NZ$40 ($25) for a meal. It's licensed or BYO, which is a saving. Open Monday through Saturday from 6:30 p.m.

READERS' DINING SELECTIONS: "In Nelson, the **Hole-in-the-Wall** restaurant is a terrific place to eat. It's run by the same couple who had the Brown House when we were here a couple of years ago, and they still serve the best food in Nelson, we think. Locals seem to agree with us, since it was crowded both times we went" (T. Jones, Seattle, Wash.). . . . "We loved **Traffer's Restaurant,** at Hardy and Trafalgar Streets" (S. Winchester, Dublin, Ireland). . . . "For an ethnic change of palette, head out to Tahuna Beach and try **Amigos Steak and Taco House,** 13 Beach Rd. (tel. 85-686), or **Chinatown,** 42 Tahunanui Dr. (tel. 86-998)" (A. E. Ellington, New York, N.Y.).

THINGS TO SEE AND DO

There's no way you're going to miss seeing **Christ Church Cathedral,** sitting as it does on a splendid elevation at the end of Trafalgar Street. And chances are good that you'll find yourself, at some point during your Nelson stay, stopping for a rest in its beautiful grounds—if you follow the lead of the locals, you'll bypass the handy benches to stretch out on the grass. That site, now known as **Church Hill,** has in the past held an early Maori *pa,* the New Zealand Company's depot, a small fort, and a tent church. The present Gothic cathedral is made of local Takaka marble; above its west door are the carved heads of five bishops, one archbishop, and King George V. The most striking aspects of the interior of the cathedral are its stained glass, particularly the rose window, and its unique free-standing organ. Open to the public from 7 a.m. to 4 p.m. daily, with extended hours in summer. Guides are available between Christmas and Easter.

Nelson's affection for the arts is exemplified in the excellent **Suter Art Gallery,** on Bridge Street by Queen's Gardens. Works by a bevy of important New Zealand painters are on display—look for the marvelous Ships Cove painted by James Webber, who sailed on Captain Cook's third voyage as official artist. There's also an outstanding collection of works by master painter John Gully, who lived here for a time—if they're not on display, they can be seen by appointment. The gallery also has a craft shop selling prints, pottery, and weaving, and a nice restaurant overlooking Queen's Gardens. The gallery has just completed a multifunctional theater that seats 160 people and has instituted an extensive program of film, theater, music, and dance; to find out what's on, check the local newspaper. Gallery hours are Tuesday through Sunday from 10:30 a.m. to 4:30 p.m. (also on Monday during school holidays).

Walkers will be in their element in Nelson and the immediate vicinity. Good **walks** abound, both in-city and in the environs, varying from an hour to a full-day's tramp. The RPO has detailed guide pamphlets from which to select those you'll have time to enjoy. Be sure to ask for *Nelson—The City of Walks,* for which there's a small charge. My favorite stroll is along **Shakespeare Walk,** which follows the Maitai River and can be picked up where Collingwood and Halifax Streets intersect at the bridge. You'll see ducks and quaint cottages and cross a pedestrian bridge that will point you back into town.

Go back in time at **Founder's Park,** 87 Atawhai Dr. (tel. 82-649), where you'll find a turn-of-the-century city in miniature and a true celebration of Nelson's commercial and industrial development. Old St. Peter's Church, built in 1874, has been moved here. My favorites are the Newmans coaches from 1923, 1947, and 1952, which actually saw years of service. The **Anchor Inn** restaurant, in a building dating from 1853, is open for meals from 11:30 a.m. to 2:30 p.m. and for tea until 4 p.m. There is a 17-minute audio-visual show and a gift shop with reasonable prices. The unique Visitors Centre, by the way, is a replica of an old mill that used to stand in Nelson where the RPO is now. The park is open from 10 a.m. to 4:30 p.m. daily, and rates are NZ$4 ($2.50) for adults, half that for kids.

Arts and Crafts

One of the great pleasures of a stop in Nelson is visiting some of its many resident artists and artisans. The RPO can give you a brochure of names and addresses of those who welcome visitors to their studios and suggested tour itineraries. I can promise in advance that it will be a rewarding experience to talk with painters, weavers, potters, and other craftspeople about the subject dearest to their hearts—rewarding, too, perhaps in that very special memento or gift you may find for sale.

Actually, even without the RPO's list, you can spend a marvelous hour or two along **South Street** with its artistic population. It's lined with small colonial homes, which have been creatively restored, and the street gives you a sense of what early Nelson must have been like. At the corner of Nile and South Streets, visit the **South Street Gallery** in an old, two-story brown house to see some of Nelson's finest pottery. It's open from 10 a.m. to 5 p.m. daily.

The **Nelson Community Potters,** 136 Rutherford St., is the hangout of talented amateur potters, and there are regular day schools (just in case you're an aspiring potter yourself). There's usually someone at work there, and many of their finished products are for sale. Drop by **Seven Weavers,** 36 Collingwood St., for prime examples of weaving from native wools. You'll find crafts happily mingling with art at the **Suter Art Gallery,** on Bridge Street.

Other interesting craft shops are the **Glass Studio,** 276 Hardy St.; and **Jens**

Hansen, a cooperative gold and silversmith workshop and sales room, 320 Trafalgar Square.

Still farther south, on the Richmond By-Pass (Salisbury Road), Paul Laird runs **Waimea Pottery Ltd.** (tel. 47-481). His ovenproof stoneware and luster-ware are sold in the Richmond showroom and throughout New Zealand, as are the unique hand-printed tiles by Colleen Laird.

Abel Tasman National Park

This extremely beautiful and popular park, named for 17th-century Dutch explorer Abel Tasman, covers 54,683 acres, extending from Separation Point, which divides Golden and Tasman Bays in the north, to Marahau Inlet in the south. A popular way to see some of the park is to take an **Abel Tasman National Park Enterprises boat trip** from Kaiteriteri and be dropped off at Bark Bay; then walk the track 2½ hours to Torrent Bay, where you'll have three hours to enjoy the area. Other boat trips provide just as much scenery, but less exercise. This area, with its sandy coves, has been called the most beautiful stretch of coastline in New Zealand. Most of the boat trips cost NZ$30 ($18.75) for adults, half that for children. There's a bus from Nelson to Kaiteriteri; the round-trip fare is about NZ$10 ($6.25).

There is a hostel, the **White Elephant,** 25 minutes from the park, at 55 Whakarewa St. (P.O. Box 181), in Moutueka, Nelson (tel. 0524/86-208); opposite the high school; the rate is NZ$12.50 ($7.80) per person. The **Marahau Camping Ground** in Motueka (tel. 0524/78-176) has tent sites for NZ$8 ($5) per person, caravans for NZ$20 ($12.50) double, and cabins for NZ$25 ($15.75) double. There is also a campground in **Totaranui,** where a park ranger is based.

If you feel like splurging (physically, spiritually, and monetarily), link up with one of the **four-day guided walks** through the park that leave on Monday and Friday; for more information about them, contact John Wilson, Abel Tasman National Park Enterprises, Green Tree Road, R.D.3, Motueka, Nelson (tel. 0524/87-801).

Southern Sights offers minibus (nine-seater) charters to the park; check with one of the hostels in Nelson or call 054/83-272.

READERS' TOURING SUGGESTIONS: "The side trip to Kaiteriteri beach and Kaka Pa Point, looking to Abel Tasman, was one of the most magnificent views on the South Island. We also took the road to Totaranui Park in Abel Tasman Park; it was fantastic at the end but the road was awful" (J. and P. Conrad, San Jose, Calif.).

Fishing

If you've ever cast a line or dropped a hook, the South Island's marvelous fishing waters are bound to be a temptation to tarry long enough to try your luck. The only problem is knowing just where, when, and how to fish all those rivers, lakes, and streams. Well, in Nelson take yourself off to **Sportsgoods (Nelson) Ltd.** on the CML Corner (tel. 89-899) to see Tony Busch and his staff. Tony knows these waters well and has guided fisherfolk from all over the world who come here just to fish with him. Tony has also written several guidebooks that lead visiting anglers mile by mile to the best fishing spots in New Zealand. His latest book, *A Trout Fishing Guide to New Zealand's South Island,* describes not only fishing areas but the geography, climate, and anglers' techniques used in the South Island. One reader (A. L. Holmes, from Denver, Colo.) wrote in praise of the book: "I have made three trips to New Zealand in the last four years, and without a guide, my fishing has been mediocre at best. I can't afford a guide every day, nor do I want one with me every day. Sometimes I enjoy just the sound of the water and my own thoughts. I have never seen such a thoroughly detailed book, and I firmly believe that anyone with a little talent at all can have a spectacular fishing vacation with Tony's book as his guide."

No matter what your time or budget requirements, the anglers at Sportsgoods can put together a fishing expedition to fit, and you may be certain you'll carry home many a "fish story" as a result.

Vern Brabant, of the **Nelson River Guides,** P.O. Box 469, Nelson (tel. 04/85-095), is highly regarded locally as a guide. He offers excellent trout-fishing forays, with a maximum of two anglers at a time. He'll take you into remote places, using combinations of helicopters, planes, and camping is in tents.

In the Vicinity

A map detailing **scenic drives** from Nelson is available at the RPO, all past points of historical significance as well as natural beauty. There are two national parks within driving distance, sheltered sandy beaches all along the coast (one of the best is **Tahuna Beach,** three miles to the south, or if it's too crowded, the beach at Rabbit Island), and several wineries open to the public (ask at the RPO for *A Guide to Nelson's Wineries*). If you don't relish being behind the wheel yourself, several coach tours and scenic flights are available. The RPO can give you current details.

One place you should definitely plan to visit is the suburb of **Stoke.** That's where you'll find the **Nelson Provincial Museum,** filled with pioneer artifacts and displays depicting the area's Maori and European history. The museum has the largest collection of historical photographs in New Zealand, with more than a million images, as well as a large historical reference library. The museum sits directly behind an elegant 19th-century stone house with dormer windows and an ornate veranda, which is known as Isel House, situated in manicured grounds (called Isel Park) set back from the Main Road. The house, with its collections of early porcelain, pottery, and furniture, is only open weekends from 2 to 4 p.m. from November to March, but the park itself is well worth a stroll to relax beneath mature trees, which came to New Zealand from worldwide origins as seeds or mere saplings in the 19th century. The museum is open Tuesday through Friday from 10 a.m. to 4 p.m., 2 to 5 p.m. on weekends and holidays.

Also in Stoke is **Broadgreen House,** at 276 Nayland Rd., a cob house (thick walls made of packed earth) built in 1855, which has been authentically restored and furnished by dedicated volunteers. Their care and attention to detail is evident all through the house, from the drawing room with its slate mantelpiece and original French wallpaper to the upstairs nursery with wicker carriages and antique dolls. Outside, the rose garden holds more than 2,500 plants, with some 250 varieties represented. Hours are 2 to 4:30 p.m. on Wednesday, Saturday, Sunday, and public holidays except for Christmas Day and Good Friday, more often in January, May, and August. Check with the RPO for extended hours.

EN ROUTE SOUTH

The choice is up to you: a full day's driving—6½ to 7 hours and an early start —will get you to Greymouth or Hokitika; or you can proceed at a more leisurely pace and stop off at Westport, which is emerging as a center for outdoor-adventure activities and a place that, though fiercely noncommercial, makes a real effort to make visitors feel welcome. You can stop for lunch in **Murchison** (the bus depot tea room is your best bet—turn left at the Hampton Hotel) or in Westport if you can hold out that long, where there's a wider choice of eateries.

If you're traveling by Newmans Coach, your driver's interesting narrative will fill you in on the history of most of the terrain you'll be covering along a road that is steep and winding at times, drops through heavily wooded mountain gorges at others, touches the sea, then turns south along a dramatic coastline, sometimes seen from high bluffs along which the road passes. If you're driving, here are some key landscape notes:

Between Murchison and Westport, you'll be following the **Buller River** much of the way. Those jagged gaps and high scarped bluffs above the wall of the gorge between Murchison and Lyell are the legacy of a disastrous earthquake in June 1929. Passing through the goldmining ghost town of **Lyell**, you'll see little left to suggest the thriving, bustling town of goldrush days. Its last surviving building, the Lyell Hotel, burned in 1963, leaving only a few faint vestiges of those turbulent times. Descending to the lower gorge, you'll be driving through flatlands, then under **Hawkes Crag**, where the road has been hewn from a sheer face of solid rock above the river, and on to a stretch of road between bush-clad walls and rocky ravines.

2. Westport

Most people zip past Westport on their way to Greymouth or Hokitika rather than bothering to turn off Hwy. 6 onto Buller Gorge Road and drive to the coast. If you do take that turnoff, keep an eye out for the **Buller Adventure Tours information Center** off to the left in a wooden house set back from the road. This is the perfect place to learn about the area's attractions, as well as stretch your legs and have a cup of tea. Westport (and food and lodging) is just eight short minutes away.

The town of Westport, 40 miles north of Greymouth with a population of 5,000, found relative prosperity as a coal-mining center after weathering the gold bust. It is served daily by Newmans coaches via the coast road and by InterCity via Reefton and a train connection. The **Buller Information Centre,** on Palmerston Street (P.O. Box 21), Westport (tel. 0289/6658), is open from 9 a.m. to 5 p.m. Monday through Friday. **Coaltown,** on Queen Street South (tel. 8204), is a mining museum with a walk-through coal mine and a multiscreen audio-visual presentation. It's open daily from 8:30 a.m. to 4:30 p.m.

Of course, the main draw here is nature, and to find out how to get on a first-name basis with it, contact **Buller Adventure Tours,** on Buller Gorge Road, State Hwy. 6 (tel. 0289/6658 or 7286); or **Norwest Adventures,** P.O. Box 356, Westport (tel. 0289/8922 or 6686). The former specializes in such adventures as jet-boating, rafting, and horse trekking, while the latter sticks to caving, tramping, camping, and fishing. Norwest has a popular trip billed as "underworld rafting"; you actually float through one of the largest caves in New Zealand, which is filled with glowworms (I'm told the experience is totally different from Waitomo). You'll find the staff on each of these tours to be young, knowledgeable, and quite bullish on Buller.

WHERE TO STAY

Westport is a small place, but its accommodations, though limited in number, may be some of the most pleasant of your trip.

Hostels

Tripinns, 72 Queen St., Westport (tel. 0289/7367), in an atmospherically old house (100-plus years), opened its doors to travelers in 1989. A five-minute walk from the bus depot, it can accommodate 40 lodgers in 15 rooms, including two doubles, four twins, and a bunkroom. The inviting lounge has a high ceiling, fireplace, stereo, and TV. There is a game room with a pool table, and the kitchen has a microwave oven. The name of the hostel is a play on manager Maurice Tipping's name (no hallucinogens here). Backpackers pay NZ$11.50 ($7.20), plus a NZ$4 ($2.50) charge for linens and blankets; the double rooms are NZ$27 ($17).

Dale's Youth Hostel, 56 Russell St., Westport, has limited accommodations but is always a hit with those who stay there, mainly because of Dale herself. The rate is NZ$10 ($6.25) per person.

Motel Flats

The **Buller Bridge Motel,** on the Esplanade, Westport (tel. 0289/7519), is a real retreat. It has ten self-contained units with a kitchen, TV, and video. I particularly like the large, grassy courtyard; kids like the play area and the rabbit and other animals that hosts Vivienne and David Jolly keep around for their guests' entertainment. There is a guest laundry, as well as a spa pool. Rates are NZ$60.50 ($37.80) single and NZ$72.60 ($45.40) double, plus GST.

WHERE TO EAT

The **Mandala Coffee House,** 110 Palmerston St., across from the fire station (tel. 7931), doubles as a gallery of local artisanship since owner Tony Ibbotson built the place and made all the tables, chairs, and even the highchairs, of rimu wood. The stained-glass lampshades were made by another local artisan. The menu changes with the seasons and includes everything from pizza to stir-fried vegetables; the soups (especially the mussel soup) and the desserts are quite good, as is the fresh-brewed coffee. Main dishes are about NZ$13 ($8.15). It's open from 8 a.m. (9 a.m. on weekends) to 10 p.m.

The place to come for an evening out in Westport is **Cristy's,** 18 Wakefield St. (tel. 7640), and it surely is conducive to lingering. The menu features local dishes of lamb and fish, as well as steak, and there are always blackboard specials. The wine is stored in an old bank vault, and there is coal-mining memorabilia everywhere. A meal will run about NZ$30 ($18.75). Come by for a drink even if you don't plan on dining. It's open daily from 6:30 to 9 p.m. Reservations are recommended. Licensed.

Drop by for a drink in the **Cosmopolitan Hotel Bar,** on Palmerston Street (tel. 6305). Surely you've been admiring the old hotels along Westport's main street, and this is a good opportunity to go inside one (and one with two fireplaces) and fraternize with the locals.

EN ROUTE TO GREYMOUTH

Turning sharply south at Westport to follow the coastline, you'll pass **Mitchell's Gully Gold Mine** only 12½ miles along your way. It's a fascinating place, not a tourist attraction but a *real* working mine, open from 9 a.m. to 4 p.m. daily except Christmas. It's been in the Mitchell family since 1866, and Ian and Helen McKinnon are the friendly miners. Back on the road, you'll soon pass through **Charleston,** where gold was discovered in 1866, leading to a population boom, with dancehalls, stores, and some 92 hotels—few reminders remain today.

About halfway between Westport and Greymouth, you'll come to one of the west coast's most unusual natural formations, the **Punakaiki Pancake Rocks.** (*Note:* Newmans buses stop here so passengers may walk down to see them.) At the top of a steep headland, a simple tea room, rest room, and shop are on the inland side of the road, along with space for parking to allow you to leave your car and follow the track across the road through native bush to the sea, where limestone structures, which look for all the world like a gigantic stack of pancakes, jut out into the water. When the seas are high and rough, water comes surging into the deep caverns below and is spouted up some 20 to 30 feet into the air, accompanied by a tremendous whoosh of sound. The surrounding area has been kept as a scenic reserve.

From the Punakaiki Rocks, the road is almost continually within sight of the sea until you turn to cross the **Grey River** and drive into Greymouth.

READER'S ACCOMMODATION SELECTION: "Peaceful **Punakaiki Camping Ground,** on the Porarari River just north of the Pancake Rocks (tel. 027/21-894), in Greymouth), has plenty of trees and picnic tables on its grounds, and from here it's easy to walk along the river and into the gorge or to rent a canoe. Choose tent or caravan sites, a bunkhouse, and some cabins" (E. F. Anderson, St. Paul, Minn.).

---

3. Greymouth

At Greymouth, it's decision-making time: whether to stop here or push on another 25 miles to Hokitika. Greymouth offers a wider choice of accommodations; Hokitika has more attractions. Greymouth does have Shantytown, a reconstructed gold mining town, but there's no local transportation to it, and it's quite possible to double back to see it from a Hokitika base. In the final analysis, your decision may rest chiefly on just how tired and hungry you are when you reach Greymouth, erstwhile "Heart of the Coast."

New Zealand's West Coast is a rugged stretch of country whose incomparable beauty has been molded and shaped by the elements—and its inhabitants are perhaps the most rugged and individualistic of a nation of individuals. Lured by Mother Nature's treasures, they have from the beginning seemed to revel in her challenges, and along with a resilient toughness have developed a rollicking sense of fun, a relaxed acceptance of the vicissitudes of West Coast life, and a brand of hospitality that is recognized (and even boasted of) by Kiwis in every other part of the country. "Coasters" are a hardy and good-hearted breed who will welcome you warmly to this unique region.

The coast's beauty and hidden wealth were entirely lost on Captain Cook when he sighted it from the sea, remained offshore, and described it in his journal as "wild and desolate and unworthy of observation." Of course, his sea-based observation could not possibly reveal the presence of nuggets of gold strewn about those "unworthy" beaches. That discovery was left for 1864, when it precipitated an influx of prospectors and miners from as far afield as California (along with a goodly number from Australia), many of whom would remain after the goldfields played out in 1867 to form the basis of a permanent population who take fierce pride in their particular part of New Zealand.

Greymouth, with a population of 12,000, keeps busy these days with coal and timber exports and the import of tourists who come to roam the beaches in search of gemstones and greenstone, fish in the clear streams nearby, and perhaps pan for gold.

USEFUL INFORMATION

The **Information Centre** is in the Regent Theatre Building on Mackay Street (tel. 027/51-01), on the corner of Herbert and Mackay Streets. Hours are 9 a.m. to 5 p.m. Monday through Friday. They can furnish detailed information about the area and book accommodations at no charge. Movies are shown Thursday through Sunday night at 8 p.m. in the building, and nightly during school holiday periods (beware Friday, when the teenage crowd gets frisky and noisy). The information center is also open to visitors from 7:15 p.m. on those evenings. Shirley Thomas runs both with great humor and helpfulness. . . . The **Trans Alpine Express** to Christchurch leaves from the Greymouth railroad station on Mackay Street. . . . The **telephone prefix** for Greymouth is 027.

WHERE TO STAY

There are many good accommodations at inexpensive rates. Motel and guesthouse operators are also very cooperative, helping you find a vacancy if your choice is filled.

Hostels

The **YHA Hostel, "Kainga-Ra,"** Cowper Street (P.O. Box 299), Greymouth (tel. 027/49-51), is about a 20-minute walk from the town center. There are 43 beds in eight rooms with some double and family rooms. This is a modern, very well-maintained hostel with a fully equipped kitchen. Book ahead if at all possible. Rates for seniors are NZ$12 ($7.50) for juniors, NZ$6 ($3.75)—plus GST.

The **Blackball Hilton,** on Main Street in Blackball (tel. Ngahere 705), has been described as "ramshackle with character," but it still manages to have a TV room, sauna, a spa pool, pickup service for two or more, and an undeniably wonderful name. Rates are NZ$12 ($7.50) for the dormitory, NZ$17.50 ($11) single, and NZ$30 ($18.75) double. There's a NZ$3 ($1.90) charge for use of the kitchen.

Cabins

Greymouth Seaside Holiday Park, Chesterfield Street, Greymouth (tel. 027/66-18), is, as its name implies, situated by the sea. On level, sheltered sites on the beachfront at the southern edge of town there are 50 tent sites, 72 caravan sites, 10 on-site caravans, 28 cabins, 10 tourist cabins, 6 tourist flats, and a backpackers bunk-house with 20 beds. Chesterfield Street is just off the Main South Road, and the camp is signposted from the Main Road. There's a modern TV lounge, kitchen, washing machines and dryers, hot showers, linen for rent, and a camp store. Grounds and all accommodations are well kept, and a courtesy car is available to and from public transport. Double-occupancy rates are NZ$13.50 ($8.45) for tent sites, NZ$15 ($9.40) for caravan sites, and NZ$29 ($18.25) for on-site caravans. Rates for double-occupancy cabins run NZ$26 ($16.25) for cabins, NZ$33 ($20.75) for tourist cabins, and NZ$48 ($30) for tourist flats; backpackers pay NZ$10.50 ($6.55) per person. Children pay half price in each case, and all rates are plus GST.

Bed-and-Breakfasts

Unfortunately, most of the B&Bs in Greymouth do not have H&C in the rooms. They are, however, homey, comfortable, and inexpensive.

Gladys Roche is the hostess at the **Golden Coast Guest House,** 10 Smith St., Greymouth (tel. 027/78-39), just back of the railway station. The red-roofed house is set in a sloping, flower-bordered lawn. The four guest rooms are bright and clean, and have heaters and electric blankets. There's a TV lounge with a pretty rock fireplace, where you're welcome to make tea and coffee whenever you wish. Bed-and-breakfast rates are NZ$38.50 ($24) single, NZ$55 ($34.50) double. The double rate for a room with continental rather than cooked breakfast is NZ$50 ($31.25); without breakfast, NZ$45 ($28.25). Add GST to all rates.

The **West Haven Tourist Lodge,** 62 Albert St., Greymouth (tel. 027/56-05), is run by Mr. Collins and is handy to the post office and InterCity and Newmans bus stations. The eight bedrooms (all with twin or double beds, except for one large family room) have electric blankets, and there's a nice TV lounge. Rates with cooked breakfast are NZ$23 ($14.50) single and NZ$44 ($27.50) double; knock off NZ$2 ($1.25) if you order continental breakfast. If you skip breakfast altogether, figure NZ$18 ($11.25) single and NZ$34 ($21.25) double, all including GST.

READER'S BED-AND-BREAKFAST SELECTION: "Perhaps our best stay in New Zealand was at the **High Street Guest House,** 20 High St., Greymouth (tel. 027/74-44), in a beautiful older house with dark-wood paneling and ceilings. The bedrooms were all bright and cheerful, and the entire place gave us the feeling of being in an English B&B. The proprietor, Mrs. Jean Thompson, fixed us a breakfast that covered *two* tables; we don't eat meat, so she gave us asparagus in cheese sauce" (A. Brehmer, Carmel Valley, Calif.).

Motel Flats

There are five modern, attractive suites at the **Willowbank Motor Lodge,** on the Greymouth–Westport Hwy. 6, just two miles north of town (P.O. Box 260),

Greymouth (tel. 027/53-39), all nicely furnished right down to potted plants. All units have been given old west-coast hotel names like Welcome Nugget, Diggers Home, and Plough Inn by the gracious hosts, Lois and Ted Gutberlet, one of Greymouth's friendliest couples, who delight in making their guests feel at home. Two-bedroom units are spacious and airy, with slanted roofs and paneled walls. Bed-sitters are more modest in size, but all have full kitchens, TVs, telephones, and electric blankets. There's an outdoor swimming pool and a free private spa pool, as well as a guest laundry with dryer. Rates are NZ$25 ($15.75) single, NZ$30 ($18.75) double, and there's a surcharge for one-night stays. For NZ$40 ($25), single or double (excluding GST), you can stay in one of two one-bedroom suites, with spa bath, full kitchen, hairdryer, lounge, and tea-and-toast breakfast served in your suite.

Aachen Place Motel, 50 High St., Greymouth (tel. 027/69-01), has ten self-contained bed-sitter units that sleep two or three, all with full kitchen facilities. All have TV, radio, shower, telephone, electric blankets, and heating, and full laundry facilities are available. It's handy to a restaurant and supermarket and a ten-minute walk from the center of town. Cooked and continental breakfasts are available. Rates are NZ$57 ($35.75) single, NZ$65 ($40.75) double, NZ$76 ($47.50), including GST. The Best Western discount applies.

You'll find the **South Beach Motel,** 318 Main South Rd., Greymouth (tel. 027/26-768), just across from the beach, a quiet location only a short drive from town. Each of the ten units comes with complete kitchen, color TV and video, radio, telephone, and electric blankets. There's one paraplegic unit, a waterbed unit, and some family units. Amenities include guest laundry, children's playground, barbecue area, and spa. Hosts Maryanne and Allan Fishburn serve complimentary tea and scones in the afternoon. Rates are NZ$48 ($30) single, NZ$59 ($37) double, plus GST. The Best Western discount applies.

A Licensed Motor Inn

A mile and a half south of town, the **Ashley Motor Inn,** 74 Tasman St., Greymouth (tel. 027/51-35), has 61 units, including 15 kitchen and six family accommodations. Rooms have TV, in-house video, carpeting, and restful wallpaper. There is a courtesy van to the railroad station and to Shantytown, but the pièce de résistance is the glass-enclosed indoor pool. It's owned and operated privately, by the Groom family, and room rates are NZ$76 ($47.50) to NZ$88 ($55).

WHERE TO EAT

One of the best budget eateries in town is the **Raceway Carvery** at the Union Hotel, on Herbert Street (tel. 40-13). Breakfast is served from 7:30 to 9 a.m., lunch from noon to 2 p.m., dinner from 5 to 8 p.m. Monday through Thursday, to 9 p.m. on Friday, Saturday, and Sunday. Roasts, chicken, fish, and salads are featured. Prices for all meals can only be described as very inexpensive. Fully licensed.

The **Bonzai Pizzeria,** 31 Mackay St., near the Information Centre (tel. 41-70), serves 16 types of pizza, including vegetarian. Besides pizza, you can get soups, sandwiches, omelets, and steaks, all at reasonable prices. The Dutch owner has shellacked European newspapers on the walls as a unique covering. Open Monday through Thursday from 11 a.m. to 10 p.m., on Friday from 11 a.m. to 11 p.m., on Saturday from 5 to 11 p.m., and on Sunday from 5 to 10 p.m. BYO.

A Splurge

If you want nightlife in Greymouth, the best you can find is a table at **Café Collage,** 115 Mackay St. (tel. 54-97), where Judith Eakin is the chef and her brother, Steve, doubles as maître d' and waiter. The dining room is lovely, with an art deco ceiling and lamps, and main dishes include lamb filet in green ginger wine and rosemary, venison medallions, and chicken livers in brandy pasta. Expect to pay NZ$30 ($18.75) for a meal. It's usually open nightly from 6 p.m. to late, though sometimes it closes on Monday, so it pays to phone ahead. BYO.

THINGS TO SEE AND DO

The star attraction at Greymouth is **Shantytown,** a reconstructed gold-rush mining town. To reach it, drive five miles south to Paroa, make a left turn, and drive another two miles inland, following a well-signposted route. The colorful town, which has been built with a keen eye to detail, contains several replicas of well-known structures like the Cameron & Co. livery stables from Hokitika in the 1860s and the Beehive store, which has been in business continually in Greymouth since 1865. Then there are true restorations, like the little wooden church with its slender bell tower, which was moved here from No Town, where it was constructed in 1866. There's also a 25-ton steam locomotive, dating from 1897, which you can ride for a small fee, bumping along in the wooden passenger cars that were the latest thing back then. For the same fare, a stagecoach will rattle you over an old bush road.

Shantytown is open every day from 8:30 a.m. to 5 p.m., with an admission of NZ$4 ($2.50) for adults, NZ$2 ($1.25) for children. (If you have no transport out here, it's almost seven times the admission fee to take a taxi round trip.)

GREYMOUTH TO HOKITIKA

The 25-mile drive south follows the coastline closely along mostly flat farmland. But look to your left, and the snow-capped tips of the Southern Alps become clearer and clearer, sharply defined against the sky, as though painted on the horizon, a teasing glimpse of the mountain splendor that awaits in a few days when you turn away from the Tasman Sea.

About 20 miles from Greymouth you'll cross the **Arahura River.** This is where Maoris found a great quantity of the greenstone they so highly prized for making weapons, ornaments, and tools. Another five miles and you reach Hokitika, where you can see artisans still working that gemstone into a multitude of items, some of which you'll no doubt take along when you depart.

GREYMOUTH TO CHRISTCHURCH

If your time in the South Island is limited, you can drive from Greymouth to Christchurch (allow the better part of a day in order to enjoy the drive to its fullest) by way of Arthur's Pass and some of New Zealand's most spectacular scenery. Just south of Greymouth, turn left onto Hwy. 73. Opened in 1866, this road was one of the last in the country to be used by horse-drawn Cobb & Co. coaches. If you come in winter, Mount Temple Basin offers a full range of winter sports; in summer, the wild mountain landscape is a marvel of alpine flowers. Regular coach service is also available from Greymouth to Christchurch.

---

4. Hokitika

As you drive into quiet, peaceful little Hokitika, you'll find it hard to believe that this was once the boisterous, rowdy "Goldfields Capital," where more than 35,000 miners and prospectors kept the dancehalls roaring and filled some 102 hotels. And because it was more accessible by sea than overland, ships poured into its harbor, even though the entrance was so hazardous that people would gather on the shore to watch unlucky ships go aground. Even so, there were as many as 80 at one time tied up at Hokitika wharfs, many of them waiting to transport the gold that poured out of the area at the rate of half a million ounces a year. It turned out not to be the endless supply they all dreamed of, and when the gold was gone, Hokitika's fortunes took another turn.

Today, you'll see only rotting remnants of those once-busy wharfs, and almost no vestiges of all those hotels. Still, Hokitika has the most attractions of any West-Coast town, and its present-day prosperity rests on farming, forestry, and tourism —likely to be much more lasting than the glittering gold. The major airport of the

West Coast is located here; there's good coach service; and you'll find it an ideal base for exploring this part of the South Island.

The Hokitika-Westlands **Public Relations Office (PRO)** is located in the Regent Theatre building at 23 Weld St. (tel. 0288/010). Unfortunately, it's not always open, due to a limited budget. If you're lucky the ebullient Heather Cowie, a long-time resident of the area, will be on hand to give you information and brochures and even arrange a visit with a local family.

The **airport booking office** is in the House of Travel (a travel agency) on Weld Street (tel. 58-134). The **post office,** on Level Street at Weld Street, is open week-days from 9 a.m. to 5 p.m.

Reminder: There is no pharmacy or bank between Hokitika and Wanaka, al-though you will find a small country hospital and a doctor in Whatoroa. Now's the time to stock up on toiletries and cash.

WHERE TO STAY

Granted, they're limited, but I bet you'll be pleased with the ones that are here. Hokitika has no youth hostel, but there is backpacker lodging at the Hokitika Holi-day Park (see below); the nearest hostel is in Greymouth.

Cabins/Campgrounds

The **Hokitika Holiday Park,** on Stafford Street, Hokitika (tel. 0288/58-172), has accommodation to suit many needs. Tent sites are NZ$6 ($3.75) per person; caravan sites, NZ$7 ($4.40) per person (half that for children); bunkhouse accom-modation for up to 14 is NZ$8 ($5) per person; backpackers' cabins with double or twin beds, carpet, table and two chairs, but no water, NZ$18 ($11.25) double, NZ$7 ($4.40) extra for a heater; tourist cabin with two bedrooms, cold-water sink, and breakfast-making facilities, NZ$27 ($17) for two and NZ$8 ($5) per extra per-son. There are two tourist flats with H&C, kitchen, and toilet for NZ$33 ($20.75) double; six motel units with kitchen and bathroom are NZ$38 ($23.75) double.

A Bed-and-Breakfast

As its name implies, the **Central Guest House,** 20 Hamilton St., Hokitika (tel. 0288/58-232), is centrally located, with banks, restaurants, attractions, and bus sta-tion nearby. All eight bedrooms are heated and have electric blankets, and the lounge has a TV and tea- and coffee-making facilities. Dinner, laundry facilities, and a telephone are also available. Owners Joanna and Brent Williamson can arrange horse treks, canoeing, scenic flights, and white-water rafting. The rates, NZ$34 ($21.25) single and NZ$54 ($33.75) double, include continental breakfast and GST. Cooked breakfast may be ordered.

Motel Flats

Top billing in Hokitika's motels goes to the **Goldsborough Motel,** 252 Revell St., Hokitika (tel. 0288/58-772). It's just across from the Tasman Sea and a short walk from the glowworm dell. Best of all, this Best Western member is run by Peg and Doug Graham, fourth-generation Kiwis. All units, bed-sitters and two-bedrooms, have fully equipped kitchens, color TVs, central heating, and electric heaters. They're all spacious and have parking at the door. There's a guest laundry, a pretty swimming pool, spa pool, and children's playground. A seven-day food store is within walking distance. Rates are NZ$60 ($37.50) single, NZ$66 ($41.25) dou-ble, plus GST. An extra adult is NZ$12 ($7.50); an extra child, NZ$10 ($6.25). Continental breakfast costs NZ$5 ($3.15). Best Western discounts apply.

Also within easy walking distance of the glowworm dell is the **Hokitika Motel,** 221 Fitzherbert St., Hokitika (tel. 0288/58-292). There are bed-sitters, one-bedroom units, and two-bedroom units with full kitchens, as well as three bed-sitters with only electric jug, toaster, teapot, crockery, and fridge. All units have cen-tral and electric heating, electric blanket, radio, TV, and telephone. There's a mini-store for essential provisions, car wash, laundry, and a courtesy car to the airport. Rates range from NZ$50 ($31.25) single to NZ$60 ($37.50) double, plus GST.

A Licensed Hotel

There's something very homey about the **DB Westland Hotel,** 2 Weld St., Hokitika (tel. 0288/58-411), and its location right in the heart of town makes it an ideal place to stay, especially if you're a bit tired of hotels that have been "glitzed" to death! Rooms here are clean, comfortable, and nicely furnished—but not fancy. And you can save a penny or two by opting for a room without private facilities. Public rooms include a lounge, dining room, and lounge bar that serves bistro meals (see "Where to Eat," below). Rooms with facilities down the hall are NZ$40 ($25) single, NZ$50 ($31.25) double; those with private facilities are NZ$50 ($31.25) single, NZ$60 ($37.50) double—plus GST.

READER'S HOTEL SELECTION: "We thought your readers should know about the **Southland Hotel,** 111 Revell St., Hokitika (tel. 0288/58-344). We had first-class accommodations. They have a laundrette and spa baths, and there are even units for the handicapped" (C. Murdoch, Aiken, S.C.).

WHERE TO EAT

Don't miss at least one stop by the **Gold Strike Sandwich Bar,** 23 Weld St. Situated in the Regent Theatre Building, they offer a variety of light meals, made-to-order sandwiches, and luscious ice cream in 16 flavors. With plenty of seating for the sightseeing footweary, this eatery (run by West Coaster Ron Hibbs) offers a comfortable rest stop combined with nutritious food and lots of friendly conversation. There's always a brisk business at the ice-cream bar, but take my advice and sample at least one of their unusual and very good sandwiches. All come on hearty, freshly baked bread, and I'm positively addicted to the venison (which, with a bowl of homemade soup, makes a lovely light meal). A local favorite is the honey, walnuts, and raisins combination, with cheese and corn also very popular. Pork, salami, and beef are also available. Sandwiches like these you won't get at home! Prices are all under NZ$5 ($3.15).

A breakfast tradition in Hokitika is to congregate at **Preston's Bakery & Restaurant,** 105 Revell St. (tel. 58-412), where the decor is small-town perfect. Eggs, toast, and bacon or sausage costs NZ$6.50 ($4.05); poached eggs and toast, NZ$3.30 ($2.05); fruit and cereal, NZ$3 ($1.90). Not that breakfast is the only meal; you can get sandwiches, steaks, and sweets, and this is a great place to load up your campervan before driving farther along the West Coast. It's open weekdays from 8 a.m. to 5 p.m. (the bakery closes at 6 p.m.) and on Saturday from 9 a.m. to 1 p.m.

The **DB Westland Hotel,** 2 Weld St. (tel. 58-411), serves terrific bistro meals in an attractive lounge bar flanked by twin stone fireplaces, with comfortable booths and table groupings. Hot plates include steak, scallops, fish, oysters, chicken, and ham, and there's a daily special. Salad plates are fresh and delicious. Prices run NZ$7 ($4.40) to NZ$12 ($7.50), and hours are noon to 1:45 p.m. and 6 to 9 p.m. In the Westland's main dining room, you can "splurge" on atmosphere while going "budget" in the pocketbook department. Lace curtains are framed by brown drapes, set off by gold-and-brown carpet, and there's a silver flower vase on each table. And on Sunday there's a smörgåsbord dinner with soup, hot and cold dishes, salads, desserts, and beverage for the grand sum of NZ$18 ($11.25) for grownups, NZ$9 ($5.60) for children. Prices are just as moderate on other nights, when the menu is à la carte.

One of the best buys in town is the lunch special at **Chez Pierre,** in the Railway Hotel on Sewell Street (tel. 58-933) and only two blocks from the bus station. For only NZ$10 ($6.25) you get soup and a main dish served with a side salad and a glass of wine or juice. And it's served in the most inviting surroundings—two dining rooms (one is no-smoking) and an open-air garden. If you come back for dinner, you'll pay more—main dishes are about NZ$16 ($10)—but chef Pierre Esquilat will make sure it's worth your while. Lamb crêpes are the specialty. Open for lunch weekdays and for dinner nightly except Tuesday from 6 p.m. to late. It's a good idea to make reservations. Licensed.

The **Tasman View Restaurant,** in the Southland Hotel at 111 Revell St. (tel. 58-344), scores high on its seafood and its view of the Tasman Sea. The fish of the day runs NZ$16 ($10), and the seafood specialties cost no more than NZ$18.50 ($11.50). Crystal and flowers are on the tables and the wood beams are rimu. It's open nightly from 6 p.m. until late. Licensed.

THINGS TO SEE AND DO

One of the primary reasons for making Hokitika your base on the West Coast is to be there after dark so you can see the **glowworms**—this is the largest outdoor group in the country—in a charming dell at the edge of town, right on the main road. The 40-foot-and-higher wooded banks are filled with sparkling clusters of thousands of glowworms, a truly awe-inspiring sight. And as interesting as are the Waitomo displays, there is something about walking down a dirt path under a natural archway of treetops and standing alone in absolute silence that makes for a mystical personal experience. There's no charge, but there's a donation box at the entrance and all contributions are appreciated by the town, which keeps this wondrous place available for us all. Best bring a flashlight for the first part of the path, but remember to turn it off when you begin to see the glowworms or they'll turn their lights off.

The **West Coast Historical Museum,** on Tancred Street (tel. 58-418), features reconstructions and relics of the "Alluvial placer" gold-mining era on the West Coast. Hastily built canvas and slab dwellings display cooking utensils and furnishings, with equipment represented by pit-sawing and a blacksmith's forge for servicing the tools needed to open up cemented wash concealing the golden treasure. In direct contrast to this sort of hardship and poverty, there are church fittings and elaborate furniture from a merchant's home, along with a typical hotel bar. There are horse-drawn vehicles on display, and pictorial records of the rich maritime trade of the river harbor. In addition, a marvelous meccano model gold dredge is operated on request, and there's a 20-minute audio-visual presentation of Westland history. Early Maori occupation is represented by authentic artifacts and jade workings. Hours are 9:30 a.m. to 4:30 p.m. weekdays, and 1:30 to 4 p.m. weekends and holidays. Adults pay NZ$2.50 ($1.55); children, NZ$1 (65¢); families, NZ$7 ($4.40).

Hokitika's Rotary Club has provided an excellent orientation base at the **lookout point** just off the road to the airport. From there you look over valley farmland to the towering peaks of the Southern Alps (each one identified by a revolving bronze pointer, which stands on a stone base) or across the town to the glistening Tasman Sea. It's a spectacular view, within easy walking distance from the center of town.

There are excellent **scenic flights** from Hokitika over the glaciers—no landing on them as some others do, but the flight is longer. The plane flies south from Hokitika to the Main Divide, over the Tasman Glacier, skirts Mount Cook, over Fox and Franz Josef Glaciers, over Okarito Lagoon (nesting place of the white heron) and large stands of New Zealand native timber. It's quite a flight. There's no regular schedule at this writing, but inquire at the PRO about times and current prices.

For **canoeing** information, contact Scenic Rafting (tel. 57-114) or South West Safaris (tel. 54-182).

SHOPPING

Don't miss the **Westland Greenstone Company Ltd.,** on Tancred Street between Weld and Hamilton Streets. The piles of rocks you see show their true color (and value) as the diamond-tipped wheels spin, cutting off slices. The workroom is open for you to wander through, watching talented artisans carving tikis and meres, fitting earrings and pins, and shaping a hundred other souvenirs from the gemstone. Then back to the showroom to consider which of their handiwork you will buy (but let me stress that you're under no obligation to make a purchase). Open from 8 a.m. to 5 p.m., 365 days a year.

You can see some intricately carved pieces from greenstone, real collector's items, at **Mountain Jade,** on Weld Street (tel. 58-007). Carving is done on the premises. In the showroom, there is also a cabinet filled with pieces designed from abalone.

The **Gold Room,** on Tancred Street (tel. 58-362; after hours, 58-946), has pendants, rings, bracelets, earrings, necklaces, tie tacs, and much more, including some beautifully set opals. Many of the items are made from gold nuggets from local gold claims. It's worth a visit even if you don't plan to buy anything.

The **Hokitika Craft Gallery,** at 25 Tancred St. (tel. 58-802), operates as a cooperative to display and sell the work of local artists and craftspeople. It's open daily and will mail worldwide.

A Dutch couple, Hans and Lida Schouten, display their considerable talents at **Genesis Creation,** 75 Revell St. (tel. 58-629). Hans works with wood, and specialties are spinning wheels, coffee tables, and stools, all made from local timber; orders taken. A weaver, Lida creates lovely woolens to sell in the small shop. They also feature the work of other craftspeople in the area, and you'll find hand-knit sweaters of natural wool (I've picked up one on every trip and treasure them all), shawls, leather goods, and pottery. The Schoutens are happy to mail packages overseas to lighten your load. The shop is open from 9 a.m. to 5 p.m. weekdays and on Saturday mornings by request. They live in the back, and you are welcome to ring at the side door should you find the shop closed.

Some of the best paintings of the South Island's West Coast are done right here in Hokitika by **Brent Trolle,** whose work is known throughout the country. You can visit him at his home, 13 Whitcombe Terrace (which also serves as gallery and studio), by calling for an appointment (tel. 57-205). I can't think of a nicer way to keep New Zealand memories alive than with one of Brent's paintings.

READER'S SHOPPING SUGGESTION: "We found a pure gray wool sweater with longenough sleeves for my tall husband at **Ken Reece and Son,** 27 Weld St. A mens-wear specialist, Ken was friendly and knowledgeable, cashed a traveler's check, and sold a heavy sweater for less than we saw elsewhere" (P. Diehnelt, Ashippun, Wisc.).

LAKE KANIERE SCENIC RESERVE

This beautiful nature reserve centered around one of the South Island's largest lakes is just 18 km (11 miles) from Hokitika—take the main highway south, but drive straight ahead instead of turning right and going over the Hokitika River at Kaniere (just say "Canary") township. If time is too short for a stop, there's a lovely 58-km (35-mile) circular scenic drive past the lake and back through Kikatahi Valley farmlands. Loitering, however, will be rewarded by beautiful, peaceful vistas of the lake ringed by unspoiled forests with a backdrop of distant mountains. You'll find an information kiosk and toilets at The Landing, where the road first comes to the lake's edge, and there are picnic tables, fireplaces, and toilets at Sunny Bight. Pick up advance information on lake and bush walks at the PRO in Hokitika, or contact the Department of Conservation, Sewell Street, Hokitika (tel. 0288/58-301). Needless to say, this exquisite bit of South Island scenery should be treated with due respect—remember that Tidy Kiwi poster!

ROSS

Nineteen miles south of Hokitika is the little town of Ross, well worth a drive over from Hokitika or a stop on your way to Franz Josef Glacier. Look for the Information Centre in a restored miner's cabin.

The **Fur Trading Post Limited** is on Moorhouse Street, the town's main thoroughfare, and it is the creation of Basil Detlaff, a skilled taxidermist, who hopes eventually to have all west-coast wildlife represented. At present there are displays of chamois, keas, and thar, as well as a live opossum, some geckos, and a working beehive. You can buy honey from that hive in the gift shop on the ground floor. Hours are 9 a.m. to 5 p.m. daily, and there's a small admission charge.

Down the street, you'll find **Ross Furs** (tel. 0288/58-108), where Mr. and Mrs. Peter Gray will show you through the workshop in which bush-tailed opossum skins are worked into coats, bedspreads, purses, and a host of other items. Prices in their showroom are often considerably below those in shops. Hours are 9 a.m. to 5 p.m. weekdays, and weekends in the summer. They will, however, open other times upon request.

Next stop is Franz Josef, 73 miles down the road.

READERS' FARM-STAY SELECTION: "Farm stays seem so expensive and hard to locate, but there is one between Hokitika and Franz Josef Glacier in Harihari—the **Wendy and John Lobb dairy farm.** The per-person price includes meals, and there is trout and salmon fishing, horseback riding, and plenty of bush walks. The Lobbs are fun, helpful folks living in an isolated, beautiful area with rain forests, glaciers, and lots of open space" (P. and W. Diehnelt, Ashippun, Wisc.).

5. The Glaciers

Glaciers are pretty impressive no matter where in the world you encounter them—tons and tons of snow crystals that have, over thousands and thousands of years, been subjected to such enormous pressures that they fuse into a solid mass of clear ice, which even greater pressures cause to move at an invisible, but inexorable, rate. What makes the Fox and Franz Josef Glaciers so unforgettable (sure to be one of your most memorable New Zealand experiences) is their descent well below 1,000 feet above sea level, framed by valley walls of deep-green bush, until they reach their terminal in luxuriant rain forests. Nowhere in the world outside arctic regions do glaciers reach such low altitudes. Fox is the longer of the two glaciers and has a more gradual slope.

On equal footing with your memories of these giant rivers of ice, however, will be those of the sunsets in these parts. From your motel lawn or window, you'll be treated to a show of great beauty. Julius von Haast, the great explorer who was the first European to explore this region, wrote of the sunsets, "New changes were every moment effected, the shades grew longer and darker, and whilst the lower portion already lay in the deep purple shade, the summits were still shining with an intense rosy hue."

ORIENTATION

The small townships of Franz Josef and Fox Glacier are only 24 km (14½ miles) apart, yet you should allow a full 45 minutes for the drive (or better yet, in my opinion, let InterCity do the driving from here on to Queenstown, leaving your eyes free to drink in some of the world's most spectacular natural beauty). Tall trees line the road, which twists from one breathtaking view to the next. If you're driving, exercise caution all the way.

The two glaciers are only a small part of the 284,000-acre **Westland National Park,** an impressive reserve of high mountain peaks, glacial lakes, and rushing rivers. It includes a fair bit of the Southern Alps, which cover more territory than the entire country of Switzerland! The park is much used for tramping, mountain climbing, fishing, canoeing, and hunting for red deer, thar, and chamois, as well as for scenic flights offered from several points.

Park rangers run **Visitor Centres** at both glacier townships, and their displays, literature on the park, and visitor activities are essential to a full appreciation of the area. From late December through January, a program of nature lectures, slide presentations, and guided walks for about NZ$4 ($2.50) per adult, less for kids, makes it possible for budgeteers to enjoy all the park has to offer with a minimal effect on the pocketbook. They also administer the four alpine huts and six tramping huts available for overnight hikers, and keep track of trampers and mountain climbers (you must check conditions and register your intentions with the rangers before setting out).

The only local transportation is by taxi, but for travel between the two townships, InterCity coaches provide dropoff service year round, Magic Bus and Southern Sights (from Nelson) in summer.

WHERE TO STAY

During peak season, accommodations are woefully short, with a greater choice at Franz Josef than at Fox Glacier. Each township has a licensed hotel; however, both are out of reach of budget travelers (the one in Franz Josef is an excellent THC and books many of the glacier walks and flightseeing trips, and sometimes has off-season special rates—see below). There's no central booking service, but the Visitor Centres can furnish a list of accommodations with current prices. All long-distance telephone calls must be made through the operator.

Hostels

The **Franz Josef YHA Hostel,** 2-4 Cron St. (P.O. Box 12), Franz Josef (tel. 754), is modern, has a spacious kitchen, new showers, and 60 beds in ten rooms, and is convenient to shops and the bus stop. Double and family rooms are available. Facilities include TV and video, a laundry and drying room, a hostel shop, bikes, and a lounge with a piano and small pot-bellied stoves. Ask about half-price nights and other promotions. Managers Terry, John, and Lillian Assen host pizza nights and barbecues. You can get breakfast and dinner seven days a week. The hostel is closed from 10 a.m. to 5 p.m. Rates for seniors are NZ$13 ($8.15), and for juniors, NZ$6.50 ($4.05), including GST. Advance booking is always advisable, especially during summer months and holiday periods. *Note:* There's a YHA shelter hostel (canvas beds, open-fire cooking, no electricity) at Okarito, 26 km (15½ miles) away in an 1870s schoolhouse—no telephone, no advance booking, and you're advised to take food in with you. If you're looking for a total escape from civilization, this is it!

The privately run **Forks Lodge and Motorcamp** is 12 miles north of Franz Josef, almost two miles from a signposted turnoff from Hwy. 6 (P.O. Box 6; tel. Whataroa 351) in beautiful forest surroundings. There are two units sleeping four to six people, one unit sleeping up to ten. Facilities include cooking rings and other kitchen fittings, H&C, and showers. It's close to good fishing and forest walks, and new owner Leslie Trowbridge is opening a puppet-opera theater. Rates are NZ$9 ($5.65) per adult, NZ$5 ($3.15) per child, plus GST. Tent sites are NZ$4 ($2.50), and campervan sites, NZ$12 ($7.50), plus GST.

The **Westland Motor Inn,** on the main street in Franz Josef (see "Serviced Hotel"; tel. 728 or 729), has converted four rooms to budget accommodation. Two are backpackers' units with three single beds in each; the charge is NZ$13.75 ($8.60) per person, and you need a sleeping bag. The other units have two single beds, a bathroom, and a telephone; the rate is NZ$25 ($15.75).

The **Fox Glacier Backpacker Hostel,** at the Golden Glacier Motor Inn on Hwy. 6, Fox Glacier (tel. 847), has heated rooms for up to four people each, with private facilities, TV, and in-house video. There is also a games room with pool table, table tennis, and darts, a laundry, and a kitchen. There are some double rooms. The hostel is right across the street from Alpine Guides. Rates start at NZ$12.50 ($7.80) and NZ$15.50 ($9.70).

Cabins

IN FRANZ JOSEF The **Franz Josef Motor Camp,** on the main road (tel. 766), is set in attractive grounds of bush and hills. There are ten basic cabins sleeping two to six persons on beds or bunks, all with good, comfortable mattresses. A new block of deluxe cabins features central heating, carpeting, and internal access to shared baths. There is no cooking in the cabins but there are communal kitchens. All are exceptionally clean, and have tables and chairs. There's an indoor swimming pool, as well as showers, TV, recreation room, and a coin-operated laundry. Six family cottages, sleeping up to eight, have H&C, stoves, crockery, cutlery, cookware, blankets, and heaters. Bedding can be rented. InterCity and Magic Bus (the backpackers' bus) coaches stop near the entrance. Cabins rent for NZ$8 ($5) per person, and deluxe cabins for NZ$14 ($8.75), plus GST.

The **Forks Lodge** (see "Hostels," above) has caravan sites in a beautiful, wooded location at NZ$10 ($6.25), plus GST, for two; children pay half price.

IN FOX GLACIER About a quarter mile from Fox Glacier township, you'll find **Fox Glacier Motor Park** (tel. 41-821), with 20 clean, comfortable cabins, some with two bunks, others with four. There are two kitchen blocks with dining rooms, three shower blocks, and a coin-operated laundry. Linen may be rented, and canned and frozen goods are available at the camp store. Double-occupancy rates are NZ$13.50 ($8.45) for tents, NZ$15 ($9.40) for caravan sites, NZ$24 ($15) for cabins, NZ$44 ($27.50) for tourist flats, and NZ$55 ($34.50) for motel units. Lodging in the bunkhouse is NZ$10 ($6.25) per person. Add GST.

A Bed-and-Breakfast

A number of readers have praised the **Callery Lodge,** on Cron Street, Franz Josef (tel. 738), for its welcoming atmosphere created by Stan and Myrna Peterson. Upstairs you'll find a nice double room, two twins, and two triples, all with shared facilities. Downstairs there are three private double rooms (Room 8 has a large bathroom with a tub), a lounge with a TV, and—to forewarn those who would not find this appealing—many trophies from international hunting trips. From the kitchen window you can see Callery Gorge, an old gold-mining valley. Rates are NZ$26 ($16.25) single, NZ$39.50 ($24.75) double, and NZ$49.50 ($31) triple with shared facilities; private rooms are NZ$51 ($32) double, NZ$53 ($33.25) twin, and NZ$61 ($38.25) triple. All include continental breakfast and GST.

A Serviced Hotel

By far the prettiest motel in Franz Josef township is the **Westland Motor Inn** (tel. 728 or 729). Centrally located on the main street, it has a licensed restaurant (see "Where to Eat," below) and lounge bar, and a beautiful guest lounge with huge glass windows and one entire wall covered by a native-stone fireplace. Grounds are beautifully planted, and just at the entrance there's an old cobble cart planted with native ferns. The 100 serviced rooms all have color TV (with video), tea and coffee facilities, private bath, and central heating. Two luxury suites have spa baths, and there are two spa pools, a games room, and a guest laundry. If you take one of the older rooms, you pay only NZ$49.50 ($31), and the amenities are the same. In the upgraded rooms, expect to pay NZ$66 ($41.25) to NZ$93.50 ($58.50), plus GST, May through September; in season (October through April), NZ$105 ($65.75) and up.

Motel Flats

IN FRANZ JOSEF There are 14 attractively decorated serviced units at the **Glacier View Motel,** State Hwy. 6 (P.O. Box 22), Franz Josef (tel. 705), a Best Western member run by JoAnne and Doug Fraser and located about 2 km (1¼ miles) north of the village. There's a small shop on the premises and a spa pool in a natural setting. Rates are NZ$68 ($42.50), single or double, including GST, and Best Western discounts apply.

The centrally located **Bushland Court Motel,** on Cron Street (P.O. Box 41), Franz Josef (tel. 757), has appealing units with high, beamed ceilings incorporating warm rimu wood. Sleeping two to six people, all are immaculate and have central heating, color TV, video, radio, and covered car ports. Smaller units are available in their Alpine Lodge Wing. There's a laundry and a children's playground on the premises. Proprietors Owen and Maggie Morris take great pains to accommodate and will even provide hairdryers and Excercycles on request. Rates start at NZ$46 ($28.75) double, plus GST.

The **Motel Franz Josef** (mailing address: Private Bag, Hokitika; tel. 742) is on the main road three miles north of the village. Quiet, trim, and tidy, it has eight one- and two-bedroom units, all with private patios facing a view of distant low hills, and all with private car ports. All are centrally heated and have TV and radio, and there's a spa pool. Mr. and Mrs. Trevor Gibb, the friendly owners, also have a small canteen with canned and frozen foods. Rates are NZ$60 ($37.50), single or double, NZ$12 ($7.50) per additional adult, plus GST.

The **Rata Grove,** on Cron Street just behind the grocery store and souvenir shop (P.O. Box 3), Franz Josef (tel. 741), is as close to the bus stop and town center as you can get. The ten units, which vary in size, are quiet and brightly lit, with a kitchen, TV, H&C, and heaters. Owners Lorraine and Reg Harris take a genuine interest in their guests, and their son, Richard, is happy to take you out and show you the local glowworm dell. Rates are NZ$66 ($41.25) single or double, plus GST. It's a Best Western and discounts apply.

IN FOX GLACIER The **Al Motel,** P.O. Box 29, Fox Glacier (tel. 41-804), sits in a valley about a mile from the township down Lake Matheson Road and is owned by Brian and Jean Mather. There are eight nicely designed and attractively furnished units that sleep two to five people. Other amenities include a laundry, barbecue facilities, a swimming pool, a nine-hole putting green, squash court, spa pool, and children's playground. A continental breakfast is available. Rates are NZ$60 ($37.50) double, NZ$11 ($6.90) for each additional adult, plus GST.

The **Glacier Gateway Motels,** P.O. Box 27, Franz Josef (tel. 41-776), adjoin the Franz Josef Motor Camp (see above). They're right at the gateway to the glacier and have splendid views of the surrounding mountains. Five units have two bedrooms and sleep up to six; two other units sleep four and have spa baths. There are covered car ports, an automatic washer and dryer, video, sauna, and spa. Rates are NZ$66 ($41.25) double, including GST.

READERS' ACCOMMODATION SUGGESTIONS: "Our most cordial welcome in New Zealand was provided by Mr. and Mrs. George Halsey at **Halsey's Motel,** P.O. Box 23, Fox Glacier (tel. 833). Not only were we given our own freshly painted and spotless apartment, but Mr. Halsey treated us to a free tour in his VW of the nearby glacier and spectacular Lake Matheson" (C. Douglas and M. Luckham, Washington, D.C.). . . . "At the **Lake Moeraki Motor Lodge,** on Hwy. 6 (Private Bag, Haast), between Fox Glacier and Haast (tel. 881 in Haast), our room was clean, pleasant, heated, and with a private bath. Dinner was served in the 'lodge,' a rustic, log-cabin structure with a games room and fireplace, where tea was served. The owners, who are Swiss, prepare and serve dinner (ours was a delicious wienerschnitzel), and since there's really no place else to eat—I think the population of Lake Moeraki is three—they also serve breakfast" (F. Munat, Middletown, Conn.).

The THC

The **THC Franz Josef,** on Hwy. 6 (mailing address: Private Bag, Hokitika; tel. 719), has in-season rates in the neighborhood of NZ$65 ($40.75)—out of the question for those of us on a budget. However, they frequently have off-season specials, which are a real bargain. Ask about the two-day special for NZ$99 ($62), which can be budget indeed. These rates are not highly publicized, but it will pay you to call ahead and inquire about current offerings if you're interested in luxury accommodations within a budget range. You just might hit at the right time.

WHERE TO EAT

There are not a great many places to eat in either township, and this may be where you do more home cooking than anywhere else in New Zealand. However, some of the following are quite good.

IN FRANZ JOSEF The **Glacier Store and Tearooms** are in a beautifully designed building right on the main street and serve light fare for lunches and teas. It's self-service, and you can lunch well for NZ$5 ($3.15) and under. The upstairs tea rooms offer fantastic views of the snow-capped Southern Alps and the luxuriant west-coast rain forest. Within the same building you can shop for food, hardware, and clothing, and adjacent to the new building is the Fern Grove Souvenir Shop, which carries a wide range of quality souvenirs, film, and a wide selection of woolen knitwear, and has a one-hour photo lab. Open every day from 7:45 a.m. to 6:30 p.m.

The **Westland Motor Inn,** at the northern end of the main street (tel. 729), has the very attractive Clematis Room, with slanted-beam ceiling and gaslight-style fixtures overhead. Wide windows look out to the mountains. The à la carte menu lists many local specialties, it's fully licensed, and has a nice lounge bar for before or after meals, where you're likely to meet a local or two, all glad of a chat. Dinner prices run NZ$15 ($9.40) to NZ$20 ($12.50), and hours are 6 to 8:30 p.m. in summer, until 7:30 p.m. in winter. You'll need to book in summer.

The THC Franz Josef's pretty **Fern Room** (tel. 719) offers an exquisite view and will cook any fish guests and nonguests alike catch (usually on Lake Mapourika) for only NZ$7.50 ($4.70) per person. Prices for main dishes range from NZ$9.95 ($6.25) to NZ$14.95 ($9.35). Quite popular is the three-course special, which costs NZ$17.95 ($11.25) and includes soup, a choice of fish or roast of the day, dessert, and tea or coffee. The Fern Room serves all three meals, and it makes a nice lunch-time destination at the end of a leisurely stroll from the village (allow about a half hour for your walk unless you're a fast walker). Breakfast is served from 7:30 to 9 a.m.; lunch, from 10 a.m. to 4:30 p.m.; and dinner, from 6:30 to 9 p.m. (If you come for dinner, arrive early enough to sit in the Gallery Lounge and watch the sun set.) Licensed and BYO.

IN FOX GLACIER The **grocery store** sells foodstuffs, hot meat pies, and sandwiches right along with camping supplies, hardware, boots, heavy jackets, and polyester shirts. The **Tea Rooms** have inexpensive grills and snacks, and **Grandma's Grub Shop,** next door, has inexpensive full meals at budget prices. All are open daily, and hours vary.

The **Fox Glacier Hotel** (tel. 41-839) serves soup, savoury, grill (a cold main course at lunch), and dessert for moderate prices.

Note: For **picnics** while you're in the area, pick up supplies at the store. You can get a hearty snack at the bus stop café in Makarora.

THINGS TO SEE AND DO

Your sightseeing at the Glaciers can be as costly or as inexpensive as your budget dictates. There are, it must be said, several sightseeing experiences that can put a large hole in that budget—and they are among the most spectacular travel experiences in the world, worth every cent of their cost. Yet it's quite possible to enjoy Mother Nature's free display and leave with an equally soul-satisfying experience that has cost you nothing. Either Visitor Centre can give you literature outlining self-guided walks, and for just pennies you can buy detailed information sheets on each. For less than a dollar there are booklets that give you a complete rundown on how the glaciers were formed, the movement of the ice, the mountains, the history of the region, and much, much more. If the do-it-yourself approach has no appeal, there are (during certain months) free guided walks conducted by park rangers, as well as free nature lectures and slide shows. If you're a biker instead of a hiker, ten-speed bikes are available from Bushland Court (tel. 757).

Glacier Trips

Now, about those expensive glacier experiences. You can do three very special things at the Glaciers: take a skiplane ride, take a helicopter ride, and go for a glacier walk.

If this is where you decide to go all out and splurge on one of the finest of all international travel experiences, take the **Mount Cook Line's skiplane** flight from Franz Josef or Fox to the top of the icefields of Fox or Franz Josef Glacier. The six-seater Cessna 185 or Pilatus Porter whisks you over lush forests and glacial moraines, with vistas of sea and ice and spectacular views of Mount Cook and Mount Tasman. You'll actually land on one of the glaciers, put your feet on the soft, deep snow covering, and perhaps have the pilot take your picture before skiing off into the horizon. The views are all the more magnificent as the sun is beginning to set when you return. Admittedly, it *is* expensive, but it's an experience that will live with you the rest of your days. The hour-long flight is NZ$98 ($61.25).

There are several shorter flights for less, as well as a wide range of other choices, with prices running all the way from NZ$86 ($53.75) up to NZ$221 ($138). The choice may not be as agonizing as you think—weather can make it for you. It's very unpredictable, and especially if your time is short, my best advice is to take the first one available. Of course, if the weather is fine, it's agonizing time again. But even if weather really closes in and neither is available, not to worry—you'll have another opportunity at Mount Cook.

There are Mount Cook Line **flightseeing centers** at both townships: at Franz Josef, phone 714; at Fox, dial 41-812. You can also book flights through both the THC Franz Josef and the Fox Glacier Hotel, and most motels.

There are a number of **helicopter flights** to the glaciers every day, including those that make a snow landing, and generally they are shorter and less expensive than the skiplane trips. The trips last 10 to 40 minutes and cost NZ$55 ($34.50) to NZ$160 ($100). Take my word for it, it's a thrilling way to get close to nature. In Fox, check with Mount Cook Line. In Franz Josef, both Mount Cook Line (see phone above) and Helicopter Line (tel. 767; or after hours, 774) offer helicopter flights.

There is another great way to experience the Franz Josef glacier, which is far less expensive than the flights and which, in my opinion, actually complements them. That is the **glacier walk,** offered by Trips & Tramps with an expert guiding you along the surface of the ice. If you're in reasonably good shape you'll be able to do the walk, regardless of age. Guides chip steps in the ice, which during warm weather is granular instead of glass-slick. You'll go up into the ice fall, walk among the crevasses, listen to the deep-throated grumble of the moving glacier. Groups leave from Trips & Tramps, and a minibus will pick you up at the THC Franz Josef, where hob-nailed boots, waterproof parka, heavy socks, and walking stick are provided, and will take you to the glacier track at 10 a.m. and 2 p.m. in summer, mornings only at other times. And the walk goes regardless of the weather! The cost of the three-hour trip is NZ$21 ($13.25); boot rental is extra. Most of the time your guide will be Rangy Tinarau, who's bound to "have you on" with his Maori humor. Rangy came here on holiday 25 years ago and just stayed on.

At Fox, in addition to a glacier walk like the above, there's a half-day **heli-hike,** when you fly by helicopter to about one kilometer (half a mile) up the glacier and walk back down. It's about the same length as the glacier walk (2½ hours), but you're on the ice longer. All equipment is provided. A longer, full-day heli-hike goes all the way to Victoria Falls, and you spend the entire day walking down the glacier (you leave at 9:30 a.m. and get back around 4:30 p.m.). You'd want to be reasonably fit for this outing, but if you really want to get to know that river of ice, this is the walk to take. Groups are small, and there's time to really explore things (this is the one the guides themselves like best).

If you're reading this book at home and the glaciers have you hooked, or if you were hooked already and are coming to New Zealand primarily to spend time at the glaciers, you might like to know that **Alpine Guides (Westland) Ltd.,** P.O. Box 38, Fox Glacier (tel. 825), offers several mountaineering courses, varying in length from seven days to two weeks. These are the guides who conduct the walks just described (check with them for schedules and prices), and their experience covers mountain and ice climbing from the Himalayas to Antarctica. Write ahead for details on physical requirements, enrollment, and prices.

Other Activities

If **fishing trips** are a big lure, contact Stan Peterson, Westland Guiding Services, P.O. Box 38, Franz Josef (tel. 750). He'll have you out on Lake Mapourika (the name means "Flower of the Dawn") in no time, and you might just come back with a 12- or 15-pound trout salmon. Whatever the size, the THC Franz Josef or the Westland Hotel will prepare it for you and serve it with vegetables and a salad for NZ$8 ($5). Stan charges NZ$44 ($27.50) per hour for up to four people in a boat and a minimum of 1½ hours. He'll also take you on **minibus tours,** including trips to the glaciers; Lake Matheson, with its scenic reflections of Mount Cook and Mount Tasman, and the gold-mining area of Okarito.

Lake Matheson, three miles from the Fox Glacier Hotel, shows up on all the postcards, but **Lake Mapourika,** 5½ miles north of Franz Josef and the largest lake in Westland National Park, deserves attention for its own arresting reflections and setting. You can swim in the lake, as well.

In Franz Josef, take a few minutes to visit **St. James Anglican Church,** the Tudor-style church whose east window frames a spectacular alpine view behind the altar. Watch for the sign just south of the Visitor Centre. If you'd like to do an hour-long **hike,** follow the sign opposite St. James Church and you're on your way.

If you managed to miss the **glowworm dells** in Waitomo or Hokitika, you can at least get the idea, on a smaller scale, in Franz Josef. Day or night, follow the sign-and rock-lined path to the heliport pad (it's across the street from the gas station). The path will tunnel through some trees and lead you down 11 steps to where you see the roots of a tree overhanging the path at a height of about four feet. Stoop down and take a peak—it's like looking at a starry night in an underground world.

---

6. Queenstown via Haast Pass and Wanaka

This is a day-long drive along a 256-mile route that takes you through some of New Zealand's most striking terrain: cool green ferns; secluded sea coves; deep-walled gorges; high, steep bluffs; alpine lakes; lagoons alive with white herons; and valleys filled with grazing sheep. Before this road was built, the only passage from east to west was an old bridle path, and at the very top of the Haast Pass there's a signpost that will point you to that path, a pretty walk back into the past. The road itself took 40 years to build, and in fact work still goes on in sections as rock slides occur. Some portions are gravel, though most are sealed and a good surface. There are steep climbs and sharp descents, hairpin curves and stretches of one-lane travel. At 1,847 feet above sea level, the Haast Pass is actually the lowest pass through the Southern Alps, very seldom blocked by snow, but peaks on either side rise as high as 10,000 feet.

A picnic lunch is ideal, as there are any number of places to stop and let your senses ramble as you eat. It's a good excuse, too, to loiter at any scenic spot that especially takes your fancy. There are roofed outdoor tables (and rest rooms) at a public picnic area about 122 miles into the journey at **Pleasant Flat Bridge.** Otherwise, the **DB Haast Hotel** (tel. Haast 827) serves a good lunch at reasonable prices (this is where InterCity and most tour coaches break the trip). Incidentally, if you are meandering and would like to see more along the way, the hotel has serviced units that go for NZ$74 ($46.25) to NZ$110 ($68.75), plus GST. If you're picnicking, save a bit for a tea break when you reach Lake Wanaka—the view, with 9,975-foot Mount Aspiring in the distance, begs a lingering look.

WANAKA

A popular resort with New Zealanders, Wanaka offers many sports activities, as well as smashing scenery. If you arrive there utterly exhausted, it makes a good overnight stopping place before going on to Queenstown.

Mount Aspiring National Park has its park headquarters in Wanaka, although the park is some 30 miles to the northwest. If you plan to spend time here, drop by the park headquarters on the corner of Ballantyne Road and Hwy. 89 (tel. 0294-3/660) for information on park activities. For accommodation reservations in the Wanaka area, it's the **Wanaka Booking Centre,** on Ardmore Street opposite the wharf (tel. 02943/7277). They handle a full range of services for travelers and can tell you about scenic flights, raft cruises, launch trips, and other activities.

Where to Stay

The **YHA Hostel** is at 181 Upton St., Wanaka (tel. 02943/7405), a central location. It offers basic rock-climbing instruction, mountain-bike rental or guided trips, and kayaking outings through its own adventure company, Down to Earth Adventures, and provides discounts for guests for horseback riding, ski rentals, and at Te Karo Wholefood Restaurant. There are 42 beds in six rooms, and seniors pay NZ$12 ($7.50), and juniors NZ$6 ($3.75), including GST.

Wanaka Motor Park, 212 Brownston St., Wanaka (tel. 02943/7883), is also centrally located and has cabins sleeping up to five, as well as caravan and tent sites. Cabin rates are NZ$14 ($8.75) per person; caravan sites, NZ$8.50 ($5.30); and tent sites, NZ$7.50 ($4.70)—all plus GST.

The **Alpine Motel,** 7 Ardmore St., Wanaka (tel. 02943/7950), has well-equipped, attractive units and laundry facilities. Rates for doubles are NZ$71.50 ($44.75) plus GST.

The **Best Western Manuka Crescent Motel,** 51 Manuka Crescent, Wanaka (tel. 02943/7773), is off Beacon Point Road about a mile from town in a quiet, peaceful garden setting with marvelous views of the mountains in the distance. There are 12 units with full kitchens, color TVs, radios, and car ports right at the door. There's a guest laundry, barbecue area, and children's play area, and in addition to cooked and continental breakfasts, there are frozen TV meals available. Rates start at NZ$55 ($34.50) single and NZ$60 ($37.50) double, plus GST.

The **THC Wanaka Resort Hotel,** P.O. Box 26, Lake Wanaka (tel. 02943/7826), sits on the shores of Lake Wanaka, looking out to the lake and mountains. The 46 guest rooms all come with private bath, tea and coffee facilities, color TV, and telephone. Those in front have either a veranda or patio. The Pembroke Room serves breakfast and dinner (lunch on Sunday), and bistro lunches and dinners are served every day but Sunday in the casual Storehouse Restaurant. There are two spa pools, and they can arrange golf, tennis, fishing, lake cruises, horse trekking, jet-boating, skiing and just about any other local activity. Rates range from NZ$65 ($40.75) to NZ$95 ($59.50), plus GST, but as is true with other THC hotels, you should inquire about any specials on offer when you plan to book.

Where to Eat

Aspiring Takeaways, 68 Ardmore St. (tel. 7803), has burgers, ice cream, milkshakes, and sandwiches at low prices and is open daily from 8 a.m. to 9 p.m.

The **Kingsway Tea Lounge**, 21 Helwick St., is one of the best value-for-dollar eateries in Wanaka, with sandwiches, soups, salads, and three-course meals at budget prices. Open from 9 a.m. to 5 p.m. six days a week, with extended hours in season.

The best place for meals is the THC's **Storehouse Bistro**, on Ardmore Street (tel. 7826). It's a rustic place featuring a brick fireplace, rough-hewn crossbeams, cushioned brick booths, and photomurals of the early-1900s Wanaka Hotel. The menu includes such main courses as fish, steak, pork, lamb, and chicken, and prices are in the NZ$10 ($6.25) to NZ$16 ($10) range. In ski season the hotel has live music for the après-ski crowd. Open Monday through Saturday for dinner and drinks. The THC also has the cozy Sundowner Bar overlooking lake and mountains, with a pianist from the dinner hour until late.

Ripples, in the Pembroke Village Mall (tel. 7413), is a cozy little place, and it's hard to say if the setting or the food is more agreeable. In summer, you can dine outside on the veranda with those wonderful views of the mountain in the distance; other times, inside is just as pleasant. The menu offers some truly innovative dishes, and it changes from month to month. A sampling includes pan-fried lamb noisettes dipped in egg and rosemary; wild pork and venison combo; smoked chicken and camembert triangles wrapped in filo pastry; and an avocado, crab, and prawn plate. The restaurant is open for dinner daily except during May, June, and November when it's closed on Sunday; during the summer it is also open for lunch. Expect to pay between NZ$30 ($18.75) and NZ$40 ($25) for a complete meal. BYO.

Things to See and Do

How to get lost and found in Wanaka? Head for the **Wanaka Maze and Puzzle Centre**, on the Main Highway (tel. 7489). Behind tall fences, there are pathways that lead somewhere and passageways that lead nowhere. The fun comes in finding your way through without becoming hopelessly lost. Most people take about 40 minutes to do that, and they do so to the tune of peals of laughter. The cost is NZ$4 ($2.50) for adults, NZ$2 ($1.25) for children. On the same grounds, you can play mini-golf or have Devonshire tea.

WANAKA TO QUEENSTOWN

There are two routes you could follow, one not open to trailers and not recommended to inexpert drivers. That 44-mile stretch of Hwy. 89 crosses the **Crown Range** and opens up fantastic panoramic views of the entire **Wakatipu Valley,** then descends into the valley in a series of sharp curves until it reaches the aptly named "Foot of Zig Zag," where you make a sharp right turn and level out to drive through farmlands all the way to Lake Wakatipu and Queenstown. The other route (the one I strongly recommend unless you're stout of heart and a whale of a driver) is via Hwy. 6 and is good traveling all the way. You'll drive alongside man-made **Lake Dunstan,** which was formed behind the **Clyde Dam.** If you take Hwy. 89, keep in mind that the liquor law actually used to state that drivers could have two drinks if going in the direction of Wanaka but only one if headed toward Queenstown.

Whichever route you choose, you may want to stop in historic **Arrowtown,** although it's just a short drive back from Queenstown (and there are good coach tours from there to Arrowtown) if you're ready to push on to dinner and bed after a long day behind the wheel.

READERS' TRAVEL SUGGESTIONS: "The 6½-mile drive to Glendhu Bay is on a paved road and offers a nice view of the mountains. However, those with a little adventure will keep going another 24 miles to the end of the road to the starting point for climbing Mount Aspiring. The mountains and views are great, the road unpaved but good. The only problem is 15 streams to cross (30 round trip), but our car did just fine" (J. and P. Conrad, San Jose, Calif.). . . . "We took the drive over the Crown Range from Wanaka and were glad we did as the Wakatipu Valley opened before us in the early evening light. It was truly beautiful and well worth the bouncing, although I think it is very wise for you to advise against the road for most drivers" (E. Angeletti, Greenville, S.C.). . . . "Shame on you! Highway 89 is *the worst road in the world!* It is not only not for the faint of heart, it's not really even for cars! One can rarely exceed 45 k/hr (unless one rents a Land Rover or truly hates the poor rental car) and Zig Zag is no less than 25 minutes of 20 k/hr in second gear going straight down a 3,500-foot high cliff!" (W. Newman, Boston, Mass.). [*Author's Note:* Well, there you have it—take it if you dare—you're forewarned, and I'll not have the decision on *my* head! Every update edition seems to bring with it still more comments about the Crown Range drive, each one voicing a very *determined* viewpoint—herewith, one of the latest.] . . . "We do not agree that Hwy. 89 is a difficult road. Its main difficulty is that it is narrow in places, but no more so than many mountain passes in Colorado. It can be easily negotiated by any careful driver and is worth at least one drive. And it is totally misleading for a reader to say that one travels straight down a 3,500-foot cliff—not so!" (S. Nelson, New Cumberland, Pa.).

READER'S DINING SUGGESTION: "On the Crown Range Road between Wanaka and Queenstown, we found the marvelous **Cardrona Restaurant,** Hwy. 89 (tel. 8153), which used to be the Hotel Cardrona. It has a fascinating history, hardwood floors, antique oak tables and chairs, patchwork cushions on the chairs, and the food is healthy and fresh—homemade sourdough bread, venison medallions, etc. Superb eating" (B. Wright, Anchorage, Ala.).

QUEENSTOWN

Queenstown is the jewel of South Island resorts—pronounced by gold prospectors to be "fit for any queen," after which they promptly christened it with the present name on a very unqueenly blacksmith's anvil. It sits, nestled at the foot of mountains called the Remarkables, on the northeastern shore of Lake Wakatipu, a 53-mile-long, 1,280-foot-deep beauty encased in a glacial bed. Its shape vaguely resembles that of a reclining figure with its knees drawn up. Maoris will tell you that's because at the bottom of the lake lies a great giant, slain by a lover avenging his lady love's kidnapping. The giant drew up his knees in pain as his body sank into the gigantic chasm that became the lake. And that, they say, explains the fact that the surface of the lake rises and falls three inches every five minutes—it's his heartbeat from far below. Scientists call the phenomenon seiche action, but what do *they* know!

Sheepherders were the first settlers in this district, and they endured the onslaught of hundreds of goldminers when the Shotover River, which feeds Lake Wakatipu, was proclaimed "the richest river in the world." The claim was well founded, for as much as £4,000 was dredged by the discoverer of gold in his first two months. When the gold played out in fairly short order the sheep men came into their own once more, and today the Wakatipu district is filled with vast high-country sheep stations, a source of less spectacular, but certainly more reliable, riches.

---

1. In and Around the Town

The lifeblood of Queenstown, with a year-round population of only 11,000, is tourism, and no matter what time of year you come, you'll find visitors from all over the world here to enjoy the lake, the river, and the mountains. From late June through September an international skiing crowd flocks to ski the slopes of Coronet Peak, whose dry, powdery snows are said to be the best in Australasia. Thus this pretty little town, far from being provincial, has a decidedly cosmopolitan air.

Cosmopolitan it certainly is, but mostly, Queenstown is just plain fun. The powers that be have, in fact, adopted as the town's official slogan "Queenstown Just for Fun"—well, I can't top that, only endorse it enthusiastically. For my money, it probably *is* the Fun Capital of this lovely country!

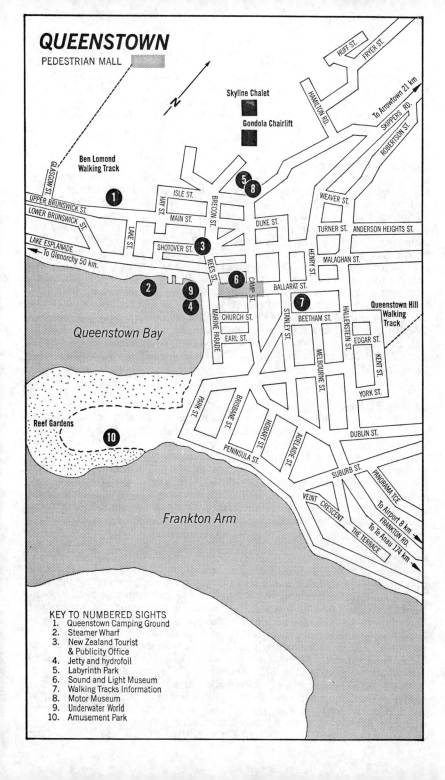

QUEENSTOWN

PEDESTRIAN MALL

Skyline Chalet

Gondola Chairlift

Ben Lomond
Walking Track

HUFF ST.

FRYER ST.

To Arrowtown 21 km

HAMILTON RD.

SKIPPERS RD.

ROBERTSON ST.

WEAVER ST.

GLASGOW ST.

UPPER BRUNSWICK ST.

LOWER BRUNSWICK ST.

ISLE ST.

HAY ST.

MAIN ST.

BRECON ST.

DUKE ST.

TURNER ST.

ANDERSON HEIGHTS ST.

LAKE ESPLANADE

To Glenorchy 50 km.

LAKE ST.

SHOTOVER ST.

REES ST.

MALAGHAN ST.

HENRY ST.

1

5
8

3

6

2

9

4

CAMP ST.

BALLARAT ST.

7

Queenstown Hill
Walking Track

MARINE PARADE

CHURCH ST.

EARL ST.

STANLEY ST.

BEETHAM ST.

HALLENSTEIN ST.

EDGAR ST.

KENT ST.

YORK ST.

MELBOURNE ST.

Queenstown Bay

Reef Gardens

10

PARK ST.

BRISBANE ST.

PENINSULA ST.

HOBART ST.

ADELAIDE ST.

SUBURB ST.

DUBLIN ST.

PANORAMA TCE.

To Airport 8 km

FRANKTON RD.

To Te Anau 174 km

VEINT CRESCENT

THE TERRACE

Frankton Arm

KEY TO NUMBERED SIGHTS
1. Queenstown Camping Ground
2. Steamer Wharf
3. New Zealand Tourist
   & Publicity Office
4. Jetty and hydrofoil
5. Labyrinth Park
6. Sound and Light Museum
7. Walking Tracks Information
8. Motor Museum
9. Underwater World
10. Amusement Park

ORIENTATION

The lakefront is the hub of Queenstown, and the street fronting the sheltered, horseshoe bay is **Marine Parade.** On the northern edge, at **Beach Street,** are the jetty, pier, and wharf. To the south are lovely public gardens. **The Mall,** reserved for pedestrians only, runs from Marine Parade for one bustling block. It is a busy concentration of activity: shops, information and booking agencies for major attractions, restaurants, the post office, and departure points for most tours. There is no local bus transportation.

Useful Information

The **New Zealand Tourist and Publicity (NZTP) Office,** 49 Shotover St., at Camp Street (tel. 28-238), is open from 8:30 a.m. to 5 p.m. Monday through Friday and 8:30 a.m. to 12:30 p.m. on Saturday. . . . The **Info & Track Walking Centre,** 37 Shotover St. (tel. 29-708), is open from 7 a.m. to 9 p.m. in summer, until 7 p.m. in winter. . . . The **airport shuttle** runs to and from the airport regularly and will drop you off or pick you up at your hotel (tel. 29-803) for NZ$5 ($3.15). . . . The **Magic Bus,** 37 Shotover St. (tel. 27-878), provides economical transport for backpackers to and from the hiking tracks. . . . The **Thomas Cook money exchange,** in the Mall at Camp Street (tel. 28-600), is open later than the banks and on weekends. . . . The **Queenstown Supermarket** is right on the Mall (tel. 27-444) and is open fairly late. . . . **Bicycle rental** is available at 23 Beach St. (tel. 26-039). . . . The **Mount Cook Travel Office** is at the corner of Rees and Ballarat Streets (tel. 27-650). . . . The **Fiordland Travel Center** is on the Steamer Wharf, Beach Street (tel. 27-500). . . . The **post office** is on the corner of Camp and Ballarat Streets. . . . To call a **taxi,** phone 27-888. . . . The **telephone prefix** for Queenstown is 0294.

WHERE TO STAY

Queenstown is filled with accommodations, many of them in the budget range, despite the fact that on the whole prices are higher here than in other places, as you would expect in a major resort area. However, it's also filled with visitors vying for these lower-cost lodgings. That means you should try to reserve before you come, be it winter, summer, spring, or fall. Having said that, let me add a bit of consolation if you should arrive without reservations: the NZTP is very helpful, and almost every information office keeps a current list of accommodations and prices, and will help you find a place to lay your head if there is one to be had. But I repeat: far better to make your reservations in advance.

Hostels

The **YHA Hostel,** 80 Esplanade, Queenstown (tel. 0294/28-413), is in a beautiful location just across the street from the lake, a ten-minute walk from the Mall. The two-story lodge-type building is designed with many windows to take advantage of the view. There are 100 beds in 17 rooms, including four twin rooms and four family rooms, two of which include private bath facilities. The hostel provides good evening meals seven days a week in summer and winter for about NZ$8 ($5), and there's a large communal kitchen. Other amenities include a laundry, drying room, and TV room. A bonus here is the fact that a large section of the hostel stays open all day. Rates are NZ$14 ($8.75) for seniors, NZ$7 ($4.40) for juniors.

Bumbles, on Lake Esplanade at Brunswick Street, Queenstown (tel. 0294/26-298), is as welcoming as its bumble-bee logo. There's room for 70; women sleep in one dormitory, men in another, and each unit has tea and coffee facilities and a refrigerator. The restaurant draws people like a magnet for roast lamb dinners, burgers, and the like, most priced from NZ$4.50 ($2.80) to NZ$6.50 ($4.05). A cottage houses the lounge with a TV and open fire. Kitchen use is from 7 a.m. to 10 p.m. Rates are NZ$13 ($8.15) per person, NZ$1 (65¢) more for a double or twin room. Linens are available for rent.

The **Pinewood Motel,** 48 Hamilton St., Queenstown (tel. 0294/28-273), can accommodate 80, and its largest rooms sleep five. There's a store on the premises, cooking facilities, and a TV room with a pool table. Pillow cases are supplied. It's a ten-minute walk from town, and managers Ken and Pat Hartshorn will pick up travelers from the bus station and take them back again if necessary. The hostel is composed of six cheerful red buildings, set against a backdrop of evergreens. The rate is NZ$12 ($7.50) per person, NZ$1 (65¢) more per person for a double room.

The **Goldfields Motel and Guest House,** 41 Frankton Rd., Queenstown (tel. 0294/27-211), has backpacker accommodation for NZ$12 ($7.50) per person and two caravans for rent for NZ$15 ($9.40), along with its bed-and-breakfast and motel-flat accommodations (see below).

Cabins/Campgrounds

Creeksyde, Robins Road (P.O. Box 247), Queenstown (tel. 0294/29-447), definitely the Mercedes of campgrounds, was blessed by the Christchurch wizard when it opened in 1988. In another life it was a plant nursery, so there are plenty of trees around, and room for 36 camper vans. The reception area is in a striking 12-sided building; there is complimentary tea and coffee in the lounge in the evenings, a spa bath (great if you've spent the day skiing), bright bathrooms (women get a hairdryer), a bath for the disabled, a kitchen, and a dining area. This is a family business, run by Toni and Erna Spykerbosch and their kids (Anya, Michael, and Uan), and they keep everything immaculate. The rate is NZ$18 ($11.25) for two, including GST.

The **Queenstown Motor Park,** Man Street (P.O. Box 59), Queenstown (tel. 0294/27-252), is about a half mile from the post office and set on well-kept wooded grounds overlooking the lake. Mountain and lake views greet the eye on every path, and the camp itself sparkles with fresh paint on its bright, airy kitchen, dining, and recreation blocks. There's a TV lounge, a provision shop and take-away bar, a laundry with dryers, and a children's playground. Basic cabins are carpeted and heated, sleep three to four in beds or bunks, and have a table with chairs, at a rate of NZ$31 ($19.50) to NZ$65 ($40.75), double or single. Tourist lodges come with H&C, toilet, shower, and tea- and coffee-making facilities, and cost NZ$42 ($26.25), double or single. There are also fully equipped motel units (including linens), at NZ$57 ($35.75) double. The 200 camp sites are NZ$7 ($4.40) per person, and 400 caravan sites go for NZ$7.50 ($4.70). All rates include GST, and there's a surcharge for one-night stays in all cabins. *Note:* Rates are reviewed for possible increase on April 1 of each year. Also, be *sure* to book ahead if you're coming between December 24 and January 10.

Motel Flats and Cabins

In a wooded, hillside setting about a ten-minute walk from town, **Mountain View Lodge,** on Frankton Road, Queenstown (tel. 0294/28-246), offers a wide range of accommodations, all of which overlook stunning lake and mountain views. There are exceptionally nice motel flats, with full kitchens, TV, radio, heater, and electric blankets, which sleep from two to four. Rates for these are NZ$75 ($47), single or double. Others, with everything except the kitchens (tea and coffee facilities only) rent for NZ$55 ($34.50) single, NZ$60 ($37.50) double. Then there's a two-story building farther up the hill, which houses ten rooms with heaters, but no H&C, each room with four bunks, carpeting, and a table and four chairs in front of a window with a lovely view. A fully equipped kitchen is shared by all, and there's a

TV lounge bar, laundry, and children's playground. You supply bedding, plus cooking and eating utensils. Rates are NZ$36 ($22.50) double, NZ$44 ($27.50) for three, NZ$52 ($32.50) for four. All rates include GST.

Mountain View Lodge also has a licensed family-style restaurant on the premises. There are candles at night; windows look out to mountains and lakes, and main-course prices are in the NZ$12 ($7.50) to NZ$16 ($10) range.

One of Mountain View's structures, the Bottle House, built in 1956, is known throughout New Zealand. Constructed entirely of 14,720 glass bottles set in sand and cement mortar, it serves as the motel office. The builder (whose identity is not revealed) avers that there's not a single beer bottle included, that he got the bottles from a dealer, and that he emptied not one himself. Cabin 7 also has bottle walls that let in light, but are slightly opaque; it's a little rundown and usually occupied by staff.

Bed-and-Breakfasts

Cathy and Jan Dickson are the friendly and helpful hosts at **Goldfields Motel and Guest House,** 41 Frankton Rd., Queenstown (tel. 0294/27-211). This complex of budget accommodations looks out to terrific views, and is just a short stroll from the center of town. In addition to six heated bedrooms with H&C and electric blankets in an attractive guesthouse, there are four chalet-type units that sleep up to three. All have H&C, tea and coffee makings, toaster, TV, and private bath with shower. A tray breakfast is included in the chalet rates, and a delicious cooked morning meal is served family style around a big wooden table in the homey dining room. At other times that dining room serves as a comfortable TV lounge (with tea/coffee facilities) that's the focal point for congenial evening gatherings. There's a guest laundry and plenty of off-street parking. The airport bus stops out front. Bed-and-breakfast rates are NZ$40 ($25) single, NZ$62 ($38.75) double, plus GST, for guest rooms. Chalets go for NZ$68 ($42.50) double, NZ$10 ($6.25) per extra person. The complex also includes motel flats with complete kitchen facilities (see below).

Sitting on a spectacular bluff overlooking the Shotover River, **Trelawn Place** (P.O. Box 117), Queenstown (tel. 0294/29-160), is the private home of Nery Howard. She not only provides two double-occupancy rooms with private baths, but also a very personal, friendly welcome that has won raves from our readers, as has Nery's cooking. Bed-and-breakfast rates are NZ$45 ($28.25) per person; bed, breakfast, and dinner rates are NZ$65 ($40.75) per person—both plus GST.

The big draw at **Queenstown House,** 69 Hallenstein St., Queenstown (tel. 0294/29-043), is the lounge with its wicker furniture, plants, and beautiful, old upright piano. Adjacent to it is the dining area where dinner is served Monday through Friday for only NZ$12 ($7.50). There are eight rooms, a few with their own sink, a laundry, showers, and a unique tub you have to *climb* into. Queenstown House is a short downhill walk into town. Rates are NZ$36 ($22.50) single and NZ$55 ($34.50) double, including continental breakfast. A cooked breakfast is available for NZ$4 ($2.50).

Undeniably, **Hulbert House,** 68 Ballarat St., Queenstown (tel. 0294/28-767), is a splurge, but if you're a connoisseur of B&Bs and antiques, you won't want to miss out on it or its friendly host, Ed Sturt, who over the years has returned the house, built in 1889, to its former glory. The house has a well-tended yard framed by a picket fence, gables, bay windows, and an ideal location overlooking the wharf and the gondolas. There are only five rooms; the doubles have their own shower. Rates, which include a filling breakfast, are NZ$80 ($50) single and NZ$110 ($68.75) to NZ$130 ($81.25) double, plus GST.

A Licensed Hotel/Motor Inn

The **Alpine Village Motor Inn,** P.O. Box 211, Queenstown (tel. 0294/27-795), is two miles from the center of Queenstown on the Frankton Road, but its scenic setting more than makes up for the drive. And if you're not driving, Dennis and Louise Winchester operate a courtesy coach to and from town several times a day and will always arrange to collect you at the bus station or airport. Set right on the lake in wooded grounds, Alpine Village offers A-frame chalets with breathtaking views of the lake and mountains on the far shore. They're furnished with tea and coffee makings, color TV, and fridge, and have central heating; and there are electric blankets for those extra-cold nights. In the main building there are ten standard hotel rooms with the same amenities. Down on the lakefront, there are 20 deluxe suites, certainly the stars of the whole complex. Provided for guests are a laundry and children's playground.

One feature that accounts for the high rate of returnees here is the lakeside cluster of heated spa pools, which are open to the lake but enclosed for privacy on all three land sides. They are entered through heated shower rooms, which provide ample dressing space. It's absolutely heavenly to emerge from the warmth into crisp lake air and sink into the soothing hot water of the pools. The spa pools are very popular with locals, especially on star-studded nights. Equally popular are the lounge bar, where an inviting brick fireplace warms body and spirit, and the licensed restaurant, with its superior menu and lovely lake view. Except during holiday periods (when they're slightly higher), rates at the Alpine Village, for single or double occupancy, begin at NZ$68 ($42.50) for standard rooms, NZ$85 ($53.25) for chalets, and NZ$100 ($62.50) for lakeside suites, all plus GST. And it's a Best Western, so discounts apply, bringing the rates even lower, and there are two-day holiday specials at bargain rates. As is true of many others, I return again and again to this special New Zealand hostelry, always with pleasant anticipation.

Motel Flats

At **Goldfields Motel and Guest House,** 41 Frankton Rd., Queenstown (tel. 0294/27-211)—see "Bed-and-Breakfasts," above, for a complete description— the Dicksons round out their budget accommodations with 17 lovely motel flats that sleep two or three. There's a bed-sitting room, full kitchen, private bath with shower, TV, and radio. All units are heated, and beds have electric blankets. Plenty of off-street parking, a guest laundry, and courtesy-car service (the airport bus also stops right at the gate). Rates range from NZ$67 ($42) to NZ$77 ($48.25), plus GST. Cooked or continental breakfast available.

The **Autoline Motel,** on the corner of Frankton Road and Dublin Street (P.O. Box 183), Queenstown (tel. 0294/28-734), is run by Pam and Stew Carter, the gracious, friendly hosts here who are always eager to help their guests with sightseeing plans. The two-story motel with roses out front has exceptionally spacious units (one family size, which accommodates up to six; the others, either bed-sitters or one-bedrooms), all attractively decorated in shades of gold and brown. All have nice views from their sundeck, but the end unit, no. 6, has the best lake view. Kitchens are fully equipped and have complete ranges. There's color TV, radio, central heating, and electric blankets in each unit. Additional facilities include an automatic laundry with dryer, hot spa pool, children's play area, car wash, and covered off-street parking. Units are serviced daily. The Autoline is a short walk from shopping and even closer to the gardens; there's courtesy-car service to the bus depot by arrangement. Rates are NZ$71.50 ($44.75), plus GST, single or double.

Dianne and Peter Smith, young and enthusiastic moteliers, designed and built **Amity Lodge,** 7 Melbourne St. (P.O. Box 371), Queenstown (tel. 0294/27-288), and their attention to comfort and tastefulness shows. Ten units, two with access for the disabled, have the bedroom tucked quietly at the back. Some have a kitchen and waterbed; all have a full bath, tea- and coffee-making facilities, and a VCR. There's a guest laundry, children's play area, and breakfast available. You may not have a stunning view here, but the surroundings and the hosts are equally lovely. Rates are NZ$88 ($55) single and NZ$99 ($62) double.

The **Garden Court Motor Lodge,** 31 Frankton Rd. (P.O. Box 572), Queenstown (tel. 0294/26-468), has eight two-level suites, with balconies, two TVs, and an emphasis on alpine views, courtesy of picture windows galore. There are also three studio suites with overstuffed chairs and a kitchenette (Room 49 is a pleasant choice). You can walk into town from here in five minutes. Rates are NZ$80 ($50) for two for a studio, and NZ$90 ($56.25) for a two-level unit, plus GST. It's a Best Western, and discounts apply.

One of the most inviting places you'll happen upon as you drive into town is the **Earnslaw Lodge,** 53 Frankton Rd., Queenstown (tel. 0294/28-728), with congenial hosts Joan and Ken McColl. It's modern, with a skylight in the inviting lobby/bar area. Five of the 19 spacious units have a small kitchen; 14 of them have bay views (for the best views, ask for the upper level). There's also a laundry and dining room, with breakfast available on request. Rates are NZ$75 ($47) single and NZ$85 ($53.25) double, plus GST.

In Arrowtown

If you're driving, you might consider staying in quaint, historic Arrowtown, 12½ miles from Queenstown.

Some 2½ miles south of Arrowtown is a real find, a bed-and-breakfast farm retreat called **Speargrass Lodge,** on Speargrass Flat Road (R.D. 1), Arrowtown (tel. 0294/21-411). It sits on 11 acres that are "as close to Scotland as you can get in the southern hemisphere," according to Denis Jenkins. He and his wife, Jenny, whom he met in catering school in Scotland, own the 6,000-square-foot home, which has three guest rooms, each with private bath; a living room with overstuffed couches and a stone fireplace; and underfloor heating. A laundry, drying room, and a Jeep are available for guests' use. Dogs, cats, ducks, hens, and sheep rule the farmyard, from which you can see the surrounding ski areas. The rate is NZ$55 ($34.50) per person, including breakfast. The Jenkins show off their culinary skills with a three-course dinner that is available for NZ$20 ($12.50).

Another good choice in Arrowtown is actually three miles from the town, eight from Queenstown—an ideal location from which to visit both. The **Lake Hayes Motel,** R.D. 2, Queenstown (tel. 0294/21-705), is on the quiet, peaceful shores of beautiful Lake Hayes. There are eight units with full kitchen, color TV, radio, and both electric and down blankets. Laundry facilities are available. In the garden there's a children's playground with trampoline and barbecue. The lake is at the bottom of the garden, good for swimming and brown trout fishing. Parking is in car ports. Rates are NZ$60 ($37.50), plus GST, single or double.

In town, the **Mace Motel** is on Arrowtown's famous Oak Avenue (tel. 0294-21/825), with six units on lawns planted with pretty shrubs. Units have two or three bedrooms, with convertible divans in the wood-paneled lounges. They will accommodate two to eight. All have kitchens, TVs, videos, electric blankets, central heating, and radios. There's a heated spa pool, children's play area, laundry, and provision store on the premises. It's 15 minutes from Queenstown and from the ski fields. Rates are NZ$60 ($37.50), plus GST, double.

Big Splurge

Without a doubt, the **Queenstown Park Royal,** Beach Street, Queenstown (tel. 0294/27-8000), has captured Queenstown's choice location—on the waterfront, with superb views of the lake and mountains. And it's just down the street from everything in Queenstown. The handsome 139-room hotel is built in set-back tiers that give a pleasant, low-key appearance to what could have been just another posh high-rise hotel. All rooms except a few in the back tier have unobstructed views, and each is tastefully decorated, comfortably furnished, and comes with two double beds, tea- and coffee-making facilities, fridge, mini-bar, telephone, TV, radio, and private bath. There's a swimming pool in the pretty inner courtyard, sauna, ski store, and drying room (no soggy ski clothes hanging around your room after a day on the slopes). In addition to the cozy third-floor bar, there's a coffeeshop with hours of 6 a.m. to 10 p.m. The hotel's gourmet restaurant, Bentley's, counts as a delicious splurge all in itself with elegant fixed-priced dinners. Room rates are NZ$215 ($134), single or double, including GST.

The **THC Queenstown Resort Hotel,** at Marine Parade and Earl Street, Queenstown (tel. 0294/27-750), created dissension when it was built because it threatened to encroach on the public gardens beside it—locals still do not frequent it. The location is ideal, adjacent to the gardens, with a courtyard overlooking the bay. The hotel rooms are decorated in restful hues of mauve, pink, and sand, and there is 24-hour room service and a complimentary laundry with soap and an ironing board. It is within easy walking distance of waterfront activities and the Mall. Its Promenade restaurant specializes in lamb dishes (see "Where to Eat"). Standard rooms are NZ$203.50 ($127), including GST, but inquire about equally comfortable lodging at the hotel's nearby annex on Horn Creek, where former condo units with fully equipped kitchens start at NZ$130 ($81.25).

READERS' ACCOMMODATION SELECTION: "Riverview Farm Lodge, P.O. Box 19, Athol, Southland (tel. 0228/8866), sits against a hill just above the Mataura River in a beautiful pastoral setting about an hour's drive from Queenstown. Sam and Liz Soper, the owners, have two young daughters and made us feel right at home. Our Laura Ashley–style bedroom and private bath were lovely, and Liz's cooking is a great experience, especially the homemade jams. From Sam we learned about sheep ranching, politics, and much of the New Zealand way of life. We left New Zealand with regret, but with a better understanding than any hotel could impart, and we have friends there now to return to visit" (J. and K. Niggemyer, Lander, Wyo.). [*Author's Note:* Riverview has undergone extensive upgrading and is now in the "Big Splurge" category, at NZ$144 ($90), plus GST, per person per night, which includes all meals and wine.]

WHERE TO EAT

You won't lack for a place to eat in Queenstown, and in any price range you choose. There are some very good, inexpensive restaurants, many of them in the Mall. Moderate prices for full meals are easy to come by, and I'll tell you about just one of the several places that qualify for a "big splurge."

The **Cow Pizza and Spaghetti House,** Cow Lane (tel. 28-588), is a cozy little stone building at the end of a lane that got its name from the fact that cows were once driven this way each day to be milked. Inside, this place probably hasn't changed a whole lot since those early days—there's a smoke-darkened fireplace, wooden beams, lots of old farm memorabilia around, and wooden benches and tables. It's a friendly gathering spot for locals, many of whom you'll rub elbows with at those long tables. As for the menu, it was *designed* for budget travelers! I counted eight varieties of pizza (including a vegetarian version) and six spaghetti dishes— and the highest price on the menu is NZ$9.95 ($6.20), unless you go for the extra-large pizza (don't unless you're ordering for two or have an extra-large appetite), which can cost as much as NZ$16.25 ($10.25). On Sunday and holidays, a small surcharge per person is tacked on. Soup, salad, homemade whole-meal bread and ice-cream desserts are also on offer. It's BYO, with a small corkage fee. Hours are noon to 2 p.m. and 5:30 to 10:30 p.m. Take-aways are available, but I strongly recommend that you eat right here—the Cow is a delightful experience, as well as excellent budget eating.

The **Cardrona Coffee Lounge** is in the Mall, and its pancakes with maple syrup (among several tasty toppings) make breakfast something special. Omelets, burgers, sandwiches, and other light fare are available. Highest price on the menu is NZ$8 ($5); most are less.

Downstairs in the Rees Arcade, you'll find the **Rees Café,** a homey little coffeeshop with friendly staff behind the self-service counter. There are red-and-white-checkered curtains at the front window, an awning over the counter, wooden booths and tables, and a relaxed atmosphere in which to eat. Choices include home-made soups, meat pies, sausage rolls, sandwiches, cakes, and pastries. Prices are in the NZ$2 ($1.25) to NZ$6 ($3.75) range.

The **Gourmet Express,** in Bay Centre on Shotover Street (tel. 29-619), bills itself as an American-style restaurant and coffeeshop, and indeed you'll find a very Americanized menu. Hamburgers, cheeseburgers, and baconburgers, club sand-wiches, pancakes, hash browns, and omelets are among the lighter fare, with heartier offerings of steak (in several varieties), fish, chicken-in-the-basket, lamb chops, roast lamb, and rack of lamb. It's a large, bright, and cheerful place with blond-wood ta-bles and chairs, and counter as well as table service. They have a children's menu, a senior citizen's (over 60) special for NZ$7.95 ($4.95), and will cook trout if cus-tomers catch it. Prices range from NZ$3.25 ($2.05) to NZ$13.50 ($8.45). It's open from 7 a.m. to 9 p.m. every day.

You can find fresh pasta featured seven days (and nights) a week at **Avanti,** 20 The Mall (tel. 28-503). There's fresh fish on Wednesday, and any day's a good day for continental breakfast for NZ$3 ($1.90). The bistro atmosphere is inviting, and in warm weather there's courtyard dining with a view of the gondolas. It's open from 8 a.m. until late. Expect to pay NZ$5 ($3.15) to NZ$12 ($7.50). BYO.

The southernmost Mexican restaurant in the world, the **Saguaro de Pablo,** up-stairs in the Trust Bank Arcade on Beach Street (tel. 28-240), features south-of-the-border decor, and modern progressive music in the background (to quote Arizonan Mike Madigan, proprietor, that's because "too much Mexican music comes a lot sooner than enough Mexican food!"). Lunch prices average NZ$8 ($5), and a full Mexican meal—choice of two from burritos, enchiladas, tacos, or tostadas, plus rice and beans—runs NZ$14 ($8.75). There's an interesting jalapeño milkshake of-fered, as well as Mexican coffee with Kahlúa and tequila, frozen margaritas, beer, and wine. Hours are noon to 2 p.m. and 6 p.m. to 1 a.m.

For inexpensive meals in a window-walled setting looking out to the lakefront, head for **Walters Retreat,** 50 Beach St. (tel. 27-180). On the ground floor of the Hotel Wakatipu, this is a pleasant, casual place that has continuous service, begin-ning at 7 a.m. and running "until late." Breakfast (served until noon) prices run anywhere from NZ$6 ($3.75) to NZ$12 ($7.50)—that's for the Kiwi Breakfast of steak and eggs. There's a whole range of hamburgers for under NZ$7 ($4.40), as well as moderately priced soups, salads, and sandwiches. For light meals, there's spa-ghetti alla bolognese, Hungarian beef goulash, and a mini-steak served with french fries. Heartier meals are in the NZ$12 ($7.50) to NZ$16 ($10) range, with choices such as steak, lamb, wienerschnitzel, fish, and chicken. Licensed.

Alpine Village Motor Inn, Frankton Road (tel. 27-795)—see "Where to Stay," above—is as well known locally for its fine **Carvery Restaurant** as for those inviting spa pools. In a lovely, candlelit room with a great view from lakefront windows, owner Dennis Winchester and his staff offer a bargain meal in anything but "bud-get" surroundings. For the grand sum of NZ$20 ($12.50)—children 12 and under pay half—you'll have a four-course dinner that begins with homemade soup, fol-lowed by starters that might include their own pâté, followed by a main course se-lected from at least three different roasts (lamb, beef, pork, etc.) and accompanied by salad from the salad bar, followed by dessert and/or cheeseboard and coffee (includ-ing good decaf). Now, that's got to be one of the best dining buys around! It's fully licensed, and a nice beginning or end to the meal is to have cocktails in the adjoining lounge with its inviting fireplace. Highly recommended, and you must book ahead.

If you've a yen (you should pardon the pun!) for something Japanese, there's the marvelous new **Minami Jujisei Restaurant** on Rees Street (tel. 29-854). Its up-stairs setting is a serene, peaceful room with traditional decor; its kitchen is under the direction of Koji Honda, a chef of distinction, and manager Tony Robertson will be happy to help you with your selection if you're not too sure about the dishes. Specialties include sushi and ise-ebi (crayfish). There's a large selection of Japanese snacks and soups, and a choice of three set meals of six courses and tea (tempura, sashimi, or steak) for NZ$27 ($17) to NZ$31 ($19.50). À la carte prices for main courses are in the NZ$16.50 ($10.25) to NZ$22 ($13.75) range. Lunch hours are noon to 2 p.m., and dinner from 6 to 10 p.m., seven days. Licensed.

HMS Britannia, in The Mall (tel. 29-600), is designed like the interior of an 18th-century sailing ship, with nets and ropes hanging from the ceiling, and lanterns and dripping candles giving off a warm glow. There may be more elegant restaurants in Queenstown, but none more pleasant than this. Owner Doug Champion and his staff go overboard to provide painstaking service and a meal prepared to order. The menu features fresh lobster, mussels, fish, steak filet, and vegetarian dishes. Expect to pay around NZ$30 ($18.75), unless you take advantage of the NZ$20 ($12.50)—that's *with* GST—special that includes soup, a main dish, and an ice-cream sundae. Open daily from 6:30 p.m. to late. Make reservations—this place is very popular locally.

Vegetarians will always find a special of the day on the menu at rustic **Westy's,** The Mall (tel. 28-635). A recent offering was spiced kumera timbal, a lovely baked mousse of creamed kumera and eggs with a cashew-nut butter with avocado fans. While this is not a vegetarian restaurant per se, the emphasis is on wholesomeness, with specialties derived, as they say, from the hoof, the tides, and the wing. I particularly like the lemon chicken with cashews. Seafood is also featured, and the homemade breads and house salads are excellent. Dinner prices are in the NZ$12 ($7.50) to NZ$22 ($13.75) range, and at lunch a selection of soups, salads, sandwiches, crêpes, etc., run around NZ$7 ($4.40). Hours are noon to 2 p.m. Monday through Friday and 6 to 10 p.m. daily. No children. BYO.

A Meal with a View

At least one of your Queenstown meals should be at **Skyline Chalet Restaurant** (tel. 27-860). You reach it by gondola, and once inside, the wrap-around windows will give you a fantastic panoramic view of the town and lake. Food service ranges from light snacks to full meals, but the star attraction is the evening smörgåsbord. The NZ$35 ($22) tariff includes your gondola round trip, meal, and entertainment (usually a band that plays for dancing). Lunch hours are noon to 2 p.m., and dinner, from 6 p.m. to midnight, daily. Licensed.

A Splurge

The **Promenade** restaurant in the THC Queenstown Resort Hotel (tel. 27-750) is unique in that it only serves entree portions, so you can sample its specialty, New Zealand lamb dishes, to your heart's, and pocketbook's, content. You've got a dozen choices and they range from NZ$7.50 ($4.70) to NZ$15 ($9.40). There are other dishes as well, including a seafood panache, beef Wellington, and grilled salmon, at about NZ$20 ($12.50). You can even pick a live crayfish (rock lobster) from the tank. The restaurant is on the mezzanine level and looks out over Queenstown Bay.

THINGS TO SEE AND DO

There is always so much going on in Queenstown, and so many things to see and do, that your first order of business should be to go by the New Zealand Tourist and Publicity (NZTP) office and pick up their *Queenstown Sightseeing* folder, which lists all current attractions, prices, hours, and booking details.

One thing you won't want to miss, no matter what time of year you come to town, is the **gondola ride** up to Skyline Point, and don't forget your camera. The view is breathtaking, and if you go at lunch or dinner you can stretch your viewing time by eating at the restaurant or snackbar (see "Where to Eat," above). The gondola operates from 10 a.m. until the restaurant closes at midnight. If you go up on the half hour, you'll arrive in time to see the thrills-and-spills film *Kiwi Magic,* starring Maori comedian Billy T. James and American actor Ned Beatty, and shown on the hour from 11 a.m. to 9 p.m. To feel as if you're in the middle of the action, be it jet-boating, tobogganing, or flying in a small plane, sit in the middle of the theater toward the front. Admission is NZ$5 ($3.15) for adults, NZ$3 ($1.90) for kids.

At the base of the gondola ride is the **Kiwi & Birdlife Park** (tel. 28-059), where, if you're lucky, you can see those illusive kiwi birds feeding and fossicking. It's open from 9 a.m. to 5 p.m.

Queenstown has two top-rated ski areas at its doorstep. **Coronet Peak,** 18 km (10¾ miles) from town, operates five lifts during winter months. In summer, a scenic chair lift, alpine slide, and restaurant are open. **The Remarkables** (named for the colors the peaks turn at sunset), 28 km (17 ½ miles) from town, has three lifts and a self-service restaurant. Both ski areas offer ski rental, ski lessons, and fast-food restaurants. Coronet Peak has a licensed restaurant as well. Mount Cook Line operates shuttle buses to both ski areas from Queenstown. Open year round, except for June.

Another "don't miss" is a **lake cruise** aboard the T.S.S. *Earnslaw,* a 1912 steamship known affectionately as "The Lady of the Lake," which makes a one-hour lunch cruise at 12:30 p.m., for which adults pay a boarding fee of NZ$19 ($12) and lunch is extra, at moderate prices; and a three-hour cruise at 2 p.m., with an adult boarding fee of NZ$28 ($17.50); children pay NZ$10 ($6.25) on all cruises. It's a leisurely, relaxing way to see the lake and mountains during lunch. The longer cruise explores the lake from Mount Nicholas to White Point, taking a 40-minute land break at **Mount Nicholas Station,** a working sheep station. There's a 6 p.m. dinner cruise with fares the same as at lunch.

From October through March, Fiordland Travel offers a way to get to Te Anau from Queenstown (or vice versa) using the "backroad." Take the *Earnslaw* across Lake Wakatipu and connect with a bus to journey along a gravel road through the spectacular open outback country of Mount Nicholas sheep station, crossing several river fjords. Passengers get to open stock gates. The trip takes about three hours and costs NZ$25 ($15.75), half price for children (those under 5 travel for free).

Or take the ten-mile, 30-minute **hydrofoil** spin around the lake at 35 mph on the *Meteor III.* Fares are NZ$18 ($11.25) and there's no need to reserve—just show up at the Main Town Pier. Check locally for departure times between 10 a.m. and 4 p.m.

In summer, the Shotover River's white-water rapids are the scene of **jet-boat trips** guaranteed to give you a thrill as expert drivers send you flying between huge boulders amid the rushing waters. They'll point out traces of goldmining along the river as you go along. Several jet-boat operators offer a variety of trips and prices. You can drive out to the river (allow a half hour), or there's courtesy-coach service from the Mount Cook World Travel Office. The jet-boat costs NZ$49.50 ($31) for adults, NZ$24 ($15) for kids. Then there's the exciting **Heli-Jet trip,** which takes you by coach out to the airport, where you board a helicopter from the trip to the river, jet-boat through then fly back to the airport. Fare is NZ$61 ($38.25) per person and you should allow 1½ hours.

If you're a motoring enthusiast, go by the **Queenstown Motor Museum,** on Brecon Street just below the gondola (tel. 28-775). Opened in 1971, the modern museum houses 50 changing exhibits in two hangar-like wings, and is managed by John and Glenys Taylor, who are happy to chat away about any of the displays, all of which are in perfect road condition and burnished to a smart gleam. There's a 1922 Rolls-Royce Silver Ghost, which once belonged to the lord mayor of London, an 1885 gentlewoman's tricycle, a 12-horsepower 1903 De Dion, and other fascinating reminders of automobile travel as it has evolved over the years. Admission is

NZ$5 ($3.15) for adults, NZ$2 ($1.25) for children 6 to 14; hours are 9 a.m. to 5:30 p.m. daily.

The lake is great for **fishing,** and the NZTP can help you get gear and guides together. The same holds true for those hardy souls eager for backcountry exploring.

Right in town—and free for everyone—is the 11-acre **Queenstown Gardens,** across from the Travelodge. There are tennis courts and lawn bowls to use at no charge, and the park is always open. Also, go by the Maori Arts and Crafts Center on Brecon Street to see a Maori carver at work.

You won't have been in Queenstown for long before finding out about **bungy jumping,** which I'm convinced is more fun to watch than to do. It means taking a 143-foot head-first plunge off the Kawarau Suspension Bridge. There's a super-strong and long bungy cord attached to your ankles so you actually stop just shy of the water (or after you've dunked your head—you can decide). You then swing back and forth about five times. The price you pay for the few minutes' of fun is NZ$75 ($49). Or you can watch the videos for free at the **Danes Shotover Rafts,** at the corner of Shotover and Camp Streets (tel. 27-318).

Believe it or not, all the above is just a sample of things to do and see in Queens-town! There are scads of tours taking in many of the above and a whole lot more. For example, there's **horse trekking** at Moonlight Stables, and. . . . But go by the NZTP and check over the complete list. They can make any reservations you require, and they'll also assist with onward accommodations and transportation arrangements.

A Day Trip

For a marvelous outing, drive 12½ miles northeast to **Arrowtown.** It was a boom town during the goldmining days, back in the 1860s, when the Arrow River coughed up a lot of the glittery stuff. Many of the original stone buildings remain, along with a stunning avenue of trees that were planted in 1867. To get a better understanding of the history of the town, go to the fine **Lake District Centennial Museum** on Buckingham Street (the town's main street) and to the **Reconstructed Chinese Camp** (don't miss Ah Lum's General Store) on Bush Creek at the northern end of town. Other places to explore are the **Royal Oak Hotel,** the oldest licensed hotel in Central Otago (you can still have a drink there); **Hamilton's General Store,** which has been in business since 1862; the **Old Gaol; St. John's Presbyterian Church,** dating from 1873; and the **post office,** where the staff dresses in period costumes.

Plan to have lunch or Devonshire tea at the **Stone Cottage,** Buckingham Street beside the museum (tel. 21-860); **The Stables,** in old stables on Buckingham Street (tel. 21-818), is fully licensed, serves bistro food, features jazz on Thursday night from 8 to 11 p.m., and is a good place to meet the locals.

If you're driving from Queenstown, come via Arthur's Point and return via Lake Hayes and Frankton for the maximum in scenery. A red **double-decker bus** that escaped from London makes the round trip from Queenstown twice a day for NZ$16 ($10); it leaves from the top of the Mall and the Earnslaw Wharf at 10 a.m. and 1:30 p.m. and returns at 11:45 a.m. and 3 p.m. (you can leave early and take the late return for maximum time to poke around).

Skiing

Despite the treasure trove of attractions listed above, however, it is skiing that brings Queenstown most alive, when skiers from around the world congregate to take to the slopes of this part of the Southern Alps from late June through most of September. There are four main ski peaks: **Coronet, Cardrona, Treble Cone,** and **The Remarkables.** All have good trails for beginners, intermediates, and expert skiers, and there is good public transport to each from town (check with the NZTP office for current schedules).

The nicest thing about skiing in Queenstown is that you don't have to be an expert to enjoy the sport. In fact, if you fall captive to the town's ski excitement and have arrived *sans* either equipment or experience, you can rent skis and take advantage of the excellent instruction offered at all four peaks. Treble Cone, in fact, has a beginner's slope just waiting for you, and you'll pay about NZ$25 ($15.75) for class instruction, NZ$50 ($31.25) for private lessons (children pay much less). Ski rental runs about NZ$24 ($15) for adults, NZ$17 ($10.75) for children. Lift fees average NZ$40 ($25) per adult, NZ$21 ($13.25) for children for a full day, less for a half day, and even less for learner lifts. Costs can be cut by taking advantage of ski packages such as those offered by Mount Cook Line in 1989 that ranged from "Starter Paks" for first-timers at NZ$40 ($25) for two lessons, rental gear, and learner's lift ticket, to NZ$99 ($62) for three days of skiing at Coronet Peak or The Remarkables. Be sure to check for such specials.

Walkways

There are several excellent walkways through the **Wakatipu Basin,** some well formed and suitable for the average amateur walker, others that require a bit more physical fitness, and still others that should be attempted only by experienced and well-equipped trampers. Ask at the NZTP office or the Great Sights office at 37 Shotover St. for information on the Sunshine Bay Track, Ben Lomond Track, One Mile Creek Walk, Queenstown Hill Walk, and Frankton Arm Walk. There's an excellent booklet entitled *Discovering the Wakatipu* that outlines these as well as others in the Arrowtown and other nearby districts, available from the NZTP office.

The Routeburn and Greenstone Valley Walks

Queenstown is the starting point for the famous Routeburn Walk, a four-day, 25-mile guided trek that takes you right into the heart of unspoiled forests, along river valleys, and across mountain passes. It's a soul-stirring experience, and suitable for ages 10 and up (and they won't say how high is "up"—reasonable physical fitness is the only requirement). You'll be bussed from Queenstown to The Divide (on the Milford Sound road), then walk to Lake McKenzie, across the Harris Saddle, past the Routeburn Falls, and on to meet the coach that returns you to Queenstown. Along the way, comfortable lodges are provided for overnight stops, and you'll be treated to some of the most spectacular views in New Zealand. Treks run regularly from November 16 through April 27 every year, and the cost in 1990 is NZ$532 ($333) for adults, NZ$440 ($275) for children under 15. Costs include all transport, meals, and accommodation. Book through travel agents or **Routeburn Walk Ltd,** P.O. Box 271, Queenstown (tel. 0294/28200). And reserve as far in advance as possible, since this trek is very, very popular with New Zealanders and groups are limited in size.

The **Greenstone Valley Walk** also takes you through scenes of natural beauty that will form lifetime memories. It follows an ancient Maori trail used by tribes who passed through the valley en route to rich greenstone lodes near Lake Wakatipu. The trail you'll walk, however, was actually cut by Europeans in the late 1800s as they opened up a route between Lake Wakatipu and Martins Bay on the Fiordland coast. Since the track passes through a valley, it is somewhat less demanding than the Routeburn Walk, but certainly no less beautiful. You'll pass Lake Howden and Lake McKellar and follow the Greenstone River through deep gorges and open valley land to Lake Wakatipu. Comfortable lodges provide overnight accommodation, and as you relax at night there are books on hand to tell you about many of the plants and wildlife you've seen during the day's walk. Your expert guides can also relate tales of the Maoris and how they once lived when they walked this valley. There are two options: the three-day walk costs NZ$495 ($309) for adults, NZ$418 ($261) for ages 10 to 15; the four-day walk is NZ$544.50 ($340) for adults, NZ$458.80 ($287) for ages 10 to 15—all including GST. The walks operate year round, and you can book through any NZTP office, travel agent, or **Greenstone Valley Walk,** P.O. Box 568, Queenstown (tel. 0294/29-572).

It is also possible to combine the two walks in a seven-day excursion that follows the Routeburn Track northbound for three days and the Greenstone Walk for three days. Costs are NZ$990 ($619) for adults, NZ$847 ($529) for children, including GST. This option is only available between November 16 and April 27 each year. Book through the Greenstone office listed above.

Check at the **Info & Track Walking Centre,** 37 Shotover St. (tel. 29-708), for information about other walks. The popular **Kepler Track,** which opened in 1989, starts in Te Anau, and has large huts and indoor flush toilets; on the **Hollyford Track,** a jet-boat will whisk you through the roughest part of the bush.

Special Events

As you may have guessed from all the foregoing, Queenstown wears a perpetual festive air. But if you happen to get here during the last full week in July, you can join the annual Winter Festival fun. There's something going on all day and into the night every single day, and some of the goings-on are downright hilarious. Take, for example, the Dog Derby (when dogs and their masters descend the slopes any way they can *except on skis*), or the dog barking contest, or . . . well, you can imagine. There are other, really spectacular, events, such as the Otago Goldfields Heritage Trail for ten days in November, the Arrowtown Autumn Festival for ten days in April, and the annual Volvo Ski Show, when expert skiing performers display ballet skiing and breathtaking acrobatic feats. There are Ski Bunnies, a Miss Snowbird, visiting celebrities, children's ski events, and fancy-dress competitions, a Mardi Gras night, and all sorts of other activities, some a bit on the madcap side, others real tests of skill. Call 27-440 for upcoming events and dates.

Milford Sound

As you'll see from the sections of this chapter that follow, I heartily recommend that you plan to visit Te Anau and go from there to Milford Sound. If, however, time or pocketbook prevent that, you should know that you're not condemned to miss that very special part of New Zealand. Inter City coaches and Fiordland Travel have excellent day-long (12-hour) trips that include launch trips on the sound (Fiordland also has a coach trip to the sound, launch trip, and plane trip back to Queenstown), and **Mount Cook Line** has somewhat pricier (but very thrilling) flight/launch packages from Queenstown.

Taking the coach in and flying out gives you an opportunity to see the scenery from two different perspectives while saving some time as well. Should weather conditions ground the plane at Milford, you can always take the coach back. The cost of this trip is NZ$183 ($114); flying both ways is only a few dollars more.

You can book through the NZTP office, the Fiordland Travel Centre at the Steamer Wharf, or the Mount Cook World Travel Centre. I, personally, am quite fond of the Fiordland trip, mostly because of their superior (luxury-class) coaches and wonderfully informed drivers (count yourself lucky if Doug O'Shea is behind the wheel!). They also furnish commentary tapes in four languages other than English. It's a long day, but a memorable one, from a Queenstown base.

All coach excursions to Milford Sound leave Queenstown at 7:15 a.m., returning around 8 p.m., and fares average NZ$95 ($59.50) for adults, NZ$49.50 ($31) for children, inclusive of launch trip. Mount Cook charges NZ$95 ($59.50) for a two-hour trip that includes tea and a short time on land at the sound, and NZ$150 ($93.75) for a four-hour trip that includes the launch cruise. The InterCity trip is NZ$85 ($53.25) with tea.

Lunch is available on most launch trips, but I'd advise packing your own.

Doubtful Sound

Captain Cook was doubtful it was a sound when he first saw it, thus the name. And the name alone is intriguing enough to make you want to go there. It's not as famous as its neighbor to the north, Milford Sound, but where Milford is majestic,

Doubtful is mysterious. Both are undeniably serene. Doubtful Sound is ten times bigger than Milford, and while it can't boast Mitre Peak, its still waters mirror Commander Peak, which rises 4,000 feet in vertical splendor.

The round trip overland to Milford is exhausting (fly one way if you can); getting to and from Doubtful is less so. Yet getting to Doubtful Sound does require four modes of transportation: a bus to Te Anau (where you should buy extra food to hold you until lunchtime and a useful booklet called *Manapouri to Doubtful Sound,* which describes everything you will see along the way), a van to Lake Manapouri, a boat across that pristine lake, and another bus to Deep Cove in Doubtful Sound— through lush forest and over Wilmot Pass, 2,208 feet above sea level, stopping along the way at the Manapouri Power Station, spiraling downward 750 eerie feet to view the seven immense underground turbines. It's like delving into the underworld and is absolutely fascinating (those who get claustrophobic don't have to do it).

Deep Cove Village, where you pick up the boat to explore the sound (another mode of transport on this trip), has a population of one—the Fiordland National Park ranger. A highlight of the boat trip through the sound comes at its end when the captain shuts off the engine in Hall Arm and you can *hear* how incredibly silent it is here. You return to Te Anau and Queenstown the way you came, without the stop at the power station. Another high point is crossing Lake Manapouri again (especially at sunset) and watching as what looks like a wall created by the many islands in the lake magically opens as the boat draws near.

Fiordland Travel is the only operator in Doubtful Sound. The price of the "Triple Trip" described here is NZ$88.89 ($55.50), half that for kids.

Note: Another difference between Milford and Doubtful Sounds is that at Milford you know civilization is nearby, with the airstrip and the THC hotel right at the boat launch. Doubtful Sound is definitely more remote. If you've never done either trip, I'd recommend Milford Sound for its sheer majesty and save Doubtful Sound as the highlight of your next trip.

SHOPPING

Queenstown has perhaps more shops of all sorts—souvenirs, knits, woolens, handcrafts, fashion boutiques, jewelry, etc., than any other one place in the country. There is one, however, that I have found to have one of the widest and most representative stocks of New Zealand goods. **Alpine Artifacts,** The Mall, has every item ever produced from sheepskin, from rugs to jackets to hats to mittens, etc., plus a fine line of leather jackets, boots, and gloves, woolens of every description, and a nice assortment of paintings by New Zealand artists. They also have silver beech spinning wheels that add a Kiwi decorative touch to Stateside decor even if you've never spun a thread in your life (completely functional, in case you *do* know how to spin). The staff here is friendly and helpful, they ship overseas with reliable insurance, and prices are competitive.

Also check out shop no. 10 and the ever-popular T & Ski in the Mall, the offerings along Beach Street, and modern, trilevel O'Connell's Pavilion, with an entrance on Beach or Camp Street. *Note:* There's no tax on goods shipped outside the country.

AFTER DARK

The two pubs favored by locals are **Eichardt's,** on the Mall, and **"Wicked Willie's,"** the unofficial name for the pub at the Hotel Queenstown.

Above Eichardt's tavern, the **Penthouse** nightclub has entertainment, which might be cabaret, disco, local bands, or even classical music. Closes at 3 a.m.

The **Dolphin Club,** a wine and piano bar at 34 Shotover St. (tel. 27-020) is another local favorite.

During ski season, private parties go on all over town in almost every hotel and motel, with friendly strangers becoming invited guests at the drop of a smile. As I mentioned in the "Where to Stay" section, an after-dark activity much favored by

Queenstown natives is a starlight loll in those lakeside spa pools out at the **Alpine Village Motor Inn** on Frankton Road (tel. 27-795) for half an hour or so. After a day on the slopes or trotting around sightseeing, it's hard to imagine anything happier!

QUEENSTOWN TO TE ANAU

It's a 116-mile drive, on good roads all the way. You'll follow Hwy. 6 as far as the grass-seed-producing **Lumsden,** then take Hwy. 94 over the summit of **Gorge Hill,** along the **Mararoa River** and through sheep and cattle country to **Te Anau,** the largest lake in the South Island. Many of the sheep stations that line the road from Lumsden on are being homesteaded by young Kiwi couples who have taken advantage of the government's Land Development Scheme. A lottery drawing determines who will be entitled to purchase at bargain prices large acreages on which the government has built a basic (*very* basic) dwelling, a paddock, and a barn. Those selected then face the difficult task of clearing and developing the land. In its natural state, this is rough, rocky terrain, and the homesteader's life is not an easy one—as you pass scraggly, poorly developed land smack up against hills and pastures that have been brought into near-manicured perfection, give a tip of the hat to those couples who have dug in and applied the backbreaking industry required to carve out a viable family life, in sharp contrast to neighbors who may have simply given in to not much more than a subsistence existence.

---

2. Te Anau

Lake Te Anau spreads its south, middle, and north branches like long fingers poking deep into the mountains that mark the beginning of rugged and grand three-million-acre **Fiordland National Park,** New Zealand's largest and, indeed, one of the largest in the world. Within its boundaries, which enclose the whole of the South Island's southwest corner, lie incredibly steep mountain ranges, lakes, sounds, rivers, magnificent fjords, and huge chunks of mountainous terrain even now unexplored. In fact, one large section has been closed off from exploration after the discovery there in 1948 of one of the world's rarest birds, the wingless takahe. It had not been seen for nearly a century before, seldom even then, and was thought to be extinct. When a colony was found in the Murchison Mountains, the decision was made to protect them from human disturbance. What other wonders remain to be discovered within the vast park, one can only speculate.

Lake Te Anau itself presents a wonder of a sort, with its eastern shoreline (that's where Te Anau—its name means "to arrive by water"—township is located) virtually treeless with about 30 inches annual rainfall, its western banks covered by dense forest nurtured by more than 100 inches of rain each year. To visitors, however, the attractions of this second-largest lake in New Zealand consist of a variety of water sports and its proximity to **Milford Sound,** 74 miles away. That sound (which is actually a fjord) reaches 14 miles in from the Tasman Sea, flanked by sheer granite peaks traced by playful waterfalls that appear and disappear depending on the amount of rainfall. Its waters and the surrounding land have been kept in as nearly a primeval state as man could possibly manage without leaving it totally untouched. In fine weather or pouring rain, Milford Sound exudes a powerful sense of nature's pristine harmony and beauty—a visit there is balm to my 20th-century soul and is the highlight of every New Zealand trip.

ORIENTATION

Te Anau's main street is actually **Highway 94** (called **Milford Road** within the township). Stretched along each side you'll find the post office, Wildlife Museum, restaurants, grocery stores, and most of the township's shops. At the lake end of Milford Road sits the **Fiordland Travel office,** where all launch trips may be booked.

Across the road and to the left from Fiordland Travel is the Waterfront Merchants Complex, with a coffee bar/restaurant, souvenir and gift shop, craft shop, and clothing boutique. Just opposite the lake, on Hwy. 94 before it turns westward to become Milford Road, are the THC Te Anau and the **Park Headquarters** (open 8 a.m. to noon and 1 to 5 p.m. every day). The **Mount Cook Line office** is on Te Anau Terrace (tel. 0229/7516).

The Milford Track

The world-famous Milford Track is considered by most dedicated trampers to be the finest anywhere in the world. Four days are required to walk the 32 miles from Glade Jetty at Lake Te Anau's northern end to Sandfly Point on the western bank of Milford Sound. To walk the pure wilderness is to immerse yourself in the sights, sounds, smells, and feel of nature left to itself—it is utterly impossible to emerge without a greater sense of the earth's rhythms. It's a walk closely regulated by park authorities, both for the safety of hikers and for the preservation of this wilderness area, yet there is no intrusion on individual response to nature once you begin the journey.

You set out from Te Anau Downs, 17 miles north of Te Anau township, where a launch takes you to the head of the lake for a fare of NZ$32 ($20) for adults, NZ$9 ($5.65) for children. You'll sleep in well-equipped lodge/huts with bunk beds, cooking facilities, and toilets, but you must carry your own sleeping bag, food, and cooking utensils. Overnight huts are manned by custodians, should you need any assistance along the way, and there's a NZ$60 ($37.50) fee for adults and NZ$55 ($34.50) for children for the three nights on the track. At Sandfly Point, another launch ferries you across Milford Sound, and the price is included in the above-mentioned fee. Upon arrival, you may elect to spend the night at Milford or to return to Te Anau, but reservations are a must, whichever you choose.

You must be over 10 years of age, an experienced tramper, and apply to Reservations, THC, P.O. Box 185, Te Anau (tel. 0229/74-11). Reservations are accepted from early November to mid-April for the following tramping season, which runs from mid-November to early April. No more than 24 people are booked to start the walk on any given day, and applications begin coming in early for specific days.

There are two ways to walk the Milford Track: as a member of an organized group or as one of the ranger-organized "Independent Walkers." THC Milford and THC Te Anau offer an excellent package plan, which includes guides, cooked meals at the overnight huts, and accommodations at each end of the trek. The 1989 fee of NZ$850 ($531) does not include GST. As an independent, you take care of all these details yourself, with the able assistance of park rangers, at a cost of about NZ$60 ($37.50).

WHERE TO STAY

Between Christmas and the end of February, accommodations are tightly booked in Te Anau (most are occupied by the week by holidaying Kiwi families), and you should reserve ahead as far as possible or plan to stay outside the township itself (possibly out the Milford Road, at Milford Sound, or at Lake Manapouri, 12 miles to the south). Other times, there are usually ample accommodations available. If you do arrive roomless, go by the Mount Cook Line office (tel. 0229/494) on the grounds of THC. Mount Cook runs a local booking service at no charge.

A Hostel

The **YHA Hostel,** Milford Road, Te Anau (tel. 0229/78-47), is a real standout, one of the most attractive in the country. It adjoins a sheep meadow in a very central location, and has 40 beds in six pine-paneled rooms with central heating, with plans to add more beds in the near future. There's a nicely equipped kitchen, a lounge (with a pot-bellied stove), dining room, and laundry, and in January, overflow accommodation is available. Rates for seniors are NZ$12 ($7.50), and for juniors,

NZ$6 ($3.75), including GST. This is the ideal place to begin and end your Milford Track Walk.

Cabins

If you want to do some tramping in the Fiordland National Park on a lesser scale than the Milford Track, park rangers will supply a map of trails and overnight hut locations. The **park huts** are basic shelters that provide a place to bunk down and cook simple fare. For those where fuel (cut wood) is provided, the overnight fee is NZ$8 ($5) per person.

Te Anau Motor Park, on the Manapouri Hwy. (P.O. Box 81), Te Anau (tel. 0229/74-57), sits on 25 wooded acres across the road from the lake. Clint and Jill Tauri, the knowledgeable and friendly owners, are very helpful to guests in planning sightseeing activities. There are a variety of accommodations here: cabins sleeping two to five; small A-frame chalets (with front decks); family cabins, which have one large bed-sitting room that sleeps five, private bath, stove and kitchen supplies, and blankets; a bunkroom with innerspring mattresses; caravan sites; and some 200 tent sites. There are four kitchen and shower blocks with laundries, indoor dining area, tennis court, games room, TV lounge, sauna, and food shop. Everything is kept in tip-top condition, and rates are budget oriented. Cabins and A-frames are NZ$25 ($15.75) double; family cabins are NZ$40 ($25) double, NZ$12 ($7.50) per extra adult, half that for children; NZ$12 (7.50) per person in the bunkhouse; and NZ$8 ($5) for tent and caravan sites, NZ$1 (65¢) extra for power points. Add GST to all rates.

About a half mile outside the town of Manapouri (12 miles south of Te Anau), the nearest starting point for the launch trips to Doubtful Sound and the Dusky Sound walking track, there are excellent facilities at **Manapouri Lakeview Motel & Motor Park** (mailing address: Te Anau Road, Manapouri; tel. 0229/66-24). Its location, ten acres directly across from the lake, is one of the most beautiful in New Zealand. There are two eight-berth cabins, two tourist cabins with kitchens, and six motel flats with kitchens, color TVs, and lake views. All units have electric heating and appealing interiors. There are also campsites and campervan power sites. Other amenities include a camp kitchen with fridge, oven, and toasters, as well as a communal dining area, sauna, children's play area, grocery shop, and a booking office for Milford and Doubtful Sound launch trips. There's even a private collection of coin-operated arcade games for guests' amusement, provided by the owners, the Nicholson family, formerly of California, and Simon Vagel, originally from Holland. Rates for cabins are NZ$13 ($8.15) on a shared basis, or NZ$16 ($10) single; tourist cabins with kitchens and cooking gear are NZ$17 ($10.75) shared or NZ$25 ($15.75) single. Camp sites are NZ$7 ($4.40) per adult, NZ$4.50 ($2.80) for children; campervan sites are NZ$16 ($10) for two adults. Motel units, which have a kitchen, a TV, and a lake view and sleep up to six people, are NZ$50 ($31.25) single and NZ$60 ($37.50) double, with NZ$13 ($8.15) for each additional person. Tourist flats (the same as motel units but without linens) are NZ$45 ($28.25) single, NZ$50 ($31.25) double. Add GST to all.

READERS' CAMPGROUND SELECTION: "In traveling to Te Anau on Hwy. 94, we stayed at the **Mossburn County Park Motor Camp,** in Mossburn, owned by a farming couple, Lex and Lynn Lawrence. They and their animals—sheep, deer, horses, donkey, Maori pigs, rabbits, goats, and chickens—are fun and appealing. The place is new, free of sandflies, and nearby is one of the most beautiful swimming holes we've ever seen. The Lawrences can also arrange glider rides" (C. and R. Greene, Tulsa, Okla.).

Bed-and-Breakfasts

Matai Lodge, 42 Mokonui St., Te Anau (tel. 0229/73-60), is only one block from the town center and lakefront, and has seven bed-and-breakfast units in a long block, with toilet and showers at one end. Rooms all have H&C, are tastefully decorated, and have heaters as well as electric blankets and comforters. The lounge has comfortable seating, and is airy and spacious. There's a separate TV lounge. You're given several choices on the menu for the fully cooked breakfast, and evening meals can be provided on request. Marilyn Redfern, the hostess, will store baggage for trampers, and cars can be parked off the street. Bed-and-breakfast rates, including GST, are NZ$33 ($20.75) single, NZ$60 ($37.50) double. Rates are reduced in winter.

Shakespeare House, 10 Dusky St., Te Anau (tel. 0229/73-49), is the home of Mike and Rosina Shakespeare (yes, they are descendants of you know who), who have long welcomed bed-and-breakfast guests to their home. They know the area well and are happy to help you plan sightseeing activities. The warm, cozy rooms are a little on the small side, but each has a shower and hand basin, and two have their own private bathroom. All rooms open onto a large conservatory, which is ideal for relaxing. The TV lounge has lovely mountain views, as does the very pleasant dining room, where an excellent English-style breakfast is served. Bed-and-breakfast rates are NZ$50 ($31.25) single, NZ$65 ($40.75) double, and NZ$69 ($43.25) double with private bath, including GST. Ask about off-season rates.

Motel Flats

Some of Te Anau's nicest motel units are at the **Redwood Motel,** 26 McKerrow St., Te Anau (tel. 0229/77-46), presided over by the friendly hosts Shirley and Allan Bradley. Its location is quite central, on a quiet residential street. There are six nicely furnished, sparkling-clean, and beautifully equipped units. All have central heating, color TV, and phone, and four even have their own washing machines (guest laundry on the premises for others). Parking is in individual car ports. There's also a three-bedroom house on the grounds with full kitchen, bath and shower, and private garden, which is ideal for families. A children's playground is also on the premises. If you arrive in Te Anau by public transport, the Bradleys will pick you up by courtesy car. Rates are NZ$45 ($28.25) single, NZ$60 ($37.50) double, plus GST. A continental breakfast is available at a small charge. Surcharge for one-night stay.

READER'S MOTEL SELECTION: "We shopped around for a while and found that the **XL Motel,** 52 Te Anau Terrace, Te Anau (tel. 0229/72-58), had the most reasonable rates. The place was immaculate, well supplied, and centrally heated. The owners, Ian and Carole Excell, were super-nice, polite, and friendly. It's across the street from the lake and within walking distance of the main street, where all the shops and the depot are" (M. Sarkissian, Miami Beach, Fla.).

Big Splurge

The **THC Te Anau Resort Hotel,** P.O. Box 185, Te Anau (tel. 0229/74-11), is located on the lakefront and is *the* superior accommodation in this area. Guest rooms all have private baths, tea and coffee facilities, color TV, and telephones. The 15 villa suites consist of a lounge, bedroom, kitchen, and bath. On-premises amenities include a restaurant, three bars, a swimming pool, spas, saunas, two guest laundries, and a travel office that can book just about any sightseeing activity in the area. Rates range from NZ$203.50 ($127) for guest rooms to NZ$330 ($206) for villa suites, all single or double occupancy, and including GST. Special packages are available off-season.

WHERE TO EAT

In the new **Waterfront Merchants Complex,** 92 Te Anau Terrace (diagonally across from Fiordland Travel), you'll find **Pop-In Catering** (tel. 78-07), a window-lined restaurant serving light meals at very moderate prices in a setting that over-looks the lake. A glass-walled conservatory affords 180° views, and I can't think of a nicer place to eat. Everything is home-cooked and -baked right on the premises. Sandwiches, meat pies, salad plates, and some hot meals are offered. At any rate, my best advice is to check this one out first. Hours are 8 a.m. to 5:30 p.m. off-season, 7 a.m. to 7 p.m. during summer months.

Bailey's, next door to the Luxmore Motel on Milford Road, is a small, cozy self-service restaurant, which also features home-cooking. It's a pleasant place in which you're likely to find locals and regular visitors. The menu covers everything from sandwiches, hot pies, and cakes, all for less than NZ$3 ($1.90); to hot meals of chicken, steak, veal, ham, and seafood for prices of NZ$5 ($3.15) to NZ$13 ($8.15). Licensed to sell wine with meals.

The setting is rustic, the food inexpensive at THC Te Anau's **Henry's Family Restaurant** (tel. 74-11). The atmosphere is much like that of a frontier saloon, with a pot-bellied stove and bare wooden tables. Grills of steak, lamb, chicken, etc., come with coleslaw and french fries, and are priced under NZ$15 ($9.40); children 12 and under pay half. It's fully licensed, and hours Monday through Thursday are 5 to 9 p.m., on Friday and Saturday until 10 p.m. For more elegant (and expensive) dinners, reserve at the THC's **MacKinnon Room,** which specializes in local delicacies, including fresh crayfish.

The THC Te Anau can pack a very good **picnic lunch** for your Milford Sound day trip or tramping, if you notify them the night before, at a price of about NZ$15 ($9.40).

THINGS TO SEE AND DO

Lake cruises are the main attraction in Te Anau, and **Fiordland Travel Ltd.** (tel. 74-16) can give you their latest brochure with current times, rates, and special concessions on launch trips. The most popular is that to **Te Ana-au Caves,** which runs year round. The tour includes an underground boat ride into the glowworm grotto in the "living" cave, so called because it is still being formed. A crystal-clear river cascades down the cave tiers at the rate of 55,000 gallons per minute, creating frothy white falls. On the second level of the waterbed you'll see the glowworm grotto. In my opinion, the day trip is preferable to the evening, since the scenic ten-mile lake cruise begs to be enjoyed in daylight.

The primary reason for coming to Te Anau is to go on to **Milford Sound** and **Doubtful Sound,** and right here I am going to stick my neck out and recommend that even if you're driving you park the car in Te Anau and book a coach-and-launch tour either through Fiordland or the THC. My reasons are twofold: first, while the road to Milford is remarkably good for such terrain, after you pass Te Anau Downs you'll need to keep your eyes straight ahead, thus missing a good bit of some of the most splendid scenery to be found this side of heaven; and second, coach drivers provide a wealth of information on the scenery through which you're passing, which adds immeasurably to the pleasure of the 2½-hour drive. Fiordland's half-day trip includes coach and cruise fares; if you book through THC, they'll arrange InterCity coach reservations. There's no way you can get to Doubtful on your own.

Waterwings Airways Ltd., P.O. Box 222, Te Anau (tel. 0229/74-05), operates two float planes, with an office on the waterfront. Their scenic flight to Milford Sound is a 1-hour-10-minute delight, at a cost of NZ$120 ($75) per adult, NZ$60 ($37.50) per child. For NZ$80 ($50) per adult, half that for children, they'll take you on a 35-minute flight to Doubtful Sound. In addition, there's a 20-minute scenic flight around Te Anau, at NZ$49 ($30.75) and NZ$24.50 ($15.25) and one for 10 minutes that costs NZ$25 ($15.75) and NZ$11.50 ($7.20), respectively. One of their best offerings is the one-hour combination Fly 'N Boat trip—at a cost of NZ$66 ($41.25) per adult, NZ$33 ($20.75) per child; they'll take you down the Waiau River to Manapouri via jet-boat, then bring you back by float plane to Te Anau by way of the Hidden Lakes. Highly recommended.

Other activities include Fiordland helicopter flights, raft trips on the Waiau River, jet-boat rides, and fishing with any one of the experienced guides available. Check with Fiordland Travel Ltd. for these or other activities, and with park headquarters for nature walks and tramping tracks. Then, head for glorious Milford Sound.

THE MILFORD ROAD

Your drive will be through fascinating geographical, archeological, and historical country, through the Eglinton and Hollyford Valleys, the Homer Tunnel, and down the majestic Cleddau Gorge to Milford Sound. To open your eyes to just what you're seeing, beyond the spectacular mountain scenery, take a tip from this dedicated Milford lover and contact **Park Headquarters,** P.O. Box 29, Te Anau (tel. 0229/75-21 in Te Anau), for information on Fiordland National Park, and ask specifically for their pamphlet *The Road to Milford,* which illuminates each mile of the way. It's a good idea, too, to arm yourself with insect repellent against sandflies, which can be murderous at Milford.

Highway 94 from Te Anau to Milford Sound leads north along the lake, with islands and wooded far shores on your left. The drive is, of necessity, a slow one as you wend your way through steep climbs between walls of solid rock and down through leafy glades. Keep an eye out for the keas, sometimes perched along the roadside trying to satisfy their insatiable curiosity about visitors to their domain. **Homer Tunnel,** about 63 miles along, is a major engineering marvel: a three-quarter-mile passageway first proposed in 1889 by William Homer, begun in 1935, and finally opened in 1940. It was, however, the summer of 1954 before a connecting road was completed and the first private automobile drove through. Incidentally, take those "No Stopping—Avalanche Zone" signs very seriously. No matter how much you may want to stop for a photo, *don't!*—it could cost you your life.

Some four miles past the tunnel you'll see **"The Chasm"** signposted on a bridge (the sign is small, so keep a sharp eye out). By all means take the time to stop and walk the short trail back into the forest, where a railed platform lets you view a natural sculpture of smooth and craggy rocks along the riverbed of the **Cleddau River.** As the river rushes through, a sort of natural tiered fountain is formed by its waters pouring through rock apertures. Marvelous! Absolutely unique! Well worth the time and the short walk.

READER'S TRAVEL SUGGESTION: "We stopped at **Gunn Lake Park** and walked through the beech forest, where everything was covered with the green velvet of mosses and lichens, to the shores of lovely Gunn Lake. We could have spent much more time here" (A. Schweinsberg, Wilmington, Del.). [*Author's Note:* Lake Gunn is the only known nesting place of the crested glebe in New Zealand. The birds construct floating nests of mosses and twigs, then weave ropes of grass to anchor them to the shoreline—for that reason, virtually no boats are allowed on the lake, and those few that are must maintain very low speeds. Just thought you'd like to know.]

Accommodations en Route

On the road between Te Anau and Milford Sound, **Te Anau Downs Motor Best Western Inn,** P.O. Box 19, Te Anau (tel. 0229/78-11), is an excellent Best Western property. There are B&B rooms with private facilities at NZ$55 ($34.50) double. One-bedroom motel flats are neat, modern units with cooking and eating utensils, fridge, electric rangette, and color TV. Rates for these units are NZ$65 ($40.75) double, plus NZ$12 ($7.50) per extra person. There's a laundry available to all guests. Also, proprietor Dave Moss runs a licensed restaurant with a local reputation for serving the largest and best roast dinner in the area at reasonable prices. As usual, Best Western discounts apply, and all rates are plus GST.

Lake Gunn Motor Inn, Milford Hwy., Cascade Creek, Fiordland (mailing address: Private Bag, Te Anau; tel. 0229/73-35 or 79-19), is the only accommodation between Te Anau and Milford Sound, and its peaceful setting is an ideal base from which to explore the Fiordland National Park. It is also very close to the beginning of both the Routeburn and Hollyford walks. The 30 luxury units have private bath, two-channel video, and piped-in music, as well as coffee and tea facilities. There's an excellent licensed restaurant serving moderately priced meals, and the lounge is a relaxing focal point for guests, who often congregate around the stone fireplace in the evening, with a tiny (but well-stocked!) bar against one wall. Lake Gunn is only about a ten-minute walk down a lovely nature trail, and there's good trout fishing for those with fishing rods in their luggage. Rates are NZ$60 ($37.50) single, NZ$72 ($45) double, plus GST. Don't, however, just plan to drop in here—reserve at least 48 hours in advance, more if possible.

---

3. Milford Sound

No matter what time of year you arrive or what the weather is like, your memories of Milford Sound are bound to be very special. Its 14 nautical miles leading to the Tasman Sea are lined with mountain peaks that rise sharply to heights of 6,000 and 7,000 feet. Forsters fur seals sport on rocky shelves, dolphins play in waters that reach depths up to 2,000 feet, and its entrance is so concealed when viewed from the sea that Captain Cook sailed right by it without noticing when he was charting these waters some 200 years ago.

It rains a lot in Milford—some 300 inches annually, more than in any other one place in New Zealand. I personally don't mind the rain, for the sound (which is actually a fjord carved out by glacial action) shows yet another side of its nature under dripping skies—the trip out to the Tasman in the rain is as special in its own way as one when the sun is shining. Ah, but on a fine day, when the sky is blue, the water reflects varying shades of green and blue and dark brown, the bush, which flourishes even on sheer rock walls, glows a deep, shiny green—that day is to be treasured forever.

In summer months, coaches pour in at the rate of 30 or more each day for launch cruises. That tide slows in other months, but the launches go out year round, rain or shine. As is the custom at New Zealand's isolated beauty spots, the THC hotel is the center of things, and in the case of THC Milford, that continues a tradition that began in 1891, when Elizabeth Sutherland (wife of the sound's first settler) built a 12-room boarding house to accommodate seamen who called into the sound.

WHERE TO STAY

The only accommodations at Milford Sound other than the THC Milford is **Milford Lodge,** P.O. Box 10, Milford (0229/8071). In it, you'll find a simple, dormitory-type lodging in gorgeous surroundings just one short, beautiful mile from the sound. It's run by the Park Board, and open only from November 7 to April 6. Basic rooms mostly hold three beds—nothing more in the way of furnishings. Five rooms have H&C; five others have showers; and the toilet and shower block is immaculate. There's also a big lounge with a fireplace, cooking facilities, a restaurant, and a free sauna. If you're thinking of walking the Milford Track, this is where many hikers spend the first night back—perhaps to prolong a too-rare close communion with nature in the wooded site. Rates are about NZ$15 ($9.40) per person.

The one "big splurge" I simply would not miss in New Zealand is at least one overnight at the **THC Milford Sound Resort Hotel,** Private Bag, Milford Sound, Fiordland (tel. 0229/79-26). The hotel sprawls along the waterfront, amid lawns and flowers and shrubs and trees that have grown twisted into stylized, Oriental-like shapes. To watch the sunset and darkness descend over Mitre Peak from the glass-walled lounge, then gather around its two stone fireplaces for the evening with other guests and off-duty staff members, is to savor this unique environment in the best of all possible accommodations. There's a comfortable patina of the years, just this side of most "luxury" decor, overlaying the lounge, convivial bar, and dining room. Bedrooms are nicely furnished, with tea and coffee makings and telephone (satellite TV is installed in rooms, and video is available each evening in the lounge). Those in front have wall-width windows to take advantage of those striking views, as well as full baths (that means bathtubs!). Rates, single or double, are NZ$130 ($81.25) to NZ$180 ($113) for guest rooms, NZ$250 ($156) for an elegant suite. Periodic specials are real bargains—in 1989 NZ$85 ($53.25) covered one night's lodging, breakfast, the launch trip, and lunch! Do splurge if you can—it's the icing on Milford Sound's unique cake.

WHERE TO EAT

You can eat very inexpensively in the nearby Public Bar, which serves pub grub. Or you can bring a picnic lunch with you from Te Anau. Food is served.

You can choose from all those things, or you can treat yourself to a very special splurge and lunch in the **THC Milford,** next to a window looking out on the sound and Mitre Peak (time is allowed between coach arrival and launch departure). The menu features the freshest of seafoods, along with soup, dessert, coffee, and cheese, and lunch will run about NZ$21 ($13.25). Add another bit for a glass of wine and dine happily in anticipation of the launch cruise ahead.

THINGS TO SEE AND DO

Milford Sound must be seen from the deck of one of the launches, with the skipper filling you in on every peak, cove, creature, and plant you pass (the narrative, filled with anecdotes, is so entertaining you won't want to miss a word!), to be fully appreciated. Both the THC and Fiordland Travel Ltd. run **cruise excursions.** There's a one-hour trip for NZ$23 ($14.50), and a two-hour cruise for NZ$27 ($17), which takes you out into the Tasman where you see the shoreline close and understand how it is that the sound's entrance escaped Captain Cook's keen eye. Even in warm weather, a jacket or sweater will likely feel good out on the water, and if it should be raining, you'll be glad of a raincoat.

If you can stay over long enough, there are some marvelous **walks** from Milford Sound. Some climb into the peaks, others meander along the shore or up close to waterfalls. Ask at park headquarters in Te Anau or at the reception desk of THC Milford. It's worth the effort to know this timeless place from the land as well as the water.

I find the tiny (2,650-foot-long) airstrip a constant source of fascination on every trip. The air controller here talks in by radio more than 5,000 planes every year, and that without the help of such safety devices as lights or radar. The perfect safety record is accounted for by the fact that pilots must be rated specifically for this airfield, so they know what they're about as they zoom down, dwarfed by those stupdendous mountain peaks. I rather suspect, also, that careful monitoring of weather conditions and a watchful eye on all air traffic within radio range have a lot to do with that record. Among the clientele are regularly scheduled Mount Cook Line flights, scenic flights, and farmers who drop down in their private planes. The airfield is a short (less than five minutes) walk from the THC, and I'll have to warn you that watching those tiny specks against the backdrop of a sheer mountain wall grow into planes that make a perfect landing can become positively addictive.

On the other side of the airstrip, another short walk will bring you to the fishing facilities on the Cleddau River, an interesting and colorful sight, since there are nearly always a few of the fishing boats tied up in this safe anchorage.

READER'S TOURING SUGGESTION: "I found the place so beautiful that I felt compelled to stay at the pricey THC!!! But worth it" (Ian McPherson, Oxford, U.K.). [*Author's Note:* This reader's comment is listed simply to validate my own admittedly "rave" comments on Milford Sound!!]

4. Te Anau to Invercargill or Dunedin

If time is short, you may want to head straight for Dunedin from Te Anau. If not, don't miss another very special place, **Stewart Island,** New Zealand's "third island," and almost as far south as you can go in this world before reaching Antarctica.

The drive to Dunedin takes about 5½ hours over good roads. Take Hwy. 94 across Gorge Hill into Lumsden, across the **Waimea Plains** to the milling center of **Gore,** through farmlands to **Clinton,** and across rolling downs to **Balclutha.** From there, it's Hwy. 1 north along the coast past **Mosgiel** (named after Scottish poet Robbie Burns's farm) to **Lookout Point,** where you'll get your first look at Dunedin. Along the way, you may want to stop in **Mossburn,** where **Wapiti Handcrafts Ltd.** on the main street (P.O. Box 6; tel. 0228/87), makes and sells deerskin fashions. They are handsome creations and slightly lower in price here than in shops around the country. They also manufacture a range of smaller items for souvenirs and gifts. As you approach Balclutha, look for **Peggydale** (P.O. Box 7; tel. 0299/82-345), an ideal stopping point for tea, scones, sandwiches, or salad plates in the lovely Tea Kiosk. Peggydale handles a wide range of handcrafts—leather goods and sheepskin products (some made in their leathercraft shop), pottery, weaving, hand-knits, etc. —even paintings by local artists. They'll send you a mail-order catalog on request.

If Invercargill is your destination, you'll take Hwy. 94 only as far as Lumsden, then turn south on Hwy. 6 to ride through rolling farm and sheep country all the way down to Invercargill.

SOUTHLAND

Invercargill is New Zealand's southernmost city, the "capital" of Southland, a region you entered when you turned south at Lumsden, extending as far northwest as Lake Manapouri and as far east as Balclutha. It is the country's coolest and rainiest region, yet the even spread of its rainfall is the very foundation of its economy, the raising of grass and grass seed, which in turn supports large numbers of sheep stations.

Its coastline saw settlements of Maoris (in limited numbers) and whalers, with frequent visits from sealers. From its waters have come those succulent Bluff oysters and crayfish (rock lobsters) you've devoured in your New Zealand travels. In fact they account for about 90% of the value of fish landed in this area.

1. Invercargill

The first thing you'll notice about Invercargill is its flatness—a bump is likely to take on the dimensions of a "hill" in these parts! Actually, that flatness is due to the fact that a large part of the city was once boggy swampland. In its reclamation, town planners have turned what might have made for a dull city into a distinct advantage by creating wide, level thoroughfares and great city parks. Invercargill is a *spacious* city. Many of its broad, pleasant streets bear the names of Scottish rivers, revealing the home country of many of its early settlers.

Among its many attractions, perhaps primary is its proximity to Stewart Island, the legendary anchor of Maui's canoe (which became, of course, the South Island, with the North Island seen as the huge fish he caught). Day trips to Stewart Island are possible any day by air and several times a week by the ferry that runs from nearby Bluff.

ORIENTATION

Invercargill's streets are laid out in neat grid patterns. Main thoroughfares are **Tay Street** (an extension of Hwy. 1) and **Dee Street** (an extension of Hwy. 6). Many of the principal shops and office buildings are centered around the intersection of these two streets. **Queens Park** is a beautiful green oasis (200 acres) right in the center of town and the site of many activities. **Southland Promotions, Inc.,** 82 Dee St. (tel. 021/86-021), serves as a local tourist office and can furnish a list of local accommodations (although they are *not* a booking agency), as well as supply sightseeing details. The **railway station** and **InterCity depot** are on Leven Street and the **post office** is on Dee Street. There is good rail, bus, and air service to and from Invercargill. Drivers will find **AA Headquarters** at 47-51 Gala St. (tel. 89-033).

WHERE TO STAY

You should have no trouble finding a place to lay your weary head in Invercargill. There are good budget accommodations in ample quantity. Advance inquiries for *hotel* accommodations should go to: Trust Hotels, P.O. Box 208, Invercargill (tel. 021/88-059).

A Hostel

The **YHA Hostel** is at 122 North Rd., Waikiwi, Invercargill (tel. 021/59-344). This is an extension of Dee Street, before it becomes Hwy. 6. There are 44 beds in the six rooms, showers, and a kitchen. There's a barbecue and picnic area available for use during the day, and the resident manager can arrange reduced fares to Stewart Island on a standby basis. He can also advise about hostel-type accommodations on the island (there are tentative plans for a YHA hostel, but no timetable as yet). Seniors pay NZ$12 ($7.50); juniors, NZ$6 ($3.75), plus GST.

A Bed-and-Breakfast

The interesting old **Gerrards Railway Hotel,** on the corner of Esk and Leven Streets, Invercargill (tel. 021/83-406), is just across from the railway station. Built in 1896 of rosy-pink brick with white trim, its façade has recently had a face cleaning and rooms have been redone. These are not fancy accommodations, but comfortable, clean, and very centrally located. Rooms with or without private facilities are available, and showers and toilets are conveniently located for those that share. Bed-and-breakfast rates for rooms without facilities are NZ$45 ($28.25) single, NZ$60 ($37.50) double; with private facilities, NZ$55 ($34.50) single, NZ$68.50 ($42.75). GST is included in all these rates. Children under 9 stay free.

Cabins/Campgrounds

The **Southland A&P Association Caravan Park,** at the Showgrounds on Victoria Avenue, Invercargill (tel. 021/88-787), has two cabins that sleep up to four, and three that sleep up to six. On the premises is a kitchen, showers and toilets, a laundry, store, car wash, and play area. There are facilities for the disabled, plus 50 campsites and 60 caravan sites. Rates for cabins are NZ$22 ($13.75) for two; caravan sites, NZ$7 ($4.40) per adult (children pay half price); tent sites, NZ$5.50 ($3.45) per adult—including GST.

At **Coachman's Caravan Park,** 705 Tay St., Invercargill (tel. 021/76-046), are 33 cabins that sleep two to four people each. The occupants have to supply their own linens, blankets, crockery, and cooking utensils. The rate is NZ$26 ($16.25) per night double. The caravan park on premises has 24 sites with hookups, a laundry, kitchen, and toilet and shower facilities. The rate is NZ$5.50 ($3.45) per person per night (plus GST), but you have to add to that a NZ$15 ($9.40) surcharge.

Motel Flats

Mitchells Motel, 85 Alice St. Invercargill (tel. 021/44-504), is a pretty brick-and-wood complex right on the edge of Queens Park on a quiet residential street. Its ten units are more like individual homes than flats, some with one bedroom, others with two. Each is nicely decorated and furnished, and has a separate living room, telephone, color TV, radio, full kitchen, and private bath. Most have at-door parking. There's also a spa pool and playground. A cooked or continental breakfast is available at a small charge. Rates are NZ$55 ($34.50) single and NZ$70 ($43.75) double, including GST. This is a Best Western so that chain's discounts apply.

The **Don Lodge Motor Hotel,** 77 Don St. (P.O. Box 208), Invercargill (tel.

021/86-125), has 23 nice self-contained units, all with parking at the door. Each unit has a telephone, color TV, fridge, tea and coffee facilities, and private shower. Cooked or continental breakfasts are available. There's also a good, moderately priced restaurant on the premises (see "Where to Eat," below). Rates are NZ$46.23 ($29) single or NZ$50.67 ($31.75) double, plus GST.

The attractive one-story blue-and-white **Tayesta Motel**, 343 Tay St., Invercargill (tel. 021/76-074), has 12 one- and two-bedroom units, each with large picture windows in the lounge, fully equipped kitchen, central heating, telephone, color TV, video, and radio. There's a laundry, play area with swings and sandpit, and at-door parking. Lola Staite is the friendly hostess at this Best Western. Continental or cooked breakfasts are available at small charge. Rates are NZ$56 ($35) single, NZ$64 ($40) double, plus GST, and discounts apply.

Only five minutes from the city center, the **Colonial Motor Inn**, 335-339 Tay St., Invercargill (tel. 021/76-058), has ten one- and two-bedroom units with private facilities, fully equipped kitchens, and a dining area. Continental breakfast is available on request. The rate is NZ$60.50 ($37.75) single and about NZ$70 ($43.75) double.

READERS' ACCOMMODATION SELECTIONS: "If travelers are going to Stewart Island by ferry, I would strongly recommend staying the night in Bluff instead of Invercargill. We stayed at the **Bay View Hotel**, directly across from the ferry departure area, and we had one of our best dinners there" (M. Lovranich, El Cajon, Calif.). . . . "In Invercargill we really struck gold when we were directed to the farm of **June and Murray Stratford**, Progress Valley, R.D. 1, Tokanui, Southland (tel. 021398/502). As hosts they were magnificent. Murray took us on his rounds checking on the sheep and new lambs, and June took us to some of the beauty spots along the 'Forgotten Coast'! They even invited friends and neighbors over to meet us. They also have a holiday house that sleeps six in three double bedrooms that they rent to families" (J. and T. Shelbourne, Paradise Valley, Ariz.). . . . **"Monticello** offers real Kiwi hospitality and a very appealing old building" (E. Ellers, Buffalo, N.Y.). . . . "We found **Lornville Lodge**, 8½ miles from Invercargill (tel. 021/358-031 or 358-762), perfect for a stopover and visit with Pauline and Bill Schuck, who own and operate a small goat and sheep farm. The surroundings are relaxing, the meals filling, and the rates are reasonable and include breakfast. There is lodging in the farmhouse as well as a self-contained cottage, and there are also campervan sites (M. and B. Humphreys, Providence, R.I.).

WHERE TO EAT

Invercargill has numerous coffeeshops offering good value. The coffee lounge in the **D.I.C. Department Store** has good morning and afternoon teas as well as light lunches, all inexpensive.

For quiche, baked potatoes with a variety of fillings, 26 different salads, nutritious hot meals, light lunches, carrot cake, muesli munch, soups, and cakes—all made daily on the premises and all very good—try **Joy's Gourmet Kitchen**, 122 Dee St. (tel. 83-985). Hours are 9 a.m. to 6 p.m. (later on Friday), and your lunch will run under NZ$6 ($3.75).

The beautiful and elegant **Grand Hotel**, 76 Dee St. (tel. 88-059), is a joy to go into, even if you don't eat. The lovely formal dining room serves reasonable dinners, with dishes starting at NZ$9 ($5.65) *Special Note:* If oysters are on the menu in any form, let that be your order. Fully licensed.

The **Hungry Knight Restaurant**, in the Don Lodge Motor Hotel, 77 Don St. (tel. 86-125), serves all three meals, all at moderate prices, and service is continuous from 7 a.m. until 10 p.m. seven days a week. The menu is comprehensive, with a nice selection of seafood, steak, chicken, etc. Lunch will run about NZ$6 ($3.75); dinner, anywhere from NZ$7 ($4.40) to NZ$10 ($6.25).

There's a bright, café air about the restaurant at **Gerrards Railway Hotel**, on the corner of Esk and Leven Streets (tel. 83-406). The menu is a mixture of native New Zealand and continental dishes and includes specialties like coquilles St-Jacques and escalopes de porc with mushroom and brandy-cream sauce, local Bluff oysters, and fresh blue cod in a lemon-and-wine sauce. Service is friendly, and your dinner bill will seldom top NZ$25 ($15.75). Dinner is served from 6:30 p.m. nightly. Licensed.

Go back in time at the **Strathern Inn,** 200 Elles Rd. (tel. 89-100), where the staff wears colonial dress and you dine in one of six dining rooms in the midst of old paintings and bric-a-brac. Local seafood dishes are the specialty, and the average cost of a three-course meal is NZ$25 ($15.75). The inn is open daily for lunch from noon to 2 p.m., and for dinner from 5:30 p.m. Licensed.

READERS' DINING SELECTIONS: "We loved the farmhouse setting at **Donovan's Licensed Restaurant,** 220 Bainfield Rd. (tel. 58-156), where the menu features game, lamb, or seafood. It's only open after 5:30 p.m. and it's worth the little bit of splurge to go" (G. Shore, Minneapolis, Minn.). . . . "In Bluff, the **Stirling Point Restaurant,** at the end of Hwy. 1, has commanding views of Fouveaux Strait and the entrance to Bluff Harbour. Local seafood dishes are delicious" (K. Goria, San Francisco, Calif.).

A Carvery Treat

Friday night in Invercargill means the carvery at the **Ascot Park Hotel**—to residents as well as visitors—so reservations are a very good idea (in fact, I heard about this feast way up in the North Island when I mentioned coming to Invercargill). The Ascot Park, on the corner of Racecourse Road and Tay Street (tel. 76-195), is a luxury hotel of the first order, and the carvery is spread in an enormous room with different levels for tables. The spread is just about as enormous as the room, with every kind of seafood currently available, endless fresh salads, great roasts for non-seafood lovers, and luscious desserts. You'll see parties of locals chatting away with visitors, and there's a party atmosphere all through the place. The price is NZ$22 ($13.75), for which you get *full* value, indeed. Highly recommended.

THINGS TO SEE AND DO

Allow at least a full hour to visit the **Southland Museum and Art Gallery** on Gala Street by the main entrance to Queens Park. The collections inside include a multitude of exhibits that will bring alive much of the history and natural resources of this area. In addition, there's a tuatarium the only place in the country you can view live tuataras in a simulated natural setting. In front of the museum, examine the section of fossilized forest, which dates from the Jurassic era of some 160 million years ago. Hours are 10 a.m. to 4:30 p.m. Monday through Friday, 1 to 5 p.m. on Saturday, Sunday, and public holidays.

Queens Park, right in the heart of the city, is just one (the largest) of Invercargill's parklands (a total of 2,975 acres) and might well keep you occupied for the better part of a day. Within its 200 acres there's a rhododendron walk, iris garden, sunken rose garden, grove of native and exotic trees, wildlife sanctuary with wallabies, deer, and an aviary, duckpond, a winter garden, an 18-hole golf course, tennis courts, and—perhaps most of all—a cool, green retreat for the senses. A very special thing to look for is the beguiling children's fountain encircled by large bronze animal statues. Over the years this beautiful botanical reserve has seen duty as grazing land, a racecourse, and a sporting ground. The entrance is from Queens Drive at Gala Street. There's a delightful Tea Kiosk for light refreshments.

Drive out to **Bluff,** Invercargill's port some 27 km (16½ miles) to the south. This is home port for the Stewart Island ferry, and site (on the other side of the harbor at Tiwai Point) of the mammoth Tiwai Aluminum Smelter (the only one in the country) whose annual production is 259,000 tons. If you'd like to tour the complex (a fascinating experience), contact **Tiwai Smelter Tours,** NZ Aluminum Smelters Ltd., Private Bag, Invercargill (tel. 021/85-999). You must be at least 12 years of age and wear long trousers or slacks, heavy footwear, and clothing that covers your arms. There's no charge, but usually tours are limited to two a week, so it pays to reserve well in advance.

There are two great **walks** in Bluff (ask the Southland Progress League office in Invercargill for the *Foveaux Walk, Bluff* pamphlet). The "Glory Walk" (named for a sailing vessel, *England's Glory,* which was wrecked at Bluff) is 1½ km (about a mile) long and passes through native bush and trees, which form a shady canopy overhead. Ferns and mosses add to the lush greenery. The Sterling Point–Ocean Beach Walk begins where Hwy. 1 ends at Foveaux Strait. It's almost 7 km (4¼ miles) long, following the coastline around Bluff Hill, with marvelous views of beaches, offshore islands, and surf breaking against coastal rocks. Parking facilities are provided at both ends of the walk, and you are asked to follow the signposts and to leave no litter in your footprints.

READER'S SUGGESTIONS IN BLUFF: "At Bluff, we visited a lookout high on a hill where you can look south over Foveaux Strait to Stewart Island and imagine Antarctica. A young man there advised us to eat at a small take-out place called **Johnsons on the Wharf.** Usually they have oysters, but not this time, so we had paua patties and mussel rolls, both absolutely delicious. Both had been minced, mixed with seasonings, rolled in crumbs and batter and fried. The paua was almost navy blue and very strange looking. It was the only place we ate it, and we loved it. Then we drove on down the coast road to the very tip of the South Island, where there is one of those signposts pointing in all directions. It was a lovely drive, and we passed an interesting house that an older couple have decorated inside and out with paua shells over the years. It was funny and quaint, but they were so pleased with it that we enjoyed the visit" (A. Schweinsberg, Wilmington, Del.).

INVERCARGILL TO STEWART ISLAND

The highlight of any Invercargill visit is a trip out to Stewart Island, about 30 km (18 miles) across Foveaux Strait. You can go **by sea** aboard the good vessel *Acheron,* maintained by Stewart Island Charter Service. It sails at 9 a.m. from Bluff on Monday, Wednesday, and Friday; the fare is NZ$30 ($18.75) per person, plus GST. The glorious, two-hour voyage crosses waters that are comparatively shallow, but they can be exceedingly turbulent. The major transport to Stewart Island, however, is via **Southern Air,** P.O. Box 860, Invercargill (tel. 021/89-129), and during the 20-minute flight, the nine-seater Britten-Norman Islander gives you breathtaking views of the coastline, changing colors of the waters below (which mark the passage of an oceanic stream flowing through the strait), bush-clad islands, and Stewart Island itself, where you land on a sealed runway and are minibused into Oban. Southern Air flies seven days a week, almost every hour in the summer; there is a minimum of three flights a day, and extra ones are added upon demand. The airline schedules even allow for a day visit if you're pressed for time. These flights are extremely popular and you should either book ahead by telephone or through travel agents or airline offices (Mount Cook Line and Air New Zealand can both make reservations) before you arrive in Invercargill. The airline can arrange accommodation or fishing trips on Stewart Island. Adult fare is NZ$57 ($35.75) each way; children pay half.

2. Stewart Island

Seen on the map, Stewart Island is not much more than a speck. But seen from the deck of the *Acheron* or from the air, its magnitude will surprise you. There are actually 1,600 km (975 miles) of coastline enclosing 1,680 km² (625 square miles) of thick bush (most of it left in its natural state), bird sanctuary, and rugged mountains. Only a tiny stretch of that long coastline has been settled, and it's the little fishing town of Oban that will be your landfall. There are about 20 km (12 miles) of paved road on the island, which are easily covered by the minibus tour, and many of the houses you see are the holiday "batch" or "crib" of Kiwis from the South Island who view Stewart Island as the perfect spot to escape the pressures of civilization. The pace here is quite unhurried—few cars, friendly islanders more attuned to the tides and the running of cod and crayfish than to commerce—and the setting is a botanist's dream. The Maoris called the island Rakiura, "heavenly glow," a name you'll find especially fitting if you are lucky enough to see the southern lights brighten its skies or to be here for one of its spectacular sunsets.

While its beauty and serenity can be glimpsed in the few hours of a day trip, I heartily recommend at least one overnight to explore its beaches, bush, and people so as to savor this very special place to the fullest. Incidentally, should you hear yourself or other visitors referred to as "loopies" by the islanders, not to worry—it'll be said with affection.

The town of **Oban** centers on Halfmoon Bay and holds a general store, post office, travel office, craft shop, hotel, forestry office, small museum, and the pier at which the ferry docks.

WHERE TO STAY

There is no reservations agency as such on Stewart Island, but pretty Beryl Wilcox and her husband, Lloyd, who operate **Stewart Island Travel,** P.O. Box 26, Stewart Island (tel. 021/391-269 or 391-293), can send you a complete list of accommodations and prices, and will do all they can to help you book. If you write from the U.S., be sure to enclose $3U.S. to cover postage. Accommodations are extremely limited, and in summer they're booked months in advance, so if your plans include a visit here, write or call just as soon as you have firm dates for your visit. It is sometimes possible to rent one of the holiday homes or apartments not currently in use, and Beryl is the one to contact. *Note:* Where a P.O. Box is not listed below, the address is simply Stewart Island, New Zealand.

Hostels

The **Shearwater Inn,** on Ayre Street in the heart of Oban (tel. 021/391-114), is an associate YHA hostel. It offers 80 beds (two to four to a room), a communal lounge, kitchen, buffet bistro, and a courtyard used for barbecues. Opened in 1989, it was the first major new accommodation on the island in 50 years. The backpacker rate is NZ$12 ($7.50) per bed (for other prices, see "Motel Flats").

Very basic "tramper accommodations" can be arranged through **Ann Pulen** (tel. 021/391-065 after 6 p.m.) or **Jo Riksem** (tel. 021/391-230). Rates are about NZ$12 ($7.50) per person per night.

Motel Flats

The **Shearwater Inn,** which opened in 1989, offers 80 beds in 28 rooms and caters to the budget-minded (see "Hostels"). Rates start at NZ$17 ($10.75), and double rooms are NZ$42.67 ($26.75), plus GST.

Ferndale Caravans, P.O. Box 117, Stewart Island (tel. 021/391-176), is on Halfmoon Bay, and has fully furnished luxury caravans with awnings, a children's playground, a kitchen, and drying facilities. Rates are NZ$50 ($31.25), single or double, NZ$8 ($5) per extra adult, NZ$5 ($3.15) per child. Add GST. Contact Lesley Gray.

Elaine Hamilton has five self-contained motel units at **Rakiura Motels,** P.O. Box 96, Stewart Island (tel. 27S), about one mile from Oban. Units sleep up to six, are heated, and have kitchens and private baths. Rates (which include GST) are NZ$70 ($43.75), single or double, NZ$11 ($6.90) per extra adult, NZ$8 ($5) per child under 12, plus GST.

A Licensed Hotel

Stewart Island's only hotel is the **South Sea Hotel,** P.O. Box 52, Stewart Island (tel. 021/391-059), run by Bruce and Sue Ford. The two-story hotel sits right in the curve of Halfmoon Bay, across the street from the water. Its public bar, bar lounge (whose windows overlook the bay), and licensed restaurant are the center of much island activity, and even if you lodge elsewhere, you're likely to find yourself in and out of the South Sea many times during your stay. Rooms all share the bath and toilet facilities down the hall, and there are exactly six singles, eight twins, two doubles, and two triples. This is the kind of charming, old-fashioned inn that seems exactly right for an island—the guest lounge, for example, has an open fire glowing on cool days, and the staff takes a personal interest in all guests (and in casual visitors, for that matter). Rates are NZ$50 ($31.25) single and NZ$75 ($47) double, with children 2 to 10 at half that. Breakfast is extra at NZ$9 ($5.65). There may be a surcharge for one-night stays. Add GST.

WHERE TO EAT

The **Travel Inn Tearoom,** adjoining Stewart Island Travel (just opposite the deer park in the center of town), serves sandwiches, meat pies, salad rolls, cakes, etc., from 9 a.m. to 3 p.m., all priced under NZ$2 ($1.25). Eat in the tea room, or take away.

The **Shearwater Inn** has basic, hearty meals at reasonable prices, by arrangement.

One of the best seafood meals I've had in New Zealand was in the large, pleasant dining room at the **South Sea Hotel.** My fish was truly fresh and fried to perfection, the salad bar was more extensive than I would have expected on an island where so much must be imported, the dessert was luscious, and the service included a friendly chat about how best to spend my time on Stewart Island. Other main courses included beef, lamb, and chicken, but seafood is their specialty, and in a setting like this it seems the logical choice. Lunch hours are noon to 1 p.m., and the set price is NZ$13 ($8.15). Dinner is served each night from 6 to 7 p.m. and costs NZ$24 ($15).

The South Sea Hotel can pack a **picnic lunch** if notified in ample time, and there's a general store where you can pick up picnic makings for a day in the bush.

READER'S DINING SUGGESTION: "Almost every eatery, including the local fish-and-chips shop, is closed in winter except at the South Sea Hotel, but you need to make a dinner reservation before 4:30 p.m." (R. Wong, Philadelphia, Pa.).

THINGS TO SEE AND DO

The only thing not to miss is the hour-long **minibus tour** given by Beryl Wilcox at Stewart Island Travel (tel. 69 or 105). Beryl will not only cover every one of those 20 km (12 miles) of paved road, she'll give you a comprehensive history of Stewart Island—the whalers who settled here, the sealers who called in (it was, in fact, the mate of a sealer who gave his name to the island), the sawmill and mineral industries, that came and went, development of the fishing industry, etc.—and will point out traces they left behind scattered around your route. She also knows the flora of the island (you'll learn, for instance, that there are 17 varieties of orchids on the island) and its animal population (no wild pigs or goats). You'll see many of the 18 good swimming beaches and hear details of the paua diving, which has proved so profitable for islanders (much of the colorful shell that went into those souvenirs you've seen around New Zealand came from Stewart Island). From Observation Point right to the road's end at Thule Bay, Beryl gives you an insider's view of her home. And questions or comments are very much in order—it's an informal, happy hour of exchange: a perfect way to begin a stay of several days, an absolute essential if the day trip is all you will have. The fare is NZ$15 ($9.40).

The **Rakiura Museum** in Halfmoon Bay features photos and exhibits that follow Stewart Island's history through its sailing, whaling, tin-mining, sawmilling, and fishing days. It also has shell and Maori artifact exhibits. Hours are 11 a.m. to 2 p.m. on Monday, Wednesday, and Friday (daily during the summer holidays). Admission is NZ$1 (65¢) for adults, NZ$.50 (30¢) for children.

Visit the small **deer park** just across from Stewart Island Travel. Small red deer are right at home in the enclosure and seem delighted to have visitors.

Just next to the deer park is the **Forest Service Office,** which has an interesting display of island wildlife in a small exhibition room. More important, the rangers there can supply details on many beautiful **walks** around Oban and farther afield. If you're interested in spending a few days on the island tramping, I suggest that you write ahead for their informative booklets on just what you'll need to bring and what you may expect. There are recently upgraded tramping huts conveniently spaced along the tracks (ranging in size from 6 to 30 bunks), but they are heavily used and must be booked with the rangers (no charge). A two-night stay is the maximum at any one hut.

Popular short walks around Oban are those to Golden Bay, Lonneckers, Lee Bay, Thule, Observation Point, and the lighthouse at Acker's Point. Ringarina Beach is a mecca for shell hounds (I have New Zealand friends who serve entrees in paua shells they've picked up on the beach here!), but your finds will depend on whether the tides are right during your visit. *Important:* If you're here on a day trip, check locally to be sure you can make it back from any walk you plan in time for the ferry or air return.

You can engage local boats for **fishing** or visiting nearby uninhabited islands at prices that are surprisingly low. Contact Phillip Smith, master of the *Seastar,* or check with Stewart Island Travel.

---

3. The Coast Road to Dunedin

You can drive from Invercargill to Dunedin in a little over three hours by way of Hwy. 1, through Gore, past farmlands and mile after mile of grazing sheep. It's a pleasant drive, and one you'll enjoy. *However,* if you have a day to spend on the road, let me urge you to follow the Southern Scenic Route along Hwy. 92 and allow a full day to loiter along the way, rejoining Hwy. 1 at Balclutha. If you make this drive, the leaflet *Drive New Zealand's Southern Scenic Route* from the Southland Promotions office, 82 Dee St., in Invercargill, is quite helpful as it details the reserves through which you will pass.

The **Southern Scenic Route,** as it is known, takes you through a region of truly unique character. There are great folds in the land covered with such a diversity of native forests that from Chaslands on you'll be in one national forest reserve after the other. Short detours will take you to the coast and golden sand beaches, prominent headlands, and fine bays.

Highway 92, let me hasten to add, is not paved its entire length—however, even unpaved portions are in good driving condition, albeit at a slower speed than the faster Hwy. 1. Picnic spots abound, so you can take along a packed lunch from Invercargill, or plan to stop in the country pub in Owaka's only hotel for lunch (stop for refreshments even if you lunch elsewhere—it's an experience you wouldn't want to miss). One very special detour you might consider follows.

Just beyond Fortrose, follow the Fortrose–Otara road to the right, and when you pass the Otara School, look for the turnoff to **Waipapa Point.** The point is the entrance to **Foveaux Strait,** a treacherous waterway that has scuttled many a sailing vessel and that is now marked by a light, which was first used in 1884. Follow the Otara–Haldane road to Porpoise Bay, then turn right and drive a little over one kilometer (about half a mile) to the **Curio Bay Fossil Forest,** which is signposted. This sea-washed rock terrace dates back 160 *million* years and is the original floor of a Jurassic subtropical forest of kauri trees, conifers, and other trees that were growing at a time when grasses had not even evolved. At low tide, you can make out low stumps and fallen logs that have been petrified after being buried in volcanic ash, then raised when the sea level changed. You can then retrace your way around Porpoise Bay and follow the signs to Waikawa and continue north to rejoin Hwy. 92 and travel on to Chaslands.

There are a few simple rules you must follow when stopping in the scenic reserves. If you picnic, you may light fires *only* in the fireplaces provided in picnic areas, and be sure to extinguish them thoroughly (only dead wood is permitted as fuel); dogs and cats may not be brought into the reserve except with permission from the reserves ranger; it is an offense to pick or damage any of the trees, shrubs, or plants in the reserves; and (need I add?) you are expected to leave your picnic area clean and tidy.

If you'd like further details about this lovely part of a lovely country, contact the **Department of Conservation,** P.O. Box 5244, Dunedin (tel. 024/770-677), or call in at the **Owaka Information Centre.**

CAMPGROUND

Papatowai Camping Ground, Waipati, R.D. 2, Owaka (tel. 0299/58-063 in Balclutha), has 25 power points and 5 sites without power. There's a kitchen with hotplates, fridge, and a pot-bellied stove; a playground; a laundry; and flush toilet facilities with showers and razor power points. The campground is handy to bush reserves and the coast, and rates are NZ$4 ($2.50) per adult, NZ$2 ($1.25) per child, plus NZ$1 (65¢) per night for power points. Open year round except June. Advance reservations are strongly advised, especially during Christmas, New Year, and Easter holidays.

From the campground, it is a short trip to the Purakanui Falls, and ten 15-minute walk from the picnic area (where there are toilet facilities) to the falls is well worth the effort.

Naish Park Camping Ground, on Charlotte Street in Balclutha (tel. 0249/80-088), has 12 sites with hookups, kitchen, toilet and shower facilities, laundry, and children's playground. Rates are NZ$7.80 ($4.90) double, NZ$1.20 (75¢) per child. From here, it's easy to get to Kaka Point, where there is good surf and patrolled swimming beaches; there are seal and penguin colonies at the Nugget Point lighthouse.

The **Brighton Caravan Park,** 331 Main Rd., Brighton (tel. 024/811-404 in Dunedin), on the coast just south of Dunedin, has 21 sites with hookups, kitchen and toilet facilities, laundry, and children's play area. It's situated beside the Otokia River, and you can rent a boat from the owners.

READERS' ACCOMMODATION SELECTIONS: "The **Rosebank Lodge,** 265 Clyde St. in Balclutha (tel. 0299/81-490), has rooms with private facilities as well as a caravan park on the grounds" (D. Stover, Atlanta, Ga.). . . . "We found the **Lake Waihola Motel** extremely reasonable for a double room; the lake and a golf course aren't far away" (A. Mays, Long Island City, N.Y.).

READERS' SHOPPING SUGGESTION: "We stopped by **Peggydale,** on Hwy. 1 about two miles south of Balclutha, with a huge collection of souvenirs under one roof. Besides finding leather goods and woolens to take home with us, we were delighted to sit down at the tea kiosk and savor some country-style food" (T. and J. London, Chicago, Ill.).

X

DUNEDIN AND MOUNT COOK

1. DUNEDIN AND SURROUNDINGS
2. MOUNT COOK
3. MOUNT COOK TO CHRISTCHURCH

You won't find pipers in the streets of Dunedin—and the citizens of "New Edinburgh on the Antipodes" are quick to tell you they're *Kiwis,* not Scots. Still, one look at the sturdy stone Victorian architectural face of the city with its crown of upreaching spires will tell you that the 344 settlers who arrived at this beautiful Upper Harbour in March 1848 could only have come from Scotland. And when you learn that Dunedin is the old Gaelic name for Edinburgh, that the city produces New Zealand's only domestic whisky, has the only kilt store in the country, and that the strains of a pipe band are common here, there's no mistaking its Scottish nature!

A reader once wrote that "very few people are lukewarm about their feelings when it comes to bagpipes—either they are very enthusiastic or they're *anti*-bagpipes." I think she's right and you might as well know up front that I am one of those enthusiasts who will drop everything at the skirl of a bagpipe and travel miles to listen to its curious music. Which fact may account in large part for the place Dunedin holds in my affections. That affection, however, is mightily reinforced by the city's serendipitous character—lighthearted chatter in pubs hiding behind somber façades, instant friendliness that belies the much-touted "dour" Scottish nature, and the spirit of fun unexpectedly discovered in almost any Dunedin gathering, the *twinkle* in Dunedin's eye. Nor is that twinkle exclusively Scottish—there's a decidedly *Irish* flavor to the fact that Science Department professors in the august University of Otago regularly choose St. Patrick's Day to conduct chemical experiments that will turn the waters of the Waters of Leith, which flow through the campus, green for most of that day!

The city's foundations were planned on the solid bedrock of a "Free Church," but its fortunes changed drastically with the goldfield discoveries in Otago, which brought thousands pouring in to bring, along with the gold speculators, the bustle of industry and commerce. From 1861 to 1865 its population erupted from 2,000 to over 10,000, and it has since that time never lost its position of prominence among New Zealand's cities. Amazingly, it has held onto its priorities of education (the first New Zealand university was founded here), conservation of its natural beauties (witness the green Town Belt, which encircles the city), and humanitarian concerns (the Plunket Society for good infant care originated here).

Dunedin, with a population of 100,000 today, is likely to be one of your most fondly remembered New Zealand cities—and you really shouldn't go away without exploring the 12-mile-long Otago Peninsula (it's pronounced "O-*tah*-go") that curves around one side of that beautiful harbor.

---

1. Dunedin and Surroundings

ORIENTATION

Most cities have a public square, but Dunedin has its eight-sided **Octagon,** a green, leafy park right at the hub of the city center that was totally remodeled in 1989. Around its edges you'll find **St. Paul's Anglican Cathedral** and the **Town Hall.** Within its confines, there's a statue of Scotland's beloved poet Robert Burns (whose nephew was Dunedin's first pastor), shady pathways, and park benches for foot-weary shoppers or brown-bagging lunchers.

The city center, at the head of **Otago Harbour,** is encircled by a 500-acre strip of land left, by edict of the founders, in its natural state, never to be developed regardless of the city's growth. Thus it is that when driving to any of Dunedin's suburbs, you pass through verdant forestland from which there are glimpses of the harbor.

The Octagon divides the main street into **Princes Street** to the south, **George Street** to the north. Most city buses leave from the Octagon at the intersection of High and Princes Streets. There's frequent **bus service** during the week, a little spotty on weekends. Fares are zoned and range from NZ$1 (65¢) to NZ$1.60 ($1), half that for children. If you buy a packet of 12 tickets, you essentially get two rides for free. The InterCity Special, for stops along the route from the bus terminal to Frederick Street, costs NZ.50 (30¢) a ride, or 12 rides for NZ$5 ($3.10). A one-day tourist ticket for families costs NZ$10 ($6.25) and allows unlimited travel on all timetable services. A smooth-working one-way street system makes driving easier than in most cities; all central streets have metered parking; and there's a municipal parking building near City Hall.

There are three very good lookout points from which to view the city and its environs: **Mount Cargill Lookout** 8 km (4¾ miles) from the city center (turn left at the end of George Street, then left on Pine Hill Road to its end, then right onto Cowan Street, which climbs to the summit); **Centennial Lookout,** or Signal Hill (turn into Signal Hill Road from Opoho Road and drive 3 km, or 1¾ miles, to the end of Signal Hill Road); and **Bracken's Lookout** (at the top of the Botanic Gardens).

Useful Information

You'll find the **New Zealand Tourist and Publicity (NZTP) Office** at 131 Princes St. (tel. 024/740-344), two blocks from the Octagon (open from 8:30 a.m. to 5 p.m. Monday through Friday). They offer a multitude of services and information. . . . Even more helpful with visitor information is the **Dunedin Visitor Centre,** The Octagon (tel. 024/774-176/177), just off George Street under the Town Hall clock, open from 8:30 a.m. to 5 p.m. weekdays, 9 a.m. to 5 p.m. weekends, with extended hours in summer. . . . The **railway station** (a sightseeing attraction; see below) is at the foot of Stuart Street, the **InterCity bus terminal** several blocks away on Cumberland Street (tel. 772-620 for train or bus information). . . . **Air New Zealand** (tel. 775-769) has its ticket office in John Wickliffe House, next to the Chief Post Office (CPO), for flight information and booking. . . . Fares on airport coaches are NZ$8 ($5) for adults, NZ$4 ($2.50) for children, and they drop you off at the Savoy, at the corner of Princes Street and Moray Place. The air-

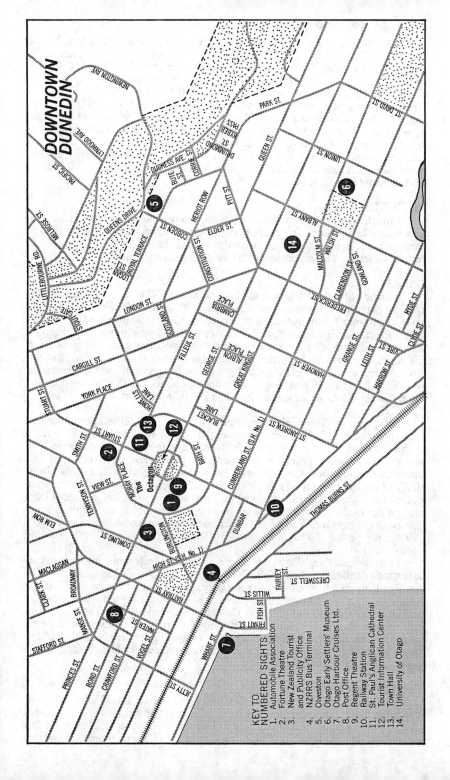

DOWNTOWN DUNEDIN

NEWINGTON AVE.
PACIFIC ST.
LYNWOOD AVE.
MELROSE ST.
LITTLEBOURNE RD.
GATE
STOUT ST.
LOGAN
ROYAL TERRACE
QUEENS DRIVE
EXETER PASS
DRUMMOND ST.
DUCHESS AVE.
BUTE ST.
CORRIE ST.
PARK ST.
QUEEN ST.
ST. DAVID ST.
ST. DAVID ST.
HERIOT ROW
PITT ST.
ELDER ST.
COBDEN ST.
CONSTITUTION ST.
ALBANY ST.
UNION ST.
MALCOLM ST.
WALSH ST.
CLARENDON ST.
GOWLAND ST.
FREDERICK ST.
HYDE ST.
CLYDE ST.
LONDON ST.
SCOTLAND ST.
FILLEUL ST.
GEORGE ST.
CAMBRIA PLACE
ALBION PLACE
GREAT KING ST.
HANOVER ST.
GRANGE ST.
LEITH ST.
CLIVE ST.
HARROW ST.
CARGILL ST.
YORK PLACE
HOWE ST.
LANE
STUART ST.
SMITH ST.
BLACKET LANE
BATH ST.
CUMBERLAND ST. (S.H. No. 1)
ST. ANDREW ST.
VIEW ST.
TENNYSON ST.
MORAY PLACE
The Octagon
DUNBAR
THOMAS BURNS ST.
ELM ROW
DOWLING ST.
BURLINGTON
HIGH ST. (S.H. No. 1)
MACLAGGAN
CLARK ST.
BROADWAY
MANSE ST.
VOGEL ST.
WATER ST.
MORAY ST.
WILLIS ST.
FAIRLEY ST.
CRESSWELL ST.
FISH ST.
WHARF ST.
RATTRAY ST.
PRINCES ST.
BOND ST.
CRAWFORD ST.
JETTY ST.
HYATT ST.
STAFFORD ST.

2
5
6
14
13
11
12
9
1
3
4
10
8
7

KEY TO
NUMBERED SIGHTS
1. Automobile Association
2. Fortune Theatre
3. New Zealand Tourist
   and Publicity Office
4. NZRRS Bus Terminal
5. Olveston
6. Otago Early Settlers' Museum
7. Otago Harbour Cruises Ltd.
8. Post Office
9. Regent Theatre
10. Railway Station
11. St. Paul's Anglican Cathedral
12. Tourist Information Center
13. Town Hall
14. University of Otago

port is a full 20 minutes from the city, which makes a taxi prohibitive at fares of about NZ$45 ($28.25). . . . **Taxi ranks** may be found at the Octagon, all terminals, and near the CPO (tel. 777-777 or 771-771). . . . The **Chief Post Office (CPO)** is at Princes and Water Streets, open Monday through Friday from 8:30 a.m. to 5 p.m. . . . The **Automobile Association** office is at 450 Moray Pl. (tel. 775-945). . . . Central 24-hour **gas (petrol) stations** are: Kai Valley Service Station, 433 Stuart St. (tel. 778-391); Downtown Motors Ltd., at the corner of Gardner and Granford Streets (tel. 771-256); and Everedi Service Station, opposite the Oval, which also sells groceries (tel. 775-566). . . . A **late-night pharmacy** (for New Zealand, at any rate), at Filleul Street and York Place, is open until 10 p.m. on Monday, Tuesday, Wednesday, and Saturday, and until 9 p.m. on Sunday and holidays. . . . The **telephone prefix** for Dunedin is 024.

WHERE TO STAY

Dunedin has many fine accommodations in almost all price ranges. It also has, however, a large student population (with lots of visitors!) and a great deal of through traffic en route to the Southern Alps and Southland. All of which adds up to *reserve in advance.* This especially holds true during summer months.

Hostels

A grand old early-1900s mansion houses Dunedin's YHA hostel, **Stafford Gables,** 71 Stafford St. Dunedin (tel. 024/741-919), with lovely flowerbeds leading up to its entrance. Centrally located close to the CPO, it is also near food stores and a large supermarket. There are 65 beds in 20 rooms with high ceilings, carpeting, and attractive wallpaper. Five common rooms include a pool room, smoking room, and TV room, and there are kitchens, a dining room, and a laundry and drying room. An in-house café offers a blackboard menu and vegetarian and meat dishes, and is open from 5:30 to 8:30 p.m. The hostel is open 24 hours, and there are no duties or linen charges. Rates for seniors are NZ$15 ($9.40); for juniors, NZ$7.50 ($4.70), plus GST.

Backpackers will put their limbs to good use to reach the **Elms Lodge,** perched high atop the city at 74 Elm Row, Dunedin (tel. 024/741-872). It has a TV lounge with a bay window and view of St. Clair Harbour and the sea, two dormitories with seven beds each and another with four beds, two double and two twin rooms, and two showers and a bathroom with a tub. Guests have access to the kitchen and laundry, and can store their food in a big cupboard. The sunny dining room is the focal point of the house. The bulletin board is filled with pictures and postcards from around the world that friendly owner Shirley Gilchrist has received from former guests. Dorm rates are NZ$13 ($8.15) per bed; double and twin rooms are NZ$15 ($9.40) per person. Bike rental is NZ$10 ($6.25) per day—good luck peddling back up the hill!

Out on scenic Otago Peninsula there are hostel-type accommodations in historic **Larnach Castle,** P.O. Box 1350, Dunedin (tel. 024/761-302 in Dunedin). The four-bunk rooms, plus showers and toilets, are upstairs in what was the hayloft of the 116-year-old stables. A kitchen is in the old groom's room downstairs, and the tables and chairs are from an old priory in Dunedin. An open fire and coal range (with radiators running from it) furnish the heating. Otherwise, the stables have been restored to their original state. Rates when you furnish linens are NZ$20 ($12.50) single and NZ$30 ($18.75) for two; linen and quilts are available for NZ$6 ($3.75) per person. Add GST to all rates.

Cabins/Campgrounds

The **Aaron Lodge Motel and Caravan Park,** 162 Kaikorai Valley Rd. (near Brockville Road), Dunedin (tel. 024/64-725), is a whole complex of cabins, cabin blocks, and motel flats on a main artery with a grassy hill out back. Seven motel flats are in front (see "Motel Flats," below), and there are 15 family rooms in two large red-and-gray cement cabin blocks. Four- or five-berthed, all are spacious, and have carpets, large wardrobes, a table and chairs, and electric heater. Beds can be curtained off for privacy. There are two modern kitchens with TVs, showers, and a laundry with dryer. Across a grassy lawn and up the hill are eight two-berth cabins with built-in beds, a shelf, and a chest of drawers; a kitchen, toilets, and showers are adjacent. There's a children's playground on the premises, and a supermarket adjacent. Rates for all cabins are from NZ$25 ($15.75) per adult couple, NZ$5 ($3.15) per child, NZ$8 ($5) per extra adult. Tent and caravan sites are also available. The Aaron Lodge is owned and managed by Margaret and Lindsay McLeod and may be reached via the Bradford or Brockville bus from the Octagon. Add GST to all rates.

READERS' CAMPING SELECTION: "About 15 minutes north of Dunedin, we found the **Waitati Farmlands Camper Caravan Park,** Waitati Valley Road, Waitati, Otago (tel. 024/22-730). It's right off State Hwy. 1, and we found it to be one of the best on the South Island, run by one of the nicest families we met in New Zealand. Jan and John Leslie are the very essence of Kiwi charm and hospitality. The park has all the amenities you'd expect, and a few you wouldn't, such as donkey rides. Nearby there are bush walks, mountain tracks, and beaches. While enjoying the peace and quiet, it was nice to know the city was close by for evening enjoyment. Ask Jan or John how to get to Murdering Bay—you're in for a treat!" (S. McGinn and C. Frodigh).

The Y

The centrally located **YWCA,** Kinnaird House, Moray Place, Dunedin (tel. 024/776-781), is a four-story, modern brick elevator building with a garden courtyard. The 120 beds are in centrally heated rooms, which include singles and doubles. Furnishings are basic, but a nice size and neatly fitted with tables and chairs, chests of drawers, and good cupboards. Floors are mostly carpeted, and bedspreads are bright and cheerful. There's a pleasant, airy dining room, a comfortable sitting room, a color TV room, and a laundry with a drying room. The Y takes casual guests for unlimited stays, has no age limits, and is open to men and women, couples and families. Lunch and dinner are available on request. Rates are NZ$30 ($18.75) single, NZ$40 ($25) double, for bed-and-breakfast, including GST. The backpacker rate is NZ$11.50 ($7.20) per night, with no breakfast or bedding. Send 20% of the room rate as a deposit.

Bed-and-Breakfasts

One of my favorite finds the last time I was in town was **Alvand House,** 3 Union St., Dunedin (tel. 024/777-379), perched at the top of a hill, with tidy, white shingles and red trim and a carnation- and rose-trimmed walkway leading to the red front door and lace-curtained windows. There are only three bedrooms, with high ceilings, carpeted floors, tall windows with stained-glass touches, a TV, electric blankets, and coffee- and tea-making facilities. Guests have the use of a washing machine and clothes line, and they often linger on the sunny porch reading the paper that the gracious hostess, Farah Jamalt, leaves out. She will prepare a Persian meal by arrangement for NZ$15 ($9.40), including wine. Room rates with breakfast are NZ$35 ($22) single and NZ$55 ($34.50) double, plus GST; an extra person is NZ$12 ($7.50).

Down the street from Alvand House is **Sheldon House Lodge,** 597 George St., Dunedin (tel. 024/775-435), named after tiny, lively hostess Mary Ming-Wong's son. (She has four other kids, some of whom you're bound to meet.) The cozy lounge has a TV, plenty of upholstered chairs, and a fridge where guests can keep food. There are laundry facilities and a variety of accommodations to choose from, each with a sink in the room; baths are shared. A family room sleeps five, and there are four double rooms and two singles. Downtown attractions are a 15-minute walk or a bus ride away. Rates are NZ$45 ($28.25) single, NZ$58.50 ($36.50), and NZ$70 ($43.75) triple.

The gabled brick **Sahara Guesthouse and Motel,** 619 George St., Dunedin (tel. 024/776-662), sports elaborate iron grillwork, is just a five-minute walk from the Octagon and is on major bus routes. Built as a hospital back at the turn of the century, it now holds 12 nice-size rooms with H&C, with one to three twin beds, all immaculate and cheerful. Room 12 is especially bright, with a stained-glass window. Behind the house, there's a block of ten motel units, four of which sleep up to five, all with kitchens, baths, telephones, color TVs, and free use of laundry facilities. The home-style breakfast includes bacon and eggs, with "down-under"–style hash browns, and they'll provide an evening meal on request. Bed-and-breakfast rates are NZ$38 ($23.75) single, NZ$58 ($36.25) double; motel rates are NZ$44 ($27.50) single, NZ$56 ($35) double. All rates include GST.

Magnolia House, 18 Grendon St., Dunedin (tel. 024/671-999), is the suburban home of George and Joan Sutherland. Set on a half acre and surrounded by native bush, the Victorian house is screened from the street by a high hedge. The house itself is quite spacious and graciously decorated, with a warm, welcoming sitting room and a drawing room that holds a piano and opens onto a sun balcony. There's central heating throughout, and bedrooms have fireplaces and antique furnishings. There are also two cats in residence and a no-smoking rule. The Sutherlands, who have lived in Dunedin for the past 25 years, are gracious hosts who enjoy helping guests plan their time in the city for the utmost enjoyment. Bed-and-breakfast rates are NZ$30 ($18.75) single, NZ$55 ($34.50) double, including GST.

READER'S BED-AND-BREAKFAST SELECTION: "**Monono,** 84 London St., Dunedin (tel. 024/778-638), must be the best-kept secret in New Zealand—a B&B experience that is more akin to a visit with wealthy but enjoyable relatives. I've spent ten times more money for a room at the Plaza in New York or the Ritz Carlton in Boston and not enjoyed such an attractive and well-appointed room in such a lovely setting" (T. Occhialino, Albuquerque, N.M.).

A Special Lodge

Many people pay Larnach Castle a visit during their stay in Dunedin, but most don't realize that the **Larnach Castle Lodge,** P.O. Box 1350, Dunedin (tel. 024/761-302), offers some of the finest, most reasonable, and truly romantic accommodation in the area. My favorite room is no. 26, where one window looks out on the Pacific coast and the other onto Otago Harbour; decorated in pink, it features a graceful chaise longue and a beautiful brass bed. Almost equally as lovely, but with only one window, is no. 20, the Blue Room. The lodge has a communal TV lounge and a fully equipped kitchen; a country store is in a village, five minutes away. The rate for rooms with shared baths is NZ$48 ($30), single or double (of these, my pick is no. 17 with its corner views); for rooms such as nos. 26 and 20, with private bath, the rate is NZ$69 ($43.25), worth the little extra.

Motel Flats

The seven motel flats at the **Aaron Lodge Motel and Caravan Park** (see "Cabins," above, for complete description), 162 Kaikorai Valley Rd., Dunedin (tel. 024/64-725), are all one-bedroom units and have electric heaters, color TV, radio, and electric blankets. All are nicely carpeted and well maintained. Rates are NZ$50 ($31.25), including GST, for one or two persons.

The **Alcala Motel,** at the corner of George and St. David Streets, Dunedin (tel. 024/779-073), is a large, attractive Spanish-style complex just a 20-minute walk from the Octagon. Each unit has a full kitchen, telephone, color TV with video, radio, and thermo-mattresses. The Motor Lodges property has a laundry, spa pool, and off-street parking. A cooked or continental breakfast is available at a small fee. A licensed restaurant and shops, hairdresser, and service station are close by. Rates start at NZ$65 ($40.75) double, plus GST.

There are 20 units at the **Dunedin Motel,** 624 George St., Dunedin (tel. 024/777-692), nine with two bedrooms, the rest with one. All are nicely decorated, and although located on a main street just a five-minute walk from the city center, units run back from the street, creating a quiet and peaceful atmosphere. All have telephone, radio, color TV, electric heater, and electric underblankets. Rates are NZ$60 ($37.50) single, NZ$70 ($43.75) double, including GST. Take the Normanby Gardens or Opoho bus.

The **Best Western Tourist Court,** 838-842 George St., Dunedin (tel. 024/ 774-270), has nine spacious units. Each can sleep three to five people, and has a full kitchen, color TV, radio, telephone, central heat, and electric blanket. There's a guest laundry, and a continental breakfast may be ordered for a small fee. Units are exceptionally well appointed, and each has an iron and ironing board. It's on a main bus line, but within easy walking distance of the Octagon. Rates are NZ$54 ($33.75) single, NZ$65 ($40.75) double, plus GST. Best Western discounts apply.

The units at **Farry's Motel,** 575 George St., Dunedin (tel. 024/779-333), are tastefully furnished, with large picture windows in all lounges. Each is centrally heated and has a fully equipped kitchen, color TV, video, radio, and telephone. Standard units will sleep up to five, and special executive suites have private spa baths, waterbeds, and video-cassette movies. There are guest laundries, a children's play area with swings and trampolines, and off-street parking. A continental breakfast is available for a small charge. Rates for all units are NZ$68 ($42.50) single, NZ$78 ($48.75) double, and NZ$14 ($8.75) per extra person; all include GST.

Formerly Farry's, the **High Street Court,** 193 High St., Dunedin (tel. 024/ 779-315), is a pretty place with a façade of white stucco and black wrought-iron trim. It also has a children's playground. If you're on foot, it's an uphill hike to the property. Accommodations and rates are the same as at Farry's (see above).

The **Alglen Motor Hotel,** 137 St. Andrew (at Cumberland Street), Dunedin (tel. 024/770-572), is only two blocks from the Octagon. Its spacious rooms come with a bathtub or shower, and three units are wheelchair accessible. There's a guest laundry, as well as a buffet lunch for NZ$10.50 ($6.55) weekdays and a Sunday smörgåsbord for NZ$18.50 ($11.50). Rooms go for NZ$70 ($43.75), single or double, plus GST.

Near the university and botanic gardens, you'll find the **Cable Court,** 833 Cumberland St., Dunedin (tel. 024/773-525), with 14 one-bedroom and three two-bedroom units and beautiful rose gardens, carefully tended by Paul Mutch, who runs the place with his wife, Robin. All the units have a comfortable living room and well-lit kitchen, plus ever-hard-to-come-by bathtubs. There are two waterbed and two disabled-access units. One-bedroom units are NZ$65 ($40.75) and NZ$68 ($42.50); two-bedroom units, NZ$72 ($45); an extra person pays NZ$10 ($6.25). Add GST to all rates.

Adjacent to beautiful St. Kilda Beach and a good children's playground, the **Beach Lodge Motel,** 38 Victoria Rd., St. Kilda, Dunedin (tel. 024/55-043), is run by Pete and Lee Nolan, who go out of their way to make this a "home away from home." The 18 units in this Best Western member range in size from bed-sitters to three-bedrooms (which sleep up to ten). All are of a nice size and contain a kitchen (continental breakfast may be ordered, and an office shop sells frozen motel meals), TV, video, radio, telephone, and thermo-mattress or electric blanket. There's a spa pool, guest laundry with dryer, a car wash, and off-street parking. For a peaceful retreat after strenuous sightseeing or a quick swim to start the day off, you couldn't have a better location than the Beach Lodge—the safe beach (with a lifesaving club station) is a 300-yard walk across a golf course and sand dunes, and there's a view of hills in the distance. The drive into the city is direct and takes about five minutes. Rates are NZ$65 ($40.75) single, NZ$70 ($43.75) double, plus GST, and Best Western discounts apply.

Within walking distance of St. Kilda Beach is the modest **Arcadian Motel,** 85-89 Musselburgh Rise, Dunedin (tel. 024/42-000 or 43-049), run by Isabelle Gerken and her winsome cousin, Wilf Radford, both in their 60s. Units—and all get morning and afternoon sun—include one-, two-, and three-bedroom accommodations and a bed-sitter, which is in the old house on the property. Guests have access to a full laundry, and markets, butchers, green grocers, and a fish-and-chips shop are nearby. Rates start at NZ$42 ($26.25) single and NZ$48 ($30) in the bed-sitter and NZ$52 ($32.50) for two in a one-bedroom unit. An extra adult pays NZ$10 ($6.25); a child under 12, NZ$6 ($3.75). All prices include GST.

A Licensed Hotel

The three-story triangular **Leviathan Hotel,** 65-69 Lower High St., Dunedin (tel. 024/773-160), is a Dunedin landmark dating back to 1898. It's on a corner directly across from the Early Settlers Museum and one block from the railway station and bus depot. The old building is in excellent condition and offers a high standard of central, budget accommodation plus 12 fully equipped suites, which are much favored by visiting M.P.s. Rooms are attractively decorated and furnished with built-in wardrobe, chest of drawers, and overbed lights. All have color TV, electric heater, and private facilities. Two family units sleep five. There's a games room with a pool table and two TV lounges. The elegant dining room serves meals in the moderate range. There's an elevator, hall telephones for guests, and a garage in the building with free parking. Rates range from NZ$56 ($35) to NZ$90 ($56.25), plus GST.

A Splurge

The grand dame of Dunedin's hotels and a favorite of visiting government officials is the **Southern Cross Hotel,** at 118 High St., (off Princes Street), Dunedin (tel. 024/770-752). It has a perfect location and the appeal of a place that's been around in one incarnation or another for more than 100 years. The standard rooms are spacious and they come with a fridge, a small table and two chairs, and a bath with a tub, shampoo, and foaming gel for NZ$120 ($75). Deluxe rooms are NZ$20 ($12.50) more. The lobby restaurant is quiet and elegant, adorned with flowers, candles, and crystal; the Exchange Brasserie is more casual and reasonably priced. If your stay falls on a Friday or Saturday night, pick a room above the second floor so disco sounds won't disturb you.

WHERE TO EAT

Make **Potpourri** (locals pronounce it "Pot-*pour*-ee"), 97 Stuart St. (tel. 779-983), one of your first choices for a meal because you'll probably want to return again and again. If you've been neglecting your vegetables, this is your chance to make up for it. Salads are NZ$1.40 (90¢) per portion, and you can order half portions. An open-face sandwich with three small salads costs NZ$5 ($3.15); fresh scones and muffins are NZ$.80 (50¢); spanakopeta with a half salad, NZ$6.20 ($3.90); and tacos, NZ$4.80 ($3). Check the blackboard for the quiche and main dish of the day. Good news for frozen yogurt lovers—it's available here. The café is open Monday through Friday from 9 a.m. to 8 p.m. and on Saturday from 10 a.m. to 2 p.m.

Dunedin residents have long treasured **Stewart's Coffee House,** 12 Lower Octagon (tel. 776-687), for its fresh-roasted coffee, espresso, and cappuccino, (you'll love the smell!); its cozy basement location—also very central—and sandwiches, which far surpass those in most such places, both in quality and selection. For example, the plain old egg sandwich becomes a curried egg sandwich at Stewart's. There's soup and a nice array of cakes and other sweets. You can, of course, get tea, but it's the coffee that's a standout, and you can buy it by the pound to enhance meals back in your motel kitchen. Open from 9 a.m. to 5 p.m. Monday through Thursday, until 6:30 p.m. on Friday.

Special Note: One of the nicest things to do in Dunedin when feet are weary and a light snack has enormous appeal is to go in to the **Methodist Friendship Coffee Lounge** (in the Methodist Mission Building, just off the Octagon), where you'll find volunteers behind the counter in a large, rather plain but cheerful room. Their motto is "talk and tea from ten to three," and they're right in our price range—two cookies and tea or coffee cost NZ$1 (65¢), and they can serve as dessert if you'd like to bring in your own lunch, as many people do. You'll be treating yourself to a refreshing, inexpensive break, and contributing to a worthy cause at the same time. Open Monday through Friday from 9 a.m. to 5 p.m.

There's a **Cobb & Co.** in the Law Courts, 53-65 Stuart St. (tel. 778-036), where you can get reasonable meals for reasonable prices. It's fully licensed, with hours from 7:30 a.m. to 10 p.m. seven days a week.

The **Terrace Café,** 118 Moray Pl. (tel. 740-686), is just across from the Fortune Theatre, and it's a real gem! By that, I don't mean this is a spit-and-polish, take-yourself-seriously little gem—on the contrary, it's a down-to-earth, as-casual-or-as-dressy-as-you-feel, sort of place that looks like a Victorian parlor. With only ten tables and seats for just 27, the Terrace comes up with a coziness that often prompts patrons to take a turn at the old upright piano over to one side. On cool nights, the fireplace glows with yet another inducement to relax as you enjoy a menu composed of great homemade soups (if they have pumpkin, you're in luck), main courses that might include deviled kidneys with bacon and mushrooms, fish curry, veal, chicken cooked in any one of a number of inventive ways, at least one vegetarian dish, Mediterranean and ethnic cuisine, crisp salads, and homemade desserts like carrot cake or chocolate gâteau. Everything is fresh, the service is friendly (as are your fellow diners —this has long been a Dunedin favorite), and your dinner tab will not exceed NZ$20 ($12.50). Hours are 6 p.m. to late, Tuesday through Saturday. You *must* reserve for dinner any day of the week. BYO.

The **Normanby Tavern,** 456 Main North Rd. (tel. 730-373), is about a mile and a half from the Botanic Gardens, and it's worth a bus or cab ride for exceptionally good food at moderate prices. This is a large, light tap room and dining room with wooden booths and tables and murals of Dunedin scenes on the walls. The menu includes fish, steaks, chicken, ham, light snacks, salad plates, or full hot meals, and portions will be generous. Lunch prices are under NZ$10 ($6.25); dinner prices, under NZ$15 ($9.40). Fully licensed. Hours are noon to 2 p.m. and 5 to 9 p.m. daily. It's a good idea to reserve if you plan to come for dinner Monday through Thursday; no reservations taken on weekends and holidays.

The Hotel Southern Cross, 118 High St. (tel. 770-752), has a very good budget eatery. The **Deli Café,** at street level, is a bright, casual eatery that's convenient for the hours it keeps—round the clock on weekends, otherwise until 5 a.m. (make that midnight in winter). It has the feel of a late-night diner, even in the afternoon. Food is served cafeteria style and there's a smoking room upstairs. You can get a snack for under NZ$5 ($3.15), as well as roasts and other hot dishes for NZ$6.50 ($4.05) to NZ$9 ($5.65). There's a 20% surcharge on anything served between midnight and 5 a.m.

Over near the university (between the Queen Mary Hospital and the campus), the **Dubliner Restaurant,** 10 Clarendon St. (tel. 775-197), provides a small, cheerful spot to eat, drink, and relax. It is reached by way of a sidewalk that takes you to the back of the house at this address, and there are picnic tables outside in the courtyard in good weather, and upstairs and downstairs seating. Everything here is homemade, with lasagne, quiche, crêpes, pizza, vegetarian dishes, and luscious desserts on the daily menu. No item is priced above NZ$10 ($6.25), and many are lower. This is a popular place with university students and other Dunedin residents, so come early or late to avoid the crowds. Hours are 11:30 a.m. to 2 p.m. Monday through Friday, plus 6 to 9 p.m. for à la carte fare.

Teas and light meals are also served at moderate to budget prices at the cozy **Lewis' Country Cottage,** 412 George St. (tel. 777-769), across from Knox Church. All the food, which includes muffins, quiche, and soup, is homemade. It's open from 8 a.m. to 4 p.m. Monday through Friday.

For a seafood meal in down-home surroundings, complete with plastic tablecloths and a linoleum floor, pay a visit to **The Best Café,** 30 Stuart St. (tel. 778-

059). It's been in business since 1937, and the hearty platters start at NZ$10 ($6.25); the hours are 11:30 a.m. to 7 p.m. Monday through Friday.

A quick mention of **McDonald's,** 230 St. George St. (tel. 790-576), simply to say that it's the biggest in New Zealand—a spacious, two-level, 350-seater with a striking double stairway. It's open until midnight on Friday and Saturday, until 10:30 p.m. weekdays, and 10 p.m. on Sunday.

One of the best food buys in Dunedin is to be found in **Heffe's,** in the DB South City Hotel, 244 King Edward St. (tel. 51-017). This is an atmospheric old pub, with collections of spoons and mugs on display. Dunedin residents love it for the convivial atmosphere, and also for the tremendous portions of roasts plus seven vegetables that come to table for about NZ$10 ($6.25). Licensed, of course, and service is seven days a week.

Chef and owner Brian Stewart runs two very good eateries in the **Robbie Burns Hotel,** 370 George St. The downstairs bar in the Robbie Burns Pub features a good array of Mexican dishes, plus roast beef, seafood, etc. There are frequent menu changes, depending on what fresh meats are available locally. Lunch only is served, from noon to 2 p.m. Monday through Friday, at prices under NZ$10 ($6.25). This place is extremely popular with locals, and your best bet to avoid the crowds is to get there exactly at noon or close to 2 p.m. **Foxy's Café,** upstairs at the same address (tel. 778-100), rambles through four rooms that look as they might have 125 years ago when the hotel was built. There are two operating fireplaces, and fittings throughout are reminiscent of days long gone. Starters include tacos and enchiladas, as well as mussels provençal; grills feature steaks in a variety of sizes and styles; and other main courses include a seafood basket, chili con carne, tandoori chicken, Italian pasta, and Mexican pancake. All grills are served with potato and side salad. Prices are in the NZ$10 ($6.25) to NZ$15 ($9.40) range on the à la carte menu. Hours are 5 to 10 p.m., until 1 a.m. Thursday through Saturday, and it's a good idea to reserve.

One of Dunedin's prettiest eateries has got to be the **Palms Café,** 84 High St., at Dowling Street (tel. 776-534). Its window walls, ornate ceiling, and two intimate dining rooms make it romantic too. A blackboard announces the day's choices; soup or chowder is NZ$3.50 ($2.20) and main dishes, such as lamb satay, vegetable quiche, or pan-baked flounder, are NZ$12.50 ($7.80). Lunch is noon to 2 p.m. Monday through Friday, and dinner, 6 to 9 p.m. Wednesday through Monday. It's strictly no-smoking and BYO.

Take time out for dinner at **Thyme Out,** 5 Stafford St. (tel. 740-467), where the changing menu features Thai beef (a local favorite), vegetable, fish, and lamb dishes. Main courses are about NZ$15 ($9.40). Owner Sue Leckie keeps the walls filled with local art, some of it for sale; take a look at her brother's unique sculpture *Relating,* which has 12 types of wood and 11 pairs of hands in it (I challenge you to find all of them). Open Tuesday through Saturday from 6 to 8:30 p.m. BYO.

If you have a penchant for sitting by the water and gazing out to sea, you'll feel right at home at **Hide Tide,** an L-shaped restaurant in the former heliport building with a dozen large windows looking onto the harbor. Ceiling fans gently stir the air in this peaceful spot, where the blackboard menu tempts with chicken, sirloin steak, lamb, pasta, fish, and seafood. Entrees are NZ$6 ($3.75), and main courses, NZ$14 ($8.75). Open Tuesday through Saturday for lunch from noon to 2 p.m., and for dinner from 6 to 9 p.m. BYO.

A Splurge

The pink two-story house at 99 Filleul St. boasts one of the best restaurants in New Zealand, practically called **99 Filleul** (tel. 777-233), the creation of husband-and-wife team Ken and Jane Greenhill. He concocts fine, inventive dishes such as grilled lamb prepared with fresh thyme and black peppercorns, spicy blackened fish, poached filet of beef with bacon and herb dumplings and fresh shiitake mushrooms. Main courses run about NZ$22 ($13.75). Be sure to order the bread basket filled with rolls and loafs made daily (walnut loaf is the house specialty). Jane Greenhill makes the desserts; top billing goes to the ginger-lemon pie, surely a first cousin to key lime pie. All the dishes are elegantly displayed on oversize black china. Dessert wines are available by the glass. The restaurant is open for lunch Tuesday through Friday from noon to 2 p.m. and for dinner Monday through Saturday from 6:30 p.m. on. BYO.

READER'S DINING SELECTION: "We discovered **Harbour Lights** seafood restaurant on the Otago Peninsula at 494 Portobello Rd., Macandrew Bay. Our meal was enhanced by a magical view of the harbor. Just be sure somebody in your party doesn't drink because the drive back is on a winding road" (R. Anderson, Charleston, S.C.).

READERS' TAKE-AWAY SELECTION: "We discovered **Glorious Food** across from the Robbie Burns Hotel, at 367 George St. (tel. 776-627). It's open until fairly late [9:30 p.m.] and has low prices and a selection that's heavy on pasta dishes, along with soup, salad, and a variety of desserts. The person on duty heated our meal for us to take back to the motel; there are a few seats inside as well" (A. and J. Guthrie, San Antonio, Tex.).

THINGS TO SEE AND DO

First of all, if you find yourself in the vicinity of Water and Princes Streets, diagonally across from the CPO, you'll be standing on what was the waterfront back when the first settlers arrived in Dunedin and what had been a Maori landing spot for many years. Look for the **bronze plaque** that reads: "On this spot the pioneer settlers landed from a boat off the John Wickliffe on the 23rd day of March, 1848, to found the city and province." It's a good jumping-off point for your exploration of the city as it is today.

Now, for all my fellow **bagpipe** fanatics, let me suggest that you try to arrange to hear the lovely instruments while you're in this little bit of transported Scotland. You may be in town for a scheduled event at which they're featured, but if not, just take yourself to the **Visitor Centre,** The Octagon, or call 774-176. They'll do their best to get you to a pipe-band rehearsal, if nothing else (which could turn out to be more fun than a formal performance!). Also ask about attending an evensong choral service at St. Paul's Cathedral or a welcoming haggis ceremony. Now that *that's* out of the way, it's on to regular sightseeing activities.

Your first order of business should be a stop by the **Visitor Centre;** consider watching their half-hour color video *Southern Adventure* for NZ$2 ($1.25); it will give you a good overview of the region and of Dunedin's attractions, culture, and that whimsical city personality I mentioned above. Also, pick up their inexpensive sightseeing map and look for their *Dunedin City Centre Walk* (it's No. 1 of the "Know the City" series) brochure to guide you around city streets.

There are terrific **scenic drives** around the city and out the peninsula, so stop by the Visitor Centre and request their brochures: Dunedin's *Golden Arrow Scenic Drive* and *The Otago Peninsula.* Both provide maps and clear directions, and the first is keyed to golden arrows along the route, which give you a good one-hour view of the city and its immediate environs. The *Green Belt* drive is closer to the city, with marked trails leading off through the bush.

The half-day **Grayline city tour** departs the Visitor Centre at 9:30 a.m. daily and shows you the highlights of the city, plus visits to Olveston and Larnach Castle for a NZ$19 ($12) fare. No need to reserve—just be there on time. **Newtons Coach Line tours** to Olveston, Glenfalloch, and Larnach Castle depart at 1:15 p.m. for a NZ$22 ($13.75) fare. Both are an excellent way to get an overall look at Dunedin.

To see Dunedin and the Otago Peninsula from the water, check with **Otago Harbour Cruises Ltd.** (tel. 024/774-215), or go by their waterfront office at the corner of Wharf and Rattray Streets to see what they have on offer while you're there. They run a variety of interesting cruises, featuring close inshore views of otherwise inaccessible Taiaroa Head, alive with fur seals and eight different species of birds.

The season runs from September until May and the fare averages NZ$23 ($14.50). The Visitor Centre can also give you details.

The small excursion train to the **Taieri Gorge** is an excellent choice for an afternoon excursion. It leaves daily at 3:30 p.m. from the railroad station. There are snacks on board and stops for picture taking, and a fine commentary is provided all along the way. And you'll be back in Dunedin by 7:30 p.m. The cost of the trip is NZ$35 ($22). The train generally operates September through April.

In the City

The **Otago Early Settlers' Museum,** 220 Cumberland St. (tel. 775-052), is a fascinating look back into the daily lives of Dunedin's first European citizens. It's just down from the railway station. Look for the sole surviving gas streetlamp outside, one of many used on the city's major streets circa 1863. Inside, there's a reconstructed blacksmith's shop; three period room reconstructions; *Josephine,* a double Fairlie steam engine, which pulled the first Dunedin–Port Chalmers express; a Penny Farthing Cycle you can actually ride (although you won't go anywhere since it's held by a frame and mounted on rollers—still fun, though); and all sorts of other relics of life in these parts many years ago. There are other hands-on exhibits, such as toys and mechanical musical instruments, and life in the 20th century is also vividly portrayed. In the Furniture Room, faded sepia photographs of early settlers peer down with stern visages at visitors—one has to wonder what they think of their progeny who wander through. Hours are 8:30 a.m. to 4:30 p.m. during the week, 10:30 a.m. to 4:30 p.m. on Saturday and on public holidays, and 1:30 to 4:30 p.m. on Sunday. Adults pay NZ$4 ($2.50); senior citizens and children, NZ$3 ($1.90).

Whether you're traveling by car, bus, air, or thumb, in Dunedin, you *must* go by the railway station (well, actually, you just *should* go by). It's a marvelous old Flemish Renaissance–style edifice, designed by George A. Troup. He won the Institution of British Architects Award for his efforts and was later knighted, but never climbed to any position lofty enough to leave behind his affectionate local nickname, "Gingerbread George." Built of Kokonga basalt, with Oamaru limestone facings, the station's most prominent feature is its large square clock tower, but equally impressive are the Aberdeen granite pillars supporting arches of the colonnade across the front, the red Marseilles tiles on the roof, and the colorful mosaic floor in the massive foyer depicting a "puffing billy" engine and other bits of railroad life (more than 725,000 Royal Doulton porcelain squares!). Look for a replica of Dunedin's coat-of-arms, stained-glass windows above the balcony (the engines on both look as if they're coming straight at you, no matter where you stand), and the plaque honoring New Zealand railway men who died in the 1914–1918 war. The lovely illuminated **Star Fountain,** which was the centerpiece of the Octagon until it was moved in 1989, now puts on its colorful musical show in front of the railway station.

Olveston, 42 Royal Terrace (tel. 773-320), on Cobden Street off Queens Drive, is a "must see" of any Dunedin visit (the Golden Arrow Drive will take you right past it). It's one of the country's best-known stately homes, fully furnished, open to the public—and it's magnificent. The double brick house is Jacobean in style, faced with Oamaru stone and Moeraki gravel, surrounded by an acre of tree-shaded grounds. A much-traveled and very prosperous couple, the Theomins, built the 35-room home in 1904–1906 as a 25th-anniversary gift for each other, and it's as much a work of art as those 270 works within its walls. The house was bequeathed to Dunedin in 1966, and has been carefully maintained in virtually its original state. There are just under 300 oil portraits in Olveston, including those of some 37 New Zealand artists. The dining room's Regency table and Chippendale chairs are still set as they were for the first Plunket Society dinner, which was held here in 1907; in the butler's pantry you'll see much of the wealth of porcelain and glass used to dress the table. At every turn there is evidence of the comfort and convenience, as well as visual beauty, built into this home. Guided tours are conducted at 9:30 and 10:45 a.m., and 1:30, 2:45, and 4 p.m. Monday through Saturday, afternoon hours only on

Sunday, and although reservations are not essential, they are given preference. Admission for adults is NZ$5 ($3.15); for children, NZ$1 (65¢).

Don't miss a visit to the **Dunedin Public Art Gallery,** in Logan Park at the end of Anzac Avenue. It holds a special collection of more than 40 works by Frances Hodgkins, Dunedin born and considered to be the finest painter ever produced by New Zealand. In addition, there's a fine collection of old masters, which includes Gheeraerdts, Landini, Lorrain, and Monet, that was given to the gallery by the de Beer family, who have a long connection with Dunedin. Open from 10 a.m. to 4:30 p.m. Monday through Friday, and 2 to 5 p.m. on weekends and holidays. Free.

Dunedin's lovely **Botanic Gardens** are at the northern end of George Street. Established in 1869, they are noted for their masses of rhododendrons and azaleas (at their best from October to December). The rock garden, winter garden, and native kohai and rata trees are also noteworthy. Morning and afternoon teas, as well as hot snacks and smörgåsbord lunches, are available in the kiosk restaurant on the grounds. No matter how rushed your schedule, you owe yourself an hour or two to stroll through this lovely, peaceful spot.

The Otago Peninsula

To explore the peninsula's 40 square miles, take one of the excellent tours mentioned above, or head out Portobello Road, which runs along the harbor. **Glenfalloch Gardens** (tel. 761-006) is a good morning or afternoon tea stop. At the 30-acre estate, allow time to wander through native bush, under English oaks, and among primroses. Glenfalloch is noted for its magnificent fuchsias, azaleas, and rare rhododendrons. Light lunches as well as teas are available in the gardens outside the chalet, with strolling peacocks occasionally fanning their glorious plumage. The gardens are open daily from 10 a.m. to 4:30 p.m., and admission is NZ$1 (65¢) per car.

Your next stop is **Larnach Castle,** Highcliff Road (tel. 761-302), about two miles north of the gardens and a bit inland (signposted). It's a neo-Gothic Victorian mansion right out of one of those old English movies, except much more grand than anything you've ever seen on film. William Larnach came from Australia in the late 1860s to found the first Bank of Otago. He began building the grandiose home (which he called "The Camp") in 1871 for his French heiress wife. It took 200 workmen three years to build the shell and a host of European master craftsmen another 12 years to complete the interior. Total cost: £125,000. Larnach's concept was to incorporate the very best from every period of architecture, with the result that the hanging Georgian staircase lives happily with Italian marble fireplaces, English tiles, and colonial-style verandas. One of the most magnificent examples of master craftsmanship is the exquisite foyer ceiling, which took three craftsmen 6½ years to complete.

William Larnach died by suicide, after rising to the post of M.P. but suffering a series of personal misfortunes—committed in his typically dramatic fashion in a committee room in the Parliament Buildings in Wellington. (Larnach's first two wives died, and his younger third wife dealt him a fatal emotional blow by dallying with his son.) After his death, the farm around the castle was sold off and the Crown used the castle as a mental hospital. It is now the private home of Mr. and Mrs. Barry Barker, who found it in a thoroughly dilapidated condition in 1967 and have spent the intervening years lovingly restoring it to its original glory. Pick up a printed guide at the reception and wander as you choose, climbing the spiral staircase to battlements, which look out onto panoramic views, strolling through gardens and outbuildings. The stables now house hostel-type accommodations (see "Where to Stay," above), but you're free to walk around its ground floor. There are also excellent accommodations in the lodge. Hours are 9 a.m. to 5 p.m. in winter, until dusk other seasons; lunch is available. Admissions (which fund restoration work) are NZ$8 ($5) for adults, NZ$4 ($2.50) for children.

Other places you'll want to visit on the peninsula include a Maori church at Otakou, an excellent aquarium at the Portobello Marine Laboratory operated by the

University of Otago near Quarantine Point, and the **Albatross Colony** at Taiaroa Head. The magnificent royal albatross, perhaps with an instinctive distrust of the habitations of mankind, chooses remote, uninhabited islands as nesting grounds. With the single known exception, that is, of this mainland colony. The first egg was found here in 1920, and a sanctuary was promptly established. Today the colony consists of about a dozen pairs each year. You *must* make arrangements to view the birds (at a respectful distance) through the Visitor Centre with a NZ$8 ($5) donation required to help with the sanctuary's maintenance.

Near the albatross colony is **Penguin Place,** where the dignified yellow-eyed penguin can be seen emerging from the surf and climbing to nests on the rocky little islet. They share with a frolicking southern fur seal colony about ten yards offshore. Binoculars are available on request. Admission is NZ$3.50 ($2.20) for adults, free for children. Book through the Visitor Centre; late afternoon is a good time to go.

A Drive North

About an hour's drive north of Dunedin, there's a unique natural phenomenon that is definitely worth the drive. On the beaches around the picturesque fishing village of **Moeraki** (just south of Hampden), huge rounded boulders are scattered around as though some prehistoric giant had used them for a game of handball. The curious rocks were, according to scientists, formed by the gradual accumulation of lime about 60 million years ago, but the Maoris claim differently. According to legend, one of the great migration canoes capsized nearby, and large gourds and kumara seeds scattered on the beach and were turned to stone; they are known as *te kai-hinaki,* "the food baskets." Now, maybe *rocks* don't sound like a sightseeing attraction to you, but just take my word for it and go by to have a look. Incidentally, if you travel from Dunedin to Christchurch by rail or bus, you'll get a good view. If you happen to arrive shortly after noon, you may be able to buy fish straight from the fishing boats coming in about that time—a real dinner-time treat.

Half an hour's drive from the city on the northern shore of Otago Harbor lies historic **Port Chalmers.** It was from here in 1884 that a ship sailed for England with the country's first shipment of frozen meat, creating an important new industry for New Zealand. A bit of an artists' colony today, Port Chalmers has a visitor center and a small seafaring museum. This area is popular for salmon and trout fishing from October to April. Drive over by taking Oxford Road out of Dunedin through the rolling hills to Port Chalmers and return via the harbor road for completely different scenery. While you're in the town, drop into **Carey's Bay Pub,** where all the fisherpeople go.

If you're driving from Dunedin to Christchurch, be sure to stop in **Oamaru** for half a day or an overnight. With its streets lined with two-story buildings and covered walkways, it looks like a frontier town, and indeed in the 1870s it claimed eight hotels, 30 grog shops, and 14 brothels. But the importance of Oamaru today is its architecture. Rightfully nicknamed the "White Stone City," it is filled with impressive buildings made of gleaming-white limestone quarried in Weston, four miles away (you can visit the quarry weekdays from 7:30 a.m. to 6 p.m., well worth the mini-excursion). Once you've walked along the main street and admired the architecture of the courthouse, bank, post office, and the fine Forrester Art Gallery, walk a little farther to the Harbor-Tyne Street historic district that the preservation-minded citizens of Oamaru have fought to save.

The **Oamaru Information Centre** is open from 9 a.m. to 5 p.m. daily; the helpful staff can provide a map and show you how to get to the basilica and the Waitaki Boys' School to see more incredible examples of how the local limestone has been put to good use. Architectural walks are organized in the summer through the Forrester Art Gallery. Save some time during your visit to Oamaru to stroll through the Public Gardens, especially Wonderland. For a quick bite, drop by **Pink's Coffee Shop** or **Willetts Tea Room,** at 83 and 163 Thames St., respectively.

For an overnight stop, I recommend the **Brydone Hotel,** Thames Street, Oamaru (tel. 0297/49-892), a tasteful blend of the old and new. Named for Thomas Brydone, who was instrumental in arranging the first shipment of frozen lamb from New Zealand, it's a gracious old building, whose older wing is full of atmosphere. Joan and Graeme Dick are the friendly managers here. Even if you don't stay the night, plan to have at least one meal at the Brydone, for under Joan's supervision, the dining room is one of the best in these parts. Bed-and-breakfast rates run NZ$45 ($28.25) per person, double occupancy. Room rates (without breakfast) are NZ$60 ($37.50) single, NZ$70 ($43.75) double. Add GST to all.

SHOPPING

Dunedin offers excellent shopping. *A few tips:* Some of the cheapest **liquor** on sale in New Zealand can be purchased at the bottle shop at the Robbie Burns Hotel, 374 George St. The markup is also slight on New Zealand wines. Open Monday through Thursday from 11 a.m. to 10 p.m., on Friday and Saturday until 11 p.m.

Dunedin has more than its fair share of gift shops, but one I can highly recommend is the **New Zealand Shop,** 132 Lower Stuart St., at Bath Street (tel. 773-379), with a fine collection of quality wool sweaters and other items, along with a large selection of T-shirts; it's open weekdays and Saturday mornings, and will open just for you if you give them a call. For leather and sheepskin items, take a look at **Hides,** 185 George St. (the **Scottish Shop** is next door), and **Hendy's,** at 108 Princes St. And just for fun (and a daydream or two?), drop by **Mooneys Furriers,** an elegant shop of elegant furs. It's in The Exchange at 126 Rattray St.

The **Golden Centre,** on George Street between St. Andrew and Hanover Streets, is a glass-enclosed concentration of shops specializing in everything from leather to woolens to women's fashions to cosmetics to gifts to books to . . . well, whatever you want, you'll probably find it here. **Moray Gallery,** 32 Moray Pl. (tel. 778-060), has an excellent selection of paintings by New Zealand artists. The **Government Book Shop,** just down from the NZTP office on Princes Street, has all sorts of publications on New Zealand (closed Saturday). Nevyn Anderson, owner of **The Bookshop,** 384 George St. (tel. 777-410), says it's a specialist bookshop, one of New Zealand's best, stocking many unusual titles as well as bestselling ones. If you've been looking for a hard-to-find title, he just may have it for you. **Daniels Jewellers Ltd.,** 72 Princes St. (tel. 771-923), has a wide variety of quality gifts, crystal, silverware, wooden items, leather items, pottery, Marlestone, and paintings by native artists. You'll also find an excellent selection of high-quality gifts at **G. & T. Young Ltd.,** 73 Princes St. (tel. 778-810). Parcels may be checked during shopping hours for a nominal fee at the Women's Public Rest Rooms in the Lower Octagon. Shops stay open to 9 p.m. on Thursday instead of Friday nights in South Dunedin and Port Chalmers.

AFTER DARK

The **Regent Theatre,** on the Lower Octagon (tel. 778-597), often has international artists such as Cleo Laine, Charlie Pride, Kris Kristofferson, Glen Campbell, Johnny Cash, and Rita Coolidge in performance. Check local newspapers or call the theater for current appearances. Tickets are in the neighborhood of NZ$20 ($12.50), but range from NZ$10 ($6.25) to NZ$45 ($28.25), depending on the show.

The **Fortune Theatre,** on the corner of Stuart Street and Moray Place (tel. 778-323), presents theatrical performances in a century-old leithstone building, which was once the Trinity Methodist Church. The southernmost theater in the world, it mounts productions of works by internationally known playwrights throughout the year in its Mainstage and Studio auditoriums. Adults pay NZ$18.50 ($11.50) a ticket; students with ID, NZ$14 ($8.75).

The **Tam O'Shanter** lounge bar in the Robbie Burns Hotel, 370 George St., is a favorite gathering spot for the younger set, where you'll find university students and the 9-to-5-ers making merry almost any night of the week. The **Plough Bar,** at the same address, has a quieter ambience, and the emphasis is on good conversation, which, while lively, is almost never loud. Take your pick, but don't miss dropping in at the Robbie Burns if you're a pub person.

Long and narrow, **Club 118,** in the Southern Cross Hotel, 118 High St. (tel. 770-752), features disco music on Thursday and Saturday from 9 p.m. to 3 a.m.; drinks are served, but no food. The club is in the old part of the hotel and retains the original ceiling.

Do as the locals do and drop into the **Clarendon Hotel,** 28 Maclaggan St. (tel. 779-095), for a drink at the end of the day. The building, which has been beautifully and lovingly restored, is no longer a hotel, only a bar and restaurant.

EN ROUTE TO MOUNT COOK

The five-hour, 206-mile drive is on good roads, leaving Dunedin on Hwy. 1 and driving north through hills and along the coastline. Some 57 miles from Dunedin, you might want to stop at the **Mill House,** in Waianakrua (tel. Maheno 515), a handsome three-story stone building, which was once a flour mill, but is now a handsome restaurant and motel complex. The colonial-style dining room is beamed and attractively furnished, and meals are reasonably priced. There's a wine license, and it's open every day except Tuesday.

At **Pukeuri,** turn inland onto Hwy. 83, where the road rises slowly to reach Hwy. 8 at **Omarama,** where you begin to see the Southern Alps glistening in the distance. At Lake Pukaki township, you turn sharply left and take Hwy. 80 along the lake and Tasman River to the glacial beauty of Mount Cook.

Where to Stay

Because of the scarcity of accommodations at Mount Cook, **Twizel** (less than an hour's drive away) makes a good base.

Basil Lodge Twizel, P.O. Box 30, Twizel (tel. 05620/671), is set amid lawns and shade trees just minutes away from shops, a skating rink, tennis courts, a golf course, and swimming pools. The complex holds hostel-style rooms, doubles, and family rooms. Hostel rooms come with pillows, pillow cases, and towels; all others are complete with bedding; and each block has centrally located bathroom facilities, as well as H&C in rooms. Meals are available, and there's also a take-away service. Hostel beds are NZ$12 ($7.50). Singles are NZ$30 ($18.75); doubles, NZ$40 ($25); and family rooms, NZ$40 ($25); plus NZ$6 ($3.75) per child. Add GST to all rates. There's a surcharge for one-night stays, but if you stay six nights, you get one free.

The **MacKenzie Country Motor Inn,** Ostler Road, Twizel (tel. 05620/869), is an attractive Best Western that has 80 serviced rooms and motel flats with a communal kitchen. On the premises, there's a licensed restaurant, bars, games room, and a guest laundry. Rates are NZ$70 ($43.75) single, NZ$80 ($50) double, plus GST, and Best Western discounts apply.

---

2. Mount Cook

Tiny Mount Cook Village is known the world over for its splendid alpine beauty and its remoteness. It sits within the 173,000 acres of **Mount Cook National Park,** some 2,510 feet above sea level and surrounded by 140 peaks over 7,000 feet high, 22 of which are over 10,000 feet. Most famous of all the Southern Alps is Mount Cook, which soars 12,349 feet into the sky. A full third of the park is permanent snow and ice, and the famed **Tasman Glacier** is the longest known outside of arctic regions—18 miles long and 2 miles wide. More difficult to get onto than either Fox or Franz Josef, it is still accessible for guided strolls or for one exhilarating downhill swoop on skis.

The park's most noted plant is the mountain buttercup known as the Mount Cook lily, a pure-white blossom with thickly clustered petals and as many as 30 blooms to a stalk. There are, however, more than 300 species of native plants growing within park boundaries. Many have been marked by park rangers so you may identify them as you walk. Bird sounds fill the air, most notably that of the mischievous kea, that curious little native parrot, which has clearly earned the nickname "Clown of the Snowline." Most animal life has been introduced—Himalayan thar, chamois, and red deer. Hunting permits are issued by park rangers.

ORIENTATION

A T-intersection at the end of the highway marks the entrance to **Mount Cook Village.** Turn left and you pass the THC's Glencoe Lodge, a modern, moderately priced motor hotel, then the lower-priced Mount Cook Motel, the youth hostel, post office, grocery shop, Alpine Guides Mountain Shop, and finally the **National Park Visitor Centre** (open daily from 8 a.m. to 5 p.m.). Rangers can give you the latest information on weather and road conditions, and it's a strict requirement that trampers into the wild must check in with them. They can also fill you in on high-altitude huts, picnic grounds, and recommended walks in the area. During summer months and school holidays, they conduct guided walks and present excellent slide shows. Turn right at the intersection and you pass Mount Cook Chalets before reaching the elegant, peak-roofed, internationally famous Hermitage.

And that is Mount Cook Village—a singularly underdeveloped pocket for mankind in this glorious alpine terrain.

WHERE TO STAY

Most accommodations—at any price level—are owned by the THC (though at this writing they are up for sale), and the pickings are poor in the budget range. One alternative, if you're driving, is to stay at nearby locations: Twizel, Fairlie, Tekapo, Ohau, Omarama, Otematata, and Kurow are all under a two-hour drive, and all have motels aplenty, with well-equipped motor camps at Fairlie, Tekapo, Omarama, Otematata, and Kurow. Needless to say, with such a scarcity of rooms, advance reservations are an absolute necessity!

A Hostel

There are 59 bunks in ten rooms at this pretty alpine-style **YHA Hostel,** P.O. Box 26, Mount Cook 8770 (tel. 05621/820). Cooking facilities are good, and there is a large common room. Best of all, the large peaked window wall frames a fair share of that gorgeous snow-capped mountain scene. Booking is essential during summer months. Rates are NZ$15 ($9.40) for seniors, NZ$7.50 ($4.70) for juniors, plus GST.

Camping

Camping and caravaning are permitted free in the park (*not* in the bush), but only at designated sites, which have water and toilets. If you use these facilities, remember that the lighting of fires is prohibited within park boundaries. Check with the Visitors Information Centre for locations and conditions. Hikers and mountaineers have the use of 12 huts in the park, all of which have stoves, cooking and eating utensils, fuel, blankets, and radios with emergency lines. Only two of these are within reach of the casual tramper—the others are at high altitudes and you would need to be an experienced, expert climber to reach them. Fees for overnight use of the huts are about NZ$10 ($6.25) per person, and arrangements and payment must be made at the Visitors Information Centre.

A Bed-and-Breakfast Lodge

Glencoe Ski Lodge, Mount Cook National Park (tel. 05621/809), is an attractive block of 57 deluxe private rooms with nicely done-up rooms, all of which have private facilities. There's a restaurant and a convivial house bar that serves as a magnet for après-ski or après-sightseeing/flightseeing gatherings. Rates are NZ$154 ($96.25) single, NZ$165 ($103) double, plus GST. One reader even ranks the Glencoe Ski Lodge above the Hermitage.

Chalets

The THC-owned **Mount Cook Chalets** (tel. 0562/809) are A-frame prefab structures, but are attractive, comfortable, and convenient, with fold-out couches and several bright chairs in the felt-floored living area. There's a hotplate, fry pan, small fridge, bathroom facilities, and electric heaters. Two curtained-off sections hold two small bunks in each, and linen is provided. It's an efficient use of space, which manages to be pleasing to the eye as well. The complex includes parking space and a laundry with washers, dryers, and irons. Rates are NZ$82.50 ($51.50), single or double. Add GST.

A Licensed Hotel

Rooms at the world-famous **Hermitage** (tel. 0562/809) can only be classified as a *Big* Splurge, but in this isolated wonderland, this may be *the* place to splurge. If you give in to that temptation, you'll pay NZ$203.50 ($127), double or single, plus GST, for rooms that qualify in every sense as "premium."

WHERE TO EAT

The **Alpine Room** at the Hermitage serves a sumptuous smörgåsbord lunch (salads, cold meats, desserts), beautifully presented, for NZ$23 ($14.50).

It also serves very good—and very splurgy—à la carte dinners featuring seafood and game.

Off the reception foyer of the Hermitage, you can get light meals, pies, cakes, sandwiches, tea, and coffee in the coffeeshop.

Budgeteers, however, will gravitate to the **food shop** opposite the park headquarters, which stocks ample supplies of dairy and canned goods, produce, frozen meats, and hot pies, and is open daily from 9 a.m. to 6 p.m.

THINGS TO SEE AND DO

No need to tell you what to see—it's all around you! And if you missed the **skiplane scenic flights** at Fox and Franz Josef, you'll have another chance here. The planes lift off some 2,000 feet above sea level to begin an hour-long flight, which includes glimpses of Fox and Franz Josef and a five-minute snow walk; the less expensive 40-minute flight surveys the Tasman Glacier only; and there are other options, as well, with fares ranging from NZ$110 ($68.75) to NZ$220 ($138).

Skiers will undoubtedly head for the Tasman, but you should know that skiing is neither inexpensive nor for those whose expertise leaves *anything* to be desired! Skiing on the glacier involves two runs of about seven miles each, with skiplanes returning you to the top after the first run and flying you out at the end of the day. Before you embark on the great adventure, you'll have to convince the Alpine Guides that you're reasonably good on skis. The 1989 price for this glorious day to add to your ski tales was NZ$395 ($247). Another possible additional expense (several, in fact) lies in the fact that you may have to wait for the weather to break, which could be a few days, and that means additional lodging, eating, and drinking expense.

All those high-priced activities (and in my opinion, they're worth every penny if you have the pennies) do *not* mean there are no budget activities at Mount Cook. First of all, the sheer grandeur of the place costs nothing and is there for all. Park rangers will furnish a map of **easy walks,** which take anywhere from half an hour to half a day—no charge, and you'll commune with Mother Nature all the way. Individual booklets are available to explain about the flora you'll be seeing.

Alpine Guides, opposite park headquarters and between the post office and the

Public Bar, rents ski and climbing equipment and can furnish guides to take you mountain climbing. There's a four-day hike, which leaves you at Fox Glacier via a transalpine crossing, a range of climbing experiences for those from novice to expert level, and special guided expeditions to the top of Mount Cook itself. These are *not,* however, budget activities. Alpine Guides, P.O. Box 20, Mount Cook (tel. 0562/ 834), can give you full details and make bookings.

AFTER DARK

The liveliest spot after dark is the **Tavern** at the Hermitage, as campers and hostelers come crowding in after a day on the slopes in all that mountain air. Open only to THC residents (which includes the lodge and chalets), the **Snowline Bar** is more elegant and features more mountain views. The house bar at the Glencoe is the **Chamois Bar and Lounge.** That's most of Mount Cook Village's nightlife—and after a day amid so many of Mother Nature's wonders, it's likely to be enough!

---

3. Mount Cook to Christchurch

This is about a five-hour drive of some 233 miles. Follow Hwys. 80 and 8 to **Fairlie,** about 93 miles. At **Lake Tekapo,** take a minute to visit the chapel, whose altar is made from a large block of Oamaru stone and features a carved shepherd. The chapel was built of rock, wood, and stone from the area, and is dedicated to early settlers. Highway 79 takes you through **Geraldine** back to Hwy. 1, through the Canterbury plains filled with grazing sheep. And across the level terrain, you'll see the spires of Canterbury's capital, Christchurch, long before you arrive.

READERS' ACCOMMODATION SELECTIONS: "Lake Tekapo is only about 30 minutes farther on a main road from Mount Cook than Twizel and offers a better location and good accommodation. The **Lake Tekapo Motor Camp,** P.O. Box 43, Lake Tekapo (tel. 0505/ 6825), has an attractive lake-frontage position with several cabins and modern motel units, as well as a park for caravans" (D. Blackburn, Glenunga, Australia). . . . "We spent two months in New Zealand traveling in a motor home with our little girl, who was 2½ years old and we found a caravan park between Timaru and Christchurch that is quite unique, the **Farmyard Holiday Park,** Coach Road, Geraldine (tel. 056/39-355). The hosts, Bob and Shirley, made us feel at home. There is a little zoo in the backyard. You can feed and play with its friendly residents" (M. and M. Avihay, Haifa, Israel).

READER'S TOURING SUGGESTION: "We stopped in **Fairlie,** gateway to the MacKenzie High Country, around noon, hoping to find a good restaurant, preferably of the health-food orientation, for a light lunch. And we did. The **Sunflower Centre,** 31 Main St., is owned by Val Parker and managed by Barry Adie, with assistance from members of Val's family, Dale and Bette. Val travels throughout the country lecturing on whole-food cooking. We were cordially welcomed into their bright, clean, and attractively decorated restaurant where luncheon and teas are featured. We enjoyed a delicious quiche and salad of home-grown vegetables and greens. A varied menu of sandwiches of whole-grain breads, fruits, salads, good hearty soups, and freshly baked quiche is offered. The adjoining section of the restaurant displays local pottery, weaving, woodcrafts, knitwear, and whole-food cookbooks" (B. Henrikson, Edgartown, Mass.).

XI

CHRISTCHURCH

1. THE CITY AND SURROUNDINGS
2. THE BANKS PENINSULA

Christchurch is as English as Dunedin is Scottish—in fact, it's more so. Gothic buildings built of solid stone are everywhere, modern glass-and-concrete buildings scattered among them like afterthoughts. London's red buses are emulated here. English trees, brought out by settlers as a bit of home, flourish along the banks of the Avon River. A primary preoccupation of its citizenry is with private gardens of the English variety. And cricket, that most English of all sports, is played by all little Christchurch boys. One of its most prized appellations is that of the "Most English City Outside England."

It is also a prosperous city—New Zealand's third largest after Auckland and Wellington, with a population of 300,000—staunchly conservative, with much to be proud of. An equitable climate (2,120 hours of sunshine annually), an airport considered to be the finest in the country, civic centers and sports arenas that outshine all those in other New Zealand cities—all are factors in Christchurch's 20th-century image.

For the visitor, Christchurch offers a variety of restaurants and entertainment, as well as excellent accommodations and more sightseeing attractions than you'll ever find time for. Seattle and Christchurch are sister cities, by the way, so if you hail from Seattle, be sure to sign the Sister City Visitors Book at the Information Centre.

1. The City and Surroundings

ORIENTATION
Cathedral Square is the center of things, the point from which to get your bearings. Above it rise the spires of the Gothic Anglican Christchurch Cathedral, from whose tower you can look out over the flat, neatly laid-out city. The Avon River runs lazily through the heart of the city, spanned by no fewer than 37 bridges as it wends its 15-mile course from Ilam (west of Christchurch) to the sea. The graceful willows that line its banks are said to have come from Napoleon's gravesite on St. Helena.

Colombo Street bisects Cathedral Square north to south and is the city's main thoroughfare. Local buses leave from the square, with zoned fares ranging from

NZ$.80 (50¢) to NZ$4 ($2.50). From 9 a.m. to 4 p.m., fares are reduced by one-half (check with the Information Centre or local newspapers), and a ten-ride concession ticket is available. The local **airport bus** costs NZ$2.10 ($1.30). Driving can be difficult until you master the city's complex **one-way street system,** and since all on-street parking is metered, one of the following centrally located municipal parking buildings is your best bet: Oxford Terrace near Worcester, Manchester Street near Gloucester, and Lichfield Street near Durham. Check locally for the locations of others.

Useful Information

Look for the **New Zealand Tourist and Publicity (NZTP) Office** in the Government Life Building on Cathedral Square (tel. 03/794-900), open from 8:30 a.m. to 5 p.m. Monday through Friday, and 10 a.m. to 1 p.m. on Saturday. . . . The **Canterbury Information Centre** is at 75 Worcester St. (tel. 03/799-629), with hours of 8:30 a.m. to 5 p.m. weekdays and 9 a.m. to 4 p.m. weekends and holidays. The *Christchurch and Canterbury Visitors' Guide* is published bimonthly by the Canterbury Promotion Council, distributed free of charge through hotels and the Information Centre, and gives up-to-date information on goings-on in the city and surrounding area. . . . The **railway station** is on Moorhouse Avenue, south of the city center; **InterCity buses** leave from here. For bus or train information, call 799-020. . . . **Newmans Coaches** leave from 347 Moorhouse Ave. (tel. 795-641). . . . The **Air New Zealand** ticket office is at 72 Oxford Terrace (tel. 797-000). . . . The **Mount Cook Line** ticket office is at 40-41 Lichfield St. (tel. 790-690). . . . The **airport shuttle bus** runs regularly and picks up travelers from hotels, motels, and backpacker lodging, with a NZ$5 ($3.15) fare. Call 669-660 anytime. . . . **Rental-car agencies** abound and one of the most economical is Renny Rent a Car, 113 Tuam St. (tel. 666-790). . . . You'll find **taxi ranks** at Cathedral Square and all terminals. To call a cab, phone 799-799 or 795-795. . . . There's a large, centrally located **post office** in Cathedral Square. . . . The **telephone prefix** for Christchurch is 03.

Christchurch Airport

Christchurch International Airport is the busiest in the country, and is located six miles from Cathedral Square, out Memorial Avenue. The **Info-service Centre,** in the domestic terminal, will book accommodations and transportation at no charge. There's a cafeteria and fully licensed (expensive) restaurant; car-rental desks; a bank with money-changing desks; a bookshop; gift and souvenir shops; a flower shop; hairdressers for both men and women; showers; and a large duty-free shop. The airport coach to Cathedral Square costs NZ$2.10 ($1.30); off-peak hours (9 a.m. to 4 p.m.), NZ$1.05 (65¢). The express bus to the airport from hotels, motels, and backpacker lodging costs NZ$5 ($3.15).

WHERE TO STAY

Christchurch has an abundance of good accommodations in all price ranges. Most are convenient to public transportation, a boon to those not driving, who will be able to consider motels because of the ease of transport. Those using the Best Western Holiday Pass will find no fewer than eight possibilities.

Hostels

The **Cora Wilding Youth Hostel,** 9 Evelyn Couzins Ave., Avebury Park, Richmond, Christchurch (tel. 03/899-199), is on a tree-shaded residential street about a mile and a half from Cathedral Square. It's a lovely old white mansion with stained-glass panels in the front door and crowned by turrets and cupolas. There are seven rooms sleeping 40, all bright and cheerful, and a comfortable lounge. To one side is a large parking area, and in the rear, a children's playground across the park. The laundry has coin-operated washers and dryers. Rates for seniors are NZ$12 ($7.50); for juniors, NZ$6 ($3.75)—including GST.

Rolleston House, 5 Worcester St. (on the corner of Rolleston Avenue), Christ-church (tel. 03/666-564), is centrally located, about a five-minute walk from Cathedral Square. The place has a cheerful atmosphere, and the bedrooms are open all day. Eleven of them hold 47 beds, and there's a kitchen, laundry, and drying room, and a dining room/lounge with piano and pool table. Rates are NZ$14 ($8.75) for seniors; NZ$7 ($4.40) for juniors, including GST.

Foley Towers (formerly the Avon View Guest House), 208 Kilmore St., Christchurch (tel. 03/669-720), is a comfortable two-story house just a short walk from Cathedral Square. There are 28 beds in 11 rooms (double and share), a lounge, laundry, and kitchen, plus off-the-street parking at this privately owned hostel. It's strictly no-smoking and no children. Rates begin at NZ$13 ($8.15), including GST.

Cabins/Campgrounds

Russley Park Motor Camp, 372 Yardhurst Rd. (on State Hwy. 73), Christ-church (tel. 03/427-021), is only two miles from the airport, close to Riccarton Racecourse, and about six miles west of Cathedral Square. Ten chalets in a green, grassy setting are all individual dark-timber structures with slanted roofs and natural light-wood interiors. All have foam mattresses, floor mats, jugs, toasters, cooker, dishes and cutlery, cooking utensils, and electric heaters. Small chalets sleep three in two single beds and one upper bunk. The large ones will sleep five in two singles, one double, and one upper bunk, and have dividing curtains for privacy, as well as a small front porch. Also available are three deluxe chalets (same as the large, but with H&C and fridge). Three tourist chalets sleep five, with two separate rooms plus kitchen, lounge, shower, toilet, two-ring rangette, electric fry pan, and blankets (linen is for rent). Amenities include a kitchen, TV lounge and leisure room, spa pool, children's play area, and a laundry with automatic washing machines and dryer. There's a food shop close by. Caravan and campsites are also available. Rates for chalets range from NZ$26 ($16.25) to NZ$34 ($21.25). The tourist chalet is NZ$45 ($28.25). Camp and caravan sites are NZ$15 ($9.40). All include GST. Sheets and blankets can be rented. Take the Yardhurst Road bus from the city.

The Y

The **YMCA,** 12 Hereford St., Christchurch (tel. 03/660-689), is a centrally located complex of two adjoining buildings—a new hostel that caters to young men and women and family groups in dormitories and single, twin, and double rooms, as well as a gym with weight-training rooms. Basic, inexpensive meals are available. Price per night ranges from NZ$10 ($6.25) to NZ$15 ($9.40); send a deposit to the YMCA, P.O. Box 2004, Christchurch, to reserve in advance. Add GST.

Bed-and-Breakfasts

Wolseley Lodge, 107 Papanui Rd. (near Bealey Avenue), Christchurch (tel. 03/556-202), is a lovely old red-and-white home set in a flower-filled, tree-shaded lawn. There are 14 rooms in this two-story house, all with H&C and nicely furnished. All have electric blankets, reading lamps, TVs, and tea- and coffee-making facilities. The lounge has overstuffed chairs and TV, and the dining room overlooks the garden. There's a guest kitchen for making tea, and a laundry with washer, dryer, and ironing board. A large parking lot is in the rear. A hot breakfast and dinner are optional, and babysitting services and economical rental cars are available. Frank and Lilly Mills are the helpful hosts in this place that feels like grandma's house. Rates for B&B are NZ$33 ($20.75), plus GST, per person (reduced rates for children).

A reader wrote me to say that she considered **Eliza's Manor House,** 82 Bealey Ave., Christchurch (tel. 03/668-584 or 664-946), "the ultimate in accommodations." I must confess I was a little skeptical—until, that is, I walked up the curving

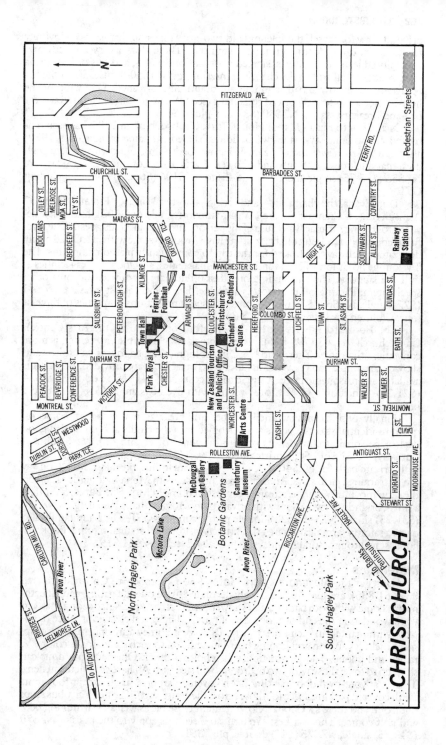

drive and saw for myself the splendid old two-story mansion that has been lovingly restored. The carved kauri staircase is magnificent. There's lots of carved woodwork, and colored lead-lite windows, stained glass, antique pieces, and bits of Victoriana scattered about all add to the charming interior of this 1860s house. Six of the ten bedrooms have private baths, and all are beautifully furnished. One wing of the house holds a moderately priced restaurant (see "Where to Eat," below). Rates for bed-and-breakfast start at NZ$60 ($37.50), plus GST.

Next door to Eliza's Manor House, **Turret House,** built in 1885, has been renovated to the same style (the two buildings shared the same owners until 1989) although it *feels* newer than Eliza's. It has ten bedrooms, eight with private facilities that include a bathtub and shower. Rates with continental breakfast are NZ$56 ($35.75) single and NZ$72 ($45) to NZ$106 ($66.25) double, including GST.

Don Evans, the charming—and caring—host at **Windsor Private Hotel,** 52 Armagh St. (off Cranmer Square), Christchurch (tel. 03/661-503), has built a devoted following, primarily because of his personal interest in all his guests. The carefully renovated, rambling old brick home has 37 rooms (some with H&C), all nicely decorated. Hallways are heated for the trip to conveniently placed bathrooms. The TV lounge holds lots of chairs and stacks of magazines, and there are tea facilities as well as a laundry. The outstanding breakfast often includes omelets or some other special item. Parking off the street is available. Bed-and-breakfast rates are NZ$43 ($27) single, NZ$63 ($39.50) double, with slight reductions for parties of three or four. Children pay half; add GST to all.

The **Hereford Private Hotel,** 36 Hereford St. (opposite the Arts Centre), Christchurch (tel. 03/799-536), just one block away from the city center, is more convenient than cozy. There's no H&C in the high-ceilinged rooms, but toilets and showers are ample and conveniently located. Tea facilities are provided. Breakfast is available at a reasonable price. A single room costs NZ$24 ($15); a double, NZ$34 ($21.25)—including GST. Shared rooms with five beds are NZ$15 ($9.40) per bed.

Finally, two charming women offer bed-and-breakfast in their private homes on quiet, residential streets. Guests are welcomed into the family at both, with a good deal of personal attention (lots of help on what to see and do). **Mrs. Roberta Conway,** 11 Clissold St., Christchurch (tel. 03/554-806), has one double room with private bath for NZ$40 ($25) per person, including breakfast. Mrs. Conway can also arrange farm stays. Almost across the road from Mona Vale gardens and on the slow-moving Wairarapa stream is the restful home of **Mrs. Ellie Bates.** She offers a small, brightly lit twin room with private bath across the hall. The charge is NZ$50 ($31.25) single, NZ$45 ($28) double per person plus GST. The Bates family also owns a salmon farm near Akaroa that attracts visitors on catamaran tours. Book this home stay through Rural Holidays New Zealand (tel. 03/661-919).

Motel Flats

Units at the **Alexandra Court Motel,** 960 Colombo St., Christchurch (tel. 03/661-855), are spacious and nicely decorated, have outside patios, and all bathrooms come with both bathtub *and* shower (important to me, since a long soak can work wonders at the end of a long day of travel). There's an electric fireplace (complete with mantel) in each unit, which makes for a homey atmosphere, and equipment includes an iron and ironing board in addition to such standards as color TV, radio, and phone. The guest laundry also holds a dryer. One-bedroom units can sleep up to four; those with two bedrooms will sleep six. All have complete kitchens. There's at-your-own-door parking, with covered carports, at all except four units (with covered parking space for those across the courtyard). The no. 4 city bus stops out front, and there's a Cobb & Co. restaurant close by, as well as a swimming pool and golf course. This is a Best Western, so discounts apply to the rates of NZ$70 ($43.75) single, NZ$75 ($47) double, plus GST.

Just six blocks from Cathedral Square, the **City Court Motel,** 850 Colombo St. (on the corner of Salisbury Street), Christchurch (tel. 03/669-099), welcomes families with children. There's a one-bedroom unit and five with two bedrooms (two large enough to sleep eight). A bonus here is the washing machine in every unit. The immaculate and spacious units all have large kitchens, separate lounge, color TV, electric heater and blanket, and bathtub, as well as shower. The lawn holds a picnic table and a children's play area, and there's a seven-day food store just across the street. Babysitters can be arranged. Rates are NZ$50 ($31.25), including GST, single or double.

The **Holiday Lodge,** 862 Colombo St., Christchurch (tel. 03/666-584), has 15 spacious and immaculate two-bedroom units, housed in two blocks on either side of a parking lot. Those in a yellow stucco building are all duplexes with bedrooms and a glassed-in sun porch upstairs. All units have color TV, telephone, radio, electric blanket, electric heater, and bath with tub and shower. There's daily maid service, a laundry, and a children's play area. Rates are NZ$45 ($28.25), plus GST, single or double. Surcharge.

True to its name, the **Southern Comfort,** 53 Bealey Ave., Christchurch (tel. 03/660-383), provides just that, thanks to the hospitality and easy-going manner of Bernard Spragg, who worked as a tour-coach driver for 20 years before going into the motel business. He can tell you all you need to know about the area's attractions. The modern units, two of which have waterbeds and four of which have microwaves, feature striking prints on the walls, TVs, videos, and in-room safes. Rates are NZ$68 ($42.50) single and NZ$72 ($45) double; kids under 4, free.

READERS' ACCOMMODATION SELECTION: "The **Ambassador's Hotel,** 19 Manchester St., Christchurch (tel. 03/667-808), was our best find in New Zealand. A large, brick bed-and-breakfast establishment, it is only a two-minute walk from Newmans bus depot and the train station and about ten minutes to Cathedral Square. A quiet double room with many toilets and showers down the hall and a full cooked breakfast was very reasonable, and the complimentary tea and cookies in the lounge at 9 p.m. was expanded to tasty, warm hot cross buns on Easter Saturday. Host Peter Ward is charming and his only concern seemed to be our comfort and convenience" (P. and W. Diehnelt, Ashippun, Wisc.).

A Big Splurge

One of the prettiest motels I've come across anywhere is the **Camelot Court Motor Lodge,** 28-30 Papanui Rd., Christchurch (tel. 03/559-124). The Camelot theme is carried out in a series of cottage-like apartments that are luxury personified. They're so spacious (they can sleep up to six) and furnishings are so posh that you may be tempted to just settle in and not leave. Some have waterbeds, and there's a lovely honeymoon suite available. In a two-story block behind these "executive suites," standard studio flats are also quite nice, with kitchen and private bath facilities. There's a cozy lounge bar on the premises, as well as an elegant licensed restaurant that serves gourmet meals. Prices range from NZ$90 ($56.25), single or double, for the studios to NZ$120 ($75) for the apartments; NZ$10 ($6.25) for each additional person. Add GST to all rates. It's a Best Western, and the discount helps a bit.

WHERE TO EAT

There are two **Cobb & Co.** restaurants in Christchurch. These are the family-style restaurants with colonial decor, which serve filling meals at moderate prices. They're fully licensed and serve from 7:30 a.m. until 10 p.m. You'll find them at the Caledonian Hotel, 101 Caledonian Rd. (tel. 666-035), and the Bush Inn, on the corner of Waimairi and Riccarton Roads (tel. 487-175).

The **Aldersgate Cafeteria,** 309 Durham St. (tel. 666-745), started out in the 1950s as a soup kitchen, and today it is still operated by the Methodist Central Mission, serving up some of the best—and certainly the most inexpensive—home-cooked meals in Christchurch. The blackboard menu changes every day, and you can eat your fill for about NZ$7 ($4.40). It's open Monday through Friday from 8 a.m. to 2 p.m. for light snacks or take-aways; hot dishes are served between 11:45 a.m. and 1:45 p.m.

Eliza's, 82 Bealey Ave. (tel. 668-584), is in one wing of Eliza's Manor House (see "Bed-and-Breakfasts"), and the room is a delight of oak paneling, red velvet draperies, and a glowing fireplace. Prices on the à la carte menu are in the NZ$8.50 ($5.30) to NZ$18.50 ($11.50) range, and dinner is served from 6 p.m. seven days a week. It's a good idea to make reservations. Licensed and BYO.

The **Oxford Victualling Co.,** at the corner of Colombo Street and Oxford Terrace (tel. 797-148), is a fully licensed restaurant in a 125-year-old building that for many years was a hotel and tavern. Nowadays it houses a complex of bars and the large restaurant that serves fish, roasts, grills, and salads at prices that will buy the main course, dessert, and coffee for under NZ$17 ($10.75)—truly one of Christchurch's best buys. Upstairs in the Skiff bar, bistro food is served from noon to 3 p.m. and 6 to 9 p.m., and in the adjacent Conservatory you can enjoy a buffet or light fare such as soup and bread or a choice of salads for less than NZ$5 ($3.15). Downstairs there's continuous service from 11 a.m. to 9 p.m. Sunday through Thursday, until 10 p.m. Friday and Saturday. A bottle shop is conveniently located on the premises.

The favorite eating and meeting spot of Christchurch locals is **Dux de Lux,** at the corner of Montreal and Hereford Streets, near the Arts Centre (tel. 666-919). It calls itself a gourmet vegetarian restaurant and serves such creative dishes as filo pastry stuffed with mushrooms, asparagus, and corn, and corn-and-coconut soup. Portions are generous; hot main dishes are NZ$8 ($5) and come with a choice of salads and cold vegetables. There are two congenial dining rooms and a tree-filled courtyard with picnic tables. Service is cafeteria style, and if there's a line, it's worth the short wait. There's music Thursday through Saturday nights. Open 11:30 a.m. to midnight daily.

A cozy, less crowded vegetarian eatery, **Mainstreet,** 840 Colombo St. (tel. 650-421), has two pretty dining areas upstairs. Main dishes are twice as expensive as at Dux de Lux (see above), but you can get a dessert or soup and a bagel for NZ$5 ($3.15). Open 11 a.m. to 11 p.m. daily.

Just behind Cathedral Square at 119 Hereford St., **Rita's Burritas** (tel. 791-060, ext. 801) is a tiny place that gives big servings—guacamole and nachos, tacos, tossed salad, and burritos, including vegetarian ones. You'll pay NZ$8 ($5) or less. Open Monday through Thursday from 11:30 a.m. to 8 p.m., Friday from 9 p.m.

For a dip into decadence, rush to **Strawberry Fare,** set back from the street at 114 Peterborough St., just off Colombo Street (tel. 03/654-897), and order a luscious dessert (that's all that's on the menu). You'll pay what you ordinarily pay for lunch—temptations such as Death by Chocolate, strawberries and cream, and banana crêpes cost between NZ$8.50 ($5.30) and NZ$12.50 ($7.80). The good news is that the coffee is a bottomless cup and two people can easily share one dessert, so go with a friend.

The elegant dining room at the **Town Hall,** on Kilmore Street between Colombo and Victoria Streets, serves a beautiful and bounteous smörgåsbord from noon to 2 p.m. Monday through Friday. Floor-to-ceiling windows look out on the sphere-shaped fountains, and the groaning board is set with an inviting display of salads, meats, hot dishes, fruits, sweets, and cheeses. The price is NZ$20 ($12.50) weekdays, NZ$22.50 ($14) at brunch and dinner on Sunday, and there's a low-cost family menu from 5:30 to 7:45 p.m. starting at NZ$13 ($8.15). From 7:45 p.m. until late Monday through Saturday, it's a full à la carte menu from NZ$18 ($11.25) per person; dancing accompanies dining on Saturday nights. All prices include GST. Licensed.

The **Gardens Restaurant,** in the Botanic Gardens (tel. 665-076), is in an octagonal red-brick building with wrap-around windows looking out to the gardens—a delightful place to eat. The garden-like interior has green rugs with white garden-type furniture and fringed Victorian lampshades hanging from the domed white wood ceiling. You can park under the trees at the Armagh Street entrance and walk over the rustic bridge to reach the restaurant. Lovely morning and afternoon teas are served, and a smörgåsbord lunch is set up under a pink awning. After lunch, take a ride on the Toast Rack, an electric tram with upright seats (whence the name), for a half-hour tour of the gardens. Tours leave the restaurant daily at regular intervals, September to May, weather permitting. The restaurant is a popular one, so it's a good idea to phone ahead to reserve. Lunch is served every day from noon to 2 p.m., but the tea kiosk is open from 10 a.m. until 4:30 p.m.

Meals at the **Coachman Inn Restaurant,** 144 Gloucester St. (tel. 793-476), are excellent value. This is an attractive room with rustic interior, lots of natural brick, heavy dark-stained timber beams, and lighting by old-fashioned lanterns. The Coachman specializes in steaks, and has won the New Zealand Restaurant Association Award of Excellence. Prices for peppered porterhouse, T-bone, garlic sirloin, lamb chops, and pork chops range from NZ$10 ($6.25) to NZ$15 ($9.40). Tender, juicy steak sandwiches are on the menu at NZ$9.95 ($6.25), and there's a nice variety of entrees and desserts. It's fully licensed, and there's an adjoining bar for a pre- or after-dinner drink. Hours are 7 a.m. to 11 p.m., seven days a week.

I'll have to confess right here that there must be a little Greek in my soul, and perhaps that colors my enjoyment of **Mykonos Taverna,** 112a Lichfield St. (tel. 797-452). However, it certainly doesn't affect my judgment of the food—and the home-style cooking here is good, from the classic moussaka to souvlakiarni (barbecued kebab with lamb, onions, and capsicums) to the flaky, sweet baklava for dessert. Once you climb the stairs in the converted warehouse and enter Mykonos, you're in an authentic taverna setting, with plain white walls, simple wooden tables and chairs, photographs and wall hangings from Greece, and candles and fresh flowers on the tables. And if you come along on Friday or Saturday, expect to find a two-piece Greek band and impromptu dancing. Prices are in the NZ$14 ($8.75) to NZ$18.50 ($11.50) range for main courses, and there's a cover charge of NZ$3.50 ($2.20) on music nights, a minimum charge of NZ$12 ($7.50) on Friday and Saturday. Bring your own wine to wash down all that good food. Hours are 6 to 11 p.m. Tuesday through Saturday, and you'd best reserve ahead on weekends.

One of the most pleasant and convenient places to eat in the city center is **Broque's,** in Noah's Hotel, at the corner of Worcester Street and Oxford Terrace (tel. 794-700). It's a pretty, relaxing room, with friendly, solicitous service. All three meals are served, and this is an especially popular lunch spot for Christchurch shoppers. The menu is an extensive one, offering light fare such as sandwiches, quiche, omelets, and cannelloni, as well as main courses of fresh fish, smoked salmon, lamb chops, steak, chicken, and the like (all served with a side salad or vegetable). Devonshire teas are served in the afternoon, and there's a supper menu from 6 p.m. to midnight seven days a week. A full cooked breakfast or lunch will run about NZ$15 ($9.40), and dinners go for NZ$30 ($18.75). Hours are 6:30 a.m. to midnight daily.

READERS' DINING SELECTIONS: "**Aldersgate Cafeteria,** 309 Durham St., started out as a soup kitchen in the 1930s, and today it serves the cheapest home-style meals in Christchurch. They have a blackboard menu that changes every day, and there are also cakes and sandwiches. It's open from 8 a.m. to 2 p.m. every day" (M. Coulthard, Christchurch, N.Z.). . . . "We love Spanish food and were pleased to find it in Christchurch, at **Pedro's,** 143 Worcester St. (tel. 797-668); the prices were reasonable, the meal filling and good" (M. Norman, San Diego, Calif.). . . . "**Home hospitality** in Christchurch is organized by Barbara Beavan, 11 Office Rd. (tel. 599-058). Someone from the group will collect you at your motel for 'a traditional meal of roast Canterbury lamb.' They ask for at least 24 hours' notice" (D. Brunk, Newport News, Va.).

Big Splurges

You'll be dining in magnificent Gothic splendor at **Grimsby's,** Cranmer Courts, on the corner of Kilmore and Montreal Streets (tel. 799-040). The marvelous old stone building was opened in 1876 as Christchurch Normal School, which operated until 1954, when it became the Post Primary Department of Christchurch Teacher's College until 1970. After that it lay vacant and was severely vandalized until developers took it in hand in 1980 to create co-op apartments in one wing and this elegant restaurant on the ground floor. You enter through heavy wooden doors into a medieval hall, thence into a high-ceilinged dining room beautifully furnished, with tables resplendent in crisp white linen, exquisite china, crystal, and silverware. Classical music plays softly in the background. Service is as elegant as the surroundings, and the food is worth every effort involved in managing a splurge meal. The cuisine is English and French, and the menu features beef steak and oyster pudding, beef Wellington, roast venison, scallops parisienne, and rack of Canterbury lamb. The price range is NZ$25 ($15.75) to NZ$33 ($20.75) for main courses. Dinner hours are 7 to 10:30 p.m. Monday through Saturday. Licensed. Highly recommended—you'll have had a "big splurge" of true elegance after a meal at Grimsby's!

Perched alongside the Avon River, **Tiffany's,** at the corner of Oxford Terrace and Durham Street (tel. 741-350), is as pretty as its picture window. The award-winning restaurant, named after the oldest daughter of the building's owner, is in a house built in 1908. It has a sophisticated, unhurried atmosphere conducive to lingering. Featured on the menu are lamb, venison, seafood, beef, and chicken. Main courses range from NZ$24 ($15) to NZ$32 ($20). Enter from the river side along the brick walkway. Open from 7 p.m. Tuesday through Saturday.

THINGS TO SEE AND DO

Your first stop should be at the **Information Centre,** 75 Worcester St. (opposite Noah's Hotel), to look over their exhaustive supply of information brochures on Christchurch and all of Canterbury. The centre is open seven days a week—8:30 a.m. to 5 p.m. weekdays, and 9 a.m. to 4 p.m. weekends and holidays. Pick up some *City Walk* brochures, especially no. 1, and the *Riverside Scenic Walk*. The Information Centre can book you on a two-hour **guided city walk;** they leave from the kiosk in Cathedral Square at 10 a.m. and 2 p.m. daily, at 1 p.m. only May through September.

Seeing the City

Cathedral Square is the hub of the city center—it will almost certainly be your orientation point, and it's great people-watching territory. If you happen to be in that area around 1 p.m., look for the Wizard of Christchurch, a colorful character (and actually a very learned individual) with very definite ideas about almost everything in the universe. If the Wizard's in town, you're in for some unusual entertainment, for which you won't be charged a cent. Christchurch treasures its "eccentrics and nutters," as the plaque outside the post office on the square attests. It's in memory of another local character, the Bird Man.

In Cathedral Square, climb the 133 steps in the 120-foot **Christchurch Cathedral** tower for a splendid panoramic view of the city and its environs. There's a NZ$1 (65¢) charge for adults, NZ$.50 (30¢) for children, or NZ$2 ($1.25) for families. The cathedral is open from 8 a.m. to 5:30 p.m. Monday through Friday, 8:30 a.m. to 5 p.m. on Saturday, and 7:30 a.m. to 8:30 p.m. on Sunday. The tower is open from 9 a.m. to 4 p.m. Monday through Saturday and from 1 to 4:30 p.m. on Sunday. For more information, call 660-046. More imposing architecturally is Christchurch's **Cathedral of the Blessed Sacrament,** also called the basilica, on Barbados Street about a 15-minute walk from Cathedral Square.

There are many good **coach tours** for seeing the city and its surroundings, one of the best and least expensive being those given by the **Transport Board's Red Buses,** which leave Cathedral Square daily. The 10 a.m. tour takes you through the garden suburbs and past impressive city buildings for fares of NZ$12 ($7.50) for adults, half that for children. Then there's one at 1:30 p.m. that takes the spectacular Summit Road to Lyttelton Harbour, with panoramas of snow-capped Alps, plains, and sea, includes a launch trip on the harbor, and makes a stop at the baronial Sign of the Takahe for tea on the way back. Adult fare is NZ$15 ($9.40); children pay half. Highly recommended.

InterCity offers a number of **day excursions,** tops among them being one to Hanmer Springs for NZ$26 ($16.25) to visit geothermal pools, gaze out at snow-capped peaks, take forest walks, or go jet-boat riding; and another to Akaroa, the quaint town of French heritage on the Banks Peninsula that was settled ten years before Christchurch, for NZ$19 ($12). If you have the time, though, I'd recommend an overnight or two in Akaroa, a real charmer. A breathtaking way to spend a day is to take the scenic **Trans-Alpine Express** train trip to Arthur's Pass or Greymouth. You can make the journey round trip by train, or come back by bus for completely different views.

You won't be in Christchurch long before you notice the **punts,** maneuvered by young men in straw hats, on the River Avon. The way to get from the bank into one of those boats is to reserve a ride through the Information Centre, then link up with a boat at one of four landings: at the Information Centre, at the Town Hall restaurant, at the Thomas Edmonds Rotunda, or at Mona Vale gardens, about a mile from downtown. The punts depart on demand from 10 a.m. to 6 p.m. October to March, until 5 p.m. in April and September, and until 4 p.m. May to August. A 45-minute ride costs NZ$10 ($6.25) per person or NZ$30 ($18.75) per family, half that for 20 minutes.

You can also take matters into your own hands and paddle a canoe down the lovely **Avon River,** which is landscaped its entire length. Canoes are for rent at about NZ$8 ($5) per hour from **Antigua Boatsheds,** Cambridge Terrace (tel. 665-885), as they have been from this same company for over a century. Open daily from 9:30 a.m. to 4 p.m.

Christchurch's flat terrain invites **cycling,** and bike lanes are marked off in several parts of the city, including parks. Parking lots even include bike racks. Join the bikers by renting from **Rent-a-Bike,** 139 Gloucester St. (tel. 664-409), opposite the Coachman Inn Restaurant; the price is NZ$2 ($1.25) an hour or NZ$7 ($4.40) a day. To zip along at a somewhat brisker pace, get some motorized wheels at **Renta Scoota,** at the same address; rates are NZ$20 ($12.50) per day, half that for five or fewer hours. If you prefer **walking,** you're in the perfect place to do it; the Information Centre can supply pamphlets mapping out scenic strolls, or simply follow the river or wander through the botanic gardens (see below).

One of the loveliest spots for photographing in Christchurch is the **Thomas Edmonds Bank Rotunda,** near Cambridge Terrace and Manchester Street. Now filled with diners rather than musicians, it's a graceful, octagonal Italianate building on the banks of the Avon. Punts on the river dock right at the landing here, to make your photos even better.

Among the interesting places to visit in the city is **Canterbury Museum** on Rolleston Avenue (tel. 668-379), which has an excellent permanent Antarctica exhibit, along with New Zealand birds, Oriental art, Maori culture, and a re-creation of a 19th-century Christchurch street. Hours are 10 a.m. to 4:30 p.m. daily, with free guided tours at 10:15 and 11:30 a.m. and 1:15 and 2:30 p.m. daily. Admission is free, although they are grateful for donations. The museum is at the entrance to the 75-acre **Botanic Gardens,** where show houses display tropical plants, ferns, mosses, and a comprehensive collection of cacti and succulents. More than one reader agrees with me that these lovely gardens should not be missed. They are particularly impressive in the spring, when there are hosts of daffodils. Keep an eye out for the huge Albert Edward oak, the first tree planted in the gardens (July 7, 1863).

Hours are 7 a.m. to sundown for the gardens, 10 a.m. to 4 p.m. for the show houses. Within the gardens, you'll find the **McDougall Art Gallery,** which holds an impressive collection of Australasian and European art, with constantly changing exhibits. Hours are 10 a.m. to 4:30 p.m. daily.

In the same area, there's the **Arts Centre,** 2 Worcester St., off Rolleston and near the museum and Botanical Gardens (tel. 660-989). A real gathering spot, it is filled with craft workshops (visit the Wool Studio), galleries (the Carpet Gallery is a unique must), restaurants, coffeehouses (the Art Centre Café is particularly inviting), a professional theater, and artists' studios. On weekends year round there is a lively Arts and Crafts Market held here, complete with musicians, booths filled with clothes and jewelry, a sampling of international cuisines, and a lively, inviting atmosphere. Festivals and other events are scheduled regularly.

The 100-acre, 15,000-square-foot **Ferrymead Historic Park,** 269 Bridle Path Rd., Heathcote (tel. 841-708), holds a fascinating collection of things from the past, including an Edwardian township, Hall of Flame, Hall of Wheels, working exhibits, and lots more. Take Ferry Road south and make the first right turn after Heathcote Bridge. If you're not driving, the no. 3 bus from Cathedral Square will get you there. It's open daily (except Christmas) from 10 a.m. to 4:30 p.m., and admission is NZ$6 ($3.75) for adults, NZ$3 ($1.90) for children (under 5, free).

Christchurch **gardens** are known throughout the country, and there is fierce competition every year between neighborhoods. To view some of these glorious gardening achievements, visit **Royds Street,** opposite Boys' High, which has won the competition for many years running. In the business community, it's the exquisite garden at **Sanitarium Health Food Company,** 54 Harewood Rd., Papanui, which comes out on top time and time again. However, just about any street you stroll will display garden patches of exceptional beauty, and if you express your delight in seeing them, the nearest gardener will have you deep in conversation in no time flat! In February there are bus tours of the award-winning gardens.

Christchurch is the American supply base and communication center for **Operation Deep Freeze,** the U.S. Antarctic Program, a scientific study program some 2,000 miles to the south. As a result, there's a steady flow of air force and navy personnel through the city. It is sometimes possible to visit, and if you're interested, contact the Public Relations Officer, Operation Deep Freeze, Christchurch Airport (tel. 583-079), at least two weeks ahead.

The **Willowbank Wildlife Reserve,** 60 Hussey Rd. (tel. 596-226), is a delightful natural park comprising a zoo of exotic animals, a farmyard of endangered breeds, and the **New Zealand Experience,** featuring native birds, including the kiwi (floodlights help you see this and other nocturnal creatures). It's a 15-minute drive from the city; take Harewood Road, turn right onto Gardiners Road and right again into Hussey Road. Open daily from 10 a.m. to 11 p.m. Adults pay NZ$6 ($3.75); children, NZ$2.50 ($1.55).

READER'S SIGHTSEEING SUGGESTION: "The Royal New Zealand Air Force Museum, on Main South Road in Sockburn (tel. 03/482-049), is a must for aviation buffs, who'll love the planes" (B. Smith, Charleston, S.C.).

Skiing

Methven, 57 miles southwest of Christchurch and 21 miles north of the agricultural center of Ashburton, lures those afflicted with downhill fever. It is the gateway to the **Mount Hutt** ski field, which is blessed with a long season, often from late May through early December. Other outdoor activities in the region include mountaineering, fishing, boating, trekking, and golf.

A Day Trip

If you follow Hwy. 1 north along the coast to **Kaikoura**—almost midway between Christchurch and Picton—you will have arrived at a place fast gaining a reputation for the animal and marine life that calls it home: seals, dolphins, whales, and numerous sea birds, including albatross, terns, penguins, and petrels. Sperm whales are most often seen between April and August; dolphins, between August and April. Seals and birds are always on hand. **Nature Watch Charters,** 94 Esplanade, Kaikoura (tel. 0513/5662), can show you around for the day; they'll even come to Christchurch and pick you up if you'd like a two-day tour. The tour leaders are American marine researcher/photographer Barbara Todd and her husband, former fisherman/farmer Roger Sutherland. **Kaikoura Tours Limited,** in the Kaikoura Railway Station (tel. 0513/5045), also provides outings. If you plan to wander on your own, just follow the Shoreline Walk along the coast to the tip of the peninsula and you should see seals and a variety of birds; the walk is almost three miles long and takes 1½ hours. Another way to reach the tip of the peninsula is via the Cliff-Top Walk, which affords panoramic views; it's three miles long and takes an hour. Kaikoura, by the way, is the only place on New Zealand's east coast where the mountains (the Kaikoura Range) meet the Pacific. The name Kaikoura means "crayfish food."

SHOPPING

There's good shopping in Christchurch, and I find prices here to be among the most reasonable in the country. For the best buy in New Zealand woolens and crafts, go by the **Arts Centre,** 2 Worcester Street (tel. 660-988). You'll find a concentration of 20 shops at the **Canterbury Centre,** at the corner of Cashel and High Streets, City Mall, with everything from jewelry, fashions, cameras, wools, a bookstore, and several eateries. The **Hide Shop,** at the corner of Gloucester and Colombo Streets (tel. 667-141), is the place to look for all sorts of leather goods, sheepskin, and woolens. Wayne and Marlene Wright have two locations of their **Garden City Antiques:** 192 Papanui Rd. (tel. 554-226) and 151 Hereford St. (tel. 516-878). Aside from marvelous old furniture you couldn't possibly fit into your luggage, they have a nice assortment of porcelain, silver, art, and jewelry—just the place to look for that special memento of your New Zealand visit. Another concentration of New Zealand products is to be found at **The Tannery,** 89 Worcester St. (tel. 665-406)—a great collection of goods, and one of the most helpful staffs in town. There's a **duty-free shop** at Cathedral Square.

AFTER DARK

For current after-dark happenings, check the *Tourist Times* or the *Christchurch and Canterbury Visitors' Guide.* Even if you're not a disco-goer, consider dropping by the **Palladium,** on the upper level in Chancery Lane (tel. 790-572), definitely New Zealand's top nightspot. The style is sparkling pseudo-deco, the light-and-laser show is electric, and the videos and music exhilarating. If you don't like crowds, show up early, at 8 p.m. Wednesday through Sunday or 9 p.m. on Monday and Tuesday; you can stay until 3 a.m. On weekends, expect to share the space with 500 people. The cover charge is NZ$5 ($3.15), or NZ$8 ($5) for a pass that will also get you into two other clubs, Caesar's and Flapper's.

A gathering place of a different kind, **Rumpole's Bar,** in the Park Royal hotel at Victoria Square, features honky-tonk piano music on Monday and Tuesday from 5:30 to 7 p.m.; the bar is fun, even when there's no music. **Dux de Lux** vegetarian restaurant has live music Thursday through Saturday nights. In the **Arts Centre,** there is a Jazz Cellar with music and dancing from 9:30 p.m. on Saturday. You bring your own wine, and there's a small cover charge.

Mykonos Taverna (see "Where to Eat," above) is an after-dark event on Friday and Saturday night if you're a lover of Greek music and dancing. And the **Coachman Inn cocktail lounge,** at 144 Gloucester St., has live entertainment on Friday and Saturday from 8 p.m. to 12:30 a.m.

The **Court Theatre,** at 20 Worcester St. (tel. 666-992), mounts plays throughout the year; past productions have included *Steel Magnolias* and *A Streetcar Named Desire.*

---

2. The Banks Peninsula

I went to **Akaroa** and the Banks Peninsula at the urging of my home-stay host in Christchurch, and I will always be indebted to her. This area has a beauty and charm all its own and I encourage you to experience it for yourself. You can drive or take a bus 52 miles from Christchurch to Akaroa (sit on the right-hand side for the best views), or for more of a tour, change to the mail-run bus at Duvauchelle and experience the beauty of the Eastern Bays (the bus departs Akaroa at 9:30 a.m. and returns at 2:30 p.m.); be assured that the driver will point out places of interest, in between delivering mail, milk, and passengers. En route you'll pass **Lake Ellsmere,** 111 square miles but only 6½ feet deep at its deepest part, and home to the Australian black swan, and **Lake Forsyth,** New Zealand's dramatic easternmost lake (you'll find an information center and rest rooms here). Stop at the Hilltop Tavern for a view of Akaroa across the harbor. The town, with a population of a scant 800, is the southernmost French settlement in the world, and New Zealand's only French inroad. In 1840 the French tried to establish a colony here, but England had just laid claim to the country in the Treaty of Waitangi. The original 63 French settlers loved the area so much, however, that they stayed on at the north end of town; French was spoken in that area until 1890. The English colonists who arrived in 1850 lived in the southern end, and to this day the street names reveal the dichotomy.

Akaroa is known for its walnuts—it was the French who first brought the trees here. You can get a sense of much of Akaroa's character by wandering along rue Lavand and rue Balgueri. Admire the winsome wooden buildings and houses dating from the 19th century, and by no means miss the cottages at the junction of Bruce Terrace and Aubrey Street (behind the Village Inn motel). The old French cemetery is just off rue Pompallier.

The Maori word "Akaroa" means "long harbor," and the water is very much a constant reality here. If you spend any time at all here, you may be overcome by an irresistible urge to try your hand at watercolors. At the very least, you'll feel as if you've wandered into one. No wonder so many artists gravitate here!

WHERE TO STAY

For a little place, Akaroa has an impressive array of accommodations, including some of New Zealand's finest offerings of bed-and-breakfast and backpacker accommodation. No matter where you stay, you'll want to linger.

A Hostel

Put on your hiking shoes. **Mount Vernon Lodge,** at the end of rue Balgueri, Akaroa (tel. 0514/7180), has the premier site overlooking Akaroa Harbour, and it's no mean feat to get to it if you're on foot. The reward is a beautiful farmyard setting with well-maintained bungalows. Each room has two levels with two beds in each level. There is a kitchen, lounge, barbecue area, and swimming pool. Horseback riding is available, and hiking is a given. The rate is NZ$13 ($8.15) per person, with a NZ$2 ($1.25) linen fee.

READER'S HOSTEL SELECTION: "**Jeff and Trish Hamilton,** on Kaik Road, Akaroa (tel. 0514/7612), welcome backpackers at their homestead. It seems to be a favorite of German travelers. Give them a call to be picked up" (C. Adair, Los Angeles, Calif.).

READER'S CABIN SELECTION: "One of the nicest campgrounds we stayed at was the **Holi-**

day Park Campground, not far from town on Old Coach Road, Akaroa (tel. 0514/7471). Besides cabins and tourist flats, there are caravans to rent" (B. Bristol, Charleston, S.C.).

A Bed-and-Breakfast

Picturesque **Glencarrig,** at 7 Percy St., Akaroa (tel. 0514/7008), was built in 1853 by the first Anglican vicor in Akaroa for his wife and six children. You'll love the large farmhouse kitchen with its drying rack and the original timberwork, the lovely single room, two double ones, all with country decor, and two sitting rooms with fireplaces. The property, which sits prettily on 1½ acres, even has a stream and mill wheel on it, and a pool. Hosts Kaye and Mike Stokes have an impressive art collection on display throughout the house. Look for Glencarrig's red roof peeking out from behind the hedgerow when you go up the hill. The rate of NZ$40 ($25) per person includes a cooked breakfast.

Motel Flats

Perched on a hilltop above Akaroa, **Mount Vernon Lodge** (see "A Hostel," above; tel. 0514/7180) has double units for NZ$35 ($22), with a NZ$2.50 ($1.55) linen fee if you only plan to stay one night. There is also a marvelous A-frame chalet perfect for a couple who wants to retreat from the world or for a family. It has a double bed looking out at the hills, two more beds upstairs, a tub and washing machine, a kitchen, and a TV. The chalet is good value at NZ$50 ($31.25) double, plus NZ$5 ($3.15) for each additional person. There is a surcharge of NZ$2.50 ($1.55) per person for one-night stays.

There are only two self-contained units at **Highfield Holiday Homes,** on rue Cachalot, Akaroa (tel. 0514/7248), so you have to reserve ahead. One unit sleeps five people; the other, six. Both have TV, kitchen, and bedding; linen, however, is an optional extra, and coffee and tea, toilet paper, and soap are provided only for the first few days. According to hosts Sue and Eric Highfield, it's quiet here, except for the birds. To find the property, drive uphill from the museum; it's the third street on the right. The rate is NZ$45 ($28.25) double, NZ$7 ($4.40) per extra person.

A Hotel

If the truth be known, a few Germans were mixed in with those French immigrants, and one of them, Jacob Waeckerle, built the **Grand Hotel** in 1860 at the entrance to Akaroa, at 6 rue Lavaud (tel. 0514/7011). Ironically, then it was called the French Hotel; it burned in 1882 but was rebuilt and renamed. Among the vestiges of the past that remain are the staircase, the coal ranges, and the foot scrapers at the entrance. The hotel has a split personality right now because the downstairs has been renovated—beautifully—while the upstairs is waiting its turn. Guests get to choose from eight rooms; Room 3 is nice and looks out onto the street below. There's a bistro/bar and restaurant on the premises, a lounge with TV and coffee and tea facilities, and a beer garden. The rate is a low NZ$20 ($12.50) per night.

READER'S BED-AND-BREAKFAST SELECTION: "Halfway through the Eastern Bays trip is an absolute must—a farm-stay with **Tad and Jill Harris** on their 900-acre sheep farm on Akaroa Road in Decanter Bay (tel. 0514/8607). It would be difficult to find more hospitable hosts anywhere, and the setting is exquisite. The Harrises have been in the farm-stay program since 1976, and the accommodation is first-rate" (J. Karst, Detroit, Mich.). [*Author's Note:* The Harrises offer *dinner,* bed, and breakfast for a quite reasonable rate.]

WHERE TO EAT

A popular place to sit and have breakfast or a "cuppa" is the **Akaroa Bakery,** on Beach Road. For lunch, choose either the **Harbour View Tearoom** or the **Montarsha Tearoom,** depending on which has the better specials posted for the day; both are on Beach Road.

The best restaurant in town is **La Rue Restaurant** (tel. 0514/7658), which was changing addresses when this book went to press, serves dinner in summer daily from 6:30 p.m. (Wednesday through Sunday in winter) and lunch on weekends from noon on. Seafood, lamb, venison, and pork dishes are on the menu. Dinner will run you around NZ$30 ($18.75); save by coming for lunch or Sunday supper.

THINGS TO SEE AND DO

Experience Akaroa Harbour firsthand on the **Canterbury Cat,** which departs daily at 1:30 p.m. year round from the main wharf (tel. 0514/7641); during the two-hour cruise you'll spot penguins and dolphins (they're in residence November to April) and visit a salmon farm.

Akaroa's land-side attractions include its fine **museum,** the best place to start your visit, especially since it doubles as the town's **information center** and can provide a good map; the **Langlois-Eteveneaux House,** part of the museum and probably the oldest in Canterbury; the **lighthouse,** which was in service from 1880 to 1980; and the **herb farm,** about half a mile up rue Grehan, open from July through April, where on the first Saturday of each month local craftspeople gather to sell their wares from 11 a.m. to 2 p.m.

A pleasant way to see this area is in the company of knowledgeable Rosemary Cuthbert Lyon, who offers a variety of reasonably priced **local tours** (book through the Akaroa Village Inn; tel. 0514/7421).

If you want to buy a book on the area or perhaps a woolen souvenir, go to **Pot Pourri,** at rue Balgueri and rue Lavaud, open from 10 a.m. to 5 p.m. daily.

And don't worry if you need cash; the **Bank of New Zealand** has a branch here.

XII

FAST FACTS FOR NEW ZEALAND

Listed below are some of those everyday practical details that can produce a first-class boondoggle if you don't have them at hand when traveling.

ACCIDENT COMPENSATION: As a visitor to New Zealand, you are automatically covered, from the time you arrive until you leave, by the same *no-fault* accident compensation plan as Kiwis. And it doesn't cost you one red cent! Benefits include compensation for reasonable expenses (by New Zealand standards) directly resulting from the accident, such as medical and hospital expenses, as well as lump-sum payments for permanent incapacity. No matter if the accident was your fault or not, you'll be covered. Be sure to note, however, that this compensation plan does not cover sickness, trip cancellation, etc. For more information, contact your nearest NZTP office. Benefits are determined by the Accident Compensation Corporation. Their head office is at Renouf House, 154 Featherston St., Wellington (tel. 04/724-434), and you should contact them immediately if you should—God forbid!—have an accident.

AMERICAN EMBASSY: The Embassy of the United States of America is at 29 Fitzherbert Terrace (Thorndon), Wellington (tel. 04/722-068). Hours are Monday to Friday from 8:15 a.m. to 5 p.m.

AMERICAN EXPRESS: The American Express Travel Service office is at 95 Queen St., Auckland (tel. 09/798-243). Other agencies around the country are: ATA Travel, Hamilton (tel. 071/82-349); ATA Travel, Rotorua (tel. 073/89-062); ATA Travel, New Plymouth (tel. 067/86-119); Century 21 Travel, Wellington (tel. 04/731-221); and Guthreys Travel, Christchurch (tel. 03/793-560). They accept mail for clients (you're a client if you have an American Express credit card or traveler's checks), forward mail for a small fee, issue and change traveler's checks, and replace lost or stolen traveler's checks and American Express credit cards.

BANKING HOURS: Banks in international airports are open for all incoming and outgoing flights; others are open from 9 a.m. to 4:30 p.m. Monday through Friday. Most banks charge a commission for cashing traveler's checks; in 1989 that was generally NZ$.05 (3¢) per check, and Countrywide Bank charged nothing at all.

CIGARETTES: You can bring in 200 cigarettes per person, as allowed by Customs regulations. Most brands for sale in New Zealand are English or European, although more and more American brands are appearing on the market.

ELECTRICAL APPLIANCES: New Zealand's voltage is 230 volts, and plugs are the three-pin flat type. If your hairdryer or other small appliances are different, you'll need a converter/adapter. Most motels and better hotels have built-in wall converters for 110-volt, two-prong razors, but if you're going to be staying in hostels, cabins, or guesthouses, better bring a converter/adapter.

EMERGENCIES: Dial 111 anyplace in New Zealand for police, ambulance, or to report a fire.

FILM: Film is expensive in New Zealand, so bring as much as you can with you. You're not limited by Customs regulations, just by baggage space. Most brands are available in larger cities. There is also same-day developing service in most cities.

HAIRDRESSING: Prices are reasonable—NZ$35 ($22) for women and NZ$20 ($12.50) for men—and neither barbers nor hairdressers will be looking for a tip.

HOLIDAYS: Kiwis love a long holiday weekend, so most holidays are juggled to fall on a Friday or Monday—sometimes including both days. They will be a big factor in the availability of accommodations, since everybody and his brother packs up and goes to another part of the country at the drop of a long weekend. Banks and most shops close for national holidays. National holidays are listed below:

January: New Year's Day
February: New Zealand Day, February 6 (the date the Treaty of Waitangi was signed)
April: Good Friday, Easter, Easter Monday (and in some counties, the following Tuesday); ANZAC Day, April 25 (the date on which New Zealand and Australian troops landed in Gallipoli in 1915)
June: Queen's Birthday (first Monday)
October: Labour Day (last Monday)
December: Christmas Day and Boxing Day (December 26)

Individual regions celebrate their date of founding with Anniversary Days, which are usually rearranged, if necessary, to fall on a Monday or Friday.

During school holidays (Christmas through the beginning of February), the entire population of New Zealand seems to be on the move. Families usually holiday together (annual office leaves fall within this period, as a rule), and many reserve as much as a year in advance in popular resort areas. There are two-week school holidays in May and in August when the same thing happens, although to a lesser degree.

KIWI: Has two meanings: if not spelled with an initial capital, it means that round-bottomed, long-beaked, nonflying bird, which has become New Zealand's symbol; when there's a capital "K," it means a New Zealander, and it's used with the utmost affection.

LANGUAGE: English is spoken by all New Zealanders—Maori and Pakeha. You'll hear Maori spoken on some TV and radio programs and in some Maori settlements, but it's seldom used in conversation in the presence of overseas visitors.

LAUNDRY: No matter whether you'll be staying in hostels or motels, there will usually be a well-equipped laundry on the premises for your use. Cities have commercial laundries, but most visitors have little need for them.

MAIL DELIVERY: New Zealand post offices will receive mail for you and hold it for a month. Just have it addressed to you c/o Chief Post Office of the city or town you'll be visiting. American Express will receive and forward mail for its clients. Allow ten days for delivery from the United States.

MEDICAL ATTENTION: Not free like accident compensation, but so inexpensive by comparison to costs elsewhere that it would almost pay to get sick while in New Zealand! Medical facilities are excellent and health care is of a very high standard. Pharmacies observe regular local shop hours, but each locality usually will have an Urgent Pharmacy, which remains open until about 11 p.m. every day except Sunday, when there will be two periods during the day it's open. You'll find them listed in local telephone directories. There's a minimal extra charge for prescriptions filled during nonshop hours. Should you need a doctor, either consult the New Zealand Tourist and Publicity (NZTP) office or prevail on your motel or guesthouse host to direct you to one. Even most small towns have medical centers.

OFFICE HOURS: Usually 9 a.m. to 5 p.m. Monday through Friday.

PAKEHA: The Maori word for "fair-skinned people," which has come to mean all New Zealanders of European descent. There's nothing derogatory in its use.

POSTAGE: It costs NZ$1.05 (65¢) to send an airmail letter or postcard to the United States, NZ$.80 (50¢) to Australia, and NZ$1.30 (80¢) to the United Kingdom or Europe. Surface mail within New Zealand costs NZ$.70 (45¢) per card or letter.

PUB HOURS: 11 a.m. to 10 p.m. Monday through Thursday, to 11 p.m. on Friday and Saturday; closed Sunday. The minimum drinking age is 20 in pubs, 18 in licensed restaurants or with parent or guardian. Children are allowed in pubs with their parents.

REST ROOMS: There are "public conveniences" strategically located and well signposted in all cities and many small towns. You'll find public rest rooms at most service stations.

Local **Plunket Rooms** are a real boon to mothers traveling with small children, for they come with a "Mother's Room," where you can change diapers and do any necessary tidying up. The Plunket Society is a state-subsidized organization, which provides free baby care to all New Zealand families, and their volunteers are on duty in the Plunket Rooms—no charge, but they'll welcome a donation.

SAFETY: Whenever you're traveling in an unfamiliar city or country, stay alert. Be aware of your immediate surroundings. Wear a moneybelt and don't sling your camera or purse over your shoulder; wear the strap diagonally across your body. This will minimize the possibility of your becoming a victim of crime. Every society has its criminals. It's your responsibility to be aware and alert even in the most heavily touristed areas.

SHOP HOURS: Usually 9 a.m. (sometimes 8 a.m.) to 5:30 p.m. Monday through Thursday, until 9 p.m. on either Thursday or Friday. Increasingly, shops are open on Saturday morning, from 9:30 or 10 a.m. until noon; most shops are closed on Sunday. Shops connected to hotels sell alcoholic beverages during pub hours, 11 a.m. to 10 p.m., but never on Sunday.

STUDENT DISCOUNTS: Not many. Expect to pay full price most places.

TAXES: Be sure to save enough New Zealand currency to pay the departure charge of NZ$3 ($1.90). A Goods and Services Tax (GST) was instituted in 1986—the amount is 12.5%.

TAXIS: Taxi ranks are located at all terminals and on major shopping streets, and you may not hail one on the street within a quarter mile of a rank. They're on call 24 hours a day, and telephone numbers are in local directories, but there's an additional charge if you phone for one. Rates vary from place to place, but all city taxis are metered (in smaller localities, there's often a local driver who will quote a flat fee). Drivers don't expect a tip just to transport you, but if they handle a lot of luggage or perform any other special service, it's very much in order.

TELEGRAMS: All telegrams are sent through the post office, either by telephone or in person. The cheapest rate is "Letter Rate," which takes about 24 hours for delivery; rates for telegrams sent after regular post office hours can be as much as double.

TELEPHONES: The area code in New Zealand is known as the STD (subscriber toll dialing); if a given number has no STD, you must go through the operator. For operator assistance within New Zealand, dial 010. For an international operator, call 0170; if you need directory assistance for an international call, dial 0172.

The most economical way to make an international call from New Zealand is to charge it to an international calling card (they are free, so get one before you go) or to dial direct. To call the United States from New Zealand, first dial the international access code, 001, then the area code and local number. Most calls, even the international ones, may be made from a pay phone booth. When you make a long-distance call from your motel, hotel, or at Telecom, expect to pay a NZ$2 ($1.25) surcharge.

There is no inexpensive time to call overseas—it's a flat rate. Within New Zealand, economy rates are from 7 to 8 a.m. and 6 to 10 p.m. weekdays and 7 a.m. to 10 p.m. weekends; no matter the day, 10 p.m. to 7 a.m. is the most economical calling time. If you call during the day, choose the afternoon over the morning; it's somewhat less expensive.

Dial 111 for police, ambulance, or fire.

TELEVISION AND RADIO: The BCNZ (Broadcasting Council of New Zealand) is the major broadcaster in New Zealand, operating TV Channel 1 and TV Channel 2, both color since 1974, and Radio New Zealand. The majority of TV productions come from Britain and America. You'll be surprised and pleased to know that commercials are never shown on Sunday, when some of the best shows are on. Television transmission hours are 10 a.m. to about midnight. News junkies may go into withdrawal in New Zealand: Channel 1 broadcasts a half hour of news at 9:30 p.m. (on weekends, make that 10 to 15 minutes of news at 9:15 p.m.), and Channel 2 provides 20 minutes of news weekdays at 5:40 p.m. For current scheduling, check the listings in daily newspapers. And to hear the country's beautiful national anthem, "God Defend New Zealand," sung in both English and Maori, tune in to Channel 1 at sign-off time.

TIME: New Zealand is located just west of the International Date Line, and its standard time is 11 hours and 30 minutes ahead of Greenwich Mean Time. A 30-minute daylight saving is permanently observed, which puts New Zealand exactly 12 hours ahead of GMT. Thus at noon in New Zealand, standard time in Sydney is 10 a.m.; London, midnight of the previous day; San Francisco, 4 p.m. the previous day; New York, 7 p.m. the previous day; Singapore, 7:30 a.m. the same day; and Tokyo, 9 a.m. the same day.

TIPPING: Kiwis don't do it. And they don't expect visitors to do it. Their theory is that all workers in their country are paid a living wage and they can jolly well live on it. Restrain that uncontrollable urge if you can—then give in to it when someone has rendered a very special service (carried a ton of luggage, come to your rescue in a puzzling situation, etc.). It's not easy for Yanks who are accustomed to tipping at every turn, but once you get the hang of the system, what a relief! And what a saving! And the nicest thing about the whole situation is that you'll get the same friendly service whether you tip or not—I once actually had a taxi driver (who had juggled my bags a few times in the course of one journey) turn down a tip!

WEATHER FORECAST: There's a "Traveller's Rundown" every morning on the radio, which gives a roundup of weather in all tourist areas. Weather reports are also given at the end of the 6 p.m. TV newscast. To unscramble those Centigrade temperatures and convert them to Fahrenheit, multiply the Centigrade reading by 9, divide by 5, and add 32°.

WEIGHTS AND MEASURES: New Zealand uses the metric system of weights and measures. Here's a quick rundown on equivalences:

Length
    1 millimeter (mm)   = 0.04 inches (*or* less than ¹⁄₁₆ inch)
    1 centimeter (cm)   = 0.39 inches (*or* just under ½ inch)
    1 meter (m)   = 1.09 yards (*or* about 39 inches)
    1 kilometer (km)   = 0.62 miles (*or* about ⅔ mile)

To convert kilometers to miles, take the number of kilometers and multiply by .62 (for example, 25 km × .62 = 15.5 miles).

To convert miles to kilometers, take the number of miles and multiply by 1.61 (for example, 50 miles × 1.61 = 80.5 km).

Capacity
    1 liter = 33.92 ounces
            = 1.06 quarts
            = 0.26 gallons

To convert liters to gallons, take the number of liters and multiply by .26 (for example, 50 liters × .26 = 13 gallons).

To convert gallons to liters, take the number of gallons and multiply by 3.79 (for example, 10 gallons × 3.79 = 37.9 liters).

Weight
    1 gram (g) = 0.04 ounces (*or* about a paperclip's weight)
    1 kilogram (kg) = 2.2 pounds

To convert kilograms to pounds, take the number of kilos and multiply by 2.2 (for example, 75 kg × 2.2 = 165 pounds).

To convert pounds to kilometers, take the number of pounds and multiply by .45 (for example, 90 lb × .45 = 40.5 kg).

Area
    1 hectare (ha; 100 m²) = 2.47 acres

To convert hectares to acres, take the number of hectares and multiply by 2.47 (for example, 20 ha × 2.47 = 49.4 acres).

To convert acres to hectares, take the number of acres and multiply by .41 (for example, 40 acres × .41 = 16.4 ha).

Temperature

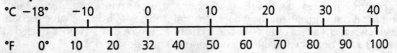

To convert degrees C to degrees F, multiply degrees C by 9, divide by 5, then add 32 (for example, [9/5 × 20°C] + 32 = 68°F).

To convert degrees F to degrees C, subtract 32 from degrees F, then multiply by 5, and divide by 9 (for example, [85°F−32] × 5/9 = 29° C).

INDEX

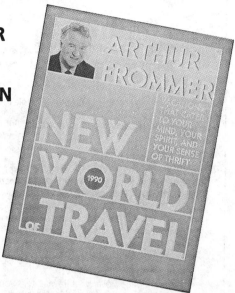

NOW, SAVE MONEY ON ALL YOUR TRAVELS!
Join Frommer's™ Dollarwise® Travel Club

Saving money while traveling is never a simple matter, which is why the **Dollarwise Travel Club** was formed 31 years ago. Developed in response to requests from Frommer Travel Guide readers, the Club provides cost-cutting travel strategies, up-to-date travel information, and a sense of community for value-conscious travelers from all over the world.

In keeping with the money-saving concept, the annual membership fee is low —$18 (U.S. residents) or $20 (residents of Canada, Mexico, and other countries)— and is immediately exceeded by the value of your benefits, which include:

1. Any TWO books listed on the following pages.
2. Plus any ONE Frommer City Guide.
3. A subscription to our quarterly newspaper, *The Dollarwise Traveler*.
4. A membership card that entitles you to purchase through the Club all Frommer publications for 33% to 50% off their retail price.

The eight-page *Dollarwise Traveler* tells you about the latest developments in good-value travel worldwide and includes the following columns: **Hospitality Exchange** (for those offering and seeking hospitality in cities all over the world); **Share-a-Trip** (for those looking for travel companions to share costs); and **Readers Ask . . . Readers Reply** (for those with travel questions that other members can answer).

Aside from the Frommer Guides, the Serious Shopper Guides, and the Gault Millau Guides, you can also choose from our Special Editions. These include such titles as **California with Kids** (a compendium of the best of California's accommodations, restaurants, and sightseeing attractions appropriate for those traveling with toddlers through teens); **Candy Apple: New York with Kids** (a spirited guide to the Big Apple by a savvy New York grandmother that's perfect for both visitors and residents); **Caribbean Hideaways** (the 100 most romantic places to stay in the Islands, all rated on ambience, food, sport opportunities, and price); **Honeymoon Destinations** (a guide to planning and choosing just the right destination from hundreds of possibilities in the U.S., Mexico, and the Caribbean); **Marilyn Wood's Wonderful Weekends** (a selection of the best mini-vacations within a 200-mile radius of New York City, including descriptions of country inns and other accommodations, restaurants, picnic spots, sights, and activities); and **Paris Rendez-Vous** (a delightful guide to the best places to meet in Paris whether for power breakfasts or dancing till dawn).

To join this Club, simply send the appropriate membership fee with your name and address to: Frommer's Dollarwise Travel Club, 15 Columbus Circle, New York, NY 10023. Remember to specify which single city guide and which two other guides you wish to receive in your initial package of member's benefits. Or tear out the next page, check off your choices, and send the page to us with your membership fee.

FROMMER BOOKS
PRENTICE HALL TRAVEL
15 COLUMBUS CIRCLE
NEW YORK, NY 10023
212-373-8125

Date_____

Friends:
Please send me the books checked below:

FROMMER™ GUIDES

(Guides to sightseeing and tourist accommodations and facilities from budget to deluxe, with emphasis on the medium-priced.)

☐ Alaska $14.95	☐ Germany. $14.95
☐ Australia. $14.95	☐ Italy $14.95
☐ Austria & Hungary $14.95	☐ Japan & Hong Kong $14.95
☐ Belgium, Holland & Luxembourg. $14.95	☐ Mid-Atlantic States. $14.95
☐ Bermuda & The Bahamas. $14.95	☐ New England. $14.95
☐ Brazil $14.95	☐ New York State $14.95
☐ Canada. $14.95	☐ Northwest $14.95
☐ Caribbean. $14.95	☐ Portugal, Madeira & the Azores $14.95
☐ Cruises (incl. Alaska, Carib, Mex, Hawaii,	☐ Skiing Europe. $14.95
Panama, Canada & US) $14.95	☐ South Pacific. $14.95
☐ California & Las Vegas. $14.95	☐ Southeast Asia. $14.95
☐ Egypt $14.95	☐ Southern Atlantic States $14.95
☐ England & Scotland. $14.95	☐ Southwest. $14.95
☐ Florida $14.95	☐ Switzerland & Liechtenstein $14.95
☐ France $14.95	☐ USA $15.95

FROMMER $-A-DAY® GUIDES

(In-depth guides to sightseeing and low-cost tourist accommodations and facilities.)

☐ Europe on $40 a Day. $15.95	☐ New York on $60 a Day $13.95
☐ Australia on $30 a Day $12.95	☐ New Zealand on $45 a Day $13.95
☐ Eastern Europe on $25 a Day $13.95	☐ Scandinavia on $60 a Day $13.95
☐ England on $50 a Day $13.95	☐ Scotland & Wales on $40 a Day. $13.95
☐ Greece on $35 a Day. $13.95	☐ South America on $35 a Day $13.95
☐ Hawaii on $60 a Day. $13.95	☐ Spain & Morocco on $40 a Day. $13.95
☐ India on $25 a Day $12.95	☐ Turkey on $30 a Day $13.95
☐ Ireland on $35 a Day. $13.95	☐ Washington, D.C. & Historic Va. on
☐ Israel on $40 a Day. $13.95	$40 a Day $13.95
☐ Mexico on $35 a Day $13.95	

FROMMER TOURING GUIDES

(Color illustrated guides that include walking tours, cultural and historic sites, and other vital travel information.)

☐ Australia. $9.95	☐ Paris. $8.95
☐ Egypt $8.95	☐ Scotland $9.95
☐ Florence $8.95	☐ Thailand $9.95
☐ London. $8.95	☐ Venice $8.95

TURN PAGE FOR ADDITONAL BOOKS AND ORDER FORM.

0190

FROMMER CITY GUIDES

(Pocket-size guides to sightseeing and tourist accommodations and facilities in all price ranges.)

☐ Amsterdam/Holland	$7.95	☐ Minneapolis/St. Paul	$7.95
☐ Athens	$7.95	☐ Montréal/Québec City	$7.95
☐ Atlantic City/Cape May	$7.95	☐ New Orleans	$7.95
☐ Barcelona*	$7.95	☐ New York	$7.95
☐ Belgium	$7.95	☐ Orlando/Disney World/EPCOT	$7.95
☐ Boston	$7.95	☐ Paris	$7.95
☐ Cancún/Cozumel/Yucatán	$7.95	☐ Philadelphia	$7.95
☐ Chicago	$7.95	☐ Rio	$7.95
☐ Denver/Boulder*	$7.95	☐ Rome	$7.95
☐ Dublin/Ireland	$7.95	☐ San Francisco	$7.95
☐ Hawaii	$7.95	☐ Santa Fe/Taos/Albuquerque	$7.95
☐ Hong Kong*	$7.95	☐ Seattle/Portland*	$7.95
☐ Las Vegas	$7.95	☐ Sydney	$7.95
☐ Lisbon/Madrid/Costa del Sol	$7.95	☐ Tokyo*	$7.95
☐ London	$7.95	☐ Vancouver/Victoria*	$7.95
☐ Los Angeles	$7.95	☐ Washington, D.C.	$7.95
☐ Mexico City/Acapulco	$7.95	*Available June, 1990	

SPECIAL EDITIONS

☐ A Shopper's Guide to the Caribbean	$12.95	☐ Manhattan's Outdoor Sculpture	$15.95
☐ Beat the High Cost of Travel	$6.95	☐ Motorist's Phrase Book (Fr/Ger/Sp)	$4.95
☐ Bed & Breakfast—N. America	$11.95	☐ Paris Rendez-Vous	$10.95
☐ California with Kids	$14.95	☐ Swap and Go (Home Exchanging)	$10.95
☐ Caribbean Hideaways	$14.95	☐ The Candy Apple (NY with Kids)	$12.95
☐ Honeymoon Destinations (US, Mex & Carib)	$12.95	☐ Travel Diary and Record Book	$5.95

☐ Where to Stay USA (Lodging from $3 to $30 a night) $10.95
☐ Marilyn Wood's Wonderful Weekends (Conn, Del, Mass, NH, NJ, NY, Pa, RI, VT) $11.95
☐ The New World of Travel (Annual sourcebook by Arthur Frommer for savvy travelers) $16.95

SERIOUS SHOPPER'S GUIDES

(Illustrated guides listing hundreds of stores, conveniently organized alphabetically by category.)

☐ Italy	$15.95	☐ Los Angeles	$14.95
☐ London	$15.95	☐ Paris	$15.95

GAULT MILLAU

(The only guides that distinguish the truly superlative from the merely overrated.)

☐ The Best of Chicago	$15.95	☐ The Best of Los Angeles	$14.95
☐ The Best of France	$16.95	☐ The Best of New England	$15.95
☐ The Best of Hong Kong	$16.95	☐ The Best of New York	$14.95
☐ The Best of Italy	$16.95	☐ The Best of Paris	$16.95
☐ The Best of London	$16.95	☐ The Best of San Francisco	$14.95

☐ The Best of Washington, D.C. $14.95

ORDER NOW!

In U.S. include $2 shipping UPS for 1st book; $1 ea. add'l book. Outside U.S. $3 and $1, respectively.
Allow four to six weeks for delivery in U.S., longer outside U.S.

Enclosed is my check or money order for $_____

NAME _____

ADDRESS _____

CITY _____ STATE _____ ZIP _____

0190

AMERICAN EXPRESS CAN DELIVER CASH AND A REPLACEMENT CARD TO YOU WITHIN 24 HOURS, AS LONG AS YOU'RE IN THIS GENERAL AREA.

No matter where you are in the world, if you lose your wallet, we can get a new American Express® Card and cash in your hands usually within 24 hours.*

If you're truly in the middle of nowhere, say the African Outback, it might take a little longer. Depending upon how many wandering hippos and fallen trees our local courier must contend with.

But more often than not, you'll have a new Card and cash the next day. Something you'd expect from American Express.

So carry the American Express Card. And no matter where on earth you go, you'll never leave civilization behind.

For assistance, call your nearest American Express office, or in the U.S. call our 24-hour number 1-800-252-3650; everywhere else call collect 602-954-1225. Don't leave home without it.®

MEMBERSHIP HAS ITS PRIVILEGES.℠

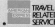

© 1989 American Express Travel Related Services Company, Inc.

TRAVEL RELATED SERVICES   *Delivery time may vary in some areas depending on transportation availability, existence of war or civil strife or other factors beyond our control. For U.S. Cardmembers only.

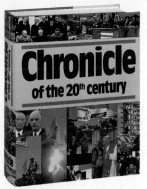
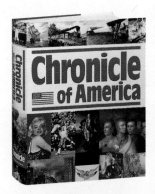

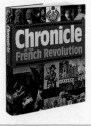